The Works of John Adams, Volume V

John Adams

BIBLIOBAZAAR

THE WORKS

OF

JOHN ADAMS.

CONTENTS OF VOLUME V.

APPENDIX.

WORKS

ON

GOVERNMENT.

A

DEFENCE

OF THE

CONSTITUTIONS OF GOVERNMENT

OF THE

UNITED STATES OF AMERICA,

AGAINST THE ATTACK OF M. TURGOT, IN HIS LETTER TO DR.
PRICE, DATED THE TWENTY-SECOND DAY OF MARCH, 1778.

BY

JOHN ADAMS.

" As for us Englishmen, thank Heaven, we have a better sense of government, delivered to us
from our ancestors. We have the notion of a public, and a constitution ; how a legislative, and how
an executive is moulded. We understand weight and measure in this kind, and can reason justly
on the balance of power and property. The maxims we draw from hence are as evident as those
in mathematics. Our increasing knowledge shows us every day more and more what common
sense is in politics." SHAFTESBURY'S CHARACT., vol. i. p. 108.

" 'T is scarce a quarter of an age since such a happy balance of power was settled between
our prince and people, as has firmly secured our hitherto precarious liberties, and removed from
us the fear of civil commotions, wars, and violence, either on account of the property of the
subject, or the contending titles of the crown."

IN THREE VOLUMES.

VOL. II.

A

DEFENCE

OF THE

CONSTITUTIONS OF GOVERNMENT

OF THE

UNITED STATES OF AMERICA.

CHAPTER FIRST.

ITALIAN REPUBLICS OF THE MIDDLE AGE.

FLORENCE.

THERE is no example of a government simply democratical;
yet there are many of forms nearly or remotely resembling what
are understood by "All Authority in one Centre." There once
existed a cluster of governments, now generally known by the
name of the Italian Republics of the Middle Age,* which deserve
the attention of Americans, and will further illustrate and confirm
the principles we have endeavored to maintain. If it appears, from
the history of all the ancient republics of Greece, Italy, and Asia
Minor, as well as from those that still remain in Switzerland,
Italy, and elsewhere, that caprice, instability, turbulence, revolutions, and the alternate prevalence of those two plagues and

* Ce qu'on appelle communément le moyen age commence à Constantin le
Grand. — *Corps Diplomatique*, Barbeyrac's Preface to vol. xxii. p. 6.

1 *

scourges of mankind, tyranny and anarchy, were the effects of governments without three orders and a balance, the same important truth will appear, in a still clearer light, in the republics of Italy. The sketches to be given of these cannot be introduced with more propriety than by the sentiments of a late writer,* because they coincide with every thing that has been before observed.

Limited monarchies were the ancient governments; the jealousies and errors of the nobles, or the oppressions they suffered, stimulated them to render monarchy unpopular, and erect aristocracies. " Ancient nations were, in one point, very generally defective in their constitutions, and that was the incertitude of the sovereignty, and, by consequence, the instability of government; which was, in all the republics of Italy, a perpetual occasion of infinite confusion. In no part of Italy, however united together, was found established an absolute hereditary monarch. By many examples, it is manifest, that kings either were created by the favor of the multitude, or at least sought their consent, and consulted the people in affairs of most importance and greatest danger. The government of the grandees, which succeeded, was rather a fraudulent or violent usurpation, than a true and proper aristocracy established by law, or confirmed by long and uncontested possession; and a popular government was never so free or so durable as when it was mixed with the authority of one supreme head, or of a senate; so that mixed governments were almost always preferred. One of the three kinds of governments nevertheless fell, when another arose; and all the Italian republics, nearly at one time, by the same gradations, passed from one form of administration to another.

" In this particular all the memorials of ancient Italy agree. They were, from the beginning, governed by kings. The Tuscans had kings; the Sabines had kings; and so had the people of . Latium; and as every city and every borough formed an independent government, these kings could not have much magnificence. Many states often obeyed the same king; for he who had the lordship of one city, procured himself to be elected the head of another. Porsenna, whom Dionysius calls King of Tuscany, because he was followed by many Tuscan nations, was

---

* Danina, *Rivoluzioni d'Italia*, vol. i. p. 41.

from the beginning only King of Chiusi. The Kings of Rome, by various means, gained the command of the Latin cities, which nevertheless, two centuries afterwards, reputed themselves still independent of the state of Rome. The King of the Veientes had the lordship of Fidena, a free city, and independent of the Veientes, in the same manner as the Visconti, Lords of Milan, Castruccio, Lord of Lucca, and the Scala, Lords of Verona, (and so many other princes and tyrants of the later ages, before the exaltation of Charles V.) made such progress in obtaining the sovereignty of many cities, which had nothing in common with Milan, or Lucca, or Verona. These kingdoms were either simply elective, or at least required the express consent of the people, howsoever often one relation succeeded to another. Neither were royal governments generally displeasing to the people; but the grandees and nobles, who were the most exposed to the caprice of the prince, both in their persons and property, studied to generate in the minds of the common people a hatred to the name of king, and to excite the desire of liberty. They flattered themselves, that if the principality, which often fell into the hands of new men and adventurers, such as Tarquin in Rome, and Aristodemus in Cuma, were abolished, they should be able to live, not only with more security and greater license, but with more authority, command, and power. In what nation, and in which city, the revolution first began, is not easy to determine; but in the course of the third century of the Roman era, one people following the example of another, this by means of one, and that of another opportunity, either expelled by violence their present kings, or desisted from electing new ones; and all Italy, hoisting as it were a common signal, changed at once its whole form of government.

"The odium of the royal name, and an enthusiasm for liberty, seized so universally, and with such energy, the whole Italian nation, that if any city wished either to continue or recover the custom of kings, this inclination was scarcely manifested before it was pointed out and reviled by the other cities, and upon all great occasions abandoned. The Veientes,[*] either from a disgust at the cabals and ambition which arose from the annual creation of new magistrates, or the better to provide for war, created afresh

[*] Liv. lib. v. c. 1.

a king; by which resolution they incurred to such a degree
the hatred and contempt of the other people of Tuscany, that,
contrary to every rule of policy, duty, and custom, they were left
alone to sustain that obstinate war with the Romans, which
ended in their ruin. In the beginning of the fourth century of
the Roman history, there is seldom or never mention made of
kings in any of the states of Italy. The whole authority and
administration of public affairs passed into the hands of the
nobility, or the senate; and that body, constituting at first the
middle order between the king and the people, became the
supreme head of the government. And although the greater
magistracies were elected by the voices or suffrages of the people,
nevertheless, all the honors and all the power of the government were collected in the grandees, who easily commanded the
votes of the electors, and who alone were the elected; for none
of the plebeians dared to pretend to offices, civil or military.
And it is too evident that, in every kind of community, the rich
and the noble endeavor, as it were, by their very nature, to exclude
the poor and the plebeians. Most of the public affairs relative
to peace or war were treated in a senate composed essentially of
patricians and nobles, who, in every thing that regarded the constitution, inclined more to aristocracy than to popular government. No city was so mean or so ill ordered as not to have a
public council, or a senate. Livy speaks of the senate, not only
of Naples, Capua, and Cuma, but of Nola, Pipernum, Tusculum,
Tivoli, the Veientes, and of others, so frequently, that it is clear
that in all the republics there was an order distinct from the plebeians, who retained in their hands the essence of the government. But the plebeians, once become obstinate, at the solicitation of the nobility, in a hatred of tyranny, had not far to go
before they opened their eyes upon their own condition, and
learned that they had done nothing more than exchange one
master for many; and they began to make every exertion to
obtain, in fact, the possession of that liberty, of which they had,
until then, obtained a taste in words, from the order of patricians
and the senate. As the multitude began to make trial of their
strength, the sovereign authority was ceded to them by little and
little, and the nobility, in their turn, were tormented and tyrannized by the plebeians. Livy observes, that, about the time of
the Carthaginian war, by a kind of epidemical malady spread

through the Italian republics, the plebeians applied themselves to persecute the nobility. Nevertheless, the order of the grandees always preserved a great part of the power; for the nature of popular government being variable, inconstant, and incapable of conducting itself, the senate and the nobility, who act with more maturity of deliberation, and with interests more united, can generally counterpoise the party of the plebeians, and from time to time overcome it. From whence it happened, that all the cities were exposed to continual revolutions of government, and very rarely enjoyed that perfect equality, which is the end of a free state; but either the favor of the people, or the necessity of the senate, devolved the principal authority on some individual, who, with or without the title of supreme magistrate, was always regarded as the head of the government. Thus we find a Manilius, head of the Latins; an Accius Tullius, principal of the Volsci; a Herennius, of the Samnites; a Calavius, of the Campanians; a Valerius, a Camillus, and a Fabius, chiefs of the Romans. And, to speak the truth, there was never any great and important success in any free state, either at home or abroad, except in those times when some one citizen held the will of the public in his own power."

But, waving the rest of these general observations for the present, let us descend to particulars, and, quitting the ancient republics of Italy, descend to those of the middle age, among which Florence is the most illustrious. As the history of that noble city and magnanimous people has been written by two authors, among a multitude of others, who may be compared to any of the historians of Greece or Rome, we have here an example more fully delineated, an experiment more perfectly made and more accurately described, than any we have examined before. We shall not, therefore, find it tedious to consider minutely the affairs of a brave and enlightened people, to whom the world is indebted for a Machiavel, a Guicciardini, and an Americus Vespucius; in a great degree for the resurrection of letters, and a second civilization of mankind. Next to Athens and Rome, there has not existed a more interesting city. The history is full of lessons of wisdom, extremely to our purpose.

We have all along contended, that the predominant passion of all men in power, whether kings, nobles, or plebeians, is the same; that tyranny will be the effect, whoever are the governors, whether the one, the few, or the many, if uncontrolled by equal laws, made by common consent, and supported, protected, and enforced by three different orders of men *in equilibrio*. In Florence, where the administration was, by turns, in the nobles, the grandees, the commons, the plebeians, the mob, the ruling passion of each was the same; and the government of each immediately degenerated into a tyranny so insupportable as to produce a fresh revolution. We have all along contended, that a simple government, in a single assembly, whether aristocratical or democratical, must of necessity divide into two parties, each of which will be headed by some one illustrious family, and will proceed from debate and controversy to sedition and war. In Florence, the first dissension was among the nobility; the second between the nobles and commons; and the third between the commons and plebeians. In each of which contests, as soon as one party got uppermost, it split into two; and executions, confiscations, banishments, assassinations, and dispersions of families, were the fruit of every division, even with more atrocious aggravations than in those of Greece. Having no third order to appeal to for decision, no contest could be decided but by the sword.

It will enable us the better to understand Machiavel, whose history will be abridged and commented on, if we premise from Nardi,* that "the city of Florence had, like all other cities, its people consisting of three genera of inhabitants, that is to say, the nobility, the people of property,† and the common people. Although some too diligently divided the nobility into three sorts, calling the first, nobles, the second, grandees, and the third, families; meaning to signify, that some of the inhabitants had come into the city and become citizens, having been deprived of their own proper country by conquest, while they were attempting to enlarge and extend their territories; others, originally of this country, had become abundant in riches and powerful in dependents, either by their own industry or the favor of fortune; and others, having been foreigners, had come in like manner to inhabit the city, but, from their primitive condition, they still retained the distinctions of lord and vassal, by habit and by fraud, both in the city and the country. And all this mixture were indifferently called nobles, grandees, and families; and they were

* *Le Istorie della Città di Firenze*, p. 1.
† Il popolo grasso, e il popolo minuto.

equally hated, contradicted, and opposed, in the government of the republic, and in all their other actions, by that party which was called the substantial people, *il popolo grasso.* The lower class of people, the plebeians, *il popolo minuto*, never intervened in government at all, excepting on one single occasion, when, with violence, they usurped it, as in its proper place will be related. Some persons made still another division of the plebeians, and not without reason; for those who possessed real estate in the city or country, and were recorded in the public books of taxes and tributes of the city, and were called the Enregistered,* esteemed themselves, and were considered by their fellow-citizens, as holding a middle station. The remainder of the lower class, who possessed no kind of property, were held of no account. Nevertheless, all this undistinguished aggregate were called the people of Florence; and the expression is still in use, as the people of Athens, or the people of Rome, anciently comprehended the whole body of the inhabitants of those cities; to which confused, and, in its nature, pernicious aggregate, as that of the head and tail always is, the body of middling citizens will always remain extremely useful, and proportioned to the constitution of a perfect republic."

As Machiavel is the most favorable to a popular government, and is even suspected of sometimes disguising the truth to conceal or mollify its defects, the substance of this sketch will be taken from him, referring at the same time to other authors; so that those young Americans who wish to be masters of the subject, may be at no loss for information.

" The most useful erudition for republicans is that [1] which exposes the causes of discord; by which they may learn wisdom and unanimity from the examples of others. The factions in Florence are the most remarkable of any. Most other commonwealths have been divided into two; that city was distracted into many. In Rome, the contest between patricians and plebeians, which arose after the expulsion of kings, continued to the dissolution of the republic. The same happened in Athens, and all the other commonwealths of Greece, Italy, and Asia Minor.

‡ Descritti.

[1] *Istorie Fiorentine di Nic. Macchiavelli, Proemio dell' Autore.* The substance of this work is here given by the author, who now and then translates a passage literally, when he desires to comment on it.

Such was the patriotism or good fortune of Florence, that she seems to have gathered fresh vigor, and risen stronger for her factions. Some, who escaped in the struggles, contributed more by their courage and constancy to the exaltation of themselves and their country, than the malignity of faction had done to distress them. And if such orders and balances had been established in their form of government as would have kept the citizens united after they had shaken off the yoke of the empire, it might have equalled any republic, ancient or modern, in military power and the arts of peace."

" The city of Florence[1] was begun by the inhabitants of Fiesole, who, situated on the top of a hill, marked out a plot of ground upon the plain between the hill and the river Arno, for the conveniency of merchants, who first built stores there for their goods. When the Romans had secured Italy by the destruction of Carthage, this place multiplied exceedingly, and became a city by the name of Villa Arnina. Sylla was the first, and, after him, the three Roman citizens who revenged the death and divided the empire of Cæsar, who sent colonies to Fiesole, that settled in the plain, not far from the town already begun; and the place became so full of buildings and inhabitants, and such provisions were made for a civil government, that it might well be reckoned among the cities of Italy.

" Whence it took the name of Florence is not so well known. Tacitus calls the town Florentia, and the people Florentines. It was founded under the Roman empire; but when that was overrun by barbarians, Totila, King of the Ostrogoths, took and demolished it. Two hundred and fifty years afterwards, it was rebuilt by Charlemagne, from whose time, till 1215, it followed the fortune of those who successively ruled in Italy; for, during that period, it was governed first by the posterity of Charlemagne, then by the Berengarii, and last of all by the German emperors. In 1010 the Florentines took and destroyed Fiesole. When the popes assumed greater authority in Italy, and the power of the German emperors was upon the wane, all the towns of that province began to govern themselves. In 1080 Italy was divided between Henry III. and the church. Until 1215, the Florentines always submitted to the strongest, having no other ambition

[1] Lib. ii.

than to preserve themselves. But as, in our bodies, the later diseases come, the more dangerous they are, so, the longer Florence put off taking a part in the troubles of Italy, the more fatal these proved.

" The cause of its first division is well known. The most powerful families in Florence, in 1215, were the Buondelmonti and the Uberti, and next to them the Amidei and Donati. A quarrel happened about a lady, and Messer Buondelmonte was killed. This murder divided the whole city, one part of it siding with the Buondelmonti, and the other with the Uberti; and as both of the families were powerful in alliances, castles, and adherents, the quarrel continued many years, till the reign of the Emperor Frederick II., who, being likewise King of Naples, and desirous to strengthen himself against the church, and establish his interest more securely in Tuscany, joined the Uberti, who by his assistance drove the Buondelmonti out of Florence; and thus that city became divided, as all the rest of Italy was before, into the two factions of Guelphs and Ghibellines.* The Guelphs, thus driven out of the city, retired into the valley, which lies higher up the Arno, where their strong places and dependencies lay, and defended themselves as well as they could; but when Frederick died, the neutral people in the city

* The former of which denominated the adherents of the pope, and the latter those of the emperor; Guelph being the name of the general of the first army for the church in this controversy, and Ghibelline that of the place of birth of the general who commanded for the emperor, about 1139.

Danina, *Rivoluzioni d'Italia.* "There flourished in Germany two principal families, the one called the Henries of Ghibilinga, and the other the Guelphs of Altdorp, which, by the marriage of Azzo d'Este with Cunegund, daughter of Guelph III., engrafted itself into the house of Este, called afterwards, for that reason, Guelfa Estense, from which are descended the Dukes of Modena, and those of Brunswick and Hanover. From the first of which families, namely, the Ghibellines, have arisen many kings and emperors, as the third, fourth, and fifth Henry. Of the other, namely, the Guelphs, there had been for many years famous dukes, who, contending for power and for credit with the emperors, had very often disturbed the tranquillity of the state. Under the reign of Henry V. these two families happily united in alliance, because Frederic, Duke of Suabia, married Judith, daughter of Henry, Duke of Bavaria, and sister of Guelph VI., who was at that time the head of the house of Altdorp."

Commentari de' fatti civili occorsi dentro Firenze. Scritto dal Senatore Filippo de Nerli, p. 2.

Historia Fiorentina di M. Piero Buoninsegni, Gentilhuomo Fiorentino, p. 35.

Annali d'Italia, da Muratori, tom. vii. pp. 150, 151, anno 1215.

Istoria civile del Regno di Napoli di Pietro Giannone, tom. iii. p. 83.

Muratori, *Dissertazioni,* tom. iii. p. 130.

Muratori, *Antichità Estensi,* parte prima, c. xxxi. p. 305.

endeavored to reunite it, and prevailed upon the Guelphs to forget the wrongs they had suffered, and return, and the Ghibellines to dismiss their jealousies, and receive them.

After they were reunited, they divided the city into six parts, and chose twelve citizens, two to govern each ward, with the title of Anziani, but to be changed every year. To prevent any feuds or discontents that might arise from the determination of judicial matters, they constituted two judges that were not Florentines, one of whom was styled the captain of the people, and the other the podestà, to administer justice to the people, in all causes civil and criminal; and since laws are but of little authority and short duration, where there is not sufficient power to support and enforce them, they raised twenty bands or companies in the city, and seventy-six more in the rest of their territories, in which all the youth were enlisted, and obliged to be ready armed under their respective colors, whenever they were required so to be by the captain or the anziani. Their standard-bearers were changed every year with great formality."

This is the very short description of their constitution. The twelve anziani appear to have had the legislative and executive authority, and to have been annually eligible — a form of government as near that of M. Turgot, and Marchmont Nedham, as any to be found; — yet the judicial power is here separated, and the people could so little trust themselves or the anziani with this power, that it was given to foreigners.

" By such discipline in their civil and military affairs, the Florentines laid the foundation of their liberty; and it is hardly to be conceived, how much strength and authority they acquired in a very short time; for their city not only became the capital of Tuscany, but was reckoned among the principal in Italy; and, indeed, there is no degree of grandeur to which it might not have attained, *if it had not been obstructed by new and frequent factions.*"

After this pompous preamble, one can scarce read without smiling the words that follow: " For the space of ten years they lived under this form of government;" especially when it appears that, during all these ten years, they were constantly employed in wars abroad, as appears by the following words: " During which time they forced the states of Pistoia, Arezzo, and Siena, to enter into a confederacy with them; and in their return with their army from the last city, they took Volterra, demolished several castles, and brought the inhabitants to Florence."

The United States of America calculated their governments for a duration of more than ten years. There is little doubt to be made, that they might have existed under the government of state congresses for ten years, while they were constantly at war, and all the active and idle were in council or in arms; but we have seen, that a state which could be governed by a provincial congress, and, indeed, that could carry on a war without any government at all, while danger pressed, has lately, in time of profound peace, and under a good government, broke out in seditions.[1]

This democratical government in Florence could last no longer; "For in all these expeditions," says Machiavel, "the Guelphs had the chief direction and command, as they were much more popular than the Ghibellines, who had behaved themselves so imperiously in the reign of Frederick, when they had the upper hand, that they were become very odious to the people; and because the party of the church was generally thought to favor their attempts to preserve their liberty, whilst that of the emperor endeavored to deprive them of it.

" The Ghibellines, in the mean time, finding their authority so dwindled, were not a little discontented, and only waited for a proper opportunity to seize upon the government again. They entered into correspondence with Manfred, the son of Frederick, King of Naples, in hopes of his assistance; but, for want of due secrecy in these practices, they were discovered by the anziani, who thereupon summoned the family of the Uberti to appear before them; but, instead of obeying, they took up arms, and fortified themselves in their houses; at which the people were so incensed, that they likewise ran to arms, and, by the help of the Guelphs, obliged the whole party of the Ghibellines to quit Florence, and transport themselves to Siena. There they sued to Manfred for aid, who granted it; and the Guelphs were defeated upon the banks of the river Arbia, with such slaughter, by the king's forces under the conduct of Farinata de gli Uberti, that those who escaped from it, giving up their city for lost, fled directly to Lucca. Manfred had given the command of the

---

[1] This alludes to the state of things existing in Massachusetts in 1786, and to the insurrection of Shays and others.

auxiliaries, which he sent to the Ghibellines, to Count Giordano, a soldier of no small reputation in those times. This Giordano, after his victory, immediately advanced with the Ghibellines to Florence, and not only forced the city to acknowledge Manfred for its sovereign, but deposed the magistrates, and either entirely abrogated or altered all laws and customs that might look like remains of their former liberty; which being executed with great rigor and insolence, inflamed the people to such a degree, that if they did not love the Ghibellines before, they now became their inveterate and implacable enemies; which aversion continually increasing, at last proved their utter destruction."

There is an admirable example of patriotism at this period of the Florentine history, in Farinata Uberti, who successfully and decidedly opposed a plan of his own party of Ghibellines and their allies, for the demolition of the city. He preserved it, however, only for his enemies the Guelphs, who, driven out of Lucca, went to Parma, and joined their friends the Guelphs in that city, drove out the Ghibellines, and had their confiscated estates for their reward. They then joined the pope against Manfred, who was defeated and slain.

" In consequence of this victory, the Guelphs of Florence grew daily bolder and more vigorous, and the party of the Ghibellines weaker and weaker; upon which Count Guido Novello, and those that were left in commission with him to govern Florence, resolved to try, by lenity and gentler treatment, to recover the affections of the people, whom they found they had exasperated to the last degree by their oppressive and violent manner of proceeding. To cajole and ingratiate themselves with the people, they chose six-and-thirty citizens out of the people of Florence, and two gentlemen of higher rank from among their friends at Bologna, to whom they gave a commission to reform the state. These delegates divided the city into distinct arts or trades, over which they constituted a magistrate, who was to administer justice to all who were in his department; and to every art a separate banner was assigned, under which they might assemble in arms, whenever the safety of the public required it.

" But Count Guido must have a tax to maintain his soldiers. The citizens would not pay it. He attempted to take back the new privilege of magistrates to each trade. The people rose in arms, chose Giovanni Soldanieri for their leader, fought the Count and his Ghibellines, and drove them out of the city. The people, having thus got the upper hand, resolved to unite the city, if possible, and recall all such citizens as had been forced to leave their homes, whether Guelphs or Ghibellines. The Guelphs returned, after six years' banishment; the late attempt of the Ghibellines was pardoned, and they were suffered to come back again; but they still continued very odious both to the Guelphs and the people, the former not being able to forgive the disgrace and hardships of their long exile, nor the latter to forget their insolence and tyranny when they had the government in their hands; so that their ancient animosities were not yet entirely extinguished, either on one side or the other."

The wrangle soon came to a crisis, and the Ghibellines fled out of the city, upon the interposition of a foreign force from Charles, King of Naples, in favor of the Guelphs.

"After the departure of the Ghibellines, the Florentines new-modelled their government, and chose twelve principal magistrates, who were to continue in authority no longer than two months, under the title of buoni homini. Next in power under them they appointed a council of eighty citizens, which they called the Credenza. After this, a hundred and eighty more were elected out of the people, thirty to serve for each sixth, who, together with the credenza and the twelve buoni homini, were called the General Council. Besides which, they instituted another council, consisting of a hundred and twenty members, equally chosen out of the nobility, citizens, and commonalty, which was to confirm whatsoever had been resolved upon by the others, and to act jointly with them in disposing of the public honors and offices of the commonwealth."

The first government of the anziani was as near a simple democracy as there is any example of; we found it, accordingly, ineffectual. The next, of buoni homini, was no better; and that could not support itself. Now we come to a new plan, which discovers, in the authors of it, a sense of the imperfection of the former two, and an attempt to obviate its inconveniences and dangers; but instead of a judicious plan, founded in the natural divisions of the people, it is a jumble which common sense would see, at this day, must fall to pieces. The buoni homini, the credenza, and the thirty of the hundred and eighty, wore an appearance of three orders; but, instead of being kept

B

separate, they are all huddled together in the general council. Another council still, of a hundred and twenty, equally chosen out of the nobility, citizens, and commonalty, was to confirm whatever was resolved on by the others. Here are two branches, with each a negative. But the mistake was, that the aristocratical and democratical parts of the community were mixed in each of them; which shows, at first blush, that there never could be harmony in either, both being naturally and necessarily split into two factions. But a greater defect, if possible, than even this, was giving the executive power, the power of disposing of public honors and offices, to a joint assemblage of buoni homini, credenza, and the two other assemblies, all in one. The consequence must be, that although every one of these four orders must be divided at once into factions for the loaves and fishes, yet the nobility, by their superior influence in elections, would have the whole power.

Unhappy Florence! thou art destined from this moment to never-ending factions, seditions, and civil wars! Accordingly, we read in the next page, what any one might have foreseen from this sketch of their constitution, " that the government of Florence was fallen into great disorder and misrule; for the Guelph nobility, being the majority, were grown so insolent, and stood in so little awe of the magistracy," (and how could they stand in awe of magistrates whom they had created, and who were ever at their devotion?) " that though many murders, and other violences, were daily committed, yet the criminals generally escaped with impunity, through favor of one or other of the nobles."

" In order to restrain these enormities, instead of twelve governors, they resolved to have fourteen, seven of each party, who should be nominated by the pope, and remain in office one year. Under this form of government, in which they had been obliged in reality to submit to a foreign master, they continued for two years, when the rage of faction again blazed out. They rose in arms, and put the city under a new regulation. This was in 1282, when the companies of arts and trades ordained, that instead of fourteen citizens, three only should govern, and that for two months, who were to be chosen indifferently out of the nobility or commons, provided they were merchants, or professed any art or occupation; and these were called priori. Afterwards, the chief magistracy was vested in six persons, one for each ward, under which regulation the city continued till the year 1342." [1]

But the course of events for these sixty years should be carefully traced, in order to see the operation of such a form of government, even in a single city. This institution, as might be expected, occasioned the ruin of the nobility, who, upon divers provocations, were excluded, and entirely suppressed by the people. The nobility, indeed, were divided among themselves; and by endeavoring to supplant each other, and aspiring to the sole government of the commonwealth, they quite lost all share in it. The priori were afterwards distinguished by the name of signori.

" There remained some sparks of animosity betwixt the nobility and commonalty, which are incident to all republics; for one side being naturally jealous of any encroachment upon their liberty and legal rights, and the other ambitious to rule and control the laws, it is not possible they should ever long agree together. This humor, however, did not show itself in the nobility while they were overawed by the Ghibellines; but when the latter were depressed, it began to appear, and the people were daily injured and abused in such a manner, that neither the laws nor the magistracy had authority enough to relieve them; as every nobleman supported himself in his insolence by the number of his friends and relations, both against the power of the signori

---

[1] " Ce fut l'an 1282 que les Florentins établirent la forme de gouvernement qu'ils ont conservée jusqu'à la chute de leur république, et qui, supprimée par Alexandre de Médicis, le 27 Avril, 1532, fut rétablie par Pierre Léopold, à la fin du siècle passé, et n'est pas même absolument détruite aujourd'hui. Je veux parler des prieurs des arts et de la liberté, dont le collège fut appelé la *seigneurie*. Depuis la paix intérieure, conclue par le cardinal Latino, Florence étoit gouvernée par quatorze prud'hommes, dont huit Guelfes et six Gibelins; mais l'état paroissoit souffrir de ce que le pouvoir exécutif étoit confié à un conseil trop nombreux pour pouvoir jamais être unanime; à un conseil qui, par sa composition même, avoit en soi les principes de la discorde, et où l'esprit de parti donnoit une place. La jalousie du peuple contre les grands nuisoit aussi à ce collège, dont plusieurs membres étoient gentilshommes; on ne cessoit de répéter que dans une république marchande, personne ne devoit avoir part à l'administration si lui-même il n'étoit marchand. Les Florentins, en effet, au milieu de Juin, 1282, instituèrent une nouvelle magistrature toute démocratique; ils en nommèrent les membres, prieurs des arts, comme pour indiquer que l'assemblée des premiers citoyens de chaque métier devoit représenter toute la république. A la première élection, on ne crut pas devoir admettre tous les métiers indifféremment à la prérogative de donner des chefs à l'état. On se borna d'abord aux trois arts que l'on regarda comme les plus nobles; mais dès la seconde élection, c'est-à-dire deux mois après, on doubla le nombre des prieurs, pour qu'il y en eût un de chacun des arts majeurs, et en même temps de chacun des six quartiers de la ville." Sismondi, *Hist. des Républiques Italiennes,* vol. iv. p. 52.

and the captain of the people. The heads of the arts, wishing
to remedy so great an evil, provided that every signory should
appoint a standard-bearer of justice, out of the people, with a
thousand men divided into twenty companies, under him, who
should be always ready with their standard and arms whenever
ordered by the magistracy. This establishment met little opposition, on account of the jealousy and emulation that reigned
among the nobility, who were not in the least aware that it was
levelled at them, till they felt the smart of it. Then, indeed, they
were not a little awed by it for some time; but in a while they
returned to the commission of their former outrages; for as some
of them always found means to insinuate themselves into the
signory, they had it in their power to prevent the standard-bearer
from executing his office. Besides, as witnesses were always
required upon any accusation, the plaintiff could hardly ever find
any one that durst give evidence against the nobility; so that in
a short time Florence was involved in its former distractions, and
the people exposed to violence and oppression; as justice was
grown dilatory, and sentence, though passed, seldom or never
executed.

"The people not knowing what course to take, Giano della
Bella, a strenuous patriot, though of a very noble family, encouraged the heads of the arts once more to reform the city. By his
advice it was enacted, that the gonfalonier should always reside
with the signori, and have four thousand armed men under his
command. They also entirely excluded the nobility out of that
council of the signori, and made a law that all accessaries or
abettors should be liable to the same punishment with those that
were principals in any crime, and that common fame should be
sufficient evidence to convict them. By these laws, which were
called Li Ordinamenti della Giustizia,"[1] (but which were in reality

[1] " Pour le maintien de la liberté et de la justice, elle sanctionna la jurispru-
dence la plus tyrannique et la plus injuste. Trente-sept familles, les plus nobles
et les plus respectables de Florence, furent exclues à jamais du priorat, sans qu'il
leur fût permis de recouvrer les droits de cité, en se faisant immatriculer dans
quelque corps de métier, ou en exerçant quelque profession. Cette exclusion fut
fondée sur la faveur que les nobles, disoit on, accordoient toujours aux autres
nobles ; c'étoit eux qu'on accusoit d'avoir paralysé la seigneurie, et l'on préten-
doit que jamais elle n'avoit déployé de vigueur, lorsque quelque gentilhomme
siégoit parmi les prieurs. La seigneurie fut de plus autorisée à insérer de nou-
veaux noms dans cette liste d'exclusion, toutes les fois que quelque autre famille,
en marchant sur les traces de la noblesse, mériteroit d'être punie comme elle.
Les membres de ces trente-sept familles furent désignés, même dans les lois, par

as tyrannical as the edicts of any despot could be,) "the people regained great weight and authority. But Giano being looked upon by the nobility as the author of these laws to bridle their power, became very odious, not only to them, but to the richest of the commonalty."

As well he might, for laws more oppressive and destructive of liberty could not have been made. Tyrannical as they were, however, they were not enough so for the people. "For upon the trial of Corso Donati, a nobleman, for a murder, although he was acquitted even under these new laws, the people were enraged, and ran to arms, and demolished the magistrate's house, instead of applying to the signori. The whole city exceedingly resented this outrage upon all law and government; the blame of it was laid upon Giano, and he was accused before the magistrates as an encourager of insurrection. While his cause was depending, the people took arms to defend him against the signori. Giano went voluntarily into banishment, to appease this tumult.

" The nobility then petitioned the signori, that the severity of the laws against them might be mitigated. As soon as this petition was publicly known, the commons, apprehending the signori would comply with it, immediately rose in a tumultuous manner; so that ambition on one side, and jealousy on the other, at last occasioned an open rupture between them, and both sides were prepared for battle ; but by the interposition and mediation of some prudent men, whose arguments with both parties were very judicious, the people at last consented that no accusation should be admitted against a nobleman, without sufficient evidence to support it.

" Both parties laid down their arms, but retained their jealousies, and began soon to raise forces, and fortify themselves as fast as they could. The people thought fit to new-model the government, and reduce the number of the signori, as they suspected some of that body to be too favorably inclined to the nobility.

"A momentary tranquillity succeeded ; but the sparks of jealousy and envy still remained betwixt the nobility and people,

les noms de grands et de magnats; et pour la première fois, on vit un titre d'honneur devenir non-seulement un fardeau onéreux, mais une punition." Sismondi, *Républiques Italiennes*, vol. iv. pp. 63, 64.

which soon broke out, on occasion of a quarrel between two
families, the Cerchi and Donati, both considerable for their riches,
nobility, and dependents.   The signori were under no small
apprehensions that the whole city would become engaged in the
dispute, and hourly expected the two parties would openly attack
each other, as soon afterwards happened, and a skirmish ensued,
in which many were wounded on both sides.   The whole city,
commons as well as nobility, divided upon it; nor did the contagion confine itself to the city alone, but infected all the country.
So ineffectual was this contemptible government of the signori
to the suppression of this animosity, that the pope was applied
to.   He sent his nuncio to no purpose, and then put the city
under an interdict; but this answered no end but to increase the
confusion; and frequent battles took place, till the whole city
took arms, neither the power of the magistracy, nor the authority
of the laws, being able to restrain the fury of the multitude.
The wisest and best of the citizens were in great terror; and the
Donati, being the weaker party, not a little doubtful of their
safety."

Such is the effect of a government of all authority in one
centre.   Here all was concentrated in the signori, chosen by the
people frequently enough; yet although the nobility were arbitrarily excluded from that council, those who were chosen were
indebted for their elections, probably to those very nobles, and
chiefly to the Donati and Cerchi.

"The Donati were the minority, upon the whole, and therefore had great reason to be doubtful of their safety.   It was
agreed, at a meeting betwixt Corso Donati, the heads of the
Neri family, and the captains of the arts,[1] to solicit the pope

[1] This is an error in translation by the author, growing out of a misconception
of the office referred to.   The words in the original are " Capitani *di parte.*"
" They were the elective heads of the Guelph party, three in number." *Italian
Republics* — Lardner's *Cabinet Cyclopædia*, p. 135, note.
  Lord Brougham describes them as the heads of "a complete party government within the government of the state.   The Guelphs chose every two months
their consuls, called *party captains,* who had their secret council of fourteen
members. their general council of sixty, three priors, a treasurer. and a prose-
cutor of Ghibellines.   There never certainly was an instance of any party feud
being in any country so disciplined and so wielded.   The vigorous administration, not only of its own affairs, but those of the republic which it governed,
was the result.   Had the Jacobin club at Paris been a more regular body, and
continued to govern in quiet times, it would have formed a second instance of
the same sort." *Political Philosophy,* part 2, p. 346.
  It is not difficult to perceive the elements of an organization in many respects

to send some person of royal extraction to reform the city." Here nature breaks out, in spite of all attempts to stifle it. A royal dignity is the most obvious thought, to extinguish animosities between nobles and commons. In this case, the captains of the arts, that is, the people, perceived it, as well as Corso and the Neri, the contending nobles. This meeting, and the result of it, was notified to the signori by the other party, who represented it as a conspiracy against the public liberty. Both sides, however, were in arms again, and Dante, who was one of the signori, had the courage to advise that sovereign assembly to arm the people; and they, being joined by great numbers out of the country, found themselves able to force the chiefs of each party to lay down their arms. They assumed an appearance of dignity, banished Corso and the Neri, and, to show their impartiality, several of the Bianchi.

"But this government had no permanent strength; the Bianchi, upon plausible pretences, were soon permitted to return. Corso, and his associates, obtained the same indulgence; but, instead of being quiet, they went to Rome, to persuade the pope to appoint a person of royal extraction, as they had before petitioned his holiness in their letters. Charles of Valois, brother of the King of France, was sent accordingly by the pope. Though the Bianchi family, who then had the upper hand in Florence, looked upon him with an evil eye; yet as he was patron of the Guelphs, and sent by the pope, they durst not oppose his coming; on the contrary, to make him their friend, they gave him full power to regulate the city as he thought best. He caused his friends to arm themselves. This made the people so jealous that he intended to deprive them of what they called their liberties, that they took arms.

"The Cerchi, and the heads of the Bianchi, having had the chief government of the city some time in their hands, and behaved with great arrogance, were become generally odious; which encouraged Corso, and others of the Neri who had fled, to return upon an assurance that Charles and the captains of the party were their friends, and would support them. Accordingly, whilst the city was thus alarmed with the apprehensions of

not unlike this, at some time or other, in the United States, the concentration of which has been thus far counteracted only by the increasing territorial surface of the country.

Charles's designs, Corso, with all his associates, and many other of their followers, made their entry into it without resistance; and though Véri de Cerchi was called upon to oppose them, he declined it, and said, ' The people against whom they came, should themselves chastise them, as they were likely to be the greatest sufferers by them.' But the contrary happened; for instead of chastising them, they received them with open arms, whilst Véri was forced to fly for his safety. Corso having forced his entrance at the Porta Pinti, drew up and made a stand near his own house; and being joined by a great number of his friends and others, assembled in hopes of a change of government, he released all prisoners, civil and criminal; divested the signori of their authority; chose new magistrates, all of the party of the Neri, out of the people, to supply their places; and plundered the houses of the Bianchi. The Cerchi, and the heads of their faction, seeing the people, for the most part, their enemies, and Charles not their friend, fled out of the city, and in their turn implored the interposition of the pope, though they would not listen to his exhortations before."

Such is the series of alternate tragedy, comedy, and farce, which was called the liberty of Florence during this "collection of all authority into one centre," the signori; in which no man of any party could be one moment secure of his life, property, or liberty, amidst continual exaltations and depressions of parties, in favor of different noble families. Although those nobles were all excluded from the government, the exclusion was but a form. Nearly all the power was in their hands, and the signori in office were only alternate tools of one noble family or another. And thus it must ever be; exclude the aristocratical part of the community by laws as tyrannical as you will, they will still govern the state underhand; the persons elected into office will be their tools, and, in constant fear of them, will behave like mere puppets danced upon their wires. But our humorous entertainment is not yet ended.

" The pope now, at the intercession of the Cerchi, sent a legate, Acqua-Sparta, to Florence, who made an accommodation betwixt the Cerchi and Donati, and fortified it by several intermarriages between them. But this spiritual policy, though deep and sound, did not answer his end; for when he insisted that the Bianchi should share in the chief offices of the commonwealth, that was refused by the Neri, who were in full possession of them. Upon this the legate left the city as dissatisfied as ever, and excommunicated it a second time for its contumacy.

" The Neri, however, seeing their old enemies in their bosom again, were not a little afraid they would use all means to ruin them in order to recover their former authority ; and both parties were still discontented, and fresh occasions of discord soon occurred. Niccolo de Cerchi and Simon, a son of Corso Donati, met and fought. The battle was so sharp and bloody that Niccolo was killed upon the spot, and Simon so desperately wounded that he died the same night."

This accident, as it is called, though an event springing necessarily from the form of government and state of parties, threw the whole city into an uproar again ; " and although the Neri were the most in fault, as Simon assaulted Niccolo, yet they were screened by the magistracy, and, before judgment could be obtained, a conspiracy was discovered betwixt the Bianchi and Pietro Ferrante, a nobleman who attended Charles of Valois, with whom they had been tampering, to persuade his master to reinstate them in the government. The plot was detected by some letters from the Cerchi to Pietro; though it was the common opinion they were forged by the Donati, to wipe off the odium they had incurred by the murder of Niccolo de Cerchi. Nevertheless all the family of the Cerchi, with many of their followers of the Bianchi party, and among the rest Dante the poet,* were immediately sent into banishment, their estates confiscated and their houses demolished by the strength of those forged letters ; after which, their party, with many of the Ghibellines who had joined them, were dispersed in different places.

" The quiet that ensued was very short; for Corso Donati was dissatisfied that he did not enjoy the degree of authority in Florence he thought due to his merit, the government being in the hands of the people, and conducted by those who were in all respects much inferior to him. To varnish over his designs and revenge with a fair pretext, he accused several citizens who had been entrusted with public money with embezzling it, and many were ignorant and credulous enough to believe that Corso

* 1298. Nerli. p. 9.

did this out of pure concern and affection for his country. The persons thus calumniated were in favor with the people, and stood upon their justification; and after many law suits and long litigations, these disputes grew to such a height that it became absolutely necessary to take up arms. On one side were Corso and Lottieri, Bishop of Florence, with many of the nobility and some of the commons; on the other were the signori and the greater part of the people; nothing was to be seen but affrays and skirmishes in every part of the city."

In such a "right constitution" as this, such a government of "the people's successive sovereign assemblies," as the signori were, the body of the nation never can be unanimous; all the most wealthy, best-born, best-educated, and ablest men, will unanimously despise and detest the government, except a few artful hypocrites among them, who will belie their judgments and feelings for the sake of a present popularity for some private ends. Those who thus hate the form of government will have numerous connections, relations, and dependents among the people, who will follow them; so that there never can be more than a small majority of the people on the side of government. Hence its constant weakness; hence it is a mere football continually kicked from one side to another by three or four principal families. Thus it appeared in this case.

"The signori, feeling their weakness, and perceiving themselves in great danger, utterly unable to punish crimes, support their friends, or curb their enemies, were obliged to send to Lucca, a foreign state, for aid, and were fortunate enough to find all the people of that city willing to come to their assistance. The tumults were composed for a time, but the signori and people were too feeble to punish the author of the disturbance."

This interval of tranquillity was no more durable than former ones.

"The pope again sent his legate, Niccolo da Prato,* who ingratiated himself with the people, so that they gave him a commission to new-model the city. In order to obtain the recall of the Ghibelline faction from banishment, he flattered the people by restoring their ancient companies, which added much

* 1303. Nerli, p. 9.

to their strength and diminished that of the nobility. But the project of restoring the exiles was obnoxious to the signori, who forced the legate out of the city, which he put under an interdict at his departure, and left in the utmost confusion.

" Two factions not being sufficient, the city was now divided and subdivided into several; as those of the people and nobility, the Guelphs and Ghibellines, the Bianchi and the Neri; and some who wished for the return of the exiles, being disappointed in their hopes, now the legate was gone, grew clamorous and outrageous, so that the whole city was in an uproar, and many skirmishes ensued. Those that were most active in raising this clamor were the Medici and Giugni, who had openly sided with the legate in favor of the exiles."

This is the first mention made of that family of Medici, who acted so distinguished a part afterwards, finally subverted the commonwealth, and changed it into an absolute sovereignty under the title of a grand dukedom, a form it still wears.

Let us look back to 1282, when this government of priori or signori, chosen every two months by the people, was established ; from thence to 1304 is only twenty-two years, in which we see a constant quarrel between the nobility and people, and between one party of nobles and another, and the neighboring states of Naples, Rome, and Lucca, in turn, called in to aid the different factions ; alternate murders, banishments, confiscations, and civil wars, as one party and the other prevailed ; and, instead of a government and a system of justice and liberty, constant anarchy, and the perpetual rolling of a mob.

In this year, 1304, Florence was visited in this lamentable manner with fire and sword. A great fire broke out, and was ascribed, as usual in such times, by some to accident, and by some to party design. Corso Donati was the only person of any distinction who did not take up arms; he thought that when all parties grew tired of fighting he was the more likely to be called in arbitrator to decide their differences. They did indeed lay down their arms, but more out of weariness of their miseries, and that they might have time to take breath, than from any real desire of being reunited and living in peace. It was only stipulated that the exiles should not be suffered to return, which was agreed to by those that favored them, merely because they proved to be the weaker side.

" New disturbances arising, the pope was advised by his legate to summon to Rome twelve of the principal malcontents of Florence. They readily obeyed the summons, and among them was Corso Donati. As soon as they were set out upon their journey, the legate acquainted the exiles that now was their time to return to Florence, as the city was then clear of the only men that had authority enough to oppose their entrance. Drawing together what forces they could, they immediately marched and entered the city ; but those very citizens, who but a little before, when they petitioned in the most humble and submissive manner to be admitted, had exerted themselves in the most strenuous manner for their return, now they saw them approach in a hostile manner, were the first that took up arms against them, and joined with the people to drive them back."

One is, however, astonished at the reflection of Machiavel, — " Such was the spirit of patriotism amongst them in those days that they cheerfully gave up their private interests for the public good," — when every page of his history shows that the public good was sacrificed every day by all parties to their private interests, friendships, and enmities.

" After the exiles were repulsed, the citizens relapsed into their former distractions ; and after much violence the governors of the commonwealth reëstablished the companies of the people, and restored the colors under which the arts had formerly been used to assemble. Their captains were called standard-bearers of the companies and colleagues of the signori, and were directed not only to assist the signori in times of peace with their counsel, but to support and defend them by dint of arms in all exigencies and commotions. To assist the two judges who had been constituted in the beginning of their state, they appointed an officer called *il esecutore* or sheriff, who was to act in conjunction with the standard-bearers and see their orders carried into execution, whenever the nobility should be guilty of any enormity or act of oppression.

" The pope died, the eleven citizens returned with Corso, whose restless ambition occasioned such troubles. In order to make himself popular, he constantly opposed the nobility in all their schemes, and which way soever he observed the people to incline, he turned all his authority to support them in it and gain their affection ; so that in all contests and divisions, or when they had any extraordinary point to carry, they always resorted to him and put themselves under his directions."

Machiavel indeed observes, " that all might now have lived in peace, if the restless ambition of Corso had not occasioned fresh troubles." But in this Machiavel is mistaken ; if Corso had not existed, the people would have found some other leader and confidant. When the people feel that the government is unable or unwilling to protect them against the oppressions of the nobles, they always seek out a Cassius, Mælius, Manlius, or Corso, to assist the old or to erect a new government that will be able and willing to protect them. It is the defect in the government and the wants of the people, that excite and inspirit the ambition of private men. To be sure, the man of any distinction who listens to the complaints of the people in such cases, whether from ambition or humanity, always creates for himself much hatred and envy among the most considerable citizens.

" In this instance, these passions increased to such a degree that the faction of the Neri divided and quarrelled among themselves. To alienate the affections of the people from Corso, they gave out, as the aristocracy always does in such cases, that he secretly designed to seize upon the government and make himself king; and his magnificent manner of living, and marriage into the family of Faggivola, head of the Bianchi and Ghibellines, made it easily believed.

" Encouraged by this, his enemies took up arms against him, and the greater part of the people, instead of appearing in his defence, forsook him and joined his adversaries. He was impeached, refused to obey the summons, and was declared a contumacious rebel. Between the accusation and the sentence there was not the interval of more than two hours. A civil war ensued ; many were killed on both sides. After a furious defence Corso threw himself from his horse and was killed. Such was the unfortunate end * of Corso Donati, to whom his country and the Neri owed much both of their good and bad fortune, one of the most eminent men that Florence ever produced."

But Machiavel should have laid the blame upon the constitution, not upon the restless disposition or turbulent spirit of

* Nerli, p. 9.

3 *

Corso; because it is impossible for a man of Corso's genius, valor, and activity, in such a government, not to be restless and turbulent; he is never safe himself, and large bodies of people are continually flattering and soliciting him, while others are threatening and persecuting him. No nation has a right to blame such a citizen until it has established a form of government that is capable of protecting him on one side, and the people against him on the other. This flimsy sovereignty of the signori was inadequate to either purpose.

After the death of Corso the exiles from Florence excited Henry * the emperor to a war against that city for their restoration; the magistrates applied to Robert, King of Naples, and gave him the government of the city for five years to defend it and protect them. This storm, after raging some time, blew over by the death of the emperor.† The Ghibellines then, under the command of Faggivola, renewed the war by making themselves masters of Pisa and committing depredations on the Florentine territories. The Florentines fought him and were totally defeated. They then applied to King Robert ‡ for another general; he sent them the Count di Andria, whose bad conduct, " added," says Machiavel, " to the impatient temper of the Florentines, which is soon tired with any form of government, and ready to fall into factions upon every accident," occasioned the city to divide again. Machiavel's severity ought, however, to have been applied to the form of government, not to the temper of the people, the latter being but the natural and necessary effect of the former. In such a government the people have no protection or security; they are continually oppressed, vexed, and irritated by one faction or another, one ally or enemy, or another, one aspiring citizen or family, or another, against whose usurpations, as the constitution affords no redress, they are obliged to recur to arms and a change of government.

" The Florentines in this case sought assistance from France and Germany, but could obtain none; they were determined, however, to carry their point, took arms, drove the Count out of the city, and sent for one Lando, of Agobbio, and made him their *esecutore*, or rather dictator or executioner, § with full

---

* Nerli, p. 10.   † Nerli, p. 10.
‡ Nerli, p. 10. Muratori, Annal. tom. viii. p. 40.
§ Nerli, p. 10. " *Bargello*," sheriff or executive officer of the law. Machia-

)ower over all the citizens. Lando being naturally rapacious and cruel went about the city with a gang of armed men at his heels, hanging up one man and then another, as those who had sent for him gave him directions; and at last to such a height of power did he arrive by the dissensions of the citizens, as to coin bad money with the Florentine stamp, which nobody had courage enough to oppose. Miserable indeed was the condition of the city at that time, which neither the bitter remembrance of the evils produced by their former dissensions, nor the dread of a foreign enemy at their gates, nor the authority of a king, was sufficient to keep united, even though their possessions were daily ravaged and plundered abroad by Faggivola, and at home by Lando.

" The nobility, most of the considerable commons, and all the Guelphs took the king's side, and opposed Lando and those who supported him; and to free themselves from so ignominious a yoke they wrote to King Robert privately, and entreated him to appoint Count Guido his lieutenant at Florence, which he readily complied with; and the other party, though they had the signori on their side, durst not venture to oppose a man of so established a reputation. But the Count soon found he had very little authority in the city, as the magistracy and the standard-bearers of the several companies openly favored Lando and his friends. Soon afterwards the citizens were reconciled and united under the king by the friendly counsel of his daughter-in-law, and Lando, deprived of his authority, was sent back to Agobbio satiated with blood and rapine.* The government of the King of Naples was continued three years longer; and, as the seven who were then in the signori were all of Lando's party, six others were added to them of the king's, and they continued thirteen for some time, but were afterwards reduced to seven again.

" About this time Castruccio Castracani † drove out Faggivola, and succeeded him in the government of Lucca and Pisa. The Florentines had enough to do to obstruct the growth of the power of this spirited and fortunate youth at the head of the

vel here introduces a characteristic of popular governments, which the author has omitted to express: " Cercando d'uno per adorarlo," " seeking after some one to worship, they sent," &c.
* Nerli, p. 11. † Ibid.

Ghibelline interest, and to defend themselves against him.
That the signori in this war might proceed with maturer
deliberation and execute with greater authority, they chose
twelve citizens whom they called *buoni homini*, without whose
advice and consent the signori were not to pass any act of
importance.   But this effort of nature to form a balance to this
simple government was of short duration; the dominion of
King Robert expired, and the government once more reverted to
the citizens, who set up the same form of magistracy that had
been formerly instituted.   The whole city was soon obliged to
march against Castruccio to the relief of Prato, and a proclamation was issued by the signori, that every exile of the Guelph
party who came in to the relief of Prato should afterwards have
liberty to return home.   This policy added four thousand men
to their army, which before consisted of twenty thousand foot
and fifteen hundred horse.   Castruccio, afraid of so formidable
a force, retreated to Lucca.   Upon this retreat great disputes
arose in the Florentine camp between the nobility and the people, about pursuing Castruccio; these disputes were referred to
the signory, which, consisting at this time of commoners as well
as of nobility, was also divided in opinion.   Upon this the people rose in a tumult and forced the signory to give way to them;
but it was now too late to follow Castruccio, and the people
were so exasperated that they would not suffer the public faith
to be kept with the exiles.   The nobility having some regard
to their honor, though the people had not, took the part of the
exiles, which produced another civil war.

" As it generally happens in all commonwealths, that after
any revolution or remarkable crisis [1] some or other of the old
laws are abrogated and new ones made in their room, so, though
the signori at first were changed every two months, yet the magistrates who were now in office, having great power, took upon
themselves to constitute a signory out of all the most considerable citizens, to continue forty months.   Their names were
to be put into a bag or purse, which was called imborsation,[2]
and a certain number of them drawn out by lot at the end of
every second month; whereas before, when the old magistrates
went out of office, new ones were always chosen by the council.

---

[1] " Dopo uno accidente."   [2] " Squittino " or polling.

As the council consisted only of the most considerable citizens, the government was before but a self-created or at least self-continued aristocracy. Now it was equally so, with this difference only, that lot was substituted in the room of choice. As the lot was not to be now renewed till after a term of above three years, it was thought they had extinguished the causes of all such disgusts and tumults as used to happen from the frequent return of elections and the number of competitors for the magistracy, not being aware how little advantage and how many mischiefs were likely to flow from it.[3]

In 1325, in a war with Castruccio, the Florentines were betrayed by their general, Raymondo. This man saw that the Florentines had been so liberal in disposing of themselves, that they had sometimes conferred their government upon kings, sometimes upon legates, and sometimes upon persons of much inferior quality; he thought, if he 'could reduce them to any extremity, they, perhaps, would make him their prince; he was very importunate with them to give him the same command in the city, that he had over their army, as he pretended he could not otherwise either require or expect that necessary obedience which was due to a general. Not being gratified, he trifled and delayed, till he was attacked and defeated with great slaughter and the loss of his own life; receiving that punishment from the hands of fortune, which his ambition and perfidy had merited from the Florentines.

"The havoc, the depredations, imprisonments, burnings, and every other kind of devastation made by Castruccio upon the Florentines after this victory, forced them to offer their government to Charles, Duke of Calabria,* son of King Robert, upon condition that he would defend them; for as that family had been used to rule over them, they chose rather to shelter themselves under him as their prince, than to trust him as an ally. But Charles, being engaged in the wars of Sicily, sent Gaultier, a Frenchman, and Duke of Athens, as his lieutenant, who new-

---

3 " La nouvelle manière de procéder aux élections, parut plus démocratique que la précédente ; elle établissoit une plus grande égalité entre les candidats. et elle appeloit un plus grand nombre de citoyens aux honneurs publics. Ce dernier avantage fut même sans doute celui qui séduisit le peuple ; il flatta la jalousie secrète des hommes médiocres, qui voyoient avec dépit un petit nombre de sujets distingués, toujours désignés par les suffrages du public." Sismondi, Rép. Italiennes.
* Nerli, p. 12.

modelled the magistracy as he thought fit. His behavior at first was, in appearance, so modest and temperate, that he gained the affections of every one.

" Charles then came in person with a thousand horse, and his presence gave some check to Castruccio, and prevented him from roving and plundering the country as he had done ; but if the citizens saved any thing abroad, it was lost again at home ; and when their enemies were curbed, they became a prey to the insolence and oppression of their friends. As the signori were entirely under the influence of the Duke of Athens, he exacted four hundred thousand florins from the city in one year, though it was expressly stipulated in the agreement made with him, that he should not raise above two hundred thousand in the whole ; besides which, either Charles or his father was continually laying some heavy tax or other upon the citizens. These miseries were still increased by new jealousies, fresh enemies, and more extensive wars, in which all the neighboring powers were involved, till suddenly Castruccio, and Charles, Duke of Calabria and Lord of Florence, both died. The Florentines, unexpectedly delivered from the oppression of one, and dread of the other, and having once more recovered their liberty, began to reform the commonwealth. They abrogated the ordinances of all former councils, and created two new ones, one of which consisted of three hundred of the commons, and the other of two hundred and fifty of both commoners and nobility ; the former was called the council of the people, and the latter the common council."

After the death of Castruccio, till the year 1340, the Florentines continued wholly intent upon their affairs and wars abroad.

" In that year new disturbances arose at home. The governors of the city had two ways of maintaining and increasing their authority ; one was, by managing the imborsations in such a manner as always to secure the signory either to themselves or their creatures ; the other, by getting judges chosen who they knew would be favorable to them in their sentences."

And how is it possible, in any simple government, to prevent such management to draw all the legislative, executive, and judicial power into one centre, and that centre a junto of aristocratics? But in this case, —

" Not content with two judges, the governors sometimes constituted a third, whom they called captain of the guards; with which office they now vested Jacopo d'Agobbio, and gave him an absolute power over the citizens. This Jacopo, under the direction of the governors, behaved with the most shameless insolence and partiality, daily injuring or affronting somebody or other. Some, who were nobly born, and men of high spirit, were provoked to such a degree, that a stranger should be introduced into the city by a few of their fellow-citizens who had the power in their hands, on purpose to insult and abuse all the rest, that they entered into a conspiracy with many other noble families, and some of the commoners, that were disgusted at so tyrannical a government, to revenge themselves; hence a conspiracy, that again involved the city in blood. By artifice and force together, the signori prevailed, and suppressed the conspiracy, beheading some, and proclaiming several other families rebels.*

" However, it did not satiate the revenge of those in adminis- tration, to have conquered and suppressed those families; but, like almost all other men, whose insolence commonly increases with their power, they grew more imperious and arbitrary as they grew stronger; for though they had only one captain of the guards to tyrannize over the city before, they now appointed another to reside in the country, and vested him with very great authority; so that any one who was in the least obnoxious to government could not live quietly, either within the city or with- out it. The nobility, in particular, were daily abused and insulted by them in such a manner, that they only waited for an opportu- nity to revenge themselves at any rate; and as one soon happened, they did not fail to take advantage of it. The Florentines had purchased Lucca; but, defeated in securing the possession of it, they carried on a war to recover it. After a long struggle, they were driven out of it, with much dishonor, and the loss of all their purchase-money. This disaster, as it usually happens in like cases, threw the people of Florence into such a rage against their governors, that they publicly insulted and upbraided them with their ill conduct and administration, in all places, and upon every opportunity.

" In the beginning of the war, the management of it had been committed to twenty citizens, who appointed Malatesta de Rimini

* Nerli. p. 14.

commander-in-chief of their forces in that expedition; but as he
executed that charge with little courage and less discretion, they
solicited Robert, King of Naples, for supplies, which he accordingly sent them, under the command of Gaultier, Duke of Athens,
who, as the evil destiny of the city would have it, arrived there
just when the enterprise against Lucca had miscarried.

"The Duke arrived at this time;* and the governors, being in
great fear of the multitude, made him conservator of the peace
and commander-in-chief, that he might have both authority
and power enough to defend them.[1] Imagining there was no
other way left to get the better of the people, who had so long
domineered over them, than to reduce them into subjection to a
prince, who, being well acquainted with the worth and generosity
of the nobility, and the insolence of the commons, might treat
both parties according to their deserts, the nobility now resolved
to take their revenge, even though it should occasion the destruction of the city. They had many private meetings to persuade
the Duke to take the government wholly into his hands, and promised to support him with all their interest and power. Several
of the most considerable commoners joined them, particularly the
families of the Peruzzi, Acciaivoli, Antellesi, and Buonaccorsi.
Such encouragement, and so fair an opportunity, inflamed the
Duke, who was naturally ambitious, with a still greater thirst of
power; and, in order to ingratiate himself with the lower sort of
people, by acting like a just and upright magistrate, he ordered a
process to be commenced against those that had been entrusted
with the management of the late war against the Lucchese; in consequence of which, Giovanni de'Medici and two more were put to
death, several others banished, and many obliged to pay large sums
of money for their pardon. This severe manner of proceeding
alarmed the middle sort of citizens, though it was very grateful
to the nobility and common people, as the latter generally delight
in evil, and the former were not a little rejoiced at the fall of
those by whom they had been so grievously oppressed; so that,
whenever the Duke passed through the streets, they resounded

---

* Nerli, p. 15.
[1] Some of the historians assign a different motive for this movement. It
was designed by the governing party to smother, under the appointment of a
more oppressive ruler, any disposition to scrutinize their own peculations and
venality. If so, they were the first victims to the shrewdness of their own policy,
for he established himself by exposing and punishing them.

with acclamations and praises of his justice and resolution, while every one exhorted him to persevere in his endeavors to detect the guilty, and to bring them to condign punishment.

"Notwithstanding the expostulations of the signori, in an assembly of all the people, the government was given to the Duke for life, and he was carried about in a chair, amidst the acclamations of the multitude; the standard of the city was torn to pieces, and the Duke's planted in its stead, at which all the good citizens were infinitely grieved and mortified, whilst those who, either out of malice or stupidity, had consented to this election, did not a little rejoice."

Machiavel's next task is to give us a detail of the Duke's tyrannical behavior, which was as wild, cruel, and mad as all other tyrannies have been which were created on the ruins of a republic. The Duke perceived the general odium he had incurred, but affected to think himself extremely beloved. He was informed of a plot against him, in which the family of the Medici, and others, were concerned; but he ordered the informer to be put to death. He cut out the tongue of Bettoni for complaining of heavy taxes, &c. His outrages were sufficient to rouse the Florentines, "who neither knew how to value their liberty nor to endure slavery," says Machiavel. But the truth is, they had no liberty to value, and nothing but slavery to endure; their constitution was no protection of right; their laws never governed. They were slaves to every freak and passion, every party and faction, every aspiring or disappointed noble; sometimes to the pope, sometimes to the King of Naples, sometimes to Lando; sometimes to one nobleman, sometimes to another; sometimes to their own signori, and sometimes to their captains of arts. If the word *republic* must be used to signify every government in which more than one man has a share, it is true this must be called by that name; but a republic and a free government may be different things.

There were now three conspiracies on foot against the Duke at once; but each conspiracy was a new system of tyranny, and aimed only at introducing one system instead of another, instead of any concert, or reasonable combination, to take down a bad government and set up a good one. The three natural divisions of society formed three different plots to set up a new tyranny, each in its own way: the nobility had one plot, the commons another, and the artificers a third. What ideas of the rights of mankind must these people have entertained! The commons had been deprived of the government, and they had no idea that the nobility or artisans had any rights; the nobility were not restored to the government, which was all they wanted; and the artisans had lost their business; but none of these orders could communicate with the others. Assassination of the Duke seems to have been all the object in view, as if that would remedy all the evils. The plots, however, were too freely communicated, and at last were told to the Duke.

In 1343 the city was all in a tumult, and "liberty, liberty!" was the cry. A war was carried on in the city, and each party changed sides several times; but, after long distractions, and much bloodshed and devastation, the Duke was blocked up in the palace, and the citizens assembled to reform the government.

Fourteen persons, one half of them of the nobility, and the other commoners, with the archbishop, had full power given them to new-model the state. The judicial department was committed to six magistrates, who were to administer justice till the arrival of the person who should be chosen to fill that office. " Greater, certainly," says Machiavel, " and more cruel, is the resentment of the people when they have recovered their liberty, than when they are acting in defence of it; and an instance of brutal ferocity happened here that is a disgrace to human nature. The people insisted upon some persons being delivered up to them, and among them a father and son; when these were brought out and delivered up to thousands of their enemies; and though the son was not eighteen, yet neither his youth or innocence, nor the gracefulness of his person, was sufficient to protect him from the rage of the multitude. Many who could not get near enough to reach them whilst they were alive, thrust their swords into them after they were dead; and not content with this, they tore their carcasses to pieces with their nails and teeth, that so all their senses might be glutted with revenge; and after they had feasted their ears with their groans, their eyes with their wounds, and their touch with tearing the flesh off their bones, as if all this was not enough, the taste likewise must have its share and be gratified." [1]

[1] It is but just to add that this was Guglielmo da Scesi, the most odious of the

This is Machiavel's description of this savage barbarity; and his words are here preserved, that it may be seen and considered that human nature is the same in a mob as upon a throne, and that unbridled passions are at least as brutal and diabolical, and unlimited power as tyrannical, in a mob, as in a monarch or senate; they are worse, for there is always a number among them who are under less restraints of shame and decency.

" When the people were thus satiated with blood, the Duke and his friends were suffered to withdraw with their effects unmolested out of Florence. After some disputes between the nobility and people, it was agreed that one third of the signori, and one half of the other magistrates and other officers of state, should consist of the nobility. The city was divided into six parts, each of which chose one of the signori; and though it sometimes happened that their number was increased to twelve or thirteen, yet they were afterwards again reduced to six. But as these six parts were not duly proportioned, and they designed to give more power and authority to the nobility, it was necessary to make a new regulation in this point, and to increase the number of signori. They divided the city, therefore, into quarters, and chose three of the signori out of each. The standard-bearer of justice, and those of the several companies, were laid aside; and instead of the twelve buoni homini, they created eight counsellors, four of each quality.

" The commonwealth," says Machiavel, " being settled upon this bottom, might have continued quiet and happy, if the nobility could have been content to confine themselves within the bounds of that moderation which is requisite in all republican governments."

It is impossible to read these grave reflections of Machiavel and Nedham, so often repeated, with patience. It would be as wise to say, that the nation might be quiet and happy under a despot or monarch, if the despot or monarch, and his ministers and minions, could be content and moderate; or that the commonwealth might be happy under an oligarchy or simple aris-

Duke's instruments of tyranny, and the judge who had lent himself to all his acts of cruelty. The son was scarcely fourteen years old, but he had made himself detested by the interest manifested in the execution of the harsh sentences against offenders. The example of the powerful is seldom copied with more clearness by those whom they oppress, than in the indulgence of their vindictiveness whenever it comes their turn.

tocracy, if all concerned in government could be content and moderate. When we know human nature to be utterly incapable of this content, why should we suppose it? Human nature is querulous and discontented wherever it appears, and almost all the happiness it is capable of arises from this discontented humor. It is action, not rest, that constitutes our pleasure. All we have to do is to guard and provide against this quality ; we cannot eradicate it.

"But the behavior of the nobility was quite the contrary," says Machiavel ; "for, as they always disdained the thoughts of equality, even when they lived a private life, so, now they were in the magistracy, they thought to domineer over the whole city, and every day produced fresh instances of their pride and arrogance, which exceedingly galled the people, when they saw they had deposed one tyrant, only to make room for a thousand."

All this, one may safely believe to be exactly true ; but what then? Why, they ought to have separated the nobles from the commons, and made each independent on the other. Mixed together in equal halves, the nobles will forever tyrannize. The insolence of one side, and the indignation and impatience of the other, at last increased to such a height, that both sides flew to arms, and the people, being most numerous, carried their point, and deprived the nobles in the signory of their authority ; the four counsellors of their order were also turned out of their offices, and the remaining number increased to twelve, which consisted of commoners only. Besides which, the eight who remained in the signory not only made a new standard-bearer of justice, and sixteen other standard-bearers over the companies of the people, but modelled all the councils in such a manner, that the government was now entirely in the hands of the people ; and we shall soon see how well it operated.

"There happened a great dearth in Florence, so that there were grievous discontents both among the nobility and common people ; the former repining at the loss of their authority, and the latter murmuring for want of bread. Andrea Strozzi sold corn as cheap as Mælius did in Rome. This drew such numbers to his house that he boldly mounted his horse one morning, and putting himself at the head of them, called upon all the rest of the people to take up arms, by which means he got together above four thousand men in less than an hour, and conducting them to the palace of the signori, demanded the doors to be thrown open to him. This attempt was too bold and rash to succeed; yet it gave the nobility fresh hopes of recovering their power, now they saw *the inferior sort of people* so incensed *against the commons.* They resolved to take arms and make use of all manner of allies to regain that by force which they conceived had been taken from them with so much injustice; and to insure success they provided themselves with arms, fortified their houses, and sent to their friends in Lombardy for supplies. The commons and the signori, on the other hand, were no less busy in arming themselves, and sent to the Sienese and Perugians to desire their assistance; so that when the auxiliaries on each side arrived, the whole city was soon in arms."

We ought to pause here and remark a combination of parties that is perfectly natural, though it has seldom occurred in the history of any nation so distinctly as to be descanted on by historians or politicians. Here is as distinct a division between the commons and the lower class as there ever was between nobles and commons. By the commons in this place are meant those citizens who in every nation of the world are commonly denominated *the middling people*, who, it must be confessed, have been in all ages and countries the most industrious and frugal, and every way the most virtuous part of the community. In all countries they have some influence, in many they have had some share in the government; but no other instance than this is at present recollected where they have ever had a sovereignty in their hands, exclusive both of the highest and lowest classes of citizens. As if it had been the intention of Providence to exhibit to mankind a demonstration that power has the same effects upon all minds, we find in this instance the Florentine commons discovering the same disposition to tyrannize over all above and all below them, as clearly as ever kings, nobles, or mobs discovered it when they had the power. The nobility drew up in three divisions. The commons assembled under the standard of justice and the colors of their respective companies, and under the command of the Medici immediately attacked one of the divisions of the nobility. At this time the Medici were only commoners; we shall hereafter see that they became nobles and sovereigns, and placed sons and daughters on some of the thrones of Europe. The action was hot and bloody for three

4 *

hours, during which they had great stones tumbled down upon their heads from the tops of the houses and were terribly galled with cross-bows below. All parties behaved with an obstinate bravery that would have done honor to any good cause; but it is unnecessary to relate all the attacks and defences and all the vicissitudes of fortune in the course of the civil war; the numbers of the commoners finally prevailed, "upon which," says Machiavel, "the people, especially the inferior sort of them, naturally rapacious and greedy of spoil, began to plunder the houses of the nobility, which they afterwards burnt down to the ground, and committed such other outrages as the bitterest enemy to the city of Florence would have been ashamed of."

"The nobility being in this manner entirely subdued, the people took upon them to reform the state; and as there were three degrees of them, it was ordained that the highest rank should have the nomination of two of the signori, the middle sort of three, and the lowest of three more, and that the standard-bearer of justice should be chosen by turns out of all three. The old laws were revived and put in execution against the nobility; and to reduce them still more effectually many of them were incorporated with the other classes.* By these means they were brought so low that they became abject and pusillanimous, and never durst rise any more against the people; so that being deprived of their arms and honors, their spirit and generosity likewise seemed to be extinguished. After this depression of the nobles, the plague, of which above ninety-six thousand people died in Florence, and a war with the Visconti, kept the city in tranquillity for a time. But the war being ended, new factions sprung up in the city; for though the nobility were ruined, fortune found other means to raise fresh troubles and dissensions.

"The bitter animosities † which generally happen between the people and nobility, from an ambition in the one to command and a reluctance in the other to obey, are the natural sources of those calamities that are incident to commonwealths; for all other evils that usually disturb their peace are both occasioned and fomented by this contrariety of dispositions. It was this that kept Rome so long divided. This also gave birth to

---

* Nerli, p. 18. Molti avviliti si fanno popolani. † Lib. III.

the factions that sprung up in Florence, though indeed it produced at last very different effects in the two cities; for the
division that first arose between the nobility and people of
Rome terminated with disputes; that at Florence only with the
sword. In Rome that was effected by a law, which in Florence
could hardly be done by the banishment and death of numbers
of its citizens. The quarrels of the Romans still added to their
spirit and military virtue, while those of the Florentines utterly
extinguished them. The former destroyed that equality which
was at first established, and introduced a prodigious disparity
among the citizens; the latter, on the contrary, abolished all superiority or difference of rank, and put every man upon the same
level. This diversity of effects must certainly have proceeded
from a difference of views. The people of Rome desired no
more than to share with the nobility in the administration of
the commonwealth; but the people of Florence were not only
desirous to have the government of the state to themselves, but
used violent measures and took up arms to exclude their nobles
from any part in it; and as the desires of the Roman people
were more moderate, their demands seemed not unreasonable to
the nobility, who therefore complied with them; so that after
some little bickerings and without coming to an open rupture, a
law was made by which the people were satisfied, at least for a
time, and the nobles continued in their honors and offices. On
the other hand, the demands of the Florentine people were so
extravagant and injurious that the nobility took up arms to support their privileges, and their quarrels grew to such a height
that numbers were either banished or slain before they could be
ended; and the laws afterwards made were calculated rather
for the advantage of the victors than the common good.

" The success of the people of Rome made that state more
powerful; for as they were admitted to govern the commonwealth and to command their armies and provinces equally with
the nobility, they became inspired with the same virtue and
magnanimity; and as the city through them grew more public-
spirited, its power also increased. But in Florence, when the
people had subdued the nobility, they divested them of all manner of authority, and left them no possibility of recovering any
part of it except they would entirely conform to their customs
and way of living, and not only submit to appear, but to be

commoners like themselves. And this was the reason that induced them to change their arms, and vary their titles and the names of their families, which was so frequent in those times among the nobility, in order to insinuate themselves into the affections of the people; so that the military spirit and greatness of soul for which the nobility had been held in such veneration, were utterly extinguished, and not by any means to be raised in the people where there were no seeds of it; by which means Florence became every day more abject and pusillanimous. And whereas Rome at last grew so powerful and wanton by the effect of its virtue that it could not be governed otherwise than by one prince, Florence was reduced so low that a wise legislator might easily have modelled it and given it what form he pleased."

The factions between the nobility and the commons, which ended in the utter ruin of the former, have been already related; but peace was not obtained. All authority was in one centre, the commons; and there were other orders of citizens who were not satisfied; the same contest therefore continued under a new form and new names. They now happened between the commons and plebeians, which were only new names in reality for a new nobility and commons; the commons now took the place of the nobility, and the plebeians that of the commons. Machiavel is as clear and full for a mixed government as any writer; but the noble invention of the negative of an executive upon a legislature in two branches, which is the only remedy in contests between nobles and commons, seems never to have entered his thoughts; and nothing is more entertaining than that mist which is perpetually before eyes so piercing, so capable of looking far through the hearts and deeds of men as his, for want of that thought. "There seemed to be no seeds of future dissensions left in Florence." No seeds! Not one seed had been eradicated; all the seeds that ever existed remained in full vigor. The seeds were in the human heart, and were as ready to shoot in commons and plebeians as they had been in nobles. "But the evil destiny of our city and want of good conduct occasioned a new emulation between the families of the Albizzi and the Ricci,* which produced as fatal divisions as those between the

---

* Erano in que' tempi così fatti gli' Albizzi e i Ricci, due famiglie popolane

Buondelmonti and Uberti, and the other between the Cerchi and Donati had done before."

It was no evil destiny peculiar to Florence ; it is common to every city, nation, village, and club. The evil destiny is in human nature. And if the plebeians had prevailed over the commons as these had done over the nobility, some two plebeian families would have appeared upon the stage with all the emulation of the Albizzi and Ricci, to occasion divisions and dissensions, seditions and rebellions, confiscations and banishments, assassinations, conflagrations, and massacres, and all other such good things as appear forever to recommend a simple government in every form.[1] When it is found in experience, and appears probable in theory, that so simple an invention as a separate executive, with power to defend itself, is a full remedy against the fatal effects of dissensions between nobles and commons, why should we still finally hope that simple governments, or mixtures of two ingredients only, will produce effects which they never did and we know never can ? Why should the people be still deceived with insinuations that those evils arose from the destiny of a particular city, when we know that destiny is common to all mankind ?

"Betwixt the two families of Albizzi and Ricci there was a mortal hatred, each conspiring the destruction of the other in order to engross the sole management of the commonwealth with less difficulty.* However, they had not as yet taken up

intra l' altre di gran reputazione e di molto seguito, per esser di parentado grandissimo, ed erano in ciascheduna di esse uomini grandi e reputati, e che aspiravano molto alli primi gradi del governo, e alla grandezza dello stato loro; e però traendo ad un medesimo segno, era tra loro l' odio, e l' emulazione, ma non già erano venuti a manifesta divisione, nè all' armi, per insino all' anno 1353. Nerli, p. 21.

* E però Uguccione de' Ricci restringendosi, come capo di quella famiglia, con gli suoi consorti, e con i primi capi della loro setta, pensarono di poter privar del governo gli Albizzi, come discesi anticamente d' Arezzo, e però tegnenti del Ghibellino ogni volta, che si ritrovasse una legge, per la quale era prohibito a qualunque disceso di Ghibellino di poter esercitare officio, o magistrato alcuno, la quel legge era disusata, nè piu s'adoperava, nè si mettava in atto, o s'osservava in modo alcuno. Nerli, p. 21.

[1] " Similar revolutions broke out at the same time in the other Italian republics. In every one the same progress was to be distinguished. The party which in all had risen to power, as democratic, no sooner felt themselves in possession of it than they turned towards aristocracy. The leaders of the rising generation presented themselves as hereditary tribunes of the people at the same time that they impugned hereditary rights." Lardner's Cabinet Cyclopædia — History of the Italian Republics, p. 187.

arms or proceeded to open violence on either side, but only thwarted each other in council and the execution of their offices."

A private quarrel happened in the market, and a rumor was instantly spread, nobody knew by whom, that the Ricci were going to attack the Albizzi; and by others it was said that the Albizzi were preparing to fall upon the Ricci. These stories were carried to both parties, and occasioned such an uproar throughout the whole city that the magistrates found it very difficult to keep the two families and their friends from coming to a battle in earnest, though neither side had intended any such thing as was maliciously reported. This disturbance, though accidental, inflamed the former animosities, and determined both sides to strengthen their parties and be upon their guard; and since the citizens were reduced to such a degree of equality by the suppression of the nobility that the magistrates were held in greater reverence than ever they had been before, each family resolved to avail itself rather of public and ordinary means than of private violence."

The intrigues of these two families to supplant each other are very curious; but as the detail of them is long, we shall leave the reader to amuse himself with them at his leisure, and come to a speech made to the signori by an eminent citizen, when affairs were become so critical and dangerous as to alarm all impartial men. " The common disease," says he, " magnificent signors, of the other cities in Italy has invaded ours, and is continually eating deeper and deeper into its vitals. All our towns for want of due restraint have run into extremes, and from liberty degenerated into downright licentiousness, making such laws and instituting such governments as were rather calculated to foment and support factions than maintain freedom. From this source are derived all the defects and disorders we labor under; no friendship or union is to be found among the citizens except betwixt such as are accomplices in some wicked design either against their neighbors or their country. All religion and fear of God are utterly extinguished; promises and oaths are no further binding than they serve to promote some private advantage, and they are resorted to not with any design to observe them, but as necessary means to facilitate the perpetration of fraud, which is even honored and applauded in proportion to its success. From hence it comes to pass that the most wicked and abandoned wretches are admired as able, enterprising men; while the innocent and conscientious are laughed at and despised as fools.

"The young men are indolent and effeminate; the old, lascivious and contemptible; without regard to age or sex every place is full of the most licentious brutality, for which the laws themselves, though good and wholesome, are yet so partially executed that they do not afford any remedy. This is the real cause of that selfish spirit which now so generally prevails, and of that ambition, not for true glory, but for places, which dishonors the possessors; hence proceed those fatal animosities, those seeds of envy, revenge, and faction, with their usual attendants, executions, banishments, depression of good men, and exaltation of the wicked.

"The ringleaders of parties varnish over their pernicious designs with some sacred title; for, being in reality enemies to all liberty, they more effectually destroy it by pretending to defend the rights, sometimes of the nobility, sometimes of the commons; since the fruit which they expect from a victory is not the glory of having delivered their country, but the satisfaction of having conquered the opposite party and secured the government of the state to themselves; and when once they have obtained that, there is no sort of cruelty, injustice, or rapine, that they are not guilty of. From thenceforward laws are enacted, not for the common good, but for private ends. War and peace are made, and alliances concluded, not for the honor of the public, but to gratify the humors of particular men. Our laws, our statutes and civil ordinances are made to indulge the caprice or serve the ambition of the conqueror, not to promote the true interest of a free people; so that one faction is no sooner extinguished than another is lighted up.

"A city that endeavors to support itself by parties instead of laws can never be at peace; for when one prevails and is left without opposition, it necessarily divides again. When the Ghibellines were depressed, every one thought the Guelphs would then have lived in peace and security; and yet it was not long before they divided into the factions of the Neri and Bianchi. When the Bianchi were reduced, new commotions arose, sometimes in favor of the exiles, sometimes betwixt the nobility and people; and to give that away to others, which we could not or would not possess quietly ourselves, we first committed our liberties into the hands of King Robert, then of his brother, next of his son, and last of all to the mercy of the Duke of Athens, never settling or reposing under any government, as people that could neither be satisfied with being free nor submit to live in slavery. Nay, so much was our state inclined to division, that rather than acquiesce under the government of a king, it meanly prostituted itself to the tyranny of a vile and pitiful Agobbian. The Duke of Athens was no sooner expelled but we took up arms again, and fought against each other with more rancor and inveteracy than ever, till the ancient nobility were entirely subdued, and lay at the mercy of the people. It was then the general opinion there would be no more factions or troubles in Florence, since those were humbled whose insupportable pride and ambition had been the chief occasion of them; but we now see that pride and ambition, which was thought to be utterly extinguished by the fall of the nobility, now springs up again among *the people*, who begin to be equally impatient for authority, and aspire with the same vehemence to the first offices in the commonwealth.

" It seems the will of Heaven that certain families should spring up in all commonwealths to be the pest and ruin of them. Our city owes its miseries and distractions not merely to one or two, but to several of those families; first to the Buondelmonti and Uberti, next to the Donati and Cerchi, and now, to our shame be it spoken, to the Ricci and Albizzi. Why may not this commonwealth, in spite of former examples to the contrary, not only be united, but reformed and improved by new laws and constitutions? *You must not impute the factions of our ancestors to the nature of the men, but to the iniquity of the times,* which being now altered, afford this city fair hopes of better fortune; and our disorders may be corrected by the institution of wholesome laws, by a prudent restraint of ambition, by prohibiting such customs as tend to nourish and propagate faction, and by substituting others, that may conduce to maintain liberty and good civil government."

This speech, although upon the whole it is excellent, has several essential mistakes. That certain families will spring up in every simple government, and in every injudicious mixture of aristocracy and democracy, to be the pest and ruin of them, is most certain. It is the will of Heaven that the happiness of nations, as well as that of individuals, should depend upon the use of their reason; they must therefore provide for themselves constitutions which will restrain the ambition of families. Without the restraint, the ambition cannot be prevented; nature has planted it in every human heart. The factions of their ancestors ought not to have been imputed to the iniquity of the times, for all times and places are so iniquitous. Those factions grew out of the nature of men under such forms of government; and the new form ought to have been so contrived as to produce a remedy for the evil. This might have been done; for there is a way of making the laws more powerful than any particular persons or families.

"As this advice was conformable to the sentiments of the signori, they appointed fifty-six citizens* to provide for the safety of the commonwealth; but as most people are fitter to preserve good order than to restore it when lost, these citizens took more pains to extinguish the present factions than to provide against new ones, which was the reason that they succeeded in neither; for they not only did not take away the occasion of fresh ones, but made one of those that were then subsisting so much more powerful than the other, that the commonwealth was in great danger.

" They deprived three of the family of Albizzi, and as many of the Ricci, of all share in the magistracy for three years, except in such branches of it as were particularly appropriated to the Guelph party; of which number Piero de gli Albizzi and Uguccione de'Ricci were two. These provisions bore much harder upon the Ricci than the Albizzi; for, though they were equally stigmatized, yet the Ricci were the greatest sufferers. Pietro, indeed, was excluded from the palace of the signori, but he had free admittance into that of the Guelphs, where his authority was very great; and though he and his associates were forward enough in their 'admonitions'[1] before, they became much more

---

* Nerli, p. 22. Fece creare una balia de 56 cittadini.

[1] This word "ammoniti" in the original is used as a technical term, and refers to a practice adopted in Florence for the purpose of excluding the Ghibellines from power. Sismondi explains it thus:

" Lorsque les capitaines de parti auroient, aux deux tiers des suffrages, déclaré Gibelin un citoyen, il leur fut ordonné de l'admonester ou avertir de ne point

forward after this mark of disgrace, and new accidents occurred, which still more inflamed their resentment.

"Gregory XI. was pope at that time; and residing, as his late predecessors had done, at Avignon, he governed Italy by legates, who, being haughty and rapacious, had grievously oppressed several of the cities. One of these legates being then at Bologna, took advantage of a scarcity, and resolved to make himself master of Tuscany. This occasioned the war with the pope.* The Florentines entered into a confederacy with Galeazzo and all the other states that were at variance with the church; after which they appointed eight citizens for the management of it, whom they invested with an absolute power of proceeding, and disbursing money without control or account. This war gave fresh courage to the Ricci, who, in opposition to the Albizzi, had upon all occasions favored Galeazzo and appeared against the church, and especially because all the eight were enemies to the Guelphs; but though they made a vigorous war against the pope, they could not defend themselves against the captains and their adherents. The envy and indignation with which the Guelphs looked upon the eight, made them grow so bold and insolent, that they often affronted and abused them, as well as the rest of the principal citizens. The captains were no less arrogant; they were even more dreaded than the signori, and men went with greater awe and reverence to their houses than to the palace; so that all the ambassadors who came to Florence were instructed to address themselves to them.

"After the death of the pope, the city had no war abroad, but was in great confusion at home; for, on one hand, the Guelphs were become so audacious, that they were no longer supportable; and, on the other, there was no visible way to suppress them; it was necessary, therefore, to take up arms, and leave the event to fortune. On the side of the Guelphs were all the ancient nobility and the greater part of the more powerful citizens; on the other were all the inferior sort of people, headed by the eight, and joined by George Scali, Strozzi, the Ricci, the Alberti, and the

---

accepter d'emploi, sous peine d'être poursuivi. De cette manière, les hommes suspects furent écartés des places, sans être soumis à une peine; mais une classe de mécontens, qu'on appela les *ammoniti* ou *admonestés*, fut exclue, en quelque sorte, des droits de cité." *Hist. des Répub. Italiennes*, vol. vi. p. 326.

* Nerli, p. 23.

Medici. The rest of the multitude, as it almost always happened, joined with the discontented party. The power of their adversaries seemed to the heads of the Guelphs to be formidable, and their danger great, if at any time a signory that was not on their side should attempt to depress them. They found the number of persons who had been 'admonished' was so great, that they had disobliged most of the citizens, and made them their enemies. They thought there was no other remedy, now they had deprived them of their honors, but to banish them out of the city, seize upon the palace of the signori, and put the government of the state wholly into the hands of their own creatures, according to the example of the Guelphs, their predecessors, whose quiet and security were entirely owing to the total expulsion of their enemies.

" But as they differed in opinion about the time of putting their project in execution, the eight, aware of the trick intended, deferred the imborsation, and Sylvestro, the son of Alamanno de' Medici, was appointed gonfalonier.* As he was born of one of the most considerable families of the commoners, he could not bear to see the people oppressed by a few grandees. With Alberti, Strozzi, and Scali, he secretly prepared a decree, by which the laws against the nobility[1] were to be revived, the authority of the captains retrenched, and those who had been admonished admitted into the magistracy. Sylvestro being president, and consequently prince of the city for a time, caused both a college and council to be called the same morning; but his decree was thrown out as an innovation. He went away to the council, and pretended to resign his office, and leave the people to choose another person, who might either have more virtue or better fortune than himself; upon this, such of the council as were in the secret, and others who wished for a

* Nerli, p. 23.
[1] That is, the Albizzi, representing the Guelph, which had become the aristocratic faction.

It was his turn to act as *proposto*, which involved the exclusive privilege of proposing new laws. Upon this singular feature of the government, the historian Sismondi justly remarks, that it was putting fetters upon the legislative power of the people's agents, which made necessary the frequent rotation of the whole, in order to prevent the chance of the authority of one becoming absolute. Neither was this check sufficient. The inability to deal with this reasonable measure in any other way than that of direct acceptance or rejection, no amendment being admissible, led to the successful appeal to the people, and the disorders and revolution that followed.

change, raised a tumult in 1378,* at which the signori and the colleges immediately came together; seeing their gonfalonier retiring, they obliged him, partly by their authority, and partly by their entreaties, to return to the council, which was in great confusion. Many of the principal citizens were threatened, and treated with the utmost insolence; among the rest, Carlo Strozzi was collared by an artificer, and would have been knocked on the head, if some of the bystanders had not rescued him. But the person who made the greatest disturbance was Benedetto de gli Alberti, who got into one of the windows of the palace, and called out to the people to arm; upon which, the piazza was instantly full of armed men, and the colleges were obliged to do that by fear, which they would not come into when they were petitioned.

" But whoever intends to make any alteration in a commonwealth, and to effect it by raising the multitude, will find himself deceived, if he thinks he can stop where he will, and conduct it as he pleases. The design of Sylvestro was to quiet and secure the city, but the thing took a very different turn; for the people were in such a ferment, that the shops were shut up, the houses barricaded, and many removed their goods for security into churches and convents. All the companies of the arts assembled, and each of them appointed a syndic. The signori called the colleges together, and were a whole day in consultation with the syndics, how to compose the disorders to the satisfaction of all parties; but they could not agree. The council, then, to hold out some hopes of satisfaction to the arts and the rest of the people, gave a *full power*, which the Florentines called a balia, to the signori, the colleges, the eight, the captains of the party, and the syndics of the arts, to reform the state. But while they were employed in this, some of the inferior companies of the arts, at the instigation of certain persons, who wanted to revenge the late injuries they had received from the Guelphs, detached themselves from the rest, and went to plundering and burning houses. They broke open the jails, set the prisoners at liberty, and plundered the monasteries and convents.

" The next morning the balia proceeded to requalify the am-

* Muratori, *Annal.* tom. viii. p. 375. Gino Capponi, *del tumulto de' Ciompi*, tom. xviii. Rer. Italic.

moniti, *the admonished,* though with an injunction not to exercise any function in the magistracy for three years; they repealed
such laws as had been made by the Guelphs to the prejudice of
the other citizens, and proclaimed rebels many who had incurred
the hatred of the public; after which the names of the new
signori were published, and Luigi Guicciardini was declared
their gonfalonier.* If those who were admonished, the *ammoniti,*
could have been content, the city was in a fair way of being
quieted; but they thought it hard to wait three years longer,
before they could enjoy any share in the magistracy. The arts
assembled again to obtain satisfaction for them, and demanded
of the signori, that, for the good and quiet of the city, it should
be decreed, that no citizen for the future should be *admonished*
as a Ghibelline, who had ever been one of the signori, or the
college, or the captains of the companies, or the consuls or syndics of any of the arts; and further, that a new imborsation
should be made of the Guelph party, and the old one burnt.
It seldom happens that men who covet the property of others,
and long for revenge, are satisfied with a bare restitution of
their own. Accordingly some, who expected to advance their
fortunes by exciting commotions,† endeavored to persuade the
artificers, that they could never be safe, except many of their
enemies were either banished or cut off."

The city continued in the utmost confusion between the two
new parties of commons and plebeians. But waving a particular detail, the essence of several years' miseries may be collected from two speeches. One is of Luigi Guicciardini, a
standard-bearer to the plebeians: — "The more we grant," says
he, "the more shameless and arrogant are your demands. If we
speak thus to you, we do so, not to offend, but to lead you to
reform; to which end we are willing that others may say to you
what will please, whilst our province remains to say that which
may do you good. Tell us, on your honor, what is there, that
you can reasonably ask more of us? You desired to have the

---

* Nerli, p. 24.

† Fu facile a Salvestro de' Medici, e a gli altri, levato che fu tumulto, vincer
la legge; ma non fu già loro così facile, nè poterano a posta loro fermare il tumulto mosso nel popolo, e nella plebe, che s'era anco sollevata in modo, che da
questo rumore ne segui l'arsione, e il sacco di molte casi. Attese la sfrenata
moltitudine due, o tre giorni a saccheggiare, e ardere quello potette. Nerli,
p. 24.

captains of the party deprived of their authority; they have
been deprived. You insisted that the old imborsation should
be burnt, and a new one made; we consented. You wanted to
have those reinstated in the magistracy, that had been *admonished;* it has been granted. At your intercession we pardoned
such as had been guilty of burning houses, and robbing churches,
and we banished many of our principal citizens at your instigation. To gratify you, the grandees are bridled with new laws,
and every thing done that might give you content; where, then,
can we expect your demands will stop; or how long will you
thus abuse your liberty? Why will ye suffer your own discords
to bring the city into slavery? What else can ye expect from
your divisions? what, from the goods ye have already taken, or
may hereafter take from your fellow-citizens, but servitude and
poverty? The persons you plunder are those whose fortunes
and abilities are the defence of the state, and if they fail, how
must it be supported? Whatever is got that way cannot last
long; and then ye have nothing to look for but remediless
famine and distress."

" These expostulations made some impression, and they promised to be good citizens and obedient; but a fresh tumult soon
arose, more dangerous than the former. The greater part of the
late robberies and other mischiefs, had been committed by the
rabble and dregs of the people; and those of them who had
been the most audacious apprehended, that when the most
material differences were composed, they should be called to an
account for their crimes, and deserted, as it always happens, by
those very persons at whose instigation they had committed
them. Besides which, the inferior sort of people had conceived
a hatred against the richer citizens and principals of the arts,
upon a pretence that they had not been rewarded for their past
services in proportion to what they deserved."

To show how divisions grow wherever human nature is without a check, it is worth while to be particular here. " When the
city was first divided into arts, in the time of Charles I., there
was a proper head or governor appointed over each of them, to
whose jurisdiction, in civil cases, every person in the several arts
was to be subject. These arts or companies, as we have said,
were at first but twelve, but afterwards they were increased to
twenty-one, and arrived at such power and authority, that in a

few years they wholly engrossed the government of the city; and because some were more, and others less honorable among them, they came by degrees to be distinguished, and seven of them were called the greater arts, and fourteen the less. From this division proceeded the arrogance of the captains of the party; for the citizens who had formerly been Guelphs, to which party those offices were always appropriated, had made it a constant rule to favor the greater arts, and to discountenance the less, and all those who sided with them; which chiefly gave occasion to all the tumults we have hitherto made mention of. And as, in the division of the people into arts and corporations, there were many trades in which the meaner sort are usually occupied, that were not incorporated into any distinct or particular company of their own, but admitted into any of the others, as they most approached the nature of their craft, it happened that when they were not duly satisfied for their labor, or any otherwise oppressed by their masters, they had no other head to apply to for redress but the magistrate of that company to which the person belonged that employed them, who, they commonly thought, did not do them justice. Now, of all the companies in the city, that of the clothiers had the most of this sort of people depending upon it; and being more opulent and powerful than any of the rest, it maintained by far the greater part of the multitude. The meaner sort of people, therefore, both of this company and the others, were, for the causes assigned, highly enraged; and being also terrified at the apprehension of being punished for their late outrages, they had frequent meetings in the night; where, considering what had happened, they represented to each other the danger they were in; and to animate and unite them all, one of the boldest and most experienced of them harangued his companions in this manner: —

" ' If it was now to be debated whether we should take arms to plunder and burn the houses of our fellow-citizens and rob the churches, I should be one of those who would think it worthy of great consideration, and perhaps be induced to prefer secure poverty to hazardous gain. But since arms have been already taken up and much mischief done, the first points to be considered are, in what manner we may retain them and ward off the penalties we have incurred. The whole city is full of rage and complaints against us, the citizens are daily in council, and the magistrates frequently assembled. Assure yourselves they are either preparing snares for us or contriving how to raise forces to destroy us. It behoves us, therefore, to have two objects chiefly in view at these consultations, — first, how to avoid the punishment for our late actions; and, in the next place, to devise the means of living in a greater degree of liberty and with more satisfaction for the future than we have done hitherto. To come off with impunity for our past offences, it is necessary to add still more to them, to redouble our outrages, our robberies and burnings, and to do our best to associate numbers for our protection ; for where many are guilty none are chastised. Small crimes are punished, great ones rewarded ; and where many suffer, few seek revenge ; a general calamity being always borne with more patience than a particular one. To multiply evils is the surest way to procure us a pardon for what has been already done, and to obtain the liberty we desire. Nor is there any difficulty to discourage us. The enterprise is easy, and the success not to be doubted. Those who could oppose us are opulent indeed, but divided ; their disunion will give us the victory, and their riches when we have got them will maintain it. Let not the antiquity of their blood, nor the meanness of our own, with which they so insolently upbraid us, frighten you. All families, having the same original, are of equal antiquity, and have been made by nature after one fashion. Let both sides be stripped naked, and both will be found alike. Clothe yourselves in their robes and them in your rags, and then you will appear the nobles and they the plebeians ; for it is poverty alone that makes the real difference betwixt us. It fills me with just concern, indeed, to hear that some of you repent, forsooth, of what you have done, and out of a qualm of conscience resolve to proceed no farther ; certainly, if this be true, you are not the men I took you for. Neither conscience nor the fear of infamy ought to terrify you ; for those who succeed in their attempts, let them have used what means soever, are never disgraced ; and as for conscience, we have no reason to give ourselves any trouble about it. Where the dread of famine and dungeons enters, as in our case, what greater terror can or should there be in hell ?' "

The speech is long, and all in the same strain. It so inflamed his audience that they determined to rise, and took an oath to stand by each other. The signori had secret information of the plot, but although they took the best measures in their power, the government had not sufficient energy to prevent or suppress the tumult. They burnt many houses and committed all sorts of outrages. If any one of the plebeians had been injured or affronted by a particular citizen, he led the mob directly to his enemy's house; nay, it was sufficient barely to mention the person's name, or to call out *"to such a man's house,"* or *" to such a man's shop."* They glutted themselves with mischief, and then, to crown all, they knighted sixty-four citizens, among whom was their favorite Sylvestro de' Medici. Their levity was very curious, for they conferred the honor of knighthood upon some of those very persons whose houses they had burnt down but a few hours before. Such is the caprice of the multitude, and so soon are their disgusts changed into favor and affection!

The behavior of the signori and the council of the people was such as might be expected from men conscious of having neither dignity nor authority derived from the laws. Before a law could be passed, it was necessary it should have the assent of the common council as well as of the signori. It was contrary to established custom for two councils to be held on the same day; so that when the signori had agreed, it was necessary to wait till next day for the common council to deliberate upon the demands of the mob. These demands were extremely grievous and dishonorable to the government; one of them in particular, that no person that was incorporated into the arts should be compelled to pay any debt under the sum of fifty ducats in two years, at which time the principal only should be paid to the creditor and the interest into the bank. Yet the signori had agreed to them, and the common council were the next morning deliberating; the multitude, naturally voluble and impatient, got together again under the palace. The law passed; but the destruction of the city was not the less expected. The signori and counsellors left the palace one by one, and the people entered it.

Hæc natura multitudinis est; aut servit humiliter, aut superbe dominatur. When the people entered the palace, Michael di Lando, a wool-comber, a bare-footed, ragged fellow, carried the standard of justice before them. " You see, my friends," said

Michael, "this palace is yours, and the city is in your hands; what would you have done now?" They unanimously cried out that he should be their chief magistrate and govern the city as he pleased. Michael, a shrewd fellow, more obliged to nature than fortune, accepted the government, with a design, however, to compose the city. To amuse the people, he sent them to search for one Nuto, the hangman,[1] and immediately issued a proclamation that nobody should dare to burn or plunder any man's house for the future; and to enforce the observance of it, he ordered a gibbet to be erected in the great piazza. The mob soon brought Master Nuto into the piazza and hung him up by one leg upon the gibbet; and as every one tore away a joint or a piece of his flesh, in two or three minutes there was nothing left of him but the foot by which he hung.

"Michael gallantly new-modelled the state, appointed new signori, and gave the rents of all the shops upon the Old Bridge to Sylvestro de' Medici; took a good share to himself,[2] and was very liberal to many other citizens who had befriended the plebeians, not only out of gratitude for past favors, but to engage them to support him in future against envy. But the plebeians thought Michael had been too partial to some of the principal commoners, flew to arms again, appointed eight heads over them, with other subordinate officers and magistrates; so that the city had now two tribunals, and was governed by two distinct administrations. They took away all honors and emoluments that had been granted to Sylvestro de' Medici and to Michael di Lando."

But Michael showed himself, in valor, generosity, and prudence, far superior to any other citizen, and well deserves to be reckoned among those few that have been real benefactors to their country. If he had been of an ambitious or self-interested disposition, the republic must have relapsed into a more intolerable degree of servitude than it was under the tyranny of the Duke of Athens; but his integrity would not suffer him to cherish any design that might be prejudicial to the good of the public, and his prudence taught him to conduct himself in such a manner as not only gained him the first place and confidence of his own party, but enabled him to triumph over that of his

---

[1] "*Bargello*," sheriff. [2] "*La podesteria d' Empoli.*"

enemies. He suppressed this new rebellion against his authority with great address and spirit; and those proceedings struck a terror into the plebeians and opened the eyes of the better sort of people, who could not help wondering at their own stupidity, that after they had suppressed the pride of the nobility, they could so patiently submit to be insulted by the very dregs and refuse of the city.

" When Michael obtained this complete victory over the plebeians, the new signori were already appointed, two of whom were of so base and abject condition, that every one seemed desirous to be rid of such infamous magistrates. As they entered on the magistracy, there was an uproar in the piazza, which was full of armed men, who shouted with one voice, ' No plebeians [1] in the signori! ' The rest of the signori, in order to appease the tumult, degraded their two associates and chose two others in their room ; they likewise dissolved the plebeian companies, and deprived all those of their offices who had any connection with them, except Michael and a few of the best of them. They also divided the subordinate magistracy into two separate jurisdictions, one of which was to preside over the greater arts, and the other over the less. For the signori it was only provided in general that five of that body should be drawn out of the less companies and four out of the greater, and the standard-bearer alternately out of each."

Sylvestro de' Medici and a few others who had promoted this new regulation became in a manner the chief governors of the city. These proceedings and this new model of government revived the old divisions betwixt the more considerable commoners and the lower sort of mechanics, which had first been occasioned by the ambition of the Ricci and Albizzi ; and because they afterwards produced terrible consequences, Machiaavel henceforward distinguishes these two factions by the names of the *popular* and *plebeian.*

" Though this constitution of government lasted but three years, it abounded with executions and banishments ; for as those who were chiefly concerned in the administration well knew there were great numbers of malcontents, both within the city and without it, they lived in perpetual fear and alarm. The

---

[1] " *Del popolo minuto.*" Machiav.

disaffected within the walls either actually did, or were supposed to cabal daily against the state; and those without were continually raising disturbances abroad by the assistance of foreign princes or republics, sometimes in one part, sometimes in another. In such a government the laws are insulted by every party in turn. Accusations were laid before the magistrates against a number of citizens for corresponding with the exiles at Bologna, concerning a plot against the city; the prisoners were examined, and nothing criminal could be proved against them. The magistrate was going to acquit and discharge them; the people rose in such a ferment of clamor and calumnies that the magistrate was forced to pass sentence of death upon them.

" Their execution occasioned fresh murmurs and discontents in the city, so that both those who had got the upper hand, and those who were depressed, lived in continual fear and suspicion of each other. Dreadful indeed were the consequences which flowed from the apprehension of the former, as every little accident furnished them with a handle to trample on their fellow-citizens, some of whom they daily put to death, or sent into exile. They likewise made several new laws to strengthen their hands, and keep those down of whom they entertained the least suspicion. These suspicions growing stronger and stronger every day, made them behave with more rigor to the other party; a manner of proceeding that only served to multiply their discontents, and to increase instead of allaying their own fears, which were not a little heightened by the insolence of Georgio Scali and Tomaso Strozzi, whose authority was much superior to that of the magistrates; and therefore they all stood in awe of those two citizens, as they knew it was in their power, if they should join the plebeians, to turn them entirely out of the administration.

" This intemperate and tyrannical manner of governing began to grow intolerable, not only to all good citizens, but even to the seditious themselves; and it was not possible that the arrogance of Scali in particular could be long supported. By delivering a friend and tool of his out of the hands of justice, by a mob, he soon furnished his enemies with a fair opportunity not only of wreaking their own private revenge upon him, but of delivering the commonwealth out of his hands, and the hands of the plebeians, who had so unmercifully tyrannized over it for three years.

" They engaged in this design Benedetto, a man of immense fortune, very humane, strict in his morals and principles, a steady friend to the liberties of his country, and sufficiently disgusted at the tyrannical proceedings of the government, so that it was no difficult matter to engage him in any measures that might contribute to the downfall of Scali. As the insolence and oppression of the principal commoners had made him their enemy, and a friend to the plebeians, so, when he saw the latter pursuing the very same measures, he quickly detached himself from them. Having brought Benedetto and the heads of the arts into their design, they seized upon Scali, and the next day he was beheaded; [*] which struck such a terror into his party, that not one of them offered to stir in his favor, though they crowded in great numbers to see his execution. When he came to suffer death, in the face of that very people who had so lately worshipped him with a degree of idolatry, he could not help complaining of the hardness of his destiny, and of the wickedness of those citizens who, by their oppressions, had forced him to caress a rabble, in which he found there was neither honor nor gratitude. He bewailed his folly in having trusted to the fidelity of plebeians, which he might well have known is ever liable to be shaken and seduced by any little suspicion, misrepresentation, or blast of envy. He told Benedetto, ' This is the last day of my misfortunes, and the first of yours.' After him, some of his chief confidants were put to death, and their bodies dragged through the streets by the people.

" His death threw the whole city into a ferment. As the city was full of different humors, every one had a separate view, and was eager to accomplish it before he laid down his arms. The ancient nobility, now called grandees, could not bear to live any longer without some share in the public honors, and exerted their utmost efforts to recover them; for which purpose they endeavored to have the captains of the party restored to their former authority. The heads of the popular faction, and the greater arts, were disgusted that the government of the state was shared in common with them by the inferior arts or plebeians; the inferior arts, instead of giving up any part of their authority, were very desirous to increase it, and the plebeians were afraid of having their new companies dissolved. From these different views

* Nerli, p. 28.

and apprehensions there was nothing to be seen in Florence but tumults for a whole year. Sometimes the grandees, sometimes the greater, sometimes the lesser arts, and sometimes the plebeians, were in an uproar; and it often happened that they all took arms at the same time in different parts of the city."

After many mischiefs, dangers, and troubles, and many consultations and conferences, a new form of government was established.* All were recalled who had been banished since Sylvestro de' Medici was standard-bearer; all offices and appointments conferred in 1378 were abolished; the new companies dissolved, and reincorporated in their respective arts; the inferior arts were not to choose any standard-bearer of justice; instead of enjoying one half of the public honors, they were now limited to one third, and those too of the lower rank. The popular nobility and the Guelphs reassumed their superiority; and the plebeians were utterly dispossessed of it, after they had held it from 1378 to 1381.

"But the new administration was no less grievous and oppressive than that of the plebeians had been; several of the popular nobility, and many of the heads of the plebeians, were banished, and among the rest Michael,† whom the remembrance of his former great merit, in restraining the fury of the populace when so licentiously plundering the city, was not sufficient to protect from the resentment of the governing party. From such impolitic proceedings in princes and governors of commonwealths, it happens that men, naturally growing disgusted with their ill-timed severity and ingratitude, often incur their displeasure before they are aware of it.

"As such executions and banishments had ever been disapproved of by Benedetto, he could not help blaming the authors of these; upon which the government began to grow jealous of him, as a favorer of the plebeian party, and one that had consented to the death of Scali, not out of any real disapprobation of his conduct, but that he might the more easily get the reins of government into his own hands. They kept a strict watch over him, and resolved to ruin him. Intrigues were soon laid, by which Benedetto was sent into banishment.‡ 'You see, my dear friends,' said he, when he took leave of them, 'in what

---

* Nerli, p. 28.   † Ibid. p. 29.

‡ Pervenne in que' tempi al supremo magistrato Bardo Mancini, uomo molto contrario alla setta plebea, e molto nemico per queste, e per altre cagioni di

manner fortune has contrived my ruin, and how she still threatens you; at which neither do I wonder nor should you: it is the lot of those who endeavor to maintain their integrity among the wicked, and who desire to sustain that which more desire to destroy. From the same principle of love to my country which once induced me to join Sylvestro de' Medici, and afterwards to separate myself from Scali, I could not forbear censuring the proceedings of those who are now at the helm, who, *having nobody to chastise them*, are likewise desirous to get rid of every one who dares to reprehend them.' He preserved his character for piety and humanity abroad, and there died. His bones were brought back to Florence, and interred there with the highest honors by those very people who had persecuted him while alive with so much rancor and injustice."

" The family of the Alberti were not the only sufferers in these distractions, for many other citizens were either admonished or sent into exile. The members of this balia having done what they were deputed for, were going to break up, as they thought it would have an appearance of modesty; but the people, hearing of their resolution, ran to arms in the palace, and insisted that they should banish and admonish several others before they resigned their authority."

" Nevertheless, to diminish the authority of the plebeians still more, the signori made a decree, that the third part of the honors which they before enjoyed should be reduced to a fourth; and, that there might be two at least in the signori, always of approved fidelity to the government, they gave the gonfalonier, and four other citizens, authority to make a fresh imborsation, and to put the names of a select number of citizens into a particular purse, out of which two of every new signory should always be drawn."

" Tranquillity now continued till 1387, when Giovanni Galeazzo Viconti, commonly called the Conte di Virtù, thought to make himself King of Italy by arms, as he had made himself

---

Messer Benedetto Alberti, e conosciuto Bardo la gelosia, che cittadini del governo avevano di quella casa de gli Alberti, con participazione de' principali della setta de nobili, fece creare una balia per sicurtà dello stato, nella quale intra le prime cose si deliberò, che Messer Benedetto fusse confinato, e il resto de gli Alberti tutti ammoniti; e furono costretti i signori per gelosia de capi della setta, che molti altri cittadini tanto popolani, che plebei, fusse confinati, o ammoniti, e per ridurre più il governo a parte nobile, e per più avvilire gli avversari artifici e popolo minuto, &c. Nerli, p. 29, 30.

Duke of Milan by treachery; but after making himself master of Bologna, Pisa, Perugia, and Siena, and preparing to be crowned King of Italy at Florence, he died.[*]

"During the war with the Duke, Maso de gli Albizzi was gonfalonier, a bitter enemy to the Alberti. He resolved, though Benedetto was now dead, to be revenged, before he went out of office, on the rest of that family, for Pietro's unfortunate end. He accused the two heads of the family of corresponding with the exiles, and took them into custody. Upon this the whole city was in an uproar. The signori called the people together, and appointed a new balia, by which many citizens, besides almost all the Alberti, were banished, and many artificers admonished or put to death, and a fresh imborsation of magistrates was made. This tyrannical manner of proceeding so enraged the arts and lower sort of people, who now saw their lives and honors wantonly taken away, that they rose in arms, some of them running to the piazza, and others to the house of Véri de' Medici, who, after the death of Sylvester, was become the head of that family, and earnestly entreated him to take the government into his hands, and deliver them from the oppression of citizens, who were daily endeavoring to destroy the commonwealth, and every good man in it."

Antonio de' Medici was most importunate with him, though they had been long at open enmity. All writers agree, that if Véri had been as ambitious as he was virtuous, he might have made himself lord of the city; but he put himself at the head of the people, marched to the piazza, and there publicly refused to do any thing unconstitutional, but prayed the signori to redress the grievances of the people.

"They highly commended him, and promised to give all satisfaction. Upon these assurances, and a reliance on Véri's word, the people returned to their houses. As soon as the tumult was composed, the signori, instead of fulfilling their promises, fortified the piazza, enrolled two thousand citizens to defend them, forbid all others to bear arms, put many citizens to death, and banished others, who had been most active in the late insurrection. The few Alberti who were left, and the Medici, thought themselves and the people deceived, and

---

[*] Nerli, p. 30.

were extremely disgusted by these proceedings; but the first
who had courage to oppose them was Donato Acciaivoli, one
of the grandees, rather superior to Maso Albizzi, who, by the
steps he had taken while he was gonfalonier, was become in a
manner the head of the commonwealth. Donato endeavored
to get those who had been sent into exile recalled, and those
who had been admonished requalified to hold their former
honors and employments. He first attempted it by persuasion,
but not succeeding, he threatened to do it by force. For this
he was cited, convicted, and banished to Barletta. Alamanno,
and Antonio de' Medici, and all those who were of Alamanno's
family, with many of the inferior arts, who had any interest
among the plebeians, were likewise banished. All these things
happened within two years after Maso de gli Albizzi had assumed
the government.

In 1397, the exiles at Bologna, spirited young men, among
whom was Antonio de' Medici, depending upon the people's
rising in their favor, determined at all events to return to their
country and assassinate Maso; but either from a terror of the
government, or prejudice against the exiles, the people would
not move; and the conspirators fled to the church, where they
were put to death.[*] This conspiracy was scarcely quashed,
when another one still more dangerous, of other exiles scattered
over Lombardy, in concert with the Duke of Milan, was discovered; but this was defeated, and the authors punished.
Then a new balia was instituted, with authority to provide
for the safety of the commonwealth. By this council, six
of the Ricci, six of the Alberti, two of the Medici, three of
the Scali, two of the Strozzi, and many others of lower condition, were proclaimed rebels; all the rest of the Alberti, Ricci,
and Medici, except some very few, were rendered incapable of
holding any office for ten years. One of the Alberti only was
spared on account of his quiet character, Antonio; but the
government was jealous of him, and soon found a pretence for
banishing him to a distance of three hundred miles from the
city; and to free the government from the continual apprehensions they lived under of the Alberti, they banished all that
family that were above fifteen years of age. These things happened in 1400.[†]

* Nerli, p. 32.   † Id. p. 33.

E

" In 1412, some of the Alberti returned from banishment, and another balia was appointed, which made new laws for the security of the state, and inflicted other penalties on the family.

" In 1414 ended the war with Ladislaus, King of Naples, whose death delivered Florence from as much danger as that of the Conte di Virtù had done."

The period from 1371 to 1434, is that which is boasted of by Machiavel as the prosperous one, but the prosperity of which he attributes to the virtues and abilities of Maso. Pisa, Cortona, Arezzo, Leghorn, and Monte Pulciano, were added to the dominion.

" All republics, especially such as are not well constituted, undergo frequent changes in their laws and manner of government. And this is not owing to the nature either of liberty or subjection in general, as many think, but to downright oppression on one hand, or unbridled licentiousness on the other.[1] "

It is very true that most republics have undergone frequent changes in their laws; but this has been merely because very few republics have been well constituted. It is very true also, that there is nothing in the nature of liberty, or of obedience, which tends to produce such changes; on the contrary, real liberty and true obedience rather tend to preserve constancy in government. It is, indeed, oppression and license that occasion changes; but where the constitution is good, the laws govern, and prevent oppression as well as license.

" The name of liberty is often nothing more than a specious pretence,[2] made use of both by the instruments of licentiousness, who for the most part are commoners, and by the promoters of slavery, who generally are the nobles, each side being equally impatient of restraint and control."

This is a truth, which is proved as well as illustrated by every page of the foregoing history, as well as by the history of almost all other republics, ancient and modern; and the next paragraph shows that Machiavel had an accurate idea of the evil, though a confused one of the remedy.

---

[1] Lib. iv. Non mediante la libertà e la servitù, come molti credono, ma mediante la servitù e la licenza. "Not through liberty and servitude, as many think, but through servitude and licentiousness." The idea is somewhat obscurely expressed, and needs the aid of the following sentence which is found translated below.

[2] Perchè della libertà solamente il nome è celebrato. "For the name only of liberty is commended by," &c.

" When it fortunately happens, which indeed is very seldom, that some wise, good, and powerful citizen, has sufficient authority in the commonwealth to make such laws as may extinguish all jealousies betwixt the nobility and the people, or at least, so to moderate and restrain them, that they shall not be able to produce any bad effect, then that state may properly be called free, and its constitution looked upon as firm and permanent; for being once established upon good laws and institutions, it has no further occasion, like other states, for the virtue of any particular man to support it."

One would be apt to conjecture from this, that Machiavel was about to propose a first magistrate, armed by the constitution with sufficient authority to mediate, at all times, between the nobles and commons. Such a magistrate, possessed of the whole executive power, with a negative to defend it, has always authority to intervene between the nobles and commons, and to preserve the energy of the laws to restrain both; and whether this executive magistrate is wise and good or not, if the commons have the negative upon the purse and the laws, and the inquest of grievances, abuses, and state crimes, that executive power can hardly be ill used.

" On such laws and principles many of those ancient commonwealths, which so long subsisted, were formerly constituted."

Rome and Sparta were, in some degree, constituted upon these principles, and in proportion as they conformed to them, they were free and happy; but neither was perfectly conformed to them.

" For want of them, others have often varied their form of government from tyranny to license, and from license to tyranny;" and for want of them, such will ever be the vibration. " For as each of those states always has powerful enemies to contend with, it neither is, nor can be possible they should be of any long duration;" and while they last, the liberty and happiness of the citizens are constantly sacrificed. " All good and wise men must of necessity be disgusted at them." So much so, that if it were not for the chance and hope of obtaining a better constitution after all the changes, any man of that character would prefer a simple monarchy at once. " Since much evil may very easily be done in the former and hardly any good in the latter; the insolent having too much authority in one, and the ignorant and inexperienced in the other." These characters of simple aristocracies and simple democracies, which succeed each other so rapidly where the third power is not introduced to control and moderate both the nobles and people, are very just; and Machiavel says what is near the truth, "both must be upheld by the spirit and fortune of one man alone, who yet may either be suddenly taken off by death or overpowered by adversity." It is a pity he had not said, parties must be upheld together by the constitutional, legal authority of one man alone, possessed of the whole executive power of the state, and then, if he is taken off by death, another will succeed; if he be overpowered by adversity, the whole state must be overpowered with him; and no form of government can be devised to warrant states against pestilence, earthquake, and famine, the inevitable and irresistible judgments of heaven.

"I say, therefore, that the model of government which took place in Florence after the death of Scali, in 1381, was at first solely maintained by the conduct of Maso de gli Albizzi, and afterwards by that of Niccolò Uzzano." This is a strong instance of the efficiency of one man, so situated as to be able to mediate between the aristocratical and democratical ingredients in society, and an argument for providing such an officer by the constitution, whose duty and business it shall always be to act the same part; nay, who shall be necessitated, from the principle of self-preservation and self-defence, to preserve the balance between them.

"The city continued in tranquillity from 1414 to 1422, eight years; Uzzano and six others had the chief authority. Those animosities, however, which were at first kindled in the city by the quarrel betwixt the Albizzi and the Ricci, and afterwards blown up to such height by Sylvestro de' Medici, were never extinguished; and although that party which had the largest share in the affections of the people continued only three years in the administration, and was turned out of it in 1381, yet as they were favored and supported by the greater part of the citizens, they could not be totally suppressed. The frequent *admonitions* and continual persecutions that were carried on against the heads of it, from 1381 to 1400, had indeed brought them very low. The Alberti and the Medici suffered most by these proceedings. Several of them had their estates confiscated;

others were banished or put to death; and those who were suffered to continue in the city were deprived of all their honors and employments, by which their party was much depressed and almost reduced to nothing. They retained, however, sharp resentments, and determined to take revenge, though under the present circumstances they thought proper to dissemble."

This administration, composed of the most considerable commoners or popular nobility, which had kept the city so long in peace, at last were guilty of two errors in point of conduct, which proved their ruin. As soon as they thought themselves safe from the attempts of the Alberti, they grew insolent and they quarrelled among themselves; two faults that have ever been committed by every single assembly, whether of nobles or commons; and which ever must be committed by all that are to come.

" Amidst their supineness, oppressions, and divisions, the Medici recovered their former authority and power. The first of this family that began to lift up his head again was Giovanni,* the son of Bicci de' Medici, who being a man of great humanity, and grown very rich, was admitted to a share in the government of the state, at which there were such extraordinary rejoicings among the people, that many of the graver sort of the citizens were not a little alarmed when they saw the old humors began to show themselves again. Uzzano represented to his colleagues † that he knew Giovanni was a person of much greater influence and abilities than ever Sylvestro had been, and that it was dangerous to promote a man of so general a reputation to such a degree of power; but the rest of the governors envied Uzzano's reputation, and were glad to avail themselves of any assistance to ruin him; so that Giovanni was set up, as it often happens, to pull down Uzzano."

When a popular assembly or a senate have the management of the executive power, disputes forever arise concerning every step in foreign affairs, and discords and factions have full play. Thus it happened in Florence upon occasion of a negotiation with Philip Visconti, Lord of Lombardy. Every faction had a different opinion. That, however, in favor of a war prevailed. Ten superintendents of the war were appointed, soldiers were

---

* Nerli, p. 34.　　　　　† Nerli, p. 34, 35.

raised, and taxes imposed, which occasioned great murmurs in the city. The taxes were said to be heavier on the poor than the rich; every one exclaimed against the oppression of the governors who had wantonly embroiled the state in an expensive and unnecessary war, only to gratify their own private interests and ambition, and to establish themselves in their tyranny. The majority of the governors at last judged it necessary to declare war, notwithstanding that the resolution still met with great opposition, especially from Giovanni de' Medici, who publicly protested against it, and occasioned a multitude of arguments pro and con. The war was unfortunate, and a battle was lost by the badness of the weather; this misfortune occasioned great consternation in Florence, especially among the governing party who had been its chief promoters; they saw the enemy powerful and elated, themselves disarmed and without allies, and what was worse, hated to the last degree by the people, who insulted them whenever they appeared in the streets, complaining of insupportable taxes, and upbraiding them with the heavy expenses of an unnecessary war.

Machiavel enumerates the taunts which fury suggested upon this occasion to an enraged and unbridled multitude. The signori called a meeting of the principal citizens, and earnestly exhorted them to use their good offices to soothe the people and appease the general indignation which their clamors had excited. Rinaldo, the eldest son of the late Maso de gli Albizzi, having secretly entertained some hopes of becoming sole governor of the republic by the merit of his own services and the reputation of his father, made a long speech in justification of the war.

A commission was given to twenty citizens to raise further supplies for the maintenance of the war, who seeing the governing party now humbled, took courage and laid the chief burden of the taxes upon their shoulders, at which they were not a little mortified in their turn. They complained of it as too heavy; but when this came to the ears of the council they took effectual care to have it collected; and, in order to make all impositions appear for the future the more grievous and hateful to the people, they gave a strict charge to their officers to collect this with the utmost rigor, and to kill any one that should dare to oppose them or refuse to pay it; and so many were murdered or wounded that it was apprehended the two parties would come

to blows; for those who had been so long in power and used to
be treated with such reverence and distinction could not bear
the thoughts of being insulted in this manner; and the other
side were resolved that every man in his turn should equally
feel the sting of these oppressions.

" The principal citizens had now many private conferences,
but Giovanni was not there; either because he was not invited
as a person in whom they could not thoroughly confide, or
refused to come because he did not approve of such cabals.

" Rinaldo de gli Albizzi made an harangue. He represented
how the government had again fallen into the hands of the people, from whom their fathers had recovered it in 1381. He
reminded them of the tyranny of those who were in the administration from 1377 till that time, in which interval either the
father or grandfather, or some near relation, of almost every one
who was then present had been unjustly put to death. That the
city was now going to relapse into the same state of confusion
and oppression, since the multitude had already taken upon them
to impose taxes; and if not either curbed by force, or restrained
by some other expedient, they would certainly in the next place
proceed to appoint such officers as they thought fit; after which
they would turn the present magistrates out of their seats, to the
utter destruction of an administration which had governed the
city with so much glory and reputation for forty-two years; the
consequence of which would be that Florence must either be
blindly governed by the caprice of the multitude, and then one
party would live in continual danger and apprehension while the
other rioted in all manner of licentiousness, or it must fall under
the subjection of some one person who would make himself
absolute lord, and perhaps tyrant over it. As the audaciousness
of the multitude was in a great measure owing to the largeness
of the imborsations, and the little care that was taken in making
them, which had filled the palace with new and mean men, he
thought the only remedy for such disorders would be to restore
the authority of the nobility, and diminish that of the minor arts,
by reducing them from fourteen to seven. This would lessen
the power of the plebeians in the councils, both by retrenching
their number and by throwing more weight into the scale of the
grandees, who would, out of revenge for old injuries, be sure to
use all possible endeavors to depress them. That wise men

always availed themselves of different sorts of people at different seasons; and if their fathers had made use of the assistance of the plebeians to humble the insolence of the grandees, now the latter were brought so low, and the former become so audacious, it would be no bad expedient to join with the grandees to lower them.

"Uzzano made answer that 'it might be done if they could draw Giovanni de' Medici into their designs; for if he concurred with them, the multitude being deprived of their head would not be able to make any opposition.' Rinaldo was deputed to wait upon Giovanni, and persuade him to join them. Giovanni replied to him that he had always thought it the duty of a good citizen to endeavor to prevent any change in the established laws. By such changes some were turned out and others brought in, and the first generally thought themselves more aggrieved than the others benefited; by which few friends and many enemies were made, mankind being naturally more prone to revenge than gratitude. That the citizens of Florence generally dealt basely and perfidiously with each other; that as soon as the promoters and advisers of this plan had sufficiently depressed the people by the help of his authority, they would certainly fall upon him next with the whole force and assistance of the plebeians, whose affections he must have lost by such a conduct, and then he would be utterly deserted and ruined. He could not help remembering the fate of Benedetto, who, at the instigation of such as conspired his destruction, consented to the severe proceedings against Scali, and soon after was sent into exile himself by the very persons who had inveigled him into those measures. That for his part he should never agree to have any alterations made in the laws or constitution of his country.'

"These deliberations when known, still added to the reputation of Giovanni, and increased the hatred of the people against the other citizens. On the contrary, Alamanno de' Medici, his relation, and Cosimo, his son, urged Giovanni to take this opportunity of humbling his enemies and exalting his friends, reproaching him with his coldness, which they said emboldened those who wished him ill to form daily conspiracies against him, and would one time or other prove the ruin of all his family and dependents; but he was deaf to all their remonstrances and prognostications, and determined to pursue his own measures.

The designs of the faction were, however, now plainly discovered, and the city began once more to divide itself into factions."

Under such forms of government there can never be an independent judicial power; all parties are either courting, or threatening, or persecuting the judges.[1]

" There were at this time two presiding under the signori in the supreme court of justice; Martino, who was one of them, was of Uzzano's party, and Paolo, the other, followed that of the Medici. Rinaldo finding Giovanni inflexible, resolved to turn Paolo out of his office, as he thought that the court would then be wholly at his devotion; but the other side being aware of this, were beforehand with him, and contrived matters so well, that they got Paolo continued and Martino discharged, to the great mortification and prejudice of his party.

" The war lasted from 1422 to 1427, and the citizens were impoverished by taxes; personal estate was now to be taxed as well as real. This was likely to fall heavily upon the rich, upon which account, before it passed into a law,[2] it was vehemently opposed by them all, except Giovanni, who publicly expressed his approbation of it, so that it was carried against them. This tax was regulated by a law made on purpose, and not left to the arbitrament of partial or interested persons; so that the more powerful citizens were in some measure restrained from oppressing the inferior sort and influencing their votes in the councils, as they had been used to do, by the threats of taxing them according as they gave their suffrages. This tax, therefore, was very · cheerfully submitted to by the generality, though highly disgustful to the rich. But as it is the nature of mankind to be ever restless and discontented, and when they have gained one advantage to be still grasping at a higher, the people, not satisfied with this equality of taxation established

---

[1] In the last chapter but one of Sismondi's history may be found some judicious reflections upon the defects of the judiciary system in the Italian republics. Although many of those pointed out by him have been remedied in the present age, the subject is not yet without its difficulties.

[2] As this tax is afterwards alluded to by name, it seems proper to add the definition which Machiavel gives of it. — " E perchè nel distribuirla s'aggravavano i beni di ciascuno, il che i Fiorentini dicono accatastare, si chiamò questa gravezza Catasto."

"And because in apportioning it the property of each one was valued to the full, which the Florentines call accatastare, (anglice, ' to lump.') this imposition was called catasto."

by the law, demanded a retrospect, by which it might appear
how much less the rich citizens had paid before, than they ought
to have done by this regulation, and by which every one should
be made to account for deficiencies."

This question occasioned very long and ingenious arguments
on both sides; but Giovanni represented to the people the bad
consequences of retrospects, and with many arguments soothed
them, till they dropped this demand.

In 1428 peace was concluded, and fresh commotions began in
the city on the subject of the new plan of taxation. " In this
juncture Giovanni fell sick, and calling his two sons, Cosimo
and Lorenzo, to his bedside, he advised them, ' If you would live
with safety and comfort, be content with such a share in the
government as your fellow-citizens confer upon you, by which
you will avoid envy and danger; for it is that which a man
arrogates to himself that makes him odious, and not what is
voluntarily given him.' He died lamented by the whole city,
for he was very charitable and compassionate. His universal
benevolence taught him to love good men and pity the evil. He
never solicited honors, though he obtained the highest. He died
possessed of immense riches,* and full of glory and reputation,
leaving his son Cosimo heir to his fortune and fame; both which
he not only maintained, but augmented."

Ambition soon kindled new wars. " The whole city was
divided into little meetings and cabals of all ranks of people, the
generality of whom were for commencing hostilities against the
Lucchese. Among the more considerable citizens who favored
this enterprise were all the followers of the Medici family; those
who opposed it were Uzzano and his party. It seems almost
incredible that there should be such a change of opinions in the
same citizens on this occasion, concerning the expediency of a
war; and yet those very persons who, after a peace that had
lasted ten years, opposed a war against Duke Philip which was
undertaken in defence of their own liberties, now strenuously
insisted upon one against Lucca, to invade the rights of others,
and at a time too when the city was to the last degree exhausted
and impoverished by the heavy expenses of the last. From
hence we may observe how much more ready mankind are to

* Nerli, p. 38.

usurp the property of others than to defend their own, and how much stronger the hope of gain is than the fear of loss. The signori assembled the common council, where the matter was debated by some of the leading men of the republic in the presence of four hundred and ninety-eight citizens."

The debate was conducted by Rinaldo on one side and Uzzano on the other; and, upon a ballot, only ninety-eight were against the war. The war was commenced and carried on with all that rapacious avarice and ambition which had begun it; and grievous complaints and accusations were brought against Astorre and Rinaldo for their behavior in it.

In 1428,[*] Niccolò da Uzzano died, and Rinaldo succeeded as head of his family and party. Rinaldo returned in a rage against the magistrates, and presenting himself before the council of war, he told them "he well knew how difficult and dangerous a thing it was to serve an unbridled people and a divided state; since the one was carried away with every rumor, the other put a malicious interpretation upon actions that were doubtful, and always punished the evil, but never rewarded the good; so that if a commander succeeded in an expedition, he had no praise at all; if he was guilty of an error, his conduct was censured by the generality; but if he miscarried, he was sure to be condemned by every one; for in the one case his own party would envy his success, and in the other his adversaries would not fail to insult him." The council endeavored to appease his resentment, but gave the command abroad to others. The war was conducted afterwards rather unsuccessfully, until they came to a battle before the town of Lucca, and were totally defeated.

"As the expedition had been undertaken almost by general consent, the people, in the utmost consternation, and not knowing where else to turn their rage, began to abuse those who had conducted the war, since they could not blame those who, by their own instigation, had first advised it, and they revived their old calumnies against Rinaldo; but the person whom they fell upon with the greatest violence was Guicciardini, who they said might easily have put an end to the war if he had not been bribed; nay, they went so far as to charge him with sending a

* Nerli, p. 39.

horseload of money to his own house, and particularly mentioned the names both of those that carried and those that
received it.   These clamors and accusations made such a noise,
that the captain of the people could not help taking cognizance
of so public a charge ; especially as he was importunately
called upon so to do by Giovanni's enemies.   Having cited him
therefore to clear himself of this imputation, he made his appearance, but with much seeming indignation and contempt of their
malice ; and his relations exerted themselves so strenuously for
the honor of their family, that the captain was obliged to stop
all further proceedings against him."

The insinuation here is very obvious that the judge was
bribed.

" In 1433 a general peace was concluded, whereby all towns
that had been taken by the Florentines, Lucchese and Sienese,
were mutually restored to their former possessors ; so that the
expense of this war was all lost.   During the course of it the
factious humors began to ferment again at home ; and Cosimo
began to act with greater spirit in public affairs, and with more
openness and zeal for the good of his friends, than ever his
father had done ; so that those who rejoiced at the death of
Giovanni were not a little damped at the proceedings of his son.
Cosimo was a man of very great prudence, of a sedate and
agreeable countenance, exceedingly liberal and humane, never
entering into any measures that would be pernicious to the
state, or even the party that he opposed, but taking all opportunities of doing good to every one, and of conciliating to himself
the affections of his fellow-citizens by his goodness and generosity.   So noble an example of benevolence greatly increased
the hatred which the public had already conceived against the
governing party, and at the same time was the best method he
thought he could take to enable himself either to live with reputation and security in Florence, or, by the interest he had with
the people, and even if necessary by force of arms, to get the
better of any persecution that the malice of his enemies might
raise against him.   There were two citizens who contributed to
promote this interest, Averardo de' Medici and Puccio Pucci ;
the one by his boldness and activity, the other by his great wisdom and experience, which added much reputation to his party ;
indeed, the judgment and authority of the latter were so gene-

rally revered, that he gave a name to the party, which was not called Cosimo's, but Puccio's party.

"In this divided state of the city, the expedition against Lucca was undertaken, which, instead of extinguishing the rage of faction, still added fuel to it; for, though Puccio's party had promoted and advised a war, yet those of the other side were chiefly employed in conducting it, as they had greater power in the government; and since Averardo and his friends could not by any means prevent this, they took every opportunity of defaming them, and calumniating their actions; so that when they met with any misfortune, it was not imputed to the superior strength or better management of the enemy, but to the misconduct and imprudence of the commissary. This was the occasion why the enormities committed by Astorre Gianni, though of themselves very great indeed, were still exaggerated. It was this sort of treatment that provoked Rinaldo to such a degree, that he left his command without permission. This was the true cause of Giovanni Guicciardini being cited to appear before the captain of the people. From hence proceeded all the charges and complaints that were exhibited against other magistrates and commissaries; and whilst those that had any foundation were always aggravated, and sometimes supported by downright falsehood, the people, out of the hatred they bore to them, greedily swallowed all, whether true or false.

"Uzzano, and the other heads of that party, perfectly well aware of these base artifices, had had several private meetings to consider of proper means to prevent the effect of them; yet they could not fix upon any expedient. It was very dangerous, they knew, to connive at them, and not less to proceed to open violence; Uzzano himself was averse to any remedies of that kind. Barbadori, seeing they were harassed in this manner, with war abroad and faction at home, made a visit to Uzzano, whom he found alone and very thoughtful in his study; and as he himself wished to see the ruin of Cosimo, he left no method untried to prevail upon Uzzano to join with Rinaldo to drive him out of the city. Uzzano replied, —

"'Common prudence would be sufficient to induce those who advise the expulsion of Cosimo to compare their own strength with his. Our party, it seems, is now distinguished by the name of the Nobility, and the other by that of the Plebeians. Remem-

7*

ber the fate of the ancient nobility of this city, who at last were
utterly suppressed in their contests with the plebeians. Our
party is divided, while that of our adversaries is compact and
entire. *Neri and Nerone, two of the chief men in the city, have
not yet declared themselves;* and it is uncertain what side they
will take. Several families are divided among themselves; and
many there are that hate us, and favor our adversaries, merely
out of envy or malice to their own brothers, or some other near
relations. Among the sons of Maso, Luca, out of hatred to
Rinaldo, is gone over to the other side; in the family of the
Guicciardini, Pietro, the son of Luigi, is a mortal enemy to his
brother Giovanni, and joins our adversaries; Tomaso and Niccolò Soderini openly oppose us, out of pique to their uncle Francisco; so that if we consider the quality of those who constitute
their party, and of whom our own consists, I see no reason why
one should be called the nobility in preference to the other. If
it is because they are followed by the whole body of the plebeians,
that very circumstance makes them so much superior to us, that
if ever we come to an open trial of our strength, we shall not be
able to stand before them; and if we still continue in possession
of the first places in the commonwealth, it is entirely owing to
the established credit of an administration which has now supported itself for the space of fifty years. But if things should
come to extremities, and our present weakness be discovered,
you may depend upon it, we should be forced out of the magistracy, perhaps to our utter destruction. Cosimo, it is true, freely
lends money to every one that wants it; not only to private
people, but to the public, upon any emergency, and to foreigners
as well as Florentines. He is a friend to such as stand in need
of protection, and sometimes helps to advance an acquaintance
to a reputable employment in the commonwealth, by the interest
which his universal benevolence has gained him among the people. What shall we be able to plead in excuse for endeavoring
to expel him the city? Shall we accuse him of being charitable,
friendly, liberal, and beloved by every one? What law condemns
charity, liberality, and beneficence? Indeed, these virtues are
sometimes counterfeited, to cajole the vulgar, by such as aspire
to dominion; but they do not appear in that light at present, nor
is it in our power to make them. We have lost our reputation
by our late misconduct; and a people naturally prone to faction,

and corrupted by continual divisions, will no longer put any confidence in us, or give credit to such accusations. If he is banished, he will return with more friends, and we shall have more enemies. If it is intended to put him to death in a *judicial manner*, that can never be effected; for, as he is rich, and the magistracy corrupt, he will be sure to escape all punishment. But if he is banished or condemned, what will the commonwealth gain by that? No sooner will it be free from the apprehensions it was under from Cosimo, but it will be liable to the same from Rinaldo. For my own part, I am one of those who never desire to see one citizen exceed another in authority; and if one of these two must seize the reins, I know not any reason that should induce me to prefer Rinaldo to Cosimo. I pray God to preserve this city from ever falling under the dominion of any one man; but if a time should ever come, when our sins shall bring that judgment upon us, I pray still more earnestly, that we may not become subject to Rinaldo. *The far greater part of the citizens, some out of stupidity, and others out of malice, are thoroughly disposed to sell their country; and fortune has been so favorable to them as to provide a purchaser.* Live quietly, then; and as to any invasion of our liberties, be assured, you have as much to apprehend from our own party as the other.'"

This speech contains a volume of instruction. The situation of such a government, where there are two parties, and no third power to balance them, is admirably described. Neri, and Nerone, who were yet neuters, are looked up to as capable, when they please, of overturning the balance, and effecting a revolution. Family quarrels are resorted to and inflamed, in order to make different branches take different sides. Though one party is called patrician, and the other plebeian, so many individuals of each desert their colors and go over to the enemy, that it is impossible to say which party is really the patrician, and which the plebeian. Timid and irresolute to the last degree, the government dares not disoblige an individual, even by punishing a crime; the government really esteeming its enemies more than its own members; and opposition approving members of government more than their own associates; all parties endeavoring to get an influence over the judges, as essential to their existence; the judicial power unavoidably corrupted,—it was easy for Uzzano to say, and perhaps sincerely, that he never desired to see one citizen exceed another in influence. But, according to Machiavel, the existence of the government had long depended upon the superior authority of Uzzano himself. And no better plan of liberty than this deplorable one of Florence can ever be preserved, without some one citizen legally vested with authority to control each in turn of the contending parties.

"Uzzano died in 1428,* and all restraint was at an end. Rinaldo now was head of the party, and was continually teazing and importuning such citizens as he thought likely to be judges, that is, standard-bearers of justice, to take arms, and deliver their country out of the hands of Cosimo; who, taking advantage of the stupidity of some, and the malice of others, would certainly enslave it. Thus Rinaldo, by endeavoring to supplant his adversaries, and they to support themselves, kept the whole city in continual alarm and suspicion; so that when new magistrates were appointed, it was presently known how many there were on one side, and how many on the other; and at the imborsations for the signori, there was nothing to be seen but tumult and uproar. Every trifling affair that was brought before the magistracy created a division; all secrets were divulged; they had no regard to justice; the good and the evil were treated alike; and there was not so much as one magistrate that did his duty.

"Rinaldo, impatient to lower the authority of Cosimo, intrigued to get Bernardo Guadagni drawn for standard-bearer,* and succeeded. He went to congratulate him, and told him how much the nobility were rejoiced to see him in possession of that dignity; represented to him the danger they were in from their divisions; and that the surest way to restore union among them was to rid themselves of Cosimo. Bernardo answered, he was fully convinced of the expediency and necessity of what he had urged, and desired him to prepare their friends to take arms.

"Bernardo then summoned Cosimo to appear before the signori. The signori assembled the people, and appointed a balia, consisting of two hundred citizens, to reform the state; and the first thing debated was, whether Cosimo should be put

* Nerli, p. 39.

to death or not. Some argued for it, others thought banishment sufficient, and many sat silent.

" Cosimo was committed prisoner to Federigo Malavolti, in the turret of the palace. From this place, he could hear the clamors of the armed men, who were below in the piazza, and frequent outcries for a balìa; which made him apprehend that his life was in danger, but much more, that his particular enemies would take some extravagant method to despatch him; for that reason, he would eat no meat for the space of four days, except a mouthful or two of bread. Federigo, observing this, bid him take courage, and eat his meat, and keep himself alive for the good of his friends and his country; 'and that you may have no more suspicion,' says he, 'I will eat with you.' Cosimo embraced him with tears in his eyes, acknowledging his generosity, and assuring him he would amply recompense his kindness, if ever fortune should put it in his power to show his gratitude.

" Federigo invited Farganaccio, a friend of the standard-bearer, to sup with him. Cosimo, after many fair words and promises, gave his guest a draught upon his banker for eleven hundred ducats, desiring him to keep one hundred himself, and present the other thousand to the standard-bearer. This he willingly undertook to perform, and gave the money to Bernardo, who then began to grow cooler and more moderate in the prosecution; so that, after all, Cosimo was only banished to Padua, though Rinaldo used his utmost endeavors to have him put to death. Averardo de' Medici, and many others of that family, were likewise banished at the same time, and with them, Puccio and Giovanni Pucci.

" Cosimo was brought before the signori, 3 October, 1433, who pronounced the sentence of banishment upon him. He received the sentence with a cheerful countenance, saying, 'that in what part of the world soever he should sojourn, his person and fortune should ever be at the service of the republic, the people, and the signori.' The standard-bearer told him, he would take care that his life should be in no danger; and having conducted him to his own house to sup with him, ordered a party of the guards to escort him to the confines of the Florentine dominions.

" Wherever he came, he was received with great honor, and publicly visited by the Venetians, who treated him not as an

F

exile, but as a person of the first rank and consequence in the
state.   Florence, being thus deprived of so great a man, and so
universally beloved,* Rinaldo saw a storm arising, and advised
his friends to collect their strength, and fortify themselves; that
so, when their enemies should rise upon them, which was daily
to be expected, they might be able to clear the city of them by
dint of force, since, it seemed, they could not do it in a judicial manner; that they must regain the affections of the grandees,
by restoring them to their honors and authority.   He was answered, that the insolence and tyranny of the grandees always
had been, and always would be, insupportable; and that it
would be madness to run headlong into a certain and slavish
subjection to them, when the danger that was apprehended from
the plebeians might only be imaginary.   Rinaldo, seeing his
advice rejected, could not help lamenting the misfortunes that he
foresaw were going to fall upon himself and his party; but
he modestly imputed them rather to the malevolence of their
destiny, than to the blindness and perverseness of men."

But both Rinaldo and Machiavel would have been much
better advised, if they had imputed all these evils to their true
cause, an imperfect and unbalanced constitution of government,
rather than to destiny or the perverseness of men.   In such a
form of government, destiny itself, without a miracle, cannot
prevent the blindness and perverseness of men.   Those who see
the clearest are forced to shut their eyes, and those who are most
upright are compelled to be perverse.

"Letters were soon intercepted from Agnolo to Cosimo, advising him to stir up a war from some quarter or another, and to
make Neri his friend; as he thought then the people would be in
want of money to carry it on.   Agnolo was banished, which did
not, however, restrain the ardor of those who favored Cosimo.   It
was now almost a year since Cosimo had been banished.   At
the end of August, Niccolò di Cocco was drawn standard-bearer
for the two next months, and with him eight new signors, all
Cosimo's friends, at which Rinaldo and his party were alarmed.
Rinaldo was for taking arms, and obliging the standard-bearer

* Partissi Cosimo di Firenze l' Ottobre, 1433, avendo lasciato di se nell universale de' meno potenti cittadini grandissimo desiderio, parendo loro esser rimesi
in preda di pochi potenti, senza speranza di capo alcuno al quale si potessero
appoggiare.   Nerli, p. 40.

to assemble the people in the piazza to appoint another balia and depose the new signori; he would get others drawn, more fit for their purpose, by burning the old imborsation, and making a fresh one, in which the purses might be filled only with the names of their friends. Strozzi, a man of a peaceable and humane disposition, and given to study rather than to faction, opposed it; and it was resolved to let the new signori enter peaceably upon the magistracy.

"Having been created by Cosimo's party, they no sooner took possession of the palace, than the standard-bearer began his office by an action which was to give him reputation, and strike a damp into such as might think of opposing him. He immediately committed his predecessor to prison, upon pretence that he had embezzled the public money; after which he began to sound his associates about Cosimo's return. Finding them well disposed to it, he communicated their design to those who were reputed heads of the Medici party, who all encouraged him to attempt it. He then cited Rinaldo and others, the principals of the other party, to appear before him, who, instead of obeying him, flew to arms. But their party was irresolute, lost its opportunity, and gave time to the signori to provide for their defence. The signori sent to acquaint Rinaldo, and those who were with him, 'that they could not conceive what was the cause of such a commotion; that if it was upon Cosimo's account, they could assure them they had no thought of recalling him.' These promises, however, made but little impression on Rinaldo, who said he would take care of himself, by turning them all out of their offices.

"*But it seldom happens that any design succeeds, where the authority of the conductors is equal, and their opinions different.* Ridolfo replied, 'That for his part, he desired nothing more than that Cosimo might not be suffered to return.' So that, all hope of success being defeated by the delay of Rinaldo, the pusillanimity of Strozzi, and the desertion of Ridolfo Peruzzi, the rest of the party began to lose their spirits and grow cool. Pope Eugenius IV., driven out of Rome by the people, was then at Florence, and interposed his mediation till he persuaded the party to lay down their arms. As soon as the signori saw their adversaries disarmed, they began to treat with them, through the mediation of the pope; at the same time, they sent privately into the mountains of Pistoia for a body of foot-soldiers, which, being joined by all the horse they had in the adjacent territories, were brought into Florence by night. Having taken possession of all the passes and strong places in the city, they called the people together in the piazza before the palace, and appointed a new balia, which, at their first meeting, recalled Cosimo, and all the other citizens who had been banished with him. On the other hand, they not only sent Rinaldo, Peruzzi, Barbadori, and Strozzi into banishment, but such numbers of others, that most parts of Italy, and some other countries, were crowded with them, to the great impoverishment of Florence, both in regard to its wealth, its inhabitants, its trade, and manufactures.

"But the pope, seeing that party which, upon his assurances and intercession, had consented to lay down their arms, entirely ruined and dissipated, was exceedingly enraged, as well as Rinaldo. The latter, however, affected to say, it would give him no great regret to be banished a city where private men had more authority than the laws.

"Cosimo, having notice, immediately repaired to Florence. It has seldom happened that any commander, though returning in triumph from victory, has been received with such acclamations and universal joy as Cosimo was by his fellow-citizens, who ran in multitudes to meet him, and saluted him, with one voice, the benefactor of the people and the father of his country." *

Machiavel begins his fifth book as if he supposed his reader convinced that the commonwealth of Florence had expired, and an absolute sovereignty in Cosimo had commenced, by grave reflections upon the changes that are incident to all governments:

"They often degenerate into anarchy and confusion, and from thence emerge again to good order and regularity. For, since it is ordained by Providence that there should be a continual ebb and flow in the things of this world, as soon as they arrive at their utmost perfection, and can ascend no higher, they must of necessity decline; and, on the other hand, when they have fallen,

---

* " Ritornò adunque Cosimo in Firenze, con tanta reputazione e con si granda allegrezza dall' esilio, con quanta, mai ritornasse alla patria sua alcun altro cittadino trionfante, da qual si voglia o possa immaginare felicissima impresa vittorioso; e benchè egli si sforzasse in tanta sua felicità, e grandezza di mantenere sempre quella civile modestia, la quale osservò in ogni sua azione mentrechè visse, ad ogni modo appariva in lui una tal maestà di principe, che meritò per pubblico decreto d' esser chiamato padre della patria, la quale da esso fu per trenta anni, pacificamente governata." Nerli, p. 43.

through any disorder, to the lowest degree that is possible, and can sink no lower, they begin to rise again. And thus there is a constant succession of prosperity and adversity in all human affairs. Virtue is the mother of peace; peace produces idleness; idleness, contention and misrule; and from thence proceed ruin and confusion. This occasions reformation and better laws; good laws make men virtuous; and public virtue is always attended with glory and success.

"At the return of Cosimo, those citizens who had been his chief friends, and some others, who had been injured and oppressed by the late administration, were determined at all events to take the government of the state into their own hands. The signori, therefore, who were drawn for the two ensuing months of November and December, not content with what their predecessors had already done in favor of their party, prolonged the term, changed the residence of several who had been banished, and sent numbers of others into exile. And this was done not only out of party rage, but likewise on account of their riches, alliances, and private connections; so that this proscription, except in the article of bloodshed, might in some measure be compared to that under Sylla and Octavius. There were, however, some executions; for Antonio, the son of Bernardo, was beheaded; and four other citizens, having left the place to which they had been banished, and gone to reside at Venice, were secured by the Venetians, who set a greater value upon Cosimo's friendship than their own reputation, and sent prisoners to Florence, where they were put to death in an ignominious manner.

" These examples greatly increased the strength of Cosimo's party, and struck a terror into that of his enemies. When they had thus cleared the city of their enemies, and such as they thought disaffected to their government, they began to strengthen their hands by caressing and heaping favors upon others. For this purpose they recalled the family of the Alberti, and all the rest of the exiles that had been formerly banished; they reduced the grandees, except some very few, to the rank of commoners, and divided among themselves the possessions of those whom they had banished. After this they fortified themselves with new laws and ordinances, and made a fresh imborsation, taking the names of all suspected persons out of the purses, and filling them up with those of their own friends. They likewise took

care that such magistrates as had the power of life and death
entrusted to them should always be chosen out of the most eminent of their party; for which purpose they ordained that the
syndics, who inspected the imborsations in conjunction with the
old signori, should have the power of appointing the new. They
left the cognizance of capital offences to the eight wardens, and
enacted that no exile should return, even after the term of his
banishment was expired, till he had obtained the consent of the
signori and thirty-four of the colleges, though the whole number
of them amounted to no more than thirty-seven. All persons
were prohibited to write or receive any letters from them; every
word, or sign, or gesture, that displeased the governors, was
punished with the utmost severity. And if there was any suspected person left in Florence, who had not fallen under their
lash for such offences, they took care to load him severely with
new taxes and impositions; so that, one part of their adversaries
being driven out of the city, and the other depressed and overawed by these means, they in a short time secured the government to themselves; and to support their power with foreign aid,
and deprive their enemies of all assistance, if they should offer to
disturb them, they entered into a defensive league with the pope,
the Venetians, and the Duke of Milan."

Cosimo is very tenderly treated by Machiavel; yet he has
impartiality enough to record the tragical story of Neri and Baldaccio.

"Among[1] those who had the chief authority in the government,
Neri was one, of whose reputation Cosimo was more jealous
than of that of any other person; as he had not only very great
credit in the city, but was exceedingly beloved by the soldiery,
whose affections he had gained by his bravery, humanity, and
good conduct, when he commanded the troops of the republic,
as he had done upon several occasions; besides which, the remembrance of the victories that had been gained by him and his
father, one of whom had taken Pisa, and the other defeated Piccinino at the battle of Anghiari, made him respected by many
and feared by others, who did not desire any more associates in
the government.

"But of all their generals, Baldaccio d' Anghiari was certainly

1 Lib. vi.

the most eminent; nor was there any man at that time in Italy,
who surpassed him either in courage, or military skill, or bodily
accomplishments; and having always commanded the infantry,
they had such an opinion of him, that it was generally believed
he could influence them to execute any purpose, and that they
would follow him in any undertaking whatsoever. This Baldaccio was very intimate with Neri, for whom he had the highest
esteem, on account of his valor and other good qualities, of which
he had long been a witness; but it was a connection that excited
infinite jealousy among the rest of the principal citizens, who,
thinking it dangerous to let him enjoy his liberty, and still more
so to imprison him, resolved to have him despatched; in which
fortune seemed to second their design."

It is very provoking to read these continual imputations to
fortune, made by Machiavel, of events which he knew very well
were the effects of secret intrigue; for there is no doubt it had
been previously concerted to get Bartolomeo Orlandini appointed
standard-bearer of justice, who, having been sent to defend the
pass of Marradi, when Piccinino invaded Tuscany, had shamefully deserted it, and abandoned all that country, from the nature
of its situation of itself almost inaccessible, to the fury of the
enemy. So flagrant a piece of cowardice provoked Baldaccio to
such a degree, that he could not help expressing his contempt of
him, both in public conversation and in letters which he wrote
to his friends, in terms that not only excited Orlandini's resentment, but made him thirst for revenge, and flatter himself that
he should extinguish the infamy of the fact by the death of his
accuser. To this resolution some other citizens (the Medici)
were privy; who encouraged him in it, and said, that by so doing
he would sufficiently revenge the injuries which he had suffered
himself, and at the same time deliver the government from the
fear of a man whom it was dangerous to employ, and might be
their ruin to dismiss.

" Orlandini, therefore, being confirmed in his purpose to assassinate him, shut up several armed men in his apartment; and
the next day, when Baldaccio came to attend at the palace, as
he did most days, to confer with the magistracy concerning the
pay of his soldiers, he was ordered to wait on the standard-bearer
immediately, which he did, without suspecting any danger. As
soon as they met, and had taken a turn or two in the gallery,

which is before the chambers of the signori, they began to talk about their affairs; and at last, coming near the door of the apartment where the armed men were concealed, the standard-bearer gave them a signal, upon which they instantly rushed out, and, as Baldaccio had neither arms nor attendants, they soon despatched him, and threw him out of the palace window, from whence he was carried into the piazza; and after they had cut off his head, his body was exposed all day as a spectacle to the people.

" This tragical event gave a considerable check to Neri's interest, and diminished the number of his partisans. The governors, however, did not stop here; for, as they had been now ten years in the administration, and the authority of the balia was expired, many began both to talk and act with much greater freedom than they thought was consistent with the security of the state. In order, therefore, to establish themselves in power, they judged it necessary to revive that court, by which they would have an opportunity of strengthening the hands of their friends, and of more effectually depressing their enemies. With this view the councils instituted a new balia in the year 1444, which confirmed the present magistrates in their respective departments, vested the privilege of choosing the signori in a few hands, and new-modelled the chancery of reformation, deposing the president, Philip Peruzzi, and setting another person at the head of it, who, they were well assured, would conform himself to their instructions. They likewise prolonged the banishment of such as they had before sent into exile, imprisoned Giovanni, the son of Simone Vespucci, and deprived all those of their honors and employments that adhered to their enemies; amongst whom were the sons of Piero Baroncelli, the whole family of the Seragli, Bartolomeo Fortini, Francesco Castellani, and many others. By such means they at the same time regained their former authority and reputation, quashed all opposition, and got entire possession of the government.

Machiavel's introduction to his seventh book, according to his custom, is full of grave reflections.

" Those are much mistaken, who think any republican government can continue long united."

So are they who think that any despotical or monarchical government can continue long united; it is as easy to form and preserve the union of a republican as of a monarchical government, and more easy. A constitution formed upon the nature of man, and providing against his discontented temper, instead of trusting to what is not in him (his moderation and contentment in power) may preserve union, harmony, and tranquillity, better than any despotism. Republics that trust the content of one assembly or two assemblies, are as credulous, ignorant, and servile, as nations that trust the moderation of a single man. And it is as true of one as the other, *ubi solitudinem faciunt, pacem appellant.*

"Differences and divisions, for the most part, are prejudicial to republics; and yet it is certain there are some that are of service to them."

The same is true of despotisms and monarchies. Divisions are hurtful for the most part, yet some are beneficial.

"Those, indeed, are hurtful that are attended with parties and factions; but when that is not the case, they tend to the benefit of the commonwealth. As it is impossible, therefore, for any legislator or founder of a republic entirely to prevent feuds and animosities in it, it ought to be his chief care to provide against their growing up into factions."

This is easily done, by distinct and independent legislative, executive, and judicial powers, and by two councils in the legislature. Factions may be infinitely better managed in such a republic, than in a despotism or monarchy.

"It must be considered then, that there are two roads to popularity in such states, the one through public stations, the other through private life. In the former, it is acquired by gaining some signal victory, by the prudent and careful discharge of an embassy, or by giving wise and successful advice in council; in the latter, by beneficence to one's fellow citizens, by screening them from the magistrates, by supplying them with money, by promoting them to honors and employments even when they do not deserve them, by entertaining the people with plays and spectacles, and by distributing largesses among them. This manner of proceeding procures followers and partisans; and as popularity thus obtained is dangerous to the state, because it is commonly applied to serve private and self-interested views; so the reputation that is acquired the other way is of credit and advantage to it, when not made a tool to party and faction,

8*

because it conduces to the good of the whole. And though emulation and envy will always spring up, even among citizens of the latter sort, yet, as they have no partisans that follow them for their own private ends, they cannot hurt the commonwealth; on the contrary, they must of necessity be of service to it, for this very emulation will naturally excite their utmost endeavors to excel each other in their merits towards their country, and make them *keep so strict a watch over one another's actions, that none of them will have it in their power to transgress the bounds of good citizens.* But the divisions in Florence constantly ended in factions, and therefore were always pernicious to the republic; nor did any one of those factions continue united any longer than it had subdued the adverse party; for when once that was done, and consequently all fear and restraint were at an end, it immediately subdivided, and split itself into others."

In truth, it is impossible that divisions, in any form of simple government, should ever end in the public good, or in any thing but faction. The government itself is a faction, and an absolute power in a party, which, being without fear and restraint, is as giddy in one of these forms as in any other. " De l' absolu pouvoir, vous ignorez l' ivresse." It must, therefore, divide, if it is not restrained by another faction; when that is the case, as soon as the other faction prevails, they divide, and so on; but when the three natural orders in society, the high, the middle, and the low, are all represented in the government, and constitutionally placed to watch each other, and restrain each other mutually by the laws, it is then only, that an emulation takes place for the public good, and divisions turn to the advantage of the nation.

" Cosimo's party got the upper hand in Florence in the year 1434; but, as there were still many very powerful men left on the side that was depressed, they yet stood in some awe of them, and therefore thought proper, not only to continue united, but to behave themselves with moderation; nor were they guilty of any misconduct or oppressive act, of consequence enough to draw upon them the hatred of the people; so that whenever they had occasion for the suffrages of their fellow-citizens to renew their authority, they always found them ready to reëstablish the chiefs of their party in any office they desired. Accordingly, from 1434 to 1455, a period of twenty-one years, they were six times appointed by the general council to fill the balia.

"There were in these times two very powerful citizens in Florence, Cosimo and Neri; the latter of whom had acquired his reputation in the public way, so that he had many friends, but few followers and partisans. Cosimo, on the other hand, having gained his authority both by his public and private behavior, had not only many friends, but partisans and dependents also; and these two continuing strictly united, never found any difficulty in obtaining whatsoever they asked from the people, as their power was founded upon the favor of the public. But Neri dying in the year 1455, and the adverse faction being utterly suppressed, this administration met with much opposition before they recovered their former authority; and chiefly from Cosimo's friends, who being now grown very powerful in the state themselves, and freed from all further apprehensions of their enemies, were likewise desirous to lower his popularity. This jealousy gave beginning to the troubles that broke out in the year 1446; for those who were then the leading men advised their fellow-citizens, when they were assembled in the general council, to take the state of the commonwealth into consideration, not to create any more balias, but to resume the imborsations, and to choose their magistrates by lot out of the purses that had been formerly filled. To cure them of this frenzy, Cosimo had no other remedy, but either to seize forcibly upon the government, by the assistance of such partisans as still adhered to him, and to crush all opposition at once; or to let things take their course, and wait till time should convince his friends that they were laboring only to destroy their own power and reputation and not his. He chose the latter expedient; for he knew he should run no risk in that, as the purses were filled with the names of such as were well affected to him, and that he might consequently take the administration into his hands again whenever he pleased. He suffered them therefore to proceed to an imborsation; but when the new magistracy was drawn, and every one thought they had now fully recovered their former liberties, the magistrates began to act in their respective departments, not according to the dictates and directions of those leaders, but as they thought fit themselves; so that sometimes the friend of one great man, sometimes the creature of another, met with an unexpected rebuff; and those who before used to see their houses filled with presents and solicitors, now had neither substance

sufficient to live upon, nor even common servants to attend
them. They likewise had the mortification to see themselves
reduced to a level with such as they had used to look down
upon with the highest contempt and disdain; and those who
before were their equals, now suddenly advanced far above them.
They had neither honor nor respect shown them by any one;
on the contrary, they were insulted and abused wherever they
went; and everybody made so free with their private characters
and public conduct that they soon begun to be aware that it
was not Cosimo, but themselves that had lost their authority.

"Cosimo in the mean time took little or no notice of these
things; but when any thing was deliberated upon that he
thought would be agreeable to the people, he was the first that
promoted the execution of it. But what struck the greatest terror into these grandees and gave Cosimo a fair opportunity of
making them repent of their past behavior, was the renewal of
the catasto, established in 1427,[1] by which the taxes were regulated and proportioned by law, and not levied according to the
caprice or pleasure of particular men. This law therefore being
revived, and officers appointed to see it executed, the grandees
having had a consultation together, went to wait upon Cosimo,
and entreated him to use his endeavors to deliver both them and
himself out of the hands of the plebeians, and to new-model the
government in such a manner that they might retrieve the reputation which formerly had made him so powerful and them so
much respected; to which Cosimo made answer, 'that he would
do what lay in his power for that purpose with all his heart,
provided it could be brought about legally and quietly, and with
the good-will and approbation of the people; but that he never
would consent to violent measures or using force of any kind.'

"They then endeavored to get a law passed in the councils for
a new balia; but finding it would not go down, they returned
to Cosimo, and besought him in the humblest manner that he
would make use of his interest to get it passed; but with this
Cosimo peremptorily refused to comply, being determined to
make them fully sensible of their error. Upon which Donato
Cocchi, who was the gonfalonier of justice, resolved to set up a
balia without his concurrence; but Cosimo raised such a spirit

[1] See p. 73.

among the rest of the magistrates, that they not only opposed
him with the utmost vehemence, but laughed at him, and treated
him with so much scorn and derision, that it drove him stark mad,
and he was carried back to his own house, raging and frantic.

"Luca Pitti,* a bold and resolute man, being now made gonfalonier of justice, Cosimo resolved to leave the management to
him; so that if any miscarriage should happen, or any odium be
incurred, it might be thrown upon the gonfalonier, and not upon
him. Luca was very importunate with the people to appoint
a balia; but perceiving it was to no purpose, he not only treated
those who were members of the councils with great insolence,
but threatened them, and soon after put his threats in execution;
for having filled the palace with armed men, in 1458 he called
the people together in the piazza, and there compelled them, by
force of arms,† to do that which they would not so much as
hear of before. After they had thus resumed the government,
they created a balia; and the new magistrates, at the instigation of a few particular persons, who advised them to support
an authority with terror which they had usurped by force, began
their administration with sending Girolamo Machiavelli and
some others into exile, and depriving many more of their honors
and employments. But Girolamo, not observing the bounds
that were prescribed to him in his banishment, was afterwards
declared a rebel; and, travelling about Italy to excite other
states to make war upon his own country, he was betrayed
and apprehended at Lunigiana, by one of the governors of that
place, who sent him to Florence, where he was put to death in
prison.

"This administration lasted about eight years, and was indeed
a very tyrannical and insupportable one; for, Cosimo being now
grown so old and infirm that he could not attend to public affairs
with his usual assiduity, the government fell into the hands of a
few insolent and rapacious men, who knighted Lucca Pitti for

---

* Luca Pitti, tenuto uomo animoso, e molto più audace, che savio, o pru-
dente. Nerli, p. 48.

† Però avendo Luca Pitti già consumato il primo mese del suo magistrato, non
lasciò passare molti giorni del secondo, che avendo disposto i signori suoi com-
pagni, et provvisto il palazzo d' arme, e di forze, e Cosimo, e gli altri della parte
essendosi provveduti, e armati in favore de' signori, fecero chiamare il popolo in
piazza e si venne al parlamento secondo il costume solito mediante il quale si
creò una nuova balià, e si ristrinse in quello lo stato, ordinandosi nuove imborsa-
zioni, &c. Nerli, p. 49.

the good services he had done the state; he had also rich presents
made him, not only from Cosimo and the signori, but from all
the principal citizens, so that he became very rich, and built
several magnificent palaces, and finished them by very arbitrary
means, extorting more and greater presents from the chief citizens, whom he obliged to furnish him with all necessary materials, and making the commonalty supply him with workmen
and artificers.

"The divisions which arose in Cosimo's party in 1455, were
for some time happily composed by his moderation and prudence;
but in the beginning of the year 1464 he fell sick, and soon after
died,* an event much lamented both by his friends and enemies;
for those who did not love him for reasons of state, seeing their
governors so greedy and ravenous while he was alive, and that
they were only restrained by the reverence they bore to his person
from proceeding to open violence, began to fear, now he was
dead, that they should be utterly ruined and devoured. They
had but little hopes in his son Piero, who, though a very worthy
man, had so weakly a constitution, and was yet so raw and
inexperienced in matters of government, that they thought he
would be obliged to comply with the measures of the others;
and there being no longer any person of sufficient authority left
to check their career, they would become every day more and
more oppressive.

"The loss of Cosimo was therefore universally regretted, and
with great reason; for, considering he was no soldier, he was the
most renowned and illustrious citizen that Florence or any other
republic in the memory of man had produced. As he surpassed
all others of his time in riches and authority, so he far exceeded
every one in prudence, liberality, and magnificence; which great
and amiable qualities made him the head of his country. Though
he showed a truly royal spirit in his great works and actions, and
was in fact the sovereign of Florence, yet so remarkable were his
prudence and moderation, that he never transgressed those bounds
of decency which ought to be observed by a modest republican.
In his little parties of pleasure, in his conversation, in his alliances,
and in every respect, he both acted and spoke like any other
citizen; well knowing that pomp and pageantry, and ostentatious

---

* In 1464, in the seventy-fifth year of his age. Nerli, p. 49.

parade, are not only of little real service, but excite that envy among men which is not incident to such actions as are done with an appearance of modesty and humility. No man of his time had a more perfect knowledge of mankind in general. In all the various revolutions of so fickle and fluctuating a commonwealth, he maintained his authority for the space of thirty-one years; for, as he was naturally sagacious, he foresaw dangers afar off, and therefore took timely care to prevent them. This great man was born in 1389. The former part of his life was full of troubles and disasters; but afterwards fortune was so propitious to him, that not only all those who adhered to him in the public administration of the commonwealth were aggrandized and enriched by it, but such as negotiated his private affairs abroad (as he had factors in almost every part of Europe) acquired great wealth; so that many families in Florence raised immense fortunes under his influence, and several others owed every thing they had entirely to his advice and assistance. He was continually laying out vast sums in churches, public buildings, and charities of different kinds. He was likewise a great patron and benefactor to learned men, and first brought Argyropulus to Florence, a Grecian by birth, and the greatest scholar of his age, to instruct the youth of Florence in the Greek tongue, and made him preceptor to his son and nephew. This writer dedicated his works to the family of Medici; namely, — his translation of Aristotle's Ethics and Physics, his own book De Regno, &c. Cosimo was at the expense of maintaining Marcilius Ficinus, the restorer of the Platonic philosophy, who translated the works of Plato, Plotinus, Jamblichus, Proclus, &c.; and he had so great an esteem for him, that he gave him a house and estate near his own seat at Careggi, that he might pursue his studies there with more convenience, and entertain him with his conversation at leisure hours."

So that he had great merit in the resurrection of letters, and perhaps in the formation of Machiavel himself, to whom the world is so much indebted for the revival of reason in matters of government, and who appears to have been himself so much indebted to the writings of Plato and Aristotle. Indeed, if ever the rise of any family to absolute sovereignty upon the ruins of a republic could be pardonable, this of the Medici, which was by real virtues, abilities, and beneficence, must be acknowledged to be an instance of it. But it never can be justified, nor ought ever to be excused, where there is a possibility of establishing a constitution well balanced and really free; and it may well be doubted whether any nation that has once been free can ever become so universally or even generally corrupted as not to be able to conduct a government of three well-balanced branches. He died full of glory, and with the highest reputation. After his death, all the states and princes of Christendom sent compliments of condolence to his son Pietro; and he has this inscription engraved on his tomb by a public decree,—"The Father of his Country." He appears to have had more merit, as well as more art, than Augustus. Machiavel is conscious that he shall be suspected of writing a panegyric upon Cosimo, rather than an historical portrait; and not without reason, for he was a dependent on the Medici family; and he has evidently hurried over some, and glossed over others of Cosimo's acts.

It is scarcely worth while to pursue this history, and relate the conspiracies which were formed against Piero and the Medici, or the suppression of them. The name of Medici had become a charm in the ears of the Florentines, like that of Hercules among the Greeks, Cæsar among the Romans, Orange among the Dutch, and others without end; and if absolute power must be established, it was as well in the Medici as the Pazzi. But Leo X. is not so excusable for not adopting a wiser plan.

"About the time of the death of Cosimo, Louis XI. of France was embroiled in a troublesome war, raised against him by his barons, at the instigation of Francis, Duke of Bretagne, and Charles, Duke of Burgundy, which they called the war for the public good.[*] It lay so heavy upon him, that he could give no further assistance to John, Duke of Anjou, in his designs upon Genoa and Naples. Hence Ferdinand of Arragon became King of Naples, and Count Sforza, Duke of Milan and Lord of Genoa; and these two having contracted family alliances together, began to take all proper measures to establish themselves and their posterity in their governments. For this purpose it was judged necessary that the king should, in the first place, make sure of such of the nobility as had taken part with John of Anjou against him in the late wars. The king made use of every artifice to

* Philip de Comines.

reconcile his nobility to him, and at last succeeded; for they saw
that if they continued in arms against their sovereign, they must
inevitably be ruined; but if they came to an accommodation with
him, or submitted to his mercy, they might obtain a pardon.
Accordingly, these noblemen made their submission to him; but
they were afterwards, upon one pretence or other, at different
times all put to death."

" In 1465, Paul the Second, a Venetian, was elected pope; and
the next year, Sforza, Duke of Milan, died, and was succeeded
by his son Galeazzo; an event that not only added fuel to the
animosities that were rekindling in Florence, but occasioned them
to burst out into a flame. For, after the death of Cosimo, his son
Peter, being left heir to his riches and authority, thought proper
to attach himself to Neroni, a man of very great power and reputation in the city, and of whom Cosimo had so great an opinion,
that upon his death-bed he gave Peter a strict charge to consult
him, and to be guided entirely by his advice in every thing that
related either to the management of his own estate or the administration of the public. In consequence of this command, Peter
sent for him, and having told him how great a confidence his
father had reposed in him, said he hoped he would assist him
both in conducting his private concerns and in the government
of the city. Neroni promised to serve him faithfully; but when
they came to examine Cosimo's books, they found his affairs in
very great confusion. Neroni, therefore, who was more influenced
by motives of self-interest and ambition than either by the friendship he had professed for Peter, or the remembrance of the obligations he lay under to his father, thinking he had now a fair
opportunity of ruining that reputation and authority to which
Cosimo left him heir, gave him a piece of advice, which, to all
appearance indeed, seemed both equitable and necessary, but
ultimately tended to his destruction. He represented to him in
how great disorder his affairs were, and what large sums of money
he would have immediate occasion for, if he intended to support
his family interest, and the reputation they had acquired of opulence and power in the commonwealth; and that there could be
no relief or expedient so proper as to call in the debts that were
owing to him, both from foreigners and his fellow-citizens; for
Cosimo, out of his natural generosity, and in order to establish
an influence at home and gain friends abroad, had always been

so ready to open his purse to every one who stood in need of his assistance, that those debts arose to a prodigious amount. To this proposal, which seemed but just and reasonable, Peter consented, and, like an honest man, resolved to make use of his own substance only in that emergency; but he had hardly called upon two or three of his debtors, before the whole city was in an uproar, every one upbraiding him with avarice and ingratitude, and loading him with all manner of reproaches and ignominious names, as if he had come to plunder them of their own property, instead of demanding payment of a lawful debt.

"Neroni, seeing the general resentment which his own counsel had excited against Peter, turned his back upon him, and entered into a combination with Luca Pitti, Soderini, and Acciaivoli, to deprive him of all power and authority in the state. The end they all had in view was the same; but their motives to pursue it were very different. Pitti was ambitious to succeed Cosimo in the government of the republic; and he became so great after his death, that he disdained the thoughts of stooping to Peter. Neroni, who knew that Pitti was not equal to so great a charge, thought, that if they could by any means get rid of Peter, the chief power must of necessity in a short time devolve upon him; Soderini was desirous that the city should enjoy more liberty, and be governed by the proper magistrates, as it used to be in former times; Acciaivoli had a particular quarrel with the Medici; thinking Cosimo had not used him well in an award between his son and his wife, and not being able to revenge himself upon Cosimo, he was now determined to do it upon Peter.

"However, they all availed themselves of the same pretext, and said, that they neither desired nor aimed at any thing further than that the republic might be governed by lawful magistrates, and not by a little junto of particular persons. The failure of several merchants about that time still increased the clamor that was raised against Peter, and gave the people fresh occasion to revile him; for they made no scruple of imputing the blame to him, and said, that the sudden and unexpected calling in of his money had been the occasion of those bankruptcies, to the great loss and discredit of the merchants in particular, and the prejudice of the whole city. Besides all which, as he was going to marry Lorenzo, his eldest son, to Clarissa de gli Orsini, everybody took occasion from thence to calumniate him; publicly declaring,

that since he could not think any match in Florence good enough
for his son, it was plain he did not regard them any longer in
the light of fellow-citizens, but was taking his measures to make
himself their sovereign. From such a temper in the people,
these ringleaders of sedition promised themselves certain success, especially as the greater part of the citizens were so bewitched
with the name of liberty, which had been made use of to varnish
over those private designs that they cheerfully listed under their
banners.

"But while these ill humors were fermenting, there were some
who, out of a real love for their country, and abhorrence of civil
discord, resolved to try if they could not stay them, for a
while at least, by turning the attention of the people upon some
more entertaining object; considering, that an idle populace is
generally made use of as a tool to serve the purposes of such as
attempt innovation. To employ them, therefore, in such a manner as might best divert their thoughts, and prevent them from
entering into cabals and conspiracies against the government,
and at the same time to console them in some measure, after
their mourning for the loss of Cosimo, who had now been dead
a year, these citizens thought it would be no bad expedient to
revive the public spectacles with which the people used to be
entertained. Tournaments also were instituted, in which Lorenzo carried away the prize from all others.

"But as soon as these entertainments were over, the citizens
returned to their former machinations with more ardor than ever;
from whence arose great troubles and divisions, which were much
inflamed by the expiration of the balia, and the death of Francis
Sforza, Duke of Milan. Galeazzo, the new duke, sent ambassadors to Florence, to confirm the treaty of alliance that had been
concluded between his father and the republic; one article of
which was, that the Florentines should pay that prince a certain
yearly subsidy. The principal of Peter's enemies took the opportunity which this demand furnished, of publicly opposing him in
council, and refused to comply with it."

We may pass over the long, though entertaining account of
the commotions, intrigues, and civil war between one party,
whose object was the ruin of Peter and the Medici family, both
in their private affairs and in their public influence, and the
other, who exerted themselves for their preservation. The last

prevailed, and the other was banished and confiscated. Some of these fled to Venice, and harangued the senate of that republic into a war against Florence and the Medici; but this war was unsuccessful; peace was soon made; and the Florentine exiles, deprived of all hopes of ever returning to their country, dispersed into different places. Tranquillity abroad succeeded; but now the Florentines were grievously harassed and oppressed at home by the tyranny and ambition of their fellow-citizens; for Peter was so disabled by his infirmities, that he had it not in his power to curb the insolence of his own partisans, or to provide any remedy; he sent, however, for the principal of them, and sharply reprimanded them. It is generally believed that, if he had lived, he would have recalled the exiles, to bridle the tyranny and rapacity of his own friends; but death, in the fifty-third year of his age, put an end to these good designs. He left two sons, Lorenzo and Giuliano, both very promising.

" Soderini was at this time the most considerable among the leading men of the state, and for his prudence and authority, in great reputation, not only in Florence, but with all the princes of Italy; so that after the death of Peter, he had the highest reverence and respect shown him by all the citizens, who daily resorted in great numbers to his house; and several states and princes addressed their letters to him, as head of the commonwealth. But as he was a wise man, and thoroughly understood his own fortune, and likewise that of the Medici, he modestly declined returning any answer to those letters; and gave his fellow-citizens to understand, that it was not to him, but the Medici, that they ought to pay their court. He assembled the heads of all the chief families in the city, and presented to them Lorenzo and Giuliano, and said, that if they were desirous to live in peace and union at home, and secure from foreign invasions, it was necessary to continue their observance to the house of Medici, and support those young gentlemen in the authority which their ancestors had enjoyed; that it was but natural to show the same regard to the family, which they had so long been used to do, and therefore it must rather be a pleasure, than a grievance, to them; for if mankind were apt to be fond of novelties, they were, for the most part, as soon disgusted with them; that it had been found much more easy to maintain a power, the envy against which was, in a manner, extinguished by time, than to raise another, which must unavoidably be subject to new emulations and speedy ruin from many causes and unforeseen accidents. Lorenzo, too, though very young, made a speech with much gravity and modesty. The citizens, before the assembly broke up, solemnly engaged to be guardians of their youth, and they, on the other hand, as solemnly promised to reverence them at all times as their protectors and parents."

After which, Lorenzo and Giuliano were looked upon as the heads of the republic, and putting themselves under the guidance and direction of Soderini, the state seemed to be perfectly composed, neither distracted by intestine discords, nor embroiled in foreign wars. But Bernardo de' Nardi soon found means to excite the ruined families, who had been exiled at the fall of Luca Pitti, to kindle another war, which was extinguished only by the destruction of the town of Prato. After this insurrection, which was suddenly raised and soon suppressed, the citizens of Florence began to sink into luxury and effeminacy. The youth, growing more dissolute than ever they had been before, and having nothing else to do, threw away their time and estates in dress, in feasting, in gaming, in women, and other such dissipations. Their whole study and emulation was to surpass each other in fine clothes.

A new war broke out on occasion of a mine of alum discovered at Volterra. Soderini thought a "lean peace better than a fat war;" but Lorenzo, thinking this a favorable opportunity of distinguishing himself, and being supported in his opinion by those who envied the authority of Soderini, his opinion prevailed, and Volterra was reduced.

In 1476 happened the assassination of Galeazzo, Duke of Milan, and the destruction of the assassins, who, as usual in such cases, were left unsupported, both by the nobility and the multitude who had at first encouraged them. Such examples ought to be warnings to princes, to reign in such a manner as to make themselves honored and beloved by their subjects ; and to others, against trusting to nobles or the multitude, except in a very good cause ; for though these may be discontented to the last degree, they will seldom stir a foot to their assistance in distress or danger.

"After the Medici had gained such an ascendant, by the

9 *

defeat of their enemies in 1466,[1] they grew so powerful, that they in a manner engrossed the government of the republic wholly to themselves; and their power was so great, that such as were disaffected to their administration, were either obliged to submit to it with patience, or endeavor to shake off the yoke by clandestine machinations and conspiracies; which being attended with great difficulties and dangers, for the most part end in the ruin of the conspirators, and only serve still more to aggrandize and strengthen those against whom they are formed. Italy was divided into two confederacies; the pope and the King of Naples were on one side; the Venetians, the Duke of Milan, and the Florentines, on the other. When Philip de' Medici, Archbishop of Pisa, died, the pope appointed Francesco Salviati, an enemy of the family of Medici, to succeed him. The signori refused to give him possession of the see. The Medici were discountenanced upon all occasions at the court of Rome, while the greatest respect and partiality were shown there to the Pazzi, a family, indeed, which at that time was one of the richest and most powerful in Florence. Cosimo, considering their opulence and quality, had married his granddaughter, Bianca, to Guglielmo de' Pazzi, in hopes of uniting the two families more strictly, and hoping to prevent all jealousies and emulation betwixt them by such an alliance.

"But so vain and fallacious are all human designs, that the event proved quite contrary to his expectation, for some of Lorenzo's friends having insinuated to him that it would be dangerous to him, and a diminution of his own authority, to throw any more power into the hands of that family, he would not suffer Giacopo, nor any of his brothers or nephews, to enjoy such honors and offices as they seemed in the opinion of their fellow-citizens to deserve. The Pazzi were so exasperated at this usage, that the Medici began to be afraid of them; and the apprehensions of the one seemed to increase in proportion to the resentment of the other; for in all competitions for places of honor or profit, the Pazzi, how much soever they might be favored by the suffrages of the people, were always sure to be set aside and rejected by the magistracy. The Pazzi, therefore, thinking it intolerable that people of their rank and fortune should be

---

[1] Lib. viii.

treated in that injurious manner, began to meditate revenge. Francesco accordingly concerted a conspiracy with many other persons, and attempted to assassinate both the Medici at church. Giuliano was murdered with such circumstances of perfidy as would disgrace the most infamous cause, much more a cause dignified with the name of liberty. Lorenzo defended himself with great bravery, and escaped with a slight wound. The insurgents rode about the town, and cried, Liberty! liberty! and called upon the people to join them. But such was the influence of the Medici, and so much were they beloved, on account of their liberality and other princely qualities, that the rest of their fellow-citizens did not desire to see any change of government. The whole city was raised, and Lorenzo safely conducted by a great number of armed men to his own house. The palace was recovered by the people, and all those who had seized upon it were either taken or killed; the streets resounded with shouts of, Long live the Medici! while the limbs of the conspirators who had been killed were either carried upon halberds, or dragged round the city; every one endeavoring to show his resentment, both in words and actions, against the Pazzi; for they not only plundered their houses, but hurried Francesco out of his bed to the palace, and there hung him up, close by the archbishop and his associates. So great was the favor and interest which the family of the Medici had gained among the people, by their prudence and liberality, that there was not a citizen of any degree whatsoever who did not go to Lorenzo, and make him an offer both of his person and fortune. Rinato and Giacopo de' Pazzi were both apprehended, condemned, and executed, with so many others, that the streets and highways were full of their limbs. None of them were much lamented, except Rinato, who had always been esteemed a prudent man, and void of that family pride which was laid to the charge of all the rest."

After the conspiracy was suppressed, and the authors of it punished, the funeral of Giuliano was solemnized with great pomp, and attended by all the citizens. He left one son, born some months after his death, and named Giulio, who was afterwards Pope Clement VII.

" The pope and the King of Naples, disappointed in bringing about a change of government in Florence by underhand machinations, now resolved to attempt it by open war; but the good fortune of the family, Lorenzo's address, and the steady attachment of the Florentines to him, carried them safely through this danger too. After the quarrels among the more considerable states were composed, in the course of several years there happened many other disturbances in Romagna, La Marca d'Ancona, and Siena; they were more frequent in Siena than anywhere else, after the departure of the Duke of Calabria, in 1488; but after many changes and revolutions there, in which sometimes the commonalty, and sometimes the nobility prevailed, the nobility at last effectually suppressing the other party, Pandolpho and Giacopo Petrucci, one of whom was in the highest repute for his wisdom, and the other for his valor, became, in a manner, princes of that city.

"As for the Florentines, they lived very happily, and in perfect tranquillity, from the end of the war till the death of Lorenzo, in 1492. For Lorenzo, having established a general peace throughout Italy by his great wisdom and prudence, had begun to turn his thoughts entirely to the aggrandizement of the republic and the care of his own family. In the first place, he married his eldest son Peter to Alfonsina, daughter to Cavaliere Orsino, and procured a cardinal's hat for Giovanni, his second son, who was not quite thirteen years of age when he was promoted to that dignity, of which there had been no example before; but he ascended by degrees through all the preferments of the church, till he was exalted to the pontificate, under the name of Leo X. His third son, Giuliano, was but an infant. He also disposed of his daughters very much to their advantage. In his mercantile affairs he was rather unfortunate; for such was the extravagance of his factors, who lived more like princes than private men, that they had dissipated the greater part of his merchandise; so that he was often obliged to borrow large sums of the public. His chief desire was to promote union among the people, and support the nobility in that degree of honor and respect that was due to them. He showed great favor to those who excelled in any art, and was a very liberal patron to learned men. He was passionately fond of poetry, music, and architecture. He founded the University of Pisa. Immediately after his death, such sparks of discord began to rekindle, as shortly broke out into a flame, and preyed upon the vitals of Italy."

Peter, the great-grandson of the first Cosimo, having entered into a league with Louis XII. of France, without the consent of the signori, was ejected by the Florentines, and retired to Venice; so that the Florentines recovered and enjoyed their ancient liberties till 1512, when Ferdinand, King of Spain, restored the family of Medici. It was again expelled in 1529. In 1530, Charles V. seized upon Florence, and made Alexander de' Medici, great grandson of Lorenzo, and who married his natural daughter Margaret, sovereign and duke of Florence. Alexander was murdered about seven years after, and having left no children, was succeeded by his brother John, whose son Cosimo was created Grand-Duke of Tuscany, by Pope Pius V. in 1569. Voltaire says, that the period while Florence was under the government of the Medici ought to be called the Medicean age, as the polite arts and sciences were then carried to the highest degree of perfection; then it was that those great geniuses, Ariosto, Machiavel, Guicciardini, Cardinal Bembo, Trissino, Casa, Bernini, Raphael, Michael Angelo, Titian, Paul Veronese, and so many others, adorned the age, and rendered their names immortal.

CHAPTER SECOND.

GUICCIARDINI begins his history of the wars in Italy, where Machiavel concludes that of Florence, with the death of Lorenzo de' Medici in April, 1492, the same year that the sagacity, fortitude, and good fortune of that ever memorable native of Coguretto, a village near Genoa, Christopher Columbus, of plebeian birth, but of noble genius, in the service of Ferdinand and Isabella of Spain,* laid the first foundation of the constitutions of the United States of America.

" The death of Lorenzo was a severe misfortune to his country, which had flourished under the influence of his prudence, reputation, and genius, in all the blessings and embellishments of a long and secure peace ; and very inconvenient to all Italy, who regarded him as a principal counterbalance to Ferdinand of Naples, and Sforza of Milan, princes as ambitious as they were powerful.

" Peter II., the eldest of his three sons, who succeeded him without contradiction, was not qualified by experience or abilities for so important a station. Deviating early from the councils of his father, and without consulting the principal citizens, he was wholly directed by Orsino, a relation both by his mother and his wife, but a dependent of Ferdinand. This new connection, so prudently avoided by his father, excited the jealousy of Sforza, and was the source of all the ensuing evils."

Without reciting the particulars of his vanity, rashness, and imprudence, especially a foolish treaty with France, which he made without consulting the magistrates, it is sufficient to say, " that, on the ninth of November, 1494, as he was going into the palace, Nerli, a youth of noble birth and great wealth, at the head of some others of the magistracy, stood armed at the gates,† and forbade him to enter. The populace, as soon as the

---

* Muratori, Annali, tom. ix. p. 367, anno 1492.
Guicciardin, lib. 6. Americus Vespucius, who began his voyages in 1497, the first two of which he made by order of Ferdinand of Castile, and the last two by order of Emanuel of Portugal, was a native of Florence.
† Nerli, p. 62. Muratori, Annal. tom. ix. p. 374, anno 1494. Fu egli dichi-

report of this insurrection spread in the town, instantly took arms. Peter, destitute of courage as well as advice, returned to his own house, where he was informed that the magistrates had declared him a rebel; upon which he fled with precipitation to Bologna, and was followed by his two brothers, Giovanni the cardinal, and Giuliano, who were likewise attainted. Thus, through the rashness and levity of a thoughtless youth, the family of the Medici fell, for the time, from a sovereign power which they had exercised for sixty years. From Bologna they went to Venice. After some time, the king, their ally, obtained a reversal of Peter's attainder, and that of his two brothers, and a restitution of their effects, on condition that Peter should not approach within a hundred miles of the borders of the republic. This was designed to prevent him from settling in Rome; his brothers were not to come within a hundred miles of the city."

After the exile of Peter and his brothers, the city of Florence attempted once more to reform its government; [*] "but," says Nerli, "the citizens who ought to have reformed the state, fell into the same error with all who had preceded them in similar enterprises, and founded the new government, as others had done whose steps they followed, upon parties and civil factions, as may be seen in the whole history of Florence, and for the benefit and convenience of the superior party and more powerful factions, and not at all for the benefit of the generality, or the universal good; and therefore it was impossible that a pacific and quiet republic should succeed, or a durable government be established. They created, however, according to the ancient custom of the city, and by means of a parliament, always a scene of violence, and inconsistent with all civil modesty, twenty Accoppiatori, or associates, with authority to imborse the signori from time to time, and to create, with other restless disturbers of the public peace, the principal magistrates; and they resolved, that Lorenzo di Pierfrancesco de' Medici, who then declared himself one of the inhabitants, de' popolani,[1] though under age, should be one

arato co' fratelli ribello, posta taglia contro le loro persone, e poscia messo a sacco il ricchissimo loro palagio.

[*] Nerli, p. 63.

[1] This translation does not quite give the sense of the original. He had been harshly treated by his cousin whilst in authority, and returned to Florence under

of the twenty; and this was accomplished by their extraordinary
reputation and influence, and thus he was made the head of the
new government; and this whole revolution changed nothing
but the head, and not at all the nature of the government."

It was in this convention, which Nerli calls a parliament, that
those elegant speeches which Guicciardini[*] has preserved, or
composed, one for Soderini and the other for Vespucci, are supposed to have been made; but it is surprising to see that neither
orator, so eloquent and able, nor yet the historian who so elegantly
reports the debate, appears to have once thought of the natural
and necessary remedy. One is for a government simply popular,
and the other for a form simply aristocratical; but neither thinks
of an equal mixture of the three forms, nor even of the two; nor
does an idea occur of separating the legislative from the executive
power. Soderini admits that, " among all writers upon government, praises have been more liberally bestowed upon the administration of a single prince, and upon that of a few of the best
citizens, than upon any popular government;" but he thinks that
" the desire of liberty is so natural or habitual in that city, and
the condition of the citizens so proportioned to that equality
which is the necessary foundation of a popular government, that
it ought, without any doubt, to be preferred to all others."   He
even thinks a question could not be made of this, " as in all their
consultations it had ever been determined, with universal consent,
that the city should be governed in the name and by the authority
of the people. But the diversity of opinions arose from this, that
some would cheerfully consent in the regulation of the convention
to that form of a republic with which the city governed itself
before her liberty was oppressed by the family of the Medici;
others, among whom he reckons himself, judging a government
so ordered to have, in many things, rather the name than the
effects of a popular government, and terrified with the accidents
which frequently result from it, desire a more perfect form, which
may preserve concord and security to the citizens; blessings
which, neither from reason nor experience, can be expected in
this city, if it is not under a government dependent entirely on

---

the amnesty to all who had opposed him. In order to avoid the odium in which
the family name was held, he caused it to be changed to that of *Popolani*, and
altered his coat of arms.

[*] Guicciardini, lib. ii. p. 41, Ven. 1574.

the power of the people. This must, however, be well ordered by two fundamental regulations. The first of these is, that all the magistrates and officers, both in the city and all its dominions, shall be distributed, from time to time, by a *universal council* of all those who, according to our laws, are qualified for a participation in government; without the approbation of which council new laws cannot be considered. Hence, it not being in the power of private citizens, nor of any particular conspiracy or intrigue, to distribute dignities or authority, none will be excluded from them by the passions or caprice of others, but they shall be bestowed according to the virtues and merits of men. By consequence, every one must endeavor, by his virtues, good manners, and by rendering himself agreeable both in public and private life, to open his way to honors. Every one must abstain from vices and injuries to others, and, in one word, from all those things which are odious in a well-constituted city. It will not be in the power of any one, nor of a few, by new laws, or by the authority of a magistrate, to introduce another government, or to pretend to alter this, but by the resolution of the universal council.

"The second fundamental regulation is this; that all the most important deliberations, as those of peace and war, the examination of new laws, and generally all those things which are necessary to the administration of such a city and dominion, shall be treated by magistrates particularly destined to this service, in a select council of the most experienced and prudent citizens, who shall be deputed by the popular council; for, as the knowledge of these affairs of state is not found in every understanding, precautions should be taken that the government may not fall into hands incapable of conducting it; and the celerity and secrecy which are often indispensable, cannot be consulted or preserved in the deliberations of a multitude. Neither is it necessary for the maintenance of liberty, that such things should be treated by large numbers; for liberty remains secure at all times when the distribution of magistracies, and the deliberations on new laws, depend on universal consent.

"These two points being secured, the government will be truly popular, the liberty of the city well founded, and a laudable and durable form of a republic established."

He then compares his project with the plan of Venice,—to

which it has not, however, the smallest resemblance,—and proceeds: "This city of ours has never enjoyed a government like this, and therefore our public affairs have been constantly exposed to frequent mutations; at one time trampled down by the violence of tyranny; at another torn by the ambitious and avaricious dissensions of the few; now shaken by the licentious fury of the multitude: and alt! ough cities are built for no end but the tranquillity, security, and happy life of the inhabitants, the fruits of our government, our felicity, our repose, have been the continual confiscations of our estates, the banishments and the executions on the scaffold, of our miserable citizens."

This is the substance of Soderini's oration, in which he is fully sensible of the tyranny and slavery of alternate factions, and the consequent miseries with which the history of Florence is filled; but, instead of proposing a rational remedy, he is for aggravating the evil. The executive power, the appointment of officers, had been the cause of discord. He now only proposes to give those appointments to the multitude, instead of a senate; to the universal, instead of the particular council; the only effect of which would be, that more heads would be turned, and more passions inflamed.

The oration of Soderini was answered by Vespucci, a famous lawyer, and a man of singular genius and address. "If," says he, "a government, instituted in the manner proposed by Soderini, most excellent citizens, would produce such desirable fruits with the same ease that they may be described, he would certainly discover a most corrupted character who should wish any other for the regulation of our country. He would be a most pernicious citizen, who should not love, without reserve, a form of republic, in which virtue, merit, and the real value of men, should be above all things acknowledged and honored. But I confess myself ignorant how it is possible to hope that a government, placed absolutely in the power of the people, can be productive of such mighty blessings. On the contrary, I well know, what reason teaches, experience demonstrates, and the authority of the greatest lawgivers confirms, that, in so great a multitude, there can never be found such prudence, such experience, and such order, as may give us room to promise ourselves the wise will be preferred to the ignorant, the good to the bad, or men of experience to those who have never seen a public transaction. For as, from an incapable and unskilful judge, it is not possible to hope for a sagacious sentence, so, from a people immersed in ignorance and involved in confusion, we cannot expect, unless by accident, prudent deliberations or rational elections. Can we believe that a multitude, inexpert, unskilful, compounded of so great a variety of geniuses, conditions, and customs, and wholly devoted to their private affairs, can possibly distinguish and know those intricate interests and duties of the public, which men of the most consummate wisdom, who are wholly inattentive to any other business, are often with great difficulty able to discern? Not to mention, that the unbounded esteem which every one entertains of himself, will stimulate them all to become ambitious of honors, it will never be satisfactory to men in a popular government to enjoy the honest fruits of liberty, but all will aspire to the highest rank, and be impatient to intermeddle in deliberations upon affairs of the most importance and greatest difficulty. For among us there is less than in any other city in the world of that modesty which yields the precedence to him who has more knowledge or more merit. Persuading ourselves, as we do, that, in reason and by right, we ought all of us to be equal in all things, the places of virtue and merit, if left in the disposition of the multitude, will be confounded; and this ambition, being diffused through the majority, will designedly bestow the most power on the most ignorant and the least meritorious; because, being by much the most numerous, they will have the most influence in a state so constituted that opinions in it are numbered and not weighed. What certainty, therefore, can you have that, although they may be satisfied with the form that you introduce at present, they will not presently disarrange the institutions the most wisely concerted, by their novel inventions and imprudent laws? And these the wisest citizens will not be able to resist. These things, at all times dangerous in such a government, will be much more so at present, because it is the nature of mankind, when they fly from one extreme, in which they have been held by violence, to rush with greater violence, without stopping at the mean, to the other extremity. Thus, he who escapes from a tyranny, if unrestrained, precipitates himself into an unbridled licentiousness, which also may most justly be called a tyranny; for a people is exactly like a tyrant, when they give to him who has no merit, and take away from him who has

much; when they confound all gradations and distinctions of
persons; and their tyranny is perhaps so much the more pestiferous, as ignorance, which has no weights, nor measures, nor laws,
is more dangerous even than malignity, which does govern itself
by some rule, restrain itself by some bridle, and satisfy itself with
some end. . . .

"Has this city ever been under the absolute government of the
people, without becoming an instant prey to discord, without
being shaken to its foundation, and without suffering an immediate revolution in the state?   Why are not our liberties secure
under the government proposed in this parliament?   All things
are referred to the disposition of magistrates, who are not perpetual, but are frequently changed; who are not elected by a few,
but, having been approved by many, are appointed, according to
the ancient usage of the city, by lot.   How then can they be
appointed by factions, or by the will of particular citizens?   We
shall have a much greater certainty that affairs of the most importance will be examined and directed by men of the most wisdom, experience, and gravity, who will govern with more order,
secrecy, and maturity of judgment, than it is possible for a people,
who are incapable of such things, to possess; a people, who are
often, when there is little occasion for it, most extravagantly
splendid and expensive; and oftener still, when there is the most
urgent necessity, so penurious and niggardly, as to rush upon the
greatest dangers and expenses, for the sake of saving the most
trifling sums."

In truth, both these speeches, with all their eloquence, were
thrown away.   Soderini was for collecting "all authority into
one centre," the people; and Vespucci into another, the senate.
Neither dared propose a separation of the executive from both,
in a first magistrate; and without that, and admitting both the
senate and people to a share, there could be no peace nor harmony
in Florence.   The question, however, was not decided by the
logic or rhetoric of either.   Few of the citizens attended the convention, and the vote would have been for the aristocracy of
Vespucci, if another orator had not intervened.

This was Girolamo Savonarola, the prophet, who declared that
he had a divine revelation from heaven in favor of a popular
government, and that Jesus Christ should be chosen King of

Florence,[*] against his own express declaration, that his kingdom was not of this world. The twenty *accoppiatori*, who had no head to keep them united, necessarily fell into a variety of factions and divisions among themselves. Perceiving their dissensions, the other citizens in general, and especially all those of the greatest reputation, who, at the election of the twenty, had not been chosen of the number, began to take courage, and raise a cry against them for the weakness of their government; and Savonarola declared, that God had constituted him his ambassador in Florence, with full power and express orders to declare his will, that Christ should be king, and that under him the city should be governed only by a single assembly or popular council. The multitude believed him, and in 1495 the twenty were all obliged to resign, and give place to the greater council and popular government;[†] and a new palace was built for them, with such ardent enthusiasm, that it seemed to be true, what Savonarola declared, that the angels had acted as masons and architects, that the work might be the sooner finished.

But this new government could no better agree than the *accoppiatori*, and for the same reason. The new great council, as well as the whole city, soon divided into three parties. The greatest and most powerful was that which depended upon Fra Girolamo, and was called the party of the Frateschi, and consisted of those who most desired, and of nearly all those who were gratified with the latitude of the popular government. The second party were desirous of having the government more restrained, and in the hands of a smaller number of the principal citizens; but they were still desirous of liberty, and, as well as the Frateschi, were in opposition to the party of the Medici. The third party consisted of those who wished for the return of the Medici, and the restoration of the old government. The views, motives, and manœuvres of these three factions, their jealousies, envies, ambition, and various schemes to supplant each other, are particularly described by Nerli, and in so natural a manner, that one would think his history written expressly to expose the folly of a government in one centre.

---

* Nerli, pp. 64, 65.
† Il consiglio maggiore, e il governo popolare. Nerli, p. 66. Che gli angioli in quell' opera s' esercitassero in luógo de muratori, ed operai, perchè più presto fusse finita.

In 1495, the Florentines met with fresh and dangerous troubles from other quarters, excited by the potentates of the league, who encouraged Peter to attempt his restoration to Florence. Peter, like all other exiles, ready to embrace every offer, imagined his own party so powerful, and the new government so odious, especially to the nobility, that he could not fail of success. He made several advances, and excited some exertions among his friends; but being disappointed of effectual assistance, he at length gave up the enterprise.

In 1497, the pope and the Venetians conceived a new project for separating the Florentines from the French. The unhappy state of their city, in which there were such great divisions among the citizens, owing to the form of their government, gave encouragement to any power that wished to molest them. For, says Guicciardini,—[1]

"In the first institution of the popular authority in Florence, there had not been introduced a mixture of those temperaments which, whilst they secured, by suitable methods, the common liberty, might prevent the republic from being thrown into confusion by the ignorance and licentiousness of the multitude. For this reason, the citizens of better rank, meeting with less respect than their condition seemed to require, the people, on the other hand, being jealous of their ambition, multitudes of mean capacity frequently assisting at important debates, and the supreme magistracy, to whom was referred the decision of the most difficult affairs, changing every two months, much confusion was occasioned in the government of the republic. To this must be added the great authority of Savonarola, whose followers were more numerous than those of the contrary opinion, and appeared to have much the greater share in the distribution of places in the magistracy, and of public honors; by which means the city becoming manifestly divided, one party still clashed with the other in all the public deliberations, as it always happens in divided cities, when *men care not how much they obstruct the common good, in the desire of lowering the reputation of the adverse party.* These disorders were the more dangerous, because, besides the long vexations and great burdens borne by that city, there was that year a very great scarcity; whence it

[1] Lib. iii.

might be presumed that the half-starved populace were desirous of a change. This unhappy disposition gave hopes to Peter, who was besides incited by some of the citizens."

With secret assistance from the Venetians, and in various other ways, he collected together a military force, and made an attempt upon Florence; but, having neither genius nor resources, he failed. His partisans committed a number of massacres in some of the neighboring towns; but his plot was discovered, and his principal friends in Florence, after full proof of the order and management of the conspiracy, were convicted and sentenced to death. By virtue of a law that was made when the popular government was established, the relations of the persons condemned appealed to the grand council of the people. The other party, apprehending that compassion for their rank, age, and numerous relations, might prevail on the affections of the people, several members of the supreme magistracy were, by pressing importunities, and almost by force and menaces, constrained to consent that, notwithstanding the interposition of the appeal, execution should be done the same night. Of what avail is law in such a government, for the protection of life or security of liberty? The most zealous sticklers for this were the favorers of Savonarola, who was reproached for not dissuading his followers from the violation of a law which, but a few years before, had been proposed by himself, as necessary for the preservation of liberty. But a dominant party, when there are but two, and no third power to balance them, is never long restrained by law, morals, or decency.

The next year, 1498, Savonarola himself was burnt, not for his enthusiastic impostures, but for preaching against the corruptions of the court of Rome, under that hellish monster of vice and cruelty, Alexander VI. This would not have been remembered here, if politics and party, rather than piety, had not produced this event, as well as the assassination of a nobleman of great influence, Francesco Valori, for being the chief patron of Savonarola, and the cause that the appeal to the popular council had not been admitted. The passions of parties, their hatred and revenge, as well as their ambition, under such unbalanced governments, lay hold of any popular prejudice, most frequently of religious zeal, and the assistance of any means, even the friendship of an Alexander and a Borgia, to aid their gratification.

"But scattering the ashes of this martyr in the Arno did not," says Nerli, "quench the flames of discord, nor heal the divisions of the city. The people remained in the same dissensions, every one quarrelling for his faction as usual;[*] and fresh disputes and dissensions arose; first, between Vitelli and the Count di Marciano; second, by reason of the difference between the King of France and the Duke of Milan; and, third, on account of elections and the magistracies."

In 1500, Cæsar Borgia,[†] having already subjected a great part of Romagna, desirous of extending his dominions in Tuscany, and having good intelligence of the disposition and divisions in the city of Florence, attempted to restore the Medici, but was diverted from the enterprise by an embassy and a round sum of money. In 1502, a rebellion, excited in the city of Arezzo, opened fresh divisions in Florence, and produced new attempts to reform the government, first, by giving a head to the greater council, and, second, by constituting a gonfalonier for life. Soderini, who had no children, had great qualities, was moderately rich, of a family of great reputation, &c., and had rendered important services to the state upon many occasions, was accordingly elected. But he had no thoughts of changing the popular government any further, and was soon found to have too much moderation for some of his friends. Rucellai, and Lorenzo di Pierfrancesco de' Medici, and some other citizens, broke off from him, would not attend his feasts, and grew discontented.

This year (1502) died the pope Alexander VI. Peter de' Medici, with some other noblemen, following the French camp after their defeat by the Spaniards at Gaeta, entered on board a bark laden with artillery, and was drowned at the mouth of the river, by the bark's sinking under her burden in a contrary wind. But these events, so fortunate in appearance for Florence, could not secure her tranquillity. The new gonfalonier for life had many parties in fermentation against him; those who desired a more popular government, and that his office should be annual, or only for three months; those of his own party, who thought him not zealous enough to make the government more aristocratical; and those who wished the restoration of the Medici, and a govern-

---

[*] Nerli, p. 81. Restò il popolo nostro nelle medesime dissensioni, e travagliato dalle sue solite sette. come si fusse prima.

[†] Nerli, p. 88. Muratori, *Annali*, tom. x. p. 1.

ment completely monarchical. All these various classes of citizens were daily observing his conduct, criticizing his administration, exaggerating his errors, and destroying his reputation and popularity.

In 1505, Bartolomeo d' Alviano invaded the country,* with a view to assist the Medici; but he was routed and put to flight. From so great a victory the citizens hoped for happiness, quiet, and repose; but the effects of it were quite the contrary, and increased the secret opposition to the gonfalonier, and the cabals of the discontented citizens. Bentivoglio, ambitious to be made captain-general, and Giacomini, to increase his popularity, united in the desire of adding the conquest of Pisa to the glory they had acquired in the late victory. The project of this enterprise occasioned great confusions in the city. The wisest and best men declared themselves against it; but such numbers were bent upon it, that the gonfalonier, either blinded by the same passions, arising from success, or wishing to counteract his adversaries, or confiding too much in Bentivoglio, fell in with it. After tedious disputes, angry accusations, and mutual reproaches in the city, the enterprise was resolved upon in the great council, with loud huzzas of the common people. A great expense was incurred in ample preparations, but the end was as unfortunate as the wiser citizens had predicted; the two principal officers destroyed all the credit of their former services, and Soderini, the gonfalonier, lost much of his reputation, more of the popular confidence and affection; and, in proportion as these fell, those who had opposed the war rose in the public esteem. The enemies of the gonfalonier increased, and their opposition, headed by the Salviati, grew more active and determined, and weakened the government to such a degree, that it was alike unable to execute the resolutions, when taken by so small majorities, to command the soldiers, to elect the council, the eight commissaries of war, or ambassadors, or, indeed, to resolve upon any thing. The two parties

* Nerli, p. 95. Muratori, *Annali*, tom. x. pp. 25, 26. " Erano i cittadini quasi tutti dichiarati a quale delle due parte più aderissero, o a quella del gonfaloniere, o a quella de' Salviati, di maniera che nel fare de parentadi, o nel concedere per mezzo de' magistrati grazie, o benefizi, o nel favorir questo, o quell' altro cittadino, che de' magistrati avesse bisogno, si scoprivano le passioni, e gl' interessi del gonfaloniere, o de' Salviati, ed in somma veniva in gara, se si dovevano pure rimutare, o di nuovo eleggere per insino a' tavolaccini del palazzo, e in ogni minima cosa si scoprivano gl' interessi delle sette." Nerli, lib. v. p. 99.

could agree upon nothing; and all the citizens were such decided partisans, either of the gonfalonier or of the Salviati, that they would not intermarry, or even give a vote for any man to any office or public favor, who was not of their side.

In the grand council, and in the city, causes enough of debate arose from day to day. In 1506, an ordinance for regulating the militia in the country, and enrolling every man from fifteen to fifty years of age under captains and colors, for frequent exercise in the military art; the demand of Alfonsina Orsini, the widow of Peter de' Medici, of the restitution of her dower, confiscated with the estate of her husband; the marriage of her daughter Clarissa to Philip Strozzi; the resignation of the Archbishop of Florence; the appointment of a successor; the war of Pisa; in 1508, the creation of commissaries; the concession of Pisa to the King of France,—all occasioned such struggles, as excited at last a conspiracy to assassinate the gonfalonier, for the purpose of introducing the restoration of the Medici. This plot was discovered, but the guilty persons had such parties in the city, and the gonfalonier was become so unpopular, that only the slightest punishment could be inflicted. As, in such a state of parties, every measure of government is opposed, another controversy arose about the continuance of the truce with Siena, which was at last agreed to upon the concession of Monte Pulciano. Various new disputes were now occasioned by the new council in Pisa. Finally, the city found that, amidst all the great transactions in Italy, by the division among the citizens, and their continual opposition to each other in every reasonable measure, they had not only very ill served their ally, the king, but had given great offence to the pope.

In 1512 was the battle of Ravenna; and after a long series of wars, in which the emperor, the King of France, the King of Spain, the Swiss, the pope, the Venetians, and all other states in Italy had been concerned, a congress was held at Mantua. " Giuliano de' Medici, in his own name and that of the cardinal, here solicited an enterprise against the Florentines. A revolution, he pretended, might be easily effected in that state, through the divisions of the citizens, many of whom wished for the return of his family. By private intelligence, which he said he maintained with several noble and powerful personages in the city, he thought a sudden attack might easily succeed; and the consequence would

be, the taking the power of Florence out of the hands of one who
depended on the King of France, and committing it to persons
who, injured and abused by him, would acknowledge no alliance
but that of the confederates. He was seconded, in the name of
the pope, by Bernardo de Bibiena, afterwards cardinal, who had
been educated in the family of Medici. An offer was secretly
made to Soderini, a lawyer, and brother of the gonfalonier, who
was then ambassador from Florence, that if the Florentines would
comply with the demand of a sum of money, the emperor and
King of Aragon should take them under their protection. The
ambassador had no authority to conclude any agreement, and
could only make his report to the republic. It was believed that,
if the Florentines had laid aside their niggardly chaffering about
the price, they might have diverted the storm; but, either through
the carelessness or the malignity of men, the cause of that city
was abandoned; and it was resolved that the Spanish army,
attended by the cardinal and Giuliano de' Medici, should march
towards Florence, and that the cardinal, whom the pope in this
expedition had declared legate of Tuscany, should call to his
assistance the soldiers of the church, and those of the neighboring
towns, whom he thought fit for his purpose. The viceroy, at the
head of the Spanish army, no sooner entered the Florentine
dominions, than he was met by an ambassador of the republic,
to know what he required of them. The viceroy demanded, in
the name of all the confederates, that the gonfalonier should be
deprived of his office, and that such a form of government should
be established, as would not give occasion of umbrage to the
allied powers; which could not be effected without restoring the
cardinal and Giuliano de' Medici to their country.

"The government of Florence was in the greatest consternation, from the divisions among the citizens, and the inclination
of multitudes to a change. A message arrived from the viceroy,
that it was not the intention of the league to make any alteration in the government or liberty of the city, but only to remove
the gonfalonier from the magistracy, for the security of Italy,
and to restore the Medici, not as heads of the government, but
as private persons, to live in all things under subjection to the
laws and to the magistracy. Various were the opinions in the
city, according to the difference of men's judgments, passions,
and fears. The gonfalonier, in a long harangue to the great

council,* offered either to resign his envied office, or to defend it
at the hazard of his life, as they should determine.

"If the Medici," says he, "have an inclination to live as private citizens, in due subjection to the ordinances of the magistrates, and of your laws, their restoration would be laudable. . . .
But let not any one imagine, that the government of the Medici
will be exercised in the same manner as before their expulsion.
The form and foundation of things are changed; educated
among us, almost like other private citizens, possessed of vast
estates in proportion to their high dignity, and offended with
none, they laid the foundation of their greatness in the affections
of the citizens; but now, bred up in strange customs, and having little insight into our civil affairs, resenting their exile, very
indigent, affronted by so many families, conscious that the
greater part of the people abhor tyranny, constrained by poverty
and suspicion, they will have no consideration for any citizen,
but will engross the direction of all affairs to themselves, and
establish their administration on fear and force, not on love and
benevolence. The city will become like Bologna under the
Bentivogli, or like Siena and Perugia."

"It was, with wonderful unanimity, resolved to consent to
the return of the Medici as private citizens, but to refuse the
removal of the gonfalonier, at the hazard of their lives and fortunes; and all hands were set to work to prepare for war, and
the defence of Prato."

The viceroy laid siege to Prato, and took it by assault, which
was followed by flight, shrieks, violence, rapine, blood, and slaughter. This sad disaster produced a vast change in the minds of
the people at Florence; the gonfalonier, repenting of his counsel,
was terrified, and became deprived at once of all esteem and
authority; others grew audacious; several young noblemen,
with one of the family of Albizzi at their head, who had been
in secret correspondence with the Medici, forced the gonfalonier
out of the public palace, and the magistrates were compelled to

---

* "Fece al popolo una orazione bellissima, che a que' tempi, e in quel caso
era molto a proposito, la quale, essendo io alloar in quel consiglio, udii quando la
fece, ed è anco molto elegantemente scritta da Messer Francesco Guicciardini
nella sua storia. Narrò in quella il gonfaloniere tutte le sue azioni di dieci anni;
dipoi offerse se, le facultà, e la propria vita per beneficio della città, e per mantenere quel libero governo, ed alla fine si rimesse tutto in quel popolo, che l' aveva posto in quel grado." Nerli, Lib. v. p. 108.

depose him.* He fled to Ragusa. Ambassadors were sent to the viceroy, with whom, by means of the Cardinal de' Medici, they easily made an accommodation. He insisted only on the restoration of his family and their adherents, as private citizens, with power to redeem, within a certain time, the confiscated estates, indemnifying those to whom they had been transferred for the purchase and improvements. The Florentines were obliged to enter into the league, pay to the emperor forty thousand ducats, and to the viceroy eighty thousand for his army, and twenty thousand for himself. They made a league besides, with the King of Aragon, under reciprocal obligations of assisting each other.

It is astonishing that the Florentines should not yet have been able to see the causes of their continual misfortunes, and the necessity of different orders, and a balance in their constitution. They now applied themselves to reform their government, to preserve their liberty, and the popular council, their "all authority in one centre," their right constitution of a commonwealth.

" To this end they enacted, that the gonfalonier should no longer be elected for life, but only for a year; that to the council of eighteen, which was changed every six months, and by whose authority the most weighty affairs were determined, should be added, for life, all those who had discharged the great offices of state, at home or abroad, that the citizens of greatest quality might always assist at their debates. At home, such as had been gonfaloniers of justice, or of the number of the ten of

---

* Tal fine ebbe il supremo magistrato di Piero Soderini esercitato da esso nove anni, e dieci mesi, e se in tale amministrazione, oltre a molte sue buone opere, avesse aggiunto quel, che anche molto più importava alla città, e a lui, l'aver tenuto più conto, che non fece, di chi veramente l'aveva condotto in quel grado, giovava forse più assai, che non fece, alla città, a suoi cittadini, a se medesimo, ed alla sua casa, e sarebbesi quel governo popolare forse anche meglio mantenuto, come si mantenne, ne primi otto anni, che si resse senza capo alcuno dopo il 1494, che non fece poi in quei dieci, che lo resse Piero Soderini. E se quel suo governo di nove anni e dieci mesi fu, ed è ancora tanto lodato, nacque da quel buono ordine, che si tenne più nello splendere, e nello stare meglio ordinata la città, che in quelli primi otto anni non si fece, e dal considerarlo più da quello, che pareva in apparenza, che da quello, che era in fatti, ed in somma il gonfaloniere non seppe mai esser principe nè cattivo, nè buono, e credette troppo colla pazienza, godendo, come si dice, il benefizio del tempo, superare tutte le difficultà, che se gli opponevano, e non bene avverti, come debbono fare i principi savi, e i buoni capi, e governatori di republica, che sempre, e ad ogni cosa la pazienza non giova, e che il tempo a lungo andare può arrecare così male, come bene. Nerli, pp. 109, 110.

the balia, a magistracy of great authority in that republic; abroad, all, who by election of the council of eighty had been sent ambassadors to princes, or had been commissaries-general in war. In all other points the laws remained without alteration. Ridolfi, a noble citizen, was elected gonfalonier for the first year; the people, as usual in troublesome times, not paying so much regard to those who were most acceptable to them for popular arts, as to a person who, by his great authority in the city, especially with the nobility, and by his own extraordinary talents, was best capable of establishing the tottering commonwealth.

" But things were now gone too far, and the enemies of public liberty were become too powerful. A suspected army was in the country, and the most audacious youth in the city were desirous of oppressing liberty. With them concurred in thought and deed, though in word he pretended the contrary, the Cardinal de' Medici; for the restoration of his family as private citizens could not have been thought from the beginning a reward worthy of so great fatigues and dangers. But now he considered that they must be universally detested by the people, from a suspicion that they would be continually exciting conspiracies against their liberty, and from the indignation conceived against the family for conducting the Spanish army against their country, and being the cause of the barbarous sackage of Prato. The cardinal was stimulated too by those who had before conspired with him, and had no honorable station in the new commonwealth. He therefore obtained the consent of the viceroy, unexpectedly entered Florence, and repaired to the houses of the Medici with a number of Italian officers and soldiers, the magistrates not daring to forbid their entrance on account of the neighborhood of the Spanish army. The next day a great number of citizens being assembled in council in the palace, and Giuliano de' Medici among the rest, the soldiers suddenly forced the gate, and rushing up stairs took possession of the palace. The gonfalonier and the magistrates were forced to submit to the will of a man whose arms were more powerful than their unarmed reverence, and at the motion of Giuliano, they called, by sound of the bell, an assembly of the people in the square of the palace. Here those who met, finding themselves surrounded by armed soldiers, and the youth of the city in arms for the Medici, consented that fifty citizens, nominated with the approbation of the Cardinal de' Medici, should be invested with the whole sovereign power of the people, which the Florentines call a balia. The government was reduced to that form which subsisted before 1494; a guard was stationed at the palace, and the Medici resumed their former grandeur, but governed more imperiously and with more absolute authority than their father Peter had done. After this manner was the liberty of the Florentines oppressed by arms, being reduced to this condition by the divisions among the citizens." [1]

" On the first of September, 1512, the new signori, without any gonfalonier or supreme magistrate, united with Giuliano de' Medici and the principal citizens of Florence, and especially with those who, having been in opposition to Soderini, or being relations or declared friends of the Medici, were the most in their confidence, to give orders for a new reformation of the city. It was thereupon ordained, by an intrigue of the signori, that a cabal of about twenty citizens should determine among themselves the mode of reformation in the state. But even in this junto many contests arose, and various projects were proposed. There were among them some who, without considering the forcible manner in which the Medici had returned, wished to reëstablish the popular government, and maintain, by all means, the grand council, at least in part, in its authority, and in order to give the government a head, would constitute a gonfalonier for one year, or two at most; they further desired, in order to give a greater perfection to the government, to make an addition of select citizens to the council of eighty, who should be as a senate of the best men for life, with a certain authority and full power, and with certain particular orders and prescribed forms. Of this opinion were the greater part of those citizens who had been in opposition to Soderini, not so much from attachment to

1 "Telle fut l'étroite et honteuse oligarchie qui fut substituée au gouvernement libre et constitutionel de la république. Le parlement sanctionna la révolution; car les seuls citoyens déterminés à tout approuver se rendirent sur la place publique, au milieu des soldats qui faisoient violence à leur patrie. La nouvelle balie prononça peu de condamnations, mais elle abolit la plupart des magistratures protectrices de la liberté; de plus, elle licencia, dès le 18 Septembre, l'ordonnance ou la milice Florentine, et elle fit désarmer le peuple. Un gouvernement que les étrangers ont établi par la violence doit craindre toute force nationale; et pour se maintenir, il doit désarmer et avilir la nation qui lui est soumise." Sismondi, Rép. Italiennes, vol. xiv. p. 268.

the Medici as for other reasons   The Medici and their most
avowed partisans, and chiefly those who, in their opposition to
Soderini, had discovered themselves the most averse to the popular state, because they did not think they could obtain pardon
from the people, could scarcely hope to live in freedom, and
were sure to have no share in the government, would, for their
greater security, restrain the state to its ancient form and
remodel it by a convention, not believing that they could
accomplish it in the ordinary way, as it had been restrained in
the house of Medici before the year 1494. After many accom-
modating manœuvres of Giuliano de' Medici, by his great
facility and kindness with those who desired a large government, and to preserve the grand council, it was concluded to
pass a law in this cabal for the reformation of this government,
and it was accordingly proposed in the grand council, and
received with great applause. For everybody was so dispirited
and so terrified with the thoughts of a convention of the people,
which was much talked of, and greatly desired by those who
wished to restrain the state into an aristocracy, that this new
law of reform was highly relished, as it lessened the authority
both of the people and the grand council.

"By the new law it was ordained, that, for the future, the
gonfalonier should be created by the grand council for one year,
should be disqualified from holding the office for five subsequent
years, and that all his connections should be excluded during
his year from holding any of the greater magistracies, such as
those of the signori, the sixteen gonfaloniers of the companies
of the people, and the twelve buoni homini. The chief magistrate
was also prohibited from holding a negotiation or correspondence with any other prince, republic, or lord, in or out of Italy;
from opening any letters addressed to the signori or any other
magistrate, without the presence of two thirds of the signori his
companions; or even any letter addressed to him alone, without
the presence of two at least of the signori, who, under the pains
of perjury, were obliged to show such letters to the other signori,
if they found any thing in them relative to the state or public
affairs. The ladies, too, and families of the gonfaloniers were
prohibited from inhabiting the palace, and from sending any letters or messages to any officer or magistrate abroad or at home;
and the gonfalonier was assigned for his whole salary four hun-

dred golden florins a year. As to the mode of electing the senate, surplusage, or optimates before mentioned, such disposition was made by this new law for the reformation of the government, that for the future, at all administrations, deliberations, and elections of magistrates, usually made in the council of eighty, all the then present signori, and all those citizens who at any time had been gonfaloniers of justice, all those who had sat among the ten magistrates for war, and all who at any time had been elected ambassadors in the council of eighty to any prince or lord in or out of Italy, should assist during their lives. And to provide for those families or societies in which there were not men of any such description, it was decreed by the law that such families might claim as far as two members, if they had the number of two, or, if they had not, one, with the ordinary qualifications, but no more ; and that such supplementary additions from the families should not amount to more than fifty in the whole, to be elected in the council of eighty, with its new addition, giving of these fifty a convenient part to the lesser arts, according to the order at that time in the city. And because Giuliano de' Medici and some of his declared friends were incapable, either by minority of age, or by having in their families two or more who came within the ordinary rules, that they might not be excluded, it was provided by the law, that by a resolution of the signori alone, eleven more, besides the fifty, might be elected, eight of whom might be under the age prescribed of forty years. In this manner was the council of eighty, with its addition, to be constituted, and in it from time to time were to be created the signori, the ten magistrates for war, and the eight for the guard, in such manner as those magistrates were wont to be elected in the greater council, observing the order of elections in the quarters of the arts, and all the forms which had been observed in electing such magistrates in the greater council. And to facilitate still further the public business, and to take away still more effectually, both from the people and the great council, the opportunity and the power of disarranging the public councils by withholding supplies of money, admonished by many past examples, the law provided, that such provisions of money and impositions of taxes for the public occasions should be passed, in the first place, in the council of eighty, by two thirds of the black votes or

11*

balls, according to the forms of balloting, and be approved in the greater council by a division of one half of the black votes, and one more. The law was passed, and the same day, in October, 1513, and in the same council, they proceeded to the election of a new gonfalonier. At the first ballot there was no choice, but at the second Giovan Batista Ridolfi was elected, and, in the presence of the council, took upon him, with the other signori, the supreme magistracy." *

This plan of reformation, however, had greatly terrified the partisans and most declared friends of the Medici, as it appeared to them they should be in great danger, when an accommodation should be made with the league, and the Spanish army should be marched out of the dominions, of being again banished from Florence, to their total ruin, that of the new constitution, and the whole house of Medici; and in this apprehension they were well grounded, for although there was in the new plan an attempt at three natural branches, yet the·executive power and the power of the purse were both left in the hands of the aristocracy, which would have instantly produced a division both among nobles and people, and the destruction of the house of Medici, as well as of the feeble popular branch of the constitution. Here was the best possible opportunity for introducing the most perfect form, by giving the executive power to one of the Medici, the power of the purse to the people, and the legis-

---

* In questo tempo, per ordine de' vincitori, fu fatto menzione nel libro publico, chiamato il priorista, del parlamento fatto, e de' Medici restituiti alla patria, a piede di quel priorato, ch' era entrato in ufficio a dì primo di Settembre 1512, essendo gonfaloniere di Giustizia Giovambatista Ridolphi, nel qual priorista, si notano tutti i signori priori, che alla giornata si fanno, et aggiunto à ciò come la nobiltà si era vindicata, e ridotta in libertà, e riformato, e stabilito il governo della città, secondo la volontà de gli ottimati, e patrizii. La quale distinzione di nobiltà, ed ignobiltà, confesso io ingenuamente non haver mai saputo fare, ancorachè io sia nato, et allevato nella medesima patria. Ma la lezzione delle presenti memorie farà cognoscere colle spesse mutazioni d' animi, e di pensieri, e delle opere, quale sia stata sempre la diversità, e la contrarietà de gli humori de' nostri cittadini. Conciosiacosachè io hebbia veduto i figliuoli discordare da padri proprii, ed i fratelli da i medesimi fratelli nell' azzioni di questa stolta favola del mondo, secondochè chiascuno è stato vinto, e traportato dall' empieto de' proprii appetiti. Nardi, lib. vi. p. 266.

"Jamais je n'ai pu comprendre, ce que c'est que la noblesse. Qu'est-ce que c'est que la noblesse?" said one of the first duchesses in France. "Ah, madame, c'est un droit divin," said a gentleman in company. "Oui, tout comme la royauté; tout de même, je vous comprend bien," replied the lady, who had too much sense to pique herself on her divinity, or to believe a syllable of the matter.

lative power to both, together with the nobility; but either no man understood the subject, or too much ambition in the Medici, too much pride in the nobility, too many prejudices in the people, or all three together, prevented it.

The election too of Ridolfi, who was thought to be, as indeed he was, a spirited man, of a celebrated house, most illustrious parentage, and of great reputation, increased their terror, especially as, in the deliberations on the new reformation, he had discovered himself much in favor of a popular life. He had been ordinarily conspicuous in the faction of Frateschi, among the first of whom he had been incorporated, after Valori, and had, in all times, conjunctures, and circumstances, favored that party which was ever in opposition to the house of Medici, as is manifest to any one who has a knowledge of those times. Whereupon many of the most open friends of the Medici, and those who most dreaded a popular government, entered into close concert with the Cardinal de' Medici, for the purpose of correcting the errors which Giuliano, his brother, by his too great facility, had suffered to slide in.

" It was not difficult to dispose the cardinal to this, as they found him, since the late reformation, under the same apprehensions, and in the same disposition with themselves; neither himself, nor Messer Giulio, prior of Capua, his cousin and a natural son remaining of Giuliano who died in 1478 by the conspiracy of the Pazzi, judging it possible securely to continue in Florence, if the government remained in that manner in the hands of the people, and at the free discretion of the citizens. Wherefore the cardinal came sometimes into the city, for he had resided in Prato when the reformation of the state was made in Florence, and took lodgings in St. Antonio del Vescovo, a place near the city, where he was visited by a multitude of the citizens, under various pretences. There, discoursing with all concerning the condition of affairs as they happened, he began with great address to represent to some that it was necessary to think of a good method for securing the state and his house; dwelling only upon general observations, and not descending to any particulars with those whom he believed to be desirous of a popular government; but consulting with his more confidential friends, and with those whom he knew to be discontented with the new regulation of the government. At last, he opened himself to a few, showing the necessity, of a convention and a balìa to a small number of citizens in whom they could confide, who might contract the state to the form in which it stood before 1494 in the hands of the family of Medici.   After these practices held at St. Antonio, the cardinal came to Florence, resolved to call a convention and contract the state; then those citizens, fitly called the blind, who had been so opposed to Soderini, began to see, when it was too late and they had no longer power to provide a remedy, that danger now at hand, which they had not been able to discern when at a distance.

" On the 16th of September, 1513, the convention was assembled, the Medici and their friends in arms having seized the palace, which had been left without a guard, because Ridolfi, when he entered on his office of gonfalonier, either from a want of jealousy of the Medici and the viceroy, who was yet with his army at Prato, or for some other reason, not only had not armed the palace, as, in order to establish the new government, it was necessary to do, but had caused it to be disarmed of the few guards which had been stationed there by the magistrates after the privation and departure of Soderini; wherefore it was easy for the Medici and their partisans to seize it.   The signori and the gonfalonier, and many other citizens, seeing the palace taken, and the absolute determination of the Medici and their armed followers to contract the state, and that they could no longer support the popular government, yielded to Giuliano de' Medici, who was in council, and had orders from the cardinal what to do.   The people were accordingly called together in convention, according to the ancient custom of their parliaments, in the piazza; the signori mounted the rostrum, and a balìa was created, that is, full power was given to fifty-five citizens for one year, with the faculty of prolonging it beyond that period according to circumstances, for the convenience and support of the state and the government, and with the faculty, moreover, of associating to themselves in the balìa such other citizens as might be thought useful to the state."

The first thing resolved on was to add eleven members to the number, making in the whole sixty-six, whose names Nerli* has preserved.   The next was to make a treaty with the league,

* Nerli, pp. 116 – 118.

and to pay well to obtain the consent of the Spanish army to march out of Prato and the Florentine dominions. An ambassador was sent to accompany the viceroy of Spain, and another, the *locum tenens* of Maximilian the emperor. A strong guard was placed in the palace; Ridolfi renounced his office of gonfalonier; all the members of the family of Soderini were taken up and dispersed about in different confinements. A plan was established for the appointment of all officers, and the sum total of power was lodged in Giuliano de' Medici, who, however, was to consult with the cardinal, with Messer Giulio, with Lorenzo their nephew, the son who remained of Piero di Lorenzo de' Medici; but when the new distribution of offices took place, fresh divisions and dissensions arose, and secret plots were discovered, whose object was nothing less than the assassination of all the Medici. Among the conspirators were many powerful citizens. The chiefs of the party were beheaded, and the rest severely punished.

"At length the pope, Julius II., died, and the cardinals in conclave,* on the seventh day, unanimously elected Giovanni, Cardinal de' Medici, who assumed the name of Leo X., aged thirty-seven. This election gave great satisfaction to all Christendom; all men expecting, from the recollection of his father's great merit, and from the fame of his own liberality, benevolence, charity, and irreproachable morals," (so says the historian, but his actions discover an ambition too powerful for his virtue.) " that Leo would prove an excellent pontiff, and, from the example of his ancestors, a lover of men of genius and learning. His first transaction was his coronation, which was performed with so pompous an appearance of his family and all the prelates and nobles from all parts, and so great a concourse of the Roman people, that Rome had never seen so proud a day since the inundations of the barbarians; the standard of the church was carried by Alfonzo d' Este; that of the religious order of Rhodes by Giulio de' Medici, all in armor, and mounted on a noble courser, for he was by nature inclined to arms, though his destiny drew him to the church. Such magnificence confirmed the vulgar in their expectations of happiness from this pontificate, which was likely to abound in liberality

* Guicciardini, lib. xi. Nerli, lib. vi. p. 124.

I

and splendor, as the expenses of that day amounted to a hundred thousand ducats; but men of better judgment were of opinion that so much pomp neither became a pope, nor was suitable to the times, which required more gravity, simplicity, and moderation.

"This exaltation of Giovanni occasioned great rejoicings in Florence,* for both the friends and enemies of the family were pleased, though for different reasons; the former from the hope of benefits and advantages, and the latter from the expectation of security, and the universal tranquillity of the city, which they thought would succeed. There remained, however, as may well be imagined, a secret discontent in the hearts of the wise, who could foresee at a distance that so much grandeur in one family, who for sixty years had held in their hands the supreme authority of the government, might in time be the means of their return, and enable them to change the state from a republic to an absolute principality.

"Upon this glorious occasion, Valori, Folchi, Nicholas Machiavel, and all the others who, on account of the late conspiracy, had been hitherto imprisoned, were liberated from the tower of Volterra; a conspiracy which, if no further attempts had been made, and the two who had been beheaded could have been restored to life, would now have been wholly forgotten. The Soderini too were all set at liberty, because the cardinal of that family had concurred with his vote in the creation of the pope. Cardinal Soderini had been gained over to this election by a promise of the liberation of his relations, and that Lorenzo di Piero de' Medici should marry his niece, the daughter of his brother Giovanvetterio; but this alliance never took effect, because Alfonsina, mother of Lorenzo, would never consent to it. To compensate for this disappointment, the pope proposed that the cardinal's niece should be married to Luigi Ridolfi, his nephew by a sister; and the cardinal at first seemed satisfied with the exchange, but it afterwards appeared that he took it very ill.

"A splendid embassy of twelve honorable and noble citizens was now sent to the new pope from the city of Florence. In all this grandeur of the house, Giuliano, Lorenzo, and Giulio de'

* Nerli, p. 124.

Medici in a few days appeared at Rome to consult with the pope concerning several of their affairs, and the division of their greatness among them; it was finally resolved that Giuliano should remain at Rome with the title of gonfalonier and captain of the holy see. By means of an alliance which he made with a lady of the blood of Savoy, aunt of the King of France, he secured to himself the duchy of Nemours, and thus voluntarily gave up all pretensions to the government of Florence. Lorenzo contented himself with the state of Florence, and soon returned to govern it in the same manner and form as his father and his other ancestors had governed. Giulio was promoted to the archbishopric of Florence, vacant by the death of Cosmo de' Pazzi, with the prospect of being made a cardinal at the first subsequent creation which the pope should make.

"In this manner, in the beginning of the pontificate of Leo, did the Medici divide among themselves the state and their own power and emoluments. Lorenzo returned to Florence, and consulted with the principal citizens about giving orders for reforming the government in all things to the state it was in before 1494, according to the intentions of the pope, resolved on in Rome. They were very attentive to hasten the general scrutiny, because of the absence of so many citizens, who, for various reasons, had gone to Rome, and, after the creation of the pope, were not in haste to return. When it was finished, imborsed, and begun to be used, a council of seventy was made by Lorenzo, for life, in the form and with the authority of that in the time of his grandfather, in 1482; and orders were also given to constitute a council of a hundred, which from six months to six months, according to the ancient custom, should be drawn. Into this council of a hundred, all who had been gonfaloniers of justice might enter at their pleasure; in it were debated and determined all provisions of money, impositions of taxes, and all laws and ordinances of most importance which had been previously approved in the council of seventy; and to enlarge their system still more, and make it more universally satisfactory, they further ordained a drawing by lot from time to time of the ancient councils of the people and the commons, which might determine on the petitions of private persons, that should be first passed in the council of seventy. In all cases which could occur, and for the security of the state, although they adopted these ordinary councils, they maintained firm the authority of their balia, which was kept constantly in being until the revolution in the state, that happened in 1527. The scrutiny ended, they created the seventy, drew the other councils, and began to make another change of the ten for war, for the eight of their new plan, in order to return every thing to the state it was in before 1494. All these ordinances were thus renewed and perfected in December, 1513, Pandolfo Corbinelli being then gonfalonier; and the seventy were elected for a term only, but with such power of confirmation that they might be said to be for life. Notwithstanding all these precautions, and the absolute power of the balia, divisions among the principal citizens still continued; some were for making the government more popular, others more aristocratical; and these divisions, which lasted till 1527,* gave much trouble to the Medici.

" The affairs of the Medici and of the state being thus settled, Giuliano began to think he had been mistaken in leaving Florence to his nephew; and Lorenzo, amidst such grandeur in his house, began to be discontented at remaining without any princely title, and at having no other than a civil rank in Florence; wherefore he shaped his course to Rome, and communicated his intention to the pope.

"He returned in 1515, determined to be made captain-general of the Florentines; and this dignity was solemnly assumed by him from the hands of the gonfalonier of justice, who was at that time Chimenti Scrnigi, in the presence of the signori, and of all the magistrates, and a great part of the people, assembled in the piazza with the staff of command, and the other public ensigns usually given to a captain-general, with the greatest demonstrations of joy and universal rejoicings. In this manner Lorenzo began to depart from the ancient manners of his family, and to lay aside in all things that mode of proceeding popularly in his dress, conversation, and intercourse with the citizens, which had ever been observed by his predecessors. Having assumed his title and magnificence, he went to Lombardy, to make his court to the King of France, who was come to Italy to establish his authority in Milan, which he had lately recovered. He became

---

* Erano i cittadini appresso a' Medici molto divisi, e dettero queste divisioni, che si mantenero sempre ne' primi cittadini del governo, di molte difficultà a' Medici per insino al 1527. Nerli, p. 129.

a great favorite with his majesty, from the desire he had of agreeing with the pope, and because Lorenzo, in all his actions and conversation, discovered an attachment to the faction of the Guelphs and the politics of France."

"Soon afterwards, an accommodation was made between the pope and the king, and the pope set out on a journey to Bologna, to have an interview with him. Passing through Florence, he made his entry into the city* with great pomp. Between the pope and. the king many things were agreed on, for their mutual defence and the maintenance of their power; and Lorenzo, because he eagerly wished to increase his importance, and obtain the title of duke, solicited the pope, under the auspices of France, to undertake an enterprise against Urbino, as it was thought the king could not fail of success, the pope having restored Parma and Placentia, two cities which Giulio had added to the state of the church when the French lost the state of Milan. But the project of an enterprise against Urbino was very disagreeable to Giuliano de' Medici, and he warmly opposed it as infamous ingratitude, considering the civilities and favors the family had received in their exile from that dukedom.

"The pope was advised to recall the Bentivogli to Bologna, and restore Modena and Reggio to the Duke of Ferrara; but Giulio de' Medici," says Guicciardini, "cardinal and legate of Bologna, whom the pope had sent to be a moderator and counsellor to the inexperienced youth of Lorenzo, moved at the infamy that would be cast on the memory of his legateship if Bologna was given up to its old tyrants, and so great a number of the nobility, who had openly declared against them in favor of the apostolic see, sacrificed to their revenge, dissuaded it.

"Giulio, though of illegitimate birth, had been promoted to the cardinalship by Leo, in the first month of his pontificate, by means of witnesses, who, preferring the favor of men before the truth, deposed, that his mother had obtained of his father Giuliano a promise of marriage. Giuliano this year came to Florence in ill health, and resided sometimes in the city, and sometimes out of it, in the neighboring cities, not without exciting great jealousy in Lorenzo, and Alfonsina, his mother, who governed in the absence of her son. The pope was in great

* Con magnifico apparato, con molta pompa, e con solennità grandissima. Nerli, p. 129.

perplexity, and could not determine whether to undertake the enterprise against Urbino, so much resisted by his brother, and so ardently desired by his nephew; and he hesitated the more, because he discovered that the King of France had consented against his inclination.   Giuliano was so ill, that he could not censure the project to the pope, excepting by his agents and letters, and Lorenzo, by his assiduous solicitations, held the king well disposed to his inclinations, and was continually about the pope with persuasions to undertake it.   The interview between the pope and the king at Bologna being finished, the former returned to Florence, apparently resolved to give satisfaction to his nephew; yet, on account of Giuliano, he proceeded to take measures for the enterprise with some circumspection.   But the disorder of Giuliano increasing, he died in March, 1516, at Badia de Fiesole, where he resided for the benefit of better air. A few days afterwards the pope left Florence, and returned to Rome."

"Lorenzo now remained, without any contradiction, in all things heir of the state, the fortune and the grandeur of the house of Medici; and being now more than ever warm in his desire to be made Duke of Urbino,* he was invested by the pope in consistory.   Lorenzo was put in command of an army, composed of the soldiers and subjects of the church and the Florentines; and the pope deprived † Francesco Maria of these dominions by solemn sentence, and gave the investiture of the duchy of Urbino, in a consistory, to Lorenzo his nephew, all the cardinals setting their hands to the bull.

"In the year 1517 certain cardinals formed a conspiracy against the pope, and the Cardinal Soderini was found among the guilty; but upon confession of their error, the pope excused them with great humanity.[1]   But upon this occasion, in order to fill up the college, he made a new promotion of cardinals, among whom were his two nephews of the Salviati and Ridolfi families.   At this time the citizens of the state of Florence

___

* Nerli, p. 130.   † Guicciardin, lib. xii.
[1] It is difficult to understand this compliment, in the face of the combination of fraud, cruelty, and avarice exposed by most of the historians in telling the story.   The curious reader can gather the particulars in the history of Sismondi, vol. xiv. pp. 432 – 439, with the authorities upon which he relies.   This writer has done the world great service in bringing the conduct of the Medici family to the test of an unswerving moral code.

were in secret very discontented, because the Duke Lorenzo,
desiring to reduce the government to the form of a principality,
appeared to disdain to consult any longer with the magistrates
and his fellow-citizens as he used to do, and gave audiences very
seldom, and with much impatience; he attended less to the business of the city, and caused all public affairs to be managed by
Messer Goro da Pistoia, his secretary. This person, either following the inclination of his own nature, or because the duke
had given him orders what to do, governed in such a manner,
and so conducted himself with the citizens, that there appeared
in him more grandeur, and more of the qualities of a prince,
and he required more honor, than any one of the house of
Medici ever had done in the sixty years that had passed between
1434 and 1494. The citizens, who had borne so much envy
against Galeotto de' Medici, found, in the example of Goro,
reason to acknowledge and repent of their error; for Galeotto,
who held from the Duke Lorenzo the same authority and the
same employment before Goro, and was besides of the family
of Medici, did the public business of the palace, and went in
person to confer with the citizens, and was satisfied with civilly
serving his patron, and with being more in reality, and less in
appearance.

"Lorenzo now made a journey to France, having made an
alliance with the king. In 1518 he returned with his lady, and
the marriage was celebrated with much pomp, rejoicings,* and
festivity. Many citizens at this time, having discovered the
inclination of the duke, and that he was determined to reduce
the state to the form of a principality, would not consent to it.
Some withdrew themselves from public affairs, despairing of the
commonwealth; others confined themselves to their houses, under
pretence of sickness; but others, having more courage and better
support, went to Rome, under the protection of the pope. The
duke, to make the last effort to dispose the pope to reduce the
state of Florence to a principality, went to finish his nuptials at
Rome, and carried with him Vettori and Strozzi, in whom he
confided, and with whom he often consulted; and after many
intrigues with the pope, they returned to Florence, determined to
reform the state. But in 1519 he died, about ten days after his

* Si fecero le nozze sontuosissime, con molta pompa, allegrezza, e festa grandissima. Nerli, p. 131.

wife, who, however, had left him a daughter, afterwards Queen
of France.

"Goro, and the citizens in his confidence, had secretly ordered
the piazza to be fortified, and the guards doubled; and had
caused to be assembled in Florence, from various places of the
dominion, a good number of their friends and confidential partisans, to assist, as occasion might happen, in the preservation of
the public security, and in observing the conduct of those citizens
who had given any cause of suspicion; and Antonio di Bettino
da Ricosoli was imborsed gonfalonier. The Cardinal de' Medici,
who arrived two days before the death of the duke, being sent
by the pope to give orders, regulated all things to general satisfaction.* After the funeral of the duke, the cardinal entered into
intimate consultations with the principal citizens, and reëstablished the government, according to the form and order which
the pope had given to Duke Lorenzo. The cardinal himself
remained, by order of the pope, in the government, to give further satisfaction to the citizens, whom he knew to be disgusted
with the proceedings of Goro in the lifetime of the duke, and the
great authority he had assumed, perhaps greater than the duke
had given him; he reduced the business of the magistrates, elections, customs of office, and the mode of expenditure of the public
money, in such a manner, that there appeared a very great and
universal joy among the citizens; and no other or greater difficulties remained to him than the usual divisions among the
citizens of the state; some of whom contended for enlarging, and
others for restraining the elections of magistrates. Wherefore,
those who wished the state more contracted, at the head of whom
was Ridolfi, opposed themselves to Salviati, who, by order of the
pope, was returned to Florence with the cardinal, and he, for
contrary reasons, was opposed to them; and because the cardinal went on, amusing sometimes one and sometimes the other
party, and supporting both, their divisions were much more
apparent at this time, and the heads of each conducted themselves with less dissimulation than they had done in the lifetime
of the duke. Indeed, the dissensions of the citizens arose in all
important affairs which the cardinal had to provide for or to think
of in his government; whereas, in the other case, in the most

* Nerli, lib. vii. p. 133.

important affairs they followed without any difficulty that which was ordered daily by the pope."

The cardinal seems to have diverted the factions from any effectual opposition to his government, by playing them one against the other, and fomenting their mutual animosities; for his government was very successful and frugal, and money was saved in it to pay off the public debts. But the war soon followed, of Pope Leo X. and Charles V., who had lately succeeded Maximilian in the empire, against the French. The cardinal was sent with his army, as apostolical legate, and went into Lombardy, leaving in his place, in the government of Florence, the Cardinal di Cortona. The affairs of the pope and emperor succeeded prosperously against the French, who lost Milan; but the pope, on the last of November, 1521, died, and finished, in the midst of so much grandeur, the legitimate succession of the house of Medici, and the male line of the first Cosimo, who by a public decree was called "the father of his country," and who, in 1434, had given rise to the greatness of his family.

"After the death of the pope, the cardinal suddenly departed from Milan, and returned to Florence, where he found that the signori had given good orders for the conservation of the state, and that Francesco Vettori, who was gonfalonier of justice, the Cardinal di Cortona, and the principal citizens in the government, had made every provision and taken every precaution for the benefit and safety of the state; and he found, too, on so great an occasion as that of a sudden and unexpected death of the pope, a ready inclination in all the principal citizens, and a universal desire among the people, to maintain the state in the hands of the Cardinal de' Medici; and all this felicity arose from his good government, which, since the death of the Duke Lorenzo, had been universally agreeable.

" Consulting now with the principal citizens, orders were given for defence in the war which Renzo da Ceri, by the favor of the French, had excited in Siena, with a view to change the government in Florence. This war was fomented by the Cardinal Soderini, and occasioned a fresh declaration against his family, that they were rebels, and involved them in greater calamities than they had suffered in 1512. During this war, many citizens began to speak without reserve of a greater degree of liberty, and a new reform of the government. They reported publicly

12 *

that the cardinal, for want of relations and a legitimate succession in his family, would be willing in a measure to dispose of the authority of the balia, and leave the government freely in the people, with a certain authority reserved to a senate for life, to consist of the best citizens, and to himself a balia for some purposes during his life; and when the principal and most suspected persons in this way were secured, although an army was still in Siena, these discourses continued and increased. Many were so eager, and so drawn away by their wishes and their love of novelty, that they began too soon to descend to particulars concerning the manner of reforming the government, which they believed and said ought to be undertaken; and they proposed the mode of electing the gonfalonier of justice; some of them would have him for life, as he had been when Soderini was elected in 1502, and others desired he might be elected annually, as Ridolfi was in 1512. Such was the zeal of many, deceived by their credulity and the ardent passions which transported them, that they began to speak more freely of the person to be elected, and Acciaioli and Vettori were named, and Gondi; but all agreed at last, the better to conciliate the cardinal, to leave the election for the first time wholly to him.

"These practices went so far, that those citizens began to be publicly named and discriminated, who were in favor of the reformation of the government, and those who were against it. That party of the citizens who had counselled the cardinal to a large and comprehensive distribution of honors, and who had ever taken the protection of the generality, appeared, upon these conversations of a reform, to give some attention to it; and that party which desired to hold the public offices and honors in few families, detested and censured those who talked of any reformation at all. The generality of the citizens stood neutral, expecting, however, with great desire, that the reform would take place. One class of young men, and especially those who had concurred in the rise of Rucellai, solicited it, and discovered themselves."

In this manner the whole city was divided and confounded; the greater part of the citizens agitated, some with hopes, and others with fears; and many ventured so far as to write various models for such a reformation, even in the presence of the cardinal. Among these, Zanobi Buondelmonti and Nicholas Machiavel sufficiently distinguished themselves. Nerli says he saw these writings, which were communicated to him by the authors at the time of these intrigues. They were also communicated to the cardinal,[1] who pretended to hold them in high esteem.[*] Alexander de' Pazzi composed a most elegant and beautiful oration, in the name of the people of Florence, in praise of the cardinal, for the restoration of the commonwealth; which Nerli remembers to have heard recited before a large company at a supper, where, having obtained a copy, he sent it to Rome to the Cardinal Salviati. These speculations proceeded so far, and were so freely discoursed on, and in so many ways, that it began to appear to the cardinal that he had permitted them to run too far, and he thought of means to restrain them; but things had gone so much beyond his intentions, he found some difficulty to resist their course.

"Fortune presented him a convenient opportunity, which was this. There had been formed, at the time of the rise of Rucellai, a certain school of young men of letters and of elevated genius, among whom was Cosimo Rucellai, who died very young, though he had excited great expectations among the literati. This society was much frequented by Nicholas Machiavel; and Nerli says he was a most intimate friend of Machiavel, and had frequent conversations in this club. These gentlemen not only amused themselves, but made a business and duty of exercising themselves in the study of history, and in making observations and reflections upon it. At their request Machiavel composed his discourses upon Livy, and his treatise of military matters. These persons went on, thinking, by an imitation of the ancients, to effect something that should be grand and noble, and render them illustrious. At length they wrought themselves up to the thoughts of a conspiracy against the cardinal, and did not well consider what Machiavel in his discourses had written to them on the subject of conspiracies. Had they done so, they would either not have engaged in the design, or, if they had, would have proceeded in it with greater caution. The heads of this plot were Zanobi Buondelmonti and Luigi Alamanni. Their intention was to assassinate the Cardinal de' Medici,

[*] E tutti suoi scritti andavano in mano del cardinale, che mostrava di tenerne conto, e di farne capitale grandissimo. Nerli, lib. vii. p. 137.
[1] The work of Machiavel, stated to have been drawn up at the instance of the pope, is analyzed and commented on after the author's manner in the fourth chapter of this volume.

and thus bring back the city to a free government, and restore
liberty to the people, as they enjoyed it before 1512. After the
death of Leo X., they sent Batista della Palla, who was in the
conspiracy with them, to Cardinal Soderini, in order to inform
him of their indignation against the cardinal, and to persuade
him, as an exile and an enemy of the Medici, to make, with
Renzo da Ceri and the family of the Soderini, such provision as
they should judge proper to conduct their designs, and to obtain
intelligence of the progress of this war. But the enterprise not
succeeding with Signor Renzo as was expected, the plot was first
suspected, and at length, by degrees, discovered by the cardinal;
the principal persons engaged in it were obliged to fly, and
were declared rebels, particularly Buondelmonti, Alamanni, Palla,
Bruccioli; and others were apprehended and beheaded; by which
means the cardinal was again secured in the enjoyment of his
government, as well as his life, and an end was put to all the
vain designs and idle discourses of a free government.

"In 1522, the cardinal contrived an interview at Leghorn and
at Florence, with Adrian the pope; in consequence of which,
Cardinal Soderini was imprisoned in the castle at Rome, and
prevented from fomenting further designs against the Medici;
and the Cardinal de' Medici became a great favorite with the
pope and the emperor. Having adjusted with the pope all his
affairs, the cardinal gave orders that Hippolito, a natural son of the
Duke Giuliano, and Alexander, a natural son of the Duke Lorenzo,
should be committed to the care of Roso Ridolfi and Giovanni
Corsi, that he might avail himself of them in time to maintain
the reputation and authority of the state in the house of Medici,
in the succession of the first Cosimo, who was called "the father
of his country," in the best manner that he could, being determined to exclude the other branch in the descendants of his brother Lorenzo. He proceeded, however, in this deliberation with
much caution and reserve, pretending to doubt of the brains as
well as heart of Giovanni de' Medici, of whom in truth he was
jealous; for, instead of meriting the contempt of the cardinal, he
had a liberality and a greatness of soul, that enabled him to
acquire the highest fame in the military art, which he had pursued from his tender years." In short, according to Nerli, who
knew him, he was possessed of every virtue and quality of a
great prince.

" In September, 1523, Pope Adrian died; and, after a long
contest in which the cardinals were two months in the conclave,
on the nineteenth of November the Cardinal de' Medici was
created pope, taking the name of Clement VII., and thus united
the sovereign authority, which he held in Florence, to the extensive power of the church; upon which happy election, as it was
called, there were great external signs of joy in Florence, in the
fervor of which an event happened remarkable enough to be
related: — In the vacancy of the pontificate many wagers had
been laid concerning the new election; among many who lost
was Peter Orlandini, and being too importunately solicited by
the winner to pay, he answered in great wrath that he would
not pay until it was determined whether the election had been
made canonically or not.   These words were reported to the
magistrates, and, after the importance of them had been considered by the cabal, Peter was summoned by the eight of the
balia, and upon his appearance was seized and beheaded in a
few hours.

" Soon after the creation of the pope, the Soderini were
restored to their country, because, although at first their cardinal
in conclave had been zealous against the Medici, his friends,
and particularly the Cardinal Colonna, had labored to reconcile
him, and succeeded so far, that his nephews were restored, and
he remained afterwards in the good graces of his holiness.
Palla Rucellai, with nine others, were sent ambassadors to render the usual homage to the new pope.   With these ambassadors the pope intrigued, as he could no longer govern in Florence,
to have one of the two young natural sons sent to govern the
city.   Some among the ambassadors and other Florentines then
at Rome were well inclined; others were timorous in disclosing
their opinions; some having notice of the secret, and of the will
of the pope, and all well knowing what the pope had determined,
in order to satisfy him, and constrained by necessity rather than
swayed by any reason or inclination, requested of his holiness
one of the young men.   The pope sent Hippolito, the son
of the Duke Giuliano, under the guardianship of the Cardinal di Cortona, because he was yet too young for so great
a government; and Ottaviano de' Medici had the care of
the family affairs and the control of the house and family of
the Magnificent Hippolito, as he was called, and as his father

had been entitled at the time of their exile, when he had the
title of Duke of Nemours.   Ottaviano was also to take the
care of Alexander, the son of the Duke Lorenzo.   In this manner were all things disposed relative to the state of Florence
and the house of Medici ; and thus they remained for four years,
until 1527, when a general scrutiny was made, which was very
extensive, and therefore made with universal satisfaction.

"In 1524, a civil war broke out in Pistoia between the parties
called Panciatichi and Cancellieri, and the Panciatichi prevailing, expelled and banished, as usual, their adversaries, and
every thing was there soon settled.   The pope did not much
interfere in the war in Lombardy between Charles and Francis,
which followed the memorable defeat of the French before
Pavia, when the king was taken prisoner and conducted to
Spain by the emperor.   In this tranquillity of foreign affairs,
the Cardinal di Cortona had, however, enough to do to cement
his government, amidst all their discontents and his own ungrate-
ful manner of treating the citizens.   For the best friends, as well
as others, did not find in the government of the pope that which
had been promised, nor those conditions and qualities of profit
and honor which they relished so much in his mode of proceeding and government while he was cardinal; nor could
the Cardinal di Cortona perceive, until in 1527 it became
very manifest, how much it imported to the benefit of the
state and the house of Medici, that he should study the character of the citizens and the principles and motives of their divisions; especially after the party, the most decided in favor of
the Medici, and of consequence the most odious to the generality, had been uncommonly weakened by the death of Alamanni,
Corbinelli, Serristori, and some others, the most warm in their
party, and the most jealous of any opposition to the present
government.

After them too Ridolfi died ; but he, before his death, by an
intermarriage with the Strozzi, had been somewhat cooled, and
dreaded a change less than formerly.   The other party, on the
contrary, were much exalted in their hopes and confidence, as
they had increased in reputation with the Strozzi, Capponi, and
Guicciardini, who, by their great quality and riches, drew after
them a strong band of honorable citizens; with these concurred
Vettori, being a relation of Capponi, and an intimate friend of

Philip Strozzi; and as to the Salviati, although Jacopo was shut up in Rome, there remained in Florence Averardo and Piero, the sons of Alamanni, the cousins of Capponi, Francesco Guicciardini, and the relations of Matteo Strozzi. Having accumulated so much favor, so great abilities, such credit, and so many intimate connections, this party began to be as bold as they were active and powerful; and Niccolò Capponi went on with the greatest reputation increasing it, as he had discovered upon all occasions such popular principles and feelings, and had acquired so much popular benevolence, that those who were desirous of innovation and a more liberal government, appeared to have found a sufficient support, whenever a proper opportunity should occur of making a change.

" These causes, however, produced no effect while the affairs of the war between the grand princes stood in suspense and unaltered, as they did during the time that the king was prisoner to the emperor in Spain. But after he had ransomed himself and recovered his liberty and his kingdom, he was more determined than ever to pursue his desire of recovering the state of Milan. It appeared to him, though he had left his sons as hostages in the hands of the emperor, that the conditions of the convention for his liberation were too hard to be observed. Not able to compose his mind, determined at all hazards to renew the war, and having found the princes of Italy in the same disposition, he agreed with the pope and Venetians, in a league against the emperor, in which the pope would have the Florentines named and comprehended. This league commenced the war in Lombardy. In the army of the church and for the pope, in place of a legate, and with the title of *locum tenens* of the holy see, was Francesco Guicciardini; the Conte Guido Rangoni, then governor of the people of the church, had the general government of the ecclesiastical state; and Giovanni de' Medici had the command of the infantry of that part abroad which was commanded by Conte Guido. There occurred in this war many dissensions between Giovanni and Guido; with the king, in his camp, was the Marquis de Saluzzo; the Duke of Urbino was for the Venetians. This war began about the year 1526.*

" The imperial generals, to divert the pope from the war of

* Nerli, lib. vii. p. 144.

Lombardy, invaded Rome itself, took the bourg of St. Peter, and plundered the palace of the pope himself; who, being besieged in the castle of St. Angelo, was constrained to make a convention to his disadvantage, and to send Philip Strozzi to Naples as a hostage for the security of the treaty, which, among other conditions, contained a definite suspension of arms. But all this success of the imperialists could not move the pope from the war. The league sent Giovanni de' Medici to the relief of Rome; but he was killed in a skirmish, which relieved the pope from his jealousy, though it exposed his capital to ruin.

"After the death of Giovanni, those citizens of Florence who desired an alteration in the government began to take courage and discover their intentions. They proceeded to sound all the citizens whom they thought proper, encouraging them to the enterprise; and at the same time the younger nobility began to desire the same with those citizens who had encouraged and counselled them, and to demand arms of the signori and the public, coloring their request with the wish by such means to be able to serve and defend their country in so great and imminent a danger as appeared in the approach of a large hostile army. They desired to be armed on no other account, and for no other end, than merely for the benefit and defence of the city. Veiled under such colors, these youths were countenanced by all that party of citizens who desired to enlarge the government, and who had taken upon themselves the universal protection of the people. But these young men entered principally into an intimate connection with Nicholas Capponi, with whom all the other citizens who desired to enlarge the government concurred; and, therefore, in the council, in the magistracy, and in all things, these youths were the favorites of Capponi, Strozzi, and Louis Guicciardini, and they took such courage as to consult with them in secret.

"Cardinal di Cortona being, as he commonly was, very slow in resolving, was ill qualified to put a stop to this secret intelligence, especially as he was obliged to wait for instructions from Rome for every measure of his conduct. The divisions among the citizens made him still more timid, which was the reason that the spirits of these youths grew bolder every day. The pope sent Gherardo Corsini to Florence to alter the fortifications of the city; but this measure was very unpopular. The news of the death of Giovanni de' Medici threw the city into the utmost consternation; and all these circumstances aided the young men in their design. The people universally, the citizens, and the young noblemen, were become very licentious in speech, very free and bold in expressing their conceits, and very tumultuous and disorderly, going in armed parties in the streets in the night, affronting the guards and disturbing the citizens with impunity. At this time the pope sent Cardinal Cibo and Ridolfi to assist Cardinal Cortona; but this had little effect.

"In 1527, when the French army turned their march towards Tuscany, the suspected in Florence began to increase, and the youth became more systematical and ardent than ever in their desire to be armed; which they now demanded with greater confidence, as Louis Guicciardini was appointed gonfalonier. Cortona assembled in council many citizens, to consult upon things of such consequence. Nicholas Capponi began with great eloquence, and without reserve, to say, that in treating of things of this importance, which concerned the safety of all, it was reasonable to hold the consultations in the palace, among a larger number of the citizens, that every one might more freely express his sentiments. Gherardo Corsini spoke in opposition to Capponi with spirit in favor of the state; and while the principal citizens were engaged in these altercations, the two armies were approaching the city. The cardinal and the Magnificent Hippolito intended to ride out to the heads of the league, and to Guicciardini, the pope's lieutenant, to concert measures for securing the affairs of Florence in their present critical situation.

" There were in the piazza many circles of young men, who anxiously waited for disturbances; and in the house of Peter Salviati a great rabble was collected of those who, a little time before, had been concerned in the nocturnal tumults which had been excited with the servants of the guard of the lieutenant of police. Within, with the gonfalonier, were those chiefs, who, at first, with more order and better council, had always managed those intrigues which were called the petitions for arms; and already in the palace were Nicholas Capponi, Mathew Strozzi, and Francis Vettori, to countenance the youths, and contrive that whatever might happen should follow in some order.

" But fortune, which had otherwise determined, caused an idle

and false report to be spread, that the cardinal and Hippolito
were gone, and had abandoned the state, as not knowing how to
maintain it any longer ; as these reports prevailed, there suddenly
arose in the piazza a confused rumor ; men bawled out the name
of Liberty ! the People ! the palace on a sudden was filled with
citizens, youths, arms, and confusion ; many began, as if they
had already conquered, to lay hands on the signori ; and those
citizens were threatened who did not say and do as this disorderly multitude desired.   The more prudent sort of persons,
elder and younger, endeavored to preserve some order, and proposed various judicious plans ; but the uproar was too great, and
violence had got possession."

    The detail of the errors and disorders is too long to be recited ;
but nothing would content the people short of a declaration that
the Medici were rebels, and the signori were compelled to this
measure.   Even Niccolò Capponi, and his colleagues, who were
present amidst such disorders in the palace, repented of the
deceit they had practised that day, and perceived that states,
which attempt to change the foundations of their government
by means of popular tumults, though they may sometimes easily
effect the alteration, will always find it difficult either to stop or
to regulate the movements of the people ; of which important
truth the history of Florence is full of fatal examples.

    " The cardinal and Hippolito, receiving intelligence of the
tumults in Florence, returned with Francis Guicciardini, and
some other respectable characters, and a military force.   They
entered into an accommodation with the rioters, and restored
the government of the Medici ; they made a new imborsation
of the signori, and imborsed as gonfalonier, in 1527, Francesco
Antonio Nori, changed some of the signori for persons less suspected, and took every prudent measure to secure the peace of
the city.   But such was the danger, that many absented themselves through fear, not believing that the pope would pardon
their behavior.   The city was in great confusion, suspicion,
and dissatisfaction.

    " At this time the army turned towards Rome, which, on the
sixth of May, 1527, was sacked by the French in their turn, and
the pope was again shut up a prisoner in the castle.   Philip
Strozzi flew to Florence with the news of the ruin of the pope,
and began to promote a change in the government ; and his

lady, Clarissa,* the daughter of Peter de' Medici, sister of the Duke Lorenzo, very gravely and boldly said to the Cardinal Cortona and Hippolito, that they ought to fly from Florence, and leave the city and republic free to the citizens.

"Upon this return of Strozzi, and in this ruin of the pope, Nicholas Capponi, Matthew Strozzi, and Francis Vettori, and all that party of citizens who had been humbled by the disorders of the twenty-sixth of April, and the other party, who were in the confidence and league of the Medici, seeing the pope ruined and a prisoner, and no hope of assistance, gave way to fortune; some through fear, and others from hopes which were held out to them by those citizens who desired a change in the state, and the ruin of the Medici. Cardinal Cortona, finding himself in such affliction, and without any assignment of money, because Philip Strozzi, who was at that time depositary of the signori, sent out of Florence Francesco del Nero, his deputy, with all the money which had been collected, a movement which was the most artful check in the whole game, made a certain capitulation between the city and the Medici, and went out of Florence with Cardinal Cibo and the Magnificent Hippolito, on the seventeenth of May, 1527, without being banished, and having the signori still in their favor, who stood firm to the government and the house of Medici to the last."

After their departure the capitulation was not observed, and Cardinal Ridolfi, who remained in Florence, was constrained to depart. In a short time a popular government was introduced, so large and licentious, that Philip Strozzi, and all those citizens who had such an inclination to the change, and who were the heads and chiefs of the plan of restoring the state to the people, were soon treated in such an injurious manner, and in so many ways insulted, that those who incline to weep over the follies and vices of their fellow-men, will have incitements enough for their tears in reading the story.

* See her speech at length in Segni, p. 8. Bisognava prima, che in tali termini si fussino condotte le cose, governarsi co' cittadini di maniera, che ne' pericoli, e nelle strettezze vostre vi si avessono a mantenere amici, e in fede, siccome ne' passati tempi si governarono gli antichi miei, che colla gentilezza, e colla benevolenza più che coll' asprezza, e col timore, si mantenevano fedeli gli animi de' cittadini Fiorentini, e poi in molti loro avversi tempi gli ritrovarono costanti; ma voi, che coll' usanze del viver vostro avete, ancora a chi nol sapesse, scoperto i vostri natali, e fatto chiaro a tutto il mondo, che non siete del sangue de' Medici (e non pure di voi intendo, ma ancora di Clemente indegnamente Papa, e degnamente prigione) che vi maravigliate voi, se sete oggi in questi travagli, ne' quali avete tutta questa città contraria alla vostra grandezza?

CHAPTER THIRD.

THE history of Segni, which was intended to record the transactions of the republic or popular state from 1527 to 1550, begins with the eighth book of Nerli, and contains a circumstantial relation of every particular. This same Segni has written the life of his uncle Niccolò Capponi. Varchi too, begins his history about the same time; so that this period is well described by a variety of historians.

"After the resolution taken by the Cardinal di Cortona, and the principal citizens in the government, to resign the authority of the balia, and to leave the state, by agreement, liberally in the hands of the people, the balia assembled on the sixteenth of May, 1527, and the provision by which liberty was restored to the people, and the government wholly conferred upon them, by the total annihilation of the balia, was received with great joy. But that, in so great a revolution, they might proceed without scandal, and ordain a government, free, pacific, and quiet, as, perhaps, those citizens, who were the principal authors of the change, and had been so zealous for it, had flattered themselves they might, (although very different effects followed, as generally happens to those who place themselves at the head of the people, and are the instruments of changing a government,) they began by giving order and form to the government, that is, by taking the power into their own hands, instead of giving it up to the people. They gave authority to the signori, the colleges, and the council of seventy, and to the members of the balia, to make, as well as they could, a deputation of thirty citizens for each quarter, giving a convenient share to the minor arts, according to the classes at that time in the city; and they ordered that such deputation should be made by ballot, among the signori, council, magistrates; and the thirty for the quarters, who were thus ballotted for by the greatest popular favor, or, in other words, who had the most black votes, should be understood to be elected; to which number of one hundred and twenty citizens, together with the said magistrates and counsellors, should be given full authority to elect all officers, meaning such as had been usually made by the council of a hundred, until the twentieth of June. All other officers were to be drawn from the ordinary purses till the same day; after which, it was determined that the council of the people, called the greater* council, should commence its authority. This greater council was arranged to have the same authority, modes, orders, and forms, which it had before 1512, but with certain limitations and corrections. The new council of *signori collegi* were to be one hundred and twenty, the supernumeraries seventy, and the balia of twenty, to whom was given authority concerning the mode of making the new gonfalonier; and the council of eighty was revived in the same form as before 1512. Then, in the abundance of their gratitude to the Medici, for permitting the popular government to be revived, they passed an indemnity to them and all their agents, and forgave Hippolito, Alexander, and the duchess, daughter of Lorenzo, late Duke of Urbino.

"At last the old balia was annulled; but the new government had scarcely assembled, before fresh dissensions arose.† Some were against observing at all the laws made as now related, especially relative to the greater council; many, without waiting for the term prescribed, favored the assembling this council, and acting in it; and some were even for beginning tumultuously, and without waiting for any limitations or corrections, and without regarding this law in any degree. Many others were for removing the signori by force before the time, though by the law they were to continue the month of June; and because the provision or law made by the balia for peaceably restoring the state to the people was not observed, as indeed it was not, and because the concession and promise made by the Medici was not strictly regarded, it was given out that they were returning with force to recover the state which they had voluntarily quitted, and which was not taken from them by force, as many had endeavored in vain to do shortly before; and many false rumors were created, propagated, and exaggerated, to terrify and confound the contending parties. These at last divided themselves

---

* Consiglio maggiore.

† Dopo questi ordini cosi dati, cominciarono molti cittadini a dividersi in molti modi, e si scopersero molte varie sette, et molte varie seditioni. Nerli, lib. viii. p. 155.

into two principal factions; the Strozzi, Soderini, &c. were the
heads of one, and Niccolò Capponi of the other.   They had a
long struggle to make the gonfalonier resign, and get possession of the palace.   The greater council was brought into being
and action before the time, and many other alterations were
made about the choice of magistrates; but a tumult in the
palace, backed by all the persuasions of Capponi, was at last
effective to prevail upon the gonfalonier to resign.   A new
gonfalonier was now to be chosen, and new regulations contrived for the election, and among a multitude of candidates,
Niccolò Capponi was chosen."

Niccolò Capponi had great qualities; but these alone were
not the cause of his elevation; it was indeed the secret influence of the Medici interest which decided the election in his
favor.   This was a very memorable example of electioneering.
It resembles in so many of its outlines all other elections, which
enter into the essence of every government in one centre, that it
is very interesting to every free citizen to consider it attentively.
Sixty electors were drawn out of the purse of the grand council,
each of whom was to nominate a citizen of fifty years of age;
and among these sixty were to be balloted for, in the greater
council, six candidates for the office of gonfalonier.   The six
who upon this occasion had the most votes, were Carducci,
Soderini, A. Strozzi, Nero, Bartolini, and Niccolò Capponi.
Each of these candidates had his distinct principles, system,
and party.   In favor of Carducci were all that part of the citizens who most dreaded and hated the Medici, who wished for a
licentious government, through which they could be revenged, by
beating down every citizen who, under the government of the
Medici, had any reputation, influence, or power.   In Strozzi
concurred a part of the same citizens, for the same reasons; but
their ardor for him was cooled by the recollection of the part he
had formerly acted against Savonarola in 1498.   In Soderini
united all those citizens who loved a government both free and
quiet, such as that which prevailed from 1502 to 1512, when
Peter ·Soderini was gonfalonier for life.   The party of Medici
were united to a man against him; with all other parties he
was upon tolerable terms.   And this is not only natural, but it
is universally found in experience, that the monarchical party is
most averse, in such conjunctures, to the aristocratical, and gene-

rally coalesces with the democratical, as these did upon this occasion in the choice of Capponi. The partisans of Nero and Bartolini were those only who hated all men who had ever held any place in government, and wished for such as were entirely new. Amidst so many competitors and such a variety of parties and views, Capponi was elected, though he had held offices of high trust and confidence under the Medici. He had in the whole course of his life, public and private, been a wise, liberal, and irreproachable citizen; the reputation of his father and his ancestors had early rendered him illustrious; he had as much resolution as he had ambition, and had maintained the character of an honest man with all; that of a free republican with the popular party, and that of a man of honor and fidelity with the Medici themselves, who unanimously fell in with his views in the election.

" Naturam expellas furcâ, tamen usque recurret."

The dominant party will, in general, in this manner prevail, though their leaders are in danishment, and even though excluded by law. Capponi had married a daughter of Philip Strozzi, and this union of their families, and even the diversity of their characters,* had contributed to increase the influence of the former. After the election of the gonfalonier, they proceeded to the choice of the signori for three months. Thus the party of Capponi carried their point, and accomplished all this weighty business by the first of June, against the regulation that the old signori should continue through the month.

" One of the first steps taken under the new government, was an appointment, by a plurality of votes in the greater council, of five citizens, under the title of syndics of the commons, to examine the accounts of all those who had handled the public money or other property from the year 1512. This was an invention of revenge and jealousy, to destroy all the friends and

* L'integrità della vita, la temperanza, la severità, la parsimonia in allevar la famiglia ferono resplendere Niccolò sopra d'ogn' altro per dignità, e per un vivo esempio di virtù : quando in Filippo un modo di vivere sciolto, l' incontinenza, la piacevolezza, la grazia, la destrezza nel trattenere gli uomini, la liberalità, la licenza, la concessione di se stesso fatta ora alla virtù, ora al vizio, ebbe forza di farlo amar sempre dalla gioventù, riverire dalla nobiltà, e accarezzare dal popolo, di tal maniera, che sebbene viveva in privata fortuna, era nondimeno come un principe. Varchi, lib. iii. p. 63 ; Segni, *Storie*, lib. i. p. 12 ; *Vita di Niccolo Capponi*, p. 2.

instruments of the Medici; and many other schemes of persecution against the party of Medici were contrived without the smallest discretion, and in spite of all the endeavors of Capponi and Philip Strozzi to prevent them. Among other schemes of persecution, the most tyrannical imaginable, which this dominant party now triumphant, practised against the minor party, was, at a time when a sum of money, (thirty thousand crowns,) was wanted by the public, to make a law that twenty citizens should be *elected*, who should be compelled to lend the public fifteen thousand crowns each."

Such is the sense of liberty and the sacred regard to property in a government in one centre!

" This popular tyranny was carried to an excess so intolerable, that Philip Strozzi, the very father of the revolution, was obliged to fly to Naples, though his brother-in-law was gonfalonier; but returning some time after with Buondelmonti, they were both imprisoned for four years in the tower of Volterra, for making opposition to the new iniquitous taxes and the administration of the syndics. Acciaioli too, who was then returned from his embassy in France, was imprisoned for being in arrear for part of a subsidy which they had imposed upon him, not only without equity, but beyond his ability. The gonfalonier could make no resistance to this popular fury, which had now got the ascendant; the great council and their three months' men, the signori, governed without control; and because they could not glut their vengeance upon the persons of the Medici, they took the images in wax of the popes Leo X. and Clement VII., and scourged and destroyed them; and the magistrates themselves were supposed to have excited the youths who were guilty of this outrage, so indecent in a catholic city; at least no measures were taken to suppress or to punish the rioters. An order was given by the magistrates, the eight of the balia, that the arms and ensigns of the Medici should be taken down in every place in the city and country, public and private, even in the private houses of the family, even from the monuments over their tombs."

All this was done, and many other invasions of their private property committed, in direct contempt of the capitulation made with Cardinal Cortona and the Magnificent Hippolito, when they resigned the authority of their balia, and voluntarily left the state to the people. It is astonishing that the people themselves should not have recollected that this courage had come into their hearts only from the present calamity of the pope, which might soon be at an end, and themselves made to feel the consequences of their present folly; but in such a tumult of popular passions there is never any reflection, prudence, or foresight. All these things happened in the first months of the new government, while the pope was in the power of the imperialists, a prisoner in the castle of St. Angelo. The plague was now in Florence, and it was difficult to assemble the councils, especially the greater council; a law was therefore made, that for the creation of officers and the expedition of private petitions, the number of the greater council necessary to be present should be only four hundred; but for the creation of the signori, the colleges, the ten of war, and the eight of the balia, the number of eight hundred must be full, as well as at the passing of new laws and the imposition of new taxes.

" In December, the pope accommodated his affairs with the emperor, obtained his liberty, and retired to Orvieto for his greater security. This event increased the number of opponents to the present government in Florence, and again brought into reputation those who had enjoyed it under the Medici. Two factions now broke out in the city. The rivals of Capponi began to raise their heads, and endeavored to render unpopular not only the friends of the Medici, but Capponi and all those who had endeavored to unite all parties for the general tranquillity. Carducci, A. Strozzi, and Soderini, now formed a triumvirate, at the head of one faction, against Capponi and his adherents; and the young men and more active partisans of each side armed themselves, both under the pretence of defending the palace. This guard, thus composed of two parties, could not be united, and gave much trouble to the gonfalonier. The pope at this time made Hippolito a cardinal. A satirical libel was composed, printed at Siena, and scattered all over Florence, in which a picture was drawn of such a gonfalonier as would be suitable to the present conjuncture; but it was in all things opposite to the character of Capponi, and very much resembled Carducci. This device excited much licentious conversation in the city against Capponi, and many projects of a new gonfalonier at the approaching election.

"These canvassings drove Capponi to a curious expedient to obtain his election. He had always maintained a good character with the friends of Savonarola the Prophet, and in this time of the plague all men were seriously inclined, and the superstitious began again to be frantic. Niccolò took an opportunity, in the greater council, to make an oration upon the times, in which, by the aid of a retentive memory, he repeated, almost word for word, one of the most terrible sermons of Savonarola, which predicted so many scourges to Italy and to Florence, and, after so much destruction, such felicity to the Florentine people; and endeavored to show that the times thus predicted were arrived. In the course of his harangue he wrought himself up to a fervor of enthusiasm, fell upon his knees before the whole assembly, and cried with a loud voice to God Almighty for mercy. His enthusiasm spread like a contagion, and the whole assembly fell upon their knees after his example, and cried out, with a voice like thunder, 'Misericordia!' as they had been used sometimes to do when attending some of the most dreadful of Savonarola's lectures; and to complete his artifice, or his frenzy, he persuaded the people, in commemoration of the tribulations, chastisements, and judgments of God, and the better to secure the felicity promised by Savonarola, that they ought to elect, for the peculiar king of the people of Florence, Jesus the Redeemer; and, as Savonarola had said in some of his sermons, that they ought to bear the ensigns of Christ, and the glorious name of Jesus, over the gates of the palace. The proposition was made in council, as soon as the gonfalonier had finished his oration, that Christ should be their king, because, according to St. Paul, God had constituted him heir of all things; and Nerli, who says he was present among so many hundreds of citizens, declares, that there were not more than twenty* white beans, or votes, against the proposition, when it was determined by ballot. Capponi, by this proceeding, made such an impression upon all orders, and gained so many partisans, that, notwithstanding all the combinations of

---

* Ultimamente fece passare una provisione nel consiglio grande, sopra di tutte l' altre notabilissima in questo genere di pietà, per la quale fu eletto Gesù Cristo Signor nostro per Re della città nostra. con tutti i suffragi di quel popolo, eccetto che di 26, che tal decreto non approvarono. Era 'l titolo di questa legge scritto sopra la porta del palazzo de' signori, in lettere d' oro, che dicevano *YHS XPS Rex populi Flor. SP QF consensu declaratus, anno, mense, die.* Varchi, p. 122. Segni, *Vita di Capponi,* p. 10.

the families of his competitors, he carried his election in June, 1528.

"In this year the pope's profound projects,* hitherto concealed with great art, began to be discovered. An ardent desire of restoring to his family their grandeur in Florence was deeply rankling in his mind; yet, by an hypocrisy too natural to that, as well as every other kind of ambition, he endeavored, by public declarations, in the most unequivocal terms, to persuade the Florentines that nothing was further from his thoughts; that he only desired the republic to acknowledge him as pontiff, as all other princes and sovereigns had done, and that they would not persecute his connections in their private affairs, nor take away the ensigns and ornaments which belonged to his family. With a commission to this purpose, he had sent a Florentine prelate as his ambassador to Florence; but as he had not obtained an audience, he solicited, through the medium of the King of France, that they would send an embassy to him, earnestly endeavoring to remove all their suspicions, and, by all appearances of candor, frankness, and familiarity in his dealings with them, to dispose them to fall in with his insidious designs. As all these devices proved unsuccessful, he exerted himself to persuade Lautrec, that as those who governed in Siena were dependents on the emperor, it would be useful to his affairs to restore Fabio Petrucci to that city; but Lautrec, from the opposition of the Florentines, would not engage in it. Failing in this way, he labored in secret with Pirro, who complained of grievances against the Sienese, that with eight hundred men, and some exiles from Chiusi, he should seize upon that territory, and endeavor by that means to govern Siena; but the Florentines insinuating to the French ambassador, the Viscount de Turenne, that the pope aimed at nothing but disturbing Florence by the means of Siena, the ambassador persuaded him to give up the movement to Chiusi.

"Capponi, the gonfalonier, held at this time † a correspondence with the pope by means of Jacopo Salviati, by which the pope intended, in time and with patience, to overcome all difficulties, and obtain the restoration of his family; but the gonfalonier intended only to amuse the pope, and prevent him from under-

---

* Guicciardini, lib. xix.   Nerli, lib. viii. p. 172.   † Nerli, p. 173.

taking any enterprise against the city with force.   Thus both
parties hoped to gain the advantage of time.   Capponi gave
hopes to the pope that the city might be disposed to agree with
him, as they had been used to do with other pontiffs, provided
his holiness would content himself to leave it in the quiet enjoyment of its liberty.   This correspondence, though conducted with
secrecy, to avoid suspicion, was communicated, however, to
several of the first citizens in the government.   Jacopo Alamanni,
though he knew the correspondence was conducted with the
privity of the government and for the good of the state, was
excited by the competitors of the gonfalonier to seize with violence Serragli, who had been sent by Salviati upon the business,
and a great clamor was excited against the gonfalonier; fresh
libels were published, and old ones reprinted; the young men
were again excited tumultuously to demand arms, ensigns, and
officers to be elected by themselves; and the triumvirate prevailed
so far as to have a new ordinance for the militia, by which an
imborsation should be made of the young soldiers, and a number
drawn from time to time, to keep the guard of the palace.

   " This was no better than making the government prisoners to
the opposition.   Alamanni at length proceeded to such violence,
tumult, and outrage against the gonfalonier, that the signori,
who were authorized by the greater council to defend the palace,
were obliged, in order to suppress this armed sedition, to order
him to be seized.   He attempted to fly, but was made prisoner,
condemned, and beheaded.   This punishment excited fresh clamors against the gonfalonier, especially among the young soldiers,
who now reproached their own leaders, the triumvirate, although
they had secretly stimulated the offence, for having concurred in
the sentence.   Perhaps to remove Carducci and Strozzi out of
the way of giving farther disturbance to the government, the first
was appointed ambassador to France, and the second to Venice.
Both declined the employment; as the laws would not permit any citizen to renounce an embassy without alleging just
impediments, to be approved by the signori and colleges, they
applied to be excused; but their reasons were not admitted, and
they fell under the punishment of admonition and other heavy
penalties.   Their arguments before the signori and colleges only
served still more to divide and distract the public councils.   At
last Carducci went to France, much against his will, but Strozzi

was condemned and admonished; and this again alienated many friends from the gonfalonier, and still further weakened his party.

But many grew weary of the endless confusions and anxieties arising from this government in one centre, and that centre the nation. Those who had been in reputation in the time of the Medici began to recover credit, and the faction of the triumvirate lost ground. "The young men, too, were divided, some warmly attached to the gonfalonier, and others as zealous against him, especially those who resented the punishment of Alamanni. The gonfalonier, trusting to a good conscience and upright intentions, proceeded in his negotiations with the pope, with the participation of his principal colleagues in government; and this he thought the more necessary, since the ruin of the French army near Naples made him suspect that the pope would reconcile himself with the emperor; and indeed the pope at this time,[*] under a countenance of exquisite dissimulation, had all his thoughts taken up with the recovery of the government of Florence, still amusing the French ambassadors and the other confederates with various negotiations, and specious hopes of his adhering to the league. Nevertheless, moved partly by the dread of the grandeur of the emperor, and the success of his enterprises, and partly by the hopes of inducing him more easily than he could the King of France to assist him in the restoration of his family to Florence, he had a stronger inclination to the emperor than to the king. To facilitate this design, he moreover most earnestly desired to draw to his devotion the state of Perugia; to which end he was believed to have stimulated Braccio Baglioni, who constantly attempted new disturbances in that neighborhood.

"In this conjuncture, a fresh altercation happened in Florence, to the great misfortune of the government,[†] excited against Capponi, at the end of the second year of his magistracy, principally by the envy of some of the principal citizens, who availed themselves of the jealousies and ignorance of the multitude. The gonfalonier, in all his administration, as well as in his correspondence, had two principal points in view; to defend against fresh attacks of envy or resentment those who had been placed in honor by the Medici, and even to communicate to them, in com-

[*] Guicciardini, lib. xix. p. 170, edit. Venet. 1574. Nerli, p. 170.
[†] Guicciardini, lib. xix. Nerli, p. 179.

mon with the other citizens, the honors and councils of the public; and, in things of no moment to liberty, not to exasperate the spirit of the pope. These points were both of great utility to the republic; because many of those who had been persecuted as enemies of the government, finding themselves in safety, would have joined heartily with the others to defend it; and because the pontiff, though he eagerly desired the return of his family, would, if no fresh provocations were given him, have less incitements to precipitation, and less grounds for those complaints he was continually making to other princes. But the ambition of many was opposed to this policy, who, knowing that they should be farther from a share in the government, or have less influence in it, if the friends of the Medici, men undoubtedly of more experience and merit, were in it, minded no other business than that of filling the multitude with suspicions of the pope and his party, and calumniating the gonfalonier, as not having a sufficient hatred against the Medici, that he might not obtain the prolongation of his magistracy for the third year. Capponi, unmoved at these slanders, and thinking it very necessary that the pope should not be provoked, entertained him with letters and private messages, as before related; a practice which was begun and continued with the knowledge and approbation of the principal citizens in administration, and with no other end than to divert the pope from taking some violent measures.

"As fortune would have it, having dropped by accident and incautiously in the council-chamber a letter from Rome, in which were some words capable of exciting suspicion in such as were uninformed of the original and foundation of the correspondence, it fell into the hands of Jacopo Gherardi, one of those who had seats in the supreme council, and were most bitter against the gonfalonier; certain seditious young men rose in arms and seized the palace, retaining the gonfalonier in custody, and calling together the magistrates and a multitude of citizens, tumultuously deliberated and resolved that he should be deprived of his office;* which decision was confirmed by the larger council. Capponi was rendered incapable; and it was ordained that the gonfalonier should be for the future but for one year, and that his salary should be reduced one half. The opposition of the

---

* Guicciardini, lib. xix. Nerli, p. 180.

triumvirate had so turned the brains of the people by their intrigues, that a great change was made in the government, and Francesco Carducci, a man proved by his past life, by his condition, and his depraved views, to be unworthy of so great an honor, was chosen in his place. Capponi was brought to his trial, and defended himself with such eloquence and ability, and showed so clearly that his conduct, instead of being criminal, had been dictated by the principal persons in government, and merely for the public good, that he was acquitted with honor, and accompanied home to his palace by almost all the nobility.

"Upon the privation of Capponi, the pope no longer entertaining any hopes but from force, sent the Archbishop of Capua in great haste to the emperor, and, as Capponi had foreseen, agreed to almost any terms that were demanded of him, in consideration of having his family restored to Florence, and a natural daughter of the emperor given in marriage to his nephew Alexander de' Medici, the son of Lorenzo, late Duke of Urbino. Him the pope intended to invest with the secular grandeur of his house, because, some time before, when he was sick and in danger of death, he had made Hippolito, the son of Giuliano, a cardinal. The emperor stipulated to give twenty thousand ducats a year with his daughter, and to reinstate the pope in the possession of Cervia, Ravenna, Modena, Reggio, and Rubiera. And thus, by their continual factions and divisions, the citizens of Florence found they had disgusted both the King of France and the emperor. Thus it usually happens, when small republics and petty princes intermeddle in the wars of great monarchs; the one in alliance thinks himself ill served, while the other, who is in enmity, is most grievously offended, and vows revenge." *

The particulars of the negotiations at Cambray; the contradictory representations of their two ambassadors, Carducci and Cavalcanti, who were of different parties; the propositions of an accommodation with the emperor, made by the Prince Doria through Louis Alamanni, and the rejection of them by the influence of Francesco Carducci, the new gonfalonier, and those citizens who were most jealous of the Medici and their party, are too tedious to relate, though they were rejected, and consequently the republic ruined, by the confused method of treating

* Nerli, p. 184.

of foreign affairs in a numerous and mixed assembly, according to the new constitution.

"The emperor now arrived in person from Spain, and all the states of Italy sent ambassadors to pay him their respects, except Florence. The triumvirate, with their new gonfalonier, were afraid that either some of the old friends of the Medici, or some of the friends of Capponi, who was at the head of the middle or neutral party, as it was called, would be sent, and by this means come again into reputation; to prevent which they not only risked the emperor's resentment, but deprived themselves of the means of obtaining intelligence of any intrigue that might be begun between the pope and him. They set on foot, however, in order, as it was pretended, to unite the citizens, a subscription and an oath, to maintain the present popular government. But although the subscription was publicly opened in a book in the greater council, many respectable citizens would not subscribe, as they knew it to be impossible to unite the citizens cordially in such a plan. The animosities of party grew warmer, and Pazzi, a friend of Capponi, of a very respectable character, was accused of uttering seditious words. The prosecution occasioned great heat. Pazzi was tried and acquitted, and Rinieri would have been imprisoned for his false accusation, if the gonfalonier and his party had not screened him from justice. In this manner did the gonfalonier, to increase his authority, and to make himself feared, seek every opportunity, and employ every means, to depress his adversaries; and if he had succeeded against Pazzi, he intended to have pursued others with still greater animosity.

"About the middle of August, the emperor arrived in Genoa, and all the rest of Italy sending him ambassadors, a fresh effort was made in Florence; and, as it could not now be prevented, the gonfalonier conceived another device to defeat it. He prevailed to have the powers and instructions so confined, especially against agreeing with the pope, that they could obtain no other answer from the emperor than, 'First accommodate your affairs with his holiness.' But this was not all the evil. In such governments nothing can be done with any degree of satisfaction to the public, but by gratifying every party; if one clamorous faction is left to excite a cry, all is confusion. Upon this occasion four ambassadors had been appointed, Strozzi, Capponi, Soderini, and Girolami, who could no more agree among themselves than with the emperor or the pope. They could never agree in writing their despatches. Soderini and Girolami, to maintain their city in the French interest and in its obstinacy not to agree with the pope in any manner, would not concur with Strozzi and Capponi in writing clearly and plainly what the emperor had said to them.

" In September, the united armies of the pope and the emperor resolved on taking possession of Perugia, and the pope gave notice to Malatesta Baglioni to depart from that city. Malatesta demanded of Florence men and money to defend it. In order to give the most pointed offence to the pope, and to make their defiance the more conspicuous, they affected to extend it not only to his person, but to the pontifical see. They resolved to send three thousand men to the aid of Malatesta, to prevent the church from recovering one of its principal territories. But, with all this assistance, Malatesta was driven out of Perugia, and marched to Florence, in consequence of an order from the gonfalonier, without the knowledge of the signori or council of ten, and against their judgments as well as the general sense of the citizens, who almost unanimously desired an accommodation with the pope. A clamor now arose against the gonfalonier and his friends, which obliged them to call to council many citizens of the other parties, whom they had long neglected, who carried a resolution to send other ambassadors to the pope, with more ample powers of accommodation. But the gonfalonier, by delaying the commission, had subtlety enough to defeat this resolution, although it had been taken with very general satisfaction; and he proceeded to take measures for the defence of the city against the confederated army. Many of the principal citizens, alarmed at these delays, harangued freely in council in favor of an accommodation; but these were insulted in the street by the youth of the gonfalonier's party, for their freedom of speech in council. This occasioned a public complaint and so much general indignation that the gonfalonier was obliged to give way and despatch the ambassadors with full powers; but he had still the art to delay the deliberations in council upon the terms of accommodation. The ambassadors met with some difficulty to find the pope, and could not agree among themselves. Soderini went to Lucca; Strozzi to

Venice; Capponi resolved to return to Florence, and labor
openly and decidedly to persuade his fellow-citizens into an
accommodation, and Girolami returned to oppose him.[*]   Capponi was taken sick, and died at Garfagnana;[1] Girolami therefore had a larger field opened to his [†] ambition to be gonfalonier,
to which end he accommodated his discourse variously to different parties of the citizens; from those whom he knew to be
desirous of peace, he disguised his sentiments, and concealed his
late conduct; to the neutral party he proposed that the city
should stand upon its defence and make the best preparations
for it, but be ready to receive, or even to propose, any reasonable
terms of accommodation on the first favorable opportunity; but
with the faction of the gonfalonier, knowing their resolution to
be fixed to see the city perish rather than yield to any accommodation, he opened himself in private without reserve, and declared
himself devoted to their system."

It is the general opinion of historians, as well as of Segni,
" that the divisions of the citizens into parties under the triumvirate, and afterwards of those persons of middle rank, who, by
means of their discord, came after them into power, as Carducci, Castiglione, and others, were the true cause of the loss of
their liberties; for these persons, though few in number, among
a people jealous of their liberties, and full of parties and various
humors, found it easy to agitate their fellow-citizens in so violent
a manner, as to make them resolve upon sustaining a siege, and

---

[*] Segni, *Vita di Niccolo Capponi*, p. 42.

[†] Infra le cagioni atte a rovinare la repubblica, una, e non la manco sono i
cittadini, che favoriti, e fattisi capi del popolo, mentrechè ora per ritenere quella
grandezza, e ora per racquistarla, cercano di fare ogni cosa, che piace alla moltitudine, nè s' avveggono, che distruggono quella libertà; e questo è confermato
con molti esempi dell' antiche repubbliche della Grecia, e più modernamente con
quelli della Romana, dove si vede, a chi considera quelle storie con buono giudi-
zio, i cittadini popolari essere stati più cagione della sua rovina, che quegli, che
favorivano l' autorità del senato.   Sienmi di ciò testimonio in prima i Gracchi, di
poi Mario, e Cesare ultimamente, i quali sebbene con oneste cagioni di sollevare
il popolo grasso, cercarono di compiacergli, ebbono nondimanco sotto questo pre-
testo medesimo nascosto il veleno, che estinse appoco appoco quella republica.
Non è dubbio, che, leggendo questa storia, si potrà conchiudere questo medesimo,
che i capi del popolo, Soderini, Strozzi, Carducci, mentrechè opponendosi a Niccolò Capponi per farsi più grandi, e venire in più grazia, indebolirono assai quel
governo. Segni, *Storie*, lib. iv. p. 102.

[1] His last words are said to have referred to the divisions by which the state
was convulsed: — " Oimè, oimè, dove abbiam noi indotta la patria nostra! "
Segni.

to render the defence glorious. And although it is not denied that the pope gave a provocation to this, and would have tried every method to recover Florence, yet the difficulties were so great, that it is not doubted he would have been contented with reasonable conditions, rather than venture on so atrocious and so impious a war."

We pass over all the marches of armies, and intrigues of negotiation between the King of France, the emperor, the pope, the Venetians, &c., which occurred before the fifth of October, 1529, when the Prince of Orange advanced before Florence, and laid siege to the city, which was now well fortified, and contained a strong garrison.

"Valori was sent by the pope as his commissary to the army, and with him went a large number of Florentine exiles, (of whom there was always a multitude scattered and wandering about all Italy, and waiting for the motion of troubled waters) who now joined the united army of the pope and emperor. As these had relations and connections in the city, an alarm was excited; and to intimidate every one from the thoughts of an accommodation, the signori resolved that five-and-twenty citizens should be declared suspected of disaffection to the popular government, and confined in the palace under a strong guard; and, to complete their plan of terror against any one who might speak of an accommodation, they cut off the head of Carlo Cocchi, for saying that it would be better to restore the Medici than to hazard the war, and for talking of a parliament." *

There is not in the whole history a fact more curious than this, as it lets us into the true character of this government. It was always called the popular government, but it was really an aristocracy; and the members of it dreaded an assembly or convention of the people, which they called a parliament, as much as they did the Medici; and soon after, the same sentence and execution was passed upon Francesco Rigogolo, for daring to speak of an accommodation.† And by these arts and means

---

* E per dare più spavento, e per mettere più terrore, a chi pur ancora volesse ragionare d' accordo, presero certa occasione contro a Carlo Cocchi sopra una querela, par la quale era Carlo accusato, ch' egli avesse detto, quando si ragionava largamente, e molto liberamente nell' universale dell accordo, *che fusse piutosto da voler rimettere i Medici, che aspettare la guerra*, e conteneva la querela, che 'Carlo in un certo modo avesse in quel suo parlare mescolato anche il nome tanto odioso al governo popolare del *parlamento*. Nerli, lib. ix. p. 199.

† Onde messono tale spavento, e tanto terrore nell' universale per cagione de'

did this aristocratical tyrant, the gonfalonier, spread such a terror among the citizens, that no man dared oppose his will; and he obtained and exercised more power than the magistrates, the cabal, (pratiche,) the ordinary council, or the laws; and he used it accordingly in the most arbitrary manner, in raising money by various illegal measures, by discarding magistrates and dissolving councils at his pleasure, and in doing all other things that an unbridled despot could do. It would be tedious, and it is unnecessary to relate all the particulars of his arbitrary conduct; of the assaults and sallies, in one of which the Prince of Orange was killed; the hopes, fears, deliberations, distresses, and famine of a siege, which does infinite dishonor to this pope, who had no right to subject the city; and of a defence which was made by the obstinacy of an aristocratical junto, for purposes of ambition equally reprehensible, though colored with a pretence of a popular government, but which was by no means conducted by the spirit of liberty, or upon any principle of a free people. On the contrary, it was conducted, from first to last, without regard to any law or constitution, and against the sense of a great majority of the people.

" The defence was sustained from October to August, on the ninth day of which month, 1530, four ambassadors were deputed to treat with Don Fernando da Gonzaga, who, since the death of Orange, had the chief command of the army, and the next day a convention was concluded. The principal articles were, that the city should pay eight thousand ducats for removing the army; that the pope and the city should give authority to the emperor to declare, within three months, what should be the form of government, 'salva nondimeno la libertà,' * with a reservation of liberty; that a pardon should be understood, for every one, of all injuries done to the pope, his friends, and

---

cittadini sostenuti, e per quelle esecutioni, che s' erano fatte, che più non era rimaso in Firenze chi pure ardisse non solo parlare dell' accordo, o della guerra, ma non era anche chi avesse in animo a contrairsi a quelli della setta del gonfaloniere in cosa alcuna. Nerli, p. 199.

* In primis, che la forma del governo abbia da ordinarsi, e stabilirsi dalla Maestà Cesarea infra quattro mesi prossimi avvenire, *intendendosi sempre conservata la libertà.* Nerli, lib. xi. p. 144. Intendendosi sempre, che sia conservata la libertà. Varchi, lib. xi. p. 429. Che la città rimanesse libera nel modo ch' ell' era, rimettendo solamente i Medici, e tutti gli altri cittadini fatti ribelli da quel governo. Segni, p. 125. Nardi, lib. ix. p. 382. Muratori, *Annal.* tom. x. p. 213, anno 1530. Laugier, *Hist. de Venise,* lib. xxxv. tom. ix. p. 385. Guicciardini, lib. xix.

servants; and that Malatesta should remain with two thousand
foot, for the guard of the city, until the emperor's declaration
should arrive."

It is made a question, whether the general who commanded
in Florence was, or was not, a traitor to his cause. Varchi is
very sanguine in the affirmative, and produces letters in evidence;
but the citizens and garrison were reduced to such extremities
for provisions, that they could not have held out three days
longer. The pope, on his part, was not very anxious to fulfil
his treaty. While the money was getting ready to pay off the
army, Valori, the apostolic commissary, in concert with Malatesta, having called together the people in the piazza, according
to the ancient custom of the city, to make a parliament, the
magistrates and others, conniving at it through fear, instituted a
new government contrary to the treaty, giving authority by this
parliament to twelve citizens,' who adhered to the Medici, to
ordain, in their own manner, the constitution of the city, who
reduced it to that form which prevailed before the year 1527.
The army received their money; the Italian officers defrauded
their soldiers, whom they dismissed to seek their fortunes without their pay; the Spaniards and Germans marched into Siena
to new-model the government of that city; and Malatesta
returned to Perugia without any further declaration from the
emperor, and left the city of Florence at the arbitrary disposition of the pontiff.

Now began the punishments of the citizens; "for those in
whose hands the government was left, partly for the security of
the state, and partly by the hatred conceived against the authors
of so great calamities, and the resentment of private injuries,
but principally because such was the intention of the pope,
brought the principal citizens concerned in the late government
to a trial, and they were sentenced to death and executed.
Others were confined, without much regret, sympathy, or pity,
from any party; for the friends of Capponi, and all the real
friends of liberty, regarded them as the cause of preventing an
accommodation, and the ruin of their country, while the Medici
considered them as their bitterest enemies. The pope sent the
Archbishop of Capua to take care of the government, who, by
the pope's orders, and to give more general satisfaction to the
citizens, caused the balia to be increased in number to one hun-

dred and thirty-six, made a general scrutiny for offices, regulated
commerce, made a new imborsation of the six magistrates,
renewed the purses, and disposed all other things according to
his inclinations.   A quarrel arose between the Cardinal Hippolito de' Medici and the Duke Alexander, and a contention for the
sovereignty of Florence; but the pope and the emperor determined it in favor of Alexander."

In 1531, the ordinance of the emperor arrived, and was formally accepted.   Many of the best citizens, some of whom had
been always friends of the Medici, with great reluctance gave
up the idea of a free government; they still solicited the pope
not to reduce the republic to an absolute principality, but they
could not agree among themselves.   Some were for a dukedom,
limited only by councils; others for restoring the state to the
form it was formerly in under the Medici; and others for a more
rational distribution of power.   But the pope was determined,
if he could, to make his family and friends secure.

In 1532, the pope's intentions were made known, and twelve
citizens were appointed to reform the state; the signori and the
gonfalonier were abolished; a council of two hundred was created, and a senate of forty-eight.   The senate of forty-eight was
to have the whole legislative and executive power, and the council of two hundred were merely to consider private petitions and
such things as should be referred to them by the senate.   Four
persons, members of the senate, were to be high counsellors of
the duke, and Alexander and his heirs were made dukes and
heads of the state.   Guicciardini's account is,* that the pope
interpreted the article in the treaty which had stipulated pardon,
not according to the sense, but the letter; not to comprehend
crimes committed against the state, but only injuries to the pope
and his friends.   Six of the principal delinquents were adjudged
by the magistrates to be beheaded, others to be imprisoned, and
a great number banished.   By these proceedings the city was
weakened, and those who had been concerned in the late troubles reduced to great necessities, and the power of the Medici
became more free, more absolute, and almost monarchical in
Florence, which remained exhausted of money by so long and
grievous a war, deprived within and without of many of its

* Guicciardini, lib. xx. p. 546.

inhabitants, its houses and property destroyed abroad, and more than ever divided within itself. And this poverty was rendered yet more distressing, by the necessity of procuring, for several years, provisions from foreign countries, since there had been no harvests nor seeds sown.

"The emperor, in declaring the form of government, neglecting the salvo of liberty, pronounced, according to the very instructions the pope had sent him, that the city should be governed by the same magistrates as in the times when the Medici ruled it, and that Alexander, who was the pope's nephew, and his own son-in-law, should be the head of the government, and be succeeded by the children, descendants, and nearest relations of the same family. He restored to the city all the privileges granted by himself or his predecessors, but on condition to be forfeited whenever the citizens should make any attempt against the grandeur of the family of Medici; inserting, throughout the decree, words which showed it to be founded not only in the power conceded to him by the people and the parties, but also on the imperial dignity and authority."

The spirit of families, and the ambition peculiar to it, is, when once thoroughly enkindled, a raging flame, extinguishable only by death. Every new gratification of it is only a fresh addition of fuel to the burnings. The passion of Hercules, Cæsar, and Mahomet, had now full possession of Clement VII.; and the domination so perfidiously acquired over that noble city, where his ancestors had laid the foundation of their power in a popularity among the basest dregs of a mob, was not sufficient to satiate it.

"The pontiff had fixed in his heart an ardent appetite for an alliance with France; his ambition and thirst for this kind of glory, which, instead of being a virtue, is a detestable vice, stimulated him the more, that, he being only of a private family, he had obtained for one natural son a natural daughter of so powerful an emperor; he now hoped to procure for his legitimate niece a legitimate son of a king of France; and he was not discouraged from this pretension by the jealousy that the King of France might form claims for his son and daughter-in-law on the state of Florence. By various negotiations he at length accomplished an interview with the King of France at Marseilles. The pontiff exerted his usual dissimulation to persuade all the world that he went to this interview chiefly to finish the peace, to treat of an enterprise against the infidels, to reduce Henry VIIL, King of England, to his duty; in short, with a single view to the public good. But he could not conceal his real motive, when he sent his niece on board the galleys which the King of France had ordered, with the Duke of Albany, her uncle, to Nizza. These galleys, after having conducted the lady to Nizza, returned to Pisa, and on the fourth of October, 1532, took the pope, with many of his cardinals, and landed them in a few days at Marseilles. He made his entry in form; the king did the same. They lodged in the same palace, and made mutual demonstrations of uncommon affection. The king, desirous of gaining the pope's heart, requested him to send for his niece to Marseilles, which the pope, though he pretended to treat first of public affairs, most cordially desired.[*] As soon as Catherine de' Medici arrived, the marriage was celebrated with Henry, the son of the King of France, and consummated immediately, to the infinite joy of the pope, who, negotiating with the king in person, completely gained his confidence and affection.

" The pope returned from Marseilles, and soon after, in 1534, he died. Alexander had taken effectual measures to disarm all the citizens of Florence, friends as well as enemies, and thought himself now secure. Philip Strozzi, however, was highly disgusted and provoked, both with the duke and the pope, because he had not been able to procure one of his sons to be made a cardinal, as his lady Clarissa had often promised him; and because two of his sons had been taken up, with some other young gentlemen, in the license of a masquerade, and committed to prison by the lieutenant of the police; and because of some quarrel that had arisen between Peter, his eldest son, and Salviati, a favorite of Alexander; in this disgust he went with his sons, as soon as he could obtain their liberty, to France. After the death of the pope, animosities increased between the Duke Alexander and the Cardinal Hippolito, and Philip Strozzi went from France to Rome; and as great divisions arose in Florence, on account of the difference between the duke and the cardinal, and their negotiations with the emperor, as had existed under the former government. Hippolito, on a journey to meet the

* Nerli, p. 270.

emperor, though in high health and strength, was taken violently ill on the road, and died, not without strong suspicions of poison. The death of the cardinal relieved the duke from all apprehensions of his intrigues; but Philip Strozzi and the exiles from Florence began to think of negotiating with the emperor, and went to Naples to meet him. Alexander too went to Naples; and great disputes arose before the emperor about the form of government, Strozzi and the exiles endeavoring to obtain a restoration of that kind of freedom which had been enjoyed formerly under the Medici. But Alexander married the Duchess Marguerita, the emperor's daughter, and returned to Florence, leaving Strozzi and the exiles disappointed.[*]

"Lorenzo di Pierfranco de' Medici had accompanied Alexander to this interview with the emperor at Naples, and there had entered into intimate friendship with Peter Strozzi[†] and the other Florentine exiles, and conceived that design of assassinating his friend and patron, which he afterwards executed with so many circumstances of cool deliberation, insidious malice, and execrable villany. He was a young nobleman, in greater favor with the duke than any other. To him, after their return from Naples to Florence, were communicated all the duke's private amours, as well as all the most important councils of the state; and, the more effectually to secure his confidence, Lorenzo had acted the part of so active an instrument, as to have drawn upon himself a universal odium among all parties in Florence, but particularly among the grandees and nobles. At the same time he held secret intrigues and intelligence with Philip Strozzi[‡] and all the exiles abroad; and at home so artfully affected an aversion to arms and public affairs, and to be so wholly devoted to his studies and his pleasures, that the duke and his courtiers called him 'The Philosopher.'[§]

Varchi informs us[||] that he received his information of this horrid action from the only persons who could be capable of relating the whole truth, because they were the only witnesses of it, and agents in it; from Lorenzo himself, in the city of Paluello, eight miles from Padua, and from Scoronconcolo, his confidant, in the house of the Strozzi in Venice.

---

* Nerli, p. 286. Segni, lib. vii. p. 199. Adriani, *Hist. di suoi Tempi*, p. 9.
† Varchi, p. 547. ‡ Segni, p. 199.
§ Segni, p. 200. || Varchi, lib. xv. p. 587.

"Lorenzo was born in Florence, the twenty-third of March, 1514, the son of Pierfrancesco di Lorenzo de' Medici, grand-nephew of Lorenzo, brother of Cosimo, and of Maria, the daughter of Tommaso di Paolantonio Soderini, a lady of uncommon prudence and benevolence, by whom, his father dying early, he was educated with the utmost diligence and care; but he had no sooner acquired the knowledge of the classics, in which his genius enabled him to make a rapid progress, than he was taken from the care of his mother and his tutor, and began to discover a restless and insatiable disposition to plunge himself into vice; and soon afterwards, in imitation of Philip Strozzi, he began to laugh at every thing divine and human, and to associate himself with persons of base condition and character, rather than with his equals. These, by continual flatteries, and fomenting his passions, led him into vice and folly of every kind, particularly into all the extravagances of brutal appetite in his amours, respecting neither sex, age, condition, nor secrecy. While he sought an intercourse with all, he affected to esteem none; yet he had an equally extravagant passion for glory, and left no empirical artifice unattempted, in his words or actions, by which he thought he could acquire a name, either of a gallant man or a shrewd one. He was nimble and active, rather thin than otherwise, and for this reason he affected to call himself Lorenzino; he never laughed; at most he only smiled. His air and action were more remarkable for grace than elegance, and his countenance was dark and melancholy. In the flower of his youth, although he was beloved beyond measure by the pope, Clement VII., he had formed in his mind a project, as he said himself, after he had killed the Duke Alexander, to assassinate his holiness. He corrupted Francesco di Rafaello de' Medici, the rival of the pope, a youth of excellent erudition and the most promising hopes, to such a degree of profligacy, that he seemed to be in a manner out of his wits; so that, having become the derision of the whole court of Rome, to avoid a greater disgrace, he was sent back as a madman to Florence.

"At this time Lorenzo fell into disgrace with the pope, and gave universal disgust to the Roman people, for another reason. One morning, in the arch of Constantine, and in other places of Rome, many ancient statues were found without their heads. The pope was so exasperated, that, not thinking of Lorenzo, he gave orders that whoever had done the mischief, excepting only the Cardinal de' Medici, should, without process, trial, or delay, be hanged up by the neck. The cardinal was obliged to go to the pope and intercede for Lorenzo, as a young man, and passionately fond, like all their ancestors, of such antiquities; but it was with difficulty he could appease the indignation of the pope, who called him the infamy and reproach of the house of Medici. Lorenzo, however, was obliged to depart from Rome, with two public proclamations after him, one forbidding him to remain any longer in that city, and the other promising not only impunity, but rewards, to any one who would kill him; and Francesco Molza, a man of great eloquence, and celebrated for his knowledge of the Grecian, Roman, and Tuscan literature, made a public oration against him in the Roman academy, in which he covered him with all the reproaches possible. With all this infamy he returned to Florence, and began to make his court to the Duke Alexander. He understood so well the arts of·hypocrisy and flattery, and counterfeited so perfectly an absolute submission to him in all things, that he made him believe he was a faithful spy upon the exiles abroad, laying at the same time, under this simulation, secret plots with these fugitives, and every day showing him letters received from one or another of them. To remove every suspicion of daring enterprise, he affected the character of a coward, and would neither exercise in arms nor wear them about him, so that the duke took a pleasure in rallying him upon his pusillanimity. He affected to be wholly devoted to books and studies, walked much alone, and appeared to have no ambition for honors, or desire of property, in so remarkable a manner, that they called him 'The Philosopher.' He complied with the inclinations of the duke in all things, and aided him in all occasions of need, especially against Signor Cosimo, his second cousin, against whom he bore an unbounded hatred, either because they were of different or rather contrary characters by nature, or by reason of a lawsuit of very great importance, which Cosimo had instituted against him for the inheritance of their ancestors. By all these artifices the duke was deluded into a confidence in Lorenzo, so perfectly secure, that, not contented with employing him as a pimp in his amours with all sorts of women, religious as well as secular, virgins, wives, or widows, noble or ignoble, young or old, he now demanded of him to procure a sister of his own mother on her father's side, a young lady of admirable beauty and equal modesty, the wife of Lionardo Ginori, who lived not far from the rear entrance of the palace of the Medici.

"Lorenzo, who waited only for a similar opportunity, represented to him that the intrigue would be attended with difficulty, though not from himself, for, in one word, all women were alike; and upon this occasion the prospect was the better, because the husband was at Naples, where he had spent much of his fortune in dissipation. Although he had never dared to speak to the lady on the subject, he affirmed to the duke that he had, and that he had found her very obstinate; but he promised that he would never cease to seduce her, by bribes, flatteries, and every species of corruption, until he brought her to condescend in all things to their will. In the mean while he was engaging, not less by actions than with words, one Michele del Tovalaccino, nicknamed Scoronconcolo, for whom he had procured a pardon for a murder he had committed, though a reward had by proclamation been set upon his head. To this ruffian he often complained of a certain intriguing personage at court, who, without the smallest provocation, had bantered, slandered, and insulted him with his jokes upon all his words and actions, but that, in the name of God——; at which words Scoronconcolo, rousing to resentment, suddenly cried, 'Name him only, and let me alone to manage him; he shall never give you another ill word or look.' Here the conversation ended for the present; but Scoronconcolo, who found himself every day more and more caressed and loaded with favors by Lorenzo, at length pressed him earnestly to name his enemy, and not to doubt of his being soon put out of his way. Lorenzo answered, 'Alas, no; the person, be he who it may, is a great favorite of the duke.' Scoronconcolo replied, in the language of a bully, 'I will assassinate him, if he were Christ himself.' Lorenzo then perceived that his design had succeeded; having invited him one day to dinner, as he often did, notwithstanding the remonstrances of his mother and the reproaches of the world, he said to him, 'Courage! courage! in that affair, which you promised me so bravely, I am sure you will not fail me; as I will never fail you, at any time, in any thing in my power. I am satisfied and resolved, but in order that we may do the business with security, I will see to getting him to a place where there may be no danger to you, and I have no doubt I shall succeed.'

"The same night appeared to him to be the most proper time, because Signor Alexander Vitelli was absent upon an excursion to the city of Castello; and he took the opportunity, after supper, to whisper in the ear of the duke, and to say to him, that at last, by the promise of money, he had disposed his aunt to comply, and therefore he must watch his opportunity to come alone, and very cautiously, into his chamber, taking particular care, for the honor of the lady, that no one should see him either enter or go out, and that he himself would go immediately for her. Certain it is, that the duke, having put on a robe of satin lined with fur, according to the Neapolitan fashion, went out to walk with four of his courtiers, whom he soon dismissed, saying, he wished to be alone; shortly after he went to the chamber of Lorenzo, where he found a good fire, ungirded his sword, and threw himself down on the couch. Lorenzo suddenly seized his sword, and winding hastily the belt round the hilt, so that it might not be easily unsheathed, laid it at the head of the duke, behind his pillow, and advised him to repose himself; he secured the door, that no one might come in, and went away to find Scoronconcolo; having done this, he said to him, in a transport of joy, 'My dear brother, now is the moment! I have shut up in my chamber that enemy of mine, and he is fast asleep.' 'Let us go thither,' said Scoronconcolo. When they were on the landing-place of the stairs to the chamber, Lorenzo turned about and said, 'Don't mind whether it be a friend of the duke or not, only mind you to secure his hands.' 'I will do it,' replied his friend, 'even though it were the duke himself.' 'Every thing is so prepared,' said Lorenzo, with a joyful countenance, 'that he cannot escape from our hands; let us make haste.' 'Let us go,' said Scoronconcolo. Lorenzo lifted up the latch and let it fall again. At the second attempt he entered, and cried out, 'Signor, are you asleep?' The uttering these words and running him through and through with a short sword was the work of the same moment. This stroke alone had been mortal, for, passing through the reins, he had perforated the diaphragm which divides the upper ventricle, where are the heart and the other vital members, from the lower, where are the liver and the other members of nutrition and of generation. The duke, who either was asleep, or remained with his eyes shut, as if he had slept, receiving such a blow, leaped up on the bed, and threw himself backwards to fly towards the door, making use of a stool

15*

which he had seized on for a shield. But Scoronconcolo, seizing
an opportunity, gave him a stroke with a knife upon the visage,
which laid open one of his temples, and clove the greatest part
of his left cheek.   Lorenzo, having dragged him upon the bed,
held him down upon his back, and bore upon him with the whole
weight of his body; and, that he might not cry out, he attempted
to stop his mouth with his fingers, saying, 'Signor, fear not.'
Then the duke, assisting himself as well as he could, seized the
thumb between his teeth, and bit it with such rage, that Lorenzo,
fallen on his back, and not able to handle his sword, was obliged
to call out for help to Scoronconcolo, who ran to his aid, and taking
his aim, sometimes on one side and then on the other, could
not strike Alexander without first or at the same time striking
Lorenzo, clasped tightly in his arms.   He then attempted to
thrust at him with the point of his sword between the legs of Lorenzo; but making no other impression than to bore the bed, he
laid his hand on a knife, which he had by accident about him,
and stuck it in the throat of the duke, turning it like a wimble.
He was already, however, very near dead from the effects of
the first blow, by which he had lost so much blood as to have
flooded almost the whole chamber.

"It ought not to be forgotten, that through the whole of this
tragical scene, while Lorenzo held him under, and he saw Scoronconcolo fumbling about him with his sword and knife to
murder him, he never once complained, or begged for mercy, or
let go his hold of that thumb, which he held firmly between
his teeth.   The duke, as soon as he was dead, slid off the bed
upon the floor; but they took him up, besmeared all over
with blood, placed him again upon the bed, and covered him
with the same pavilion with which he had concealed himself
before he first fell asleep, or made a show of being asleep; which,
in the opinion of some, he designedly did, because, knowing himself unskilful in the ceremonies of politeness, and the lady whom
he expected, a mistress in elegant conversation, he wished in this
manner to avoid the necessity of exchanging fine speeches with her.
Lorenzo, after he had disposed of the duke, not so much to see
whether they had been heard, as to restore himself and recover his
spirits, much exhausted by fatigue, placed himself at one of the
windows which overlooked the broad street.   Some persons in
the house, particularly Madam Maria, the mother of Cosimo, had

heard a noise, and a trampling of feet; but no one had stirred, because Lorenzo, with this view, had, for some time before, been used to bring into this chamber companies of his comrades, drinking, rioting, and making a show of quarrelling, crying out, 'Murder! treason! you have killed me!' and other exclamations of that kind.

"When Lorenzo had restored himself, he made Scoronconcolo call one of his footmen, named Freccia, and show him the dead body, which he recognized with such astonishment and horror, that he was with difficulty restrained from crying out. To what purpose he did this he neither explained to the historian, nor was he able to conjecture, unless it was upon the same principle, that nothing which Lorenzo did, from the moment of the death of Alexander to the time of his own death many years afterwards in Venice, ever succeeded, or appeared to be well judged. He took from Francis Zeffi, his maitre d'hotel, a small sum of money, all that he had by him in cash; and taking with him the key of the chamber, he left the house with Scoronconcolo and Freccia, and having previously obtained from the Bishop of Marzi a license for post-horses, under color of going to his country seat of Cafaggiuolo, to see Giuliano, his younger brother, who, as he pretended, had written to him that he was at the point of death with the cholic, went directly to Bologna, where he dressed his thumb, which was found marked for life, and there related to Silvester Aldobrandini, the judge, the whole transaction. But the judge, thinking it a romantic fiction, would not believe, and very imprudently neglected to take any notice of it, until the arrival of the Chevalier Marsili, who, with some others, went in pursuit of Lorenzo.

"The latter, in great haste and fatigue, arrived at Venice on the Monday night, and with much ado convinced Philip Strozzi that under that key, which he held out to him, he had locked up the Duke Alexander, with his throat cut, and dead of many wounds. Philip, at last believing him, embraced him, called him their Brutus, and promised him that he would marry his two sons, Peter and Robert, to his two sisters. Lorenzo excused himself for not having assembled the people after the death of the duke, for three reasons. One was, that he had been to the houses of several of the popular citizens; but some had not heard and others had not believed him. Another was, that he had left it in commission with Zeffo to open the chamber early in the morning, and go in quest of Giuliano Capponi, and other citizens, lovers of liberty, and tell them what he had found there.   Thirdly, that Scoronconcolo had not ceased to stimulate him to depart, saying to him every minute, 'Let us save ourselves; we have done but too much.'   But thus much is certain: that as no conspiracy was ever so deliberately meditated, nor more completely executed before, so none was ever so stupidly and vilely conducted after the fact; nor was there ever any one from whence resulted effects more contrary or more hurtful to the perpetrator, and more prosperous and profitable to his enemies, the first of whom, without all controversy, was the Signor Cosimo.

"I will not dispute," says Varchi, "whether this act was cruel or compassionate, commendable or blameworthy, since no man can resolve that question, and give a true answer to it, who does not know for what reason, and to what end, Lorenzo was induced to commit it.   If he was urged to so great an enterprise, not simply at the hazard of the government of Florence, which, upon the death of the duke without legitimate descendants, would have fallen to him, but also of his own life, in order purely to deliver his country from a tyrant and restore her liberty, as he affirmed, I should think that no praises that could be given him would be high enough, and no rewards could be bestowed upon him which would not be below his merit."

Is it not astonishing that such a historian should admit of a doubt, whether the motives of Lorenzo could be good ones? Is it possible to read his own history, and not see that this struggle was merely between different branches of the same family of Medici for the sovereignty, and that there was not a ray of public virtue or love of liberty left in any of them? Strozzi, the rival family of Medici, had married a Medici, and could not bear that Alexander should rule.   His character was too vile to be redeemed from infamy by his hypocritical affectation of republican simplicity, and his renouncing all titles but that of Philip; but he had great family connections, and was countenanced by France, and therefore might possibly recover his influence and power in Florence.   This made it dangerous for the historian to · mark the conduct of Lorenzo with that decided indignation which it merited.

"Some were of opinion that he was moved to this action merely by the malice of his nature, and the depravity of his own heart; others thought that he ventured on this danger to cancel the ignominy of the two Roman proclamations, and the oration made against him by Molza; others thought him agitated solely by desire to make his name immortal, an ardent passion, that with all his crimes and vices, had always incredibly tormented him."

The right of a nation to depose a tyrant, and to destroy him if he cannot be otherwise deposed, is as clear as any of our ideas of right or wrong. In the Roman republic it was made an early and a fundamental law, by the aristocratics however, that it should be not only lawful, but meritorious and glorious, to kill a tyrant; and Brutus therefore acted the exalted part of the best citizen. But if the right of single citizens, when good and virtuous, and intending only the public good, to kill a tyrant was as clear as that of treading on the head of an adder, or hunting down a devouring wolf, it would by no means follow that one tyrant might claim a right to destroy another, merely to take his place.

The people of Florence were now so totally devoted to the Medici family, that there was no party among them but what was headed by some branch of it; the blood of the Medici must in all events govern them; and the difference between them was worth very little. Strozzi and Lorenzo were worse than Alexander; and the only tolerably good man among them was Cosimo, whom they all hated, but whom Providence was pleased to call to the government in this awful manner. The silly tales of prognostics, the enthusiasm of the disciples of Savonarola, and the confusions and terrors among the principal people upon the first suspicion and final discovery of the duke's destiny, are not worth repeating.

"The council of forty-eight were assembled, but were not agreed in opinion. Canigiani proposed, that in place of the deceased duke, Giulio, his natural son, should succeed; but there was no other person present, who did not either smile at his folly or express indignation; for besides that the child was not five years old, this was known to be the inclination and secret motion of Cardinal Cibo, Lorenzo's brother, who wished to be the tutor, and therefore governor of the city. After him, the Signor

L

Cosimo de' Medici was proposed, who, knowing nothing of what had happened, was at Mugello, fifteen miles from Florence, at his country-seat of Trebbio. At this nomination all appeared to be struck, and looking at one another, seemed ready to accept it, every one knowing that Cosimo was the next heir after Lorenzo, according to the declaration of the emperor; but Palla Rucellai, without doubt in favor of Philip Strozzi, to whom he was attached, warmly opposed this proposition, and said, that so many citizens, and of such consequence, were abroad, that nothing of importance, especially so great an affair, ought to be determined on; and notwithstanding all that was urged by Francesco Guicciardini, and Francesco Vettori, he persisted obstinately in his objections, and occasioned some confusion in council. At another day, however, Cosimo was elected head of the commonwealth, accepted the trust, and behaved in it with so much wisdom, that those who, from his moderate and composed behavior before, believed him to be possessed of but mean abilities, were constrained to confess, that God had granted him discretion with the dukedom."

Intelligence was scattered throughout all Italy, with incredible celerity, of the death of Alexander; and, by all the Florentine exiles, the name of Lorenzo di Pierfrancesco de' Medici was exalted in praises to the skies, not only as the parallel of Brutus, but greatly surpassing him. Varchi wonders that so many citizens of great prudence, and especially Guicciardini, who conducted the whole of this election, should have suffered themselves to be so far blinded and transported by their ambition or avarice, or both, as not to see what they were about. Indeed, no man is ever to be praised, perhaps never to be justified, in consenting to the surrender of a free government; and Guicciardini appears much to blame for not endeavoring to newmodel the commonwealth upon this occasion. But most probably he knew what Varchi himself confesses,* that the Florentines were at this time all either avaricious or ambitious, and the major part of them proud, envious, and malicious; and therefore that none of them could be trusted by him or by each other. He probably believed that delay, or any attempt to restore liberty or reform the constitution, would only give an opportunity to

* Varchi, p. 621.

Strozzi, Lorenzo, and the exiles, to assume the dukedom in reality, under the alliance of France; he moreover probably thought it impossible, among an ignorant people and so many corrupt factions, to amend the constitution, and that a sovereignty in one was preferable to their old fluctuating aristocracy, disguised under the name only of a popular state.

The exiles were still restless, and endeavored to excite fresh wars against their country; but Cosimo, by his abilities, address, and activity, defended his authority, and was afterwards confirmed, not only as head of the state, but as duke and sovereign. And here ended the shadow of a free government.

Let the reader now run over again in his own mind this whole story of Florence, and ask himself whether it does not appear like a satire, written with the express and only purpose of exposing to contempt, ridicule, and indignation, the idea of " a government in one centre," and the " right constitution of a commonwealth?" If he suspect that this mean sketch is in any degree varied by prejudice from the truth, let him read over any historian of Florence, as Machiavel, Guicciardini, Nerli, Nardi, Varchi, Villani, or Ammirato, and then say, whether it is not a libel upon Turgot and Nedham. From the beginning to the end, it is one continued struggle between monarchy and aristocracy; a continued succession of combinations of two or three parties of noble, rich, or conspicuous families, to depress the people on the one hand, and prevent an oligarchy or a monarchy from arising up among themselves on the other. Neither the first family, nor any of the others their rivals, made any account of the people, excepting now and then for a moment, for the purposes of violence, sedition, and rebellion.

Instead of devising any regular method for calling the people together, with a reasonable notification beforehand of the time, place, and subject of deliberation, a little junto of principal citizens concert a plan in secret among themselves, give notice previously to such as they please, their own dependents and partisans, order the bells to be rung, and a little flock of their own creatures assemble in the piazza. There the junto nominate a dozen or a score of persons for a balia, to reform the state at their pleasure; no reasonable method of voting for them, no instructions given them; the people huzza, and all is over.

What ideas are here of the rights of mankind? what equality is here among the citizens? what principle of national liberty is here respected? what method is this to obtain the national sense, the public voice? Can this be called the voice of God?

When the balia is appointed, what is the question before them? Is there any inquiry how the government can be made a fair, equal, and constant representation of the nation, and a sure instrument for collecting the public wisdom? The imborsations are made, and eight hundred names are put in the purses. These alone are citizens; all the rest are to have no vote. These appoint the signori, a small council, for the ordinary administration, and the gonfalonier, who has no more power than a doge of Venice, nor so much dignity. The great council is the centre in which all authority is collected, and he who had most influence in it governed in reality, whoever were the signori or the gonfalonier; consequently, the council and signori too were always divided into parties, at the head of whom were always two of the most noted families; and the only question really was, which should be first. As the waves and winds determined, sometimes one and sometimes another prevailed, and took vengeance of their opponents by banishments and confiscations. The executive power was sometimes managed by the signori, and sometimes by the grand council; the judicial power was always the tool of the prevailing faction. Was there one year, one moment, in the whole history, when the citizens could be truly said to enjoy the blessings of liberty, equality, safety, and good order?

If you fix your eye upon any period, from the beginning to the end of the republic, and suppose the gonfalonier possessed of the whole executive power, with a negative upon the legislature, the signori and grand council made separate and independent branches of the legislature, though elected periodically by the people, and the judges made during good behavior, would not those terrible disorders have been prevented? The negative to the gonfalonier is not proposed, because he is a wiser or a better man than others, but merely as a constitutional instrument of self-defence; without it, he cannot defend the legal authority which the constitution has given him, but the executive power will be pared away, or wrested out of his hands, by the encroaching disposition of human nature in the two houses. If he wantonly uses his negative for other purposes, a case that can rarely happen, a new gonfalonier must be appointed; but if his ministers are made responsible for the advice they give him, the two houses will always have a remedy. An honest representative of the commons will always have another remedy, by withholding supplies.

As this account of Florence was introduced by some reflections of a modern author, it cannot be concluded with more propriety than by some others from the same able and liberal writer. In his Parallel of the Italian Republics of the Middle Ages with those of Ancient Italy, he says,[*] "Whoever shall read in the Annals of the Cities of Lombardy and in the Chronicles of Tuscany, how the people passed so frequently, both in external wars and in civil factions, from battles to peace, and from domestic life to arms and hostilities, and that perpetual succession of accords, rebellions, and tumults, will be apt to believe that he sees, copied under different names, the wars of the Romans with the Latins and the Volsci, the continual quarrels of the plebeians with the patricians, and the animosities of the senate against the tribunes; and sometimes it will happen to him, that in reading, for example, the Florentine History of Scipione Ammirato, he will think he has in his hand a translation into his own language of Livy. The manner of proclaiming and prosecuting war, and of concluding peace, which was practised by the ancient Italians in the time of Camillus and of Pyrrhus, is not very different from that which we observe in the age of Frederic II. and the Manfreds; and, in the internal concerns of the cities, both in the one and the other period, the cruelty and the pride of the nobles towards the plebeians, and the injustice of the people in their demands, as soon as they had discovered their own strength, and had begun to lay their hands on the government, were equal. The one and the other were animated with the same spirit, agitated by the same humors, and subject to the same revolutions. That supreme love of their country, which, on occasions of public danger, silenced and appeased their private quarrels and enmities, reigned equally at all times in both; the same simplicity of manners, the same severity of life, the same patience of poverty and fatigue. To this is to be added,

* Danina, *Rivoluzioni d' Italia*, lib. xii. cap. v. vol. ii. p. 241.

the use and exercise of arms, by which every little nation, if it cannot make extensive conquests, at least may preserve its own liberty. Finally, he will observe with pleasure, how, after the ancient Italians, and those people who in the middle ages arose from the ruins of the kingdom of the Lombards and of the second western empire, the cities which appear to have had the narrow-est territory and the most modern original, not only maintained their freedom for a long time, but increased in power and domi-nion; whereas the most able and the most ancient passed more easily under the yoke, either of tyrants of their own, or of foreign powers. We shall see, in like manner, a great resemblance in the fortune of the tyrants of the ancient Italian cities and those of the republics of Tuscany and Lombardy, in the age of Frede-ric II. and the following; and may very well find reasons to compare Ezzelino of Romagna with Tarquin the Proud; the Marquis Oberto Pelavicino, Buoso-da-Doara, and Martino della Torre, with Porsenna, King of Chiusi, and with other like princes or supreme magistrates of the ancient Tuscans, Latins, Campanians, and Samnites. From which we have shown that the free and independent cities passed sometimes under the yoke of some powerful citizen, who made himself the master, or under the dominion of a tyrant of some other neighboring city; so that a signor of Padua, of Milan, or of Verona, obtained the govern-ment of many other cities of Lombardy, equally free and inde-pendent."

CHAPTER FOURTH.

MACHIAVEL, from his long experience of the miseries of Florence in his own times, and his knowledge of their history, perceived many of the defects in every plan of a constitution they had ever attempted. His sagacity, too, perceived the necessity of three powers; but he did not see an equal necessity for the separation of the executive power from the legislative. The following project contains excellent observations, but would not have remedied the evils. The appointment of officers in the council of a thousand would have ruined all the good effects of the other divisions of power. There is some doubt about the time when it was written; Nerli and Nardi think it was addressed to Clement VII., but the English editor supposes it was Leo X., and his opinion is here followed.

About the year 1519, Leo X.,* being informed of the discords that were ready to break out in Florence, gave a commission to Machiavel to draw up a plan for the reformation of that state. He executed this commission with great abilities, and the most exquisite subtilty of his genius; and produced a model, in the opinion of some, of a perfect commonwealth. The sovereign power is lodged, both of right and in fact, in the citizens themselves.

"There are three orders of men in every state, and for that reason there should be also three ranks or degrees in a republic, and no more; nor can that be said to be a true and durable commonwealth, where certain humors and inclinations are not gratified, which otherwise must naturally end in its ruin.

"Those who model a commonwealth, must take such provisions as may gratify three sorts of men, of which all states are composed; that is, the high, the middle sort, and the low."

Machiavel by these observations demonstrates, that he was fully convinced of this great truth, this eternal principle, without the knowledge of which every speculation upon government must be imperfect, and every scheme of a commonwealth essen-

* *Discourse upon the proper Ways and Means of reforming the Government of Florence.* Eng. edit. vol. iv. p. 263.

tially defective. Taking this fundamental principle along with us, let us give an abridgment of this valuable discourse.

"The reason why Florence has so often changed its form of government is, because there never was yet either a commonwealth or monarchy established there upon true principles. A monarchy cannot be stable, where the business, which should be directed by one,[1] is submitted to the determination of many; nor can a commonwealth be durable where humors are not gratified, which must otherwise be the ruin of it. Maso moulded the republic into a sort of aristocracy,* in which there were so many defects, that it did not continue above forty years, nor would it have lasted so long, but for wars which kept it united. The defects were, that power was continued too long in the same persons; that the elections were subject to fraud and underhand practices; there was no check upon the grandees, to deter them from forming parties and factions, which are the destruction of a state. The signori had but little reputation, while they had too much authority; they had a power of taking away the life and property of any citizen without appeal, and of calling the people together to a conference whenever they pleased; so that instead of being a defence and protection to the state, they were rather an instrument of its ruin, when they were under the influence of any popular or ambitious man; raw young men of little experience and abject condition, were introduced into the signori; but what was of the last consequence was, that *the people had no share at all in the government.* All these defects together occasioned infinite disorder and confusion, and if wars had not kept the state united, it must have been dissolved long before it was.

"This form was succeeded by that of Cosimo. Afterwards the city endeavored to resume the form of a republic, but the measures taken were neither calculated to gratify the humors of all the citizens, nor had sufficient force to correct them; so far from being a true and perfect commonwealth, a gonfalonier for life, if an able and bad man, might easily have made himself absolute lord; if a weak and good man, he might have been pulled from his seat, and that establishment overturned. There

---

[1] "Dove le cose si fanno secondo che vuole uno, e si deliberano con il consenso di molti."

* *Hist. of Florence*, b. iii. See page 66 of this volume.

was not strength in that government to support the standard-bearer, if a good man, nor to check and control him if a bad one. The reforms which were made were not with any view to the public good, but to strengthen and support different factions in their turns. Even the ends of faction were not answered, because there was always a discontented party, which proved a very powerful instrument in the hands of those that were desirous to effect any change or innovation in the state.

"No form of government can be devised that will be firm and lasting, which is not either a true principality, or a true commonwealth. All intermediate forms between these two extremes will be defective; for a principality can only be ruined one way, and that is, by descending into a commonwealth; the same may be said of a commonwealth also; for the only way by which it can be ruined, is by ascending to a principality. All intermediate forms may be ruined two ways, that is, either by ascending to a principality, or descending into a commonwealth; and this is the cause of their instability.

"Those who model a commonwealth must make such provisions as may gratify three sorts of men, of which all states are composed, that is, the high, the middle sort, and the low; and though there is a great equality among the citizens of Florence, yet there are some there who think so highly of themselves, that they would expect to have the precedence of others; and these people must be gratified in regulating the commonwealth. These people then will never be satisfied, if they have not the first rank and honors in the commonwealth, which dignity they ought to support by their own personal weight and importance. It is absolutely necessary to gratify the ambition of all the three several ranks of people; which may be done by electing sixty-five citizens, of not less than forty-five years of age, in order to give dignity to the government, fifty-three out of the highest class, and twelve out of the next, who should continue in the administration for life, subject to the following restrictions: — In the first place, one of them should be appointed gonfalonier of justice for a term of two or three years, if it is not thought proper to appoint one for life; and in the next, the other sixty-four citizens, already elected, should be divided into two distinct bodies, each consisting of thirty-two; one of which divisions, in conjunction with the standard-bearer, should govern the first

16 *

year, and the other the next; so that they would be changed alternately every year, and all together should be called the signoria.

"After this, let the thirty-two be divided into four parts, eight in each; every one of which should reside three months in its turn with the standard-bearer, in the palace, and not only assume the magistracy with the usual forms and ceremonies, but transact all the business which before passed through the hands of the signori, the council of eight, and the other councils, all which must be dissolved. This should be the first member, or rather the head of the state, and by this provision the dignity of the signori will be restored; for as none but men of gravity and authority will ever sit there, it will be no longer necessary to employ private men in the affairs of state (which is always of prejudice to any republic) since the thirty-two who are not in office that year may be advised with upon occasion, sent upon embassies, and made useful in other functions.

"Let us now come to the second order in the state. Since there are three orders of men in every state, there should also be three ranks or degrees in a republic, and no more; upon which account it is necessary to prevent the confusion occasioned of late by the multiplicity of councils in our city, which have been established, not because they were conducive to good order, but merely to create friends and dependents, and to gratify the humor and ambition of numbers, in a point which yet was of no service to liberty or the public, because they might all be corrupted and biased by party. The council of seventy, that of a hundred, and that of the people and commonalty, should all be abolished; and, in the room of them, I would appoint a council of two hundred, every member of which should be not less than forty years of age; a hundred and sixty of them to be taken out of the middle class, and the other forty out of the lowest, but not one out of the sixty-five. They should also continue for life, and be called the council elect; which council, in conjunction with the sixty-five, should transact all the affairs that used to be transacted by the above-mentioned councils, now supposed to be abolished, and vested with the same degree of authority, and all the members of it appointed by your holiness; for which purpose, as well as to maintain and regulate these provisions, and others that I shall mention hereafter. it is necessary that a degree of authority, equal to that of the whole collective body of the people of Florence, should be vested by a balìa in your holiness and the Cardinal de' Medici, during the lives of both; and that the magistracy of the eight di guardia, as well as the balìa, should be appointed from time to time by your holiness. It is likewise expedient, for the support of your authority, that your holiness should divide the militia into distinct corps, over which you may appoint two commissioners, one for each.

"By these provisions two out of the three classes may be thoroughly satisfied. It remains now to satisfy the third and lowest rank of the citizens, which constitutes the greater part of the people. For this purpose it will be necessary also to revive the council of a thousand, or at least one of six hundred citizens, who should nominate all the magistrates and officers, in the same manner they used to do formerly, except the above sixty-five, the council of two hundred, the eight di guardia, and the balìa. Without satisfying the common people, no republic ever yet stood upon a stable foundation.

"The state being thus modelled, no other provisions would be wanting, if your holiness and the cardinal were to live for ever; but, as you are subject to mortality, it is necessary, if you would have the republic continue firm and strongly supported on every side, in such manner that every one may see himself perfectly secure, that there should be sixteen standard-bearers appointed over the companies of the citizens, which may be done either by your own authority, or by leaving the appointment to the great council, remembering only to increase the number of the *divieri*, assistants to the gonfalonier and commanding detachments of the people under him, that so they may be more spread over the city, and that none of the gonfaloniers should be of the sixty-five. After their appointment, four *proposti* should be drawn out of them by lot, and continue in office one month; so that at the end of four months they will all have been *proposti*. Out of these four, one should be drawn, to reside for a week only with the eight signors and the gonfaloniers in the palace; by which rotation all the four will have kept their residence there at the end of the month. Without the presence of this officer, the said resident signori should not be allowed to pass any act; nor should he himself have any vote there, but only be a witness and inspector of their proceedings, to which he may be suffered to

put a stop till he has asked the opinion of all the thirty-two together, and had the matter fully discussed by them.   But even the
thirty-two, when all together, should not have power to resolve
upon any thing, except two of the said *proposti* were present,
who should have no further authority than to put a stop to their
resolutions for a time, and report them to the council elect; nor
should that council have a power of resolving upon any thing,
except six at least of the sixteen gonfaloniers, and two *proposti*,
were there, who should only have the liberty of taking the matter
out of the hands of that council, and referring it to the great
council, provided that any three of them should think it necessary
so to do; and as to the great council, it should not be allowed
to meet, unless twelve of the gonfaloniers and three of the *proposti* at least were there, who might give their votes in it like the
other citizens.

" This order should be observed after the death of your holiness
and the cardinal, for two reasons: In the first place, that, if the
signory or other council should either disagree in their resolutions,
or attempt any thing against the public good, there might be
somebody vested with a power to take the matter out of their
hands, and refer it to the people; for *it would be a great defect in
the constitution, that any one set of magistrates, or single council,
should have a power to pass a law by its own authority alone, and
that too without any remedy or appeal;* upon which account it is
highly necessary that the citizens should have some proper officers,
not only to inspect their proceedings, but even to put a stop to
them, if they seem to be of pernicious tendency.[1]

"Besides this, in order to give such a degree of stability and
perfection to the commonwealth, that no part of it may shrink
or fail after the decease of your holiness and the cardinal, it is
necessary that a court should be erected upon occasion, consisting
of the eight di guardia and a balia of thirty citizens, to be chosen
by lot out of the council of two hundred and that of six hundred
together; which court should have a power, in criminal cases,

[1] The other reason is omitted, which is singular, as it appears to have some
bearing on the reasoning of the author.
" The other reason is, that, in depriving the generality of the citizens, by suppressing the signory as is now done, of the power to be of the signori, it is necessary to restore to them a grade which may resemble that of which they are
deprived; and the one proposed should be such that it is greater, more useful to
the republic, and more honorable than that was."

of summoning the accuser and accused to appear face to face before it in a certain time.

"Such a court is of great use in a commonwealth; for a few citizens are afraid to call great and powerful delinquents to account, and therefore it is necessary that many should concur for that purpose, that so, when their judgments are concealed, as they may be by balloting, every man may give his opinion freely and in security.

"The highest honor that can be attained by any man, is that which is voluntarily conferred on him by his countrymen; and the greatest good he can do, as well as the most acceptable to God, is that which he does to his country. None are to be compared to those who have reformed kingdoms and common-wealths by wholesome laws and constitutions; but as there have been but few that have had an opportunity to do this, the number is very small that have done it. This kind of glory has always been so much coveted by such as made glory the sole end of their labors, that when they have not had power either to found or reform a state, they have left models and plans in writing, to be executed by others, who should have, in future times; as Plato, Aristotle, and many others, who have shown that, if they did not found free states themselves, like Solon and Lycurgus, it was not owing either to ignorance or want of good-will to mankind, but to want of power. Heaven, then, cannot bestow · a nobler gift upon any man, nor point out a fairer road to true glory.

"If things continue as they are, whenever any commotion or insurrection shall happen, either some head will be appointed in a sudden and tumultuary manner, who will rescue the state by violence and force of arms, or one part of the citizens will open the council of a thousand again, and sacrifice the other without mercy. In case either of these events should happen, your holiness will be pleased to consider how many executions, how many banishments and confiscations must of necessity ensue; a reflection which must surely shock the most hard-hearted man alive, much more a man of that remarkable humanity and tenderness which have always distinguished your holiness. The only way, then, to prevent these evils, is to establish the several classes and ordinances of the commonwealth in such a manner that they may support themselves; and they will always be able to do this when each rank has its due share in the administration, when every one knows his proper sphere of action, and whom he can confide in; and, lastly, when no one has any occasion to wish for a change of government, either because his ambition is not thoroughly gratified, or that he does not think himself sufficiently secure under such an administration."

CHAPTER FIFTH.

SIENA.

THE antiquity of the city of Siena is proved by the notice of Pliny, Tacitus, and Ptolemy, if not by another circumstance mentioned by its historian, namely,—the splendor of certain families among its citizens,* nobility being only an ancient virtue, accompanied with the splendor of riches. The tradition, that it was first planted by Remus, can hardly be supported by the single circumstance, that the ensigns of the city are a wolf giving suck to two infants.

Siena was built by the ancient Tuscans, whose province was anciently inhabited by the Umbrians, who were driven out by the Pelasgians from Arcadia, who were afterwards driven out by the Lydians from Asia, five hundred and sixty years before Rome was built. These, from Tirrhenus their king, were called afterwards Tirrhenians; and because they used in their sacrifices great quantities of frankincense, *thus*, they were called Thuscans, and their country Tuscany, by others called Etruria.† Livy represents the Etrurians as abounding in wealth, and filling the whole length of Italy, from the Alps to the straits of Sicily, with their fame; and, in another place, represents the Tuscan empire as much more ancient than the Roman.‡ They inhabited twelve cities; the form of their government was a confederacy, like that of the modern Swiss, Dutch, and Americans.

"The twelve cities, peoples, or divisions of territory rather, were called Lucumoni, from the magistrates annually chosen to govern the whole province of Tuscany. Twelve annual magistrates were chosen, one by each city, to govern the whole province, called Lartes and Lucumones; the names of these cities were Luna, Pisa, Populonia, Volterra, Roselle, Fiesole, Agillina,

* Siena dallo splendore delle famiglie s' era nobilitata,—essendo proprio la nobiltà una antica virtù accompagnata dallo splendore delle ricchezze. *Historia del. Sig. Orlando Malavolti, de' fatti, e Guerre de' Sanesi, cosi esterne, come civili,* p. 4.

† Malavolti, p. 9, 10.

‡ Tuscorum ante Romanum imperium late terra marique opes patuere; mari supero inferoque, quibus Italia insulæ modo cingitur . . . . Ii in utrumque mare vergentes incoluere urbibus duodenis terras.

Vulsino, Chiusi, Arezzo, Perugia, and Faleria, the ruins of which
are near to Viterbo. In the same manner was the republic of
the Achaians afterwards formed by the Greeks, the twelve cities
of which are enumerated by Polybius. Not unlike this republic
of the Tuscans was that of the Latins, who, upon public occasions, assembled in a certain place under Mount Albanus, called
the Forest of Ferentina; where, having deliberated in council
upon their affairs, they gave the charge of the execution of their
resolutions to two praetors.* It is true that sometimes, at the
exchange of magistrates, the Tuscans, varying the form of their
government, by agreement among themselves created a king;
and each one of the twelve peoples of the twelve principal cities
concurred to give him a minister, whom the Romans afterwards
denominated a lictor. And of so much grandeur, and so illustrious an example, were the government, the ceremonies, the religion, and the other qualities of the Tuscans, that Romulus, in
imitation of them, in giving laws to the Romans ordained, besides the habit of the robe and the cloak, the curule chair, and
the same number of ministers, determining a corresponding number of lictors. This is told us by Livy: 'Et hoc genus ab Etruscis
finitimis, unde sella curulis, unde toga praetexta sumpta est,
numerum quoque ipsum ductum placet, et ita habuisse Etruscos,
quod ex duodecim populis communiter creato rege, singulos sin-
guli populi lictores dederint.'

"With this mode of regimen, and this form of government,
with their union and virtue, the Tuscans augmented their empire
so greatly, that it extended to the Alps, which separate Italy from
France, and from one sea to the other; one of which was named
from them the Tuscan, and the other the Adriatic, from the city
Adria, which was their colony, and under their dominion. Having
acquired all that part of Italy which was afterwards called Cisalpine Gaul, in order to hold it more securely, and give room to
their people, by relieving Tuscany of so great a number of inhabitants, they sent into it twelve colonies. In this manner they
proceeded, augmenting and amplifying their empire on every
side, for seven hundred and thirty years, until, in the reign of

---

* Concilium Latinorum erat ut omnes Latini nominis rerum communium causâ
ad Lucum Ferentinæ, qui erat sub monte Albano, coirent, ibique de summa rep.
consultarent, ac duobus praetoribus rem universam Latinorum committerent.
Sigonius, upon the authority of Dionysius.

Tarquinius Priscus, the Gauls took possession of that part of Italy, which they called Cisalpine Gaul, one part of which was afterwards called Lombardy, and the other Romagna. Then the empire of the Tuscans began to decline, because on one side they were combated by the Gauls, and on the other by the Romans; and having, by the abundance of wealth, become ambitious and avaricious, discord, following the train of those vices, changed the form of their government, and destroyed their prosperity; and this empire, which, by its union and good order, had grown up, and, computing from its beginning to its dissolution, subsisted more than a thousand years, easily ruined itself by means of contentions, occasioned by habits adverse to the virtues by which it had been gained. Dispossessed by the Gauls of all their territory beyond the Apennines, and continually molested in Tuscany by the Romans, they were no longer united in the defence of each other, by reason of the variety creeping into the form of government in the separate cities, occasioned by ambition, avarice, and luxury; vices opposed to each other, but powerful to ruin a great empire. When they saw the most manifest danger of the ruin of the whole, they exerted all their force, but were no longer able to defend themselves. The other Tuscans, from an indignation against the Veientes for having separately elected a king, looked on with indifference while the Romans subjected that people. Livy says, the Veientes, to avoid the tedious contentions of ambition, which was sometimes the cause of dissensions, created a king, and thus gave great offence to the other peoples of Etruria, not more by their hatred of that form of government, than from their detestation of the man.*

"Tuscany, after long wars, many victories and defeats, and the destruction of a great number of citizens, was finally subjected to the dominion of the Romans, by Q. Fabius Maximus Rutilianus. They, to secure the province against rebellions and tumults, sent a colony into it; and finding Siena in the centre of the twelve cities, and the situation strong, they sent thither their colony and garrison, under the first consulate of Curius Dentatus, two hundred and ninety years before Christ.

"The Tuscans remained quietly under the government of the

* Veientes contra, tedio annuæ ambitionis, quæ interdum discordiarum causa erat, regem creavere; offendit ea res populorum Etruriæ animos, non majore odio regni, quam ipsius regia. Livy.

Romans, until the invasion of Italy by Asdrubal, when they were accused of having held a secret correspondence, and given assistance to the Carthaginians. After that great victory of the Romans, in which Asdrubal, with fifty-six thousand of his men, was slain, Marcus Livius was sent to Tuscany, to inquire which of the twelve cities had assisted the Carthaginians, who reported, that he found nothing against Siena. Tranquillity, thus restored, continued under the Roman government till the social war, when the inhabitants of almost all Italy waged war with the Romans for the privileges of Roman citizens. This war cost the lives of a very great number of men, and ended with the ruin of Arezzo and Chiusi, two of the principal cities of Tuscany, from whence many families removed to Siena, as a place of more security, both on account of its being a Roman colony, and as it had ever discovered more fidelity to the Romans than any other Tuscan city."

We may pass over the conversion of Constantine, in a dream of a standard, (gonfalone,) with the motto ἐν τούτῳ νίκα; his division of the empire, by retiring to Byzantium, into two, the Grecian and Roman, or eastern and western; the decline of the western empire; the capture of Rome by Alaric, King of the Goths, in 412; the sacking of Rome by Odoacer, King of the Herulians and Thuringians, in 475, the first of the barbarous kings, who drove out Augustulus, annihilated the empire, made himself King of Italy, and so established his power, that the western empire remained vacant for three hundred years, till the time of Charlemagne, though Justin, after the victories of Belisarius and Narses over the Goths, sent Longinus into Italy, with the title of exarch, a kind of first magistracy, which continued one hundred and seventy years, through a succession of thirteen.

" Longinus having found that the several cities had undertaken to govern themselves, each one having created its own magistrates, sent a governor, not to rule generally in the province, but to each city of any considerable consequence. To these governors he gave a new name, that of dukes. The first that he sent to Rome was called a president, but those who succeeded him were called dukes like the rest. This title of duke, from the name of a military office, was reduced to the name of a dignity, which, at this day, is the principal one in Europe after the royal dignity. And thus, all the time that Narses remained in Rome, after the

expulsion of the Ostrogoths, the cities of Tuscany governed themselves by their own magistrates, acknowledging no superior, until
the arrival of Longinus, in 566. He, with his new governors or
dukes, debilitated the forces, and destroyed the reputation of the
empire, and the confidence of the people in their own militia, to
such a degree, that the Lombards, under Albinus their king,
found it easy to ruin Tuscany, which they conquered, plundered,
and oppressed, sometimes under the general power of their kings,
and sometimes under an officer, sent to command in particular
cities. These Lombards, from their proud hatred of the Romans,
endeavored everywhere to change the laws, customs, manners,
and especially the language. In their time the Latin language
in Italy was corrupted into that speech now called the Italian,
which is no other than the Latin corrupted by a mixture of
the barbarous speech of those very Lombards, and some other
nations, who governed in Italy after them; as the French and
Spanish are similar corruptions of the Latin, the first by a mixture with the language of the Franks, and the last, with that of
the Visigoths and other barbarians. The Lombards held the
domination of the major part of Italy more than two hundred
years, when they were totally subdued.

"Desiderius, who, from a Duke of Tuscany, had made himself
King of Italy, was the last Lombard king, and was totally defeated, and sent prisoner to Lyons in France, by Charlemagne,
in 773. This great monarch having taken Pavia, which was the
principal city and royal residence of the kings of the Lombards,
proceeded to many other strong places, which were held by governors of castles and garrisons in the service of the king, or of
particular lords of these places; those which surrendered, and
swore obedience, were left under the command of their lords, but
those which resisted, and were reduced by force, were given by
Charlemagne to some of his barons or nobles, in reward of the
services and merits they had shown in the course of the war.
More of the cities of Tuscany defended themselves than of any
other parts of Italy, because they were better fortified, and therefore more French noblemen were left here. These married with
original families in Siena, and from those matches have issued
the greatest part of the noble families which have been and still
are in that city. They continued afterwards, many hundreds of
years, to be lords of the same castles, until, by continual discords,

many families not only lost their estates and commands, but
became extinct, as will be shown in the sequel.

" Charles, for the greatness of his soul and the multitude of
his victories, received the surname of Magnus, and was made
Roman emperor. As Longinus had brought into Italy the title
of dukes, the Lombards those of marquises and castaldi or bailiffs, the French now imported that of counts. Charlemagne,
having arranged all things to his mind in Italy, set out on his
journey to return; and passing through Siena, and being moved
with the relation which he heard from those noblemen whom he
had left there, of the fidelity and other good qualities of that
people, and being touched also by their petitions, he made them
free, and determined that they should not be subjected to the
king or any other power. This is the reason that, in the division
of Tuscany, afterwards made between Louis the Pious and Pascal the pope, in which it was declared that Arezzo, Chiusi, Volterra, Florence, Pistoia, Lucca, Pisa, and Luna, should be reserved
to the emperor, and Orvieto, Bagnarea, Viterbo, Sovana, Populonia, Roselle, Perugia, Sutri, and Nepi, should belong to the
ecclesiastical state, Siena is not found among the former or the
latter. Being free and independent, it was left in the enjoyment
of its liberty; and as the nobles had procured from Charlemagne
so great a favor, the people, in gratitude to them, and ignorant,
no doubt, of any better form, left the government to them, and
suffered an optimacy[1] to be established. Siena was a long time
governed by these noblemen; and, as long as the signori consisted
of these successors of Charlemagne in Italy and the empire, all
remained quiet in this city, as well as in the rest of Italy. This
tranquillity continued to the time of Arnulphus, the last emperor
of the house of France, who was approved by the pope. At this
time, ambition, discontent, and ill humor began to arise in Italy,
from the weakness of the successors of Charlemagne. Berengarius, Duke of Friuli, and Guido, Duke of Spoleto, aspiring to
the empire and the kingdom of Italy, took arms against the
emperor; Berengarius succeeded, declared himself emperor, and,
by the favor of the Roman people, was made King of Italy; in
which dignities he was succeeded by Berengarius II. and III. A
contest, however, arose between the princes of Italy, France, and

---

[1] Un regimento d' ottimati, "an aristocracy."

Germany, for the empire and the kingdom of Italy, which continued sixty years; and a Saracen invasion having been defeated
by Albericus, he was declared Duke of Tuscany by the pope, and
acknowledged no superior in the emperor or others. Contentions
soon arose between him and the pope; and the Hungarians, taking advantage of them, made inroads into Italy, plundered Tuscany, and ruined Volterra. The Romans, judging this calamity
to proceed from the discords between the pope and Albericus,
assassinated both. Such was the malignity of these times, and
Christian princes had deviated so far from a virtuous conduct,
and had become a prey to ambition, avarice, and pleasure, (powerful ministers to every kind of wickedness,) that they determined,
through these means, and without scruple, to occupy those dignities which their ancestors had acquired by religion, charity, and
every Christian virtue; they lived in continual discords and bloody
wars among themselves; and the people, after their example,
having adopted their follies and vices, and embroiled themselves
in the same dissensions, found themselves ruined. Having neither forces nor courage to defend their country, the Hungarians
committed, in a short space of time, greater ravages in Tuscany
than the other barbarous nations had been able to do in three
hundred years.

"The Saracens, too, or Moors, broke in and destroyed the sea-
coast of Siena, and took Jerusalem and Spain, until at last they
were defeated by Charles Martel in Italy, in 930, and by Ferdinand
III. in Spain, in 1216. The city of Roselle was ruined by them,
and its inhabitants fled to Siena, which made it necessary to
enlarge the bounds of the city, and take in the ancient castle
Montone, built at the time of the King Porsenna of Chiusi,
who, desirous of assisting Tarquin the Proud in his restoration
to Rome, sent to his aid two hundred infantry and fifty cavalry;
the former, taken from the castle Montone, were commanded by
Bacco Piccolomo; and the latter, taken from the Old Castle, by
Perinto Cacciaconte. From these two captains are descended
the two most ancient families in Siena, those of the Piccolomini,
and those of the Cacciaconti.

"Otho, the first emperor of the German nation, but the second
of that name, expelled the last of the Saracens, and left an officer
in Tuscany, who governed it in his name, with the title of Vicar
of the Empire. The successors of Otho followed the same prac-

17 *

tice; but Siena, by the indulgence of Otho, maintained its independence under the government of its nobles, and its liberty was afterwards confirmed, with ample privileges, by Otho III. of the German nation, who had been served in his enterprise by a company of gentlemen from Siena, and to it was presented a new ensign of the white lion. Both the first and the third Otho left many of their gentlemen in Siena, from whom are descended several of the noble and powerful families in that city, where they continued a long time, behaving virtuously and honorably in the service of their country. All the inhabitants of the city and territory, living then in union and harmony, were comprehended under the name of the People, which has since, from a general denomination, become a particular and peculiar name of a faction called Popolo, the citizens being divided into parties. Although the body of the city increased on every side, both in numbers and riches, it was nevertheless unable to enlarge its boundaries or extend its jurisdiction; for, having on one hand the lands of the church, and on the other the territories of the emperor, it could not go beyond its own limits.

"At this time much industry and many artificers were introduced, by means of an extensive commerce. Besides other noblemen, the Count Bandinello de' Bandinelli, having agents and correspondents in many parts of the Levant, imported large merchandises, to his own great profit as well as the public utility, employing and maintaining a multitude of people in every kind of labor. He was in a great measure the instrument of directing this people to merchandise. The same Count Bandinello, moreover, being consul, and desirous of displaying the consular dignity and authority, gave orders that two commanders, or officers, on all occasions of solemnity or ceremony, should go before the consuls, with rods in their hands and fringes at their breasts, after the similitude of the lictors, who walked with their bundles of rods and with their axes before the consuls of Rome. He also ordered, that to the trumpets should be fixed those streamers of white and black taffety, which have been ever since used by all the supreme magistrates who have succeeded in the place of the consuls; and that the fifers and trumpeters, with the rest of the family and servants of the magistrate, down to modern times, in the public palace, should be clothed in blue and green.

"About the year 1059, contentions arose between the Emperor

Henry III. and the pope, who decreed him an enemy to the church, and interdicted him his empire and kingdom; which quarrel was the reason that the cities of Tuscany began to be agitated with seditions. Some of them declared in favor of the emperor, and others, rebelling against him, adopted republican governments, and attached themselves to the pope, by whose assistance they hoped to defend themselves against the emperor, who would have oppressed them. From this division originated the desire in the minds of the people to increase their forces, that they might the more easily resist the emperor, if he should invade Tuscany with a design of reducing them to his obedience. To this end every city and castle endeavored to make itself master of those in its neighborhood, or at least to draw them to its alliance, which involved them in frequent wars, and was the original of those discords and enmities with which many cities of Tuscany were long agitated, and which proved the ruin of some, though it augmented the greatness of others.

" The Italians having long remained under the obedience of the German emperors, and having very rarely been employed in their wars, either by them or their captains, neglected, in so long and inactive a kind of servitude, the regulations of their militia; but now, in danger of oppression from Conrad I., the cities, in order to defend themselves, ordered a kind of chariot to be built, and called it *il carrocio*. It was covered with rose-colored cloth, with a large pole in the centre, on which was displayed a white standard, with two scarlet stripes, in a cross, at the middle of it; and on every side of the carriage stood a man, who held in his hand a cord fastened to the top of the pole, that neither the force of the wind nor the weight of the standard might incline it one way or another. The chariot was drawn by oxen covered with white, although they varied the colors according to the prevalence of factions in the city. The care and command of this chariot was given to one of the most experience and ability in war, who became the captain; and to him, for the purpose of increasing his authority, a shield and a sword were given by the public. But in the times which followed after the Emperor Frederick I., this was the office of the podestà;* and he was accompanied with eight trumpets and one priest. In this manner the cities of

* The Italian writers in Latin call this office and officer, both, by the name of *potestas.*

Lombardy, as well as Tuscany, sent out their people to war, without entertaining any soldiers in pay; for those who were ordered out to war in those times, in Italy, went at their own expense, so great was their affection to their country, as in the beginning the Romans did. Wherever the triumphal chariot was found, there were the head-quarters of the captain, like the prætor's among the ancients. With this manner of making war, confiding in the power of the faction it followed, and living by plunder, each city was ambitious to increase its dominion, and declined no opportunity which occurred of opposing itself obstinately to the most powerful princes and veteran armies, for the defence of its own dignity, and that of the party to which it was devoted.

" Deriving from these motives, and from successful enterprises, great courage and ardor, when Henry III., with his antipope, besieged Gregory VII. in his castle, and, for fear of Robert Guiscard, on his march to succor the pope, retired to Siena, Florence took the part of the pope, and Siena that of the emperor; and from this principle arose that irreconcilable hatred and enmity between these cities, which lasted so long, and produced so much war and bloodshed. Upon this occasion a memorable battle was fought, and a signal victory obtained by the army of Siena over that of Florence. Certain persons in this engagement had been the first to begin the action, and behaved themselves so bravely in it, that it was adjudged that their conduct had been the principal cause of putting the Florentines to flight. The republic, in reward of their merit, and to incite and inflame by this example the minds of others to act nobly in the service of their country, erected, by a public decree, a very high tower by the sides of their houses. The Greeks and Romans, by decreeing statues to them, used to honor those who performed similar achievements in the service of the republic, by this means rendering their memories immortal; and they were more or less honored, according to the position in which the statue was placed, and the height and grandeur of the statue itself; wherefore they made some larger and others smaller; some on horseback, others on the ground; and to make the glory of others still more illustrious, they sought the most eminent artists, and placed the statues on columns,*

---

* Columnarum ratio erat attolli supra cæteros mortales. *Pliny.*

knowing that columns, anciently dedicated to men, were marks
of honor, and conspicuous tokens of immortal glory. Moved
by these old examples, they who governed the city of Siena
having, by the long domination of the barbarians in Italy, lost
the arts of sculpture and painting, which were held in so high
estimation by the ancients, as well as by the modern civilized
nations, and not being able, for want of artists, to make statues
or columns to honor these brave and virtuous citizens, ordered
those towers to be built. After which precedent, for similar
merits and services, many others were afterwards erected; among
which that of the Malavolti was built by the public, in memory
of the virtue of Philip Malavolti, captain of Siena in the Christian army of Clement III. This, like many others which had
been raised before, was habitable; and although they were erected
only as memorials of the honor due to greatness of soul, they
were afterwards employed very often as fortifications for offence
and defence, by the several parties, in their civil wars; permission was granted by the public, to many gentlemen, to build
towers at their own expense, as testimonials of the nobility and
splendor of their families; and until, long afterwards, they were
taken down by order of Charles V., and the materials employed in a castle which that tyrant built for himself, they were
so large and so high, as to be seen from a great distance, and
made a most beautiful appearance.

In the union of the Christian princes, in 1099, against the
Saracens, and in the army engaged in the enterprise against
Jerusalem, the city of Siena had a thousand men, under the
command of Dominick and Boniface Gricci, noblemen of Siena. Henry IV., after the death of Henry III., coming to
Rome for the crown, in 1110, renewing the discords with the
pope Pascal II., and Gelasius his successor, and marching to
Rome with his armies, excited afresh the ill humors in Tuscany. But these not having much energy, did not at that
time produce effects of moment; yet, stirred up from time
to time by the discord among the great princes, and other
accidents, though they seemed at times to be quieted, they
broke out again, and were never wholly extinguished; they
rather went on increasing, and at last, discovering themselves
with greater malignity, they grew, from particular disputes between one city and another, to the most general and sanguinary

factions of all, or the greatest part, of the territory of Tuscany,
and all the rest of Italy, making alliance among one another, of
those who were of the same faction, against other leagues
among the factions who were their enemies.   One party having
taken the name of Guelphs, and the other of Ghibellines, these
parties and divisions were not only between one people and
another, but, to complete the ruin and destruction, they spread
into the same city, and sometimes into the same family, till
there was not a spot of earth to be found whose inhabitants
were not divided, and on which the citizens did not frequently
meet in arms against each other; as it happened in 1137, and in
1147, between the noble houses in Siena, in which private
interests and party passions had infinitely more energy than the
interest of the public.   Although the nobles had so long governed
and preserved this republic in peace, they now most imprudently
suffered themselves to be blindly led on by ambition.   This civil
discord having entered, and been increased and artificially fomented by the heads of those plebeians who had attached themselves, some to one nobleman and some to another, in the city,
they began to endeavor in turn to expel one another by violence
from the city.*

By this means, coming frequently to blows, and meeting often
in arms, they gave occasion to the plebeians, who wished nothing
better, to study the means of taking the government, by little
and little, out of their hands, in the firm hope of being able to
obtain it, if not entirely, at least in part, to themselves; for the
gentlemen being in arms, and each party afraid of being overcome by the other, strove to acquire friends and adherents among
the plebeians, whom they now called by a more decent appellation of the People.   That they might be able with stronger
forces, to conquer their enemies, or at least secure themselves
from being conquered by them, neither party was willing, by
refusing the people a share in the government, to make them
their enemies.   They agreed therefore to give them a third part:
wherefore, when they first appointed two consuls of noble houses,
who should annually govern the republic, it was ordained, that
for the future they should appoint three, two of them to be
noblemen taken from each faction, and the third from the

* Plebs est cæteri cives sine senatore. *De Verb. Signif.*

people; and sometimes they made the number six, observing
the same distribution ; and this is the reason why many persons
have believed that certain families, which at this day are of the
order of the nine,* finding that their ancestors were made consuls
in those times, were originally noble, not knowing that the people,
from whom the order of nine had their original, participated at
that time, by a third part, in the government, and that from
some of those popular families, who at that time held the consulate, are descended those of the nine.   The nobles, who at
this day are denominated in Siena gentlemen, and who anciently,
being very powerful, were sometimes called grandees, are sprung
from a part of those ancient families, who in the first institution
and ordination of the republic took upon them the government,
which, with large additions to the city and its dominions, they
held till the year 1137, when the plebeians, or more properly the
people, first began to enter into a share of the government of the
state and police of the city; by this means, although those who
had been in public offices and dignities had acquired nobility to
their descendants, they had not yet assumed the name of nobles
or of gentlemen.

Although in Siena, as in all the other cities of Tuscany,
the popular faction long prevailed over the nobles, they followed, as the most favorable and least invidious, the name of
the people ; and thus, leaving uncorrupted the ancient nobility,
perhaps to avoid the distinction of greater and lesser, like that
of nobles and patricians among the Romans, they busied themselves in those factions, through which, at different times, they
began to ennoble themselves; the people in process of time
divided into three parties, one of which was called the people
of the smaller number, who were those of the order of the
nine; the second, the people of the middle number, who were
called the order of the twelve; and the third, the people of
the greater number, called the order of reformers, including all
the lesser people,† combined with some of the ancient houses,
under this denomination, were the most numerous, as will be
largely shown in its proper place.   Subsequently to these three
popular factions, out of those who were afterwards accepted into
the government and acquired civil rights, together with those

---

* Dell' ordine de' nove.   † Il popolo minuto.

few houses who would not follow the above-named factions, another order was created, which was called the order of the people;
and these, however they may since have been ennobled, have
taken no other name than that of the popular faction. So of old
in Rome it happened, that the patricians and ancient nobles had
always the name of nobles, and the plebeians, (so called by the
Romans,) although they had been consuls and dictators, and had
enjoyed triumphs, were ever called plebeians, until some families were added to the number of patricians by the emperors,
Julius Cæsar, Augustus, and Claudius. The greater part of the
families of nobles, who were denominated by Romulus the
greater race, and of those who were added by Tarquinius Priscus, and were afterwards called by Lucius Brutus the lesser
race, being already extinguished, this distinction was preserved
in the Roman senate, where the fathers were understood to be
those who were of patrician houses, and fathers conscript those
who had been added and recorded in the number of senators;
and thus plebeians sometimes, by concessions of princes, acquired the name of nobles. These orders were in all respects
contrary to those which were used at this time in the cities of
Tuscany, which, being governed by the multitude, did not admit
the nobles to honors, nor to the administration of the republic,
if they did not, first renouncing their nobility, acquire the privilege of being of the people; such was in that age the odium
against the name of nobles among those who governed the
republics of Tuscany, from the jealousy and terror that were
entertained of their greatness; and this we may well suppose
was the main reason why those first popular characters, and
the others who followed after them, did not care to acquire the
name of noblemen or gentlemen; on the contrary they exerted
themselves with all diligence, by the laws and by all their
actions, by extermination and destruction of one family after
another, totally to destroy the memory of all the noble houses
of the gentlemen, in such manner that the greatest part of them
are extinguished. Among the few that remain are the Bis-
domini, the Tegolei, the Floridi, who were original inhabitants
of the city, and lived in that third of it which was called
the Old Castle, with many other noble families enumerated.
In another third of the city, named the Third of Saint Martin,
the noble families of Jazzani, Trombetti, Guastelloni, Sanse-

donii, and others dwelt; in the remaining third, called the third of Camullia, lived the Gallerani, Scricciuoli, Arzochii, Mignanelli, &c. There was another distinction of five families, who were counts, and lived indifferently in any part of the town, which were called the greater houses, as the Counts Ardenghesci, Guiglieschi, Scialenghi, Cacciaconti, and Valcortese. There were other families who, because very numerous, had the privilege of having two members from each family in the magistracy, while the rest could have but one, as the Piccolomini, Tolommei, Malavolti, Salimbeni, and Saraceni; and in the same proportion they might have seats in the council of a hundred gentlemen, to whom, in this reform of the state, fifty popular members were added. This council was renewed once in two years, and sometimes every year; and was elected by the general council, one member from each family, with ample authority. In this council, which was to assemble at least once a month, they consulted upon all affairs of the most serious nature and the greatest importance.

"Under this form of government Siena continued for some time, and, following the imperial party, they had a mind to possess themselves of the castle of Radicofani, then held by the church, pretending that it had been given to the bishop and people of Siena by the Count Manente de' Visconti di Campiglia, before 1138; but this expedition failed. In this year the inhabitants of Siena and the Aretini united with the Conti Guidi, whose castle of Monte alla Croce they relieved from a siege of the Florentines. The Conti Guidi were lords of many castles in Casentino and one part of Valdarno, and had been decorated with the title of counts by Otho the emperor, after he had liberated Italy from the lordship of Berengarius III., when one of the family who came with him from Germany, married a lady of Florence, from which marriage descended the house of Guidi."

We may pass over the bloody wars and variety of victories and defeats between these two cities of Siena and Florence; but when Frederick Barbarossa came into Italy, they made a truce, and new laws and confederations were made between the people of Tuscany.

"The Florentines, Lucchese, Pratensians, and lords of Carfagna, entered into one league; and the inhabitants of Siena,

Pisa, Pistoia, Aretina, and the Conti Guidi into another; and because the Sienese had shown themselves, in the dissensions which had happened in times past between the popes and the emperors, favorable to the empire, the Pope Adrian, attentive to the arrival of Frederick, with much solicitude completed the fortress, and part of the walls of the territory, of Radicofani. In 1154, Frederick was crowned at Rome, after long disputes with the Romans, and returned to Germany in 1155. The Sienese, by sympathy, being of the same faction, acquired a jurisdiction over Poggibonzi, an eighth part of which castle had been given them by the Count Guido Guerra. This castle was afterwards, in 1268, taken by Charles, King of Naples, and given to the Florentines, and by them demolished, as always friendly or subject to the Sienese, and a receptacle of Ghibellines. In 1158, Frederick came a second time into Italy. The Sienese, being at variance with the Counts of Orgia, and other lords, their neighbors, who held many strong castles very near to Siena, some of which were demolished by the Sienese, the lords of these castles were desirous of rebuilding them; but Frederick granted to the Sienese the privilege, that neither those counts, nor any other lords, nor their successors, should rebuild any castle or fortress, within twelve miles of their city."

As it is a sketch of the laws, their vicissitudes and variations, that we are attempting, we have nothing to do with wars or disputes between popes and antipopes, the church and the empire, nor with the accessions of Staggia or Orgia to Siena. In 1167, Frederick returned to Italy, and confirmed all the privileges and donations which had been before made to Siena. The fourth, fifth, and sixth journey to Italy, and all the wars, and truces, and peaces, between Florence and Siena, may likewise be omitted; though in the last, which was in 1184, he found enemies in the Sienese, his old friends. According to some writers, this strange revolution was in 1186, and the causes of it deserve to be examined and explained.*

Charlemagne, as has been before related, left the government of Siena in a single assembly of hereditary nobles, who, no doubt, as they had procured the independence of the city by their inte-

* Malavolti, lib. iv. p. 36. Giovanni Villani. *Croniche Fiorentine*, lib. v. Muratori, *Rer. Italic. Scrip.* tom. xv. *Chronica Sanese*, di Andrea Dei. Muratori, *Dissertazioni*, 50. Muratori, *Annal.* tom. vii. anno 1186, p. 56.

rest and intercession, thought it their own, and entailed on their posterity forever. While the people considered these rulers as their benefactors, to whom they owed so much; while the nobles were united, and the city continued with constancy faithful to the emperors, all went smoothly on; at least, no history appears to the contrary; but in a course of time, when the nobles became divided into parties, each of which courted the people, not so much from humanity, patriotism, or love of liberty and equality, as because their bones and sinews were wanted in the civil wars, the people, with very good reason, began to demand a share and to take a hand in the game. But how? Not in any proportion which could give them a control, or a power of self-defence, or even much influence; but by claiming one in three consuls, and fifty in one hundred and fifty senators. Absolute power was still in the noble hundred, and the people, by their members, only became nearer witnesses of their own insignificance, and of the arbitrary disposition of their noble masters. This, therefore, of course, irritated the people, and gave them able leaders, while it increased the motives of the factions in each party of the nobles to caress them still more.

" In consequence of this, the public councils and conduct, in 1186, began to be unsteady, and a strong faction appeared for the pope against the emperor. Philippo Malavolti, Palmerio Malagalla, and Guido Maizi, were this year consuls. The Guelphs had acquired so much influence as to shut the gates against the emperor desirous of passing through the town, and even to attack and defeat his army; but as soon as he was prepared to punish them for this offence, certain orators were sent to him by those in the government, to excuse the fault, and to beg his pardon. They said, the resistance to his majesty had been occasioned by the fury of the people, who arose in a tumult, very much against the will of their governors, who had always been faithfully devoted to him. The emperor received them graciously, and confirmed their privileges under some severe conditions; moved however to this grace, according to the custom of great princes, more by his own interest than by any confidence he had in their professions; but as he was now intent upon an enterprise into the Levant against the Turks and Saracens, he wished to leave all things in tranquillity in Italy. Intending, on his return, to make himself master of the kingdom of Sicily and Naples, he was desir-

ous of preserving peace in the cities of Italy already friendly to
him; and by reconciling the others, to acquire more friends and
followers, who might assist him, and remove all obstacles to his
enterprise.   With this view he sent Henry his son, already
elected King of the Romans, into Italy, with great pomp and
authority, who pretended to be favorable to the Sienese, and
granted them the power, under the imperial authority, to elect
consuls, as they had been long used to do; but those who should
be elected, were obliged to accept the investiture of their consulate, without expense, from the king himself, or the emperor, or
their successors, if in Italy; if not, from their legate or vicar in
Tuscany; and if there should be no imperial legate in Tuscany,
the consuls elect were obliged to go in a body, or a part of them,
or send an ambassador, to demand the investiture of the emperor, or whoever should be King of the Romans.

"In 1187, Jerusalem was besieged by Saladin; and Siena sent
five hundred of her young men, under the command of Philip
Malavolti, in the Christian army raised for its relief.   Henry, on
his return from this expedition, was declared by the pope emperor, and invested with the kingdom of Naples and Sicily, upon
condition that he would recover it from Tancred, the son of
Roger IV., of the house of Normandy, heir of William, King
of England, who died in this crusade.   While the pope and the
emperor were occupied in this enterprise, and all Italy was filled
with arms and rumors, and so many gentlemen of Siena were
absent in the wars, the people of Siena thought they had a
favorable opportunity to endeavor with safety to take the government of the republic out of the hands of the consuls, and, by
a reformation of the state, introduce a new form of popular
government.   The plebeians, tumultuously rising, with great
impetuosity flew to arms; but the gentlemen, who had foreseen the insurrection, assembled in the public walks, provided
with attendants and arms, that they might be able to oppose
the people, and defend the dignity of the government.   The
heads of the popular faction, perceiving that their design could
not succeed by force, put a stop to the tumult, but stood
armed in several parts of the city.   The most respectable
citizens of each party, meeting half way between the two
bodies, effected a reconciliation so far, that both sides agreed to
lay down their arms; and it was agreed, that if any one would

demand or request that any thing should be corrected or reformed
for the public service, he should propose it civilly, without the
din of arms; and if it should be judged an error or a grievance
by the council, there should be no difficulty in obtaining its
amendment or redress; and with copious reasoning, they demonstrated the disorders which must arise from exciting the mob,
with arms in their hands, to demand new laws, because, always
naturally desirous of seeing new things, they are never contented
with what they possess; and having obtained one object of pursuit, they suddenly look for another, setting neither bounds nor
laws to their appetites; upon every little accident, which is
always in the power of any one to excite, they fly, according to
their present passions, prejudices, necessities, or inclinations, to
robberies and conflagrations, many examples of which have been
seen in Siena, as well as other cities; and no method of suppressing an unbridled populace has been hitherto invented, without manifest and universal danger.

" They moreover took into consideration, that, from the vicinity
of Florence, in times so agitated, both parties ought to be sensible into what ruin they might fall, while they were engaged at
home in contending with each other; and had it not been for
this danger, the nobles were, at that time, so superior in power
to the plebeians, that they would not have submitted to this
insolence, nor let escape this opportunity of putting an end to
such seditions, by chastising the authors of this. They only
advised the consuls to call together the council the next day.
When together, they deliberated and debated upon a variety of
subjects; but, after many contests, they concluded upon nothing
but this: in order to satisfy the ambition of two or three persons who aspired to be consuls, it was determined, that,
instead of three consuls, there should in future be six, observing the same distribution of two thirds noblemen, one third of
whom were to be of the Ghibelline faction, and one third popular members. By this measure they quieted the minds of the
ambitious and envious for this year. But the year following, at
the new election of consuls, fresh innovations would have been
attempted, if, at that time, those Sienese gentlemen, who had
been to Asia at their own expense, had not returned in triumph,
to the universal joy of the whole city. This event quieted the
minds of those who were inclined to civil discord. As the crea-

tion of six consuls had produced no other effect than to increase
the difficulty of assembling them together, and of concluding
deliberations by deciding questions, it was now resolved to have
only three; and in this way they went on, varying the number
according to the times and the business."

In 1194 and 1195, the commerce of the city was much increased by emigrants from Milan; the manufactures in wool
were introduced; the great fountain and aqueduct was built,
as well as the palace.

" In 1197, the Conti Scialenghi were made to submit and swear
allegiance to Siena, for all the lands and castles, as il monte
Sante Marie, Montebello, Monte Martino, Monte Bernardo,
Monte Franco, &c., and the Cacciaconti, Cacciaguerra, Tancredi,
Guido, Ranieri, Bernardino, Aldobrandino, Renaldo, Counts of
Scialenghi, were admitted citizens of Siena. The inhabitants
of Asciano also submitted. The Count Napoleone de' Visconti di Campiglia, the Counts Guiglieschi, and the Counts
Ardengheschi, also capitulated. The inhabitants of Montalcino,
who had frequently excited quarrels between Siena and these
counts, now discovered much animosity, and preparations were
made for war, to bring them to submission; and, that civil dissensions might not interrupt the enterprise, and to quiet the
minds of many, who desired that military matters should be
separated from the civil and political, and that the consuls
should have nothing to do but attend to affairs of state and
government of the city, they made an election of a foreign
nobleman, who, with imperial authority, should have the care of
all civil and criminal causes, having judges, assessors, and other
officers in his family convenient for such an office.

" This magistrate they called podestà, from the power and
authority granted to the cities of Italy to create such an officer
by the Emperor Frederick I., at the peace of Constance, in 1183,
and to the Sienese in particular, by Henry VI. in 1186, when
he came into Italy as vicar to his father Frederick. And besides
the judicial authority, in civil and criminal causes, the podestà
had the government and command of the army in case of war.
The first who was elected podestà of Siena was M. Orlando
Malapresa of Lucca, for one year, and he entered on his office
the first of January, 1199, according to the order of the city.
The Sienese were desirous of an accommodation with the Flo-

rentines, that they might not be molested by them in the enterprise they meditated against Montalcino."

The discords among the princes of Germany upon the election
of an emperor, and the revolution of empire in Constantinople,
are not much to our present purpose.

"In 1201, a perpetual alliance, offensive and defensive, was
concluded between Florence and Siena, Philip Malavolti being
podestà, by which the inhabitants of Montalcino were declared
enemies of both.   In 1202, the army of Siena made themselves
masters of their fortress and territory.   The Counts Ardenghesci
refused to furnish their quota to this expedition, which excited
the resentment of the city against them, and at length a war.
The cities of Tuscany, that lived and were governed as republics, remained long without any palace, or other public place in
which they could assemble their magistrates and councils; they
were therefore summoned to meet sometimes in one church, and
sometimes in another, varying with the changes of the chief
consul, until the establishment of the office of the nine, at which
time a palace was built.   For the first magistrate usually collected the rest in his own parish church, as the Romans long
congregated their senate, sometimes in one temple, sometimes
in another, according to the nature of the business on which
they were to deliberate.

"Another quarrel soon arose between Florence and Siena, at
the conclusion of which the latter were obliged to relinquish
Poggibonzi, whose inhabitants praised the Florentines very
highly, while they reproached the Sienese with bitterness.   The
arbitrators, or agents, who settled this dispute, were very ill
received on their return; and the praises of Florence, which
they heard repeated, displeased them as much as the reproaches
of themselves.   These excited great heats, resentments, and
personal altercations, not only among the common people, but
among all the noble houses which had given their opinions
against making the cession of Poggibonzi.   The disputes upon
this occasion went so far, that many personal enmities grew out
of them, and parties frequently came to blows and bloody combats in arms, by which many factions were generated, who,
frequently fighting with each other, produced a number of atrocious actions and scandalous crimes.   The wisest men, those

who consider more the end than the beginning of things, a character peculiar to prudent men, were hardly able to invent a remedy, or by the interposition of the public authority to preserve the peace. The city remained a long time wonderfully agitated, the citizens having no confidence in one another, standing in continual suspicion, and daily expectation of further disorders, tumults, and seditions. These distractions delayed the expedition against Monte Pulciano, which however was at length, in 1204, undertaken; when dissensions arose among all the cities of Tuscany upon the question, whether Monte Pulciano was within the dominion or country of Siena. It was customary to settle such disputes by a congress or parliament of rectors, from all the cities of the league or company of Tuscany; and such deputies were now appointed, who, after hearing the parties, and examining witnesses, determined in favor of Siena.

"It was a custom of the emperors to maintain a vicar in Tuscany, who lived and held a court in San Miniato Altedesco, who gave an account of the causes where an appeal was had to the emperor, and received the rents, taxes, tolls, customs, tributes, and other gifts, all which the jurists call by one word, *regalia;* and when it happened that the emperor sent no vicar to the province, he sent nuncios to particular cities, and called them counts of those places to which he sent them, with the same authority. This method of collecting together and making a congress, which was used in those times by the cities of Tuscany, was generally very useful to the whole province, because the *rettori,* (so they called the representatives who composed the congress,) as soon as they understood that a difference had arisen between one city and another, although they were sometimes of different and contrary factions, exerted themselves, according to the obligations of their magistracy, with extreme diligence, to bring them to an accommodation; and if sometimes their endeavors to adjust the difference did not succeed, and the war was prosecuted, the congress nevertheless stood firm, and the rectors did not fail to do every thing in their power for the universal benefit, and at all times appeared together in parliament for the public business which occurred, and to make their elections, at the stated periods, of new rectors; for they had no authority when alone in their respective cities, but only while

they were assembled in one body. As it was their duty to be
always attentive to the common interests, if so many people,
for their private ends, excited by the ambition of dominion, or
by avarice, two qualities very unfriendly to peace, had not left
off this federal order, the ruin of so many republics had not
perhaps been effected; but as the men of that age were little
accustomed to reflection, and had less prudence in providing for
futurity, they were still less solicitous to leave, by the means of
letters, the memory and history of their times, so that only a
confused notion of a few particulars remains at this day, not
only of this confederation, but of an infinite number of other
great events and institutions.

" In 1206, the discords followed between Philip of Suabia and
Otho of Saxony, and their contention for the empire, in which
Philip was superior; which were followed by wars with the
Saracens, and between Siena and Florence, in which the army
of the former was defeated at Montalto.

" In 1209, the king of the Romans came into Italy, and confirmed the privileges of Siena, particularly those of electing
consuls, coining money, and administering justice, reserving
appeals, and other conditions expressed in the grant of Henry; but
declaring, that neither Jacomo, Aldobrando, and Henry, sons of
Aldobrandino Giuseppi, and other nobles who held signories in
the county of Siena, nor their subjects, should be under the
podestà of the city. The consuls endeavored to divert the
minds of the people, now at peace with Florence, by employing
them in rebuilding the castles, and restoring the strong places
belonging to the republic; but they found it impossible to suppress or divert the ambition of the popular multitude, who,
feeling themselves relieved from foreign wars, would be employed
in domestic seditions. As they were at liberty to choose the
podestà, either from foreigners or from the nobility of Siena, the
choice was generally made from among the latter. The people
thought, that the introduction of this office had rather been a
loss than an acquisition to them ; and that the nobles, by means
of it, had aggrandized themselves. They insisted that this should
be corrected in the order of choosing the podestà ; and to remove
all occasion of dissensions, and maintain the public tranquillity,
the gentlemen concurred, in 1211, in a new law, that the podestà
should, for the future, always be a foreigner."

It is easy to see that the pride of most of the nobles concurred with, if it did not excite this popular humor; for the jealousy and envy of the nobles can never bear to see one of themselves elevated much above the rest. Regardless of equality among the people, and irreconcilable enemies to any appearance of it between the people and themselves, they must always be peers, or equals among one another; and when a king, or any other first magistrate, must be placed over them, they always prefer the introduction of a foreigner to the elevation of one of their own body.

" But it does not always happen in these cases, that by taking away the cause, the effect is removed. Those who are grown inveterate in the habits of dissension, without having any regard to the public good, and without the least cause of complaint, will find means of interrupting and disturbing good order. The people had obtained whatever they demanded, yet they would not lay down their arms; and the multitude appearing in continual insurrections, some terrible catastrophe was apprehended, and would have occurred, if the nobles had not likewise resorted to arms, and, with a great concourse of those who wished for peace and order, had not marched through the city. This procession spread a terror among the seditious, who, from fear, laid down their arms, and returned to their houses. Upon this the government was reassumed, and confirmed by the punishment of many of those who had been the heads of this commotion. The first who was created podestà, according to the new law, was M. Guido di Ranuccio da Orvieto.

" In 1221, Frederick II., after his coronation, having granted many favors to several lords and cities of the Ghibelline party, renewed and enlarged the privileges of Siena, of administering justice, of paying the *gabelle* or imposts only at the gates of the city, of coining money, and of exemption from all customs and tributes in the country. These exemptions and privileges perhaps occasioned a demand of similar favors which was at this time made by the territories tributary to Siena, such as Chiusi, Montelatrone, Montepinzuto, Potentino, Luriano, Vico, the lands of the abbey of St. Antimo, and other places. But as this demand occasioned a civil war, and Siena raised a force both of horse and foot, which they were ill provided to resist, they capitulated.

"In 1222, the Count Ranieri da Travale, originally of the Morea, in the Peloponnesus, was made a citizen of Siena, and annexed the lands and castles he had purchased to their dominion. From him are descended the Counts of Elci, Montingegnoli, and Fuosini. But the city, when it was not at war with Florence, nor against the pope, nor engaged in crusades, nor in rebellion against the emperor, was almost continually engaged in disputes and wars with the mountains, castles, and lords in its neighborhood, though in alliance with it, or under its dominion; and whenever a moment of perfect peace occurred, seditions and tumults broke out. With the conquest of Grosetto, and an increase of jurisdiction, Siena had excited much envy in a part of those cities of the Guelphs, in Tuscany, Florence, Lucca, Orvieto, and Perugia, which were in a league against the other confederation of the Ghibellines, which were Siena, Pisa, Arezzo, and Pistoia. The former took measures to oppose the Sienese in their favorite enterprise against Monte Pulciano, and this occasioned a series of altercations and wars, not only among these cities, but with the lords of the mountains, too long to be related; but at last Monte Pulciano was taken, and peace concluded.

"The cities of Tuscany, now in profound peace, and all apprehensions of its interruption removed by the presence of the emperor in Italy with a powerful army, the Sienese thought themselves secure from the stratagems as well as invasions of their enemies. This sense of security awakened in the minds of the multitude in the city of Siena the same desire of making themselves masters of the internal government of the republic, which at former times they had entertained. The principal heads of this faction, in their consultations on the project, and discoursing on the means of carrying it into execution, found among themselves a great variety of opinions, from whence arose violent dissensions. From this two circumstances occured, which prevented the scandalous disorders that usually happen in such cases. The first was a delay of the conclusions and resolutions; the second was, that in this interval it was not possible to keep the plot so secret and concealed, that no intimations should be given to the nobility of what was meditated to their disadvantage, and the manifest danger of the whole city, if to such an end the people should recur to arms. When the

nobles had discovered and considered the situation and the danger they were in, not only from these commotions, but from the
hatred which, in the wars of so many years with Florence and
Orvieto, they had provoked in the minds of the inhabitants,
from such prudent considerations it was determined to treat
civilly with the popular party, without the din of arms, lest they
should be involved at once in a war both at home and abroad;
and as the popular party, from the same motives, concurred
with the nobles, that the innovation should be made when in
their civil robes rather than in armor, it was agreed that the
council should be assembled. Here they deliberated and debated
on the mode of reforming the government of the city. As the
popular party saw no possibility of obtaining to themselves
the government exclusively, as they had at first projected and
reasoned among themselves, they demanded, that, in addition to
their third part in the council and magistracy, it should be left
to the discretion of the council themselves to choose the other
part of the magistrates, and fifty more members at least of the
council, out of the nobles or people, at their pleasure. To this
the nobles would not agree, and many of them opposed it with
such efficacious reasons, as made it appear unreasonable to the
popular party themselves, and the petition was neither granted
nor countenanced by many votes. Tolommei, Malavolti, Buonsignori, and Gallerani, were the principal speakers among the
nobles; and their eloquence was employed to persuade the popular party, that they ought to be contented with the share they
already enjoyed in the republic, and esteem themselves under
obligations to the memory of their grandfathers, who had so
benevolently embraced them, and taken them into their society;
and having received so great a favor from the nobility, who had
received them into an equality with themselves, it would have
been a more rational and becoming conduct to have demonstrated
their gratitude, by acknowledging the benefaction, and coöperating harmoniously in the public service, in the imminent danger which they saw over the commonwealth, rather than excite
every day fresh seditions. They might well know that those
who had held the government hitherto, were not men of so poor
capacities as to have occasion, in the administration of the
republic, for the assistance of so great a number of new men,
for the most part useless, or more properly pernicious, by their

contracted understandings and small experience; that their project was the more alarming, as they proposed to make the magistrates so very numerous; because it had been seen, in numberless examples, and experience had found it an infallible observation, that states had been seldom well governed by the multitude, in whose deliberations, besides other imperfections, the opinion of the most ignorant and incapable weighs as much as that of the most prudent and experienced. Those cities which had rashly committed the government to the multitude, had, to their misfortune, more frequently experienced revolutions in the state, than those which restricted the government to a few; for although, to a superficial view, the equality of the citizens in the public deliberations, where the votes are numbered, but neither weighed nor measured, might appear a just and reasonable thing; yet to any man who maturely reflected on the subject, it must appear in a very different light.

" As to the mode of making the elections of magistrates, if it were possible to concede to the people the share they demanded, these orators demonstrated that it must prove pernicious to the commonwealth. The method proposed was a way to take from the council the free power of creating the magistrates, the proposed law imposing the necessity of creating one third of them from one faction exclusively, and taking away the discretionary right of electing those who, according to the occasions and times of war or of peace, might be the best qualified to discharge the duties of their office. It was affirmed, that in a very little time it would be seen, that not only the nobles, who had from the beginning ruled, and with so much virtue and dignity aggrandized their country, but even that those popular families, which, for a space of a hundred years, had honorably governed and prospered with them, would by this innovation be thrown out of the government. That this invention, as now proposed, it was easy to be perceived, had no other end in view than to introduce a government of new men, by pulling down those who had hitherto maintained it; because, as the council in the election of officers was bound by necessity always to elect a third portion from the popular order, it might, and would soon happen, that of the other portion, either all, or at least a part, would be popular members, new persons, and unexperienced in administration; and the nobles, and those accustomed to government, would be

deposed, to the grievous loss and misfortune of the public.
When it was admitted that every citizen, without distinction,
might be admitted to honors and to government, is it not better
that the council should have the free faculty of making their
elections of persons apt for their offices, that men may be excited
by this motive to habituate themselves to honorable exercises
and virtuous courses? That to impose the necessity of electing
another, who knows that he must be elected at all events, is to
take away from him every incentive to virtuous behavior. This
would be precisely the way of bestowing honors on sloth instead
of virtue, and to give the establishment of magistrates to the
laws, not the appointment to the council, who will be, for the
most part, forced to make the election contrary to their judgments and inclinations; an indignity too great to be offered to
that senate.

"This harangue was answered, on the part of the popular
faction, by William Gollucci, who said, that the nobles ought
not to disdain to have the people associated with them in the
government of the commonwealth, among many other reasons,
because they very well knew they had it not now in their power
to say, what had been affirmed by their grandfathers, when in
the beginning they refused to admit the people to any share,
that popular men are not fit to exercise magistracies, nor to rule
in the councils of the city; for having, since 1135, governed in
concert with them, participating only in a third part, they had
given such assistance, that the city was greatly increased in
dominion, riches, and population, as was evident to all men; so
that their society might be said to have been of the greatest
public utility; and the same benefits, and still greater, might be
expected in future, when, instead of a limitation to a third part,
there should be no bounds prescribed. It very rarely had happened that any city had arisen to grandeur, if it had not admitted
the people and the other subjects to the administration of the
commonwealth, and to the magistracies. 'This,' said he, 'was
the ruin of the Lacedæmonians and the Athenians, who, although
they were most valiant in arms, would have found their republics
of little energy and short duration, if they had excluded their
subjects from the hopes of rising, by their arms and other virtues,
to honors and public magistracies. What was it that elevated
Rome to its superlative greatness, more than their having given

the rights of citizens to privileges and honors, to all in Italy who
submitted to their empire? What can stimulate your own citizens to greater alacrity in the service of the public, than the
hope of arriving, by their good behavior, to the highest honors
of the republic, and the knowledge, that if in war they place
themselves in the post of danger, they are sure to do it for their
own proper utility, as well as for that of others? What interest
can you believe will make them more ardent, animated, and
intrepid, in any public enterprise? We know, moreover, that no
government can be properly styled a republic, which does not
comprehend all the people of the city.' By these reasons he
endeavored to persuade the senate, that is to say, the council,
that the demand made by the people was as much for the public
service in general, as their own in particular; and as to that
which had been said by the grandees against receiving new men
into the government, he replied, that as all other things, how
ancient soever they might be, had a beginning, so it was
with nobility; 'as, for example, we may say, as you know very
well, that next to the original nobility of our city, with Charlemagne, when he delivered Italy from the domination of the Lombards, the Malavolti and the French gentlemen, who since have
called themselves Baudinelli, came, who were received, not only
into the number of the citizens, but into the ranks of the nobles
and patricians of Siena; after that, with Otho I., when he expelled the Berengarii from Italy, the Salimbeni, the Tolommei,
came, who in like manner were enumerated among the nobles and
grandees of this city; and in times more modern, many others,
who were lords of several castles of this state, as the Scorcialupi,
who since have called themselves Squarcialupi, those of Tornano,
of Valcortese, of Berardenga, Scialengha, and many others, who
all enjoy the title of nobility. Finally, our grandfathers were
admitted to the government in 1135; and if we, their descendants, have retained the name of popular, it does not follow that
we have not acquired nobility. For what reason then, if your
ancestors have accepted foreigners and ultramontanes, and even
conquered lords and landholders into their peerage, should not
you receive your own proper fellow-citizens, those who are born
free within the same walls with yourselves, and run the same
fortunes with all others? You will say, because they are not
noble. We however say, that all those others in this kind of

nobility were not more noble than at this hour these are, who,
by means of public dignities, have acquired nobility, or than
they will be who shall come into the government after us; and
as we shall be an example for them, so will they be to those who
may come after them; and the city will be able, by this means,
to preserve for a longer time the nobility of her citizens; and, as
it is natural that whatever has a beginning must have an end,
new noblemen will succeed from time to time to those who may
fail, and the land will be better peopled, and more powerful.'

"A short replication to these arguments was made by Rinaldo
Alessi, who said, that if the people, since they had participated
in the government, had remained more quiet, it was possible the
city might have made some notable acquisition; but, as every
one knew, the continual seditions which the popular party had
excited, had raised their inordinate desires, and disposed them
more to civil wars than to wars with their hostile neighbors; and
that those acquisitions which they had made had been obtained
rather by the incidents of the times than by any other reason;
that the ancient gentlemen who came formerly with Charlemagne and the first Otho, when they were invited, many centuries ago, to inhabit this city, had the signories of many castles
given them in reward of the illustrious actions which they
performed for the service of the empire, by Charles and Otho;
and that more splendor and nobility had accrued to the republic than to them by their coming to inhabit it. And the same
thing was true of the other lords of this dominion, who, according
to the accidents which have occurred, have been made gentlemen of Siena, the city being aggrandized and ennobled by the
acquisition of their families, castles, and signories."

By these speeches we see that neither the aristocratical nor the
democratical orators aimed at any thing more than a government
of all authority in one centre; but the legislative and executive
power were to be lodged in one assembly. The nobles wished
to have the whole house to themselves, and the commons wished
the same thing, though each party temporized and modified their
language with some regard to the other. The loaves and fishes,
the honors and emoluments, were what they all sought; more
than liberty, safety, or good order; more than the commerce, arts,
or peace; more than the prosperity, grandeur, and glory of their
country. Not one of them thinks of giving all the executive

power to the podestà, with a weapon to defend it; not one thinks of dividing the sovereign legislature into two assemblies, giving to the nobles and people an equal share; yet, without these arrangements, every intelligent reader of their history at this day perceives that all the projects of either party for amendment would only increase the evil, by inflaming the ill humor.

"After many discourses, made by several persons of both parties, the grandees became sensible that, if they should recur to arms, and defend the dignity of their stations, they might, in the war which they expected with Florence and Orvieto, and from the difficulty of obtaining money, put all in danger, by refusing to concede something to accommodate their civil discords; they therefore concurred in the opinion that prevailed, that the council should make the election of thirty citizens, fifteen of each party, who should have authority to propose a new form of government, since it appeared that the magistrates, called the consuls, after the introduction of the office of the podestà, that of the four purveyors, and the chamberlain of Biccherna, were no longer of any authority at all, and that there was a necessity to think of making a magistracy of a greater number of men, and of more authority concerning the affairs of the state and the administration of the republic. The thirty persons who were invested with this full power, or, as the Florentines called it, this balìa, having discoursed and deliberated some time upon the subject of their commission, and wishing to give satisfaction to the public, as well as gratify the ambition of many individuals, by constituting a numerous magistracy, proposed to the council to institute a magistracy of twenty-four, to be elected by the council out of the whole body of the people, or the citizens at large, on condition that a greater number should not be nominated or voted for from one faction than from the other; and as it was understood that the Emperor Frederick was soon to leave Italy, and it was expected the Florentines would soon attack them or some of their dependencies, the measure soon obtained; the four-and-twenty magistrates were immediately created, and they entered on their offices with great spirit, by making preparations for war against the Florentines and the other Guelphs."

This revolution, if a bare change of the number of first magistrates, without any change in the sovereignty, can be called one, was in 1232, while the emperor was at Ravenna.

The Sienese were now involved in constant wars with their
neighbors till 1238, when the discord between the pope and
the emperor revived the animosities of the ancient factions of
Guelphs and Ghibellines in Tuscany, as well as in many other
parts of Italy, and with greater hatred and animosity than ever;
nor was there any people who were not infected with this destructive contagion, by which, without having any other cause
of quarrel, they fought with each other with mortal enmity; not
only one city against another, but the same city, divided into
these factions, combated itself; each party had not only different
ensigns, under which they marched out to war, but they distinguished themselves by the color and wearing of their clothes, by
their gait and air and gestures of the body, and by every other
the smallest circumstance; so that, at the first aspect, a Guelph
might be known by a glance of the eye from a Ghibelline. These
were not the only divisions among the Sienese, but, since the
introduction of the magistracy of Twenty-four, a new diversity
arose among the citizens, and a new distinction of party names.

" This government did not please all, and those who approved
it assumed the name of the Twenty-four, and those who were
dissatisfied took the name of the Twenty-seven. Hatred and
resentment increased among them to such a degree, that in 1240
they flew again to arms, with most violent commotions of the
whole city, the slaughter of multitudes on each side, with innumerable robberies, burglaries, plunderings, and conflagrations of
houses and palaces, and other crimes committed by the plebeians.
But, as the rabble in favor of the Twenty-four appeared to be
the strongest, this magistracy survived the lawless attempts to
destroy it, and preserved authority enough to elect M. Aldobrandino di Guido Cacciaconti podestà, who, by his prudence
and the public authority, reduced the city to some degree of
obedience to the laws."

The secret was, that the pope and the emperor were to the republics of Italy, what Sparta and Athens had been to those of the
Peloponnesus. Each must have a party in every city; if the
nobles were on one side, the people would be on the other, and
vice versa; and every art of seduction was employed by one
power or the other on both.

The Sienese were now plunged in new wars, which continued,
almost without interruption, till 1258. " The cities of Tuscany,

which, in the discord between the pontiffs and emperors, had followed the imperial party, and were denominated Ghibellines, after the death of Frederick II. were greatly oppressed by the other cities, which, having followed the ecclesiastical party, were then superior, and were distinguished by the name of Guelphs; but since Manfred, overcoming the forces of the pope, had made himself master of the kingdom of Naples and Sicily, he took the Ghibellines in the province of Tuscany into his more immediate protection, and placed Siena at the head of that party. As Florence was the head of the Guelph party, each city in its turn was an asylum for the exiles of the other; which, in addition to the jealousy, envy, emulation, and selfish views, common between neighboring nations as well as cities, proved a continual provocative to war."

These wars and rebellions of their mountain castles, which it would fill volumes to describe, will be passed over. Yet it may be proper to mention the rebellion of Monteano and Montemassi, when the Count Giordano demanded in the senate that one third of the city should be armed and sent out, because a form of their constitution is upon this occasion explained.

"Although the Sienese were zealously inclined to comply with the request of Giordano, and thought the expedition very interesting to their country, they would not depart from the ancient order; when any expedition was proposed, for the subject to be maturely considered, it must have been proposed in the council of the credenza, and consulted on, three times, on three several days, in the general council, before any thing could be determined. Upon this occasion a deputation was appointed to attend the army, consisting of the podestà, the captain of the people, the first three members of the office of Twenty-four, and twelve good men, *buoni huomini*, deputed by the commons. The soldiers and officers in these expeditions served without pay, in imitation of the Romans, who, for three hundred and forty-nine years, continued to go out to war, every one at his own expense."

This is universally alleged by historians as a proof of their love of their country; but it may as well be considered as a proof of their poverty and their ignorance, for there is no example of it among rich and well-informed people; it would be indeed unjust and unequal. As the provisions and apparatus were found by the public, and plunder was made wherever they went, it is very probable that the most of their armies were better fed and more profitably employed abroad than at home, as manufactures were little known, and commerce and navigation in their infancy.

" In the year 1259, ambassadors were sent to the King Manfred by the council of the *credenza*, who from the council general, or the senate, which signified the same thing, had the authority deputed to them to give commissions and instructions to ambassadors. The council of *credenza* was a secret council, as its name imports, in which were secretly treated those things which were to be proposed to the general council, which, representing the whole city, had greater authority; but no proposition could be made, if it had not first obtained in the council of *credenza*.

" This is very remarkable; the sovereignty was in one single assembly, the general council; the leading members, however, had influence enough to get themselves separated from the body by its own act, all secret affairs committed to them, and nothing permitted to be brought into the general council without their previous approbation. This arrangement was afterwards imitated by the grand dukes. In the council of the people, nothing could be treated which had not previously been treated in the consistory, and by them proposed.

"Another council obtained in Siena, which has been mentioned before, called the council of assembly, of fifty members for each third, which, at stated periods, was changed by the general council, and limited by them in authority." So that the whole sovereignty, the whole legislative, judicial, and executive authority, was literally in one centre, that of the general council; and all other assemblies, councils, magistrates, and officers, were only committees and deputies of that body.* In this council of credenza the secret treaty was made with the Count Giordano, and ambassadors sent with his to Manfred.

In the year 1260, the memorable battle of Monte-aperto was fought between the Florentines and Sienese, in which the latter obtained a complete victory, and reduced Florence to the brink of destruction. At this glorious period, when their great rival Florence was reduced to such extremities as to be obliged to submit to the emperor and the Ghibellines, and make peace

---

* Malavolti, lib. i. della Seconda Parte, fol. 7 and 8. *Croniche Sanese*, Ap. Muratori, *Rer. Ital. Script.* tom. xv. pp. 29, 30, &c.

with Siena upon her own terms; when so many other people and territories were daily submitting to their jurisdiction, and ambassadors of congratulation were arriving from all parts, is it not surprising that union and harmony at home should not accompany such transports of joy as appeared in every part of their dominions? Yet, in a government so constituted, a dispute among a few young gentlemen at a bath of Petriuolo was sufficient to divide the whole city.

" In this rencounter one Baroccino di Bencivenne Barocci, a youth of the popular order, was killed by M. Robba Renaldini. Of this homicide M. Bennucio Salimbeni was also accused, who, besides being banished together with M. Robba, and both having their palaces demolished by the fury of the people, because Bencivenne, father of Baroccino, was of the magistracy of the Twenty-four then governing the city, and through the hatred which the people bore to the nobles, was condemned in a fine of twelve thousand pounds, and rigorously held in prison in irons, till his father Salimbeni was obliged to pay it. So rigid a punishment, transgressing as they thought all bounds of justice, provoked some of the nobles, who would not remain exposed to the discretion and insolence of the multitude, daily excited in commotions against them; so they left the city, and retired for safety to Radicofani, a place by its situation sufficiently strong. Upon this the magistrates declared them of the party of the Guelphs, which provoked them to overrun, with some troops of horse and their followers, the dominions of the republic in the country, and plunder the lands of their enemies. For it was by their instigation they believed the magistrates had been induced to pass a decree so pernicious and prejudicial, not only to them, but to the whole city, by the divisions which must arise from it among the citizens, reviving the hatred of factions, both of Guelphs and Ghibellines, nobles and people, which through the fear of foreign wars all parties had united unanimously to bury in oblivion, to their infinite advantage in the late war against their national enemies. From this disorder, arising out of that leisure, idleness, and insolence, which, after the overthrow of their external enemies had taken the place of fear, factions and parties took occasion to revive their enmities, and to study to offend, provoke, and injure one another. Having learned in Siena the mischief which had been done in the country by the fugitives, now become exiles,

o

a strong force of German troops, as well as the militia, was sent out, both cavalry and infantry. After an obstinate engagement, and many slain on both sides, among whom were several persons of consequence, the exiles were defeated by superior numbers, and the discipline of the German troops."

This was in 1262. The history proceeds with accounts of rebellions and submissions of one and another of their mountains, castles, signories, and other little dependencies, and of the persecutions of their exiles and the Guelphs; and all things in this period are done in the name of the commons of Siena, till the year 1266, when "many ill humors began to appear again in the city; and by the accidents which had occurred, so great a change had been produced in the minds of the multitude, that it appeared to the major part of those concerned in the administration, that, for the universal satisfaction, it was become necessary to remodel the government in a better form. To this end sixty citizens were elected." But by whom? Not by the people, or citizens at large, nor by a convention of their deputies, the only legitimate expedient for framing a new constitution, but by the general council. "Into this number of sixty were elected, indiscriminately, both grandees (for so the nobles were now called) and popular men, with authority to reform the city by new regulations, by which they were to introduce universal peace and tranquillity among the citizens. But a contrary effect was produced; for it seeming to the popular party as if the sixty, in the many months spent since they assembled, had been making provisions favorable to the nobles, they assumed that these had been made to their prejudice and damage, and rose with astonishing noise and tumult; and rushing impetuously in arms to the palace of the bishopric, where the sixty were congregated, and setting fire to the gate, they constrained them to renounce the magistracy; many of them, both of the popular citizens and of the nobles, returning privately to their houses, through fear, went out of the city. Others, taking arms, endeavored to defend the public honor and their own; among whom were many of the houses of Tolommei, Salimbeni, Piccolomini, Accarigi, and other families, who, combating in a variety of places, after having done and suffered much injury, causing the death of many persons of every party, and not longer able to resist so great a multitude, were forced to depart from Siena, together with M. Inghirano, captain of the people, who in this contest had shown himself favorable to the magistracy of the Sixty. As soon as they had departed, they were declared rebels and enemies of their country, their estates were confiscated, and the palace of the Tolommei demolished, as well as another of the Piccolomini, and the tower of the sons of Salimbeni, and the houses of Accarigi. The instrument of all this ruin was one Master Lutterio, who is named without a surname; and another, named Ferrucio, was sent as a commissary to Campriano, to demolish the palace of Ranuccio Tolommei, &c. In this new sedition, excited by the multitude against the magistrates of the Sixty, though it was not properly a quarrel between Guelphs and Ghibellines, nor entirely between the nobles and the people, those who had before been driven from the city took it up and united with the exiles of the Guelph party, who, incited by the favoring victory of King Charles, and uniting with the Orvietans and the Counts Aldobrandeschi, did infinite damage in the dominions of Siena, and in a few days made themselves masters of the lands of Monte Pulciano, of Torrita, Menzano. Cerreto, and many other places, which, rebelling against the city, surrendered to its exiles. The greater part of Tuscany, by these and similar divisions, stood in constant trouble and danger. Moved by this consideration, the citizens of Siena who held the government, desirous of reuniting and reconciling their exiles, that they might preserve the state from still greater confusions, sent ambassadors of the Ghibelline party, one of whom was the bishop of Siena, to Rome, to the pope Clement IV., praying his interposition to conclude a peace between them and their exiles and confederates. The pope accepted the office of mediator, and a peace was concluded August 2, 1266, and confirmed by all parties, with promises of mutual forgiveness."

New connections were formed with Charles of Anjou, King of Naples, and fresh wars engaged in, which kept the minds of the citizens employed, though the Sienese and the Ghibelline cause met with defeats and disasters, which reduced it so low, that Siena was left alone to support it. This adversity, however, had one good effect. "On the fifteenth of August, 1270, it produced a peace between the Guelphs and Ghibellines in Siena; and the twenty-four magistrates, with twelve *buoni homini* of the commons, meeting in one assembly, agreed that in future the government should be administered by thirty-six magistrates, of nobles and commons in equal portions, with the title of The Thirty-six Governors of the City and Community of Siena. This was followed by a league with Florence, under the auspices of Charles, King of Naples. The party of the Guelphs was now so powerful, and the Ghibellines so depressed, that the Sienese, who, like all other people under governments so constituted, with parties nearly equal in numbers, wealth, and merit, without any mediator between them, always stood on the brink of sedition, turned the scale rather in favor of the Guelphs; and these, as soon as they felt their power, rose upon the Ghibellines, and drove them out of the city.

" Understanding that King Charles was at Viterbo, they sent ambassadors to congratulate him on the happy success of affairs in Tuscany, who presented him with four thousand five hundred golden florins in behalf of the republic, the Guelphs being desirous, upon this their first appearance in power, to show their gratitude; and a diet of Guelph ambassadors was soon held in the castle of Florence. The Sienese Ghibellines in exile were nevertheless troublesome, appearing in many places in arms, and ravaging the country, till the Guelphs marched out, fought, and routed them. When this was done, they in their turn took vengeance, by demolishing the castles and towers of the Ghibellines, both in the city and country. In 1272, the pope Gregory X. again interposed his mediation, and obtained the restoration of the Ghibellines both in Siena and Florence; and the stipulation, promising them protection, was ratified by the college of thirty-six governors of the city and commons of Siena."

But the minority is never happy; indeed, they are always oppressed by the majority, where there is not a separate executive and an independent judicial, whose interest as well as duty it is to be impartial between them. In a little time the Ghibellines, who were returned to Siena, found by experience the truth of this observation. They found that they had not the same privileges* with others, nor the same chance for honors, nor the same security of their reputations, as when formerly they had shared the government with the Guelphs. Living in little credit,

* Tanto fù sempre piu potente il favor, che la Giustitia nelle città partiali, com' è stata quasi sempre la città di Siena. Malavolti, lib. iii. part ii. p. 44.

having small hopes of any change in their favor, and knowing that they had no security for their property, liberty, or lives, but in the mercy of the major party, they returned into the country of Siena, and, joining with the Ghibelline exiles from Bologna, renewed the old troubles and the usual party rage. They raised forces, excited rebellions, and formed alliances with little territories and signories, till they were able to meet a party of the army sent out against them in 1277. These they defeated at Pari, and took many prisoners, among whom was Ridolfo, the captain, whom they beheaded. The news of this skirmish and defeat threw the Sienese army into such a sudden panic, that they betook themselves to flight, without having seen their enemy, and without any military order returned to the city. Such an excess of timidity, such an infamous cowardice, though it is not unprecedented nor uncommon even among the bravest troops, could not fail to occasion great indignation in Siena.

"When the multitude considered how easily the enemy might, if they should have the resolution to follow their advantage, enter the city itself, and join their partisans there, they rose in a tumult, and ran with great fury to the defence of the gates, and stood in arms all the rest of that day and the following night. In the morning, finding that the enemy had less ardor to follow than their own army to fly, they laid down their arms, but went about the streets of the city, discoursing in much ill humor, that the divisions of the nobles might very easily prove the ruin of their country, if some remedy was not discovered; and they declared that they would no longer be disturbed by exiles, nor compelled, by the discords among the gentlemen, to be forever in war, and in danger of losing their lives and their property. It appeared to them that, for the common tranquillity, a peace ought to be concluded, as proposed by the pope's legate, who had been sent to recommend a reconciliation between the people of Tuscany. The Sienese of the Guelph party, who governed the city, influenced by these murmurs, the legate's exhortations, and a weariness of civil war, which held them in continual agitation and danger, both in their public and private affairs, agreed at last, in 1279, to a peace with their exiles, who, without any further noise of arms, and to the universal satisfaction of all parties, were restored to their country and their honors, under the podesterate, or, as they chose to call it, the signory of Matthew de' Maggi of Brescia."

In the next year, 1280, in the podesterate of Alberigo Signoregi of Bologna, the palaces of the Incontri were burnt and demolished by the fury of the people, instigated by the Guelphs; a convulsion which originated in the usual source, the divisions and enmities among the gentlemen, and produced the usual effect, an idle and useless attempt to reform the government, by restraining the power to fewer hands, without dividing and separating it into its natural departments. The thirty-six magistrates were now reduced to fifteen, as if the number of members, not the nature of their power, had done the mischief; and it was ordained that no gentleman could be of the number of fifteen, but all must be popular men; as if noble demagogues and popular demagogues were not all equally absurd, ambitious, proud, and tyrannical, when they have no necessity to be wise, modest, humble, and equitable. This decree was as tyrannical as any that can be conceived; for if it were admitted that a descent from a line of benefactors to their country was no merit, nor any argument for employing a citizen in public offices, surely it is no demerit, nor any argument for excluding him. The reason assigned for it was, that the pride of the nobility increased and accumulated by their bearing the public authority, and that they ought not to have the power to make their pride and arbitrary dispositions more intolerable, nor, by their divisions among themselves, to disturb so frequently the public peace and quiet of the other citizens, as they had done in times past; as if the pride of new men were not equally or even more exalted by power, their dispositions apt to become more arbitrary, and their divisions even more intractable and furious, which is the certain truth of fact.

" These fifteen new magistrates were called the governors and defenders of the commons and people of Siena; but by this arbitrary institution they neither quieted themselves nor reunited to them the exasperated minds of the nobles. Without considering the damage which, in the divided situation of their principles, opinions, and affections, would result not only to themselves, but to the whole city, weakened to such a degree by its divisions, that malignant humors and irreparable animosities must be generated from fresh hatreds and revenge, and without seeing

that the exaltation of the popular faction, patronized as it was
by the supreme magistrates, would prove their depression, the
Guelphs and Ghibellines, in a few months after, again flew to
arms; and part of the multitude taking side with the Guelphs,
many of the faction of Ghibellines were driven out of the city, at
the head of whom was M. Niccolò Buonsignori, a man of great
reputation, and in great credit for his valor with the soldiers and
princes of those times. His fame had procured him many followers of the Ghibelline faction; and having received information
that the Ghibellines who, after his departure, had remained in
Siena, were grievously oppressed by Orsini, the podestà of that
city, he wished to deliver them from such injustice, and vindicate
their cause. By the aid of the Counts of Santa Fiore, from whom
he had no small number of men, he approached one night to the
gate, to which the Ghibellines in Siena, with whom he had an
understanding, rushed; and having suddenly made a breach, he
entered the city. Guided by several citizens, with their assistance
he fought all night and the next day; but was finally driven out
again. The battle upon this occasion between the parties was
general, for the bells of the commons, which were upon the
tower of Mignanelli, had rung to arms, and the people had
very generally risen. Danger was affronted on all sides, and
the struggle was furious. Although the Ghibellines had by
force of arms made their way to the market, the Guelphs put
them to flight, massacring some, and making many prisoners,
leaving among the dead M. Jacomo Forteguerri, who was one
of the heads of the faction. Niccolò found himself surrounded
with a host of his enemies; but, although on horseback, he
retreated, defending himself with that fierce intrepidity that so
commonly appears in civil wars, and went out of the city
through the same gate, accompanied by great numbers of the
nobles of Ghibelline houses, as the Forteguerri, Paliaresi, Salvani,
Ugurgieri, Ragnoni, and others, who would not remain in the
power of an enraged enemy, and retired to the territory of Rigomagno. This was on the fifteenth of July, 1281. Matthew
Orsini, the Roman, being podestà, was afterwards sent by the
magistrates of Siena, the fifteen governors and defenders of the
commons and people of Siena, with an army composed of the
men of the third of San Martino, and other people summoned
from the other thirds, to attack the Ghibellines in Rigomagno.

Here the exiles had fortified themselves, and, when attacked, as they had expected, defended their strong-hold with great bravery; but at length they were forced to evacuate it, and leave the ground to the Guelphs, who having, at the expense of much slaughter on both sides, got possession of it, razed the walls, and cut off the head of Neri di Belmonte, a captain of the Ghibellines, whom they had taken prisoner, in retaliation for a similar severity committed by them on Ridolfo della Treguena, a few years before, when they defeated the Guelphs at Pari.

"In 1282, the Count Silvatico de' Conti Guidi was podestà, and the Sienese, the other castles of their state being intimidated by the examples made at Rigomagno, sent them orders not to receive the exiles, nor any other Ghibellines, but to resist them in arms, to demolish the walls of Monte Fallonica, those of St. Agnolo in Colle, and those of Monticiano, in which territories M. Niccolò Buonsignori had attempted to make a stand, and from which he made a predatory war upon Siena for some months, with several exiles from that city and other places. Martin IV., a Frenchman, succeeded to the pontificate, and by his favor King Charles regained his former credit in the cities of Tuscany, and was restored to the dignity of senator of Rome, to the infinite dissatisfaction of the Ghibelline party, who upon this occasion were wholly deprived of any share in the government by the triumphant Guelphs, both in Siena and in many other cities."

And this is ever the object of a prevalent faction or a decided majority, to monopolize the whole government to themselves, by the total exclusion of the minority; and when possessed of the whole legislative, executive, and judicial power, they drive into exile, confiscate, behead, and oppress in every way, without control.

"The Sicilians broke out in rebellion against Charles; and while his forces were employed in attempting to reduce them, the Sienese of the Guelph party, who governed the republic, to prevent their Ghibelline exiles and rebels from attempting some innovation under favor of the revolution in Sicily against King Charles, the head and protector of the Guelphs, sent a new army into the country to persecute and plunder the Ghibellines; and this year the fifteen governors and defenders of the people and commons of Siena, the consuls of the merchants, the consuls of the manufacturers in wool, the signors of the other arts, the signors gonfaloniers of the companies, and the captains of the country, were all congregated together with the podestà in the general council, and a treaty made with Ranieri de' Conti d' Elci and several other lords.

"A war continued between Charles and Peter, King of Aragon; and in 1283 Charles died, which again raised the hopes of the Ghibellines, and excited them to arms in Romagna and in the territories of Siena, where they did infinite mischief, sometimes approaching and entering the city itself. At last an army was raised, and they were put to flight. If this vigorous exertion had not prevented them, they were in a fair way of regaining the ascendency in the city, where great discontents prevailed; for the government, in 1280, having been placed entirely in the hands of the popular party, as has been related, the gentlemen could not with quiet minds submit to it; and although, by the divisions among them into Guelphs and Ghibellines, they were disunited among themselves, it was much feared by the ruling party that, when the enemy should approach the city, they would endeavor, with the assistance of some of the popular men, (for these too were divided,) to make themselves masters of some part of the state with their arms, although they had not been able to obtain it by their beans. The Sienese, in determining all questions in their councils and among their magistrates, made use of beans as votes, white ones for the affirmative and black for the negative. The governing party, knowing that, by the death of Charles and the other mishaps which followed it, the party of the Guelphs was much debilitated, thought it necessary in this year, 1284, to make many new provisions for the security of the state; among which, as they could not confide in the multitude, they thought to restrain the government to a smaller number of persons, it appearing to them that they could more securely confide in a few, whose abilities, being more united, would have greater energy than those of many, and that they might more easily agree among themselves, treat with greater secrecy, form their resolutions, and decide upon execution for the defence of the state. After long and angry controversies, they gained the concurrence of the nobles in one opinion, though little satisfactory to them, that the fifteen magistrates should be reduced to nine; and this was the original of the order of the

20*

Nine in Siena; and, that they might with more convenience attend upon the public, without being interrupted by their private affairs, it was ordained that they should continue for two months continually assembled in the same palace, and live at the expense of the republic; and it was declared that in this office, denominated 'The Nine Governors and Defenders of the Commons and People of Siena,' although the nobles were to have a part in all the other magistracies, no noblemen could be elected. The statute says, ' De numero dominorum novem, vel ipsius officii officialis non possit aliquis de aliquo casato civitatis Senensis, nec aliquis nobilis de civitate, vel jurisdictione Senensi. Domini novem, qui sunt, et esse debent defensores communis et populi civitatis Senensis, et districtus, ac jurisdictionis ejusdem, sint et esse debeant de mercatoribus, et de numero mercatorum civitatis prædictæ, vel de media gente.' "

The nature of the animal is nowhere revealed in stronger characters than in this curious record, where a government in one centre, and that centre a group of merchants, with unblushing heads, exclude not only all the plebeians and lowest class of laborers, but all the artists, mechanics, and men of the three liberal professions, and all the landholders of the country, and monopolize every thing to themselves, as they would monopolize a merchandise or forestall a market. There appears a ridiculous variation of the numbers of this magistracy for many years together, as if they thought the faults of the government, which every one felt, were owing to this circumstance; and the same fickleness appeared in all the other cities of Italy, particularly Florence, where the number of priori was once three, then six, afterwards twelve, presently eight.* This form of government was as detestable to the plebeians as to the nobles; and the wars between Genoa and Pisa, and the expeditions against rebellious lords, and the death of four princes in this year, 1285, Charles, Philip, Peter, and Martin the pope, could not prevent the Ghibellines and the common people (il popolo minuto) of Siena from uniting against the Nine.

---

* Quare quatuordecim virorum officio, qui mixti ex utroque genere, civitatem regebant antiquato, priores artium creavere, tres ab initio creatos constat, postea sex, inde duodecim, mox octo; publicis ædibus inclusi, nec aliud quicquam, quàm de republica cogitare jussi sunt, et sumptus ex publico eis præbiti, tempus autem hujus magistratus bimestre constitutum est. Leonardo Aretino, in Malavolti, lib. iii. part ii. p. 51.

"For, on the succession of Honorius IV. to the papacy in the place of Martin, and after the death of Charles, his son being a prisoner to the Aragonese, weakness appeared among the Guelphs; and the Ghibelline exiles of Siena, assisted by the people of Arezzo, were encouraged to take by surprise a Sienese castle, named Poggio a Santa Cicilia, which they fortified; from hence, with troops of horse, they made continual incursions and depredations, not only upon the country of Siena, but other confederated cities of the Guelph party, until the Sienese, after a siege of six months, unable to take it by force, had reduced it by famine, in 1286. A great number of prisoners were made, and, after demolishing the walls, delivered to the podestà to be punished. The people, however, were so oppressed by their popular mercantile government, and so much preferred that of the nobles, that they took their part, rose in convulsion, joined the Ghibellines in arms, with great impetuosity rushed to the palace, and compelled the nine governors and defenders of the commons and people of Siena, and their podestà, Bartolomeo de' Maggi of Brescia, to deliver the prisoners into their hands, to be conducted to the house of the bishopric, to save their lives. But no sooner had they come out of the palace than the Guelphs, who by order of the magistrates had been summoned, and united with the soldiers of the guards and garrisons, a kind of standing army maintained for the defence of the state, proceeded to oppose and affront the Ghibellines, who, with the popolo minuto, had excited this sedition; and finding that these, thinking the prisoners safe, had begun to disperse, they attacked them with great fury, slew many, put the rest to flight, recovered the prisoners, and cut off their heads, to the number of sixty-five, among whom were several principal characters."

The union of the plebeians, the popolo minuto, with the nobles and Ghibellines, against the government of the commons and Guelphs, is not less remarkable than the distinction established by their very title between the commons and people. Both are perfectly natural, for the popolo grasso can never bear to be mixed with the popolo minuto, any more than nobles to be confounded with commons; and the union of the laborers and mechanics with the nobles, against a government of dogmatical merchants, by whom they were oppressed, was as natural as that which has so often happened, of the people with a monarch, against the tyranny of nobles and patricians. The general sense of the city upon this occasion appears to have been in favor of the nobles, and their opportunity was lost merely by the weakness of the human understanding, which seldom knows how to seize with promptitude and decision the critical moment that decides so many great events. The Ghibellines were not, however, suppressed; they continued to assemble in the country, and unite in bodies from various cities, and commit frequent depredations, laying waste the country both of Florence and Siena. These civil wars continued, without interruption, between the cities and their exiles, with various fortune, till 1292, when Siena became so weak, and the government so tyrannical, as to force the nobles to sell their lands, houses, and castles, to bear the expense of defending that government from which they were so arbitrarily excluded. Prosecuting the war abroad against the Ghibellines, and plundering the nobles at home, they suppressed both at last, and began to entertain lofty thoughts; at the public expense they built magnificent palaces for the signori of the commons of Siena, to give the government more authority, majesty, and strength, and the more effectually to trample down the pride of the nobility.

"To this end, as the ambitious desires of men are insatiable, although Siena was at full peace, and without the least suspicion or apprehension of the Ghibellines, the nine magistrates, who had the absolute power of the city, taking occasion of the many private enmities and personal hatreds which had grown up, and were habitual and even hereditary between many noble families, ordered that four hundred men should always stand in arms in each third of the city, on the pretence of obviating any scandalous rencounter that might suddenly arise between one family and another. To these standing guards they gave arms and ensigns, with orders that, at the ringing of the bells, they should all march to the piazza; and a complete arrangement of orders was given, that at the call of the magistrates they should be ready to quell the scandals and quarrels which, to the great danger of the public as well as private persons, they said, arose from the discord of the gentlemen; and to prevent the gentlemen in such cases from moving on horseback or otherwise, they placed at the head of every street, and even at every corner, an enormous iron chain, to be drawn upon occasion across the street, and prevent their passage. Under this color of preventing disorders and tumults, to be occasioned by the discords among the noble houses, the popular party were thus armed without opposition, not so much to prevent the pretended disorders, as to secure themselves from any attempt of the nobles, if ever they should unite to reinstate themselves in their dignities, and obtain a restoration to that share in the government which was their undoubted right."

For the consciences of these mercantile demagogues must have taught them, that if the nobles had no more, they had at least an equal right with themselves, or any others, to participate in government; and thus those public arms, which had been provided by their ancestors for the conservation of their country and their liberties, were now most insolently converted into the weapons of civil war, and turned by the cunning of one party against the rights of another; and whether this plague of the city of Siena, and all the other republics of Italy, was produced by the natural pride of the nobility, impatiently borne by the people, or by the immoderate jealousy and envy of the people, or whether by both together, it was not the less fatal to all the Tuscan republics, by conducting them to that destruction, to which all republics have been devoted when subjected to any government in one centre, whether that centre be the unbridled licentiousness of the multitude, or the ambitious and avaricious discords of the few.

" The nobles were at this period persecuted, not only in Siena, but in all the other cities of Tuscany, and deprived of all share in government; and those who were in power held in such detestation the very name of nobility, that, thinking the judgments of others would keep pace with their own passions, they ordained by public laws, that such as would formally and solemnly renounce their nobility, and declare that they were *no gentlemen,* should become qualified to be in the government, and to be admitted into the supreme magistracy; in such contempt were held, at this time and by these men, those advantages and that character, which in other places have ever been most ardently desired and sought, at every hazard of life and fortune, and which the sons and descendants of these very merchants have with so much avidity since claimed, insisting on being entitled to the rank and title of nobles and gentlemen, merely because descended from magistrates holding the power of the state.

" Having thus excluded all gentlemen from the administration
of the republic, and extinguished all their hopes of ever recovering it, these tyrants, the nine magistrates, had the assurance to
constitute a new regimen, which, under the name of a popular
government, tended more to give the power to a few, than to
distribute it generally ; and this restriction to a few, although it
was injurious and oppressive to some, is said to have been more
useful to the state, and of longer duration, than if it had been
relaxed in favor of the many."

Perhaps it is universally true, that if the whole government
must reside in a single assembly, it is more safe, peaceful, and
durable in a few hands than in many, an aristocracy than a
democracy.

" Having modelled the government according to their own
passions, interest, and convenience, they proceeded to subdue
the rebellious mountains and castles in the country. It was in
this year, 1299, the house of Austria had its origin, in the
elevation of Albert to the empire. The wars against the Turks,
and in Sicily and Flanders, occupied the spirits in some degree
till 1302, when the many enmities among the noble houses in
Siena were renewed with as much boldness and violence as
ever, which occasioned frequent tumults and continual agitation
in the city ; parties meeting in arms, sometimes upon one incident
and sometimes on another, and many of all sides falling victims to their fury ; and, from the number of clients and adherents to these families, all the orders of government for maintaining in each third of the city an armed guard were not
sufficient to preserve the peace ; and the magistrates feared they
would not long be able to keep the nobles out of the government; they therefore thought it prudent to try another method.
When any quarrel broke out, the nine magistrates sent for the
heads of those families which were engaged in the brawl, and
endeavored to reconcile them ; and in this way they succeeded,
in some degree, to reconcile the Malavolti and Salimbeni, the
Gigli and Squarcialupi, the Piccolomini and Pelacani, the Tegolei and Malavolti, and many others.

" The major part of the Guelph cities of Tuscany, in 1303,
were delivered from the discords and dangers which they had
with the Ghibellines, in consequence of the victory obtained
over them at Campaldino ; but having nobody to fight with, as

if they were incapable of quiet and impatient of rest, the Guelphs divided themselves into two factions, the one called Bianchi, and the other Neri. This pernicious distinction had its beginning in Pistoia, in the family of the Cancellieri, whence, spreading through many other cities, it infected the whole province of Tuscany, and part of Romagna. The city of Siena, though naturally inclined to divisions, preserved itself some time from this venomous contagion, chiefly by the constant occupation it already had in the quarrels between the people and the gentlemen, which would not allow time for new contests. This division, however, broke out in Florence, very near them in neighborhood, where, after many skirmishes in arms, the Bianchi were overcome by the Neri, and expelled from the city; and all the influence of the pope, with his spiritual armor, could not reconcile them. The Bianchi now in exile, though Guelphs, united with the Ghibellines, and, assisted by the Aretines and Bolonese of the same faction, made an attempt, in 1304, upon Florence; but some cavalry, sent from Siena, put them to flight."

The detail of altercations and civil wars, within and without, between these complicated and contradictory mixtures of Neri and Bianchi, Guelphs and Ghibellines, nobles and commons, from this time to 1309, is too minute to be related, although there was no pause, no interval of quiet. In this year the quarrels between the nobles, particularly the families of Tolommei and Salimbeni, arising merely from their envy of each other, and their emulation in feasting and entertainments, broke out anew. Though excluded from government, though plundered in property, these families had still admirers, followers, and adherents among the people, who made them formidable to the magistrates, and gave them influence to weaken the government, more than they possibly could have had with their whole share in a well-constituted state. All the nobles, with their followers, who were very numerous, as well as the multitude of people, their friends and adherents in the counties or signories in the country, became divided by this private quarrel into two parties. Wonderful was the jealousy of those in government, and their apprehensions for the safety of the state; and to secure it, as they pretended, from all danger that might arise, to repress the temerity and pride of the seditious, they ordained, that for every company, in town or country, which consisted, in all, of forty-two

since the nobility were excluded, there should be appointed one
captain and one gonfalonier, as there used to be anciently, when
the city raised an army for the field; that this militia, whenever
any tumult was to be apprehended, and in all other emergencies,
should hold their men in arms (but none of the nobility were to
be admitted among them, as they were in former times, when
the companies were of fifty-nine) and together, under the command of the gonfalonier of the Third, should march in all haste
to the palace with their public ensigns, and there execute the
orders which should be given them by the magistracy of the Nine.
For the same purpose they organized three centurions, three commanders of brigades, and eleven vicariates, each of whom had
his own distinct ensigns and colors.

"But by this whole system of forty-two armed companies,
their captains, gonfaloniers, and centurions, formed *in appearance* for the common service, and under color of suppressing the
feuds of the grandees, the principals of the party who governed
the city, thought to pursue their own inordinate desire of reducing the government to a smaller number of persons, by means
of the public arms, of which, through this artifice, they made
themselves masters. They therefore prohibited not only the
noblemen, but many of those popular persons who had, many
years before, ennobled themselves, and acquired the name of
families, to enjoy the benefit of the law which, in the beginning
of the present form of government had been made, that those
who would renounce their nobility, and reduce themselves to the
popular order, should be capable of being magistrates. Taking
advantage of a little tumult on the twenty-sixth of May, 1310,
which they themselves excited, they sounded the alarm, and
called together at the palace their whole military force; and instead of proceeding to suppress riots, or punish criminals, it was
there declared, by those citizens who had arrogated to themselves
the whole government, that those families which were named
in writing should never be of the number of popular families,
but they and their descendants, forever, should be understood to
be grandees, and incapable of serving in the office of the Nine,
then the supreme magistracy, as all of the Ghibelline party had
been rendered incapable before; and this practice was common
at this period in all the other cities of Tuscany, as well as in
Siena, whenever the governing party had a mind to exclude any

man from the magistracy, to make him a grandee, which is the same thing as a noble. Ninety families were *admonished*, as the phrase was, that is, rendered incapable of the magistracy, for being noble, or for being made and declared so — a number that comprehended all the families of any distinction or consideration.

"Having thus reduced the government to a small number, by excluding everybody but themselves, they became very assiduous in attending the magistracy, in order to make the most of it; and in a short time they acquired so great an authority, so much wealth and power, that they became formidable not only to the nobles, but to that part of the people which was not admitted by them into the government. Holding down all others, they established their own power in the state so oligarchically, that, like other despots, they were obeyed by every one from fear. The Ghibelline exiles, however, made frequent inroads upon their territories; and the disqualified families had so many friends, that these nine magistrates were kept in continual alarms. In 1313, some of the nobles appeared to have so much influence, that the government thought it necessary to reënact and republish their militia law, and the law of exclusion of all the nobles and grandees, depriving them of all the honors, offices, and privileges of the commons. They sometimes thought themselves so secure that they might recall their exiles, then would suddenly seize and imprison them; and were generally employed in foreign or domestic wars, or in quelling some rebellion, till 1315, when a fresh quarrel broke out between the Tolommei and Salimbeni, two noble families, and produced tumults and battles in the streets, in which much blood was shed, and the city thrown into such confusion, that the militia, when called out, would not, or could not, obey the orders either of the magistrates or their own officers. The whole people took arms, and sided with one party and another, some for government, some for the Tolommei, some for the Salimbeni, till the Nine issued a proclamation, that, upon penalty of life and fortune, both parties should appear in their presence, before a candle, which they had burning, should be consumed.

"Wars and tumults occupied the citizens till 1318, when, upon the disbanding the army at the peace with the city of Massa, the troops and the people in general, who expected to have plun-

dered it, were very discontented, and two classes of tradesmen,
the smiths and the butchers, began a riot in the city against
their captain, calling him traitor, and collecting tumultuous
bodies of the multitude. The captain, finding himself in great
danger, contrived to escape their fury, in which he was favored
by some noblemen, who, by entertaining the people with soft
words, composed their anger; and, as they had neither any head
nor guide, they were easily persuaded to go home. Although
this tumult was quieted in appearance, the minds of the citizens
were much altered, and there was danger of fresh commotions.
To avoid greater inconvenience, seeing that the greater part of
the plebeians stood in arms through fear, with their shops shut,
to defend themselves from punishment, the magistrates absolved
them from all penalties incurred by those who had been in
arms in the late tumult, and commanded, under grievous penalties, that every one laying down his arms should return to
his business. It would have been a remarkable thing, if, in
a factious city, like Siena, quieted as it was from foreign
wars, new seditions and civil wars had not been fomented
within; but discontents with the government were now universal. The nobility, the plebeians, and the middling people,
being all excluded from the government, excepting the nine,
were all oppressed and all provoked. The doctors, as they called
the judges and notaries, were of a rank and character as nearly
in the middle between the nobles and plebeians as any. These,
excited as much by the persuasions of the other persons, as
moved by their own interest, came forward and demanded or
petitioned the Nine to be admitted into the government of the
city, and to be declared capable of serving in the supreme
magistracy of the republic. Reasons the most solid and cogent,
as they thought, were urged by them, to show that their pretensions were but just and reasonable. It appeared to the nine
signori, that this petition was impertinent, and an offence that
merited not only correction, but a severe chastisement; and having rejected it with much bitterness, they decreed the punishment of which those should be adjudged worthy, who, from such
interested motives, should seek to disturb the civil orders, and
interrupt the common quiet of the city. The doctors and notaries they dismissed from their offices, and declared them incapable
of holding any office in the city or country. This high-spirited

edict excited the indignation and despair of the doctors and notaries, and they entered into a conspiracy with the butchers, smiths, and other plebeians, to assassinate the whole nine, with all their adherents, take possession of the palace, make themselves masters of the state, and appoint one of the Tolommei, who favored the enterprise, podestà, another nobleman captain, a third proconsul, and thus to distribute all the offices of state among their leaders in the conspiracy.

"With this intention, on the twenty-sixth of October, 1318, the conspirators arose in a tumult, raised a loud cry against the nine, and demanded, with arms in their hands, a participation in the government; but they were soon met by a large body of cavalry and three hundred infantry, who were then kept in pay, to be sent to Genoa in the service of King Robert, and whom the nine magistrates, having some intimation of this enterprise, not willing to trust their own guards alone, had ordered out, for their security. A furious battle ensued, and much bravery was displayed on both sides; but as the commotion had been excited by the plebeians themselves, and was encouraged but faintly by the nobility, chiefly with a view to try their strength, the forces of government prevailed; yet the plebeians sustained the shock with more firmness than was expected; and if they had been judicious enough to wait till the regular troops were gone to Genoa, would have carried their point. The greater part of the gonfaloniers, centurions, and captains, concurred with the multitude, in desiring to acquire the benefits of civil life, and the rights of citizens; but the magistrates were favored by one part of the gentlemen, who were not well pleased that the government of the city should be reduced totally into the hands of the plebeians, and thus obtained from Florence some forces, under the command of one Bingeri Rucellai, by whose assistance the multitude, being first disheartened by the non-appearance of their leaders, were finally dispersed. Some of the leaders of the butchers, &c. were beheaded, and Rucellai rewarded with the ensign of the white lion, the arms of the people of Siena.

" When the tumult was quieted, and the city purged by the punishment of the principal delinquents, the nine sent succors to King Robert at Genoa, and to the Guelphs at Brescia, Cremona, and Perugia; and thus they became employed in all the wars abroad; but even this was not enough, in 1324, to prevent

the feuds between the two noble families, the Tolommei and Salimbeni, whose hatred produced many murders and assassinations, many other single combats, besides general and more
sanguinary actions between parties of their followers in the
streets, both by night and by day. In 1325, the Guelphs were
defeated by Castruccio Castracani, Signor of Lucca, near the
castle of Altopascio, where he made a great slaughter, and many
prisoners, and brought both Florence and Siena into imminent
danger; but this was not sufficient to prevent another tumult, in
which the podestà took one part, and the captain another; many
were insulted, some slain, nor was the disorder suppressed without grievous fines and capital punishments.

" In 1326, Walter, Duke of Athens, vicar of the Duke of Calabria in Florence, came to Siena, and demanded the signory of
that city, in the same manner as he had obtained that of Florence. The demand appeared to the citizens very strange,
though they treated him with great magnificence. They thought
it proceeded from a very bad principle, and worse intention, considering the sincere and affectionate attachment which they and
their ancestors had ever, with the utmost veneration, demonstrated for his house, and the great and many tokens of fidelity,
which might be known from their actions towards King Robert,
Kings Charles I. and II., and towards all their connections on all
occasions; and as it appeared to them, that they were outrage-
ously insulted, and by him from whom they least expected it, they
suddenly rose in a great tumult in arms, and, drawing the chains
across the streets, shut up their gates, lest the Florentines should
send a reinforcement. They not only prepared for defence, but,
their suspicions increasing, also to attack with all their forces, the
lodgings of the duke himself at the bishop's palace, and give
battle to his people. Such a commotion and concourse of so
numerous an armed multitude, under so many standards of their
companies and vicariates, demonstrating that in this the city was
united, and not divided, as had been represented to the duke,
upon the supposition of which division he had founded his demand, spread a terror among his followers; and demanding to
speak with the magistrates, it was agreed, that the requisition
of the duke should be referred to a senate. Such an assembly
was accordingly congregated, to the number of four hundred and
eighty senators, who, after long debates, having regard both to

the liberty of the republic and the honor of the duke, determined that Charles, Duke of Calabria, should have, for five years, and no longer, power to elect the podestà of Siena from the number of three, who should be proposed to him by the people of Siena; that he should not, however, be called podestà, but vicar of the duke, on condition that every vicar, before he should take upon him the office, should take an oath to observe the laws and statutes of the city of Siena; and the citizens well knowing of how much detriment to cities are divisions and animosities, the duke easily persuaded the Salimbeni and Tolommei to make a truce for five years."

In 1328, the nine magistrates made a census, or description of the families of the city, third by third, and there were found eleven thousand seven hundred and eleven heads of families in the whole, nobles, grandees, substantial people, and lesser people all together. The calamities of famine and pestilence, as well as war and sedition, which happened in 1329 and 1330, though the magistracy of nine discovered too much insensibility, and too little activity, to relieve the people, we pass over as evils not proceeding immediately from the form of government, and too afflicting to humanity to be related.

In 1331, a fresh affray happened between the two great families of Salimbeni and Tolommei. The inveteracy with which ancient and honored families take hold of a nation, and become interwoven with each other and the whole people, so that it is impossible to get rid of their influence, appears very strongly on this occasion. Though excluded and robbed, they could not dispute without setting the whole city to disputing. The rencounter between two noblemen, in which one was killed, produced the assassination of another, and the whole city took the part of the one or the other, and tumults and commotions in arms threatened universal ruin, till the government issued a proclamation against the two principal actors, offered rewards for their lives as assassins, and raised a force to confirm it, which obliged them to fly to Ferrara, where they and the other Tolommei, their descendants, were long afterwards known by the nickname of The Assassins. But this could not prevent fresh tumults and homicides in Siena, between the same families in 1332; nor others between the Malavolti and Piccolomini, in 1333, which were renewed in 1334, notwithstanding the employment the city had, through this whole period, in foreign affairs. In 1335, the league was renewed between the Guelph cities, and particularly between Siena and Florence. In 1337, an accommodation was attempted between the quarrelsome nobles, but without much effect; but in 1342 their ungovernable passions broke out again in homicides and general tumults.

"In 1343, the Duke of Athens attempted to promote his own ambitious views of obtaining the sovereignty of Siena, by pretending to mediate between the nobles and the nine, and to reconcile them with each other; but his dissimulation was not profound enough to deceive either party. In this year there were three conspiracies at once against the Duke of Athens at Florence, and the government of Siena sent ambassadors to his assistance; but the people in their fury had committed great disorders and many homicides, and finally besieged the Duke in his palace for a time, and then drove him out of the city; after which, by the advice of the Sienese ambassadors, they reformed their government, instituting eight priori, four of them noble, and four popular; but this form was soon demolished, and the government became as popular as that of Siena itself; the nobles were excluded, and tempted to renounce their nobility, in the same manner, and with the same whimsical, odious, and vicious effects.

"In 1344, the Counts of Santa Fiore, and the Visconti de Campiglia were made citizens of Siena, and subjected their lands to the republic." In the year 1346, another memorable commotion happened. "Such is the nature of the people, that, ever desirous of seeing new things, they frequently hold in contempt those that are present; governed more by their wills than their prudence, and excited by vain hopes and immoderate desires, they are too often easily stimulated to enterprises, which, if regarded with an eye of reason, would be found impracticable. The government of the nine, by the length of time, by their arbitrary exclusions, and by their more arbitrary restriction to so small a number, were grown so odious, not only to the nobles, but to a great part of the multitude, that neither could patiently bear that a few popular men should enjoy every thing, and be masters of all men, when it appeared to them that others had more merit. From conversations and consultations they proceeded to action, and many popular men having associated

under Spinelloccio Tolommei, they rose in a mighty tumult."
There is no room to doubt that they would have risen long
before, and not have suffered such a government to stand a
month, nor indeed to be erected at all, if the Tolommei and
Salimbeni, the Malavolti and Piccolomini, could have agreed
who should be the leader. The divisions of the nobles among
themselves had alone lost them the government, and prevented their recovering it. The people in those days, and in
that city, were utterly incapable of planning or executing any
enterprise whatever. "A noisy uproar of ' Down with the
Nine!'* ran through the city; but the insurgents, not having
been able to force the palace, and having in vain attempted to
enter several houses of the nine magistrates, which were well
guarded, some of them entered the house of Berto di Lotto,
where there happened to be an entertainment, and found John
Foscherani, one of the principal men in the government. Him,
with his son, who exerted himself nobly in defence of his father,
they slew. The perpetrators of this murder, intimidated with the
apprehension of punishment for what they had done, and perhaps made cowards by remorse of conscience, rushed out of the
house, and committed themselves to flight for safety; the rest
retired to the houses of the heads of the conspiracy, thinking to
assemble a great number of their partisans, and again to try
their fortune. This attempt, however ill-digested and unsuccessful, excited a terror in the magistrates, perceiving that a part of
the nobility had concurred in it, and fearing they had not force
sufficient to suppress it. They found means, however, to defend
themselves, by a strong guard, in the palace, till they received
assistance from Florence, and other places in alliance with them,
which enabled them, by means of the captain of war, to apprehend the conspirators, many of whom were beheaded, and others
declared rebels; after which, they entered into a new league with
the popular government of Florence, for mutual support against
such insurrections. This convention was concluded between
the syndics of the commons of Florence, and the syndics of the
commons of Siena, each party obliging itself to aid, favor, and
support, with their councils and arms, the other, and in every
way to operate for the conservation and maintenance of the

---

* Muoiano i Nove.

peace between them, and the internal tranquillity of each, under the office of the signori, priori of the arts, and the gonfalonier of justice in Florence, and that of the signori of the nine governors and defenders of the commons and people of Siena, declaring that whatever conspiracy or insurrection should be made against the magistrates or government of either city, should be understood to be made against the other, and its whole force exerted for the destruction of the conspirators.

" In 1348, another confederation was formed in Siena between the cities of Florence, Siena, Arezzo, and Perugia, and a large army raised by them; and in 1352, another against the Visconti. In 1354, being at peace, and without much apprehension of any foreign war, there did not fail to arise in Siena persons who spent their time in exciting new discontents as well as fomenting old humors, which they hoped would soon arise to seditions and civil war; for those who, with the authority of the Nine, had so long governed the city, had acquired, together with great power and immense riches, much envy among their fellow-citizens. This envy and resentment had, upon many occasions, given birth to conspiracies and various enterprises for wresting the authority out of their hands; and although they had defended themselves, and punished the principal delinquents, they had never been able to eradicate the seeds of sedition so effectually but that many remains of it were left in the minds of their adherents, which went on continually increasing by time, till the magistrates were seriously apprehensive that the common people would attach themselves to Charles, the emperor, and by his assistance depose them. Desirous of possessing themselves first of his favor, and moved by the persuasions of one of the Salimbeni, whom, on account of his enmity to many of the noble houses, they had taken into their confidence, they sent ambassadors to Charles, to offer him the obedience of the city; and, so ill a counsellor is fear, the majority, much against the judgment of many of their colleagues, were for submitting freely, without any exception, or making any conditions, hoping by his assistance, or at least without offence to him, or opposition from him, to reëstablish their authority; not considering, that having always been Guelphs, and by so many offences provoked the past emperors, particularly Henry VII., his grandfather, it would be impossible for him to judge whether they submitted from any motive other than fear or necessity, or to confide in their fidelity. But the hour was come when this form of government must be changed into another. "Charles having in all appearance benignly accepted the offer, dissimulating his intentions, came to Siena; and soon after his arrival, the little people, *il popolo minuto*, by Charles's orders, and guided by the Tolommei, Malavolti, Piccolomini, Saraceni, and even some of the Salimbeni, with a great and universal commotion of the whole city, rose and drove out of the public palace the nine magistrates, not without robberies and murders committed by the rabble, who burnt the caskets and boxes in which were kept the ballots of the nine magistrates, which every two months were drawn, one by each magistrate, for two months to come. Charles, by whose consent and orders this novelty had been committed, gave a commission to twenty citizens, twelve popular and eight noble, to think of a new plan of government. The twenty elected for this purpose, in three days, ordained that a new magistracy should be instituted, of twelve popular members, and entitled The Twelve Signori, governors and administrators of the commonwealth of Siena, to be elected four from each third of the city, and, as the nine had done, to reside in the palace at the public expense, and to be changed every two months, with full authority in every respect to administer the government of the republic, in company, in all their deliberations, with twelve noblemen, four for each third, who might inhabit the city in their own houses, without being obliged to live in the palace, except when they should be summoned to assemble with the twelve signori for the public service and despatch of business, as it should occur; and this number of noblemen were called *the College*, without whom the signori could not come to any resolution, or enter on any deliberation relative to the government of the city. A council, moreover, of four hundred citizens was ordained, one hundred and fifty of whom were to be nobles, and two hundred and fifty populars, (of those, however, who had not been of the office of the nine,) who were to be elected and changed every six months, and this was called the *General Council*. The Emperor Charles IV., after he had taken the crown, returned from Rome, and remained some days at Siena; where, finding little good understanding between the people and the nobility, he took occasion from their discord to attempt to make himself master of the city and the state, and to invest it in the Patriarch of Aquilea, his natural brother. To this end he courted the people, making many demonstrations of benevolence, with many favors which he did them in public and private; and he so operated upon them that they were content to give him the sovereignty, and put him in possession of the fortresses; and the patriarch having in this manner taken the government of the city, the twelve signori and the noble college finished their office. The emperor, felicitating himself that he had provided his brother with a beautiful dominion, took leave of Siena, and went to Pisa. There, entering into negotiations to make himself master, as he had done at Siena, he met with some difficulties, which soon multiplied upon him, in consequence of the novelties which sprung up in Siena; where one party of the citizens, not able to support the sovereignty of the patriarch, which trampled down the nobles and first populars, and studiously strove to aggrandize the common people and the multitude, upon whom he justly thought his greatness depended, arose in arms, closed the gates of the city, and demanded that the magistrates of the signori of the twelve governors and administrators should return and reside in the palace, and, together with the college, reassume the government of the republic; and that the chains which used to be drawn across the streets, but on the entrance of the emperor had been taken away, should be replaced. Three days the city stood under arms, before they obtained of the patriarch their demand. At length the magistrates were reinstated and the chains replaced.

A new rumor was then spread in the city about certain strangers who had been taken up, because they said that they had come for the service of some noblemen. The common people, from jealousy, and suspicion of plots and machinations, would have had them hanged; but the nobility, with many of the* greater people, defended them. Upon these occasions there was no adequate mode of deciding such questions but by arms; to these they accordingly resorted, and the twelve signori sent to Pisa to demand aid from the emperor, who was found in great perplexity; and fearing that, by the inconstancy of the people, the patriarch might meet with some fatal accident, he answered, that, upon condition they would consult his brother's safety, they

---

* Molti de' maggiori populari.

might model their government as they should think proper; that he would not take any part, as he had no particular knowledge of their disputes. The prisoners were therefore only confined, and the patriarch voluntarily renounced the sovereignty to the twelve magistrates, who were already returned to the palace, and the day following restored the fortresses, and joined the emperor in Pisa, leaving the city and state free, and the government, which he had held for a few days, in the hands of those magistrates from whom he received it.

" In this manner the government of the nine came to an end, who had governed with so much boldness from 1283, when this form had its beginning, under the protection of the King of Naples and the union of the Guelph cities in Tuscany, and, it must be owned, aggrandized the republic;[1] and those very men of the popular side who had been of the nine, were not only deprived, with all their descendants, of the capacity of being in the government of the twelve, but it was by a law enacted that, in the volume of the statutes, the word *nine* should be erased, and the word *twelve* written in its place; in such abhorrence were they now held by all men." These decrees of the new government, it is true, were as arbitrary as any of the former; but the whole history of this republic is but a series of changes from one unbalanced party to another. " The citizens who had held the last government were nicknamed *the nine;* and this name descended by inheritance to their posterity, and gave rise to the order of the nine, and became the principle of those divisions, which went on increasing among the people of this city, and became so sanguinary as to make them forget the distinctions of Guelphs and Ghibellines, nobles and populars; for after the government of the republic became again entirely vested in the hands of the populars, and then again restricted to a few, the desire constantly increased in the multitude, first to participate, then to monopolize the whole, as happened in the creation of the twelve, who became eligible exclusively from the *popolo minuto.*

---

[1] A Sienne, le gouvernement n'étoit plus dans les mains du peuple; une oligarchie roturière, sous le nom d'ordre des neuf, s'en étoit emparé. Quelques ambitieux avoient profité avec artifice du mode d'élection aux magistratures, pour concentrer en dépit des lois et de la constitution, l'autorité entre les mains de quatre-vingt-dix citoyens. Dans l'intérieur, ils se maintenoient contre la haine des nobles et du peuple, par la corruption et la brigue. Au dehors, ils espéroient s'agrandir par la perfidie. Sismondi, *Répub. Ital.* vol. vi. p. 222.

"The emperor returned to Germany, and the Sienese soon
found their new system as defective as the former.[1] The whole
government was still in one assembly; and though the nobles
were less than half of it, they appeared to have the whole power,
as they always will when mixed with the commons. The noblemen proceeded in their offices too arbitrarily; the splendor of
their birth and riches, accompanied with the public authority,
acquired them too much credit, too imposing an influence; and,
in their usual strain, according to the lofty pride of their natures,
they must needs govern all things. In order to carry into effect
their desire to reduce them, as well as to establish their own
authority, the popular party would forthwith have gone to arms,
had not an unexpected accident compelled them to change their
purpose. In the expulsion of the nine, the dependencies of the
state, seeing so great an alteration in the city, and that those
who had been used to command were deprived of all power, and
persecuted with so much cruelty and rancor by the other citizens,
thought that by such divisions the public must be too much
weakened to defend the city, much less the state. Embracing
this opportunity, Grosetto, Massa, Montalcino, Monte Pulciano,
Casole, and other lands in the jurisdiction of Siena, refused obedience to the magistrates of the city, and to the patriarch, during
the few days that he held the sovereignty. The new government,
and especially the nobles, were very zealous to send out forces
to suppress these rebellions, and succeeded against Massa; but
the inhabitants of Monte Pulciano attempted to practise a deceit;
they sent a false letter to the twelve, promising submission, in
order to amuse them, while they were in reality carrying on their
military operations. This letter was delivered to the twelve
signori, who, without calling in the twelve of the college,[2] as,
according to the constitution, they ought to have done, opened
and read it; and perceiving, by many manifest circumstances,
the imposition, they hanged up in the piazza him who had
brought the letter. The multitude were collected together by
this execution, and the nobles were much exasperated that the

---

[1] Ainsi, la révolution avoit changé les personnes qui gouvernoient, elle avoit
changé leur nombre et leurs titres; mais elle avoit conservé tous les mêmes principes; et sur les ruines d'une oligarchie roturière, elle en avoit élevé une autre
plus roturière encore. Sismondi, *Répub. Ital.* vol. vi. p. 234.

[2] The twelve nobles. See, for the nature of their office, p. 249.

letter had been opened and such business done without their knowledge, and contrary to order. The popular leaders of the day took occasion of this commotion to accomplish their own desires; sallied out with a great noise of arms; put themselves at the head of the mob; went to the houses of many noblemen and of the nine, with intention to put all to pillage, and force the noblemen to renounce the magistracy of the college; and would have proceeded to infamous lengths, if the gravest and most moderate citizens had not appeared, and persuaded the nobles to obviate all inconveniences by renouncing the government, in which they had discovered the best and sincerest intentions towards their country, and not more arbitrary dispositions than the popular men. The council next day ordered that three noblemen only, one for each third, should be admitted into the government, with the title of the Three Defenders; but these in a few days were deposed. That similar tumults might not happen every hour, and throw all things into confusion, they concluded to give a head to the twelve magistrates and the public arms, by whose orders alone the gonfaloniers, captains of companies, and centurions were to move. Instead of a captain of the people, whom they used to elect among foreigners every six months, they ordained that some citizen of Siena should be elected every two months; that he should be of the popular party, and one of the twelve administrators and governors, at whose deliberations he should be present as a member. The captain was afterwards commonly elected in addition to the number of twelve. The government thus organized, they proceeded against the rebels.

"Before the end of the same year, 1355, the plot of Gano di Benedetto Macellaro, and his friends, was discovered. These were the principal heads of the plebeians, the little people,[1] that very faction that governed the city. Considering that, by the inconstancy of their own multitude, it might happen to their government of twelve as it had happened to the nine, they determined, for greater security and firmness to the state, to reduce the government into the hands of one man, who, from his wisdom, virtues, and the public authority, might, by crushing

---

1 " *Il popolo minuto.*" The English words *little* and *great*, constantly used by the author, are not free from ambiguity. In modern politics, conservative and radical come nearest to the ideas.

all seditions, consolidate and maintain it. Signor Meio di M.
Jacomo Tolommei, who they knew had been always favorable
to the plebeians, and desirous of making himself powerful by
this means to defend their liberty, was selected by them as the
man of the people ; to him they communicated their intentions,
and found him very well disposed to conform. Other writers
have said, that the first motion came from Meio, who persuaded
the heads of the plebeians to confer with their friends ; however
this might be, they were all seen frequently together in the
house of Meio, to consult upon measures for the execution of
their plan. The visits so often made by so many plebeians to
this house were observed; and the twelve magistrates conceiving
a suspicion, gave orders to the conservator, who had been introduced instead of the captain of war in criminal matters, to
imprison Gano, and the others, who were heads of the conspiracy. Upon examination they confessed, that it was their
intention, for the public good, to take the government from the
twelve, and give it to Meio Tolommei, who might more easily
preserve the city free from seditions and civil wars. Gano's
head was struck off; and the others, who enjoyed the favor
of some grandee, a thing that in ill-constituted cities is eternally
superior to justice, were confined ; but Meio and many others,
who had fled from Siena, were declared rebels, and his palace
was demolished.

" In the year 1357, the Emperor Charles IV. confirmed all the
privileges of this popular government, and made the magistrate
who governed the city of Siena vicar of the emperor.

" In 1362, Giovanni de' Salimbeni, upon receiving some injury,
or at least taking some offence at the government, made himself
the head of a conspiracy of many noblemen and many of those
popular men who, as of the magistracy of the nine, had been
admonished, and rendered incapable of office, to take the government out of the hands of the twelve, and restore it to the nine.
But the secret was revealed to so many, that one at last informed the government; the plot was ordered by the twelve to
be inquired into, and a very great number of considerable people
were seized, some beheaded, others banished, and others imprisoned;" and all this without any regular process of law or
formality of trial.

" In 1363, a new magistracy was created, and called the Regulators, who had the care of revising the accounts of those who had the management of the public money, to see that the commons were not defrauded.

" In 1365, fresh quarrels arose between the Malavolti and Tolommei, and a plot was discovered of the Piccolomini against the government of the twelve; and these families were subjected to heavy fines for their punishment, probably because the government had not strength to inflict a severer chastisement. And this timidity appeared to be well founded in another instance the same year, when their ambassadors returned from Rome, one of whom, being attached to the nobles, had given offence to the twelve, by speaking freely against them in his absence; he was cast into prison; but the government were not able to punish him with death as they intended, for the noblemen appeared in arms to defend him."

These instances, with many others, show, that however arbitrarily or severely the nobles and most revered families are excluded, they will ever have a controlling influence over the government, when in one assembly of commons only, sometimes by secret practices, at others by open force. Indeed, such families are always in reality the heads of the factions that tear the state, though, in appearance, they have no share in it, as was seen more plainly the next year, when those twelve who had the government in their hands were afflicted beyond measure with fears of new animosities and insurrections against them.

" They found themselves divided into two factions, one called the Caneschi, and the other Grasselli, the former the favorites of the Salimbeni, and the other of the Tolommei. Knowing that the nobility were irritated by the late imprisonment of their friend the ambassador, and by the design which the twelve had discovered, by means of false testimony, to take his life and confiscate his estate, if he had not been defended by the nobles, they looked out for foreign aid, and sent to the pope to obtain it; they sent also ambassadors, some noble and some popular, to the emperor, to sound his disposition towards the republic. Among these was John Salimbeni, a man of prudence, very useful to the state, and in high reputation abroad. His death at this time was a public calamity; for the twelve, dreading the union of the noble houses, artfully introduced and excited among them every provocation to arms, to keep them divided, and excite one family against another. The nobles, at last perceiving the malicious artifice, secretly united among themselves, and, simulating a greater hatred to one another than ever, on the second of September, 1368, they, with their friends and adherents, armed themselves as if they intended to come to a decisive battle against each other. They then with one impulse turned their arms against the magistracy of the twelve, drove them out of the palace, taking possession of the arms, and, without putting any to death, made themselves masters of the city and the state.

" At once they new-modelled the government, ordaining a magistracy of ten noblemen, and three of those popular men who had been of the nine; took possession of the fortresses, and sent ambassadors to the emperor to obtain his confirmation of their new authority; but they found that ambassadors from the twelve and those plebeians who still adhered to them, had arrived before them, to solicit Charles's aid to recover their power; and had filled the court with slanders to such a degree as to move the emperor's compassion in their own favor, and his indignation against their antagonists. He therefore amused the ambassadors of the latter with false promises, while he sent Malatesta di Rimini to reinstate the former; a design in which, by the treachery and ambition of the Salimbeni, he succeeded. As soon as it was known in Siena that Malatesta, with his forces, was approaching in the neighborhood, the little people, in the interest of the twelve, arose suddenly and tumultuously in arms, and, with the assistance of the Salimbeni, forced open the gates to admit the imperial army, not without an obstinate battle, however, which continued the whole day, (September 24, 1368,) and great slaughter.

" The government was thus again taken from the nobles, their houses plundered, and themselves driven out of the city to their castles in the country. The multitude of plebeians having tasted the sweets of public honors, power, and riches, combated furiously upon this occasion; and having, by the aid of Malatesta and the Salimbeni, been victorious, they reformed the system. Excluding the nobles, they instituted a council of one hundred and twenty-four popular men, whom they called The Council of Reformers, because to them was given authority to reform the constitution. Sixty-one of these were of the plebeians, or little people; thirty-five of those popular men who had been in the office of the twelve, and twenty-eight of those who had been in the office of the nine, or of their descendants or associates. These governed with the participation of Malatesta, who was in Siena the lieutenant or vicar of the emperor after the expulsion of the nobles. This party having held the government of the state and inhabited the palace of the signori twenty-two days, reorganized the magistracy of the twelve, adding five of the little people, and four of the twelve, to three of the nine, who had been in the magistracy of the consuls together with ten gentlemen; and determined that these should be called *The Twelve Lords Defenders of the People of Siena.* They made a new box of magistrates, in which they put fifty-one ballots, in each of which was contained a magistracy of twelve citizens, with the distribution before mentioned of five, four, and three." By this we see that a complete aristocracy was established, and a very narrow one too, such as may well be called an oligarchy, by this faction of the little people, or plebeians. The choice of magistrates was confined to fifty persons only. " They created also a general council of six hundred and fifty popular men, preserving the same proportion of five, four, and three, to continue till January next. To this council they joined another, called The Council of the Companies, to the number of two hundred and forty; and this is the first time that in the public books was written and preserved the memory of the divisions among the people; and thus, by creating magistrates expressly and avowedly by distributions of factions, of orders, and of mountains, as they did afterwards, they made their discords immortal. Animosities, kept alive by these records, not only cost the lives of an infinite number of individuals in the frequent and bloody innovations which followed, but finally proved the destruction of the whole commonwealth, and the establishment of the domination of one man."

So says the historian; but whether these records had existed or not, the calamities, and the issue of them, would have been the same, provided they had not changed their government from one assembly to two, and separated the executive authority from both. Scrambling for loaves and fishes, in an assembly of people, or representatives, or nobles, or in a mixture or union of both, will forever have the same effects.

" These reformers annulled all the deliberations and decrees
made by the late magistracy of the nobles, except those which
contained the liberation of the banished and condemned. Wishing to reward the noble house of Salimbeni for the benefit
received from them, they gave them, in honor and recompense
of their perfidy against the other nobles, five castles; and moreover, with privileges proportioned to their merit, they made
them popular citizens, that they might be capable of being in
the magistracy. The Salimbeni were the first who followed the
example of Manlius, the first of the Romans, who from a patrician made himself a plebeian, and from a similar caprice, renounced his nobility, that by the aid of the plebeians he might
make himself master of the liberties of his country."

So says the historian; and it is true there is a remarkable
resemblance between the rivalry of Manlius and Camillus, and
that of the Salimbeni and Tolommei; and both examples are
equally demonstrative of the dangers and evils of a sovereignty
in one assembly. There will ever be two rival families to tear
the vitals of the state, and one or the other, perhaps both, will
sacrifice truth, right, honor, and liberty, to obtain the ascendency.

" The nobles, now chased from the city, met at Cerreto Ciam-
poli, to consult what they ought to do to regain their situations
in the city. The magistrates of the twelve having intelligence
of this assembly, declared six noblemen of the house of Cerretani rebels, which obliged them, with the others, to look out for
some strong place to make the seat of war. As they were to
be treated as enemies, one part of the Tolommei took possession
of the castle of Montieri, another that of Traguanda; the Malavolti occupied Castiglione, the Piccolomini Batignano, and
others, other castles, from whence they began to make war upon
all the country of Siena, to intercept the supplies of provisions,
to demolish the mills, and to carry their depredations to the very
walls, holding the people in continual alarm and terror, and the
city in a manner besieged, so that few had the courage to go in
or out. The twelve defenders, in order to disunite the nobles,
pardoned all the others, and banished only the Tolommei, Malavolti, Piccolomini, Cerretani, Saraceni, and Forteguerri, to the
distance of twenty miles in the country, in lands subject to the
emperor, upon penalty of life and fortune for disobedience. This
proclamation was not obeyed, and an army was sent, under com-

mand of the podestà Simone da Spoleto, selected by Malatesta, to recover from the noblemen the lands they held of the commons of Siena; but they returned without success, to wait a better opportunity.

"It appeared by this time to the order of the twelve, that they had been immense losers by the change of government; for whereas, prior to their deprivation through the nobles, they had enjoyed it all, sharing with no one, at present they only shared a third part; and being stimulated by ambition, which oftener measures things by its will than its prudence, they did not consider those dangers concealed under their immoderate desires. They persuaded the little people, that by joining with them they could easily exclude by force the order of the nine from the regency. The people, joining them in arms, soon put the plot in execution; but these, finding success so easy, were incited, before laying down the arms in their hands, in their turn to think more of their own convenience, profit, pleasure, and utility, than of their honor, integrity, or the public good, so that without ceremony, they deprived the twelve of their share in administration; and burning the gate of the palace, and the major part of the public books, with a great noise, and universal convulsion of the city, they dragged out of the palace the three of the nine, and the four of the twelve, who occupied the office of the lords defenders of the people of Siena.

"To avoid more scandalous excesses, and to put an end to the tumult of the people, who would not be satisfied nor quieted without a new order to reform the government of the city, by transferring it to the little people, or (to distinguish them more clearly from those other popular men who had been of the party of the nine and of the party of the twelve) to those who were truly the plebeians and altogether new men, because (as the plebeians said in Rome, when, in high wrath against the nobles, they created Terentius Varro consul) those plebeians, who had already been ennobled by serving in the government, despised the lower plebeians (*la plebe bassa*) more, and showed themselves more inimical to them, than the ancient nobility, Malatesta entered the palace, and selected eighteen of the little people, who, together with the five of the same sort who remained in the palace of the twelve defenders, and three gonfaloniers of the thirds of the city, and four of the house of Salimbeni, were to reform anew the government of the republic. These, meeting, without loss of time, in the consistory, which is the apartment where the signori usually assembled, with Malatesta, adopting the advice of M. Reame di M. Notto Salimbeni, made an election of ten of the little people, who, with the five who had remained in the palace, were to exercise the office, now augmented from twelve to fifteen, of defenders of the people of Siena, until the beginning of January next, with the same authority those had had who exercised the office of the twelve governors and administrators of the republic of Siena before the second day of September last. Thus the new magistrates were all made of popular men, who had not been of the nine, or of the twelve; and to the eighteen reformers, and the others ordered by Malatesta, they added a certain number, by the distribution of the companies, who, with the fifteen lords defenders, made the number of one hundred and fifty reformers, all of the lesser people, who, with ample authority given them by Malatesta, as imperial vicar, were to reform the government.

" The twelve now perceiving their error, and that, by attempting to usurp power from others, they had lost their own, sent, with the privity of the Salimbeni, to negotiate with the emperor yet remaining at Rome, to the end that, when passing on his return through Siena, he might effect their restoration to their former state. The popular men of the greater number, still denominated in the public books The Little People, having information of that effort of the twelve, and considering that, if the twelve should unite with the nobles and the nine, and be assisted by the arms of Charles, they might easily make themselves masters of the city, and seize the government, thought it more prudent to yield a part by consent, than run the risk of losing the whole by force. Moved by this consideration, (such is the inconstancy of the multitude!) the reformers ordained that the party which had been dragged from the palace should return, and occupy their offices with the fifteen defenders till the first of January, at which time they were to join in the ballot, and draw, from the boxes already made by the other reformers, three popular men, of whom the one who should have the most votes in the council of the reformers was to be captain of the people. This person proved to be Matteino di Ser Ventura Menzani, so that the magistracy consisted of the number of fifteen, of whom eight were of the little people, four of the twelve, and three of the nine. They declared, moreover, that the gonfaloniers of the thirds of the city, different from the gonfaloniers of the companies whom they were to command, should be called Master Gonfaloniers, and should always be of the little people, like the captain of the people; and the three counsellors of the same captain should be taken, one from each sort of people. This captain, with his counsellors and master gonfaloniers, had full authority in fact, though not according to the orders in the statutes, and a discretionary power in all criminal cases, but not in civil. From this reform, the order of Reformers had its first original; for this name of reformers remained afterwards in those popular men who were of the council of the last reformers, and descended to their posterity, as it happened before to the nine and the twelve, all of whom had their origin from the people. This tripartite division appeared to the reformers to be a most powerful cause of divisions and discords, which they wished to prevent; therefore they ordered these distinctions to be annulled, and the whole people to be united in one body, and, when in any writing there should be occasion to mention the little people, it should be called the people of the greater number; that the party of the twelve should be called the people of the middle number; and the nine, the people of the lesser number;* but although the names of the factions were changed, the substance of things was not united."

As these distinctions arise from that constitution of human nature, and course of its passions, which legislation is not yet perfect enough to alter or to remedy, but by making the distinctions themselves legal, and assigning to each its share, whatever it may be hereafter, the same discords remained among the popular men, and preserved always the same distinctions in the public books.

* This record is very curious, and worth inserting. "Item considerantes, dicti providentes, quod ex divisione populi, civitates destruuntur, et annihilantur, et magnam divisionem præbet ordo, factus per alios reformatores, quo cavetur, quod officiales eligantur per quinque de populo parvo, quatuor de gente duodecim, et tres de gente novem, eoque ubi debet populus esse unitus, sit tripartitus, et ideo provideretur, quod dictum capitulum et ordinamentum sit cassum, et sit totus populus Senensis unicus, et unum corpus censeatur, et, siquando in aliqua scriptura esset mentio facienda de populo parvo, dicatur de populo majoris numeri, et si de gente duodecim esset facienda mentio, dicatur de populo mediocris numeri, et si de gente novem, dicatur de populo minoris numeri."

"They ordained further, that of the officers of merchandise, or chamber of commerce, there should be two of the people of the greater number, one of those of the middle number, and the other of the lesser number, while the nobles should remain out of the city; but in case they should return, instead of one of the two of the greater number, a nobleman should be elected; and this rule they followed in after times, electing one nobleman and three popular men; and by this order it became a declared point, that the nobles were not comprehended in the people, but were distinct from them. They further ordained (correcting the order given concerning the mode of electing the three popular members, who were to be joined to the twelve of the ballot to be drawn every two months, to make the number of fifteen defenders) that a hundred for each third should be put into the boxes by the council of reformers, and that, in drawing for magistrates, eight should be drawn for each third; and they made many other provisions to consolidate, as they said, the popular state, which were very displeasing to the twelve, who could not endure that the nine should be restored, and the greater part of the government should be taken out of their hands. They could not sit easy under this mortification, but, with the favor of the Salimbeni, they frequently stirred up fresh tumults, which Malatesta with his soldiers had trouble enough to suppress. The twelve, with the Salimbeni at their head, still restless, applied to the emperor, and made him great offers to assist them in new-modelling the government. The emperor would not agree without the consent of the senate or general council, which was sometimes upon great occasions called together. Being assembled at this time to the number of eight hundred and sixty-nine, they refused their consent; but, by a vote of seven hundred and twenty-one, confirmed the present form, imposing grievous penalties upon all such as should speak or act any thing against it, or attempt any alteration in it.

"The twelve, perceiving that they could not succeed in this way to obtain their unconquerable desire of mastering the government, deliberated upon the means of securing by arms what by intrigue and fraud they had not been able to acquire; they flattered themselves that, by the interest of the family of Salimbeni, they could procure the aid of Cæsar's arms. While, through the discord thus excited, the public in Siena remained in this fluctuating state, the nobles in exile made frequent inroads into its territory with their cavalry, plundering and burning at their pleasure, and holding the city in a manner besieged. The emperor, taking advantage of this, labored with both parties to lay aside their animosities. A truce was agreed on, and arbitrators or mediators to settle the pretensions of all parties. The mediators assembled in a church, but the twelve and the Salimbeni studied to prevent their determination. The people and the nine were willing the nobles should return. The twelve and the Salimbeni persuaded the emperor to negotiate with the pope to send a legate, because, seeing the people and the nine concur in the return of the nobility, it appeared to them they should be too inferior in force and influence to their enemies without the aid of foreign arms.

"Parties remaining in suspense and suspicion of one another, neither dared to lay down their arms. At last it appeared to the twelve that, by favor of the imperialists and the pope's legate, they had acquired enough to be superior, and, not willing to lose the opportunity, they made Niccolò Salimbeni their head; and with many foreign troops they began the uproar, with a great show and noise of arms, crying, *Down with the traitors of the nine, who wish to restore the nobles!* They ran through the third of the city, and having met Scotto di Minuccio, who was captain of his company, they killed him, because he had given his opinion for confirming the boxes of ballots and the government; and proceeded to the houses of several families of the nine to assassinate them. Not finding them, because they had fled for safety, the twelve, with their mob, ran through the whole city, plundered the houses of the nine, and then marched to the palace; with the connivance of Malatesta, who appeared in the piazza with his armed men, they drove out the three of the nine who were of the fifteen lords defenders; and, aspiring at a complete victory, they made the emperor move from the house of Salimbeni, where he was lodged, by giving him hopes that, if he went in person to the palace, he would have the city at his devotion. On the other hand, the remaining magistrates, seeing three of their colleagues dragged out of the palace, excited to indignation at the insult, and at the danger they were in of losing the government, suddenly caused the bell to be rung, sounding to arms; and so great a multitude of people assembled in arms in the piazza, and in such a fury, that the captain of the people, taking courage to turn with his colleagues upon the twelve, the Salimbeni and podestà, drove them out of the palace.

"The battles which ensued in the city were obstinate and bloody; splendid feats of valor were displayed on all sides; but they are unnecessary to be related. The government was finally triumphant; at least their military commander had all the power of a dictator. Negotiations were soon opened between the principal men and the emperor; and it was concluded that the same government should stand, under the emperor as its sovereign lord, and the city should be considered as a vicarage of the holy empire. But of what avail are treaties, or decrees, or agreements, when the government remains in one assembly? The emperor was scarcely gone out of the city, before fresh plots and treasons of the twelve and the Salimbeni were discovered, and new tumults against the nine. The lords defenders, together with the council of reformers, to put a stop to these disorders, were obliged to create a new office, which they called the Executor; and they gave him great authority in criminal matters, even to proceed discretionally, and without observing the orders of the statutes. But with all this there was no security in town or country; and justice was so corrupted, that an infinite number of assassinations and robberies were committed with impunity.

"Certain travellers at last were robbed and murdered in the neighborhood of the castle of Monteriggioni; and several men from the castle ran out with their arms, took four of the men who had committed the robbery, and, without sending them to the city, or waiting for any trial, hanged them on the spot; and as this example was followed by the people in the country, the roads began to be more secure; but in the city the insurrections still continued. The executor having caused all the popular men who had not been banished or declared rebels to return into the city, it happened that one Niccolò di Guelfo, of the order of the nine, killed Paolo di Legacci, and wounded two others of the order of the twelve, who, happening to be present, attempted to defend him. At the rumor of this, a great disturbance arose, and numbers of people collected and fell into skirmishes, in which many were killed. To quiet this commotion, the lords defenders placed guards of soldiers in the palace, in the piazza, at the gates, and many other places, confined eight of the principals of the order of the nine, and sixteen of the order of the twelve; and the delinquents having fled, the tumult subsided. Propositions of an accommodation between the nobles and populars had been made by the mediation of the Marquis of Monferrato; but, as little progress was made in it, and the nobles were impatient, they took the castle of Batignano, and approached to Monte Pulciano, with the exiles from that territory," (for every village had its disputes between the great and the little, and its revolutions, triumphs, and banishments,) "who had intelligence with the popular party within, by whose aid they entered, and made prisoner of Jacomo de' Cavalieri, who had made himself lord of the place. Intending to save his life, they threw him into prison; but the plebeians, not satisfied with deposing him and plundering his property, and in order to satiate their revenge for the injuries they thought they had received from him, went the next day to the prison, and, breaking it open, cut him to bits; and every one took a piece, as is customary with meat at market. The nobles were so enraged with the people for this, that they fell upon them, killed many, and drove others off the territory. When they had done this, they set up another government, and that a popular one," (which is remarkable enough,) "and departed.

"The Marquis of Monferrato, who had undertaken the mediation at the request of both parties, but saw that all his pains to restore harmony between the nobles and populars would be in vain, departed from Siena and went to Florence, whence he communicated his award to Malavolti, who represented the nobles, and to Guerrieri, who was ambassador for the popular men who governed the city. The decree, however, as he had foreseen, was accepted by neither party. One article was, that the Salimbeni should release to the republic the castles which had been given them; and that they should no longer keep the standard with the arms of the people, nor the infantry, which the magistrates had given them for the guard of their persons. By reason of this, a part of the people, who followed the faction of the twelve, made a tumult, declaring that they would not degrade the honor nor lessen the grandeur of the Salimbeni; and several persons of consequence were killed in this riot. At this time the castle and land of Pian Castagnaio was taken by the Count di Nola, captain of some men of the church; and it was said that

the Salimbeni, contrary to their compact with the commons of
Siena, when it was given to them, had sold it. This report
produced tokens of great dissatisfaction among the citizens in
general, and especially when the same count, within a few days,
reduced the lands of San Salvadore to his obedience, and held it
as if he had been its sovereign. Moved at this loss, the fifteen
lords defenders sent an ample force and recovered it. It now
appeared to the Salimbeni that the popular men, by the loss of
Pian Castagnaio, were disgusted with them, and had not the
same confidence and affection for them as they usually had before
this accident happened; wherefore, considering what might occur,
being enemies of the other nobles, and not very acceptable to the
popular men, they solicited the Florentine ambassadors, who
were in Siena, to treat of peace between the nobles and those
who governed the state, and of a reconciliation between them
and the other nobles; and in a short time both points were
accomplished, with little satisfaction, however, to those who
governed the state, though in appearance they pretended the
contrary.

"While the Florentines were treating of a peace between the
nobles and commons of Siena, Odoardo di Mariscotti, thinking
the proceedings too slow, and desirous to hasten them, began,
from a castle of his, to infest the roads with his highwaymen,
robbing and assassinating the merchants and others who tra-
velled that way, which incited the magistrates to send out an
army, and take and demolish his castle, destroying many of his
people, and bringing him prisoner to Siena. The same army,
the day after, marched to Campriano, where they subdued
another band of the nobles, employed in intercepting provisions
in their way to Siena. Campriano they took by assault, and
destroyed the fortress, after having slain in the action three of
the house of Tolommei, three of the Piccolomini, two of the
Scotti, and one of the Mariscotti, with many others. The castle
of Cotone was obliged to capitulate; Castiglione fought nine
hours incessantly, and in the battle lost some of the Tolommei,
and some of the Malavolti, and many others of the nobles; but
the place was taken, plundered, and burnt; after which the army
returned to Siena with a great number of prisoners. There did
not remain many of the nobles united together, capable of doing
much damage to the dominions of the republic.

" On the other hand, the popular men, the more to consolidate their power, having seen the unanimity of the nobles through the order of the last reformers, erected a company, whom they called the Grand Family of the People, which should endure to perpetuity among those popular men who should be elected by the reformers for the conservation of the popular state of the city, and of the company itself, into which no nobleman could be received. Every member was to take an oath to observe the rules ordained for the maintenance of both the state and the society; and many exemptions and immunities were granted them. Every one whose name was subscribed to the association, was to hold the arms of the people painted upon some conspicuous place of his house; from which institution, the white lion is seen at this day, over the doors of many houses. They had also the privilege of bearing the white lion in their own proper arms, and many persons availed themselves of it, as is seen in the arms of many families still remaining. All who were not of the association of the people were forbid to bear it in any manner. These and other regulations being made, desirous of preventing the incursions, and repairing the damages done by the nobles in the country, they collected a numerous force, went to their castles, and seized sometimes upon one and sometimes upon another, not meeting any power that could resist them, till the republic of Florence, to whom, on the thirteenth of May, 1369, the difference between the people and the nobles had been referred, made their report, to the great satisfaction of both parties.

" This award was dated the last of June, 1369, and, among the other articles of the peace, the nobles were to be restored to their country, and be made capable of all the magistracies of the commonwealth, except those of lords defenders, gonfaloniers, and counsellors; and this was ratified by the popular men in a general council. The nobles in ten days ratified it on their part, to the wonderful satisfaction of the city and the state, as they hoped to put an end to so many miseries. The reformers afterwards, for the maintenance of the peace, as they said, ordained grievous penalties for any one of the nobles who should offend any of the people, and it was made capital to strike or draw blood from any one of the council of reformers; and to show that affairs which interest many ought to be made known to

and managed by many, wishing to increase the number of that
council, which was not at that time more than one hundred and
fifty, on the twenty-second of August, 1369, they added to it
those of the little people, who had been of the first reformers
after the expulsion of the nobles, and those of the same people
who had been of the lords defenders since January, 1368, or
should be in future, and the master gonfaloniers whilst this box
lasted ; and wishing to reform the council of the people, it was
ordained by the general council, that all the people, of whatever
number, who shall have been of the lords defenders, or of the
twelve governors, after the twenty-third September, 1368, should
be understood to be of the council of the people ; and from this
the practice began, which continued as long as the republic, that
those who had been of the signori should be of this council.

"It was likewise ordained, that when any thing should obtain
in the council of the people, which ought to be proposed to the
general council, and the bell was ordered to ring for a general
council, the council of the people being in session, the members
of the council of the people should be members of the general
council ; and by this order the general council was converted into
the council of the people, and was no more assembled during
the commonwealth. The public was very much in debt, and
had not the means of satisfying its creditors ; it was therefore
ordained, that all those who had lent money to the commons,
and ought to be reimbursed, should be arranged in three different
books, according to the distinction of the thirds of the city, and
made creditors, each one, in the sum total of his credit, with
orders that the chamberlain should pay at the rate of ten per
cent. every year to each creditor ; and this union or consolidation
of the public debt was called *il monte*, the mountain, or the
lump ; and this practice was afterwards repeated upon various
occasions ; and these were the provisions, which were punctually
paid off by the chamberlain in the time of the republic, but
were imitated afterwards, merely to abate the debt of every one,
who had lent money in the ordinary loans."

We see by this, that in those days republicans had some
regard to honesty and the public faith, and the infamy of de-
frauding creditors was left to the absolute monarchy.

"The number of the reformers being increased, their authority
increased every day, and with it the desire of reducing the office

of lords defenders wholly to the little people, called the people
of the greater number. To this end, in 1370, they excited certain tumults among the journeymen and laborers in the woollen
manufacture, inhabiting the coast of Ovile, the very lowest
of the people, who, meeting frequently together, called themselves the Company del Bruco, because such was the ensign
of that country;[1] many of these, having taken the occasion
of some quarrels with their masters in the woollen trade, and
guided by one Dominico, a dealer in old clothes, raised a
great uproar, beating some and threatening others; being armed
and in great numbers, as it was a year of scarcity, they turned
to the houses which had the reputation of having some grain;
and, through fear, it was given out to them. This quieted
them until three of their leaders were taken up by the authority
of a senator, and upon examination, confessed crimes enough to
condemn them to death. Upon this all those of the company
del Bruco, arose again in arms with a very great noise, ran to
the palace of the senator, and with menaces of burning him in
his house, insolently demanded the three prisoners. They then
began furiously to fight with the officers of justice, and to collect
materials for applying fire to the gate. The captain of the people,
who was Francesco Naddo, perceiving the danger in which the
senator was, and that the city was all in arms, took the resolution,
in order by the public authority to prevent the disorder from increasing, to go in person and endeavor to suppress it. With his
standard and trumpets before him, he arrived at the palace of
the senator; but finding it impossible to allay the fury of the
plebeians otherwise, he made the senator set at liberty the three
prisoners, and returned to his palace, believing that the company
would lay down their arms as they had promised.

"But having come off conquerors in this warfare, and forced
justice herself, they acquired so much presumption, that, running
with great violence to the gate of the palace of the signory, and
finding it locked, they attempted in several ways to force it;
they raised a loud clamor, that the four lords of the order of
the twelve, and the three of the order of the nine, should be
banished; but finding them well defended, they ran to the palace
of the Salimbeni, to avail themselves of their assistance and

---

[1] A caterpillar.

authority. Having in the way encountered Nannuccio di Francesco, who had been a few months before captain of the people, because he had upon that occasion favored the order of the twelve, they slew him. The Salimbeni would not move nor intermeddle in this sedition. They therefore took from them the colors with the ensign of the people, which, as associates of that faction, they still held at their window, although they had made a peace with the other nobles. From the gonfaloniers of Camullia and San Martino they likewise took their standards, and having given them to others, they returned to make a fresh attack upon the palace; and being repulsed from thence, they sent a party towards Camullia to attack the house of the Salimbeni, against whom they were bitterly enraged, because they would not concur in this revolution. Meeting a company of noblemen of the houses of Salimbeni, Malavolti, Tolommei, Renaldini, and others, in considerable numbers, who had made a great exertion, and taken arms to quell this tumult of the plebeians, the parties went to action immediately, the noblemen were many of them killed, and the rest routed; and although many men were appointed to endeavor to quiet the disturbance, they not only found no means of suppressing it, but they found it impossible to prevent it from increasing every moment in violence; until one morning, in the month of July, the company of the people arose in arms with the company del Bruco, and dragged from the palace the four lords who resided there, of the order of the twelve, and three of the order of the nine, instead of whom seven others of the larger number were elected by the people, to reside with the eight who remained in the palace, and fill up the number of fifteen signori.

"But suspecting that, by having thus brought into their own hands the whole government of the city, the other citizens would be provoked to make an alteration, the council of reformers, to whom full power had been given by the general council, resolved that the names of those of the twelve and the nine, who had been pulled out of the palace, should be returned into the box of the freemen, so that they might be drawn another time to occupy the same office, and enjoy the same privileges, as if they had remained in the palace two months entire. The order of the twelve, however, not being satisfied with this regulation, conspired with some of the nine, aided by the captain of

the people, who, although he was himself of the popular order
of the greater number, was of an elevated spirit, and could not
bear, that the state should be reduced, in his time, with such
indignity into the hands of men of such base condition, entered
into the conspiracy, sent them the master gonfaloniers, with
their arms, who united with the conspirators, and on a sudden
attacked those of the company del Bruco, in their own houses,
on the coast of Ovile, and, before they had time to get their
arms and make a stand, slew a great part of them; and they
were exasperated into such rage and fury, as to have no consideration of age or sex, but to murder without distinction all
who came in their way.

"At the same time the company of the people having risen,
fought in the piazza and in several places of the city, with great
ferocity, and the twelve, with their conspirators, remained in
many places superior; but a stone, cast from the tower of the
palace, fell upon the gonfalonier of San Martino, who, with
his company, returned from the coast of Ovile, was fighting in
the piazza, and struck him to the ground; and every one, who
saw him, believed him to be dead. By this accident his party was
seized with a panic and fled, and gave an opportunity to the
popular party to gain the superiority, and break and rout the
conspirators. A part of the principal leaders of the conspiracy
were taken prisoners, together with Francino, captain of the
people, and Magio Calzolaio, gonfalonier of the third of the city;
and on the first of August, 1371, without letting them finish the
term of their magistracy, a most miserable and horrible example
was set, by cutting off their heads publicly in the piazza; at the
same time, they beheaded many others; but the two other gonfaloniers, having saved themselves by flight, were declared rebels,
with many others, and a new reformation of the state was resolved on.

"The reformers made a new box of magistrates for five years,
continuing the office of the fifteen defenders, of whom twelve
were popular men of the greater number, who were afterwards
called reformers, and three popular men of the smaller number,
who were those of the order of the nine, and in place of Francino, as captain of the people, Landino Fabro was substituted.
Confirming the usual order, they resolved, that the president of
the council of reformers, who was changed every third day,

should act with the lords defenders and with his counsellors, although they had joined in the magistracy four of the little people, in place of those whom they took away of the twelve, to give a more decisive superiority to their faction. They admonished and disqualified all those of the people of the middle number who had been of the twelve, and twelve families of the people of the lesser number, who had been of the nine, and some of the people of the greater number, who had been numbered among the reformers, and had agreed with the twelve. Two hundred and twenty-eight were condemned in pecuniary penalties; and all those who were condemned were called, without distinction, *Fini*. A number of men, both horse and foot, sent by the Salimbeni for the service of the twelve, arrived at Torrenieri, but learning the turn of affairs, returned back. Almost all the lesser artificers afterwards joined themselves to the number of the reformers; and for the security of the state they had from Florence a hundred cavalry. The public, by great expenses and little government, being without any appropriation of money, that they could avail themselves of, the reformers introduced the practice of selling the public revenue, besides the confiscations and penalties, for three years, which did not obtain more than three hundred and eighteen thousand golden florins. This commencement of the usage of selling the public revenues, which was continued from this time, was the reason why the public was always in debt; selling for a small price, which was not sufficient for the necessary expenses, illegal practices were the consequence, and from thence new seditions, which finally accomplished the ruin of the republic. The twelve did not cease to stir matters to the prejudice of the reformers, because the capacity of being in the magistracy was now taken from them. For security, their arms were taken from them, and placed in the chamber of the commons, and the captain of the people seized many of them on suspicion, who were in great danger of losing their heads."

The year following the conduct of the twelve occasioned the same suspicions. The nobles themselves were never more impatient of exclusion, nor more eager to try every expedient to recover their share in the state. The nobles, indeed, were not only injured, but had a right to complain. The twelve were injured, but they had only that wrong done to them which

they had set against the nobles, and they ought to have recollected,

> " Nec lex est justior ulla
> Quam necis artifices arte perire suâ."

But if the rule of doing as you would be done by were the rule
of life, and observed by all men, there would perhaps be no
need of government at all.

" The twelve, to be sure, did not think their own case and that
of the nobles parallel, but were indefatigable in insinuating,
sometimes into one, and sometimes into another of the little
people, that it was neither profitable to them, nor honorable to
the public, to suffer those reformers to *tyrannize* over the city;
and they frequently succeeded in drawing over to their side partisans, with whom they proceeded to consult of the means of
carrying their intentions, to take the government out of the
hands of the reformers, into effect. They opened themselves
to so many, that at length the machination was discovered, and
numbers taken up; among whom was Ser Cecco d'Andrea, the
man of the highest reputation with the twelve, who was beheaded; and of the others, some were imprisoned, others fined,
and those who had escaped by flight were banished; and Ser
Agnolo d'Andrea was condemned, because, having made a
dinner for some of his friends at his country-house, no reformer
was invited." Other instances of the grossest prostitution of the
judicial power were attempted by the vulgar tyrants, who now
had the sway. "Giovanni Calzettaio, who was one of the
council of reformers, prosecuted one of the twelve for striking
him. Niccolò Rosso da Terano, the podestà, upon examination
of the parties face to face, found evidence of the malicious fraud
of the reformer, who, to give a color to his false accusation, that
the other had broke the law, by which it was made capital to
strike or draw blood of a reformer, had struck and drawn blood
from himself. He had the integrity to imprison the complainant,
and finding him to be so abandoned a fellow, and many charges
brought against him of atrocious crimes, he adjudged him to
have his head cut off under the gallows, since it was not lawful
to hang him, being one of the reformers."

Justice, it seems, though attempted, was not yet so prostituted
but that many others were chastised for enormous crimes; but
the most of the criminals being of the people of the greater

R

number, who were the dominant faction, and held the great part in the government, tumults were generated in no small numbers among the multitude.

"But when Antonio di Orso and Deo Malavolti were imprisoned and beheaded for having carried off a young woman, though with her own consent, and half a dozen other noblemen executed for other crimes, the plebeians were pacified and softened by the blood of so many nobles, and that insurrection, which had been raised to save the lives of the condemned plebeians, was quelled.

"When all were returned to their habitations, and their arms laid aside, the senator, Louis della Marca, ordered four of the heads of the late sedition to obstruct the course of justice to be seized, and sentenced them to be hanged; others he imprisoned, and some were fined. The senator, among so many controversies, rumors, and tumults, as occurred during his administration, although *ex debito justitiæ* he had been obliged to order so many executions, ran a great risk of being murdered in those popular seditions of multitudes, who were offended by him, and both himself and his family were under no small apprehensions."

In such a state of society the human heart pours forth all its turpitude, and all parties appear to be equally abandoned. "The signor of Perolla, a castle of the Maremma of Siena, died, and left an only daughter heir to the estate and the lordship. Andrea Salimbeni, who was a relation, went to visit the young lady; by some fraudulent stratagem, which is not explained, he put her to death, made himself patron or tyrant of the place, and, with a gang of people under his command, committing robberies on the highways, and all the neighboring places, rendered it unsafe to pass in that quarter. The report of this was soon carried to the Sienese, who sent out a body of men, under the command of the senator, and the twenty-third of April, 1374, took the place, and carried Salimbeni, with twenty-eight others, prisoners to the city. Sixteen of these in a few days were beheaded by order of the senator; but either from respect to the family, or from fear of their power, he did not proceed against Salimbeni. Upon this the company del Bruco again arose in arms, with the other plebeians, and, running to the palace, with threats demanded of the lords defenders that justice should be done upon Andrea Salimbeni. The captain of the

people, the two priori, and their colleagues of the lords defenders, found themselves so mean in spirit, so infertile in council, so
unskilful at their own game, that not knowing any better way
to prevent the evil from increasing, they gave authority to
Noccio Sellaio to do in that emergency, whatever he should
judge useful to the commonwealth. Noccio snatching eagerly
at this opportunity, by which he thought to gain the hearts of
the plebeians, and by their favor raise himself to power and
superiority above his fellow-citizens, entered into the palace of
the senator, and sitting down in the midst of an immense
crowd, on the bench from whence sentence was usually given,
condemned Andrea Salimbeni to death, and ordered his head to
be struck off before the public. Intending to dispatch Pietro da
Massa in the same manner, he was prohibited by the major part
of the reformers, who began to perceive his design, and to see
the error which the lords defenders had committed in giving him
such an authority; and although he had at his heels the company del Bruco, and the other lowest plebeians, they revoked
the power that had been given him. This measure excited
a great tumult in the city; but the reformers, being united, were
able to quiet it.

"Niccolò and Cione Salimbeni, with others of the same
family, and their associates, moved with indignation and grief
at the outrage which had been committed upon Andrea, took
from the commons of Siena the castles of Montemassi and Boc-
cheggiano, and with large companies went about, committing
depredations in the country. The reformers, to make preparations for recovering their lands, and for making head against
the Salimbeni and their followers, created a new magistracy of
ten citizens, to superintend the conduct of the war. The first
provision made by this new council of war was, to imprison
twenty-six citizens of the order of the twelve, and condemn
them in twelve thousand golden florins, which were immediately
paid." Was the robbery of Salimbeni worse than this? "They
next sent to demand aid of Florence and Lucca, and obtained
it; but ambassadors were sent from Florence, Perugia, and
other places, at the same time, to make peace if possible, knowing
that their own discontented and distracted factions were ready
to break out; but the Salimbeni would not listen to any thing,
because the ten had sent an army in force to the castle of Boc-

cheggiano, with instruments for destroying the walls, cranes, mortar-pieces, and other things which in those days were used in war to fortify estates. On the other hand the Salimbeni, having collected together many of their friends and adherents, watched a convenient opportunity, sallied out from their lands, and attacking their enemies without the least expectation, broke their order, put them to flight, took many prisoners, plundered their camp, and burnt all the frames, bastions, buildings and instruments they found there.

"As soon as this defeat was well known in Siena, the relations of those many citizens, who remained prisoners, ran in arms to the houses of the Salimbeni, and seized all they could find of those families, that they might hold them as hostages to redeem their own relations. Neither the plague nor famine, both of which raged this year, 1374, could prevent continual plots of the Salimbeni and the twelve to recover the government of the city, and constant skirmishes and wars between them and the reformers and lords defenders throughout all the territories of the republic. In the year following, ambassadors were sent from several friendly cities, to persuade peace between the reformers and the Salimbeni. The reformers, desirous of lessening the number of their enemies, in 1379 restored all the rebels who had been denominated *Fini*, and banished in the time of those seditions, which were made by the gonfaloniers and the twelve. The nobles, however, were employed in forming parties in the country, and in negotiations with their friends in the neighboring cities, till, in 1384, they were able to meet the reformers in the field, and give them a complete overthrow; and if they had pursued their victory, such was the astonishment and panic of the reformers in the city, they might have made themselves masters; but in this their fortune befriended them. Finding they were not pursued by their enemies, they assumed some vigor and courage, gave orders to guard the gates and suppress the seditions which were moved in the city against them, and sent abroad for foreign aid.

" Florence, Pisa, Bologna, and Perugia, hearing of so great a change, and fearing greater civil discords, sent ambassadors to Siena, to endeavor to reunite the nobles in exile, and the popular men who governed the city; but, after trying every mode of negotiation, and every proposition of accommodation, with both parties, they found they could make no impression upon either, and returned home. It was the opinion of the reformers, that the Florentine ambassadors, from some interest of their republic, in their secret negotiations with one party and the other, had been the cause that the peace had not been effected, as, from both sides appearing to be weary of the war, was generally hoped and expected. The time was come when the magistrates, the lords defenders for the months of March and April, were to be drawn; and the council being assembled, and the ballots drawn, Giovanni Minucci, one of the lords defenders, proved to be captain of the people. When the council dissolved, they perceived no small tumult made by the citizens of the order of the twelve, who said, they did not know for what reason the power of participating in the honors and cares of government was taken from them, rather than from other popular men, and that they no longer would tolerate the abuse; and although the disturbance appeared to subside for the present, the twelve, fomented by the gentlemen, who were very active, and had made themselves masters of a great part of the dominion, and who promised the twelve, in all events, to assist them with men, arms, and provisions, to the utmost of their power, for the common service against the reformers, did not cease to demand, with great animosity and many threats, that a place should be given them in the magistracy.

" These motions of the twelve, favored by the nobles, gave much molestation to the heads of the government; and therefore, that they might not have to defend themselves against too many enemies, on the twenty-third of March, 1384, in the morning, they assembled the council, and obtained that the twelve, in the new draught, should have a part in that magistracy, by increasing the number from fifteen to eighteen; but, as experience has ever proved, gratitude shown and remedies applied out of season, have little effect. When the council was finished, at noonday, Cestelli, a seditious man of the order of the twelve, was taken up by the ministers of justice. He refused to obey, and calling with a loud voice for assistance, multitudes of the twelve and the nine hastened, at his cry, to his relief, and took the prisoner by force from the officer, who had already drawn him from the hill to the piazza. Upon this riot, Materazza and Nerini, accompanied by a great number of reformers, interposed,

partly by their authority, and partly by their arms, to recover
the prisoner. They fell with great impetuosity upon those who
had rescued him, and denouncing vengeance and death on the
twelve and the nine, as obstructers of justice, cried, ' Long live
the Reformers!'   At this cry the whole city rose at once in
arms, and, with those of the twelve and the nine, went to the few
noblemen who remained in Siena; having taken the entrance
of the piazza, they prevented the plebeians from passing in to
the aid of the reformers, and, from the houses of the Scotti and
Saraceni, annoyed the multitude of reformers, who were fighting
in the piazza against their friends. The contest had become general
in various parts of the city, and it appearing to the nobles, the
twelve, and the nine (as the major part of the plebeians ran to the
service of the reformers) that they had the disadvantage, they
began at the instigation of a Jew to cry, ' Peace! Peace!'   At
the hearing of this word, industriously echoed in various parts of
the city, a great number of the little people, distinguished from
the plebeians or the rabble, wearied out with so many seditions,
and united with the nobles and their adherents, ran with great
fury to the prisons, broke them open, and set at liberty all the
prisoners, among whom were M. Uguccione and Niccoluccio
Malavolti; these, taking the lead of the multitude, attacked the
army of reformers, and, urged on by the keen desire of vengeance for the injuries received, combated with such intrepidity
as to drive them out of the piazza, after having made a great
carnage, and many prisoners. They instantly entered the palace,
and, although the people within made a gallant defence, took
possession of it, and drove out the lords defenders and reformers,
not only from the palace but the piazza, and took from them the
administration of the republic, both in the city and the country.
This revolution was followed by the usual train; more than four
thousand men of the faction of reformers, chiefly artificers, in a
few days were sent into exile; and, what is worse, when in the
course of a few years their affairs were accommodated, not the
tenth part of them returned to their country."

Thus ended the government of the faction of reformers, and
this new species of sovereignty in one assembly; but only to be
exchanged for another, consisting of nobles, twelves, and nine.

" The exiles of all these three parties now returned in great
numbers from all the neighboring cities, provinces, and countries,

and brought with them a strong body both of cavalry and infantry. We may now expect to see the government shining with the splendid names of Salimbeni, Malavolti, Piccolomini, Tolommei, and all the rest; but we have no reason to expect justice, liberty, order, peace, or common decency.

"The new government was instituted in a new magistracy of ten citizens, to be changed every two months, and entitled the Lords Priors Governors of the City of Siena, into which number were to be admitted four popular men of those who had been of the twelve, four of those who had been of the nine, and two of the people of the greater number; of those, however, who had not been of the council of reformers nor of the lords defenders; and thus the people were divided into four factions, the Nine, the Twelve, the Reformers, and the People, and of these discordant materials in one assembly, were the legislative, executive, and judicial powers to be composed; and this mode continued till 1387."

The order passed in a general council, establishing the new regimen, in 1385, and the scrutiny for magistrates was made for eight years, and the names put into the boxes, a practice which was analogous to that in Florence, which they called imborsation, which was putting the names into purses, to be drawn out upon occasion. Those who had now the most votes in the general council were assorted together in forty-eight ballots, one of which was to be drawn every two months. The first draught was now made, and the lot produced a ballot, in which were the names of Andrea, Cicerchia, and eight others. These took upon them the magistracy of lords priors governors, on the twenty-eighth of March, 1385. "The tumults were quieted, the soldiers disbanded, the fortresses of the dominion rendered to public commissaries, many remunerated for their services, fireworks played off, and many feasts made, and incredible manifestations of joy, and ambassadors sent to all confederated cities to inform them that the city was delivered from the tyranny of the rabble, and the palace cleansed, which had been once thought an Augean stable. Twelve of the principals of the conquered faction were put to death by the course of justice, and thirty sent out to the frontiers, and the major part of those who had fled, declared rebels and enemies *pro more revolutionum;* and by order of the council of petitions, under authority given them by the general council, their castles were restored to the Salimbeni. But the envy of fortune, according to the historian, and the malice of their constitution, according to truth, would not suffer this felicity to be enjoyed for one year. The Tolommei were now returned, and living in the same city with the Salimbeni; and this fact alone, under such a plan of government, would be enough to give the reader an anticipation of what would be the consequences. Conspiracies were formed in the country among the friends of the exiles, and by companies of depredators, who began to be troublesome and to do mischief in the dominion. The Florentines, too, began to set up claims upon parcels of territory; and while this dispute was in negotiation between the ambassadors of the two people, a plot was discovered, to the great terror of those who governed the city, commenced by a part of the family of Tolommei, who, in concert with some popular men, who intended to restore the reformers, had drawn towards the city certain foreign troops, in an irregular manner, from different places, and entertained them secretly in several of their fortresses. These troops, hearing that their destination was discovered, and the plan impossible to be executed, as many citizens were already imprisoned on account of it, retreated, and the prisoners confessing the truth, were condemned to death. Yet the lords priors, with the rest of their faction, (for the government was never any more than a faction,) were in trouble enough, knowing the danger they were in from the divided minds of their fellow-citizens, and from the hatred and immortal enmity which the Florentines appeared to bear them. This storm was averted by submitting the dispute with Florence to the mediation of Bologna, and by the cession of many lands.

"One conspiracy was scarcely suppressed, and a foreign war declined from fear of themselves, before another was discovered of greater moment, and a more pernicious nature than the first, excited by M. Spinello Tolommei, and a great number of reformers and others, who had such intelligence in Siena, that it seemed to them easy to effect a revolution, and make themselves masters of the state. But, as many examples both ancient and modern demonstrate, conspiracies made by a multitude, through the variety of interests of those who are comprehended in it, have seldom attained their intended end; and the greater part of conspirators have lost their lives and their fortunes, because the design has been revealed by such as had rather be rewarded with security, than stand in danger of their lives, when a suspicion has gone forth in the public; so conspiracies of lesser numbers have been equally unfortunate, through the want of power to carry them into execution. The reformers, excited by Spinello Tolommei, were betrayed by one of their associates; and one of their chiefs, Nanni di Dota, was beheaded; but Tolommei was too powerful a man for such a government to dare to make an example of; he was therefore admitted to a treaty with the magistrates. Soon afterwards the Count Guido di Santa Fiora submitted to the commonwealth, and after him Monaldo di Visconti di Campiglia.

"Another conspiracy was discovered in Siena among the reformers, under the conduct of the same Spinello Tolommei. A spy, whom he sent with a letter to his correspondents in the city, was intercepted, threw himself out of a window in despair, and was killed in the fall, and a few of the conspirators were beheaded. The city, by these continual plots, so often discovered, was kept in constant terror, as was every village and castle of the whole dominion; for example, in the castle of Casole a violent sedition was awakened; the Casolans were divided into two parties, and coming to arms among themselves, skirmishes happened every day, and many were killed and more wounded. The same mischievous divisions were suffered too in the city of Massa. Monte Pulciano, likewise, was governed by a single assembly of signori, who by their divisions occasioned similar seditions and civil wars among themselves, and their different parties excited a long war between Florence and Siena; at the conclusion of which the Florentines, by their intrigues, laid the Sienese under many disadvantages; and these would have been greater, if at this time it had not been known that the Sienese were in intimate correspondence with Giovan Galeazzo Visconti, Lord of Milan, who, after having taken the city of Verona, had, with a great increase of his power, taken the city of Padua, and made prisoner of Francesco da Carrara, who was lord of it.

"On the twenty-sixth of November, 1387, to give some satisfaction to the people, who began again to show signs of discontent, it was determined in Siena that to the number of the ten lords priors there should be added one of those popular men who had been reformers; and it was declared that, when mention

24*

should be made of those persons who were of the reformers, and who might be admitted to occupy the office of the signori, and who called themselves of the people of the larger number, it should be understood to apply to their fathers, sons, brothers, by the masculine line; and those who had been admonished between 1371 and 1384 should be comprehended in the number of the other popular men, who had not been of the reformers nor signori; and if any of the monte of the nine (for this was now the name of distinction) or of the monte of the twelve had been of the said reformers, they might be signori for the monte of the people of the greater number; but he alone should be considered as of the reformers, and not any of his ancestors, descendants, or connections; as these should all remain in the monte (heap, lump, or collection) of which they had been before. They ordained, moreover, that of the chamberlains and notaries, who were eleven in number, four should be of the nine, four of the twelve, and three of the other popular men. And whereas in the other magistracies there used to be in each two nobles, one of the twelve and one of the nine, there should now be added one popular man, who had not been either of the nine or of the twelve, and thus in each of those magistracies there should be two nobles and three populars; that is to say, as it is expressed in the record of the deliberation of the council, ' one of the nine, one of the twelve, and one of the other populars;' and of these other populars, one at one time was to be of those who had been reformers and of the signori, for the monte of the people of the greater number, and one other at another time of those of the same monte, who were not of the reformers nor the lords defenders; and by these provisions, those who held the government in their hands studied to conciliate the friendship of the little people, and take away, in some degree, the occasions of conspiracies. And, that they might not alienate from their government the minds of the nobles, they resolved that all the podestaries and ordinary captainships, such as the captainship of Maremma, Montagna, Valdichiana, and others, should be given to the nobles, and to no others; and when occurrences should oblige them to send abroad extraordinary captains, they might send part of them from the nobles and part from the populars; and this order in favor of the nobles was made perpetual.

" These and other regulations were not sufficient to satisfy all, nor yet the hostile designs of Florence, nor the victory obtained by Niccolò Piccolomini over the Brettoni, to divert the people of Siena from their discontents; so that on the eleventh of May, 1388, another amendment of their constitution was attempted. The apprehensions of foreign war as well as domestic broils increased; and to facilitate the public deliberations, that they might not upon every occasion have to call a general council, they introduced a council of substitutes, and called them the *Simiglianti*, with the same forms and the same authority which the council formerly had in the times of the twelve and the nine. This council comprehended all those who had been of the lords priors governors, and those who had their names in the boxes of the same magistracy, to whom, that they might not appear to be diffident of them, they afterwards added twelve noblemen, elected from the nobility in general; and to gratify and oblige those of their citizens who were abroad, and prevent them from joining their enemies within and without, they gave a pardon to those rebels who had been confined for six months, and had observed their limits, and, although their time was not expired, gave them leave to return to the city; those who were confined for a year, might return in two months; and those who were confined for more than a year, in six months.

"At this time, Batista Piccolomini returned from Milan, who had been sent as ambassador there; and with him was sent M. Giovanni della Porta, treasurer of the Lord Giovan Galeazzo, with orders to raise and take into pay as large a number of soldiers as possible; and to this end the treasurer sent his paymasters, with the Count Ugolotti Bianchiardi, who, having been sent with the ambassador by Giovan Galeazzo, for the service of the city of Siena, went to Marca, and engaged in the pay of Visconti, M. Brogliole and Brandolino, each with a hundred cavalry, and ordered that Boldrino da Panicale should form another company.

"The Florentines carried on their intrigues with so many factions in the state, and discovered a disposition so hostile, and designs, or at least desires, of making themselves masters not only of Monte Pulciano and the other dependencies, but of Siena itself, that the government thought it advisable to hasten their deliberations upon a subject they had in contemplation for several months, a league and confederation with Giovan Galeazzo Visconti, Lord of Milan and Conte di Virtù. This prince, since he

possessed Verona and Padua, had intended to take possession of
Bologna, which had been sometimes under the dominion of the
house of Visconti; and because the Florentines, as confederates
of the Bolognese, had sent them assistance, and favored them as
much as they could with their armed men, took upon him the
protection of the city of Siena, and promised her ambassador to
assist her, and sent the Signor Paolo Savelli, with three hundred
lances, upon whose arrival uncommon rejoicings were shown in
the city. Galeazzo engaged in this warfare, not so much for the
service of Siena, as to have an opportunity of maintaining the
war in conjunction with them, upon that side, against the Florentines, that they, having employment enough to defend their
own houses, might not be able to send succor to Bologna; and
by this means to endeavor to make himself master of several
places in Tuscany, from whence he might hope, by maintaining
the divisions and most ardent hatred, which went on every day
increasing, on account of Monte Pulciano, and the injuries the
Florentines and Sienese committed against each other, to make
himself master of the province, and at length King of Italy, an
ambition he had long entertained. To this end he entered into
negotiation with the ambassadors of Siena; and on the twenty-
second of September, 1389, the treaty was signed. The articles
were, that the league should continue ten years; that common
cause should be made in a war against Florence; that Galeazzo
should maintain during the war, which was to be declared in
fifteen days, seven hundred lancemen, with three horses to each
lance, in his pay in Tuscany, for the service of the commons of
Siena; and the Sienese were to have three hundred in their pay
in the same manner, with two hundred cross-bowmen; that if
their enemies should send forces from Tuscany into Lombardy,
it should be lawful for the count to avail himself of these his
forces, but that Siena should not be obliged to send her forces
out of Tuscany; that the count should not be obliged to make
war or defend the Sienese against any other enemies than the Florentines; that any other community of Tuscany might be admitted into this league; that all the cities, lands, fortresses, and
places which by the league might be acquired in this war, should
belong to the republic of Siena, if it had any previous pretensions
to the dominion of it; otherwise, every one should be left to its
liberty, upon condition of holding the league and their allies for

friends, and their opposers for enemies, and of giving hospitality, passage, and provisions, on paying for them, to the people of the league. Galeazzo might make peace, truce, or armistice with the people of Florence, including the commons and people of Siena, with all their lands, cities, and subjects; but the Sienese could not make either without his consent; and the ratification was to be on both sides exchanged in three months.

"A war ensued, which lasted till 1389, and was then concluded by a peace, and a confederation between many republics and princes; the Conte di Virtù, Florence, Bologna, Perugia, the Marquis of Ferrara, Siena, the Lord of Mantua, the Lords de' Malatesti, Lucca, the Count di Montefeltro, Pisa, &c. This confederation, however, was not well observed; and the inhabitants of Monte Pulciano, particularly, violated it, as was supposed, at the instigation of Florence. This occasioned not only a ratification of the former treaty, but the formation of a new one between the republic of Siena and the Signor Giovan Galeazzo Visconti, Conte di Virtù, Lord and Imperial Vicar of Milan. The county or earldom of Virtù is a state in France, in the province of Champagne, which was given by King John in dower to Isabella his daughter, married to this Prince Giovan Galeazzo Visconti, which acquired him the title of Conte di Virtù; and of which marriage was born Madame Valentina, wife of Louis, Duke of Orleans, brother of Charles VI., King of France, who had in dower the same Conte di Virtù, and the city of Asti in Piedmont; of Charles, their first-born, Duke of Orleans, was born the King Louis XII; of Giovanni, their second son, Count of Angoulême, was born Charles of Angoulême, father of the King Francis I. These successors of Valentina pretended, after the death without issue of Giovan Maria and Filippo Maria, their brothers, sons of Giovan Galeazzo, that the state of Milan belonged to them; and for this reason the King Louis XII. and the King Francis I. afterwards made that celebrated war in Lombardy, and recovered and lost several times over the duchy of Milan.

"To return from this digression,—on the ninth of November, 1389, the treaty was ratified and exchanged between Siena and the count; yet a fresh conspiracy was discovered in the city, excited by Spinello Tolommei in banishment, and the reformers, in conjunction with foreigners, and Monte Pulciano again rebelled; but the arms of Siena, aided by the count and his captain, Charles

Malatesta, were triumphant at home and abroad, and this year the first bombardment ever seen in Tuscany was practised. Upon some little reverse of fortune, when the count lost the fortress of Padua, and when, to the calamities of war, those of pestilence and famine were added, in 1390, the noble families of Salimbeni, Tolommei, and Malavolti, unable to bear one another, and some of them still less willing to submit to a superior, resumed their old employment of exciting seditions. Florence wanted peace, and the pope exhorted it. The families of Tolommei and Malavolti, still jealous of the Salimbeni, and their superior influence and favor with the count, began to stir up discontents. In their opinion, it was neither profitable nor glorious, nor even honorable for the republic to waste itself on all sides for the service of the Count Galeazzo, who, in the greatest exigency of the war, had, by withdrawing his forces, left it a prey to the enemy. From this specimen of his conduct, the Sienese could only expect, if he had been or should be victorious, a servitude which they would find very bitter and irksome. Every one who was not blinded by an immeasurable hatred, which the vulgar had conceived against the Florentines for the injuries they had done the republic, must already see the disposition of the count; and especially since the arrival from Milan of the Marquis Andreasso Cavalcabò, of his privy council, to take upon him the office of senator of Siena, to which he had been elected. The marquis had demanded, with great ceremony, in the name of his master, and on his behalf, that, for the common utility, the dominion of the city of Siena should be given to him. This embassy caused a wonderful change in the minds of all those who desired that their country should remain independent and free; and the more, as they knew that the generality of the citizens, without listening to any arguments against it, and without any consideration of futurity, or of the nature of princes, never content with a middle flight, and never long to be depended on, were not only inclined to it, but had prepared a petition to the general council, that an answer should be given to the count's ambassador in these words: 'We are content; and, as a singular favor, we supplicate his lordship that, from his benignity, he will be pleased to take upon him and accept the dominion and government of the city of Siena, its country and district, and of us his devoted children and servants; and that he rule and govern us as to his excellency shall seem convenient;' and, descending to particulars, they added and affirmed, 'We are ready to give and confer upon him the city of Siena, its country and district, with its simple and mixed empire, and to transfer to him liberally the lordship and govern- ment of it, so that he may freely dispose of it, in all things, as of the city of Milan, or Padua, or any other the most submissive to him.'

"The contents of this petition, although at first prepared in secret, had reached the ears of those who endeavored to promote peace with Florence and the public tranquillity, wonderfully irritated their minds, and incited them to show to their fellow- citizens the incredible damage to the city which must arise from such an unlimited submission; and to foretell that, in a little time, when they should begin to experience the bitterness of servitude to such as are born and bred to liberty, they would in vain repent of their levity, rashness, and error. They recalled to the recollection of the citizens the great virtues of their fathers and other ancestors, which had defended their country, preserved their liberties, and transmitted both to them; and with how much generosity, bravery, and magnanimity, they themselves had defended it in arms against Charles IV., when present in Siena in 1368 with a powerful army. That they were under the most tender obligation to transmit the sacred trust to their posterity; and this they might easily do, to the inestimable benefit of the city, by a peace, which they had the power and opportunity to make. That when they should be delivered from the calamities of foreign war, and the yoke of tyranny which hung over their necks, they should be at leisure to make provi- sions of grain against the famine, and to find alleviations of their distresses from the plague.

"To these reasonings of the Tolommei and Malavolti were opposed those of the Salimbeni, who, having been long favorites of the Ghibelline party, were mortal enemies of the others, who were Guelphs. Moved by the interests of faction more than those of the public service, having procured the petition to be heard, and the decree passed and proclaimed by the council, in order to oppress the opposite party by arms, when they had not been able to answer their reasons, they drew over to their side M. Giovan Tedesco, head of the Ghibellines in Arezzo, with his cavalry, and marched through the city, accompanied with a

great multitude of people of their faction, and proclaimed the
name of Giovan Galeazzo Visconti, Conte di Vertù and Lord of
Milan, protector, and chief of the Ghibelline faction in Lombardy, and slew in this sedition twenty men of the followers of
the adverse party, and made many prisoners; among whom was
Niccolò Malavolti, who, though he had often honorably acted for
the service of the republic, was, with many others, beheaded.

"The other members of the families of Tolommei and Malavolti, with many of their followers, left the city, and retired to
their castles. The people of Siena, wearied out of patience by
being the dupes and tools of two or three ambitious families,
were easily led by one of them to rejoice in placing a master
over all. They were now so inclined and disposed to servitude
to one, in preference to a few, that, blinded with anger, they
would not see the evident ruin which must come with the
destruction of public liberty; and neither themselves nor their
leaders knowing the true cause of their divisions and misfortunes, nor any remedy by which union and liberty might be
reconciled by law, they humbly solicited the subjugation of their
country, and the privilege—of passive obedience.

"On the fifteenth day of March, in the same year, the record
was approved in the general council, and authority was given to
the lords priors to appoint a syndic, and a deputy of the commons of Siena, to execute all that was contained in the resolution, and to deliver the keys of the city to the commissaries of
the Count Galeazzo, with its absolute dominion, without pact or
convention of any kind."

The example is here complete; and although the tyranny of
the Visconti was afterwards overturned, various forms of a republic attempted, exiles sent out and recalled as usual, yet, as the
executive power was always left in an assembly, and inveterate
factions were not legally separated from each other, nor empow-
ered to control each other, the same divisions, seditions, and civil
wars were perpetual, till the same weariness induced the people
again to confer the sovereignty on the Grand-Duke of Etruria,
where it remains to this time. It is not easy to conceive what
further experiments can be made of a sovereignty in one assembly,
or how the consequences to be drawn from them can be more
decisive. Whether the assembly consists of a larger or a smaller
number, of nobles or commons, of great people or little, of rich

or poor, of substantial men or the rabble, the effects are all the same,—*No order, no safety, no liberty, because no government of law.*

It is often said, that the republics of Greece, Rome, and Tuscany, produced in the minds of their citizens great virtues; an ardent love for their country, undaunted bravery, the love of poverty, the love of science, &c. But if a little attention is bestowed upon the subject, these will be found to be very feeble arguments in their favor. It was not the love of their country, but of their faction. There were in every city three factions at least; every citizen loved one third of his fellow-citizens, and hated the other two thirds. It is true that, in such a state of things, affection for friends strengthens in proportion to the fear and hatred of enemies; and the desire of revenge becomes as strong a passion, and demands gratification as imperiously as friendship, and perhaps even more. How was it possible, when men were always in war and danger, that they should not be brave? Courage is a quality to be acquired by all men, by habit and practice. When scenes of death and carnage are every day before his eyes, how is it possible that a man should not acquire a contempt of death, from his familiarity with it, especially if life is made a burden, by continual exertion and mortification? The love of poverty is a fictitious virtue that never existed. A preference of merit to wealth has sometimes existed under all governments; but, most of all, under aristocracies. This is wisdom and virtue in all. But can much of this be found in the histories of any country, that was not poor, and obliged to be so? Can we see much of it in Florence and Siena? The love of science and literature always grows where there is much public deliberation and debate; and in such governments, where every faculty as well as passion is always on the stretch, great energy of mind appears. But there is a form of government which produces a love of law, liberty, and country, instead of disorder, irregularity, and a faction; which produces as much and more independence of spirit, and as undaunted bravery; as much esteem of merit in preference to wealth, and as great simplicity, sincerity, and generosity to all the community, as others do to a faction; which produces as great a desire of knowledge, and infinitely better faculties to pursue it; which, besides, produces security of property, and the desire and opportunities for commerce, which the others obstruct.

Shall any one hesitate then to prefer such a government as this to all others? A constitution in which the people reserve to themselves the absolute control of their purses, one essential branch of the legislature, and the inquest of grievances and state crimes, will always produce patriotism, bravery, simplicity, and science; and that infinitely better for the order, security, and tranquillity they will enjoy, by putting the executive power into one hand, which it becomes their interest, as well as that of the nobles, to watch and control.

CHAPTER SIXTH.

" The Tuscans were an ancient and original people of Italy, whose power was so considerable, that they extended their dominion from one sea to the other. These people, some ages before the foundation of Rome, built twelve cities, and among them Bologna, which was made the capital of the kingdom.[*] Some years afterwards, when Constantine, from his reverence for the holy see, had transported the throne of the empire to Byzantium, and the majesty of the emperors was become, from its distance, little respected by the Italians, many cities, and Bologna among the rest, in 382, instituted a republic. Claterna, a neighboring city, at the distance of twelve miles, which had been built also by the Tuscans, likewise erected an independent republic; but first an emulation arose, and afterwards a war, in which the Claternates were subdued, and they being as discontented with their obedience to the citizens of Bologna, as they had formerly been with that to their king, they were received, according to the custom of the Romans, into the country of the conquerors. This city was afterwards ruined by the barbarians so entirely, that no vestige of it remains but in history.

" In 961, Otho,[†] Emperor of the Germans, came into Italy, delivered it from the yoke of the Berengarii, obtained of the pope the crown imperial, and, with general applause, the title of Otho the Great. This prince, perceiving that the cities of Italy, from their natural generosity of sentiment, and their distance from the emperor, could not be held in subjection, conceded to many of them their liberty, reserving a light tribute.

" [‡] Bologna obtained, with a sort of preëminence, and with a smaller tribute, her usual liberty, with the privilege of electing

---

[*] Bombaci, p. 2.

[†] Muratori, *Annali*, tom. v. p. 397, anno 961 – 2.

[‡] Conseguì Bologna con maggiori preëminenze, e minori gravezze la esperimentata libertà con facoltà d' eleggere i magistrati con mero, e misto impero, e conforme all' instituto di Ottone, con tre sorte di consigli diede forma alla sua republica, con titolo di comune. L' uno fù il consiglio di Credenza che era quello de' consoli, e de gli altri magistrati; l' altro fù il particolare che comprendeva i

her magistrates with a mixed authority; and, conformably to the
institution of Otho, gave a form to her republic, with three
councils, with the title of a community. The one was the
Council of *the Credenza*, which was that of the consuls and the
other magistrates; the other was called the Special Council,
and comprehended the nobility; the third was called the General
Council, and was that of the people, which, without the power
of suffrage, was assembled, in order to be present at the administration of the oaths to the magistrates, and other similar
public appearances."

In this constitution there is a shadow, and no more, of three
branches. The people, who ought to constitute an essential
part, were excluded from all influence, and only called out occa-
sionally to look at their rulers, and gratify their senses with
shouts of acclamation. The *credenza* and the nobility formed
an aristocracy, in which the magistrates were appointed, and
the administration conducted. It seems to have been an imitation of the Roman consuls and senate, without even the poor
expedient of a tribune to control them.

In 1153, the cities of Italy began to elect pretors, whom they
named podestà or bailiffs; and, excited by their example, the
citizens of Bologna elected Guido Sassi to that magistracy, and
invested him publicly with the sceptre and the sword of justice.
This was a reduction of the divisions of the republic to that
union which is the effect of the government of a single person,
against the corruption of which they endeavored to provide by
the college of consuls, and by the brevity of annual magistrates.

"Felsinus, King of Tuscany, was the founder of the royal
city of Bologna, the mother of arts, sciences, and studies, and
the nurse of laws, and, after his own name, called it Felsina.
This city, which the Italian authors delight to describe, is situated at the foot of the Apennines, in the middle of the Emilian
Way, in the forty-fourth degree of latitude, between mountains
and plains equally beautiful and fertile; in the north a fruitful
plain in the east the river Savena, in the west the Rhine; not
far from the sea, and in the neighborhood of lakes and rivers

nobili; il terzo fù il generale, et era quello del popolo, quale però senza podestà
de' suffragi, si raddunava ad esser presente a' giuramenti de' magistrati, et ad
altre somiglianti apparenze. *Historie memorabili della Città di Bologna* ristrette
da Gasparo Bombaci, p. 9.

abounding with fish. The air is temperate, and the country plentiful of every thing necessary and useful to human life.[*] This glorious city was made by the kings of Tuscany the metropolis of their dominion, and the seat of their residence. Their empire indeed extended only over the twelve cities, of which this was the first; the others were Veii, Chiusi, Cortona, Populonia, Tarquini, Vetulonia, Volterra, Volsena, Roselle, Perugia, Arezzo, and Fiesole."

In the year 1123, the form of the republic of Bologna, the state of the city, and the customs of the citizens, were as follows. Those who shall read their history, will easily perceive that this republic did not, in those ancient and rude times, administer the city scientifically, nor conduct skilfully the affairs of war. "They elected three councils, a special council, a general council, and a council of credenza, in the authority of which, with their magistrates and judges, the supreme government consisted. The special council was elected annually in this manner. In the beginning of December the special and the general council were convoked, either by the consuls or by the pretor, according as one or the other of those officers happened to be in the government of the republic, in presence of whom, every one of the council, observing the order of his tribe, made his election and his drawing by lot. For this purpose, there stood before a tribunal two urns, in one of which were placed to be drawn as many tickets as there were men of that tribe present in council, and on them their names were written; in the other were as many blanks, except ten written upon by the hands of two brothers, hermits of St. Augustin, deputed by the council for that purpose. When the drawing was to be made of the first tribe, a boy of the age of twelve years, or less, drew a ticket from the principal urn, and the person whose name came out presented himself at the tribunal; the boy at the second urn drew another ticket, and if by chance it was blank, that person was excluded from the election of the council; but if the ticket was written upon, he became an elector; and this method was followed, until the ten black or written tickets declared the ten electors of that tribe. This being done, the same was repeated by the men of the other tribes, one by one, until forty men, that is to say, ten for

---

[*] Ghirardacci, *Historia di Bologna*, p. 2.

25 *

each tribe, were electors.　Then the forty electors retired to a secret place, and elected six hundred men, that is to say, one hundred and fifty for each tribe, excluding, however, the mean and poor artisans, occupied in low and base works, and minors of eighteen years; neither was any one obliged to accept of this office.　And these six hundred men then presented themselves as the special council.　In the same manner and order, in substance, in three days, the council of *credenza* was elected; but all the doctors of laws, without other qualification or appointment, might enter this council, and that of the six hundred.　After three days more, the general council were elected exactly in the same mode; but he who had been an elector in one council could not be an elector in another.　These councils assembled sometimes all together, and at other times separately, according to the nature of their business, and they assembled at the sound of a bell or trumpet.　There were provided by these councils three bells, the lesser, the middle, and the greater; for the special council the smaller bell was rung, for the council of credenza the middle, and for the council general the greater.　It was forbidden to the consul, or the pretor, to convoke the councils, if he had not previously ordered the business which was to be treated by the chancellor to be written in a book provided for that purpose. When the council was collected, the chancellor publicly proposed the subject that was to be considered; and, this done, the orators, who were four, and stood near the tribunal of the magistrates, reasoned in public.　A like privilege was granted to the orators of the magistrates, who were also four; but this only touching the business of the magistrates, and their opinions, in answer to the question separately put to them, were written down, and called the resolution or division.　It was sometimes tolerated, when it appeared to be necessary, that private or individual magistrates should harangue in council, who, mounted in a pulpit, with a loud voice delivered their opinions; and upon the questions proposed by them a division was made, or a resolution taken.　These divisions were made in various ways.　Sometimes the opinion of every one was taken in secret, and written down by a notary, successively; at other times every one gave his vote openly and audibly, and frequently the decision was made by white and black beans; now, those of one opinion went to one side and those of a different judgment to the other;

then one party stood up, and another sat down; and in these cases the voices were counted by the ministers publicly. The will and resolution of the council being determined, the decree was published, and recorded in a book, and another council could not be convoked till this decree was made. A number of notaries were employed; some to write the speeches and opinions, others to publish the decrees, and others to receive the laws. Such were the usages of the councils of this republic, which was honored with the name of commons, or community.

"Of the magistrates, some were ordinary, others extraordinary; the ordinary were created and deputed every year in the republic, and were called the magistrates of the court; the extraordinary were those who were deputed for some extraordinary business. The principal ordinary magistrates were the consuls of the community, or the pretor instead of them; the consuls of justice, the judges of the community, the attorney-general, the judges of appeals, the judges of new crimes, the judges of the office of exiles or outlaws, the judges of new causes, a judge who was the executioner of sentences, and the questor; and they all had their soldiers and notaries. The extraordinary were the legates, curators, and syndics.

"The same mode was observed in the choice of consuls as of counsellors. The election of pretor was in this manner. In the month of September the councils, general and special, were called together at the pleasure of the magistrate; but before they convened, the day and hour that each tribe was to go out to the choice by lot was published; and, in the manner already described in the election of counsellors, the forty men were drawn from one and the other council assembled, excluding, however, the magistrates; these forty suddenly retired to a secret chamber, where they were locked up from the consuls of the state and the merchants and bankers, that no one might, by word or letter, corrupt them; and if, through the whole night and the next day, by consent at least of twenty-seven of them they had not created a pretor, they lost the authority to elect; and the next day the pretor convoked the general council and the council of credenza, and from one and the other were deputed forty men, as before; and if these, to the number of twenty-seven, could not agree, the election and deputation of the pretor was referred to a suffrage or joint ballot of the general council and council of credenza. The pretor might be elected from any city, at the pleasure of the council, provided he was not a relation of any of the electors as far as the third degree, nor possessed a real estate in Bologna or its territory, nor was less than six-and-thirty years of age; and it was an injunction always to elect a man of reputation, virtuous, noble, and wise. Of right, according to the statute, a pretor could not be elected from the place of the antecedent pretor; yet this was sometimes practised; but he must not be his relation.

"The election ended and published to the councils, public letters were written to the pretor elect, requesting his acceptance of the honor that was offered him; and upon the day when he made his entry into the city, he was met and honored by all the people. The pretor had the same prerogatives and authorities which the consuls had; and therefore, according to the times, the republic was governed sometimes by consuls and sometimes by pretors; and sometimes there were at once both consuls and a pretor, as appears by instruments signed both by the consuls and a pretor in the years 1177 and 1179. It appears, that instead of consuls, the citizens sometimes turned to an election of a foreigner for a pretor, to compose the discord which arose between those of the citizens who abused their liberty, to the end that they might call delinquents to account, and punish with more severity, and not fluctuate so easily from love or hatred, fear or favor. But because for the most part the pretors were not skilled in the laws, at first two, and afterwards four judges of the law were called to aid them; and the pretors were decorated with high hats, long swords, and a sceptre, to denote their power (*potestà*); and from this they were afterwards vulgarly called podestà. Besides the consuls or the pretor, in whom resided the sum total of the republic in peace and war, certain other magistrates, as has been mentioned, governed, and the mode of electing them was the same. Two tribes were called out to the lot one day, and the two others the next; and the deputed electors were prohibited to choose a father, son, brother, or any other relation, and moreover such as were inept, unskilful, or incapable of such government; and according as any one was elected, he was proclaimed with a loud voice in council. To obviate all frauds which might be attempted, the ten written tickets being drawn, all the rest were examined in presence of the council, to see that there were no more than the law allowed. It was provided by law, that no one could elect or proclaim a magistrate, who did not pay twenty pence into the purses of the treasury, which were exacted by the pretor; and it was forbidden to any one to accept of the office, if he had not been out of it one year. None could be elected, but by that tribe in which he had his domicil; and every one who entered on a magistracy, took an oath to exercise his office with integrity and fidelity.

"Besides the magistrates already mentioned, there were those of the soldiery; the mode of electing whom was the same, but the government different. The *command in chief* was given to the consuls or *to the pretor*. The officers of the army among the cavalry, in the infantry, of the people, and lastly of the *carroccio*,[1] were different. The officers or prefects of the foot, of the horse, and of the people, because they carried a standard, (*gonfalone*,) were called gonfaloniers; and each one in his tribe was elected by his fellows, in the manner before described. Moreover, some citizens served on foot, and some others on horseback; and those who performed the service of their own accord, did it more willingly than when deputed by commission of the magistrates to that purpose. Wherefore, when any enterprise was undertaken by the military order, every one, whether of the foot or the horse, according to the necessity, went out under his own standard or ensign; and if the service required a greater appearance, each gonfalonier of the people led out his own tribe; and then it was said, that the people were gone out. It rarely happened that all the tribes went out at once; but at one time, the infantry of one tribe; at another, the cavalry of another; now one whole tribe, and then another. All the men were enrolled in the militia, from eighteen years of age to seventy, at which age men were released from all public offices, so as to be even rejected from the council. And if by accident any old man, who exceeded that age, inconsiderately entered the council, the election was annulled. In every parish, those who kept horses for war were described or registered in companies, by deputed muster-masters. These companies, some of which were registered by tens, and some by twenty-fives, according to the number

---

[1] See page 199.

of the soldiers described by the muster-masters, at certain periods conducted their horses to officers deputed for the service, to be reviewed and approved; and notaries took down their names, with their furniture, and the quality of the horses.

"Military expeditions were of two sorts; one with squadrons or legions of light horse, the other with regular armies; and great was the difference between being ordered out upon an excursion of troopers, and an expedition with the army. Because of the frequent excursions of the cavalry, it was ordained that in every tribe there should be public marshals or blacksmiths, and every master of a burgh should have ready and in order all the instruments for shoeing horses, to the end that the cavalry passing that way, and having occasion, might be always served. The treasurer paid a certain stipend to every magistrate, and kept an account of the public revenues and all expenses. The revenues consisted in tributes, gifts, and tolls or customs. The gifts were upon the gates, bankers, lands, mills, oxen, &c.; and if the revenue was not sufficient for the expenses of the war, a tax was imposed, by order of the council, upon polls and estates, according to every man's possessions and incomes. Thus much concerning the ordinary magistrates.

"The extraordinary were always elected by the pretor, as the ambassadors, directors of public works, and the syndics. No magistrate could go upon an embassy; and to any one who was sent out of the territory upon an embassy, they assigned three horses, two notaries, and one cook. If the embassy was to the pope or the emperor, the expense, attendants, and servants, were ordered at the discretion of the council. A commission was given the ambassador in writing, and the whole legation was governed by instructions. It was ordained in general terms, that no one should petition or *seek* to be created of the number of magistrates; and if any one was known to *seek* it, his conduct was publicly related in council, and it was reproached to him as the greatest infamy. The officers of state, with the title of *podestà*, with their judges and notaries, were elected partly from the mountains, and partly from the plains or low lands. The castles which were subject to the Bolognese elected also their own consuls, and, when they were commanded, went to war with them, and carried various standards. All the burdens and tributes were much heavier upon them than upon the citizens, excepting only some persons who, for particular merit, had been exempted by the council.

"There were many colleges or companies in the city, as that of the merchants, the goldsmiths, and the artificers. The merchants and goldsmiths created their own consuls, and the companies of artificers appointed their own treasurers; and those who were able to do it assembled together in associations for the promotion of commerce and improvement in the arts. The people and the city afterwards increasing, there were elected certain colleges of arms, one called that of *the Lombards*, another *della Branca*, and another *del Griffone;* and these had the care of the arms of the republic, and were decorated by the city with many privileges; and the foreigners who were of these companies were made citizens of Bologna, if they had been householders in the city ten years, and might be of the council of the commons, stewards of companies, and magistrates, equally with other citizens. The greatest part of the laborers in the country were slaves of the nobles, from which servitude, however, they were afterwards liberated, the community paying a certain sum of money to their masters.

"All these particulars of their constitution were found in the ancient customs, or the privileges granted or confirmed by the emperors, or in the decrees of the councils, or in the laws of the city; the former were called *reformationi*, the latter *statuti*. The decrees were those ordinances which, at the prayer of the pretor, were adopted by the councils, or made by him and approved by them. The laws were no other than the ordinances made by the legislators, who were called *statutieri*. No ordinary magistrate was of these legislators, but they were deputed, according to the wants of the city, from time to time, and, after the example of the Athenians, reviewed the old laws, and altered, amended, accommodated, and reformed them, according to their judgment. The laws which these legislators made were reported to the council, by them recited publicly to the people, and written in the volumes of civil law, which to this day are called the *Statuto*. This constitution was preserved till after the year 1250.

"The houses were of wood, without much ornament or skill in architecture; and from this cause they were frequently exposed to terrible fires. Among all the buildings, the most noble objects were the steeples built upon the churches, and the towers built

by all the principal citizens. The frequent fires, and the common
calamities of Italy, the deluges of water, and the frequent exiles
of the citizens, are supposed to have destroyed many objects, and
buried in oblivion many facts worthy of eternal remembrance."

There are greater traces of an artificial and scientific legislation
in this constitution, than in either that of Florence or Siena;
nevertheless, all authority, legislative, executive, and judicial,
was in one council; for, when the special and general council
met together, they acted as one, and when one met alone, it
acted as sovereign; the podestà, and his judges and notaries,
were only deputies of the council. Although so much pains was
taken, by mixing lot with choice, by rotations, and other prudent
precautions, to prevent ambition, faction, and sedition from entering, all was ineffectual.

Omitting most of the wars, foreign and domestic, we may
select a few instances from whence the operation of this form of
government may be evinced.

"Henry V., as he was called, but of Germany the Sixth,[1] after
his succession to his father Frederick, passing through Bologna
with Constantia his wife, in his way to Rome to receive the
imperial crown, was magnificently received by the people, and
entertained by Gerardo, Bishop of Bologna, in the bishop's palace;
in acknowledgment of his kind reception, he gave to Gerardo the
title of Prince, which was afterwards retained by the bishops of
Bologna. Henry was not only crowned as emperor, but with
much ceremony invested with the kingdom of the two Sicilies,
as the inheritance of his wife Constantia.

"In the next year, Gerardo, Bishop of Bologna, by his favor
with the emperor and the pope, and the privileges he had obtained
for the city, was grown into such reputation for justice and virtue
with all men, that he was constituted pretor with great popularity,
and in the beginning of his dignity he contracted a friendship
with Albert, the Count of Prato, and made a treaty for mutual
defence. Gerardo having the first year administered in such a
manner as to be thought a bright example of a good and moderate ruler, seemed a little afterwards to be changed in his whole
nature, began to desire innovation, and openly to favor the plebeians, oppressing the nobles and first men of the city. This

---

[1] Ghirardacci, lib. iv. p. 101.

gave occasion to grave disorders and seditions; for the patricians, who had conferred the office upon him, and were accustomed and habituated to the command of others, could not easily tolerate this injury and the evident partiality of the pretor; so they assembled in the palace, and created twelve consuls, men of great authority in Bologna.

"Gerardo, hearing of the election of consuls, was in high wrath, and began to threaten them with his frown; but they quickly published to the people that he was deposed from the office of pretor. Giacomo Orsi, a powerful citizen, and a favorer of Gerardo, collected a company of armed men, and attempted to oppose the resolution of the consuls and patricians; whereupon Specialino Griffoni, not less celebrated in letters than in arms, and one who was studious and intent upon maintaining the republic, turned round to the nobles, and harangued them as follows: 'Is it consistent with our duty or our honor, fellow-citizens, to suffer that authority which for three hundred years and more we have enjoyed, of directing this our republic, to be wrested from us by a private person, placed by us alone in the government of it, for the general safety of the city? Shall we submit to become like the vilest populace, esteemed of no importance or authority, and subjected to that Gerardo, to whom we are and forever shall be objects of jealousy and terror, so long as our republic shall remain safe and sound? Rouse up your spirits at once; never think of bearing this insupportable tyranny; and let the object itself, and the opportunity of the moment, stir you to this enterprise, infinitely more than my words; and accept of me, according to your pleasure, either as a soldier or a captain in the service to which I am willing to devote my soul and body.'"

Amidst all this aristocratical thunder, the still voice of reason and experience whispers to a candid reader the probability that the nobles were more tyrannical than Gerardo; that the people were impatient under it; Gerardo disposed to alleviate their burdens; and the nobles thence alarmed with the apprehension of a master over themselves, rather than over the people.[1]

---

[1] Cette première indication de leur jalousie, ce premier appel à la décision des armes, sur les droits des deux ordres rivaux, étoit cependant, pour eux-mêmes, d'un bien dangereux exemple: car ils n'étoient pas les plus forts. Le peuple pouvoit à son tour recouvrer, par les mêmes moyens, l'influence qu'on lui ravissoit, il pouvoit les chasser eux-mêmes de la ville. Sismondi, *Rép. Ital.* tom. 2, p. 285.

"The speech being ended, he seized his arms, and, accompanied by the consuls and the greater part of the nobles, marched to the bishop's palace. Giacomo Orsi, with those devoted to him, opposing them in arms, they came to action; but Giacomo, not being able to resist the impetuosity of the assailants, with great difficulty saved himself, with Gerardo, by flying from the city. The consuls, disappointed by their flight, were the more exasperated; and seeing Orsi out of their power, they declared him a rebel against the republic, confiscated all his property, and ordered his house and tower to be razed to the ground."

Such decision delivered the city for the present from this violent sedition, and with as much virtue as that which delivered the Roman patricians from Mælius or Manlius.

"But the next year, under new consuls, although it appeared that the sedition of Gerardo was quieted, and that no disposition remained for innovation, yet all on a sudden, on the first of July, some of his abettors proceeded from words to blows with some of the adverse party, in which affray Pietro Scannabecchi lost his right hand, and Scannabecco Ramponi lay mortally wounded, among many others both killed and wounded. The day after, both parties prepared their arms, and came to battle again in the palace of the community; when Giuseppe Occelletti and Tomaso Toschi da i Gieremei, supporters of Gerardo, were slain; whereupon the consuls were again obliged to take arms against Gerardo, who, having taken possession of a castle called Sorresano, had there fortified himself. They sent out Guglielmo Malavolti, a consul, with a chosen band of soldiers, who conducted himself with so much skill and bravery, that he drove Gerardo from his fortress, and burnt his castle. In a short time the Emperor Henry, by a decree, liberated the bishop Gerardo, whom he called his *Prencipe*, from the *oath of calumny*,[1] and permitted him to exercise his functions in all his causes, and those of the bishopric, by an administrator, or other legitimate person.

"The next year, 1195, it seems they tried the experiment of a pretor again," (that is to say, as we may conjecture the family of Gieremei and their party prevailed in the public councils to carry this point,) "and Guido Cino was elected. But as he followed, in his administration, the steps of Gerardo, after having done

[1] "Henrico per Decreto liberò Gerardo in tutte le cause del giuramento della calonnia." This was an oath prescribed by the civil law.

intolerable things against many persons, he was dishonorably deposed from his office, and accused of an infinite number of iniquities; and, attempting to fly, he was made prisoner by those whom he had offended, all his teeth were drawn out of his head for his punishment, and then he was set at liberty. In his place, Guido da Vilmercato, of Milan, was appointed.

"In 1202, civil discords arose in the city, by which Bologna was not a little troubled and afflicted. The first disorder that occurred, arose from an ancient enmity between the Asinelli and the Scannabecchi. These two factions meeting in the high street, with a sudden and impetuous onset engaged in arms, and many were killed and wounded on both sides. This quarrel was composed by the interposition of the pretor and the other nobles; but another soon arose from some private offence; for Giovanni Tettalasini had killed Guido Pepoli. This enmity between these two families continued forty years before it was pacified.

"In 1212, upon some public occasion, among a great concourse of nobility on horseback, Gieremia Malavolti, falling from his horse, was killed, to the grief of the people and the emperor."

And, probably to the equal joy of the nobility.

"In the year 1218 there were in the city of Bologna ten thousand scholars at the academy for the study of the law; in such reputation was that university.

"[1] The quarrel between Frederick the emperor and Gregory the pope, revived in Bologna the party distinctions of Guelphs and Ghibellines, drawn from Germany in the time of Henry IV. Not only some cities favored the emperor, and others the pontiff, but in the city of Bologna the citizens arrived at that degree of extreme madness, that, in hatred of each other, they strove to deprive each other of their lives and fortunes together. Sons became enemies to their fathers, and brothers to brothers; and, as if it was not enough to shed their own blood, like mad dogs, they proceeded to demolish houses, and to burning the cities, the trees, and the corn. This diabolical pestilence produced such an aversion to each other, that they studied to distinguish themselves in all things; in their clothes, in the colors they wore, in

1 Ghirardacci, lib. v. p. 146.

their actions, their speech, their walk, their food, their saluta-
tions, their drink, their manner of cutting bread, in folding their
napkins, in the cut of their hair, and innumerable other extravagances equally whimsical. A plague truly horrible, a flame
wholly inextinguishable, which proved the extinction of many
noble families, and the ruin of many miserable cities.

"The next year, under the pretorship of Uberto Visconti, a
cruel war arose out of a violent sedition. Godfrey, Count of
Romagna, favorite of Frederick, took Manzolino, a castle of
Romagna, and drove out from it the prefect of Bologna. This
officer's return stimulated the people to a violent revolt, because
every one lamented that the castle had been lost by the neglect or misconduct of the pretor, and that of those who governed
in the city; and in such manner did this indignation, conceived
in the hearts of all, increase, that, seizing their arms against the
will of the republic, they collected together in the piazza, immediately made one Giuseppe Toschi their leader, a man not only
bold but rash, and, with the loudest cries, ran tumultuously to
the palace of the pretor, where Giuseppe demanded the standard
of the people, and the armed guards of the palace, declaring
that he would go out and meet the enemy, and prevent his committing further depredations on the territory of Bologna. The
pretor refused his demand; but Giuseppe, consulting only his
own temerity, broke open the gates of the palace, forced his
entry into it, ransacked every thing, and burned all the papers of
the pretor. In order to acquire more favor with the people,
he turned out all the public tables, rung the bell, contrary to the
will of the pretor and the guards; and having thus collected
all the people armed in the piazza, he had the *carroccio* brought
out, and ordered all things for a war. He then arranged four
thousand infantry under Bornio Gieremei, whose tool he probably was, eight hundred cavalry under Orso Caccianemici and
Prendiparte Prendiparti, and four hundred men at arms under
Alberto Galluzzi and Lodovico Ariosti.

"In this curious manner a foundation was laid for a change in
the commonwealth, and an institution of the People. They
called by this name, *The People*, the new republic placed in the
hands of the people, whose superintendents were the prefect of
the people, the *antiani*, the consuls of the merchants, and the
masters of colleges. According to Thomas Aquinas, the *antiani*

were instituted in the cities of Italy, as the tribunes were in Rome, that they might take the part of the plebeians; but after this Giuseppe, whom they created prefect of the people, no other prefect is mentioned till 1255. The Florentines and the Genoese having ordained a republic of the people about the same time, introduced also the prefect of the people and the *antiani;* and this popular government was sustained, with its proper councils, to whom the prefect and the *antiani* were governors, the pretors and judges of the pretors remaining as they had been before that time; six *antiani* were created from all the four-and-twenty tribes; and the use and creation of these *antiani* continued as long as the republic, their number only being increased, as well as that of the consuls of merchants and masters of colleges.

"By this change of government the republic became involved in two wars at once, with Imola and Modena; and the people of Bologna, finding their affairs not succeed to their wishes, rose in a tumult, and killed Rolando Formaglini, superintendent of Piumazzo, because his fortress was taken by the enemy, they having suspicions that he had betrayed it for money.

"The animosities of the Guelphs and Ghibellines mixing with the disputes between the nobles and commons, produced such convulsions in all the cities, especially in those adhering to Frederick, that in Modena, Reggio, Parma, Cremona, Bergamo, and Pavia, those who favored the church were finally expelled by the power of their adversaries, and driven into exile; and Bologna still continued to be agitated with seditions, as well as with disputes with the bishop and the pope, by whom the people were excommunicated.

"In 1234,[1] was settled the controversy with the bishop, but a greater tumult than had ever been known arose, on account of Alberto Lambertazzi, who being in the piazza, and seeing Gabriel Sanzio his enemy, killed him. This homicide put arms into the hands of a multitude of citizens. Although the pretor, not having the criminal in his power, declared him an outlaw, the relations and friends of the deceased did not the less greedily watch for a severe revenge. As they saw that the party of the Lambertazzi were upon their guard, and went about pre-

---

[1] Ghirardacci, lib. vi. p. 156.

pared, with a great retinue of armed men, they consulted upon
modes of getting into action. Meeting one day with Alphonso,
the brother of Albert, they came to a rude scuffle together, in
which much blood was shed, and more mischief would have
been done, if the interposition of the pretor had not interrupted
it; but this broil was the beginning of discords and seditions
which lasted a long time."

The hatred between the most considerable families had grown
so inveterate, — having continued, with few interruptions, for
forty years, namely, from the death of Guido Peppoli, — that much
bloodshed was apprehended; but John of Bologna, a famous
preacher, coming into the city, preached peace, charity, and
benevolence, to his immortal honor, with so much success, that
a kind of reconciliation was made between the families of Del-
fini and Malataschi; Torelli and Andalò; Griffoni, Artenisii,
and Castel de' Britti; Galluzzi and Carbonesi; Lambertini and
Scannabecchi; Pepoli and Tettalasini; who had been constant
enemies; and several intermarriages were contracted among
them.

"In the year 1211 is found the next mention of the *antiani* of
the people, who presided in the instituted republic of the people, and moderated in two councils; one called the little council, which they, with the consuls of the merchants and goldsmiths, masters of the arts and of arms, the gonfaloniers of
the people, and of the *collegi*, and their counsellors, composed;
and the other called the grand council, in which they were again
found, with the other larger number of counsellors; and all that
was by these ordained was perpetually to be observed; so that
all laws were made, executed, and judged by the majority of
this single council, or by persons deputed by them."

The same original and essential fault that had occasioned
their miseries, and continued to increase them.

"In 1248, secretly making great preparations for war, and
calling to their assistance the March, Romagna and Azzo da
Este, they created eight noblemen to conduct the war against
the Modenese; these were Alberto Galluzzi, Lambertazzi, Prendiparti, Samaritani, Scannabecchi, Ariosti, Guido Gieremci, and
Cattellani. For captain-general they elected the Marquis Azzo
da Este; but he being infirm, to show his gratitude to the
senate, sent them three thousand cavalry and two thousand

foot. Gieremei had command of half the men at arms, and Lambertazzi of the infantry."

It appears from this, that though the government was called popular and the people, that the people was no more than an aristocracy, and that the nobles were not excluded. The two families of Gieremei and Lambertazzi were very near the head of the republic, and, as we shall soon see, most eagerly contending for the foremost station.

" An obstinate battle was fought, in which great exertions both of skill and bravery were shown, and a complete victory obtained by the Bolognese, and King Hentio[1] taken prisoner. In 1254, the treaties with the Marquis da Este and the commons of Ferrara were confirmed in the council general and special of the commons of Bologna. The next year the republic adorned itself with a new magistrate, Ricardo Villa being made pretor; but because the pretor was the superintendent of the republic of nobles, which was called *The Commons*, it was now their pleasure that there should be a prefect, or captain of the people, who should govern the popular republic called *The People*. This dignity had been laid aside a long time, though it had been the original title of the first magistrate, but was now revived, and Giordano Lucino was elected to it. Separating the functions, it was ordained, that the pretor should have the authority and jurisdiction of the city, and be superintendent of the councils of the commons, and that the captain should administer in war abroad; that within the city the councils of the people should govern, and confer in the public business with the *antiani*."

" In the year 1257, a transaction was completed, which alone ought to be sufficient to immortalize the republic of Bologna. There is, among the records of that city, a book entitled ' The Paradise of Pleasure,' which contains the decree of the third of June, 1257, by which all the slaves and villains were manumitted, and annually taxed in a certain quantity of corn, which was consigned to the care of an officer, already instituted and called the pretor of the sack, who was appointed in the same manner with the pretors of the castles. This law, at first prepared by legislators, was recited and approved by the councils

---

[1] The son of Frederick.

of the people, assembled, according to the usage, by the ringing of bells.   The record is in substance, — ' In the beginning God Almighty planted a paradise of pleasure, in which he placed man whom he had created and clothed with a white robe of innocence, giving him a perfect and perpetual liberty; but the wretch, unmindful of his own dignity and the divine munifi- cence, tasted of the apple forbidden him by the commandment of Heaven, and thereby dragged himself and all his posterity down into this valley of misery, poisoned the human race, and most miserably bound it in the chains of diabolical servitude; and thus, from incorruptible it was made corruptible; from im- mortal, mortal; subjected to continual vicissitudes and most grievous slavery.   God, however, beholding that the whole world had perished, had compassion on the human race, and sent his only begotten son, born of the Virgin Mary, who, coöperating with the grace of the Holy Ghost, to the glory of his own dignity, breaking the bonds with which we were held captive, restored us to our primitive liberty; and therefore it is very justly questioned, whether men, whom nature from the beginning pro- duced and created free, and the law of nations only subjected to the yoke of servitude, ought not to be restored to the blessing of manumission.

" ' These men have been a shame to the cause of liberty.   In consideration of which, the noble city of Bologna, which has always fought for liberty, recollecting the past and providing for the future, in honor of Jesus Christ, our Lord and Redeemer, has redeemed, with a price in money, all those who, in the city of Bologna and its bishopric, were found confined in a servile con- dition, and after a diligent examination, decreed them to be free; ordaining that no one, constrained in any kind of slavery, in the city or episcopacy, shall dare to remain or be detained in it, to the end that so great a mass of natural liberty, redeemed by a price, should not be liable to be corrupted by any remaining mix- ture of slavery, as a moderate fermentation corrupts the whole mass, and the society of one evil depraves many that are good. In the time of that noble man and podestà, D. Accursius of So- rixana, whose reputation spreading far and wide, shines like a star, and under the examination of D. Jacob Grataceli, his judge and assessor, whose skill, wisdom, constancy, and temperance, recommend him to all men, the present memorial is made, which

by its proper name ought justly to be called PARADISE, containing the names of all the masters and all the slaves, both male
and female, that it may appear by what servants and maids
liberty is acquired, and at what price; to wit, ten pounds for
those of more than fourteen years of age, whether men or
women, and eight pounds for all under that age, to every master
for every one whom he holds in servitude.   This memorial was
written by me, Conrad Sclariti, a notary, deputed to the office
of servants and maids; and may it remain to posterity a monu-
ment of this transaction." *

Amidst the melancholy gloom of factions and licentiousness,
of injustice and cruelty, of fraud and violence, such a gleam of
humanity, equity, and magnanimity, is refreshing.   It shall be
left to our own reflections, the first of which will undoubtedly
be a wish to see a paradise of pleasure in each of the United
States of America.

[1] " The temporary reconciliation of the nobles had produced
prosperity and success to the republic; but as the constitution
remained the same, and war alone had preserved the benevolent
impressions of John the preacher, as soon as that was over the
seditions of the citizens again disturbed all their quiet and felicity.   The Galluzzi, Lambertazzi, Artenisi, Britti, Carbonesi,
Scannabecchi, all noble families and greatly esteemed in Bologna,
could no longer restrain their passions, and, as the historian very
justly observes, God knows how they could have restrained
them so long.

" The Lambertazzi were the first to set fire to the train of
jealousy and indignation, hatred and revenge, and to begin the
ruin of their country.   Provoked by some words, reported to
them by their flatterers, and perhaps invented or exaggerated,
they took arms, and coming fiercely to action with the Gieremei,
a great quantity of blood was shed on both sides; they would
have proceeded to greater extremities, if Ramponi, a man in
high esteem, had not dexterously interposed, and by his wisdom
and courage, brought them to an accommodation; yet the quarrel continued to break out at times, and prevailed even among

* Ghirardacci, lib. vi. p. 194.
In a copy of this work which Thomas Brand Hollis presented to the author,
he specifies the recording of this act as meriting immortality for it.
[1] Ghirardacci, lib. vii. p. 197.

the scholars. One of the tribunes of the city was dangerously wounded, and Raimondo, a Genoese, was beheaded, but this did not end the disorder. The Galluzzi and Carbonesi took up the dispute, and several horrid murders were committed, and several of the dependencies of the republic, taking advantage of the opportunity, or excited by partisans, rebelled."

The disorder lurked, however, in some degree of secrecy till 1260, when it broke out again, and the parties began to collect together companies of idle vagabonds, and on a thousand occasions endeavored to come to action.

" Finally, the Gieremei went out in arms against the Lambertazzi, the Galluzzi against the Carbonesi, the Lambertini against the Scannabecchi, and the Artinesi against the Britti. They continued engaged a long space of time, each party assisted by the families of its adherents. The pretor, with all his court and forces, was obliged to turn out, and partly by his menaces, and partly by some small remains of reverence for authority, he put a stop to this most sanguinary and horrible rencounter, and obliged those who remained alive to return to their houses.

" In 1264, these intestine broils were renewed, particularly between the families of Lambertazzi and Gieremei, and while many were anxious to make peace between them, and were occupied in contriving the means of it, the Lambertazzi, little inclined to any accommodation, by exerting all their influence and intrigues, on purpose to offend the Gieremei, procured that Peter Pagani, a powerful citizen of Imola, should be made lord of it, to the end that he might expel from thence all the friends of the Gieremei, and demolish all their houses, a commission which he fully executed. Imola, thus revolted from the obedience of Bologna, drove out Giacopino Prendiparte of Bologna, or, as others say, killed him, who was commissary and governor in the name of the city of Bologna. This action so displeased the senate, that they suddenly sent out a powerful army with the *carroccio*, under the pretor, and obliged the usurper and his men to evacuate the post. But before this enterprise was finished, another tumult happened against the judges, one of whom, Uguccione, was assaulted and killed, and the parties were again upon the point of coming to a bloody decision, and it required the whole court in arms to disperse the tumult.

" Before the end of the year, another tumult arose in Imola, where the Bricij, principal leaders of that city, favorers of Cujano and Saffatello, had secretly introduced many men, and drove out of the city the Imindoli, their enemies or rivals. But the people were so displeased with this violence, that they rose upon the Bricij and their followers, drove them out of the city at the point of the sword, and recalled the Imindoli. The senate, on the news of this fidelity, bestowed the highest praises on the people, and to reward them, by removing the cause of such inconveniences, ordered that for the future they should have no pretor at all, and that all their differences should be brought before the pretor of Bologna, to be adjudged with equity and celerity, upon condition that they should pay the auditors or judges who should hear their controversies five hundred pounds a year. All this was cheerfully accepted by the people of Imola," as much preferable to continual quarrels in arms, to determine whether the Gieremei or Lambertazzi should have the appointment of one of their instruments to be a pretor among them.

"Clement VI. among the first acts of his pontificate, invited into Italy Charles of Anjou, brother of St. Louis, King of France; and Uberto, Count of Flanders, general of Charles's army, passed into Italy with forty thousand men. Bologna, with Milan, Bergamo, Verona, Mantua, and Ferrara, joined the church and France; four thousand men, under Guido Antonio Lambertini, a noble Bolognese, joined the crusade proclaimed by the pope against Manfred.

"The Lambertini indulging their enmity against the Bocchetti laid a plot one day to kill one of them, and thinking to find him in a certain place, where their spies had informed them he was, they went to seek him, but he was gone. In their return they met one of the Scannabecchi; letting loose their malice against him, they killed him and fled. The pretor, informed of their crime and flight, issued a proclamation against them, rifled their houses, and to intimidate other malefactors, burnt them to the ground. Finding by these continual homicides that the government was too weak to restrain the parties, a new magistracy was created in the city, of three men, who were to hear and prudently examine the differences among the nobles, and endeavor to appease them. Andalò, Malavolti, and Ramponi, all men of great candor and singular prudence, were chosen. Andalò was of great authority with the Ghibellines, Malavolti with the

Guelphs, and so was Ramponi. These, without respect of persons, judging with impartiality, had a wonderful effect in the city, and by great mildness composed many discords and long enmities, particularly between the Asinelli and Scannabecchi, among whom a great deal of blood had been spilled, and who had been a long time enemies; and, in a word, brought the city to a degree of tranquillity.

" It was this year that, hearing of the defeat and death of Manfred, the Ghibellines in Florence began to tremble, and the Guelphs to triumph. That city chose two pretors from Bologna, the same Malavolti and Andalò, and erected their council of thirty-six Guelphs and Ghibellines, divided the city into seven greater arts, and gave every art its gonfalonier; and this year Dante the poet was born.

In 1267, " Charles Calzolaio, finding a young man in Bologna in bed with his wife, killed him, to maintain his own honor, but was taken into custody, and sentenced to death by the pretor, as one who, contrary to the laws, had taken justice into his own hands. This sentence appeared to be unjust to the other Calzolai, who tenderly loved their brother Charles, and they united together, mutually pledged their faith to each other to rescue him, and taking arms, went to the palace of the pretor, and forcibly delivered Charles from his prison. This excited in the city a mighty tumult, and so intimidated the pretor, that he concealed himself in a place of safety. The commotion subsided by the exertions of the consuls, and the fury of the Calzolai subsided so far, that the senate ventured to inquire who were the authors of the tumult; but the heads of it were by this time escaped from the city, so that the company of the Calzolai were only fined in a sum of money. To this uproar succeeded another still greater, between the Lambertini and Scannabecchi, in which many were left wounded, and many slain; among whom was Bartolomeo Guidozagni, a friend of the Lambertini. This tincture of blood enkindled the minds of the two parties to vengeance to such a degree, that, like mad dogs,* they thought of nothing but persecution, murder, and extermination; and they collected their friends, both within and without the city, together to this effect. The consuls in office,

---

* Come cani arrabbiati. Ghirardacci, p. 212.

to whom information was given of the danger, published a proclamation, that no man should be introduced or let into the city, if he were not previously known to the deputies appointed to superintend, who might know by that means the reason of his coming, and oblige him to lay down his arms. This prudent precaution in a few days quieted the factions, and the consuls, thinking the late disorder too light to be very severely punished, only made an example or two in each of the families, by confining one of the Lambertini in Mantua, and one of the Scannabecchi in Florence; and because the consuls saw the violent enmities which prevailed among many noble families, which were in danger of increasing every day to mortal rancor, they availed themselves of the resolution and prudence of Andalò and Malavolti, lately returned from Florence, by electing them to compose the peace of the city, giving them ample powers for that end. And this measure succeeded so far, that the Lambertini and Scannabecchi, the Gozzadini and Arienti, Guidozagni and Orsi, Calamatoni and Sangiorgi, Bianchetti and Pizzigotti, and many other noble families, were reconciled, in the presence of the consuls in the palace, with much satisfaction to the whole city. But as no measure of the executive could be taken without offence to some part of such a divided executive authority, the consuls, by annulling all the condemnations in the late disturbances, excited the indignation of the pretor Dandolo, so that he resigned his office. The consuls, who were not sorry for it, appointed Aurelio Rocca dalla Torre, of Milan, in his stead."

In this instance, as in many others, before and after, being obliged to appoint a foreigner for their first magistrate, to avoid the certain seditions and rebellions that would have been excited by the adverse party, if any natural born citizen, however distinguished by merit, had been raised to this eminence, among his jealous peers.

" In 1268, Alberto Caccianemici, for some offensive words of his nephew Guido, son of his brother Gruamonte, which were reported to him, without examining the truth of the information, in a fit of impatience for vengeance, called his two sons to him, and ordered them to go and put their cousin to death. His orders were executed with great inhumanity." But, in such a state of government and parties, the laws are overborne by

popular and powerful individuals, and there is no justice to be
had against them in a regular prosecution; so thought the
people in this case, and therefore took upon themselves the
punishment of so atrocious a cruelty, by rising in arms, and
demolishing their houses.

"In 1269, another instance of a similar but more important
nature happened. The captain of the people governed severely
in his office, and did not do justice to the people, as they said;
and this provoked the wrath of the people so far, that they
deposed him. The pretor took this deposition in ill part, and
thought that the principal authors of it ought to be punished,
at least in some small degree, to discountenance such irregularity. But this irritated the people so highly, that, perceiving
his danger he thought it prudent to fly; and a new pretor, as
well as captain, were appointed. Thus the discontented nobles,
although they could not, from their opposition to each other,
obtain the first offices in the state, had it always in their power,
by secret machinations with the people, to excite tumults, and
distress, embarrass, and depose the foreigners who held them.

"There is an example of generosity in the gentlemen of Bologna, in the year 1270, too much to their honor, amidst all their
quarrels, to be omitted. A great scarcity prevailed in all the
cities of Tuscany and Lombardy, and the people of Bologna
were reduced to extreme misery by famine. Upon this occasion all the noblemen, and other rich men of the city, had the
charity to open their stores, and expose all their corn and grain
to the people; and, not satisfied with this, they united together,
collected all the money they had, or by their credit could borrow,
and offered it to the senate, that it might be sent to Romagna,
and other distant provinces, to procure a supply of bread for the
city. This benevolent effort, however, produced an accidental
ill effect; it occasioned a rivalry in the markets for grain between Bologna and Venice, which produced resentments, re-
taliating imposts and duties, and at last a war, in which the
Venetians were conquered.

"But the city of Bologna could not enjoy its triumphs in
peace; malignant spirits in secret scattered reports and calumnies to disturb the public tranquillity, sometimes against one
illustrious citizen, and sometimes another. These rumors coming
to the ears of the senate, they exerted all their skill to discover

whether the crimes alleged had been committed or not; but, after all their diligence found no evidence, but idle suspicions. Nevertheless the senators and people, taking the hint from these endeavors to excite disorders, judged it would be useful to create a new magistracy of three men, of the best lives, and most wisdom, to preserve the quiet of the city, and to administer justice, by rewarding the good, and chastising the insolent disturbers of the peace of others. To this end ample authority was given them to bear arms, and to take with them armed men; to imprison delinquents, and accommodate all disputes which should arise; and these were called the Magistrates of Peace. The three chiefs divided their people into three military classes; one was called that of the *Lombardi*, and to this was committed the red standard, with the figure of Justice holding a drawn sword in her hand; the second was called *the Griffin*, and to this was consigned the white standard, with a red griffin; the last was called *della Branca*, to which was allotted the white standard, with a red lion holding a sword in his right paw. These companies were greatly esteemed in the city, and much honored by the senate, who granted them signal privileges, registering the magistrates as true and noble citizens.

" While this new magistracy was wholly employed in the preservation of the honor and peace of the city, and daily reconciled the minds of the citizens, the rancor of private animosity broke out again in the murder of Philip, called *il Bologna*, one of the company *della Branca*, by Soldano de' Galluzzi, who fled, which beyond measure displeased the senate; not having the murderer in their power, in order to give complete satisfaction to the company, they published a capital proclamation against him, and demolished to their foundations all the houses he had both in town and country. By this exemplary punishment alone would the irritated minds of the company, who had arms in their hands, be pacified."

The next year it appears by the records, that, besides the pretor and captain of the people, four and twenty wise men (*sapienti*) were elected, six for each tribe, out of all the tribes of the city, by the *antiani*, to preserve the companies of the city. They elected also four citizens to oversee the plentiful supply of the city; and five and twenty other wise men to superintend the fortresses and castles in the country, as well as some things relative to the government in the city. All these inventions, dictated by distress, and the feeling as well as fear of the evils of discord, were only aggravations of the evil, as they only divided the executive power still more, without dividing the legislative; whereas the direct contrary ought to have been the remedy, namely, they ought to have united the executive power, and divided the legislative, and by that means have produced that trinity in unity, which is neither a contradiction nor a mystery, but is alone efficacious to curb the audacity of individuals, and the daring turbulence of parties. The judicial power, independent of all, is able to encounter any man or combination of men, without recurring to such rigorous measures, inconsistent with liberty, as these new magistrates in Bologna were obliged to adopt. In order to purge the city of its many popular disorders, they were obliged to forbid a great number of persons, under grievous penalties, to enter the palace; nor was it permitted them to go about the city, nor to bear arms. All this they were obliged to do to prevent collections of people in the streets. Afterwards some of the first people of the city were banished, and confined to certain places abroad, and, upon pain of death, sentenced to depart the city in three hours. It is provoking to read the perpetual cant of these historians, such as, that, in this year 1273, Bologna, having compelled the Venetians to peace, and ruling over Imola, Faenza, Forli, and the castles of Romagna, in peace, and by fear, might have become great and glorious by the valor of its citizens, if civil discords had not begun again to commit their cruel ravages. These dissensions, on the contrary, proved the ruin of the city, and were the cause that, by little and little, she lost her ancient authority and grandeur, and from a patron she became a client, from a mistress a subject; a miserable fall, which began in this manner.

"There were in Bologna two most noble families, the Gieremei and the Lambertazzi, between whom, not only the party prejudices of Guelphs and Ghibellines, but a rivalry for power and preëminence in the state, had long subsisted; but neither party animosities nor family jealousies were able to prevent Imelda, a daughter of Orlando Lambertazzi, a most beautiful young lady, from entertaining a partiality for Boniface, a son of Gieremia de Gieremei, a very handsome young man, who was desperately in love with her. This mutual passion thus increas-

ing in their hearts from day to day, the two lovers at last found
an opportunity to meet. The lady's brothers being engaged in
some amusement at the house of the Caccianemici, having information of this interview, went to their sister's chamber, and
finding Boniface there, fell upon him with poisoned weapons,
and in an instant pierced his breast and his heart, their miserable sister flying in despair from their fury. Having committed the murder, they concealed the body in a sink, which
ran under some apartment in the house, and fled from the city.
The murderers having departed, Imelda, full of apprehensions and
terrible presages of what she should discover, ventured to return
to her chamber, and seeing upon the floor a rivulet of blood, she
followed its direction, and opening the place where her lover lay
she threw herself on the delicate body, still warm and bleeding,
and distracted with tenderness and grief, applied her lips to his
wounds, and drew in the poison with his blood; and whilst
sorrowfully lamenting the loss of her lover, the poison spread
over her whole frame to her heart, and Imelda fell dead in his
arms."

A catastrophe so tragical could not be recited on a stage without affecting in the most sensible manner the most unfeeling
audience. The discovery of it to the public in Bologna could
not, one would think, but melt the most obdurate heart of faction, and soften the savage monster to humanity; but the effect
of it was so contrary to this, that it wrought up the hatred between the two factions to a mortal contagion, which increased
and spread till it ruined and enslaved the republic.

" Whilst the unfortunate fate of Boniface and Imelda depressed
the spirits of the two noble families, the senate understanding
that the city of Forli had rebelled, and that the Aigoni, according
to the stipulation, were not restored to their country, called the
council together, and the question was proposed, Whether they
ought first to march against the rebels of Forli, or merely to
restore the Aigoni to Modena? The Lambertazzi advised, that
the first attention should be given to the cause of the Aigoni;
and, on the contrary, the Gieremei advised, that they should
first endeavor to subjugate Forli. The parties, not agreeing in
opinion, they began to fall into confusion. Finally, the council
of the Gieremei prevailing, the army was sent out, and laid close
siege to Forli.

27*

" The following year, the senate, having much at heart the reduction of Forli, resolved, in order to chastise so great a disobedience, to order out the *carroccio*, and all their army. The pretor entered the senate to take leave for his departure to the war, and there found Antonio Lambertazzi laboring to convince them that the enterprise against Forli would not succeed. After having urged many arguments, he began to speak slightingly of the honor of the Gieremei, who had carried this point against him. Gieremeo Gieremei, who was present, provoked at his insolence, gave him the lie, and by mutual agreement they went out of the palace into the piazza, where they drew their swords and began to combat. A great crowd of the two factions soon gathered about them, and fell to fighting all together, so that much blood was shed, and the battle grew more hot, and greater numbers collected; when Gozzadini and Cavaliere, with many others interfered, parted the combatants, and the Lambertazzi returned to their houses. The pretor, who went with the people to the tumult, wishing to put some restraint of fear upon both parties, ordered four of the houses of each party to be demolished; but this severity had little or no effect; for having grown more bitter than ever against each other, they were almost every day in arms and action together. As this revolt was already divulged to the circumjacent cities, the companies *della Branca*, of *the griffin*, and of the *Lombardi*, understanding that the Guelphs of Modena, and the Ghibellines of Forli, intended to come in to the aid of the two parties, took arms and, together with the people, posted themselves to guard the passages of the city; receiving intelligence that the Guelphs of Modena were on their march, they went out to meet them, and put them to flight at the point of the sword. The Count da Panigo, who had armed himself in favor of the Lambertazzi, hearing of this defeat of his friends, made his escape from the city; but his people were put to the sword by the company *della Branca*, who afterwards razed to the ground all the houses, not only of the count, but of his followers. The Ghibellines from Forli, friends of the Lambertazzi, hearing of the slaughter of the Modenese and the followers of the count, made by the soldiers *della Branca*, suddenly retreated. These civil wars in Bologna were scarcely divulged abroad, when all Romagna, taking advantage of the occasion, rebelled; and for this reason the senate, together with the pretor and the companies, posted themselves at all the ways, to make peace between these two factions; in which enterprise they fortunately at length succeeded, and, after much reasoning and persuasion, they obtained hostages from both sides, and thus the city was quieted.

" While this peace was in treaty, the principal heads of the rebellion of Imola, of Faenza, and of Salarolo, dreading the resentment of the Bolognese at Forli, saved themselves by flight. The Bolognese were indeed formidable, for they were collecting a powerful army to march into Romagna. When it was embodied, and the pretor of Bologna attempted to go out upon the campaign, Antonio Lambertazzi, forgetting his plighted faith, and disregarding the fate of the hostages delivered, flew out again in arms to prevent the *carroccio* from going out, and recommenced a plentiful effusion of blood. This sedition was the most terrible of any that had ever yet happened; it lasted forty days without intermission; so that Bologna became a haunt of murderers, and the streets ran down with human blood; the property of all men was subjected to depredation, the edifices were ruined, and the grandeur and glory of the city trodden under foot.

" The Lambertazzi, at last overcome, fled the city, with all their accomplices, and went to Faenza, leaving their houses and palaces a prey to the people, which, shortly, were all levelled with the ground; and because the pretor and captain of the people had always held a good understanding with the Lambertazzi, they were now deposed from the magistracy, although it is universally agreed that the judgment and decrees of the former were unexceptionably impartial and upright. Fifteen thousand citizens were banished, whose names are distinctly written in a book among the records in the chamber of Bologna. These persons, scattered in various places, planted new families, as the Guerrini in Forli, the Bazzani and Sacchi in Parma, the Malpighi in Lucca, the Carrari in Ravenna, the Buoninsegni in Terni, the Maffei in Rome, the Bagarotti in Placentia and Padua; from which families have arisen men famous both in arms and letters. The Lambertazzi sought an asylum in Faenza and in Forli, and fortified themselves in both those cities; but the Gieremei, not content with having driven them out of the city, endeavored to chase them from the places where they were received; wherefore, that they might not be taken by surprise, they sent to their friends in every place, particularly to the Count di Montefeltro, the Counts of Modiana, and to others of their faction, for succor. The banished citizens of Ravenna, being united with those of Forli, Ariminum, and other places, went to Forli, and from thence to Faenza, and there fortified themselves, and a little afterwards drove out the Manfredi; and passing afterwards to Castel San Piero, and from thence to Salarolo, where the Manfredi had resorted, and having taken the castle, many of their enemies were put to death, and many made prisoners and sent to Forli, among whom was Alberico Manfredi.

"At Bologna, many of the faction of Lambertazzi were imprisoned; and as a report was spread that a powerful succor was arrived to the Gieremei, the Lambertazzi, with their wives and children, fled to the mountains, and from thence to Faenza, where, with the assistance of their friends, they began to collect forces. The Gieremei, receiving information that the Lambertazzi were preparing to return to Bologna, consulted in council upon the project of going out first in search of them. The resolution was taken with great precipitation, and they marched out with the *carroccio* with great spirit to Romagna. The Ghibellines, who were apprized of their approach, went out suddenly to meet them in arms, and the Guelph party were defeated, leaving three of the Gieremei dead upon the field, and Alberghetto Manfredi mortally wounded and a prisoner. This reverse of fortune spread a terror in Bologna; but, dreading a total loss of their city, they exerted themselves to the utmost to fortify it, and had recourse again to their confederates and friends, and in a short time assembled a strong army. It is unnecessary to enumerate all the places and parties from whence each side drew its aids; but the *carroccio* again went forth, and was again met by the Lambertazzi and their allies, when another terrible engagement ensued, and again the Lambertazzi remained victorious. Two thousand men were slain, among whom were a great number of the principal nobles. The Lambertazzi pursued their victory into the territory of Bologna, where they put every thing to fire and sword, destroying vines, trees, corn, and houses, and took a great number of castles, and, it is supposed, might have made themselves masters of the city, such was the panic in it, without striking another blow; but, thinking they had done enough for the present, they returned to Faenza.

"The Bolognese, finding their affairs unfortunate, both at home and abroad, deliberated on sending to King Charles for assistance, and two ambassadors accordingly went, Passaggieri and Prendiparti. Many citizens displayed their public spirit in defence of the city and senate, and subscribed large sums to defend their liberty; Passaggieri, for example, was so attached to the Gieremei, that he gave six thousand pounds for the common good. The senate by proclamation ordered, that every citizen possessed of a horse should have him recorded in a book, that they might know what assistance the militia might have in case of extremity, and the name of every man who then owned a horse is very carefully preserved as a family distinction.

"The Lambertazzi,[1] after their victory over the Gieremei, did not fail to make incursions into the country of Bologna every day, disturbing now one place, and then another, in such a manner, that there was not a castle, village, or city, of that party, that was not infested, or threatened with their arms. The Bolognese, apprehensive that the evil might extend itself too far, and that the people, wearied with so many calamities, might revolt, and having before their eyes what Rodolph the emperor had done, they began to meditate a surrender of the city to the pope; ambassadors were appointed, who were courteously received, and their petition attended to, at Viterbo. The pope was vastly pleased with the submission of Bologna, and she acknowledged the church and the pontiff for her patron. The instrument is dated twenty-ninth July, 1278, by which the ambassadors, 'in the name of God, and of the podestà, captain, council, and commons, recognize the dominion, diction, law, jurisdiction, power, and principality of the city, territory, and district in St. Peter, the keeper of the key of the kingdom of heaven, and in Nicolas III., and his successors, Roman pontiffs, reserving the laws and rights of the city, territory, and district.'

"Although the Gieremei discovered an obstinate aversion to any kind of peace or reconciliation with the Lambertazzi, the pope conceived a great desire of uniting Romagna and Bologna in his interest, and, after long negotiations to that purpose, he succeeded in persuading both parties to listen to his proposals,

---

[1] Ghirardacci, lib. viii. p. 233.

U

and submit to his decision. The constitution of the pope Nicolas III., 'upon the reformation of the peace of the Bolognese, to wit, the Gieremei and Lambertazzi,' was made, and the prisoners on both sides set at liberty ; and in 1279, the two factions of Gieremei and Lambertazzi were assembled once more in the piazza of Bologna, in presence of the cardinal legates of the pope, appearing in great pomp and splendor. The families of the party of the Lambertazzi and of that of the Gieremei were all recorded by name, and, after long orations made by the cardinals, the instruments were signed, and the oaths of perpetual peace and friendship taken by them all."

The proceedings, as they remain on record, are very voluminous, and it is not possible a peace should be made with more solemnity or less reserve; but of what avail are pious exhortations, charitable resolutions, or solemn oaths, against inveterate passions in unbalanced governments?

In 1280, "the Lambertazzi, who could not live under the operation of the secret venom of their personal hatreds, which daily corroded their hearts, making little account of the peace made, or the penalties imposed, burning with desire to imbrue their hands in the blood of the Gieremei, having taken their arms, flew to the piazza, and finding there a great number of their enemies, fell upon them with a sudden fury; after a long combat, they pushed the Gieremei out of the piazza, and made themselves masters of it, and would have easily possessed the palace, if the captain with two thousand men, had not rushed into the midst of the danger, and with the Caccianemici, Lambertini, Ariosti, Prendiparti, and other friends, opposed them, and, at the point of the sword, driven them back, and pursued them out of the city. The battle on both sides was bloody, and many principal men were killed in it, after performing prodigies of valor. The Lambertazzi, thus again driven from the city with their arms, retired to the mountains with great loss, and the Gieremei proceeded to the old work of ruining their houses, within and without the city ; and having issued a proclamation against a great number, they sent others into confinement, according to the usage in such cases in those times. Berthold, the count of Romagna, the pope's nephew, immediately summoned all parties to appear before him, and give an account who were the aggressors in the late revolution, and prevailed upon the Gieremei and Lambertazzi to give hostages to perform the award for settling their differences; but before the affair could be finished the pope died, and Berthold restored the hostages to the Guelphs, but the Lambertazzi not acting to his satisfaction, he carried theirs to Rome.

" Bologna now remaining in the hands of the Gieremei, four officers were immediately created, whose duty it was to preserve the peace of the city, and to them was given the highest possible authority; and they began their operations with so much prudence and firmness, that their proceedings gave great satisfaction to the citizens, and with whatever they ordered or desired the people complied with affection and confidence, excepting some of the followers of the Lambertazzi, who not being able to bear the sight of the city at peace, while their party were driven out of it, began, by slow degrees and secret practices, to consult of measures to make themselves masters of it, and restore their banished party. For many days they discoursed together in secret upon this project, and hoping that fortune might for once favor and assist them, they determined finally to assault the piazza; and because all the city was in security, and lived in peace, they readily persuaded themselves, that by surprise their design would succeed. One day, at the hour of dinner, issuing out in arms, and crying with a lively accent, *The people and the church !* they seized on the two mouths of the piazza. The Gieremei, as soon as they were alarmed, ran out with the people in general with arms in their hands, and coming to a fierce engagement with their enemies, after a plentiful effusion of blood, drove them out of the city to the mountains, to go from thence to Faenza and dwell with their friends.

" The city of Bologna now purified of all tumults, the senate attended to the fortification of all the fortresses and castles in the country, placed strong garrisons, and furnished plenty of provisions, and all things necessary; and the commanders placed in them, we may well suppose, were all good Guelphs and Gieremeites. The Lambertazzi having taken refuge in Faenza, and partly in Forli, those who were in Faenza, following the activity, ardor, and boldness of their genius, began to live with so much liberty, that it appeared as if Faenza was their own. This conduct was observed, and excited not only much censure, but the greatest malevolence in the citizens, and, among others, in Tibal-

dello Zambrasio, one of the most noble in Faenza. This nobleman, seeing himself exposed to the ridicule of the town, on
account of a pig which the Lambertazzi had made so free as to
take from him, and because they had threatened his life for
demanding the restoration of it, grew into such a rage, that he
swore he would lose his life, or have satisfaction. After talking
much of various projects, he at last determined upon one
which he had never talked of at all. He pretended to be
seized with a melancholy humor; went strangely out of his
house sometimes, flying the company of his friends and relations; appearing in the streets uncommonly thoughtful; sometimes talking to himself of a variety of things, and muttering
imperfect sentences. Having held this course of life for some
days, his infirmity became divulged through the whole city. · In
a few days more, without confiding his secret to his father or
any other, he counterfeited the part of a complete idiot; and his
behavior was so wild, whimsical, and extravagant, that he appeared both to his father and brother to be wholly bereaved of
his understanding. It threw his family into distress, and the
whole city into the utmost astonishment, to see a nobleman who
had ever shown so much prudence as to be held in high esteem,
fallen suddenly into such misfortune and disgrace, though so
worthy of compassion. In a few days more he took from his
own farm an old mare, wholly worn out, and reduced to a mere
skeleton; and having shaved her with a pair of scissors, trans-
formed her into such an object as excited the laughter of every
one who saw her. In this condition he led her into the city,
and there turned her loose. The boys soon collected about the
animal, and beat and terrified her till she ran, with all the strength
and spirit that remained in her, throughout the whole city, and
occasioned a general hubbub wherever she went.

"The Lambertazzi, knowing nothing of the notorious fact,
any more than of the secret motive, were alarmed with suspicions that their enemies were rising, seized their arms, and ran
about to every place where they heard the loudest shouts and
noises. Finding it was only an idle populace insulting Tibaldello's mare, they joined with others in the laugh, and returned
to their houses. The same pageantry having been repeated
more than once afterwards, the Ghibellines became so secure,
that when they heard a similar cry, they said it was 'only Tibal-

dello's mare.' Rising at length to the third stage of counterfeited madness, Tibaldello ran about the streets in the night, and cried out, 'To arms! to arms!' and taking in his hands the padlocks and bars of the city gates, which were sometimes carelessly left, he raised a very great multitude and a mighty rumor, so as again to alarm the Lambertazzi, and drive them to their arms; but, finding it another freak of Tibaldello, they threatened him severely if he should make any more such disturbance, and returned. By these whimsical movements, frequently repeated, he so effectually quieted the suspicions of the Lambertazzi and Ghibellines, that upon any such uproar they laughed with the rest, and made themselves merry with the crazy whimsies of Tibaldello. With so much art and perseverance was the folly simulated, that all suspicions were quieted, not only in the Ghibellines, but in the whole city; and the belief of his irrecoverable folly was universal.

"Having pursued his plan thus far with success, he opened himself in perfect confidence to a very faithful friend, made him acquainted with his design, and desired him to prepare with secrecy two habits of monks, in a sack, and meet him the next day in a forest in the neighborhood of Faenza. This was done; and at the hour prescribed they met, Tibaldello having gone out of town with all the appearance of a madman, disguised like a falconer, with two dogs attending him, and a hawk in his hand, to the high diversion of every one that met him. Arrived at a lonely place in the forest, he set his dogs and his hawk at liberty, and, with his faithful companion, putting on the habits of friars, that they might not be known by any whom they might meet on the road, and travelling all night, at the opening of the gates in the morning they arrived at Bologna, and took lodgings at the house of Alberto Battagliucci. To Guido Ramponi he related all that had passed, explained his intentions, and by his favor obtained an introduction to the council of secrecy. Here he opened his whole design, and the desire he had to chastise the Lambertazzi; and showed them of how much importance it was to them to embrace the present opportunity to remove from their sight and their apprehensions those enemies of their city and people, who were constantly employed in schemes of mischief against both. This counsel was received with pleasure by the whole body, and the business was referred to the four superintendents of peace, under oath to keep it secret. To these

Tibaldello methodically communicated his plan, and demanded only for himself, and all the family of the Zambrasi, and Ghirardone, his faithful friend, and his family, to be made citizens of Bologna; and engaged to send hostages as security for what was to be done. The offers of Tibaldello were very satisfactory to the pretor, and Guidottino Prendiparte pledged himself for the family of Zambrasi. The four superintendents made him relate the method and means by which every thing was to be conducted; and the stratagem appearing to be practicable, they again took an oath to keep the whole a secret.

"The business concluded on, they dismissed Tibaldello, who was to procure the hostages; so, setting out the same evening, he reached Faenza at the opening of the gates, and entered the city without being known by any one. Arrived at his house, he found his whole family in great affliction. To his aged father alone he related in order the progress he had made by means of a feigned madness, in his plan against those who had taken little account of the honor of his family and blood. The father, with joy beyond expression, and a thousand embraces of his son, caused to be assembled in his house all their relations, to whom, in an eloquent and prudent harangue, Tibaldello related his actions and designs. All with one voice and one heart offered to devote themselves to vengeance on the Lambertazzi. Tibaldello, to whom an hour appeared a thousand years, till he could see an end of his enterprise, the next day secretly sent his three brothers,—namely, Zambraso, Guido, and Fiorino, to Bologna, conducted by Ghirardone, informing the four superintendents of what they were to do, and of the hour when their soldiers ought to appear at Faenza. The hostages received, the council assembled, digested every particular, and secretly gave orders that all the passes should be secured, that no one might be able to send intelligence of any thing that happened.

"On the twenty-third of August, 1281, the army of Bologna was formed, and marched out of the city in order, with all the Guelph party; by a forced march the whole night, they were early in the morning at the gate appointed; finding it open, they freely entered the city, and were conducted to the place intended for action. The Zambrasi had embarrassed and stopped up the streets where they thought proper; and Tibaldello, as usual, feigning to make a noise with the padlocks at the gates of the houses of the Lambertazzi, in truth fastened many of them within, so that they could not go out. The whole apparatus being ready, he set up a cry of *Long live the church!* and *Down with all the traitors!* and while he was terrifying the city with this horrid outcry, the Bolognese, with the utmost security, made themselves masters of the piazza of the city. The Ghibellines, followers of the Lambertazzi, hearing the noise of voices and the sound of arms, rang the bells, assembled a great number, and hastened to the piazza, there to fortify themselves; but, finding the Guelphs already in possession, they began the conflict."

The particulars of this engagement, the danger of one and intrepidity of another individual, are not now material. "The action was sharp and bloody; and after mighty feats of valor on both sides, and many killed and wounded, the Lambertazzi were defeated, and such as could, obliged to fly into the country; all who could not, were put to the sword. Nine of the principals fled to a church or monastery for sanctuary, but were there miserably put to death. Besides five hundred prisoners, a multitude of others wretchedly perished in the sinks and ditches.

"The Bolognese, having obtained the victory, and by means of it the complete dominion of Faenza, pardoned the Faentines, but confiscated all the property of the Lambertazzi and their adherents, both within and without the city. Finally, they appointed a new pretor and a sufficient guard, and triumphantly conducted Tibaldello Zambrasi, his father, and with them Zambraso, Guido, and Fiorino, the hostages, and their sister and other relations, to Bologna, who were all made by the senate not only citizens, but nobles. The same honors and immunities were conferred on Ghirardone and his relations, to all of whom the senate gave houses and possessions, and they enjoyed the most respectable offices in the state. As the victory was the twenty-fourth of August, the senate ordained an annual festival of St. Bartholomew's day, in perpetual commemoration of Tibaldello; in which his pig, his mare, his hawks, dogs, friar's dress, and city keys, were all transmitted, in sculpture and marble, to the amusement and astonishment of posterity.

"The nobles of the party of Lambertazzi, who were still remaining in Forli, sent ambassadors to the pope to obtain peace, but they could accomplish nothing; the pope not only refused to receive them, but ordered them to return. The Gieremei sent ambassadors, and they were admitted to an audience, and received with dignity; and by their persuasions the pope sent Giovanni Appia, a French gentleman, a counsellor of King Charles, with eight hundred cavalry, to recover Forli. The pope made him Count of Romagna, and he went with the ambassadors to Bologna, where he was received with great honor; where he remained, however, but a short time; for having in 1282 despatched what belonged to his office, he took with him two of the tribes of the city, and marched into the territory of Ravenna. From thence he wrote to the republic of Forli, commanding them to send out of their city the Count Guido da Feltrio, and all the foreigners; but he was not obeyed, because neither the Count nor the Lambertazzi, to whom he wrote at the same time, were willing to go."

Their refusal gave occasion to another long war, and to all the fire and sword, stratagems and massacres, as well as carnage in battle, that usually attended all their wars. But though these evils also originated in the same source, the imperfect constitution of Bologna, they may be passed over.

"It seems there were still some persons left in Bologna of the name of Lambertazzi, one of whom, in 1285, came to blows with one of the Scannabecchi under the piazza, which occasioned another rising of the people in arms. They were both put to flight, but overtaken in the country, and beheaded; and all the party of the Lambertazzi were again declared rebels, and all their families banished to a certain distance in the city, and confined to places assigned them. The wise men (*sapienti*) afterwards made a provision, that all those of the party of the Lambertazzi who had taken an oath of fidelity to the church and the party of the Gieremei, according to a general regulation made in the council of the commons and people of Bologna, should be cancelled from the book of the exiles, excepting those who, since taking the oath, had gone to live in Faenza, Forli, and other places, and united themselves with the enemies of the people of Bologna; and with this reservation, that none who had been of the party of the Lambertazzi at the time of the first commotion, should be of the council, or hold any office. This regulation gave great satisfaction to the city, and a general tranquillity.

"But the government had not strength to preserve the peace. In 1286, a private quarrel, however, happened, probably from the general state of parties, in which Gualradi, of the company *della Branca*, was killed. The government was neither able to punish the murderer nor to prevent the people from taking it upon themselves in their own way. They took arms for revenge, and ruined all the houses, towers, trees, and other property of the persons guilty or suspected, both in the city and out of it, and of all their relations. But the new government could not long remain quiet. The council of eight hundred, and the people, having their eyes fixed upon the general utility of the city and its district, that all things might be governed with consummate prudence, gave orders to the sapienti to examine how a new council might be established, of two thousand persons, of sufficient wisdom, charity, and property to support the weight of the commonwealth. The sapienti, elected by the antiani and consuls, having maturely deliberated and debated, ordained that the new council of two thousand should be elected by ballot in that council; that is to say, that a hundred electors for each tribe should be appointed, each of whom should have the election of five members of the new council; that each one should be not less than eighteen nor more than seventy years of age, and should be truly of the party of the church and of the Gieremei of the city of Bologna, and so held and reputed in the time of the first commotion which happened in the city; that he should not be a servant,* a puppet-showman, a porter, nor a foreigner, &c., nor a constant inhabitant of the country of Bologna, and should have been a constant resident in the city for twenty years; should be rated to the public taxes, and have paid his share of the public collections; should be known in the lists of the public factions, but should not be a clergyman or ecclesiastical person, nor of any other city, castle, or land which has favored the Ghibellines or the party of the Lambertazzi. If there were any one at present in the council, in any of the cases enumerated in this order, he could not be chosen by any elector whatsoever; and if he obtained a ticket as an elector, he could not vote himself in any manner. No one could be elected contrary to the preceding form, under penalty of banishment and a fine of twenty pounds for every one that should vio-

---

* "Non sia servo, burrattino, brentatore, fachino, nè fumante, o forestiero." p. 270.

The translator omits to notice a remarkable qualification which precedes these, " che sia senza macchia d' infamia alcuna."

28 *

late it, and for every offence; and any one who should be elected contrary to this order should not take the oath of a counsellor, nor proceed to choose another, under the same penalty. Every election made against it should be null, and any one might inform secretly or openly of a breach of this law, and obtain the penalty. The antiani, consuls, and doctors of laws and their notaries should be of this council *ex officio*, in addition to the number of two thousand; but no one was to be a member who was not a native of the city. The senate then caused to be distinctly recorded, in three books, the names of the banished Lambertazzi, repaired the *carroccio* and its standard, and painted it with the portraits of six saints, and laid out upon it no less than thirty pounds and ten pence."

Many other regulations and precautions were taken by the triumphant faction of the Gieremei, to fortify themselves in the government, and exclude, in the most decided manner, every man who had any tincture of, or connection with, the opposite party; but still there were not wanting many seditious persons, insidiously meditating to undermine their tranquillity, and to favor those who were held to be rebels against them; so that the senate were frequently alarmed, and full of apprehensions of the total ruin of the city.

They saw that almost the whole country was one continued tavern of the banished (*banditti*); and, to put some restraint upon their temerity, purge both the city and country of such a dangerous plague, and quiet the seditions of the nobles, they assembled the antiani, consuls, and all the sapienti, made many ordinances against the banished rebels, to the end that no fresh revolution might be attempted; and made it a capital crime to attempt or propose, or even to speak or reason about their restoration or pardon.*

* There is another anecdote in 1288, which, although it remains in mysterious obscurity, may yet be alleged as an instance of those extravagant characters, irregular events, and atrocious actions, which always abound in such governments, render the protection of the laws precarious, and life and liberty insecure. "Ambassadors had been sent by the republic to Forli, and to the Count of Romagna; and other ambassadors were sent to the Marquis of Este, to congratulate him upon his interposition to promote an accommodation between the citizens of Reggio, who were truly of the party of the church, and to beg that by his counsels and mediation he would prevail upon Bettino Galluzzi, elected captain of Reggio, to hearken to reason, and restore some merchandises taken at Rubiera from Bolognese merchants. Lamberto Bazzilieri, a Bolognese, had contracted friendships with many persons in the court of Obizzo, Marquis of Este, and

In the beginning of the year 1289, all their prudence appeared
to be ineffectual; for in their own faction, and in the new government, were two parties still, the nobles and plebeians, and a
tumult arose between them.   The senate, the pretor of the preceding year, and the people, became involved in the dispute, till
the pretor thought his life in danger, and secretly went away from
the city with many of his friends.   The want and the necessity
of representatives of the people was felt at this time; and whether it was to obtain information, or to throw off a burden of
care and labor, or to gratify some aspiring individuals, or to
please the people, or to extend their influence, or whether all
these motives concurred, the antiani, assembled in the chamber
of the pretor, considered among themselves what ought chiefly
to be done relative to the war at this time to be carried on in
conjunction with their confederates; and they ordained that two
wise men, of exemplary lives, should be elected from each tribe,
who should examine, and, in concert with them, the antiani,
inquire in what state were the stipendiaries of the commons of
Bologna, and see whether the soldiers had their horses according
to law, and whether provision was made of money to pay salaries,
wages, &c.   But who was to elect these wise men?   Not the
people; not the tribes themselves.   This would have made two
centres; and all authority must be in one.   The antiani themselves therefore elected them; and in the afternoon the antiani
and the wise men assembled together, and consulted generally

frequented familiarly all the courtiers of that prince; so that he was held to be
one of that court. Finding Obizzo at table one day at dinner, Lamberto, without
being observed by any one, approached very near the person of the prince, drew
his dagger, and, with a rapid and malicious force of his arm, gave him an unexpected stroke across the visage. Azzo, the prince's son, and all the other courtiers and citizens present, laid their hands upon their swords, and rushed upon
the malefactor to put him to death; Obizzo, though his face was covered with
blood, had the presence of mind to command them to desist, but ordered him to
be put to the torture. to make him confess from what motive, and at whose instigation, he had made such a desperate attempt. After a long and cruel examination on the rack, he declared that he had not done it by the orders, or at the
desire, or by the advice of any one. nor excited by any hope. nor in consequence
of any previous conversation or thoughts, but that he had been urged on by a
sudden fury. This confession not being credited, he was examined again repeatedly, but, with the same constancy and fortitude, persevered in the same confession; nor could all his torment extort from him any other answer. Finally,
bound to the tails of four asses, he was dragged through all the city of Ferrara,
and afterwards hanged." This action is an example of that contempt of life,
that inveteracy of resolution, and that immovable fortitude, which is sometimes
inspired by the inflamed passions of party; but his denial is by no means a proof
that the plan was not concerted.

about the soldiers; and it was concluded that the number in pay ought not to be diminished, but rather increased; and that particular attention should be given to the collection of the revenue upon several articles, as grain, salt, mills, &c., that money might be had in season to pay the soldiers their stipends, &c.

But there is not time nor room to pursue this relation. It must be sufficient to add, that affairs went on in this curious manner to the final catastrophe of all such governments, an establishment of absolute power in a single man. There were in Italy, in the middle ages, a hundred or two of cities, all independent republics, and all constituted nearly in the same manner. The history of one is, under different names and various circumstances, the history of all; and all, excepting two or three that are still decided aristocracies, had the same destiny, an exit in monarchy. There are extant a multitude of particular histories of these cities, full of excellent warning for the people of America.* Let me recommend it to you, my young readers, who have time enough before you, to make yourselves masters of the Italian language, and avail your country of all the instruction contained in them, as well as of all the art, science, and literature which we owe to Greece, Italy, and Palestine, countries which have been and are our masters in all things.

* By all of them is verified the observation of a liberal writer, quoted before: "These republics were all exposed to almost daily revolutions; and seldom did the system of administration continue a whole year the same." Danina, *Revolutions of Literature*, c. v. sect. 10.

A

DEFENCE

OF THE

CONSTITUTIONS OF GOVERNMENT

OF THE

UNITED STATES OF AMERICA,

AGAINST THE ATTACK OF M. TURGOT, IN HIS LETTER TO DR.
PRICE, DATED THE TWENTY-SECOND DAY OF MARCH, 1778.

BY

JOHN ADAMS.

IN THREE VOLUMES.

VOL. III.

A.

DEFENCE

CONSTITUTIONS OF GOVERNMENT

OF THE

UNITED STATES OF AMERICA.

CHAPTER SEVENTH.

ITALIAN REPUBLICS.

PISTOIA.

"THE Roman republic, according to its custom* of putting judges in all places under its dominion, sent to Pistoia a pretor, who had the whole jurisdiction, civil and criminal, over the city; reserving always, according to the tenor of the Roman laws, obedience to the magistrates of that commonwealth. This jurisdiction, acquired by the Roman republic over the city of Pistoia, passed to the Roman emperors, and from these, into the power of the Goths and the Lombards, and successively of those who, from time to time, were lords (*signore*) of Tuscany; and it has continued, down to our times, under the same tie and obligation of dependence. It is very true, that the province being

---

* Memorie Storiche della città di Pistoia, raccolte da Jacopo Maria Fioravanti, nobile Patrizio Pistoiese. Edit. Lucca, 1758, cap. ii. p. 15.

liberated from the government of foreign nations, and its governors (*dominatori*) having permitted the people to make laws
and create magistrates, the authority became divided; hence,
when the concession was made to the Pistoians to create magistrates, to take the name of consuls, and to form the general
council of the people, they were permitted to expedite, by the
authority of these, many things in their city; reserving always,
nevertheless, the sovereignty to their lords.

" This concession of governing themselves by their own laws,
obtained by the provinces of Italy, was the pure liberality of
Charlemagne,* at a time when, having delivered them entirely
from the government of the barbarians, he placed them under
the command of one of his royal ministers, with the title of
marquis, or of duke. Under this system of government Tuscany was comprehended, which had its dukes and marquises,
who governed it. But as it was the custom of Charlemagne,
and, long after him, of his successors, to send to the cities of
this province two subaltern ministers, one with the name of
castaldo, or governor, and the other with that of count, which is
as much as to say, judge of the city, who held his courts of justice either alone, or in conjunction with the castaldo, and very
often with the bishop of the place, as the bishops were assessors
and officers, deputed as vassals of the king or the emperor; so
the city of Pistoia was a long time ruled and governed by this
order of castaldi and counts.

" Otho II., having ascended the imperial throne, and having
conducted the affairs of Italy with little good fortune, the people began to think it lawful to lose their respect, and to fail
in their veneration for the imperial commands, and the cities
advancing in their inclination for liberty, many of them began
to reassume the title of consuls, which had been extinct under
the Lombards; and if these had somewhat of a greater authority, nevertheless, they were not exempt from the jurisdiction of
the dukes and marquises, or from the sovereignty of the kings
and emperors.

" A greater spirit of independence arising in the minds of the
Italians, in the time of those great discords between the empire
and the church, diminished to such a degree the esteem of the

---

* Sigonius, *De Regno Italiæ*, lib. iv.

people towards the emperors, solemnly excommunicated by the pontiffs, that a great part of the cities of Italy, estranging themselves by little and little from their obedience, began to conduct themselves like independent states, in entire freedom. This happened in the time of Henry IV. and V.; and the disobedience increased still more, when all the German forces were engaged to sustain, in Germany, the competition between Lothario II. and Conrad the Suabian, for the throne of Cæsar. Then the cities, taking advantage of the distance of those who had power to bridle their arrogance, began to be insolent;[*] then they began to lift up their heads, and to do whatever seemed good in their own eyes; then they thought it lawful to appropriate to themselves many of the rights of royalty due to their sovereign; and believing themselves able to shake off the yoke of superiority, they attended to nothing but to their present advantage, and to extend the limits of their usurped liberty. But with all this, they were never able to extinguish the nature of their subjection, nor the obligation of dependence; for Frederick I. passed over to establish and regulate their privileges, in the convention of Constance, and the rights of royalty which had been then usurped. And the people were held to an annual census,[†] and obliged to perform certain royal and personal services.

In the twelfth century, the cities, after the similitude of ancient Rome, all reassumed the title of consuls, and began, some sooner and others later, to make their proper statutes, and establish their popular government. Though it is not possible to ascertain the precise time when the institution of consuls was first made in Pistoia, they are, nevertheless, found named in the statutes of 1107; and of these there were two, called the *Consul of the Soldiers*, and the *Consul of Justice*, taken from the nobility of the place, and were called the *Greater Consuls*, to distinguish them from the plebeian consuls of the second class, called the *Lesser Consuls*, or *Consuls of the Merchants*, taken from the common people. Their authority, and sometimes their number varied; but there was ever to be one more of the popular than of the greater consuls.[‡] The election of these magistrates

---

[*] His diebus, propter absentiam regis, Italiæ urbibus in insolentiam decedentibus .. Otho of Frisingen.

[†] Sigonius, *De Regno Italiæ*, lib. xiii.

[‡] Unus plus de popularibus quam de majoribus.

was made every year by the people, with the intervention of all the governors (*rettori*) of the arts of the city; and they governed, with a council of a hundred of the better sort of citizens, administering justice both to the laity and the ecclesiastics. This council, besides its extraordinary assemblies, was obliged to meet in the months of March, May, July, and September, after a previous intimation, given by the consuls, of the business to be done; and for the result of this assembly, all determinations upon things of most importance must wait; and all laws, resolutions, and deliberations, first proposed and digested in the smaller council by the few, must be here confirmed or rejected."

Here again is a constitution of all authority in one assembly. The council of a hundred was sovereign. The consuls, though they had the command of the army, and the judgment of causes, could do nothing in administration by themselves, or with advice of their little council. They had no negative upon any deliberation or resolution of the great council; and, on the other hand, the people had no negative, not even the poor protection of a tribunitian veto. Accordingly we read, in the next paragraph, that

" The power of the people having greatly increased, by means of their usurped liberty,[1] the factions had become numerous, and so much the more intractable and seditious, as the incentive of power was become the greater. In 1155, the emperor Frederick I., after having reduced Milan to his obedience, and received the oaths of fidelity from all the other cities of Italy, and, among the rest, from those of Tuscany, in order to obviate the continual tumults which arose, judged it necessary to institute the office and dignity of podestà, and to send to the government of those cities gentlemen from among the foreign nobility, with that title. This commission of podestà operated to the damage and diminution of the influence of the consuls, because in this magistrate was vested the whole judicial power, both in private and civil causes, and in those which were public and criminal; and therefore the podestà was the ordinary judge in the city,[*] with full power, dominion, and authority to govern, command, and

---

[*] Con tutta la balià, impero, e potestà di governare, comandare, e castigare. Fioravanti, p. 18.

[1] The historian seems to have had little notion of natural rights.

chastise, granted to him by the emperor, to whom, as their legitimate sovereign, the people had recourse in cases of appeal, and in all denials of justice.

" From its subjection to this minister, in the earliest times of the institution of his office, the city of Pistoia was again oppressed; and, as the nomination was reserved directly to the sovereign, so the officer was changed as often as the times seemed to him to require. The discords and dissensions having become softened by length of time, Pistoia acquired the right of election of this minister, who obliged himself, in many things, to follow the various ordinances and resolutions of the consuls. This election of the podestà was made by the Pistoians in virtue of a municipal law consented to by the sovereign; the person elected remained in office only six months, and was chosen by the council of the people, as it was called, that is, the council of a hundred, with the intervention of all the *rettori* of the chapels, and of the arts. The podestà was bound to carry with him judges skilful in the laws, notaries, two companies of militia, horses, and servants, and other followers; and these officers were obliged in all things to render their accounts. It was customary to confer this dignity of podestà upon the chief citizens. The consuls or the podestà, jointly or severally, had no authority to impose taxes, to consent to war, peace, truce, or alliance, without the council of the people, which consisted of a hundred citizens, elected in the proportion of five and twenty for each of the four gates or quarters of the city, with the addition of all the *rettori* of the chapels, and of the arts."

In other words, the podestà, consuls, council of a hundred, and rectors of the chapels and arts, were all collected in one assembly, to determine on grants for money, peace, war, truce, alliance, &c., and all questions were determined by the vote of the majority, which necessarily made that tempestuous and capricious government in one centre, against which we contend.

"And to the podestà, for his regulation in the exercise of his office, were given by the city fourteen counsellors, and two judges; one *de lege*, that is to say, doctor of laws; the other *ex usu* or *de usu*, which they interpreted, a protector of the commons; and two advocates for arguing each cause. With the opinion of all these, he decided upon those things which affected the honor or utility of the public, as, after having made his election of these

attendants, he was obliged to stand by their advice.* This
podestà, in early times, superintended not only the secular, but
the ecclesiastical government; but in process of time the city
became governed by three, namely,—the consuls, the podestà, and
the bishop; for the bishop had profited of the violent dissensions
that prevailed in the city, to draw to himself various rights
and jurisdictions, as has happened in other nations.

" The lordship of the podestà, therefore, having preponderated
over the authority of the consuls, these were gone, when the
office of captain of the people was created. This institution
happened in Pistoia, when the Guelph party, by an increase of
their numbers and strength, acquired the superiority of the Ghibellines; at which time, the lordship was taken from the podestà .
with a great concourse and tumult of the people, and nothing
was left him but the charge of hearing and determining civil
causes. Twelve anziani of the people were then instituted, and
the authority of the consuls was transferred to them.

" The last appearance of the consuls in the records of Pistoia,
is in 1248, and the first of the captain of the people, in 1267;
when it is said in the statute, that the captain of the people was
the first ruler of the city, and the primary defender of its rights,
and that he ought chiefly to watch over the conservation of the
peace; that he was the judge of appeals, and of all causes in
the second instance; that he had cognizance of crimes; that he
governed with supreme authority, united with that of the anziani;
that he kept a court, of the same kind as that of the podestà,
but more numerous; and that the city gave him, for ornament
and defence, three hundred of the best and ablest men, who,
taking an oath of fidelity to him, stood continually in his service.† The election of this ruler was to be made by the anziani,
in the person of some foreigner, and not of any citizen of Pistoia, notwithstanding, some of the primary citizens did in fact
obtain this office, as appears by the records. Yet the anziani
were sworn not to elect any man of Tuscany, or of the city of
Pistoia, of its district, or other place adjoining to the city or its

* His oath was, Et petam a consiliariis toto tempore mei dominii de rebus,
quæ mihi videbuntur expectare ad communem honorem, et utilitatem nostræ civitatis Pistorii. Fioravanti, pp. 18, 19.

† Volumus quod eligantur trecenti boni homines de populo Pistoriense, de
melioribus et potentioribus, pro manutentione et defensione Capitanei. Rubrica
cento della Legge del 1274.

bishopric. The words of the law, in the twelfth rubric of 1267, are, ' Nos anthiani populi Pistoriensis, juramus, sine aliquo intellectu nobis dato, vel dando eligi, vel eligi facere nobis, et Pist. unum bonum et virum prudentem majorem XXX. ann. in nostrum capitaneum populi devotum, et fidelem ecclesiæ, qui non sit de civitate Pistorii, vel districtu, et qui non sit de Tuscia . . . vel de aliqua terra, quæ confinet cum civitate, vel episcopatu, vel districtu Pistorii.' And this dignity of captain of the people was in such reputation, that, in some places, princes were chosen, and sometimes even the pontiffs; and such personages, by means of their vicars, often exercised it.

" The captain of the people, therefore, being the conservator of the peace, and the defender of the rights of the city, the Pistoians, to give him a strong arm to bridle those who had unquiet and restless brains, thought it necessary to create certain companies of armed men, who, at the sound of a bell, should be obliged to assemble in the piazza, in order to execute the orders which should be given them by this officer and the *anziani*, without whose permission they were not allowed to depart. These companies were called by the name of the Equestrian and Pedestrian Orders, because they were composed of both horse and footmen. They were afterwards augmented to twelve, in the proportion of three for each quarter, which embraced an infinite number of people; and every company had two captains, one *gonfalonier*, whose office was to carry the standard of his company, and four counsellors; and it was the duty of the captain of the people to procure the election of these officers, as is asserted in the statute of 1267, rubric 19: ' Teneatur capitaneus *del popolo*, primo mense sui regiminis, eligi facere duos capitaneos, unum gonfalonerium, et quatuor consiliarios pro qualibet compagnia civit. Pist. pro factis ipsius compagniæ.' And in the additional laws of 1286, eight priors were added to these companies, two for each quarter; and other orders were made for the good regulation of this militia.

" The twelve *anziani* were created with the same authority and full power which the consuls had held; but the precise year cannot be ascertained. The number of members of which the new magistrature was composed, appears by a law of 1267: ' Ordinamus quod duodecim anthiani populi civit. Pist. sint et esse debeant in civitate Pistoria.' These twelve magistrates were renewed every two months; and afterwards, as appears by a law of 1277, it was established, that the *anzianate* should not continue longer than one month; and this magistracy of the *anziani* was elected by a council of the people of two hundred, by the *rettori* of the arts and their counsellors, and by the captains, gonfaloniers, and counsellors of the companies of the people, and by the *anziani pro tempore.* The head of the *anziani* was, in the primitive times, called *prior*, and not *gonfalonier.* The prior being the first dignity among the *anziani*, each member enjoyed it in rotation for an equal number of days, (as the president's chair of the States General is filled by all the members in turn, for one week, at the Hague.)   This prior had great authority, as appears by a law of 1267, written in the thirty-seventh rubric: 'Anthiani teneantur facere, et faciant inter se, unum priorem de ipsis anthianis adjectum ipsis, sicut eis videbitur de tempore, cui cæteri anthiani pareant, et parere debeant, et obedire; et qui contrafecerit puniatur a priore anthianorum.'   Although the name of gonfalonier appears in the records of some of these years, yet certainly he was not the head of the *anziani*, but of the arts; thus, in the law of 1283: 'Item capitaneus debeat spendere et assignare gonfalonem gonfaloneriis electis, vel eligendis, ab unaquaque arte et populo .... ita quod unaquæque ars suos gonfalonerios et officiales habeat.'   From this it clearly appears, that these gonfaloniers were the heads of the arts, and not of the supreme magistrature of the *anziani;* which gonfaloniers were elected by the council of the people of two hundred, by the *rettori* of the arts, and their counsellors, and by the captains, gonfaloniers, and counsellors of the companies of the people, and by the *anziani* for the time being.   These *anziani*, sitting together with the captain of the people, and the general council of the people, promulgated laws and statutes, gave execution to all the laws, civil and criminal, performed and conducted all the most important affairs relating to the government, and restrained the nobles and plebeians with the fear of punishment within the limits of respect and obedience." *

That is to say, all authority, legislative, executive, and judicial, was collected together in one single assembly.   But how they restrained the nobles and plebeians to obedience, we shall soon see.

"In the year 1329, these *anziani* are called in the records

* Fioravanti, p. 21.

Imperial Counsellors, (*Consiglieri Imperiali*,) a remarkable title, obtained probably from the Emperor Louis, of Bavaria, when, after the death of Castruccio, he placed one of his imperial vicars over the custody of the city of Pistoia. The dignity of gonfalonier of justice was probably instituted in the year 1295, because in the next year, 1296, in the acts of council it is recorded, ' De consilio et consensu et auctoritate dominorum anthianorum et vexilliferi justitiæ populi, et auctoritate ducentorum consiliarorum.'

" The new law of 1330, names a gonfalonier of justice, and eight *anziani*. ' It is resolved, that the *anziani* of the commons, and people of the city of Pistoia, be, and ought to be, eight only, namely,— two for each gate or quarter, and one gonfalonier or justice for the whole city. . . . . The said lords, the *anziani*, and the gonfalonier of justice, and their notaries, shall be and ought to be of the best popular men and artificers of the city, and not of any house of the grandees.' * And the authority of the gonfalonier of justice was placed upon an equality with that of the *anziani*. The law ordained, that, ' wherever, in the statutes of the commons and people, mention is made of the *anziani*, the same shall be understood of the gonfalonier of justice, although it be not written ; and in all things, and everywhere, he shall have the same authority, and full power (balia) as has one of the *anziani*, besides his proper office.' And to show that the gonfalonier of justice was not, in the beginning, superior to the *anziani*, it appears that, after the introduction of that office, they continued to appoint, in the usual manner, a prior of the *anziani*, with the same authority and preëminence before described. The law of 1330 says, ' And the *anziani* and gonfalonier of justice, after they shall be congregated in their palace, and shall have taken their usual oaths, shall constitute one prior from among themselves, for such time as they please, to whom all the others shall obey, under the penalty, &c. So that each of the *anziani* and gonfaloniers of justice shall be prior, according to the proportion of time they shall be in office.'

" The gonfalonier, by the duty of his office, was bound to send out, with the consent and participation of the *anziani*, the stand-

* Dicti domini anthiani, et vexillifer justitiæ, et eorum notarii, sint et esse debeant de melioribus popularibus et artificibus dictæ civitatis, et non de aliqua domo magnata. Fioravanti, p. 21.

ard of justice, to assemble the armed militia, and go out to execute process against any of the grandees (*magnati*); 'which
gonfalonier of justice,' says the law, 'shall be bound by the obligation of an oath, and under the penalty of five hundred pounds,
upon the commission of any homicide, to draw forth the standard of justice, and, together with the captain of the people, to
go to the house of the grandee committing such homicide, or
causing it to be committed, and to cause his goods to be
destroyed, and not to suffer the said standard to repose, until all
the property of such delinquent shall be totally destroyed and
laid waste, both in the city and the country; and to cause the
bell of the people to be rung, if it shall seem expedient to the
lords, the *anziani*, and the gonfalonier of justice, or the major
part of them; and all the shops, stores, and warehouses, shall
be shut immediately upon the commission of such homicide,
and shall not be opened till execution shall be done as aforesaid.
But in all other offences perpetrated against the person of any
man of the people by any grandee, it shall be in the discretion
of the said lords, the *anziani*, and the gonfalonier of justice, or
the major part of them, to draw out the said standard or not.'
Such a rigorous kind of justice, as it regarded the grandees, who
gave themselves a license to commit excessive disorders against
those of the commonalty, was thought to be best adapted to
their insolence. And to undeceive those who may imagine that
in Pistoia, at that time, the title of grandee was a respectable
title, and distinctive of the true nobility of the place, it is necessary to have recourse to the common municipal law, which says,
that the *magnati* (grandees) were all those, of whatever condition, who, abandoned to an ill life, offended the commonalty,
and held the city and country in inquietude; they for this reason
were called *Magnates*, became separated from public affairs, and
excluded entirely from all magistracies and offices, and subjected
to very rigorous penalties. By the laws of the years 1330 and 1344,
to be declared a *grandee* was rather an infamy than an honor. The
words of the law are these: 'But if it shall happen that men
of any race, or noble house, or any one of them from such a
a noble house or stock, born of the male line, or any others, live
wickedly and flagitiously against the people, hurt the men of
the people, and terrify and disturb their peaceful state, or shall
endeavor to do so by themselves or by others, and this shall be

made known by public fame to the captain of the people and the *anziani* and gonfalonier of justice for the time being; these magistrates, at the petition of any of the people of Pistoia, shall be obliged to propose to the council of the people, that such a noble house or progeny, such a man or number of men, thus defamed, be written and placed in the number of grandees, and be accounted as such.'* And as the Pistoians were driven to great perplexities to maintain in peace and quiet, their popular government, and in order to punish severely all those who should take the license to disturb the pacific state of their city, they proclaimed this penalty on all delinquents, by a law of the year 1418, rubric 9. 'But if it shall happen that any one of any noble house or race, or any one of any other condition, shall live wickedly and profligately, or shall commit or attempt to commit any such crime or misdemeanor against the people, and the pacific state of the people of the city of Pistoia, they shall be recorded in the number of grandees, and accounted as such.'" [1]

To such extremes of caprice and violence, destructive of all liberty and safety, are such governments naturally and necessarily reduced.†

" The city of Pistoia had also in its regimen a syndic. This was an officer who was called an Elder, or Syndic-General,

---

* Scribantur et ponantur in numero magnatum et potentum, et pro magnatibus et potentibus habeantur. Fioravanti, p. 22.

† The devices on the standards, seals, and coins of the republic, as well as all other antiquities, are not within the design of this essay; but there was on one of their standards an idea that contained the truest emblem of their government; a lamb pursued by a wolf, with the motto, *Pace, richezza, superbia; guerra, povertà, umiltà;* Peace, riches, and pride; war, poverty, and humility. If the wolf is construed to signify the majority, and the lamb the minority, as there was neither a shepherd nor shepherd's dog to interpose between them, the resemblance is perfect.

[1] "A peine l'indépendance des cités avoit été reconnue par l'empereur, que le peuple crut qu'il étoit temps de se faire rendre compte du pouvoir des gentils-hommes, qui jusque alors avoient administré ses affaires avec autant de patriotisme que de bravoure et de talent. Cette défiance nouvelle se dirigeoit contre des hommes qui auparavant avoient bien mérité des républiques; toutefois il ne faut point l'attribuer uniquement au développement de l'ambition et à la vanité des plébéiens, ni les taxer d'ingratitude. Dès que le danger qui menaçoit les villes avoit été écarté, les intérêts des nobles et ceux du peuple avoient cessé d'être communs. Les premiers, n'ayant plus en vue la défense publique, s'étoient livrés de nouveau à leur projets d'agrandissement et à leur ambition de famille. Une indépendance solitaire leur convenoit mieux encore qu'une liberté partagée avec des bourgeois; et s'il falloit rechercher la faveur d'une puissance à laquelle ils ne vouloient point obéir, ils aimoient mieux faire leur cour aux empereurs qu'au peuple." Sismondi, *Hist. des Rép. Ital.* tom. 2, p. 236.

who must be forty years of age, and live forty miles from the city. His duty was to look over the accounts of the podestà, the captain of the people, the anziani, and all the magistrates and officers of the city and its district, when they resigned or were dismissed from their charges. There were, moreover, according to the law of 1402, judges of appeals in all causes, civil, criminal, and mixed; and to them belonged the cognizance of all disputes and regulations concerning provisions; they also superintended the sumptuary laws, against all luxurious excesses in the dress and ornaments of the ladies; and they entertained a number of notaries, and a numerous family and court, for the execution of all services appertaining to their offices.

"The city of Pistoia being in this state of government, in 1355, the Emperor Charles IV. arrived at Pisa, and the citizens appeared before his imperial majesty, and gave him the demonstrations of vassalage and obedience due to the sovereignty which he held over their city. The emperor confirmed to them all the privileges granted by his august predecessors; and desirous of fixing the reputation and reverence for the dignity of the gonfaloniers of justice, he enlarged their authority, as well as that of the *anziani;* and wishing to make the Pistoians enjoy, quietly, a sort of liberty, he gave them, by a diploma of the twenty-sixth of May, the faculty of living and governing themselves, according to their laws and laudable customs, in a free, popular state, under the regency of the anziani and the gonfaloniers of justice, declaring both the anziani and the gonfaloniers, for the affairs of Pistoia and its dominion, his vicars, and vicars of the empire, for the whole term of his own life. "The anziani," says the diploma, "and the gonfalonier of justice of the people, and commons of Pistoia, who now are, and for the time to come shall be, in office, and no others, we constitute our general and irrevocable vicars, for the whole term of our life, with the full administration in the city, country, and district of Pistoia, and in all its lands, castles, and places. Pistoia maintained itself in this state of a republic as long as Charles IV. lived; and, taking advantage of the distance and negligence of his successors, it persevered in the same government until the year 1401, when the Emperor Robert, by his charter, declared the gonfalonier and priors of the arts of the city of Florence his vicars, and vicars of the empire, and gave them the government of Arezzo, Volterra, Pistoia, and the other places of Tuscany."

But in the interval between these periods, the Pistoians were never quiet; for, governing themselves in what they called a free popular state, they were for reducing all to a level, and thought, or pretended, to make all the citizens enjoy equally the public honors and offices of their city.

"In this state of things, the rebellion of Sambuca was fomented by some of the citizens of Pistoia, at the head of whom was Riccardo Cancellieri, who had made himself master of several castles in the mountains; from whence he made inroads on the whole territory of Pistoia, and kept the inhabitants in continual alarms, with the design of delivering his country into the hands of John Galeazzo Visconti, Duke of Milan. Upon this occasion the imperial vicars in Florence sent, for the protection of Pistoia, two thousand infantry, some cavalry, and three commissaries, who, calling together the general council, imposed upon the counsellors the necessity of doing whatever was required of them, that they might not incur still greater miseries. In the first place, they required that every resolution and statute of liberty, and every condition, article, and confederation, which the city had, should be annulled; and then, by another resolution, that they should subject themselves to the people of Florence, with liberal authority to govern Pistoia at their discretion. This proposition of the Florentines was ill relished by the Pistoians; and while the council was debating on it, the soldiery took possession of the piazza and palace of the *anziani;* and having understood that no resolution had passed, they began with drawn swords in their hands to cry, "Florence for ever!" (*Viva Firenze!*) and to threaten the counsellors. Thus intimidated, they by an ample resolution suddenly surrendered the liberty of their city to the Florentines, from that day, the tenth of September, 1401, to the calends of January, 1402, to the end that they might apply a summary remedy to the evils with which they were agitated and oppressed. Thus say the books of reformations in Florence; and then were painted the lions, the ensigns of Florence, upon the palace of the syndic of the city of Pistoia.

"It was not long before these imperial vicars, availing themselves of the authority given them by the emperor, and of that given them by the Pistoians themselves, sent to Pistoia four commissaries to reform the public offices. These, desirous, as they said, of smoothing the passions of the chiefs which had disturbed the quiet of the city of Pistoia, proposed that the forms and orders of the city of Florence should, as much as possible, be imitated; and that the twelve *buoni homini* should be called the Twelve of the College; and that the supreme magistracy of the *anziani* should be no longer denominated the *Anziani* of the People, but the *Priors* of the People; and, not making any innovation in the gonfalonier of justice, that he should retain the same name. The prior of the *anziani* was to be called *Proposto* or President of the Priori, according to the words of the reform, 'And the priors shall have among themselves one president continually, who shall continue three days in this manner. After the oaths of office shall be taken, they shall cause nine votes, with their names, to be put into a purse by a notary, one of which shall be drawn out for a president, and so successively during the term of their office.'

" The Florentines having thus limited and restrained the privileges of the Pistoians, or made the election of the *anziani*, and given them the name of priors, they made eight purses, in the proportion of two for each gate, and regulated themselves according to the plan in 1376; in which year, to take away the scandalous names of the two factions of Bianchi and Neri, Whites and Blacks, two companies were instituted, one called the Company of St. John, and the other of St. Paul, and one prior was drawn for the gate of one company, and another for the other; and the gonfalonier of justice was drawn, at one time from the company of St. John, and at another from that of St. Paul. This manner of drawing the magistracy of the *priori* was changed in 1427, when they began to be drawn from two different purses, the first and the second.

" In 1417, the Pistoians, considering that in so great a change of affairs they ought to make some advancement of the dignity of the gonfalonier of justice, ordained that the first place in rank should no longer be held by the president and rector of the city, but by the gonfalonier. Thus says the law, ' That the gonfalonier of justice shall always hold the more dignified place, and after him the president; and in like manner, in going out, with the rector and other officers of the city of Pistoia.' This law was ratified by the law of 1437; and from this it followed, that in 1463 they began to make for the president, who was to continue in that office, a purse by itself; as it was determined, in 1471, that for the future two should be drawn from that purse, and the oldest man of them should be the first to occupy the president's place, unless the younger were a doctor of laws; and this was called the purse of the president; the first of whom had the power of speaking and answering first in all meetings; which power however ceased, in the first president, in the year 1492, when it was determined, that the right of sitting and speaking first should, in all occurrences, be enjoyed by the gonfalonier of justice; and thus this office of gonfalonier of justice, . rising continually in dignity, began by little and little to be desired by the nobles; and, by common consent and a public decree, it became confined to the nobles alone.

"The supreme magistracy of the *priori* becoming a little civilized, the purse of the president got to be considered as the first after that of the gonfalonier of justice, and that of the priors which was the first became the second; but, because four subjects were drawn from this, it was called the Purse of Four; and the other, which was called the Second of the Priori, became the third, and was called, from this time, the Common Purse, in which all citizens qualified for offices should remain, at least for the period of one renewal, although by his condition of birth, merit, and age, he might be qualified for a purse of higher rank. When it was afterwards established, that the descendants by the male line, of men of rank, and of presidents, should no longer enter upon the office of prior through that purse, but through that of four, the same was called no longer the Common Purse, but the Third; whence, by virtue of this new order of magistrature, we read, in 1475, of one gonfalonier of justice, two presidents, four of the first, and two of the second purse, and one notary, with the preference to the gonfalonier of sitting first, given him by the law of 1474, which says, 'The gonfalonier shall obtain the first and most dignified place.'

By the few memorials that remain in the archives of Pistoia it appears, that there have been many and various councils of citizens, for the regulation of the public affairs of the city, in which councils the supreme authority of government resided; and before the construction of the public palace, all these coun-

cils were assembled in a church, at the election of the head of
the supreme magistracy of the *anziani*. The council of the
people, from the year in which the *anziani* were instituted, until
1477, had the privilege to make the renewals of the magistrates
and public officers of the city; in which year it was ordained,
that such renewal should be made by those who had been drawn
gonfaloniers of justice, and workmen of St. James. These
riformatori began to be called men of rank (*graduati*) for being
arrived at the first two grades and honors of the city, which at
that time were the offices of gonfalonier of justice, and of a
workman of St. James; and, for the first time, they are found
thus named in the reform of 1483; from which time it was
established by law, that two of each family should assist, to
make the renewal of public offices, and that the number of
thirty-three should be sufficient to make the renewal with va-
lidity. And this order of the *graduati*, or men of distinction, is
that by which, at this day, the nobility of the city of Pistoia is
most clearly distinguished. In the year 1521, the assigned number of the graduati to make the renewal of the public officers
failing, there were elected certain citizens, of the other noble and
popular families, to whom was given the name of *Arruoti;* and
it was established as the duty of these to assist in making the
renewal; and this lasted till 1580.

" In the times of the consuls we read, that there was a council
of a hundred citizens, who were chosen by four men of good
fame, twenty-five for each of the four gates of the city; without
this council, neither the consuls nor the podestà could determine
any thing; and when there arose a question of peace, war, or
taxes, besides the council of a hundred, all the *rettori* of the
chapels and arts assisted."

And as upon these occasions the consuls, podestà, counsellors of the hundred, and rectors of chapels and arts, all met in
one assembly, and determined all things by a majority of votes,
which, as has been before observed, made it a government in
one centre (an aristocracy in reality, though a popular state in
name) and consequently some two or three families must always
be at the head of it, and constantly contending for the superiority, this kept the people in perpetual contention.

" There was another council, as appears by the records, formed
of fourteen citizens, and of all the doctors and advocates, which

was destined to counsel the podestà; as he himself, after having made his election of them, was obliged to regulate himself by their advice. Such was his oath; 'And I will consult my counsellors, through the whole time of my government, in things which shall appear to me to regard the common honor and utility of our city of Pistoia.'"

As neither the podestà nor this council had any negative on the legislative council of a hundred, yet, since the podestà had the choice of the members of the smaller body, that was no doubt composed of his friends in the council of a hundred, in which case it is plain that the same persons and families must have had the chief influence and direction of affairs in both; so that this executive council had the same centre with the legislative council.

" It is further found, that in the first times of the government of the twelve *anziani*, namely, in 1267, there were two councils, one of forty counsellors of the captain of the people and of the *anziani* who were required to be of an age above forty years, and their office continued six months; and they resolved upon all propositions which were proposed to them by the captain of the people and the *anziani*, provided they were not contrary to the laws and regulations of the commons and people. The other council was called the *Council of Two Hundred Counsellors of the people;* and in the assemblies of this council assisted all the aforesaid forty, and, moreover, all the captains, gonfaloniers, and counsellors of the companies of the people, and all the *rettori* and counsellors of the arts, and all those who had been *anziani*."

The fabric of this government, and its spirit, was the same with the former, only the name of captain of the people was substituted for that of podestà, and a council of forty was substituted to that of fourteen, and a council of two hundred to that of one. The alteration therefore was not at all for the better.

" After 1330, there was one council, called the General Council; this was formed of a hundred citizens, namely, fifty popular[1] men, and fifty grandees (*magnati*). In this council assisted all the members of the council of the people, all the gentry, all the doctors of laws, and all the physicians of Pistoia, matricu-

---

[1] " *Popolari,*" the common people as distinguished from the nobles.

lated in the college of physicians. But this council had of itself
no authority, and could do nothing without the council of the
people. In like manner, after the same year, 1330, the principal
council of Pistoia was that of the people, in which assisted all
the *anziani*, gonfaloniers of justice, and their notaries, and two
hundred popular citizens; and none of the grandees could be of
this council. They were elected fifty for each gate. The authority of this council was supreme and sovereign, to make and
repeal laws, impose and take off taxes, &c. In·more ancient
times, as appears by the rubric 62, of the law of 1267, the
council of the people had consisted of six hundred citizens; but
because such a multitude generated confusion, it was reduced
to two hundred in 1270.

"But the government of longest duration in Pistoia was that
of the eight priors of the people, and one gonfalonier of justice;
and this body was called the *Supreme Magistracy of the City*, and
was renewed every two months, from the four purses, in the palace
of its residence. When they proceeded to draw these magistrates,
with solemn pomp, the box was taken from the treasury of St.
James, within which were locked up, with four keys, all the
votes of the magistrates of the city, and it was carried in procession, accompanied by the magistrates of all the colleges, with
trumpets sounding, into the public palace. Here the gonfalonier
of justice was drawn from the first purse, who was the head of
this magistracy, and not only enjoyed the supreme dignity, and
the preëminence in place, robes, habitation, and in all other
respects, but answered in the namè of the public; and although
in public affairs he could not rule alone, there was always allowed him a right of freely entering when he would into the
greater council, and into all other councils and colleges where
any matters of importance were under deliberation, and there
give his opinion, his reasons, and his vote. This gonfalonier
was a man of gravity, from his age; and that he might be
respectable in all points, it was required that he should be of an
ancient family;* and he who enjoyed this supreme post enjoyed
a jewel, held in veneration by the people, and in great esteem
by the nobility. There were then drawn from the other purse
two persons, who were called presidents; and these were some-

---

* Si richiede lunga, e continovata chiarezza di sangue.

times of a middle age, and sometimes old men, and for the most part, after giving proofs of their wisdom in this station, they ascended, either by means of their birth or their merit, to the rank of gonfalonier. From the other purse, called the purse of four, were successively drawn four subjects of the prime nobility, or at least of middling condition, who, for the most part, were in younger age; and from this purse, some by their birth, and some by their merit and their age, passed up to the more dignified purse of the presidents, and sometimes to the rank of *graduati*, or men of distinction. In the last place were drawn two persons from the third purse, in which were contained the names of all the citizens who had not made any advancement in the other purses, or had been of families worthy only of the purse of four, and among these were found those who exercised civil and liberal arts; and these did not diminish the dignity of the magistracy, but rather gave occasion to maintain the union between the plebeians and the nobility; for with this compensation, the former remained long quiet, without any insurrection. This magistracy had in the service of its ministry a chancellor, who was a notary public, and was drawn from a purse destined for that purpose. This magistracy began their offices on the morning of the first day of the month, in their senatorial robes. Each of the priors wore a robe of scarlet lined with red damask, vulgarly called a gown (*lucco*), with a hat or bonnet lined with a cloth of black silk, with its ribbon and tassel of black crape, and upon the left shoulder a large knot of crimson satin, which was commonly called *becca;* and the chancellor wore a gown of black cloth, lined with red cloth, without the knot upon the shoulder, but with a hat similar to those of the priori, whose duty it is to draw up and sign the acts of this magistracy; but the gonfalonier of justice was clothed with a robe of red velvet, with a similar shoulder-knot, and his head was covered with a broad hat, of a noble appearance, the name of which is *tocco*.[1]

" This magistracy, thus clothed and ornamented, after the discharge of the old magistracy, took the oaths of office, in the public view of the people, in the larger piazza, and under the ample covering of it, built in 1332 with the revenues of the ex-

[1] In the original work, the author deems the hat of importance enough to justify an engraved representation of its form.

cise, or *gabelles*, of the four quarters of the city; and, after having taken the oaths, they went in procession, with the standard of justice, to the chapel of St. James the apostle, protector of the city, and thence to the palace of their residence, which was spacious enough to receive, in the year 1536, the Emperor Charles V., in all the forms of majesty. None of the component members of that magistracy could go out privately; but only when in some determined function was it permitted to the whole body of the magistracy to go out of their palace with solemn pomp. This magistracy resided with its chancellor, night and day, in the palace, to the end that all public business might be despatched with the greater vigilance, for the good government of the city; and they drew from the commons a sufficient appointment, both for the maintenance of their tables, and of six and twenty persons destined to their service, and for the honorable management of the furniture of their palace, the linen for their persons and households, and of their plate, and all other things necessary for their use in the time of the government. This magistracy also entertained a chaplain, with a handsome salary."

We may pass over the tedious description of feasts and public processions, and say,—

" That the gonfalonier of justice was the head, not only of the supreme magistracy, but also of all other subaltern magistracies which were in the commonwealth, and without him there could not be convened any council of the citizens, to engage in any public deliberation. This magistrate, while the public residence continued, was attended, whenever he went out of the palace, by a retinue consisting of one person, who, with the title of fiscal, resided in Pistoia, of one assessor, versed in the profession of the law, of the captain of infantry, of two architects of the palace, of the steward of provisions, of the chancellor *del danno dato*, of the master of the house, and of six and twenty servants; and in the performance of religious ceremonies, and in some of the principal assemblies, this magistrate had a retinue of magistrates and nobility, which gave him more splendor than a crown.

" The magistrates, upon whom depended the right government of the city of Pistoia, are, besides those already named, all these which follow; some determine upon public affairs, others preside in judicature, others superintend the common, others private interests; these watch over health, those over plenty; some attend to the preservation of the peace, and others to politics.[1] These magistrates are the twelve *collegi;* six for petitions; two for the works in the palace of the supreme magistrates; the two companions; the captain of infantry, who in ancient times was called by the name of captain of the families of the *anziani,* and who, in primitive times, was called by the name of *votalarche,* the institution of which office was most ancient. The six laborers of St. James, besides other commissions, held the care of the markets, and were, exclusively of all other magistrates and lawgivers of Pistoia, the judges and overseers of all offences touching provisions, and constituted the first magistracy of the nobles; because he who is denominated a laborer of St. James enjoys the noble rank of the *graduati,* a dignity and charge of equal nobility, although of different function and command, with that of gonfalonier of justice, as this office confers the character and distinction of nobility both upon the person and the family. There are also the four officers of the pious house of wisdom; the four *operai* of the holy virgin of humility; the magistrate over the rivers and roads; the laborers of St. John and St. Zeno; the magistracy of *buoni homini* over the prisons; the ministers of the *Monte di Pietà*; the ministers of salt; the ministers of pledges deposited; the approvers of the excises; the purveyor for the commons; the four over civil suits; the two over the restitution of taxes; the two over the public schools; the deputies superintending the poor; the deputies for the assessment of taxes; the magistrates of abundance; the magistrates of health; the judges of controversies relative to beasts; the four peace-makers; the ministers of the trumpet; the eight reformers; the ministers of the commons; the ministers of the customhouse; the syndics of the *rettori;* the deputies over the workhouse of the poor; the auditors; the college of judges; the notaries; the *rettori* of the arts; the tribunal of damages done; the clerks who assist in civil suits; the magistracy of three judges, who are foreigners; but at present, as the public revenues are farmed out, these are suspended, and in their place the treasurer of the city is introduced to decide the controversies of the people, with the

---

[1] "alla politica," the general policy.

liberty of appeal to the grand ducal chamber at Florence, in cases of denial of justice. The appeal from civil causes, determined by these magistrates, is sometimes to the supreme magistracy of the *priori* and the gonfalonier of justice of the city, in the name of whom, and under the impression of whose seal, the public decrees are despatched.

" There is, moreover, a council general of the people, formed of sixty citizens, and their office continues six months; at this council the priors of the people, the gonfalonier of justice, the twelve *collegi*, and the six for petitions assist. This council holds the supreme authority of the city, and has jurisdiction over all the magistrates who transgress their offices, and has the faculty to treat and despatch the most important affairs of the state of Pistoia, to make and repeal laws, name ambassadors, dispense offices, lay on and take off taxes, and to give all assistance to the other magistrates, who have their peculiar duties; and each member may oppose a decision on any question under deliberation, that it may be referred to another session, to be approved or rejected on mature consideration.

" For the most weighty business of the government, there is a council composed of the old and new council of the people, the priors of the people, the gonfalonier of justice, the twelve of the college, the six of petitions, all the *graduati*, the resident officers of the pious house of wisdom, and all the resident gonfaloniers, who decide as to the majority appears most useful and advantageous for the public good. Here all the most momentous affairs and causes most interesting to the public are digested.

" There is also a council of *graduati*, which had its beginning in 1483, and is composed of two persons for each family, of those persons, however, who actually enjoy the dignity of the *graduati*, which is the first of the honors of the city; and three and thirty members are sufficient to form a valid council, to which it belongs to promote persons and families to the citizenship of Pistoia, and to public offices and honors. Every five years, this council, together with the gonfalonier of justice, and the eight reformers, put to a secret vote all the persons who enjoy the citizenship of Pistoia, and reward or condemn them, as justice requires. They renew the imborsations of public offices and honors, and give or take away from all as they please;

examining well the grades of citizenship, of nobility, of antiquity, merits and demerits in all persons and families, over whom they keep a watchful eye, in order to prevent all occasion of confusion, disorder, and disturbance, which might happen through the discordant pretensions of the citizens ; and thus guarded and established, they come from time to time to the distribution of those offices for which there is occasion.

" Pistoia has also its dispenser of laws, (*giusdicente*,) the duty of whom is to take care of the peace and tranquillity of the citizens, and to distribute justice, both according to the municipal laws, and conformably to the will of the sovereign ; and from ancient times his post was occupied by the podestà, introduced by the emperors into all the cities of Italy ; and because that, in the league that was called the confederation of Tuscany, concluded in 1197 between many places and cities of that province, for their common defence against the rights, or at least claims, of the emperor, in order to stretch the limits of their liberty,[1] Pistoia had her place, and elected, according to the tenor of the association, her head, with the title of captain, to whom were confided, as the law required, all her affairs and pretensions, therefore, in 1200, it is said that Pistoia had for her captain one by the name of Gualdaccio ; from which year, until 1529, there was always elected by the Pistoians, and by those who had the government of Pistoia, a governor, (*rettore*,) together with the podestà, for the good direction of the affairs of that city.

" Afterwards it happened, that in the great tumults between the factions of the Panchiatici and the Cancellieri, there were elected by the Florentines thirteen commissaries, to establish the peace between them ; and among the multitude of things which they did in 1502, they annulled the office of captain, and created that of commissary ; and thus in some years the officer was called *commissary*, and in others *captain commissary*, and in others they returned to the old name of *captain*. In 1529, the Pistoians, finding themselves in great difficulties, doubtful whether they should be able to govern themselves, and dreading the devastations of the army of the Emperor Charles V., which was near their confines, sent ambassadors to Bologna, to supplicate Clement VII. who was then in that city, that he would condescend

---

[1] " per dilatare i limiti della loro *usurpata* libertà."

to defend their city from the imminent danger, and take it under his protection; and they delivered him the keys of it; which the pontiff, in his own name, and in the name of the emperor, who fought for the obedience of the Florentines, and the other cities of Tuscany, with great alacrity accepted, and immediately sent Alexander di Gerardo Corsini for the government and custody of Pistoia, with the title of commissary; and therefore it followed that a podestà or captain was not elected afterwards, with the exception of three years, but one magistrate alone, with the title of commissary-general, as was ever after the custom.

" The Emperor Charles V., having, in 1530, reduced the Florentines and their confederates, by force, to submission to the empire, and restored in Florence the house of Medici, who had been banished by their fellow-citizens, consigned to them the government and dominion of Tuscany. Pistoia did not hesitate a moment in its obedience to the new regent of the province, by which ready submission they obtained from him the privilege of continuing to govern themselves according to their own laws and laudable customs; and they continued to receive, in place of a podestà and captain, a commissary-general for their defender and governor; for all the time that the government of the house of Medici lasted, in order to maintain the charge with suitable dignity, it was their custom always to confer it on some senator of Florence.

" The government of the house of Medici terminating in the year 1737, by failure of the succession, it was conferred, by the Emperor Charles VI., on Francis III., Duke of Lorraine and Bar. This new lord of Tuscany, pursuing the same system of government of the house of Medici, has continued to furnish the city of Pistoia with a commissary-general, if not a senator, respectable at least for his nobility, who, regulating the government by the laws of the city, has always enabled it to enjoy a perfect tranquillity.

" Francis II., grand duke of Tuscany, in 1749, conceiving a good opinion of Pistoia, as a city of merit, and in all things respectable, and wishing to raise its dignity and honor, annulled the office of commissary-general, and confided the government to a minister, with the title of governor." *

* Fioravanti, p. 38.

In a city, where every interest seemed to be guarded by particular magistrates, where so many changes were made in their form of government in order to find one which would please and satisfy the people, one might expect to find happiness, if it were possible that it should exist where legislative and executive powers were confounded together in one assembly. But if we go over again the several periods of the history of Pistoia, we shall find that similar causes had the same effects.

"At the end of the eleventh and beginning of the twelfth century,[1] civil discords in Pistoia generated much misery; and many families, fearing that they should have still greater evils to suffer, determined to abandon their country; and, as a lesson to their mad and cruel fellow-citizens whom they left behind them, they caused an inscription to be engraved on the inside, on the gates, 'Habbi pazienzia,' (have patience,)" a motto that ought to be written over the door, and engraven on the heart, of every citizen in such a government, "and went to inhabit other countries.

"Italy beginning, in 1112, to be infected with the contagious disease of the factions of the Guelphs and Ghibellines, destructive insurrections and tumults were raised in Pistoia; and the citizens, infected with a spirit of cruelty against each other, without fear of human or divine chastisement, attended to nothing but party quarrels, and mutual slaughter and murder;" and these contests involved the city in continual wars, foreign and domestic, till the year 1235, when "the podestà, a wise man and a nobleman of high rank, exerted all his prudence, vigilance, and solicitude, to repress and compose the tumults of the nobles and popular party, who, on account of the government, were grown unusually fierce and insolent; but not being able to reconcile differences so inveterate, nor prevent the cruelties which both parties, regardless of his menaces and punishments, daily committed, the city was thought to be in evident danger of total desolation. As some of the citizens had given assistance to the Conte Guido de' Conti Guidi, who was become odious to other citizens as a supporter of Ghibellines, tumults were multiplied, till the city was at length divided in two, and they came to a fierce battle. As one party would not mix with or depend upon

---

[1] Fioravanti, cap. x. p. 164.

the other, each one elected its podestà and consuls, as if they had been separate cities; and a war was maintained between them for years with such fury, as set all laws, human and divine, at defiance, till, exhausted and humbled on both sides, they were forced to have recourse to Rubaconte, podestà of Florence, under whose mediation a peace between them was concluded, with a detail of articles, to the performance of which Florence became guarantee. In consequence of this mediation and peace, Pistoia returned, for a short time, to her flourishing condition; so that not only the greater powers admired her felicity, but the most formidable of the other cities stood in awe of her. But, oh miserable vicissitudes of ill constituted governments!* to the confusion of the citizens of Pistoia, the other cities, by some intervals of peace and union, grew powerful. Pistoia alone, by the continuance of quarrels, factions, and civil wars, was reduced to weakness in command, honor, and fortune."

It was not long before the old disputes revived, and continued till 1251, when the pope was obliged to interpose, and negotiate a new peace between the parties in Pistoia. But this peace could not be effected till long wars, a great destruction of lives, and a general desolation of the lands and cities, by the various leagues and alternate confiscations of the rich and the poor, the nobles and commons, Guelphs and Ghibellines, had fatigued and exhausted all parties.

" In 1260, the Ghibellines of Pistoia, Florence, Volterra, and Prato, could no longer bear the insolence and impertinence of the contrary faction. They therefore formed a union with their friends in the other cities, raised armies, and renewed the wars; and, after many sharp conflicts, and at length the sanguinary battle of Monte-aperto, they turned the tide of fortune and the torrent of popular passions in their favor, till all Tuscany became Ghibelline, excepting Lucca and the Florentine exiles. At the instigation of the Conte Novello, vicar of King Manfred, Pistoia, Florence, Siena, Pisa, Volterra, Saminiato, Colle, Prato, and Poggibonzi, raised a standing army to make war upon Lucca, because this city was the asylum of their fugitives." This army was maintained only by the imposition of general and very heavy taxes, did infinite damage in the country, and at

---

* "Ma oh misere vicende del mondo!" Fioravanti, p. 219.

last, in 1267, obtained a peace between Pistoia and Lucca, upon conditions, one of which was, that each city should pardon the other all the injuries, molestations, discords, offences, damages, rapines, homicides, devastations, and conflagrations, that had been committed.

" In 1268,[1] the Guelphs in Pistoia were much displeased that the heads of the Ghibellines, banished and driven out from their city, should, under Astancollo Panciatichi, have fortified themselves at Lucciano, a castle under the eyes of Pistoia; therefore they ordered Cialdo Cancellieri, their podestà, to go out with an armed force and dislodge them. Panciatichi, having penetrated the designs of the Guelphs in Pistoia, fearing that he could not resist the assault of his enemies, because he was inferior in force, and without hopes of succor, abandoned the post, and went to Pisa, where he united himself with his confederates; so that Cancellieri, finding the castle empty of inhabitants, plundered and demolished it, and caused the Panciatichi to be banished as the heads of that faction, whose estates were all confiscated.

" The party spirit of the citizens of Pistoia having, in 1270, in some measure subsided, by means of the government of the Universal Pacificator of Tuscany,[2] they set about a reformation of their magistrates; and considering that a multitude always generate confusion, they reduced to two hundred their general council, which had been composed before of six hundred members, and created many new magistrates and jurisdictions, to bring into order the affairs of their government. But in 1284, there arose again most grievous disorders, by reason of the ill administration of justice; and the general council elected the wisest citizens, to make another reformation and new laws, and to bring about a reconciliation among the principal citizens who disturbed the public tranquillity. But all their regulations were ineffectual; for in the next year, 1285, fresh disturbances were perceived in the city of Pistoia, occasioned by certain families, who, by means of copious wealth, and the adherence of numerous friends, followers, and relations, aspired to govern the city at pleasure; but as the wisest men exerted themselves, that their public affairs should depend only on law and justice,

---

[1] Fioravanti, c. xv. p. 229.　　[2] Charles of Anjou, King of Naples.

not upon the passions and caprice of individuals, they called together the general council. These endeavored to render those families odious and unpopular, as well as the title by which they were distinguished; and to this end ordered, that they should be declared "grandees," (*magnati*,) who by their influence and power disturbed the public tranquillity; and to be declared a grandee became equivalent to being declared a seditious person, impertinent, and separated from the public government of the city.

"The dominant party ruled the Guelphs so arbitrarily, committed so many robberies upon them, and burned and destroyed so much of their property, that these became desperate, and joining the exiles from many cities, raised an army, which obliged the Pistoians, and the governors of other cities, to raise another to oppose it, at an expense of a general imposition of taxes upon all the necessaries of life. The two armies met in the plain of Campaldino, and a memorable victory was gained by the Guelphs; and fire and sword were again scattered wide in consequence of this.

"In 1290, another fierce tumult arose in Pistoia, between the most illustrious families, occasioned by a sword cut, given by Mone Sinibaldi, upon the face of Gio. Vergiolesi. Upon this signal there was a general insurrection; and it cost all the art and resolution of the government, to do justice, to prevent another general battle; for civil discords were beyond measure increased, and the people, without any bridle, were in the utmost danger of desolating the city, and leaving it empty of inhabitants. The exiles in the mean time took their stations among the mountains, where they fortified themselves, and made incursions from time to time, robbing, plundering, burning, and murdering, without control.

"Another insurrection, in 1296, came very near accomplishing the final ruin of Pistoia; it ended in a bloody battle, in which many persons lost their lives, and the parties remained as inveterate and cruel after as they had been before it. Insurrections and tumults continued so frequent, that the bishop fled for fear, the merchants could do no business, and revolutions, insolence, robberies, assassinations, daily happened;* and such dis-

* Le rivoluzioni, le insolenze, le rubberie, li assassinamenti, che giornalmente accadevano, &c. Fioravanti, p. 243.

trust was fixed in the minds of all men, that all lived in continual fear and suspicion. These apprehensions were carried to such a length, that each one shut himself up in his house, with the friends he could collect, where he fortified himself; and those who had not towers to their habitations erected them.* Sixty towers were erected in this single city, some of which still remain elevated above the houses, some are now covered with roofs, others since included in the buildings as they have been enlarged, and others, from time to time, have been ruined and destroyed in the subsequent wars. It is to be noted, that, by law or by custom, towers might not be erected but by the nobility, and these had their measure; so that, to avoid envy, they could not exceed a limited height. But at this time the insurrections of the citizens and of the people of the castles in the high lands increasing, seditious and perverse people were found everywhere, which gave occasion and motives to all the citizens to think of their houses; and they began, through the whole state, to proceed to exemplary punishments, without regard to the age, condition, or sex of the persons, and thus, in a short time, they remedied so many evils and tumults; and besides the quiet that resulted to the city, the stimulus had an effect on the castles, in the mountains, — namely, Cavinano, Lizzano, Popillio, Piteglio, S. Marcello, Mammiano, and others, — to make that universal peace which is mentioned in the archives of the city."

But the disorder was not confined to the common citizens in town and country, it originated in the divisions among the men of birth, fortune, and abilities, in the government.

" The contests for superiority among the *anziani* themselves, in 1298, arose to such a degree, that from argument, intrigue, and oratory, they proceeded to blows, and, after a rude encounter, the weaker party fled to the public archives, and shut and secured the door in the faces of their pursuers. Those without, finding it impossible to pursue the affray, determined to take their vengeance by fire; accordingly, setting fire to the archives, those within remained, together with all the papers, files, and records, a prey and a triumph to devouring flames."

This terrible event, as may well be believed, produced still greater tumults and confusions, which were terminated at last

* Fioravanti, p. 244.

by a calamity of another kind, more terrible, if not more destructive, a continuance of earthquakes for eight days together,
which shook down houses and towers more effectually than the
inhabitants were able to do. This event, which was believed by
some to be a judgment of Heaven for the animosities of the
citizens, it was hoped would promote peace and benevolence
among them; but they soon revived, with more wickedness
than ever, their ancient dissensions.[1]

The family of Cancellieri, at this time having most influence,
both by the riches they possessed, and by their great numbers,
amounting to a hundred men in arms, as brave as they were
haughty, were become formidable to all the other families in
Pistoia, to such a degree that all, both in the city and country,
stood in fear of them. It happened that Carlino di Gualfredi,
and Dore, or Amadore, the son of William Cancellieri, being
together in a cellar, where they had drank too freely, fell into a
squabble, in which Dore was beaten and insulted with outrageous language, which offended him so highly that he meditated a cruel revenge. Going out of the wine cellar in this
temper of mind, Dore went, late as it was at night, and laid
himself down in a corner of the street by which Carlino was
used to pass, and there happening to see Vanni, the brother of
Carlino, on horseback, without thinking of his innocence, gashed
him in the face by a blow with a target, and by another stroke cut
off part of his left hand. In this deplorable condition Vanni was
carried to his father, who, seeing his son thus barbarously treated,

---

[1] "A vingt milles de Florence, sur la route de Lucques, au pied des Ap-
penins qui séparent la Toscane d'avec le Modénois, est bâtie la ville de Pistoia.
Malgré la fertilité de son territoire et sa riante situation, cette cité n'a point ac-
quis d'illustration par sa population, sa richesse, son commerce, ou sa puissance;
mais en revanche la violence de ses révolutions, et la haine profonde des partis
qui la divisèrent, répandirent un levain de discorde sur le reste de la Toscane et
presque de l'Italie, et suscitèrent pour une offense privée et une querelle de
famille, une guerre universelle. Le peuple de Pistoia est peut-être le peuple
le plus violent, le plus emporté, le plus factieux dont l'histoire nous ait conservé
le souvenir. C'est un peuple qui semble avoir eu soif de guerres civiles; il ne
fut point désaltéré de sang même après avoir réduit sa patrie à n'avoir qu'un rang
obscur parmi les villes d'Italie; il ne se reposa point sous le joug du despotisme
qui, étouffant toutes les passions, détruisant tous les intérêts, endort presque
toujours les peuples dans le repos de la mort; il continua de combattre après que
la liberté, le gouvernement, la gloire, ne pouvoient plus exister pour lui; tel
qu'un des géans de l'Arioste, dans la chaleur de ses batailles, il oublioit qu'il étoit
mort. Exemple à jamais mémorable de la fureur insensée que les noms seuls peu-
vent encore inspirer aux hommes, lorsqu'il ne subsiste plus aucune des causes
qui avoient excité leur discorde. Sismondi, *Rép. Ital.* tome iv. p. 94.

was so inflamed with resentment, that, disregarding all laws divine and human, he began to meditate his revenge. At this moment the extravagance of his son was reported to William, and affected him with such grief and disgust, that he thought of averting any unfortunate consequences by an act of submission; and he sent his guilty son to the father and brothers of the man he had injured, to ask their pardon in his own name and in that of his afflicted father. But all in vain; for scarcely had Gualfredi cast his eyes on Dore, when he seized him, and, without regard to the goodness of his father, cut off one of his hands upon a horse manger, and gashed him in the face, in the same manner as had been done to Vanni his son. By this atrocious deed, done in cool blood and a sober hour, the father and brothers of Dore were so exasperated, that in order to obtain some signal revenge, they united the force of their friends and relations, filled the city with brawls, discord, and murder, and divided not only the family of Cancellieri, but the whole city, into two parties.

"The Cancellieri were at that time very numerous, very rich, and in near degrees of blood related and allied; some of them were derived from the lady Nera, and others from the lady Bianca, both of them wives of M. Cancelliero, the first author of the surname of this family; but now, no longer regarding their consanguinity, they became so perverse as to attend to nothing but the destruction of each other; and reviving the memory of the ladies, from whom the ancestors of Carlino and Dore had their original, the followers of Carlino took the name of Bianchi, and the followers of Dore, that of Neri; and the people being already infected with diabolical passions, the Ghibellines took the part of the Bianchi, and the Guelphs that of the Neri; and from this time the two factions of the city began to be called Bianchi and Neri, and frequent bloody battles were fought in the city between them.

"* The whole people in the city and country became divided into Bianchi and Neri, and the mutual slaughters of men, and burnings of houses, came very near to ruin the country. There was not a person who was not obliged to assume one of these

---

* Ferretus Vicentinus. lib. ii. apud Muratori, tom. ix, *Rerum Italicarum Scriptores.* Muratori Annal. tom. viii. pp. 2, 3. Cosi le maledette Sette si andavano dilatando per tutta la Toscana.

names, and side with one of the parties. Recourse at last was
had to Florence, to assist the magistrates in controlling these
parties; and the heads of the parties were banished, all except
Bertacca, far advanced in age, and one of the knights of St.
Mary, an order which had been instituted by Urban IV. to
pacify the factions. It was confined to the nobility, invested
with white robes with a red cross, and two red stars in a white
field; but with all its pomp and sanctity, had very little influence to correct the errors of an imperfect government.

"The Cancellieri took refuge in Florence, those of the Neri in
the house of the Donati, and those of the Bianchi in that of the
Cerchi; and thus infected Florence at last to such a degree, that
those party distinctions became as common and as mischievous
in that city as in Pistoia. At this time the Tuscans, holding
themselves free from all subjection to the empire,[1] and regulating all things according to the caprice of parties unbalanced in
their governments, the pestiferous venom of faction spread
wider every day in the minds of the people. Each side aiming
at nothing less than the other's total destruction,[2] had for its object the ambition of domineering without control. With this
maxim, which is characteristic of the seditious, these factions
joined in the city of Florence to trample on the laws; and the
Bianchi party succeeded in driving out by force the Neri, and
assumed the mastery of the city."

But before the end of the year, another revolution was effected
both in Florence and Pistoia, and the houses of many of the
principal people levelled with the ground.

[1] The Italian author is at least consistent in his views of the nature of popular
rights. He says, —
" Essendo in questo tempo i Toscani *usurpatori* degl' Imperiali diritti."

[2] There was a refinement in the degree of their malignity which deserves
notice in a history of ill-balanced governments.
" Un principe odieux paroît avoir été constamment admis à Pistoia ; c'est que,
pour que la vengeance fût complète, il falloit qu'elle ne tombât pas sur l'offen-
seur; car si elle n'atteignoit que celui-ci, elle n'étoit qu'un châtiment, qui. propor-
tionné à l'offense, et attendu, ne pouvoit causer une douleur assez profonde à
ceux dont on vouloit se venger. La première offense étoit tombée sur un innocent: pour que la réciprocité fût complète, il falloit que la seconde atteignît un
homme également innocent."
" S'il y avoit dans l'une ou l'autre famille un homme que ses vertus fissent
respecter et chérir de tous, ou même que son caractère paisible eût éloigné des
dissensions civiles, et eût rendu comme inviolable au milieu des fureurs de la
guerre, c'étoit lui que le parti contraire désignoit pour sa victime ; et il ne croyoit
savourer tout le plaisir de sa vengeance, que lorsqu'il avoit bravé pour commettre
le crime la sauvegarde des loix, et tout respect divin ou humain." Sismondi, *Rép.*
Ital. tom. iv. pp. 98 - 100.

"The Florentines, among whom the Neri governed, in 1302, suspecting that the Bianchi, now banished from their city, would, with the assistance of the Bianchi who ruled in Pistoia, rise again with new force, entered into a combination with Lucca for the total destruction of Pistoia; and a war succeeded, which lasted many years, and extended to all the cities of Tuscany, introducing the distinctions of Neri and Bianchi, and several revolutions in all of them."

But the war against Pistoia was maintained by Florence and Lucca in concert, till Pistoia was taken, its country divided, and its people persecuted and oppressed, until, finally, they refused to receive a podestà from Lucca and Florence. This occasioned another army to be sent against them.

"The [1] Pistoians then called in the mediation of Siena; by whose decision it was ordained, that the podestà and captain of the people for Pistoia should not be chosen by the Lucchese and Florentines, but by the Pistoians themselves, provided that the election should always fall upon some citizen of Florence or Lucca. This award was supported by the Tedici, Ricciardi, Rossi, Lazzari, and Sinibaldi, and others, their followers, against the will of the Taviani, Ughi, and Cancellieri, and their adherents, both among the grandees and people. This difference of opinion occasioned quarrels and dissensions. The three families could not bear that the five families should *lord it over the city; each of these parties, therefore, striving to drive out the other, without regarding the expense or inconvenience, assembled their friends and forces, marched through the country, laid waste, combated, and assassinated, in defiance of all government. But in the end, the Taviani having fallen into an ambuscade in the midst of their enemies, near a river, some were killed, others made prisoners, and the rest dispersed as fugitives; and their fortress, della Pieve di Montecuccoli, now called Valdibura, and the church of St. Simon, where they had been used to retreat, were sacked and burnt.

"In 1316, the Pistoians conceived a jealousy of the prosperous fortune of Uguccione, not only on account of a signal victory he had obtained against the Guelphs, but because he had been made lord of Pisa and Lucca, and had it in contemplation to

---

[1] Fioravanti, c. xviii. p. 260.   * Signoreggiassero la città.

reduce Pistoia to his power.   But dissimulating their fears, and to make him friendly and benevolent to their city, the Pistoians chose him for their podestà.   Coming to Pistoia, he restored the Cancellieri, the Taviani, the Ughi, and Sinibaldi.

" In 1317, the Pistoians, by reason of the turbulence in Tuscany, put themselves under the protection of Robert, King of Naples.   Castruccio Antelminelli, captain-general of the wars of the Lucchese, having conducted to a happy issue many enterprises for that community, thought of reducing to its dominion the city of Pistoia, by the means of its Bianchi exiles; but after many skirmishes and mutual ravages of each other's territory, a battle fought between him and Giulione, who commanded the Pistoian forces against him, in which a decisive victory was obtained by the latter, produced a treaty of peace between them, one article of which was, that the exiles should be restored; the Neri consenting to this rather than risk a renewal of the war.

" In 1321, Uberto Cancellieri executed the office of podestà in the city of Padua, to the greatest satisfaction of that people. And the same year, Matteo Panciatichi gave clear proofs of fidelity and courage in the office of commissary of Romagna, under Clement V. and the people of Florence."

From 1321 to 1330, the history of this republic is filled with wars, seditions, and intrigues, all set on foot by the different contending parties, in order to elevate some individual, a favorite, or a tool of their own, for the sovereign of the state.   The simple heads of the story must suffice.

" Castruccio commences a destructive war upon the frontiers, to obtain the sovereignty of Pistoia for himself.   The people of Pitteccio betray their castle into his hands to favor his designs, being probably inclined to that party; the leaders, however, were beheaded for treason by the Pistoians.   Amidst these calamities, Ormanno Tedici conceives the design of making himself the sovereign of Pistoia.   The want of rain for eight months, and the devastations of war, had occasioned a famine in Pisa, Lucca, and Pistoia.   Upon this occasion, Tedici, and Vanni Lazzari, both rich and powerful, as well as proud and ambitious men, and consequently jealous of each other as rivals, appear upon the stage; their intrigues are full of all that duplicity and hypocrisy, which is universal on such occasions.*   Tedici persuades the Pistoians

* Fioravanti, lib. xix.

to a truce with Castruccio, and seizes the piazza and palace of the *anziani* with his partisans; is made lord of Pistoia, reforms the magistrates of the city, and concludes the truce with Castruccio, much against the will of the other party. Having gone through all the ceremonies of a revolution, that is to say, reversed every thing, recalled exiles, &c., and governed the city fourteen months, his nephew, Philip di Fortebraccio Tedici, a youth full of ambition, conspired to take away the sovereignty from his uncle, and assume it to himself. To this end, he began by corresponding with the Guelphs in exile, and by infusing into them a belief that his uncle entertained a secret correspondence with Castruccio, to deliver Pistoia into his hands. The nephew, by other artificial discourses and simulated manners, exerted himself with the Guelphs to depose his uncle, and restore all the banished and scattered members of the Guelph party. His fictions were credited, the resolution was taken with alacrity, they united themselves with the impostor, and, the better to obtain their desires, communicated their intentions to Neruccio Conte de Sarteano, a Guelph gentleman of prudence and sagacity, and requested his counsel and assistance; who, deceived by the relation of facts, so well invented and colored by Philip, acknowledged, that if remedy was not immediately provided, Pistoia would fall into the hands of Castruccio; and offered them his cavalry, and promised to exert all his force to obtain the ends they desired. The uncle discovering the conspiracy, complained to his nephew, who roundly asserted it to be a fiction of malice; and went immediately to the heads of the plot, told them that the abbé his uncle was informed of all, held a short consultation with them, in which it was resolved to rise at once, and carry into execution what they had intended. The conspirators assembling in the morning, and taking arms in season, rushed with Philip to the piazza, scattered the guards, by putting to death all who resisted, took the place, ran through the city, assaulted the palace of the *anziani*, occupied the gates, and garnished the walls with their people, and Philip remained lord and sovereign of Pistoia. This done, Philip called together the council of the people, obtained the title of. captain, and taking the sovereignty of the city on himself, reformed it with new *anziani* and magistrates, and, governing severely, made himself feared by all men.

x

" The Abbé Tedici, having lost the lordship of Pistoia, and
eager to regain the possession of it, machinated with his other
nephews and adherents to throw out of the window of the public palace his nephew Philip; and going with his followers to
the palace, he was introduced alone to a conference with the
artful Philip, by his express order, who immediately ordered the
gates to be shut against the other conspirators, and with a very
few words again imposed on his uncle, and made him prisoner.
Philip, thus liberated from the snares of his uncle, suddenly
renewed the truce with Castruccio.   He conducted his negotiations, both with Florence and Castruccio, with so much duplicity, that he deceived both; there are few examples of deeper
simulation, more exquisite address, or of selfish knavery of a
blacker dye, than he practised with his uncle, with the Florentines, and Castruccio.   After obtaining of the Florentines the
creation of his son a knight of the golden spur, three thousand
golden florins for himself, and noble matches and rich dowries
for his two daughters, of the Florentines, he married himself to
Dialta, the daughter of Castruccio, and delivered Pistoia into
his hands.   Castruccio immediately informs the Emperor Louis
of Bavaria of his new acquisition; and Louis sends to this
great man, so faithful and ardent in his service, a commission to
govern Pistoia as his imperial vicar.   Florence makes war to
recover the city; but is beaten by Castruccio, who receives the
emperor afterwards in Pistoia, and is made by him duke both of
Lucca and Pistoia, and soon after dies."

If he had lived, the example would probably have here been
complete; the continual altercations of the principal families
having completely overturned the constitution, and introduced
an absolute monarchy.   But his death opened a door for still
further contentions.   " M. Vinciguerra di Astancollo Panciatichi,
prefect of the royal militia of France, and a general in the wars
of Normandy, came into the service of the Florentines at this
time, with the character of general, and rendered himself memorable to posterity, and most grateful to his family, by building
in four years, his superb palace in Pistoia, in the parish of St.
Matthew.   The sons of the deceased Castruccio thought,[1] by
the favor of the Vergiolesi, Chiarenti, Tedici, and other powerful

---

[1] Fioravanti, chap. xx. p. 286.

families in Pistoia, to get themselves acknowledged as sovereigns of that city; and to this end procured an armed force to take possession of the piazza and palace of the *anziani;* but the imperial vicar, with his four hundred German guards, and by the favor of the Muli, Gualfreducci, and Panciatichi, families sufficiently powerful, gave battle to the sons of Castruccio, and drove them out of Pistoia, into the mountains of Lucca.

" The Florentines, taking advantage of the divisions and confusions in Pistoia, excited their people suddenly to war, and went and laid siege to Carmignano; and after many fierce battles for fifteen days it surrendered, which made the Florentines, with the Guelph exiles, very insolent, ravaging the country, preventing the farmers from sowing their grounds, and threatening even the walls of Pistoia.

" In this state of things, there arose in Pistoia two potent factions; one originated in the house of Vergiolesi, and the other in that of Panciatichi. The Vergiolesi adhering to the government of the imperial vicar, through fear of the four hundred Germans who were in Pistoia, induced a good part of the people to refuse their consent to a peace with the Florentines and Guelphs. The Panciatichi, with their followers, not judging the sentiment of the Vergiolesi good and useful for the city, esteemed it more advantageous to make peace, than to maintain the country in subjection to the avidity of the Bavarian and his ministers. But the other party determined to interrupt the treaty, by exciting the city to an uproar, and by parading the streets with their Germans, by whom many of the people were assassinated. Finding themselves thus ill-treated, the people, collecting together, fell upon these Germans. A skirmish followed, so serious that many were killed, many surrendered prisoners, and those who escaped were obliged to fly with their vicar to Lucca. In the mean time Ricciardo di Lazzaro Cancellieri, a Guelph exile from Pistoia, secretly assisted by the Florentines, and rendered powerful both by the money and the bravery of his Guelphs, understanding the disunion in Pistoia, marched into the mountains of Pistoia with great terror, to acquire possession of some confiscated castles of his party. This occasioned great disgust and alarm to all the city, and roused Giovanni Panciatichi to go out with his faction to oppose him; who attacking his enemy with great spirit, prevented him from making himself the lord of that extensive country. The Panciatichi, then, the Muli, and the Gualfreducci, pushing the advantage they had gained, and suspecting some treason from the Vergiolesi applied themselves at once to cut off the means to such designs. With all diligence they procured from the *anziani* an assembly of the general council, by whom all the sons and relations of Castruccio, Philip Tedici, Charles his son, with all their families, were banished and imprisoned out of Pistoia, and all their goods and estates confiscated; and to make sure of the imprisonment or the death of the Tedici, a reward was offered of five hundred florins of gold. This done, they made peace with Florence, and four knights of the golden spur were made by the Florentines, two of the family of Panciatichi, one of the family of Muli, and one of the Gualfreducci, in gratitude for their important services; and both cities submitted to the church, and banished the emperor."

The common people about this time began to be weary of the cabals of the principal families, but were too ignorant to contrive any method to restrain them, but that which always renders them still more desperate and destructive to the community, an attempt to bring all upon a level.

" The fashion at funerals had become so expensive, that every one exceeded his proper abilities in making a show; and the. Pistoians, not without giving occasion for ridicule, attempted to regulate the expense upon such occasions, by decreeing a uniform moderation for all. At the same time, considering the blessings and advantages of equal and clear laws, and that the people by the means of them are rendered tractable, and less haughty and audacious, they prepared certain statutes and provisions for the good government of their city. And as it appeared to them, that some of the principal families arrogated an undue share in the management of public affairs, and were disposed by force to oppress the commonalty, they determined that all offences against the latter should be severely punished, and that the next noble relation of any grandee should be obliged to pay any pecuniary mulct which should be inflicted, in case his estate was not sufficient to discharge it; and in case the delinquent was sentenced to a capital punishment, and escaped by any means from justice, his next relation among the grandees should be held to pay a thousand pounds."

Although nothing can be conceived more inconsistent with liberty, equity, or humanity, than these laws, yet the terror of them is said to have procured a momentary tranquillity; especially as certain companies of armed militia of the popular party were instituted in the four quarters of the city, to force them, arbitrary, oppressive, and cruel as they were, into execution. But this militia was not long able to control the spirit of disorder, and it became necessary to provide a stronger bridle for unquiet and seditious spirits, and a new and most rigorous law to beat down their arrogance and insolence.

"The plebeians at this time feeling themselves the true and real grandees, and at the highest summit of power, ordained by a law, that all those, of whatever condition they might be, who should give themselves up to an evil life, and give offence to the commonalty, and disturb the quiet of the city or country, should be, as a punishment for their actions, denominated "*grandees*," (*grandi, e magnati*,) and excluded from the magistracies, and all management of public affairs, and be subjected to more severe punishments. It is true that the nobles had still some share in the government, because the plebeians, that they might not make too many enemies at once, did not seek to exclude all from public offices, but selected from the number divers houses of the most pacific, and the greatest lovers of justice, and placed them among the popular men, to take away their power from the others, and secure it to themselves. No nobleman, however, adopted by the commonalty was permitted to make any ostentation of his nobility; so that if any one of the popular men was made a knight by any prince or republic, he was suddenly deprived of his office; whence many of the nobles, who wished to enjoy all the benefits of the commonalty, were obliged, by a simulated respect to the plebeians, to lay aside their arms and surnames, to distinguish themselves from their connections remaining among the grandees. Other nobles there were, who chose rather to be excluded from all public offices, and live exposed to the rigorous laws of the grandees, than to lay aside their arms or surnames, jealous of obscuring the ancient hereditary splendor of their ancestors. In this, however, they were deceived, for the principal popular men took care to preserve their distinction, by a law, " That if by a statute nobles were made plebeian, they do not lose by that their nobility;" that the advantage of being of the people accrues to them besides; and by another law, declaring many to be *magnati*, it is subjoined, "the rest we understand to be of the people, although born of noble race and progeny." From this it was contended, that those were deceived who measured the antiquity and nobility of their own or other families by the rule of the enjoyment of the principal magistracies.

"In 1332, several of the most powerful families, arrogating too much authority in public affairs," or, in other words, being found by the plebeians to have too much influence for them to be able to control, "such dissensions and disturbances arose, that it was thought necessary to declare them in the number of the grandees; and accordingly, it appears by the records, that the Cancellieri, Gualfreducci, Muli, Ughi, Panciatichi, Taviani, Ricciardi, Tedici, Sinibaldi, Tebertelli, Vergiolesi, Rossi, Lazzari, Forteguerri, Visconti, Foresi, and others, that is, all the principal families in the nation, were declared to be *magnati*, stigmatized with that odious appellation, and excluded from all share in public offices.

"In this year severe sumptuary laws against effeminate luxury were made by the council, the solemnities and expenses of weddings were regulated, and the clothing of men. Extravagant fashions in these things had tempted most people to exceed their revenues, had multiplied debtors, and rendered dubious and difficult the credit of merchants. Certain wise citizens were authorized to prepare regulations of this kind; and they succeeded in making such wise laws, that frauds and abuses became less common.

"Yet the caprice and instability of this government appears very remarkable at this time; for although the Cancellieri were the year before recorded for grandees, yet in 1333, Ricciardo Cancellieri was declared a knight by the council of the people of Pistoia, and was feasted at the public expense. When any one was made a knight by any sovereign, or any city, he became suddenly noble, although he had not been so by birth; for birth, at that time, was neither necessary to nobility nor to knighthood. The ceremony of arming the knight was made with great solemnity, receiving the military girdle from the other knights." *

* Fioravanti, p. 301.

In 1336, the Pistoians lamented the death of their most beloved citizen Cino, their greatest lawyer and judge, the master of Bartolo and Petrarch.

In 1342, Pistoia was obliged to capitulate with the Duke of Athens, who held the government of it three years, and ruled it as tyrannically as he did Florence.

In 1344, the government was recovered from the Duke of Athens; and,

" To remedy the infinite tumults which were daily excited by the power of the families of the *magnates*, who, by their riches and adherents made their authority and influence prevail, it was ordained, that in time of any tumult or uproar it should not be lawful for any man of the people to enter the house of any grandee, and if by chance any one should be in such a house at such a time, he should immediately quit it, that he might not be under the temptation to assist the grandee, upon pain of the loss of all public offices, and confiscation of all his goods. And no one of these powerful families, whom they branded with the name of *grandees*, could go into the service of any prince, city, or republic, if he had not first obtained the permission of the general council, on pain of being declared a rebel; and that the families of the grandees might be known to all, the following description and declaration of them was made and published by thority, namely, — ' Omnes de domo Cancellariorum, omnes de domo Gualfreducciorum, Tediciorum, Lazarorum, Viscontorum, Panciaticorum, Ugorum, Mulorum, Tavianorum, Sinibuldorum, Vergiolensium, Rubeorum, Ricciardorum;' which grandees, in time of any tumult or strife, must not go out of their houses, unless called by the captain, or the gonfalonier, and *anziani*.

" The Pistoians, informed of the robberies, assassinations, and havoc, which were daily committed by certain rebels in the above mountain, and of the treasons plotting by those of Serravalle against the peace and quiet of the commons of Pistoia, did not neglect to use the necessary expedition to chastise the insolence of the former, and to divert the malignity of the latter; against the former they sent out a body of soldiers, who put the rebels to flight, and pulled down their houses; against the latter, they promulgated severe laws, with a promise of a thousand pounds reward to any one who would accuse an accomplice of treason."

To show the inefficacy of all such democratical despotism, as

the declarations of grandeeism against the principal families
in a community, Frederick Cancellieri, surnamed for his great
vaìor Barbarossa, had influence enough to obtain so great a distinction, and so popular and honorable a post as the command
of the troops raised and paid by Pistoia, to go upon the expedition for the conquest of the Holy Land; Angiolo Cancellieri
was made a bishop, and rose fast in the church; and Niccolò
Cancellieri, as captain of the Florentines, acquired immortal
glory by besieging in his own palace, and deposing from the
government of Florence, Walter, Duke of Athens; and Marcello
Cancellieri also made himself illustrious as a divine, and obtained
the place of auditor of the chief court of judicature at Rome."

So much of the time of the husbandman, the artisan, and the
people in general, was taken up in war at home and abroad, and
the fields were so often laid waste, that it was impossible to
obtain a constant and certain supply of provisions for the people. The consequence of this was famine and the plague, two
other evils in those days springing, with innumerable others,
from their imperfect government.

" The plague and famine, which, in the course of the past
year, had nearly deprived Pistoia of inhabitants, at length ceas-
ing, the few that remained were so grieved and astonished at
such a calamity, that one would have thought their minds too
much softened and humbled to engage again for some time in
their nefarious tumults; but the few surviving citizens found as
much disunion and animosity among them as ever. Fresh disorders arose, and there was no possibility of restraining the indignation and fury of the two families of Panciatichi and Cancellieri,
who, upon some dissatisfaction arising among them, fell into such
quarrels, that, as each party had many adherents, many murders
and much slaughter followed; and much greater would have
ensued, if the people had not gathered to separate the combatants, and compelled them to retire to their houses.[1] To prevent
the prevalence and increase of these disorders, the citizens called
together the general council, by whom it was ordered that diligent inquisition should be made after the heads of the tumult,
and a rigorous prosecution was commenced against Richard
Cancellieri, and Gio. Panciatichi, the heads of the two families;

[1] Fioravanti, chap. xxii. p. 314.

who, although they humbled themselves, and asked pardon for the error they had committed, and made an entire reconciliation with each other, were condemned in a fine of five hundred lire each, to be paid to the commons of Pistoia, and were obliged to ratify by an oath, in full council, the peace they had made between them. But notwithstanding all this, neither of the families really laid aside their bad temper towards the other; for their principals having, rather from the fear of justice than a desire of tranquillity, made the peace between them, they daily applied themselves to provide arms and men, and finally proclaimed themselves openly to be mortal enemies to each other. This gave rise to the factions of the Panciatichi and Cancellieri, from whence arose such actions and events as brought final ruin on themselves, their relations, their friends, and the city itself.

" I reflect with astonishment and stupefaction," says Fioravanti, " that the Pistoians, abandoning, without cause or reason, their native sagacity, and becoming factionaries, should have fomented the passions of these two particular families; have set the boasting of preëminence over one another before the public peace; and have employed all their forces against the tranquillity of liberty in that city, celebrated through the whole world for men illustrious in arms, in letters, in sanctity, and wisdom; prudent in her laws and in her government to such a degree, that foreign republics had made a model of her laws. Nevertheless, thus it was; giving themselves up a prey to their griefs and afflictions, they deprived themselves of all repose, and making the passions of a few common to them all, lost their liberty and their government; blessings, which till this time had been preserved, not without the envy of their rival cities! "

This writer needed not, however, have been so much surprised, if he had considered the nature of man, and compared it with the nature of a government in which all authority is collected into one centre. An attentive reader will be surprised at the boast of that tranquillity and liberty hitherto enjoyed; and will be at a loss to find one moment in the whole history where there could have been any degree of either.

Arbitrary laws of exclusion and disqualification, and awkward attempts to expose to popular odium the principal families, made without the least modesty or equity by a popular majority, will never have weight enough with the people to answer the

32 *

design of them. Those families will still retain an influence
with the people, and have a party at their command very nearly
equal to that of the majority; and being justly irritated and
provoked at the injustice done them, will never want a disposition to attempt dangerous enterprises.

" The family of the Cancellieri, though stigmatized and disqualified as grandees, were still held in great esteem, among all
ranks, for their riches and numerous adherents. Richard, the
head of the family, stimulated by his own resentment and ambition, and no doubt excited by his partisans, had the presumption
to entertain thoughts of making himself sovereign lord of his
country. Courting the people to this end by his liberality, affa-
bility, and courtesy, he waited only for a favorable opportunity
to acquire it. Having filled his house with a large number of
persons, his countrymen and foreigners, he suddenly marched out
with these and his relations to assault the piazza and the palace
of the *anziani;* but being met by the captain of the company of
the *anziani,* with his men, and with these many of the grandees,
and a multitude of the common people, adherents of the Panciatichi, the Cancellieri were repulsed with great spirit, and perceiving their lives in great danger, they fled and shut themselves
up in the house of the Bondacchi, their friends. Their faction,
seeing themselves left without a head, in disorder and defeated,
fled in despair out of the city by the gate of St. Mark. The
Panciatichi, having thus conquered Richard, proceeded with
great violence to burn the houses of the Cancellieri. Richard
was outrageous at the destruction of his houses and the flight
of his followers; but being informed that they were waiting for
him in the country, he scaled the walls in the night, went out to
meet them, took the castle of Marliana, and there fortified himself.

" With the Cancellieri on their flank, and Gio. Visconti, Archbishop of Milan, and Lord of Bologna and all Lombardy, in
their neighborhood, both with parties desirous of making them
lords of Pistoia, the Pistoians were obliged to put themselves
under the protection of Florence, upon certain conditions. Richard Cancellieri, hearing of this, went to Florence, and with
plausible reasons made it there believed that the Panciatichi
held a secret correspondence with Visconti, to deliver Pistoia
into his hands. The Florentines thought they might as well
govern Pistoia themselves, and have it wholly at their devotion,

and immediately gave Richard the command of horse and foot, to go and subdue it. The attack was made in the night, and would probably have succeeded, if the ensigns of Florence had not been imprudently displayed, which so enraged the Pistoians, that resolving to die rather than submit, they repulsed their invaders."

The Florentines sent a formidable reinforcement; but the Pistoians defended themselves with intrepidity till they assembled their general council; and although Gio. Panciatichi was infamous as a *grandee*, he was still the soul of the republic, and no other man had enough of the confidence of his fellow-citizens to be sent ambassador, and entrusted with their salvation. He executed his commission, convinced the Florentines that they had been deceived by Cancellieri, and made an honorable peace; and in 1352, the Pistoians effectually assisted Florence in defending itself against the army of Visconti of Milan.

" In 1353, the attention of all parties was turned to peace, to put an end, once for all, to the troubles of Italy, and it was finally concluded between all the Guelph cities of Tuscany, namely, Florence, Siena, Pistoia, Perugia, Arezzo, city of Castello, and others, of one side, and Gio. Visconti on the other, with certain pacts and conditions; among which Visconti freely released into the hands of Pistoia the castles and fortresses of Piteccio, Torri, Treppio, Fossato, Monticelli, and Sambuca; and on all sides all the exiles were released. By virtue of which article, the families of the Ammanati, Tedici, Vergiolesi, Gualfreducci, and others, were restored to Pistoia, and all their property was restored to them.

" Richard Cancellieri, nevertheless, in 1354, being still obnoxious to the Panciatichi, did not cease to strengthen his party, by soliciting the friendship of those who might be useful to his views. To this end he formed an intimate friendship with the captain of the Florentine guards, of whom he expected to make an essential use in all occurrences. But the Panciatichi, jealous of this intimacy, complained of it bitterly to the Florentines, who, to please them, dismissed their officer, but at the same time exhorted the complainants to live quietly, and lay down their arms; for that at all events, and at any expense, as authors of the peace between the two families, they were determined to maintain it. At this time, some disquiet arose between the different members of the Cancellieri family, one of whom, Pievano, joined the Panciatichi, and brought an accusation before the Florentines against Richard, that he meditated some great treachery against them. A rigorous investigation was instituted, Richard being found innocent, the accuser and the heads of the insurrection were severely punished, while he was honorably acquitted."

The emperor Charles IV. made a grant to the Pistoians to govern themselves by their own laws and laudable customs, in a free popular state, under the guidance of the *anziani* and gonfalonier of justice, whom he made perpetual vicars of the holy Roman empire. That this sketch may not be protracted to an immeasurable length, we may pass over the rebellions and wars between 1355 and 1376, at which time,

" The dissatisfactions among the citizens of Pistoia were so increased, by the renewal of officers in 1373, that tumults arose, and to such a height were they carried, that the Florentines, who desired no more than to become lords of Pistoia, or to see it destroyed, because it was rich, noble, and powerful, thought it a favorable opportunity to strike in with their meditated designs. Under the specious color of peace and quiet, they annulled the late renewal; and by new laws, under pretence of taking away the scandalous names of the two factions of the Panciatichi and Cancellieri, divided the officers into two orders, calling one *the company of St. John*, and the other *the company of St. Paul;* so that a moiety of the citizens, exclusively of the grandees, who had not enjoyed the benefit of the imborsation, was now imborsed in the purse of the company of St. John, and the other moiety in the purse of the company of St. Paul; and to obtain the supreme magistrate four were drawn, one for each quarter, from the purse of St. John, and four, in the proportion of one for each quarter, from the purse of St. Paul; and the gonfalonier was to be drawn alternately, once from one purse, and another time from the other. And because the company of St. John was protected by the Cancellieri, it immediately followed that it declared itself of that faction; and that of St. Paul, protected by the Panciatichi, declared itself openly of the faction of Panciatichi; and in this manner, instead of extinguishing the fire, it increased to such a degree, that it spread not only in the city, but through all its territory; and Pistoia was reduced to a condition so deplorable, as to be obliged to abandon all domestic society and familiarity, every one being suspicious not only of his neighbors and relations, but of his bosom friends."

In 1383, all ranks of people exceeded their abilities in expenses at funerals, and in other effeminate luxury; sumptuary laws were made against extravagant expenses; but the historian confesses, that although he thought there was reason for them, yet, as he could not read them himself without laughing, he feared he should do no good by relating them.

" The Pistoians having bestowed all their endeavors and studies to obtain a peace with Bologna, with whom they had long been at war on account of boundaries, now hoped to live happily; but they were again tormented with insurrections, attended with rapine, burnings, and murders innumerable.

" The news arrived in Pistoia, in 1390, that John Galeazzo Visconti had sent against the Florentines an army of twenty thousand men, under the command of Jacopo del Verme."

This war lasted several years, and was brought upon the city by its divisions.

" The Pistoians had now been eight and forty years in some sense dependent on Florence; for in 1350, after the great commotions, they had entered into a stipulation, by Richard Cancellieri their fellow-citizen, with the people of Florence, to keep forever a purse of six Florentines taken from among the popular party, out of which should be drawn their captain of the people. In this year, 1398, for the sake of a more intimate connection and familiarity with the commons of Florence, it was farther stipulated, that for the future the podestà of Pistoia should be a Florentine."

Continual animosities had occasioned in the minds of the citizens such weariness, grief, and compunction, that it is impossible to read, without commiseration, their awkward attempts to reconcile themselves with one another, and to extirpate the civil discords, with which Pistoia was furiously agitated. The whole people, of every age, sex, and condition, were persuaded to go in procession through the city, clothed in white sacks, to ask mutually each other's pardon, and to cry " *Misericordia e pace!*" (mercy and peace) and there can be no doubt that a momentary benevolence, and many acts of Christian charity, must have been produced by a pilgrimage so solemn and affecting; but the de-

fects in the constitution of their government were not amended
by it, and the troubles of the people soon revived.

The jealousies of the Cancellieri and Panciatichi[1] revived,
and proceeded to such lengths, that in 1401, Richard Cancellieri,
to revenge himself, began a secret treaty with Visconti Duke of
Milan, to deliver the city of Pistoia into his hands, that he
might govern it with his absolute power, and exterminate the
faction of the Panciatichi. The plot was discovered, and Richard
and all his children declared rebels, and their houses reduced to
ashes. Richard in the country joined with other exiles, and
burned the houses of Panciatichi. The Pistoians were now so
alarmed with the danger, from the Visconti and Cancellieri in
concert, that they were obliged to put themselves into the hands
of the Florentines. The Cancellieri carried on the war, however,
with so much spirit and success, that, although the Duke of
Milan died in 1402, Richard was able, in 1403, to obtain a peace,
by which the state of Pistoia was obliged to restore his family
to all their estates, and make good all their losses. The Panciatichi agreed to this, that the consent of all the leaders might
be obtained to lay this burden on the people, by whom the
damages done to the Panciatichi too were to be repaired.

"In 1420, it was ordained,[2] that in the renewal of magistrates
and public offices, the families who had been stigmatized with
the opprobrious name of *grandees* should be restored to the
rights of citizens, and share in the management of public affairs.
But these, beginning with their usual impertinence to labor that
every thing should be done as they would have it, and all offices
disposed by their influence, quarrels and dissensions among the
citizens arose, by which the whole city fell into the greatest
agitation; whence it was necessary, for the maintenance of the
public peace, to exclude them afresh from public affairs. These
families were the Panciatichi, Rossi, Sinibuldi, Ughi, Taviani,
Vergiolesi, Lazari, Cancellieri, Ricciardi, Visconti, Gualfreducci,
and Tedici.

"The ladies indulged in great expenses in the furniture of their
houses, and in the superfluous ornaments of their persons and
families. The general council thought it necessary to interpose,
and prohibit all clothes to be lined with foreign furs, or to be

---

[1] Fioravanti, cap. xxiv. p. 342.   [2] Chap. xxv. p. 351.

embroidered with pearls, gold, or silver, or other expensive and superfluous decorations; and because all former laws for the same purpose had been found ineffectual, they were now renewed with most rigorous penalties."

In 1455, a civil war broke out in the territory of Pistoia, called Alliana, between the Cancellieri and Panciatichi, which spread into the city, and went to such furious lengths that the ladies themselves took arms, and fought with as much bravery as the gentlemen, to revenge the slaughter of their relations; and before this commotion was ended, the slaves, or what they call the the vassals or villeins, took arms. And no method to restore peace could be devised, till Florence was requested to send four commissaries, who compelled the Cancellieri and Panciatichi to take an oath to be peaceable. Yet insurrections, tumults, and civil wars, continued in 1476, and indeed, with very little intermission, till 1485.

"In that year[1] Baldinotto Baldinotti, foreseeing that Lorenzo de' Medici might possibly arrive at the sovereignty of Pistoia, considering the great reputation, influence, and authority, which he enjoyed in that city, laid a plot to take him off. As a lover of the liberty of his country, he thought it just and honorable to go with his own son, and lie in wait in the way between Poggio and Cajano, by which he knew Lorenzo was to pass, in his journey to Pistoia, to the feast of St. James. But the confidants of Lorenzo having discovered the design, the conspirators were without delay apprehended, carried prisoners to Florence, and there punished with death."

Another civil war between the Cancellieri and Panciatichi, attended with its customary cruelty and devastation, occurred, and was not composed till the Florentines summoned four of each party, and compelled them to give security, that for the future no quarrels, murders, burnings, or robberies, should be committed in Pistoia. But this answered the end only in part, for the parties went out of the limits of the state, and there committed all sorts of cruelties on one another; and in 1490, the civil war was renewed in the city.

"On the death of the Emperor Frederick III., Maximilian, his son, succeeded to the throne of the empire; but delaying his

---

[1] Fioravanti, p. 367.

entry into Italy, he gave occasion to Louis Sforza, tutor of the Duke of Milan, to invite Charles VIII., King of France, to come to the conquest of Naples. Upon this occasion the Pistoians threw off their subjection to Florence, or rather broke off the connection. But this acquisition of liberty and independence had a short duration; for the Pistoians knew they could enjoy no tranquillity under their own government, and with their own parties; after two years negotiation, they agreed to a new convention in 1496.

"The families of the grandees, or *impertinents*, as they were called, revived their pretensions to be admitted to the honors and public offices of the commonwealth; but as this was contrary to the popular will, and the passions and interest of their leaders, tumults ensued.[1] The pretensions of these families were countenanced by the Florentines; but the popular men in the plenitude of their power, opposed it with so much resolution, that nothing new was effected.

"Plague and famine raged in Pistoia to such a degree, that some were in hopes the citizens would put an end to discord and sedition, and at least endeavor to enjoy peace; but the people, trampling under foot all laws, human and divine, began to renew, both in the city and the country, their oppositions and enmities, which proceeded to such feats of arms and mutual slaughter, that they were again obliged to have recourse to the Imperial vicars in Florence, to interpose and put an end to those strange accidents which threatened the total destruction of the country.

"The dissensions of parties in the city and its territory being somewhat abated, the citizens began to flatter themselves with the hopes of quiet;[2] but neglecting to provide a remedy against the emulations of private interest, in individuals and families,

---

[1] The original meaning of Fioravanti seems not to be accurately adhered to in this place.

"In tempi sì calamitosi, anche le Famiglie Magnate, o impertinenti come si disse, si fecero sentire con la loro pretensione di essere *contro ogni volere de' popolari* ammese agli onori, e ufizi pubblici, e a tale effetto principiando a tumultuare, obbligarono i Fiorentini a proteggere la loro pretenzione; ma i Pistojesi *opponendosi a sì impertinente domanda* fecero sì, che riconosciute da' Fiorentini per buone le ragioni de' Popolari, non restò per allora innovata cosa veruna." p. 374.

The historian's opinion of the cause of the evil in this instance is plain enough. The next paragraph explains the other side of the question.

[2] Chap. xxvii. p. 376.

by separating the executive power from the legislative, rivalries arose, which produced such ruin, both to the country and the contending families, as has been deplored by all subsequent generations. The fact was, that by the death of Buonaccorsi, a director of a hospital of St. Gregory, it was necessary to proceed to the election of a successor. On the tenth of October, 1499, four subjects or persons, had been balloted for, and approved as suitable, by the general council, among whom the one, who should be confirmed and approved by the bishop of Pistoia according to the law, was to obtain the office. The council having discharged their duty in the nomination of the four, the ordinary proceeded to reject two of them, one after another, and left the competition undecided between Piero Terchio and Bernardo Nutini, each of whom endeavored to interest his friends in his favor. Terchio was protected by the Panciatichi, and Nutini by the Cancellieri. The bishop was at Florence, whence it happened that Salimbene Panciatichi caused his friend Terchio, to be confirmed, as director of the hospital, by the Canon Jacob Panciatichi, under color of his being the apostolical legate; and sending to Florence for the approbation of the bishop, the good prelate promised to comply. The Cancellieri hearing of this, went also to Florence to supplicate the bishop not to approve the election; but the bishop, who wished to keep his word, would not listen to them. Seeing that they could not move him from his promise, they applied themselves to obtain solicitations of his friends and relations, with such assiduity and importunity, that the irresolute [1] prelate was at last induced to comply with their request. The Panciatichi, understanding the strange resolution of the prelate, had recourse to the priori of the people and the gonfalonier of justice of their country, and obtained an order, that the possession of the hospital should not be given to Nutini, who had the smaller number of votes, but to Terchio, who by right ought to have it; and Terchio, accompanied by some of the Panciatichi, was placed in the government of the hospital.

The Cancellieri, returning from Florence with the confirmation of the bishop in the person of Nutini, carried him to the hospital to give him possession, but found the place occupied;

[1] " Dolce," *amiable*, frequently signifying the same with the word used in the text.

whereupon, returning to Florence, they carried their complaint to the *rettori;* and, after much altercation between the parties, it was determined that the affair should be decided in a court of justice, and the cause committed to two lawyers. The judges determined that Nutini had been elected and canonically confirmed, and he was accordingly put into the office, against all that could be said or done by the Panciatichi, who, upon pain of being declared rebels, were obliged to abandon the hospital, which they had held well guarded, and give way to the execution of the sentence. The Cancellieri were made insolent by their victory, and, sometimes by words, sometimes by actions, assumed a haughty superiority over the contrary party; who, considering themselves derided and insulted not only by the Cancellieri but by the bishop, went about venting their passions among the people; whence it happened, that hostilities beginning between these two families, they never ceased till they ruined the city of Pistoia.

" The Panciatichi could not erase from their minds the many and great injuries they had received from the Cancellieri, and now meditated a cruel revenge. On the fifth of February, 1500, they unexpectedly assaulted, under the greater piazza, Baccino Nutini and others, and having mortally wounded Giorgio Tonti, they set to running through the whole city, and murdering all the Cancellieri, excepting some who had taken refuge in the palace of the lords priors. The Cancellieri who survived were not at all intimidated, because, having many adherents, it was easy for them to rouse the plebeians against the Panciatichi; quick at their instigation, these showed themselves fierce persecutors of that faction, for, arming themselves, all shouted ' Vengeance! vengeance!' and in the tumult a multitude of the Panciatichi and their adherents were killed upon the spot. Matters became so exasperated, that both parties thought of nothing but mustering as many followers as they could. In May the Panciatichi assembled a great body of men, and seized the piazza, and more than half the city fortified themselves in the balconies, steeples, and towers, and devoted their whole time and attention to preparations for war. The Cancellieri on their part, with followers equally numerous, fortified themselves in the other side of the city, and were assisted by such numbers of men, who came in from the mountains and plains in the coun-

try, that they composed a large army. In such a scene of
turbulence, suspicions were so frequent and dangerous, that it
became necessary for every man to declare himself; for both
parties adopted the same maxim towards the moderate men
and neutrals, ' If you don't show yourself our friend, we will
show ourselves your enemy.'[1] There was not a man, finally,
who did not take a share in all the injuries and insolence of a
party ; and frequent battles, sometimes in one street, and sometimes in another, both by night and by day, disturbed the whole
city so, that there was no time for the people to take any repose.

"In this state of things there arrived at Pistoia two commissaries, with five hundred men, sent by the Imperial vicars in
Florence to put a check to the impetuosity of faction, who
entered by the gate of Caldatica, and, taking possession of the
most important and advantageous posts, gave orders to all to
retreat and abandon their arms. These orders were scarcely
promulgated, when there unexpectedly appeared a large body
of armed men to the assistance of the Cancellieri, which had
been sent by their adherents in Bologna ; and, on the other side,
a number of men from St. Marcello, and other neighboring
countries, came to the succor of the Panciatichi. And neither
party choosing to give way to the other, they began, in the face
of the Florentine guards, to strike each other so cruelly, that the
faster their forces increased, the more were multiplied the insults,
arsons, murders, and slaughter.

"The commissaries seeing all things rushing to destruction,
ordered the heads of both parties to appear at Florence, and
that the soldiers, both foreign and domestic, should leave the city
upon pain of being declared rebels, and they extended the same
threat to all who should entertain them in their houses. The
Panciatichi were disposed to obey; but the Cancellieri, who
were favored by one of the commissaries, continued insolent,
and those who had been summoned made a jest of the orders,
and refused to move; whence those ministers, seeing themselves
little respected, and less obeyed, returned to Florence. The
soldiers had left the city, and the heads of the factions, seeing
themselves deprived of their strength, set themselves to enlisting
the plebeians on their side, and a great body of people eager

---

[1] " Se tu non ti mostri nostro amico, dunque tu sei nostro nemico."

for slaughter stood ready to begin a new affray. As the death
of Giorgio Tonti had been displeasing to the Cancellieri, they
could not forget it, nor conquer their desire of a bitter revenge;
with this view they occupied, with all their people, the piazza
della Sala, and leaving a number to guard it, went with the rest
to the little square of the Trinity, to pull down the houses of
the Cellesi, and then that of one of the Panciatichi; after which
they laid siege to the palace of Gualtieri Panciatichi, which they
briskly beat down; then running through the city, they killed
Francis Nutini, and plundered his house, with that of Gabriel
Visconti, Bernard Cellesi, Matthew Cellesi, and setting fire to
all of them, they ran to attack the house of Astorre Panciatichi,
from whence those of its faction fled, and this house remained
in the power of its enemies, who stripped and robbed it. They
then burned the houses of the Centi, those of Gio. di Francesco,
and Thomas Balducci, and that of Gori, archdeacon of St.
Zeno, and auditor of the bishop Pandolfini. After so many
pillages, burnings, and demolitions, they returned to the piazza,
and rifled all the shops and stores of the Panciatichi, with whom
they engaged in a bitter conflict, and a large number on both sides
perished. At this instant a powerful reinforcement of men arrived to the Panciatichi, who without loss of time renewed the
attack upon the Cancellieri, and both parties fought in the
parish of Our Lady of the Lily, and in that of St. 'Michael,
with such desperation, that a great number on both sides were
killed and wounded, and if a great rain had not parted the combatants, it seemed as if the whole race would have been here
exterminated. But upon this occasion a truce was concluded.
The heads of these factions were now summoned to Florence;
thirty of them went, and were immediately thrown into prison.
A rigorous prosecution," as it is called, "was commenced against
them. Some were acquitted without any conditions of peace or
truce; others were punished by imprisonment; some by seques-
tration of their property, and some were banished."

" This decision extinguished no part of the flames of revenge;
on the contrary, the rigor practised against some, and the lenity
to others, gave rise to still greater insolence; and in the face of
the Florentines themselves, and in their own city, some of the
acquitted Cancellieri committed excesses as outrageous as before.
Introduced by some of the malignant into Florence, secretly, at

the shutting of the gates, they set themselves to search for Andrew and Salimbè Panciatichi, to assassinate them; and favored by the obscurity of a foggy air, after two o'clock at night, they found it easy to put Salimbè to death, though Andrew had the good fortune to escape, by hiding himself in a joiner's shop. For this atrocious crime seven were outlawed; but they having been reinstated in Pistoia, in defiance of justice, the factionaries soon came to another rupture; they confounded all things in such a manner, that there no longer remained any who dreaded the divine, much less human justice; but scattering their strife through the plains and mountains, nothing was heard of but quarrels, treachery, conflagration, and murder. The two factions were at length weary of such inconveniences and fatigues, and, to prepare themselves to combat with greater vigor, they made for a short time, and with common consent, a truce; each party increased its supply of arms, men, and provisions; and the Panciatichi, desirous of victory, invented several new instruments and machines of war, and fortifying themselves with these, thought themselves invincible.

" The Cancellieri, as well as the Panciatichi fortified themselves with forts and bastions of timber, and machines of war, and stood well upon their guard in their posts. The Panciatichi, no longer able to restrain themselves, set in order all their people, made Palamidesse Panciatichi, and Bartolomeo Cellesi, their leaders, and arranged all their posts, officers, and soldiers. But while they were occupied in these dispositions, they unexpectedly found the opposite faction ready to meet them; the battle was fought, and the Cancellieri obtained a bloody victory, because the Panciatichi were abandoned by a large body of Lombards, whom they had hired for their defence. They did not, however, lose courage, but reassembling their partisans, and rallying their soldiers, they appeared again in a short time, with greater numbers and ferocity than ever; and the engagement being renewed, for the short time that it lasted, was so terrible and fatiguing, that both parties, exhausted and faint, were constrained to retire with their wounded men to their posts.

" The Cancellieri having taken some repose, and, considering that they had the countenance of the new Florentine commissaries, by whose advice those of their associates had been restored to Pistoia, who had been banished from Florence for the murder

33 *

of Salimbè Panciatichi, assumed fresh courage to attempt every means for the destruction of the Panciatichi. On the ninth of August they scoured all the streets and squares of the city, and wherever they found a Panciatichi they murdered him. They put to death also Bernardino Gai, and mortally wounded the Conte di Rigolo Bisconti; but many of the Panciatichi, thinking it their duty to avenge themselves, fell with such impetuosity upon the rear of the Cancellieri, as obliged them to retire. In this state of things the Florentine commissaries cited to appear before them ten persons of each party; who, though they made their appearance, were detained in the palace of justice, and exhorted to peace, or at least to a temporary truce, would not accept of any of these proposals; therefore the commissaries, not knowing what to do with them, dismissed them. Animated rather than terrified by this weakness of authority and the judicial power, they recalled all their followers confined in various places, and providing themselves again with arms and assistants, renewed the war. Such was the ardor, violence, and force of the Cancellieri and their party, that they excited great terror, not only in the country parts, but in all the city. Not content to have taken possession of all the councils, and assembled them to govern as they pleased, and rendered their people disobedient to all law, but they also sent them, with the utmost license, through the country, to ravage, plunder, and burn the villages and habitations. The men of prudence and reflection, seeing such destruction and so much ruin, and foreseeing more, exerted themselves to obtain an election of eight citizens, to whom were given the whole authority of the general council," or, in other words, they were made dictators, "that they might find a remedy for so great confusions, and do whatever should be necessary or convenient for restoring the public tranquillity.

" In the meanwhile the clergy were aroused, and with uncommon zeal exhorted the people in private, and fulminated from the pulpit against all this ungodliness and unrighteousness of men; but all this apostolical benevolence, added to the unlimited power of the eight dictators, were insufficient; men's ears were deaf, and their eyes blind, to every thing but the malignity of their own passions, and every one continued to do whatever seemed right in his own eyes. They recalled into Pistoia all the banished men, with numerous troops of their adherents; these filling the city with bad men, and bringing fresh force and vigor to the respective parties, they prepared to commit new excesses. The Panciatichi, finding themselves at liberty, and loosened from all restraint, went, on the thirteenth of August, unexpectedly, to batter down the houses of Giuliano Fioravanti, that of Jacob Peri, that of Antonio Popoleschi, and many others, upon which occasion many were wounded; Francis Panciatichi, and John Astesi, with many others of inferior condition, were killed. On the fifteenth of August they went to batter down the house of Biagio Odaldi, but these making a resolute resistance, many were wounded, and the rest obliged to retreat; but returning the next day, to attack it, they labored to such purpose, that partly with force, and partly with fire, they took possession of the house. They went next to the palace of Neri and Thomas Fioravanti, and finding no resistance they took it and filled it with their men. They assaulted too the houses of the Celate, Salincorni, and Curradi, and not being able to take them, set fire to them, and burnt five warehouses of Antonio Ambrogi; they entered into the house of Lorenzo Gatteschi, but there they were obliged to fight a long time, and the engagement became general, so that it was impossible to ascertain the number of the killed and wounded of the two factions, but there was not a street in the city which was not incumbered with dead bodies, and polluted with human blood.

"Intelligence of the strength of the Panciatichi had been communicated by the Cancellieri to their friends, who, on the morning of the seventeenth of August, with a hundred cavalry, and two hundred infantry, appeared suddenly at the houses of the Cellesi, by whom so brave a defence was made, that they were repulsed; but after taking a short repose, they returned to the assault, took the house, plundered it, and set it on fire. They went next to the houses of Antonio Ambrogi, to the two houses of the Cioci, to that of Vincenzo Mati, and burned them, with many others, and retook those which had been hitherto occupied by the Panciatichi, who finding themselves obliged to abandon the houses of Andrea Fioravanti, and Antonio Popoleschi, consigned them, in desperation, to the flames. But while the party of the Cancellieri were busy in this mischief, they were attacked, in two places at once, by the Panciatichi; and scarcely was the action begun, when, perceiving their disadvantage, they retreated behind the church of St. Anthony, and set fire to the house of Nicholas Godemini; from thence they went to the Old Gate, and attacked the houses of the Bracciolini in the piazza, where, meeting with a bold resistance, they went with great anxiety to find the commissaries, and demanded of them the possession of the hospital del Ceppo, which was then governed by one of the Panciatichi, otherwise they would set fire to it. The Panciatichi had already two hundred country-men of the Plain, under the command of Michelino Jozzeli, and that of Lisca, who, posted for the guard of the hospital, were determined to perish rather than abandon it. The commissaries seeing so many people assisting the Panciatichi, would not openly espouse the request and attempt of the Cancellieri, but pacifying them with soothing words, they gave orders to M. Criaco, the captain, who, in behalf of the Florentine Imperial vicars, with five hundred soldiers guarded the piazza, in their name to take possession of the hospital, under the pretence of preserving it from so much fury. The captain, with one hundred of his soldiers, marched to the hospital, and employed all his art to obtain possession of it, but was answered by the Panciatichi, that they would not go out of the place alive. Upon this the commissaries in person went to the hospital, and acknowledging that it must require great feats of arms to take it, talked so fair to the Panciatichi, that these delivered it up to them. It was, however, unexpectedly pillaged by the Cancellieri, and then placed by the orders of the commissaries, in the power of the supreme magistrate of the city, by whom possession being taken, regulations were made for the good government of it, and the administration given to four prudent citizens.

" A little afterwards the commissaries and the bishop undertook to persuade the party of the Panciatichi not only not to seek the control of the hospital, but also to absent themselves some time from the city, and in that manner to remove the cause of so many disorders, and endless evils which threatened to succeed. These orders, or this recommendation, were given to Bastiano and Vincenzo Bracciolini, of that faction, who immediately held a conference with Andrew and Antonio Panciatichi, their leaders. These thought fit to obey, first demanding security for their houses and other property, which was

promised them by the commissaries. They made haste to
communicate these particulars to all their factionaries, who,
adhering to the opinions of their principals, collected together
all their property of value, and carried it towards the church of
St. Paul, and there filled up the whole street which leads to the
gate Caldatica, and stood well upon their guard. The Cancellieri were in the contiguous street, with four hundred soldiers
from Bologna; but fearing to risk a battle, the Panciatichi
marched out of Pistoia without receiving injury, followed by the
Cellesi, Rossi, Franchini, Forteguerri, Fabroni, Bisconti, Bracciolini, Brunozzi, and many others of equal rank and condition.
The gates were instantly shut, and the walls lined with men by
the Cancellieri, who from that eminence, scoffed at the retreating
faction, with impunity and without danger.

"The Cancellieri remained in Pistoia, and it is not possible to
relate the abominable iniquities and cruelties committed by them
in the height of their triumph, insolence, and power; ranging the
whole city without control, they attended to no other business
or amusement but to ruin, burn, plunder, and ravish, whatever
of the Panciatichi they could find, and he who could commit
the most atrocious deeds was the most esteemed, admired, and
applauded. In this manner was the public faith, and the solemn
promise made to the Panciatichi, fulfilled and performed! To
the principal palace of the Panciatichi they set fire; the houses
of the Brunozzi, Cellesi, and many others contiguous to them,
were dismantled; the beautiful habitations of John, Oliver, and
Virgil Panciatichi, with many other places and houses filled
with grain, corn, wine, oil, and timber, were burned; and all the
summer-houses, shops, and stores, and every other building
which belonged to the Panciatichi; in one of which was found
in bed the Count di Rigolo Bisconti, ill of the wounds he had
received in some of the late engagements; the Count was without ceremony, thrown out of the window into the street," not
by a common rabble, but by Ceccone Beccano and Gio. Taviani, men of distinction and consequence. "They afterwards
made search in all the steeples and towers, as well as through
all the churches, for refugees of the other faction, and, wherever
they found any, they drove them out, robbed them, and sent
them to their houses; and so enormous was the evil committed
by the Cancellieri factionaries, that by the end of the twentieth

of August they had burned more than two hundred houses and stores, and all of the principal sort, contrary to the promises and solemn faith passed to the Panciatichi by the commissaries; and thus a beautiful and charming city was become a receptacle of assassins, of robbers, of murderers, and of men of every evil deed."

While the faction of the Cancellieri thus tyrannically domineered in Pistoia, that of the Panciatichi would have done the same if they had been in the city, equally without control. "In their state of banishment, they still meditated the oppression and destruction of their rivals, and to this purpose collected men, and fortified themselves on the plains in the country. Not being able to obtain the countenance and assistance of the Florentines, but rather being threatened by them with their displeasure and chastisement, they set themselves, with all their forces, to maltreat the country with their robberies, arsons, homicides, and imprisonments, in such a manner, that making frequent excursions into the mountains, they soon reduced all the territory of the Pistoians to a miserable and deplorable state. At the same time the Cancellieri, no longer knowing what to steal, or whom to rob, went on inventing new affronts for the Panciatichi, or those whom they suspected to favor that party, who remained in Pistoia. As the city was full of malicious people, who could not contain themselves, they went frequently out of the gates, and stole cattle and other property from the Panciatichi in the country, till all the Panciatichi, who were near the bounds of the city, were obliged to retreat into the plain, and unite with their associates; here they began to think of checking the power of their enemies; and all being eager to return to their houses, they thought it a duty by force to put a bridle on the arrogance of their adversaries, and reduce them, once for all, to subjection. To this purpose they erected a strong bastion near the bridge of Bonelle, and another in the neighborhood of the bridge *alla Pergola*, and fortified themselves at St. Angiolo, at St. Bastiano, at the great house of the Forteguerri, at Tenuta, at Magia, at St. Nuovo, at Tizzana, and made other fortifications, with preparations of munitions of arms, provisions, and men, from the mountains and from Lucca, who came to lend them assistance; and by these means they held all the country in subjection, and all the contrary faction in terror.

" The Cancellieri seeing the preparations made by the Panciatichi, and apprehending some unexpected assault, without delay, made preparations necessary to remove these factionaries effectually from the country. Collecting together a body of four thousand men, of their own and the Bolognese, they went out to attack, at the same time, the two bastions near the bridges. The Panciatichi were astonished and panic-struck at the sight of so many men, and giving themselves up most shamefully to flight, the assailants, in less than one hour, had complete possession of both bridges, and dismantled both the bastions. Proceeding to St. Angiolo, which was guarded by Bartolomeo Cellesi, an intrepid officer, and experienced in arms, they fought a most bloody battle, in which Cellesi himself was killed; for this brave commander falling from his horse, was assassinated, and his head, severed from his body, was fixed on the bow of a saddle, and carried to Pistoia, there to be exposed to mockery and insult; at the sound of the trumpets it was placed upon the architrave of the well of the great market, that the people might demonstrate their joy and triumph over it, and there it was kept three days. This inhuman exultation was the beginning of ill fortune to the Cancellieri; the indignation of the Panciatichi was so excited by the scoffs and taunts offered to Cellesi, and by the shameful repulse in an assault of an enemy's bastion near the river Brana, that, whilst the Cancellieri were shouting ' Victory!' and returning without order, and with a great booty to Pistoia, the Panciatichi, making a commander of Franco di Meo Gori, a man of a very numerous family in Terruccia, proud and fearful, but fortunate, and accompanied by four of his brothers, and other relations, in all about a hundred persons, followed in the rear of those who thought themselves victorious, to the grove of elms, and there retaking the plunder routed the party. Many were slain, more made prisoners, and the rest, scattered in various places, returned late and in disorder to Pistoia. The Panciatichi having obtained so signal a victory, proceeded, under their captain, Franco, to Tizzana and Magia, and there summoned all the people of the party to arms, and stood night and day in good order and well guarded. The Cancellieri, seeing the increasing force of the Panciatichi, despaired of dispossessing them of the plain, and therefore employed all their craft to effect a separation between the Panciatichi in the country, and the Panciatichi in the city, in order to weaken the faction; in the course of two months they accomplished their design, and a truce was concluded between the Panciatichi in the country and the Cancellieri in the country, which occasioned great feasts and rejoicings in Pistoia.

"This truce, however, had but a short duration; parties began again to rage, and mutual slaughters were renewed; and although the Florentines knew that the territory of the Pistoians was no longer manageable, on account of the continual murders and assassinations committed in it by night and by day, yet they would not, or knew not how to put their hands to any effectual remedy; and although they ordered into confinement for three years, upon pain of rebellion for returning to Pistoia, all the families of Bisconti, Panciatichi, Cellesi (except that of Bernardo,) Fabbroni, Matteo Brunozzi, Rossi, Forteguerri, Bracciolini, Cioci, and Gherardi, and many others specified, to the number of two hundred, yet it was not possible that this banishment should have any effect; because many Florentines, their friends, besides favoring and assisting them with money and other effects, obstructed the execution of it, which was the principal cause that the Panciatichi consolidated themselves on the plain, with the firm resolution not to depart from it. The Panciatichi, nevertheless, were not a little anxious, when they knew that the commons of Florence were against them; and the Cancellieri were not less disturbed with fears when they saw their enemies in possession of the dominion of the country; so that they were obliged to consider themselves as besieged in Pistoia, rather than as lords of it; wherefore, reflecting that there was no blessing more necessary than peace, it was determined by the general council, that they ought to have recourse to the Most High with pious and holy works, and to this end orders were given to the laborers of St. James the apostle, that adequate alms should be given to all the religious orders, that they might by their prayers supplicate Heaven to send peace and union among the citizens."

All this was very commendable and proper; but to depend upon these prayers alone, without changing their constitution, was as irrational and presumptuous, as for the crew of a sinking ship to pray for preservation, without working the pumps or stopping the leaks.

Accordingly, in 1501, they were found to have been ineffica-
cious;[1] "for the execrable factions, in a still greater effervescence
of cruelty, made use of every cunning stratagem, and attempted
every means to destroy themselves and their country. The Cancellieri, dreading that the Panciatichi might return to Pistoia, determined not only to hold them at a distance from the city, but to drive
them, with all the force they could possibly assemble, quite out of
the country; and to this purpose, having taken into their pay three
thousand foot, drawn from the country, the mountains, from Valdinievole, from Prato, and other places, and fifty cavalry, early in
the morning of the fifth of February, they sallied out with these
forces, well armed, from the gate Caldatica, and went, one thousand men towards Montemagno, and two thousand towards St.
Angiolo. These last arrived at St. Angiolo, entered the church,
spoiled it of every thing valuable, and set it on fire; and because thirty of the Panciatichi, who were posted as guards in the
steeple, knew it was impossible in any manner to defend it, they
gave the signal of their being besieged by a flag, as had been
previously concerted with their friends in the neighborhood. Suddenly three hundred Panciatichi, compacted together in the form
of a squadron, under the command of their captain, Franco Gori,
using every artifice to avoid being discovered by the enemy, threw
themselves by surprise into the middle of the Cancellieri, and in
a short time broke and defeated to the number of two thousand
persons. This victory was so advantageous to the Panciatichi,
that three of them only were wounded, and one killed, while the
Cancellieri lost more than three hundred and fifty killed, a pro-
portionable number wounded, and many were made prisoners;
and those few who escaped, threw down their arms, and in small
numbers and great disorder fled towards Pistoia. This splendid
victory, with the acquisition of a great booty, obtained by the Panciatichi, animated them not to shrink from any inconvenience or
fatigue to prosecute the abasement of their enemies; wherefore,
without loss of time, taking, to deceive their antagonists, a pair
of colors which had been seized in the last battle, they paraded
with this on their march, and went to attack the other Cancellieri, who, at Santo Nuovo, had besieged their associates the
Panciatichi, then guarding it; but the Cancellieri, advertised, by
means of a lady, of the artifice, fled, with the enemy almost at

[1] Chap. xxviii. p. 385.

their heels; and hastily coasting round the cliffs of Casale, took
the road towards Collina and Fontana, and in confusion, disbanded, and covered over with mire, reached Pistoia. This retreat
took up the whole night. This flight of the Cancellieri occasioned
no small damage to the innocent Panciatichi who had remained
in security in Pistoia; because, such fugitive Cancellieri as returned to their country, had no other thoughts than to revenge
themselves wherever they could, by scouring the city, with arms
in their hands, and falling upon those unhappy people; they assassinated in the piazza a countryman, and Felice di Marco, who
were of the Panciatic faction, and the others, wounded and
beaten, by flying into the fortresses and palace of the rettori,
escaped their fury, and saved their lives.

" The Panciatichi upon the plain in the country, having been
informed of the treachery committed upon their companions in
Pistoia by the Cancellieri, conceived against that faction an indignation beyond all credibility greater than ordinary; so that,
after a little repose from the fatigues lately suffered, they prepared to persecute their enemies with greater ferocity. Hearing
that some of them had built a strong bastion in the township of
Casale, from which fortification they daily made inroads among
the inhabitants, and committed much mischief, they went, on the
twenty-fourth of March, and took the bastion, the Cancellieri who
guarded it shamefully flying. Others of the Cancellieri, in Casale itself, taking post in the church and in the belfry, after a
sharp conflict, were overcome by Michelino Jozzelli and Charles
Nicolai, many of them cut to pieces, many others wounded, and
the rest pursued over the mountains, where they left their arms,
and fled with precipitation. Others, in the meadows of Vignole
and of Agliana, were stripped and totally dispersed; others, at
the bridge of Bonelle, suffered a perfect defeat, in which many
were slain, and the rest fled in disorder. The Panciatichi, seeing their affairs succeed so happily, prepared themselves for
greater enterprises, and calling together all their people, they
went against the castle of Momigno, took it, and set it on fire.
They then took Vinacciano, and burnt all the houses of the
Cancellieri; and the houses of the Panciatichi having been a
little before burnt by the Cancellieri, this place by the last conflagration became entirely desolate and destroyed. Nor was the
damage less that was done at Montegastoli, in the country of

Fontana, of Collina, and of Gabbiano. The Panciatichi then fortified themselves at Montebuono, and did infinite damage from thence to the party of the Cancellieri, who, taking Giacche-rino, built by the families of the Panciatichi, made a stand against their enemies, and there followed in this neighborhood burnings of houses and murders of people. At length the two factions descended towards the long bridge, and came to battle, which was continued for some time with obstinacy; but the Cancellieri, having the worst of it, at last fled.

"The few good and wise men who remained, considering the miseries and destruction which resulted to the city of Pistoia and its territory from the two unbridled factions, exerted them-selves to assemble the general council, by whom two citizens were elected, to see that all malefactors should be chastised and punished. But a provision of this sort could never be sufficient to intimidate a number of factionaries so powerful; it accord-ingly only animated them to greater fury; for the persons elected being poorly attended, and provided with little power or force, how could they be able to restrain a desperate people, who re-quired extraordinary rigor, and much greater energy, to render them quiet, pacific, and obedient? This was so well known to those ungovernable people, that it rendered them more fierce, proud, and insatiable of revenge, so that the Cancellieri, seeing themselves overcome in battle, determined to accumulate a great quantity of money, in order to provide men to conquer the force of their enemies. To this end, they burthened the city of Pistoia with the payment of twenty thousand ducats of gold; they sold the effects of St. James, to the amount of four thousand crowns; they pawned, for eighteen thousand crowns more, at Bologna, the chalice of gold of the chapel of St. James, which weighed twenty-two pounds; they sold two angels of silver, a fathom and an half in height, and a pair of candlesticks which were worth five hundred crowns; they took a most beautiful basin, and an ewer of silver, of the value of four hundred crowns; moreover, they coined into money other silver basins, and an image of the Virgin, and another of St. John, of pure silver, which were of St. Zeno, and all the dishes and basins of silver which were in the palace of the supreme magistrate; they took from the Monte di Pietà six thousand ducats, and one thousand five hundred from the House of Wisdom, and made up a sum of forty thousand crowns."

In the age and country where these things were done, this robbery of churches, of saints, and angels, this plunder of holy relics, was sacrilege and impiety of the deepest dye, enough to have shocked and revolted the city in any other circumstances; but the spirit of party made it all lawful to the Cancellieri and their followers.

" They made Mancino of Bologna their captain, one of the bravest soldiers of those times, hired fifteen hundred foreigners, of infantry and cavalry, and called in all their friends from the mountains and country, so that Pistoia was so full of soldiers, that all the houses could scarcely hold them.

" In the mean time, the Panciatichi party neglected nothing to procure all the advantages in their power; encouraged by one Pazzaglino, of Serravalle, they attempted to take that castle, in which by means of that traitor they succeeded, and they fortified themselves in the post which guarded Valdinievole and in the steeples of the churches of St. Stephen and St. Michael. Both parties being in want of provisions, made excursions to the adjacent country, reaped the grain, pillaged cattle, and sometimes burnt houses and killed inhabitants, till they reduced the places to a most miserable and deplorable state. Having in this manner provided themselves on both sides with men, arms, and provisions, the Cancellieri were anxious to undertake some enterprise with the body which they had hitherto kept in pay at so great an expense and with so little effect. After a consultation, part remained as a guard in the city, and part went out to the mountain. Six hundred infantry and fifty cavalry went out, well armed and in good order, and attempted an assault, in two divisions, upon Brandeglio and Castellaccio, but were discouraged by a brave defence. They then turned towards Cireglio, and making a fierce attack, they easily carried it, plundered it of all that was valuable, and utterly destroyed it by fire. They then went to the church, which, with its steeple, was full of people and of property; they laid siege to it in such a manner, that those who guarded it became irresolute about defending it; but, encouraged by the women who had taken refuge there, who, like generous amazons, took arms and repulsed the enemy, they placed in security the goods, and in a short time regained the post, which the men alone would have abandoned. The Cancellieri, filled with shame and disgrace, returned to their main body, and advised their companions to return to Pistoia; but when they began their march, they were so persecuted by the Panciatichi, that the killed and wounded exceeded by far those who in confusion returned to the city. Then it was that the Panciatichi hastened to Berrignardo, Borghetto, and Piazza, and burnt all the houses of the Cancellieri; and such were the damages done that day by the factionaries, that more than one hundred and fifty houses of both parties were burned down.

"Those of the party Panciatichi, who had entered into the castle of Serravalle, thinking themselves in security, stood negligently on their guard in that post; intelligence of which being sent to the contrary party, they sent, with great haste, six hundred soldiers upon an enterprise against the place. Two hundred took post around it, and the four hundred others, introduced by some in the place into the castle, began to rush everywhere without control, so that the Panciatichi, taken by surprise, retired to other strong posts in the neighborhood. Early in the morning, the Cancellieri approached the steeple of St. Michael, and took it by a vigorous assault. They afterwards battered that of the church of St. Stephen; but perceiving that it was not to be carried without some delay, they set fire to the church, from whence the flames ascending to the balcony, soon burnt those who held it. They intended, moreover, to have attempted the acquisition of the citadel, in which the greater part of the Panciatichi were shut up; but a reinforcement of five hundred infantry, and one hundred cavalry, arriving to those in the fort, and reinforced farther with three hundred men from the mountain, and two hundred from Lucca, conducted by Michael Jozzelli, who had taken the most important posts without the walls, the castle was besieged in such a formidable manner, that the Cancellieri lost all hopes of expelling the contrary faction from that place The Cancellieri in Pistoia, however, hearing the situation of their companions in the castle of Serravalle, sent, at the approach of evening, three hundred infantry and fifty cavalry, with plenty of provisions, to reinforce and refresh them; but scarcely had these soldiers met the others at the foot of the mountain, when, repulsed and pursued by the Panciatichi as far as the long bridge, they were obliged to submit to the loss of twenty persons, many arms, and all their provisions.

"In the mean time there came to the assistance of the Panci-

atichi, Martino Ciuti with two hundred men, the Captain Franco
Gori with three hundred, and many others, who, uniting with
those already there, amounted to three thousand, who attacked
that castle on the side of the citadel, in which the companies
had taken refuge; but seeing all their attempts were rendered
vain, one hundred of the most alert approached to the gate with
such impetuosity, that they made a breach, and let four hundred
men into the castle, who attacking the Cancellieri in the rear, in
less than an hour killed more than three hundred, and made
more than one hundred prisoners, and permitting the foreigners
to escape by a shameful flight, gained a large booty of goods,
money, arms, and horses.   The Panciatichi having obtained this
noble victory, the citizens of that faction began to think of endeavoring to return to Pistoia; but were dissuaded by their friends
of the country, who would not consent.   They all went therefore together to their usual posts upon the plain, with their prisoners and rich plunder.   If they had attempted to return to
Pistoia, they would not have been opposed, for the factionaries
in the city were so impoverished, that many had gone out of the
place; and although the bells of the people were rung that day,
not one person appeared in the piazza.

  " There succeeded many more affrays and slaughters, burnings
and depredations, to relate all of which in detail would be endless.   Great were the damages done the same day by the Panciatichi in Alliana; but by the treacherous misconduct of their
captain, Martino Francese, they were disgracefully repulsed, had
many killed and many wounded; and, what was more to be
dreaded, the Cancellieri carried thirteen of their heads in triumph
to Pistoia, and by that means revived the courage of their companions, almost sunk in terror and despair.   Great was the
slaughter of their enemies, and numerous the burnings of houses
committed by the Panciatichi of Montagnana, the seventh of
July, at Momigno.   The tenth of July, the Panciatichi of Brandeglio collected a large number of men from the plain and the
mountain, and burnt all the houses of the Cancellieri which were
at Satornana, and at St. Felice, and plundered the property and
the cattle.   The twentieth of July the Cancellieri burnt in Pistoia eight houses and six shops of the Bracciolini, and set fire
to three houses of Gio. di Franco, and demolished the house of
Francisco Cellesi, near St. Prospero.   The twenty-eighth of July,

the Cancellieri went to Montebuono, a town of the Panciatichi, took it by treachery, and burnt it, after having made twelve prisoners; whom they conducted to Pistoia, led into the hall of a house inhabited by Giuliano Dragucci, where they strangled them, and threw them out of the window. This, which they called justice, they compelled a priest to execute, who was in the number of the prisoners, and then they put the priest to death in the same manner. Much destruction was made by fire on the thirtieth of July, in the commons belonging to the house of the bishop, and in other places, by the Panciatichi; but no less were the evils committed the same day by fire by the Cancellieri in the township of Bonelle; and in so many other places were such excesses committed by the two factions, that they reduced Pistoia to be the most unhappy among all the miserable cities of Italy; its whole territory was one scene of burnings, murders, and captivity of men, and the citizens themselves were become the talk and the scorn of the whole world. The Florentines, who, as imperial vicars, had some pretensions to interfere in the government of Pistoia, derived from the Emperor Robert, had neglected till they reproached themselves, to attempt any salutary remedy to so many evils.

" In the beginning of August, the Cancellieri, the faction which had now the dominion in Pistoia, considering that the Panciatichi were masters of the country, and were well furnished with provisions, while the city was in danger of famine, assembled in the public palace to deliberate; and they concluded it would be for the advantage of their country, and of both parties, to make peace with the Panciatichi. This resolution was soon communicated to the Panciatichi, who suddenly consented to treat. At this time the Florentines offered their mediation, proposed articles, and sent troops to keep order, &c."

The particulars of this negotiation were curious enough, but this essay is already too long. The wisest and most prudent men in the city held secret communications, sometimes with one party, sometimes with the other, and then with the Florentines, till at last they prevailed to have a general council called. This consisted wholly of Cancellieri, for the Panciatichi were still in the country, and consequently the demands of the latter were thought too considerable. Such controversies arose, even among the Cancellieri, that it was feared nothing would ever be concluded. Some juggling monkish trick at last succeeded; a dove, white and black, (*bianca e nera,*) after the similitude of the arms of the Panciatichi family, flew down upon the seat of the supreme magistrate, and gave manifest signs that the Most High was in favor of peace; the hard hearts of the Cancellieri relented, and peace was made. The great affair of the appointment of a director of the hospital was settled, by giving each party alternately the appointment. The Panciatichi were restored to the city; all crimes and atrocities were pardoned, and to be forgotten. Eight citizens were to reform the government in such a manner, that the gonfalonier, and all the other officers, should be equally drawn from each faction; and the families enlisted under the Panciatichi on one side, and under the Cancellieri on the other, were all named and recorded.

"Seditions and tumults had ceased; the two factions enjoyed in Pistoia a tranquillity that they believed would be lasting; but the habits of discord were not eradicated, passions were not extinguished, and the parties were not balanced. Accordingly, in 1502, the symptoms were discovered of a hidden gangrene; the Cancellieri pretended to have been exempted by the general council, from accounting for what they had taken from the commons and from pious places; and the Panciatichi demanded to be refunded in part, if not in the whole, of the damages done by fire to their houses; but as the general council, and the other offices of the city, were composed of an equal number of subjects of the two factions, one party refused to approve of the petition of the other. This exasperated their minds to such a degree, that the usual factions arose, and proceeded to blows and to arms. They were soon separated by the Florentine troops of cavalry and infantry, who were posted as guards in Pistoia, and obliged, without laying down their hatred, indignation, and rancor, to return to their houses; there they prepared to give a fresh scope to their passions; and the Cancellieri, as the most powerful, causing to be taken out of the hands of the Panciatichi the fortresses they held, began anew to prepare for driving them altogether out of the state of Pistoia.

" The Panciatichi, penetrating the designs of the Cancellieri, made no delay in providing men, and each party introducing them by night, stood waiting the chance to execute their ill designs. On the twenty-fourth of February, the Cancellieri, in three divisions, fortified themselves, with three hundred men at the gate of Guidi, with two hundred and fifty on the hill in the street of St. John, and with two hundred and fifty in the street near St. Dominic. A party of the Panciatichi coming in from the country, occasioned the battle to begin; but the Panciatichi outnumbered, and almost surrounded by their enemies, were compelled again to abandon the town with precipitation and disorder.

"The Panciatichi, thus expelled a second time from the city, dispersed in divers places on the plain; and the Cancellieri remaining lords of Pistoia, suddenly shut the gates, and went with unbridled rage to plundering, burning, and destroying all the remaining houses and substance of the Panciatichi. They robbed and burned the houses of the Rossi, Forteguerri, Cellesi, Radda, Bambolino, Doffo, Gualfreducci, as well as the Panciatichi, and many others. Meditating still greater cruelties, they ran in great fury to the public palace, and all those of the magistracy who were of the party of the Panciatichi, whom they could find, they most cruelly put to death. In this state of things, those who presided over the administration of justice, supported by the Florentines, attempted to provide a remedy against new combinations, and made the disturbers lay down their arms. To make an example, they hanged Puccino Puccini, whom they found guilty of the murder of the supreme magistrates; and declared thirteen others outlaws, whom they condemned for high treason, for the contempt shown to the supreme authority; these were driven out of Pistoia, and fled to Montale.

"This rigor of justice, however, instead of restoring quiet to Pistoia, served rather to hasten its ruin; because the Panciatichi fortified themselves with bastions of wood, well furnished with arms and men, near the bridge di Bonelle, by means of which they controlled the whole city, and kept the minds of the Cancellieri in constant agitation, till the pride and ferocity of the two parties suffered not a day to pass in the city or the country without rencounters, burnings, and slaughter.

"The Panciatichi, being thus fortified at Bonelle, and other places of the plain, concluded to make an exertion of all their possible strength totally to destroy the contrary party; to this purpose, early one morning, they separated into several divisions, traversed that extensive country by different routes, and after a

few hours all met together to assault sixteen houses belonging
to the Tesi, Mati, and other Cancellieri families; these they
stripped of the most valuable effects, and burnt to the ground.
The Cancellieri hastened in great numbers to prevent so great
a misfortune; but the fury and the strength of the Panciatichi
were such, that, after having killed and wounded many, they
obliged the rest to fly. Their flight animated the Panciatichi to
set fire without delay to all the houses in that vast plain, and,
produced a conflagration, which the historian could compare to
nothing better than the opening of one of the mouths of hell.*

"Pistoia, being in this deplorable condition, and deprived of
all succor and assistance, was filled with people given up to a
licentious way of living, without fear of divine, and much less
of human justice, who committed continual insolence and wickedness of every kind. Wherefore many, knowing the great
damage which resulted to their country, instigated the general
council to elect one of the wisest and most learned citizens, with
supreme authority, to administer full and summary justice, in
order to find a remedy for so great disorders, and extinguish so
great a fire by punishing every fault, and reducing the people to
the necessity of embracing peace and tranquillity. The council complied with the petition of the principal citizens of the
place, and taking all authority from the podestà and captain,
conferred the title of doge upon Mariotto di Peraccino del Guida,
a doctor of laws living at Porta Guidi, and gave him all the
authority of the council itself. Mariotto assumed the government of the city, acted with so much rectitude, that no man
could complain of his partiality, and introduced so much tranquillity into the city, as to excite the jealousy of Florence,
which feared that it might thereby be defeated in the end it was
aiming at.

"But the Cancellieri, as being those who had been the occasion of the exaltation of Mariotto, desirous of demonstrating
their superiority in all matters, soon gave occasion to the general
council to apprehend fresh evils. They therefore appointed for
the doge three of the wisest and most prudent citizens for his
counsellors, that, amidst such dangers, he might be animated
and assisted to relax nothing in repressing the pride of restless

* Sembrava essersi aperta in quelle parti, una bocca di inferno. p. 394.

spirits, and that he might be more ardent in reducing the people to order and quiet. All these endeavors, however, availed little; for Jacopo Savello coming to Pistoia with a hundred men in arms, on foot and on horseback, in aid of the Cancellieri, these determined to go out to the attack of the Panciatichi. Uniting three hundred men to the soldiers of Savello, they issued out of the city in two squadrons, one of which went to assault the houses of the Giacomelli, and the other went towards the abbey of Pacciana, where, having routed a hundred cavalry of the Panciatichi, they returned to unite with the other division, and both went to work to rob the houses of every thing valuable, and then to set them on fire, and put the inhabitants to the sword. In the mean time the party of the Panciatichi, numerous in armed men, marching suddenly in front of the enemy, thought to revenge themselves for their past defeat, by the total extermination of the Cancellieri. But, because the river Ombrone, which lay between, hindered the two parties from coming to a fierce battle, frequent skirmishes ensued on its banks, which after a long time appearing about to terminate to the disadvantage of the Cancellieri, this was the reason that, intimidated by the force of the contrary party, they hastily retired, with Jacopo Savello, towards Alliana; and in the confusion they abandoned the greatest part of their arms. This general depredation ruined the crops, and the country was afflicted with a severe famine, which obliged Savello to leave Pistoia.

" The Cancellieri of Cavinana, desirous of restoring to Igno the Cancellieri, their companions, who had been banished from thence, assembled a body of men, who, joining with two hundred and sixty persons, on horseback and on foot, that came out to their assistance from the city, advanced to make trial of their strength; but, meeting with their fellow factionaries from the mountain, and making up five hundred foot, and one hundred horse, they all directed their march towards Pitellio, and encamped near the old parish church, where they waited two days the arrival of other forces, to make a united assault upon that castle. Not seeing them arrive, and fearing that succor might come to the Pitellians from their friends in St. Marcello, they laid aside their meditated enterprise, and returned to their homes.

" The Panciatichi of the mountain, finding themselves dis-

turbed by the Cancellieri, thought it a duty to revenge themselves; and collecting for that purpose one hundred and fifty
men at Cutigliano, began to scour the country and commit
depredations. They were encountered with a great booty, and a
sharp engagement ensued, and, after three hours, the Panciatichi
thought it convenient to leave their prey, and retreat, to save
their lives, to Lizzano. The Cancellieri, having recovered their
property, and observing the retreat of the Panciatichi into certain
houses of Lizzano, marched into it. Then the Panciatichi of
Lizzano, for fear of the contrary party, who were increased to
five hundred persons, and thinking to save their property and the
furniture of their houses, deposited them in the church and its
steeple, to which also the women and the men retired. The
Cancellieri arriving in Lizzano, and finding all the houses abandoned, pillaged all that was left in them, and then burnt them.
They then laid siege to the church and steeple in so close a
manner, that there was no space left for the Panciatichi to
escape. The Cancellieri sent notice to their fellows in the
city, country, and mountains, to send them immediate succor,
that they might have dead, or prisoners, their confined enemies.
One thousand five hundred men appeared, and took away from
the besieged all hope of assistance. In this desperate situation
there was no proposal of surrender or capitulation. The Cancellieri repeatedly assaulted their enemy; but they obstinately
defended themselves, and often wounded the assailants. These
at length renewed the enterprise by fire, and attacked both the
church and steeple in that manner. Those in the church could
no longer endure the raging flames, and all retired into the steeple. This place not being capacious enough for all, many were
suffocated with the heat and smoke. The Panciatichi, reduced
to this state of misery, were by some of the Cancellieri promised
their lives if they would surrender. Eighteen of the besieged
took advantage of these fair words; but scarcely were they in
the power of their enemies, when they were perfidiously put to
death; none of the rest would surrender, but resolved to perish
in the balcony. The besiegers, seeing this courageous resolution,
increased the fire under the balcony in such a degree, that the
flames arising around and above it, many of the poor wretches
within it, tormented with smoke, and heat, and pain, sunk under
their misery; and the more they deafened the square below with

their cries, the more their inhuman enemies exerted themselves to distress them.

"The party of the Panciatichi of the plain, advised of these miseries in which their friends of the mountains were involved, and not able to endure the horrid excesses which were committed, expedited, under the command of Toso, the brother of the Captain Franco Gori, at once to Pupillio four hundred infantry, and one hundred cavalry, who giving notice to all the factionaries of the mountains, that they might come to the relief of their friends, in a short time had an army of a thousand men and more, besides a large number of cavalry. Taking possession of proper posts, and making suitable fortifications, Toso, by a great shout, gave a signal of the succor arrived to the poor victims besieged in the balcony. The Cancellieri, when they discovered this reinforcement, sent parties suddenly to repulse them, who found them so well fortified, that any attempt against them must be ineffectual. Succors from all parts arriving to the Panciatichi, the Cancellieri found it necessary to raise the siege, and retire without risking a battle. The besieged who survived the pain, hunger, and other miseries, came out of that steeple and balcony, where more than one hundred and twenty were found dead by the heat, thirst, and hunger; and their liberators, not caring to pursue their fugitive enemies, only set fire to their houses, by which new conflagration there was not a house left in these two beautiful villages.

"The Panciatichi having avenged the wrongs done to their friends, took the road of St. Marcello, to return to the plain; but one hundred and fifty of them deviating without military order, were unexpectedly attacked by the people of Calamecca; and not being able to defend themselves, they found it convenient to save their lives by taking their flight in the night. This event instigated the Panciatichi to increase their forces, to destroy entirely the contrary party; and hiring to this end, troops from Ferrara, Modena, and Lucca, they brought together four hundred infantry, and one hundred cavalry, who, continually increasing, gave cause to the Cancellieri to prepare for new battles; the whole country was so excited, that from the great preparations of both parties for war, nothing remained to be expected but to see the utter ruin of those places.

"In this miserable state of things, Louis, King of France, excited the Florentines to interpose. They elected thirteen commissaries, and gave them full power. These prohibited all to wear arms, and cited the heads of the factions, both of the Panciatichi and Cancellieri, in the city, country, and mountain, to appear at Florence on the twentieth of August. Of the heads of the Panciatic faction who appeared at Florence in obedience to the order, were six of the principal men of the Panciatichi family, four of the Cellesi, four of the Bisconti, seven of the Brunozzi, three of the Gherardi, and four of the Rossi. Bartolomeo Panciatichi, M. Goro Ghieri, and Captain Giuliano Gherardi, with seven others, refused to come, and incurred the penalty of banishment as rebels. Of the heads of the Cancellieri party, there appeared in Florence in obedience to the citation, two of the Cancellieri, three of the Gatteschi, three of the Ambrogi, two of Perraccino, three of the Melocchi, three of the Tonti, and two of the Odaldi; nine refused to go, and were declared rebels. Six of the heads of the Panciatichi on the plain appeared, and four of those on the mountain, and an equal number of the Cancellieri from each. As soon as they appeared in Florence, seven of the Cancellieri, and six of the Panciatichi, were committed to prison, and all the rest forbidden to leave Florence on pain of banishment as rebels.

" The Florentine commissaries then took all public offices, and the public revenue, out of the hands of the Pistoians, and imposed heavy fines on the leaders for breaking the peace. Upon examination it was found, that more than four hundred houses had been burnt in the city, and more than sixteen hundred in the country."

The rigor of the Florentines[1] preserved the peace but a short time, for in the next year the two factions of the Cancellieri and Panciatichi broke out into another civil war, as violent and destructive as ever. But let us pass over the particulars, and mention only a few circumstances.

" The Florentines again made peace in Pistoia by their commissaries, imprisonments, fines, and other severities, which the Pistoians were too much exhausted to resist. In 1505, the Pistoians petitioned Florence to be restored to the honors, offices, and revenues of the city; and it was granted.

---

[1] Chap. xxix. p. 401.

" The Pistoians were such friends of the house of Medici, that they had the address to escape, at the time when the Spanish army invaded Prato, and committed such cruelties and devastations there.

"John de' Medici was made pope, and assumed the name of Leo X., and the Pistoians made such rejoicings upon this occasion, and sent such congratulations by their ambassadors to the pope, and to Julian his brother, and Lorenzo his nephew, as recommended them to favor.

"In 1514, the families of Panciatichi, Cancellieri, Ricciardi, Gualfreducci and Vergiolesi, who in 1369, had been forbidden to have, obtain, or exercise the offices and dignities of the city of Pistoia, its country, or mountains, supplicated, with others, to be admitted to public offices and honors. Their petition was repeatedly rejected by the council; but at length, by the influence and intercession of the pope, Leo X., they, their children, and descendants, were restored and admitted to all the honors demanded."

Is there in history a more curious fact? These families were, by an obstinate, arbitrary, and stupid law, excluded from all offices and share in government; yet it was impossible to establish a government that could control them, and they disposed of all offices, and the whole government, divided as they were into two parties, struggling for the whole time, and butchering each other, that one of them might rule the whole.

One spark of malignity remained concealed in the minds of the factionaries, the Panciatichi and Cancellieri, and in 1515 broke out in a furious flame, extending into the plain and the mountains. From tumults and murders both parties proceeded to make preparations of men and arms, to revive the civil wars in all their horrors. But the Florentines, that is to say the Medici family, interposed with such energy, as restored the public tranquillity; in order to preserve which they drew off many of the turbulent spirits, by taking them into their service as guards, &c.

"After the death[1] of the Emperor Maximilian, Charles of Austria, King of Spain, was elevated to the throne of Cæsar, and was called Charles V. Upon this event the Pistoians ex-

---

[1] Chap. xxx. p. 410.

pected some innovations, but the emperor was prevailed upon
by Leo X. to make no change in the government of Tuscany;
on the contrary the emperor confirmed to the Florentines the
privileges of the state, authority, and lands, of which they were
in possession.

"Giulio de' Medici was seated on the pontifical throne, and
called Clement VII. The Pistoians did honor to his elevation
by great rejoicings, and by an embassy of congratulation; which
produced a letter from the pope full of paternal affection for the
city of Pistoia, and abounding in praises of the citizens who
composed it."

The ascendency of the Medici family was not, however, sufficiently established to prevent a civil war from breaking out
again in Pistoia between the Cancellieri and Panciatichi.

"An obstinate battle was fought between them, which lasted
seven hours, and the Panciatichi were again obliged to leave the
city, and go into the country to their usual mischief. They
returned in a short time with additional force, fought the Cancellieri again, and obtained a victory, not without a multitude
of killed and wounded on both sides. After this new tumult
many prayers were appointed in Pistoia, to obtain the extirpa-
tion of civil discord. The insurrection was soon heard of in
Florence, and Niccolò Capponi, whose prudence was esteemed
equal to his valor, was sent as commissary, with an army,
to suppress it. With great difficulty, and much severity, he
succeeded in making a peace, or a truce, between the two
parties."

In 1527, the same factions revived their hostilities, but the
leaders were seized and sent to Florence, and imprisoned, and
mulcted in fines so severe as intimidated others. Charles, Duke
of Bourbon, with a large army of Spaniards and Germans,
approached the Alps of Tuscany, and threw the Pistoians into
an uncommon agitation; but a great fall of snow obliged him
to divert his course from Pistoia to Rome.

"The Florentines having, in 1527, banished the Medici, and
taken down, with great impetuosity, the arms of that family
from every place in the city, Charles V., in 1529, took upon
himself the obligation of entirely reëstablishing that family in
that city; and to this end he commissioned Philibert, Prince of
Orange, to lay siege to Florence with a large army of Italians

and Germans. The Florentines made great preparations for defence, not only of their city, but also of Pistoia. They sent into it five companies of infantry, and placed each gate of the city under a company, and the piazza under the fifth, all under commanders in whom they had confidence. But all these exertions of the Florentines for the security of the city of Pistoia, and to maintain it at their devotion, appeared, even to themselves, to be vain and of little moment, if the good-will of the two factions of the Panciatichi and Cancellieri could not be obtained; and as the Cancellieri were already naturally inclined to their views, they courted and complimented the Panciatichi as the most powerful, and as the adherents to the Medici; and to accomplish their purpose they called to Florence some of the heads of that party, and, admitting them into their council of war, affected a great esteem for their judgments and opinions in things of the greatest importance.

"The Pistoians, however, placed little confidence in those who at this time had the sway in Florence; they therefore created a new magistrate over all affairs of the war, and gave him ample authority to do every thing for the advantage of the city. This magistrate esteemed the five companies insufficient for the defence of the city, and sent to Florence for more; but he was answered, that the troops of Charles V. were approaching to lay siege to Florence, and that the forces of their enemies increased every day, so that they had enough to think and to do for their own defence; that the Pistoians must therefore make use of the means they had for their own salvation; and to this end they gave orders to their commissary, who resided in Pistoia in behalf of the commons of Florence, that he should release freely into the hands of the Pistoians the balia of their city, that they might both govern and defend themselves; and to their soldiers, posted as guards, to return with all possible expedition to Florence. These orders of their principals were suddenly executed by the commissary and podestà. Pistoia remained free from the yoke of the Imperial vicars, provided itself with men, arms, and provisions; but dreading the army of Charles V. on one side, and the Panciatichi being known to favor the Medici, they sent four ambassadors of that party to offer the keys of the city to the pope, and pray his intercession with the emperor that his army might not enter their territory.

35*

Many of the citizens, intimidated by the uncertainty of the times, absented themselves. " Not being able to foresee the end of the war, the advising council adopted another measure, the appointment of ambassadors to Florence to obtain a recon- sideration of their resolution. This produced such a rage in the Panciatichi party, that one of the ambassadors, Tonti, was assassinated, and a riot instantly ensued, in which eighteen of the Cancellieri lost their lives, and the whole party was driven out of the city, and their houses plundered and burnt, particu- larly the celebrated palace of that family near St. Luke's. The principal actors in this mischief having made a rich booty of money and jewels, fled to Bologna, where they were most gra- ciously received and pardoned by the pope.

" At this time the real extinction of the faction of the Cancel- lieri followed; because the Panciatichi, favorites of the pontiff, as adherents of the house of Medici, assumed such vigor, that enraged not only against the Cancellieri of the city, but of the country, both on the plain and in the mountains, they sacked, burnt, and destroyed, the greater part of their houses, spreading ruin and devastation as they went, in Cavinana, Lanciole, Cu- tigliano, Spignano, and all the other castles and possessions of the Cancellieri. The people of Serra, followers of the Panciati- chi, burnt the castle of Calamecca, which held for the party of the Cancellieri; these were so inflamed with resentment, that, with the help of some companies of Lombards, they compelled their enemy to fly, some of whom retreating for safety into the church of Crespole, were there besieged, and all put to death; others retired to the belfry, and there fortified themselves, so as to hope to escape the fury of their persecutors, but in vain, for the assailants, disappointed of their vengeance by the sword, resolved to obtain it by famine. The Panciatichi being reduced to this state, one of their most daring soldiers, named Appol- lonio di Dante, to deliver his companions from the hands of their enemies, precipitated himself from the tower, and his cloak taking the wind, he descended with no other injury than a slight hurt in one of his arms. Running first to Serra, and then to Pistoia, he roused one of the Cellesi to march, with a good body of soldiers, to the relief of the besieged. After this, Pitellio, Pupillio, and Mammiano, by turning to the party of the Panci- atichi, suffered no other damage than the loss of a multitude of their inhabitants, who were driven from their habitations as adherents to the Cancellieri."

The pope, Clement VII., accepted the gift of the city, and by a letter or charter, directed to his beloved sons, the priors, gonfalonier, and people of the city of Pistoia, sent his pontifical commissary to take possession. The Panciatichi had now exterminated the Cancellieri, and obtained the power of governing; but it was at the expense of subjecting both themselves and their country to a foreign power and another rival family.

Charles V., the twenty-eighth of October, 1530, constituted Alexander de' Medici governor, not only of Florence, but of all Tuscany, to the extreme joy and satisfaction of Clement VII. Thus pope and emperor, Guelphs and Ghibellines, Bianchi and Neri, Panciatichi and Cancellieri, were at last all brought to unite, as all such constitutions of government ever have united, at last, in a government of all authority in one centre, but that centre a worthless, however artful, despot.

" The Pistoians were in hopes, that at least under an absolute prince they might enjoy a little tranquillity; but in 1531 the usual disgusts between the two factions of Panciatichi and Cancellieri began to spring up. Although the former, by the partiality of the house of Medici, were indulged in all their caprices, yet finding themselves now increasing in strength, nothing would satisfy them but the total expulsion from the city, and the complete destruction, of all that belonged to the Cancellieri. Tumults and slaughter arose, and no man had the knowledge or the will to provide a remedy.

" Alexander de' Medici took possession of his principality in Florence; great rejoicings were made in Pistoia, and four ambassadors sent to present the congratulations of their city, and recommend it as having been always faithful lovers of his family. The forty-eight senators, instituted in Florence this year under Alexander, pacified the two factions of Panciatichi and Cancellieri, and those persons and families who remained of the latter faction returned to the city, to the joy of all.

" Alexander distinguished Pistoia from all other places under his dominion, for its great affection and sweet love to his family, by giving orders that all the business of Pistoia should be addressed immediately to himself in person.

" Charles V., having ascertained the untruth of the accusations of tyranny brought against Alexander de' Medici by the Florentine exiles, made a visit to Pistoia, where he was received and entertained in the public palace.

"Alexander took it into his head that commissaries and governors were destructive to a state, and therefore abolishing the office, he disarmed the inhabitants as inclined to tumults, and appointed ten noble Pistoians to govern their city. On the sixth of January, 1536, Alexander was assassinated by Lorenzo, and Cosimo succeeded. When the news of this assassination arrived in Pistoia, the heads of the Panciatichi party assembled, and, after mature deliberation, concluded that the present was a convenient opportunity for destroying totally all remnants of the Cancellieri party. To this purpose they excited an insurrection of all their factionaries, under color of maintaining the city of Pistoia in its devotion to the house of Medici. They made leaders of Gio. Cellesi and some others, and with a great multitude scoured the city, and in a very short time assassinated fifteen. Many others, hoping to secure themselves, took post in the fortresses, but, betrayed by the commanders, who let in the Panciatichi, they were miserably deprived of their lives. The partisans of the Cancellieri, seeing that they could not resist the fierce assaults of the contrary faction, went to hide themselves, some in the towns, some in the monasteries, and others in subterraneous places; others went out of the city, found a leader, and hazarded a battle with their enemies, in which many were killed, and others afterwards burnt in steeples. Many, who had foreseen such an event, had before retired to Montale and Montemurlo, places of their faction; so that the Panciatichi remaining masters without control in Pistoia, sacked, burnt, and destroyed all the houses, shops, and stores, which remained of the contrary party in the city.

Cosimo I. had ascended the throne of Tuscany, and ambassadors were sent from Pistoia to congratulate him. At the same time the factionaries of the Cancellieri, who had taken refuge in Montale, constituting as their leader the Captain Guidotto Pazzaglia, their compatriot, and a head of the Cancellieri faction, who, now aged and weakened by many military fatigues, had retired to his estate called the House in the Wood,* fortified

* La Casa al Bosco.

by a thick and high wall, and defended by a high and strong
tower, entreated him to engage in their defence, and obstruct the
approaches of the Panciatichi. Pazzaglia took under his command all the factionaries of his party, and, by a secret correspondence which he had with Philip Strozzi, increased his
numbers to four hundred men, whom he quartered in his own
habitation. From this post they took the license to go out frequently to the annoyance of the Panciatichi, and gave them
much disturbance and many apprehensions. The Panciatichi,
to make a diversion and a division of the forces of the opposite
party, which every day increased in power, went and commenced
a cruel warfare with the Cancellieri of Cavinana. These were
made uneasy, and retired to their steeples, where they made a
brave defence. At this time the commissary took the resolution
of bridling the parties by authority and with rigor; but the Panciatichi, who were more than a thousand men in number, in contempt of justice, and sparing neither age, nor condition, nor sex,
executed in a short time a cruel vengeance on their adversaries
by fire and sword; and going on every day increasing in ferocity,
they increased their murders, rapines, and fires, till they reduced
Cavinana, St. Marcello, Crespole, Calamecca, Lanciole, Pupillio,
and other places, to spectacles of desolation. Many of the
Cancellieri, perceiving that fortune was not favorable to them,
retired to the parish church of Cutigliano, and there fortified,
stood upon their defence, without losing their presence of mind,
waiting from the brave Captain Luca Giacomelli some convenient succor, by which they might once more attempt an attack
upon the rear of the Panciatichi, who, to increase their power
both in numbers and situation, had taken a post very near them.
These disorders were very displeasing to the Duke Cosimo de'
Medici, and he took great pains, by means of his commissary,
to restore quiet to the Cancellieri, to which the Panciatichi at
length consented. Nevertheless the church was scarcely opened,
when they burst into such a furious rage, that they fell upon
every one of the Cancellieri, and cut them to pieces. Cosimo
was not discouraged, even by this outrage, from using other
means to restore quiet to Pistoia, and at last reduced some part
of it to good order. But the faction of the Panciatichi, having
no longer any of the Cancellieri on whom to vent their rage,
turned all their hatred and indignation against one another.

A 2

The faction became divided into two, which rushed into such persecutions of each other, that innumerable quarrels and murders succeeded. The example was followed among their connections in Florence, which gave occasion to the *rettori* of that city, who dreaded greater disorders, to draw the two parties to a truce.

"At the same time the Duke Cosimo was exactly informed, that the Captain Pazzaglia received daily additions to the numbers in his house; and that by the assistance of Philip Strozzi, and the other exiles, many were induced daily to go into his service, and the terror had of this great captain was thus increased. Desirous of providing against every sinister event, which he foresaw might occur, not only from the great number of men who were assembled at the House in the Wood, but from the thousands of men which Pazzaglia at the sound of a bell was able to raise, the duke, after having in vain attempted to gain him by means of some friends, sent Otto da Montauto, with a thousand infantry, to attack the House in the Wood, and make prisoners of its garrison.

Montauto by forced marches sat down before the place, but he was early discovered by Pazzaglia, who, always vigilant, saw every thing and thought of every danger, and was fiercely repulsed. Montauto, perceiving the enterprise to be difficult which he had thought so easy, sent to his brother Frederick, who commanded the guards in Pistoia, for immediate succor. The prompt arrival of this aid alarmed Pazzaglia, who, finding himself besieged by a great number of soldiers, and not hearing the bell of Montale, which he had ordered one of his officers to ring, to assemble the assistance he expected from that and other places, ventured out of his habitation, clothed and armed like a soldier, and with a joyful countenance went to meet his besieger, and demanding safety for himself and his soldiers, put himself into his hands. Montauto received Pazzaglia with a smiling countenance, and knowing him to be humane, generous, and polite, he knew not how to refuse his demand. They both entered the House in the Wood, where they refreshed themselves so splendidly, that Montauto, admiring still more the greatness of soul of Pazzaglia, could not without tears conduct him to the presence of the duke. Cosimo had enough of policy as well as generosity to receive him like an intimate and confidential friend. He took him to his most private consultations, and decided on no affair of state without his advice. The duke, perceiving that the ten noble Pistoians, assigned to govern the city, had not fulfilled the obligations enjoined upon them, or preserved good order, restored the use of the ancient offices of podestà and commissary. He promoted to these offices men of moderation as well as of spirit, and thought by their means to remedy all disorders; but there still remained enough of the citizens inclined to quarrel, to keep the city in tumults, and to degrade all justice.

"Niccolò Bracciolini had insinuated himself into favor with the duke, by having revealed to him a conspiracy of the Salviati, Ridolfi, Strozzi, and Valori, and was appointed to the command of certain companies of infantry which were in garrison there. This officer, recollecting that Francesco Brunozzi had been averse to include him in the last truce made between the factions by the mediation of the Florentines, conceived the design of taking bitter revenge of all the Brunozzi family. For this purpose he put himself at the head of his adherents, collected a considerable body of armed men, besides those which Gio. Cellesi held concealed in his house, ready for any orders, went through the city in search of Brunozzi, and having found him, deprived him of his life. He proceeded to set fire to his house, and all the other houses of the family, but was obliged to get possession of them at the point of the sword. The Brunozzi made a brave defence, but were inferior in numbers, and three sons of Francesco were left dead, and the rest fled to some obscure place. Not satisfied with this, Bracciolini proceeded to the country houses of the family, with a soldiery as tyrannical as himself, and there committed all imaginable cruelty, burning and destroying every thing. For this cruel revenge he was afterwards condemned to pay to the surviving Brunozzi only two thousand five hundred ducats for damages.

"At the same time many exiles from Florence, desirous of deposing from the throne of Tuscany the Duke Cosimo de' Medici, in order, as they pretended, to set their country at liberty, collected together at Mirandola four thousand infantry, and three hundred cavalry, and gave the command of them to Piero Strozzi, who took for his colleague Baccio Valori, and came with one division towards Pistoia, and halting at Montemurlo, waited for the rest of the army. The party of the Cancellieri, who there expected them, received them with transports of joy; and having repaired the citadel, and furnished the castle with every necessary, they all, being fifteen hundred men in number, thought of nothing else but doing infinite mischief to the party of the Panciatichi. They burned Satornana, Valdibura, Uzzo, and Capo di Strada, carrying off from all a rich booty. Taking no account of the government of Florence, the Cancellieri made every effort to reënter Pistoia, and the exiles from Florence had no other view than to deliver their country from the government of the Medici; so that all were agreed to assemble men, provide arms, and collect money, that they might be able by force to wrest the command from the Duke Cosimo. That sovereign, informed of this, and that those in rebellion against him were fortified with much care, every day increased in force, and did great damage, ordered Alexander Vitelli, Otto da Montauto, and Piero Pipicciano, that they should depart in the night from Florence with their troops, three thousand Spaniards, and two regiments of Germans, and go to the assault of Montemurlo; and that the force of the enemy might be diverted and disunited, he ordered the captain Frederick da Montauto, then in Pistoia, to unite the force of his companies with those of the party of the Panciatichi; and the same night, with cries and fires, spread terror in the neighborhood of Montemurlo, that the party of the Cancellieri might be necessitated to abandon it. The party of the Panciatichi, adhering in all things to the will of the duke, united with the forces of Frederick da Montauto, and in a dark night set in an uproar the country of Alliana, and from thence went to burn the houses of the abbey of Pacciana. Setting fire to a multitude of ricks of hay and stacks of corn belonging to the common people, they constrained the Captain Bati Rospigliosi, the Captain Francesco Gatteschi, the Captain Francesco Arferuoli, the Captain Luca Giacomelli, with many others of the exiles, to abandon Montemurlo and the neighboring places, to go and succor their factionaries of the abbey at Pacciana. A severe and obstinate battle ensued, in which, in the end, the Panciatichi were superior, with the death of sixty persons of both parties, among whom were numbered the Captain Mattana, with five soldiers of Cutigliano, who were enough to put in doubt the victory. The head of Mattana was carried to Pistoia, and, amidst the exultations and rejoicings of his adversaries, carried to the piazza as a spectacle to all. This detachment of the exiles being at break of day, the first of August, 1537, defeated, Vitelli and Montauto, knowing that the principal heads of the rebels were in the citadel, went to the attack of Monte-murlo, and finding it in all parts ill manned, they animated their people, and assaulted the fortress, which, after a resistance of five hours, was carried. Pietro Strozzi, attempting to make his escape, fell into the hands of the besiegers; a thousand men of both parties were slain, and Philip Strozzi, Baccio Valori, Francesco degli Albizzi, and many others, were conducted prisoners to Florence, where, as rebels both to the state and the empire, they were put to death. This was the establishment and the basis of the grandeur of Cosimo I. de' Medici, who afterwards, on the thirtieth of September, obtained a most ample diploma from the Emperor Charles V.

"Upon this memorable victory the Pistoians congratulated the duke with an excess of joy by their ambassadors; and the party of the Panciatichi, who had rendered all possible assistance, recollecting that the Cancellieri of the House in the Wood had taken refuge in the parish church of Cutigliano, when that place was sacked by the Captain Vincenzo di Poggio, and the proud towers which were there were ruined to the foundation, now hastened with such ferocity to the assault of that church, that, after a long and good defence, the besieged, without hope of succor, surrendered at discretion to their enemies, who, uniting with those of Valdibura, of Cireglio, and of Uzzo, their adherents burned more than thirteen hundred houses of the Cancellieri, in the towns of Bigiano, the abbey of Pacciana, Chiazzano, Satornana, Calamecca, Crespole, and Lanciole.

"The emperor preparing in Lombardy for battle against Francis I. King of France, and relying on the valor of Pietro Strozzi, general of the Italian infantry, the Pistoians were agitated with fears, and made great preparations for defence.

"The controversy between Pistoia and Lucca, about the boundary between them near Pupillio, being adjusted, the Duke Cosimo was desirous of establishing the peace of the city; and for this object, with menaces and efficacious admonitions, he did not cease to press the obstinate citizens to submit to a regular life, and reduce their affairs for once to good order and a state of tranquillity; but as the Pistoians, in their unbalanced state, had no other consolation than to stand immersed in dissensions, quarrels, and discords, they paid no attention to the sovereign councils, but went on, more and more boisterous, wicked, and seditious, destroying the good order of government, reducing every thing, without control, to the advantage of their private interests and the wantonness of their wild caprices.* The indignation of the duke was at last excited against these obstinate brains, whom he thought it his duty to tame, by taking from them all the honors, public offices, and revenues of the city, as well as the institutions of charity, and to shut up the palace, the residence of the supreme magistrates. With this view he elected four commissaries for the affairs of Pistoia, and gave them full authority to fulfil his determination. All this was ordained and established at the instigation of certain citizens of Pistoia, and all the efforts of the people were made idle; since, by the tenor of the sovereign command, all the magistracies and offices of the city were suppressed, and the administration of the entire revenues and institutions of charity was consigned to Taddeo Guiducci and Christopher Ranieri, with the title of *Proveditors General,* who received into their possession all the movables of the public palace; and the supreme magistrates who had resided in it were dismissed. Six citizens were deputed, with the title of *Proveditors of the Commons,* to whom the palace was committed; these, with the resident commissaries, and not otherwise, assembled to treat of the affairs of their city. These having held the office a certain time, it was permitted to the Pistoians to draw six subjects from a purse destined to that use.

"But the duke [1] apprehending that these new regulations would excite insurrections, sent a body of soldiers, only three hundred and fifty in number, to disarm the citizens, and rein in the seditious and the wicked; amplified the fortifications, and furnished them with every necessary. Many of the Pistoians now considered themselves as slaves, and thought their nobility debased by the privation of all the honors, public offices, and revenues; they thought it inconsistent with the dignity of

---

* Sempre più tumultuanti, e facinorosi, e sediziosi, guastando il buon ordine del governo, riducevano quello, senza freno ai vantaggi dei propri interessi, e disordinati capricci.

[1] Chap. xxxii. p. 432.

their blood to lead a life so obscure and inglorious; they therefore retired from the city, and went to inhabit in other places;
hence the city was in danger of depopulation, became defective
in many arts of convenience and necessity, and nothing was
heard but sighs, groans, and lamentations. The few inhabitants
who remained, knowing the great damage which had resulted to
their country from this resolution of the duke, were never satisfied with venting their reproaches and curses against those who
had advised it;" and they would have attempted more such
great things as compose the whole history of their country, if
many had not been disheartened by the rigor of the new government.

"All the soldiers in garrison at Pistoia being, in obedience to
the orders of the sovereign, gone, with all other persons of note,
to Florence, to make their honors and acclamations on the happy
marriage of the Duke Cosimo with Leonora, the daughter of
don Peter of Toledo, Marquis of Villa Franca, and Viceroy of
Naples, the Cancellieri esteemed the opportunity convenient to
rise and take vengeance on the Panciatichi. As all the soldiers
were gone, and everybody was turned to Florence, the Cancellieri resolved to enter the city in the night, and kill all the Panciatichi, without pardoning or sparing one, that there might not
remain the least memorial of them. They hired people from
various places, of every quality, and some of the most brave,
intrepid, and desperate; and having gained over to their party
many in the city, that they might, at a critical moment, open the
gates, they introduced, in small numbers at a time, many of their
most desperate men, and quartered them, in perfect secrecy, in
the houses of their adherents and partisans. They elected for
their Captain Giovanni Tonti, who entered the service in the
night of the fifteenth of June, put in order more than four hundred soldiers, and marched with them to the gate of St. Mark,
at Pistoia, where the walls were lowest, there giving the concerted signal to those within, that with their knowledge he might
enter the city unknown to their enemies. At the signal of
Tonti, those who were upon the walls suddenly let down one
of their men, with orders to say to those without, that they had
waited four hours, and because day approached, many had
retired to their houses for fear of a discovery; and that therefore it would be advisable to delay the enterprise till the next

night. Hearing this, Tonti sent immediately one of his aids to desire those upon the walls not to depart, and instantly consulting his colleagues, he found but one for waiting till the next night. Transported with impatience, Tonti at once cried out to his soldiers, ' Follow me ; now is the time to show our courage!' and placing a ladder against the wall, mounted to the top, from whence, whilst grasping at a stone, in order to climb over the wall, he fell with it headlong into the ditch. His people, hearing the noise of his fall, but not seeing, by reason of the darkness, what had happened, suspected that they were discovered, and that Tonti had been repulsed by the contrary party. Those, therefore, who had ascended on other ladders turned back, and gave themselves to flight, very few remaining for the defence of Tonti; among these, the most spirited and the most faithful pressed to see what had happened, and discovered Tonti, with one thigh broken, half dead in the ditch; understanding the truth from him, they placed him on a ladder, and, with the assistance of his brother, carried him to a house in the neighborhood as a place of security. In this state of things, Simon Gatteschi, and Philip Ghelardini, persons of great zeal and activity, prepared to carry on the enterprise. Confiding much in the assistance of those in the city, they hastened early, with thirty followers, to the gate of St. Mark, and finding it open, entered the city, and marched to the piazza. As many of the Panciatichi as they found they killed, which raised a great uproar in the city, and intimidated the people so much, that all retired to their habitations. The heads of the Panciatichi observing that the rioters were very few, and that none in the city gave them assistance, took courage, and making, by order of the commissary, a hasty collection of men, they began with these to pursue the others with so much spirit, that some of them fled out of the city, went towards Cireglio and Cavinana, there made a rich prey, and escaped into Lombardy. Others were taken and severely punished, and afterwards all the accomplices of the conspiracy were by a public proclamation declared rebels ; thus ended the tumult. The commissary afterwards ordered many of the Cancellieri party to be arrested, who were about fifty in number, held them three months in prison, put some of them to the torture, by which he discovered the truth of the fact, and then set all at liberty, without condemning any.

"All contradiction and opposition being suppressed, and the harvest being plentiful, the Pistoians thought no felicity superior to theirs, and they held it lawful to forget the past by immersing themselves in a sea of pleasures, by the allurements of which they were seduced into a very vicious and expensive life.

" Cosimo perceiving that the privation of honors and offices had decreased the population of the city, and diminished commerce and the revenue, esteemed it his interest, as well as that of the public, that the city should be restored to its primitive state. On the thirtieth of March, 1547, he made a concession forever in favor of the Pistoians, of all the honors and public offices, and all the privileges, which were established in the year 1496, in the convention with the Florentines. The purses were soon formed of the usual magistrates, and all the persons worthy of that preëminence and those honors had their names imborsed, and the individuals were drawn with universal rejoicings.

" The representation of the faction of Cancellieri, under the name of Dormentoni, and that of the Panciatichi, under that of Risoluti, made by some, among the sports and shows of the Carnival, with habits and ornaments proper to that age, through some injurious words thrown out in jest among them, occasioned disorders of so serious a nature, that there was great danger of reviving the ancient animosities and insurrections; but the Duke Cosimo caused to be arrested the inventors of those masquerades, intimidated their followers, and restored the public tranquillity; and, to make the greater impression on the people, and secure their quiet for the future, he punished the prisoners in an exemplary manner.

" The government continued absolute[1] in the family of Medici till the year 1737, when, upon the death of John Gaston I., the last grand duke of that family, without issue, the family became extinct. Don Carlos, King of Naples, in his own name, and Philip V. King of Spain, not only in his own name, but also in the name of the infant don Philip, and don Louis, and the other sons whom he might have by the Queen of Spain, renounced all right and pretence, which they or their descendants might have to the succession of the grand dukedom of Tuscany, and transferred all such rights, actions, or pretences, to Francesco di Leo-

---

[1] Chap. xxxviii. p. 494.

36 *

poldo, Duke of Lorraine and Bar, his heirs and successors; and Pistoia soon swore allegiance to the new sovereign."

And here ends another most splendid example of the blessings and felicities of a republic without three orders forming a mutual balance! It is quite unnecessary to excite the resentment, or flatter the vanity, of any individuals or families in America, by mentioning their names; but if you begin at New Hampshire, and proceed through all the States to Georgia, you will at once be able to fix your thoughts upon some five or six families in each state, some two of whom will, in the course of fifty years, perhaps of five (unless they are restrained by an independent executive power, three independent branches in the legislature, and an independent judicial department,) be able to divide the state into two parties, one generally at the head of the gentlemen, the other of the simplemen, tear one another to pieces, and rend the vitals of their country with as ferocious animosity, as unrelenting rancor and cruelty, as ever actuated the Cancellieri and the Panciatichi in Pistoia. And it will not be the fault of these individuals or families; they will not be able to avoid it, let their talents or virtues be what they may; their friends, connections, and dependents, will stimulate and urge them forward, by every provocation of flattery, ridicule, and menaces, until they plunge them into an abyss, out of which they can never rise. It will be entirely the fault of the constitution, and of the people who will not now adopt a good one; it will be the misfortune of those individuals and families as much as of the public; for what consolation can it be to a man, to think that his whole life, and that of his son and grandson, must be spent in unceasing misery and warfare, for the sake only of a possibility that his great grandson may become a despot![1]

---

[1] It is scarcely necessary to point out the mistake which has been here committed by the author as to the probable course of things in the United States. Neither does the escape from the danger here referred to seem to have been so much due to the establishment of the form which he advocates, as to that radical equality of condition which the law and custom of equal distribution of inheritances everywhere establishes. Sixty years have passed away, and such a thing as family influence has not as yet produced the smallest perceptible effect upon the political movements of state or nation.

A highly plausible, if not entirely sound view of the progress of government, making the regard for family one of the intermediate stages of civilization, is given by Dr. Arnold in the appendix to the first volume of his edition of Thucydides.

A further elucidation of the author's views on this point will be found in his letters to John Taylor of Caroline, now for the first time published, at the end of this work.

CHAPTER EIGHTH.

CREMONA.

"CREMONA[1] had persevered under the government of consuls until 1180, when she changed the form of her government, reducing all the authority of the consuls to one person alone, who, from the supreme power which was given him, was denominated a podestà. The election of consuls had occasioned such contests among the principal families (as none could be elected to that dignity who were not citizens) that it was now ordained by law, that none should be elected to the office of podestà who was not a foreigner, and a citizen of some other city, as should be agreeable to the council, provided he was not related by blood to any of the electors, had no real estate in the city or country, and was arrived at least to thirty-six years of age; and, above all things, they sought for men of prudence and most eminent reputation, to whom, as soon as they were elected, they sent letters by a public order, praying them to accept the dignity offered them; and on the day when they made their entry into the city, with a public concourse and acclamations, they were solemnly met and received by the whole people. They carried in ceremony the ensigns of their authority, the furred cap, the long sword, and the rod or sceptre.[*] And because for the most part they were men of military talents, rather than skilful in the laws, they conducted with them judges expert in the legal science, by whose means they tried all causes civil and criminal, and assembled the council when it was necessary. After this change of magistracy from consuls to a podestà, which, however, was of short duration and little stability, as they created sometimes a podestà, sometimes consuls, and at other times both together, there occurred in the state and republic of Cremona many and very great disturbances.

"Cremona in 1183, sent her ambassadors to Placentia, where all the ambassadors of the other cities of Lombardy, the

---

[*] Il capello, e il stocco, e la verga, ò scettro.
[1] Dell' historia di Cremona d'Antonio Campo, Cavaliero, pittore, et architetto Cremonense. In Milano, 1645. Libro secondo, p. 26.

March, and of Romagna, were assembled together with the ambassadors of the emperor, and King Henry his son, in May. At this assembly it was concluded, that all the cities should send their ambassadors to the diet of Constance, a principal city of Germany, to establish the peace negotiated between the emperor and the cities. On the twenty-fifth of June, 1183, was established, ratified, and confirmed, that peace, so solemn and so celebrated, which, from the name of the city where it was made, was called the peace of Constance; a correct copy of which treaty is to be found at the end of the fourteenth book of Sigonius, of the kingdom of Italy.[*]

"Such was the instability of the government, that the city returned, in 1190, to the administration of consuls. They in the next year elected a podestà again, who led them out to war, but was unfortunate, and this made them weary of a podestà; and the next year they created consuls, and consuls were annually elected until 1195, when they returned to a podestà."

All this is perfectly natural; the people were distressed by the contest of the principal families when they had consuls, and therefore wished to have a foreigner as a podestà to keep them in order. The principal families, however, struggled for consuls, that they might have the rule; and one party prevailed this year, and the other the next.

"The consuls, in 1198, to supply the city with water, dug a well, and built a conduit of water, which was afterwards called the Murmur, from the complaints of the people against the expense of it, which were so great, that they rose in tumults, and insisted on choosing a podestà. Cremosino Oldoino was accordingly appointed, and governed jointly with the consuls to the end of the year."

Any one may pursue at his leisure the particulars of the changes from consuls to podestà, and from podestà to consuls, till the year 1209, when, upon the appointment of consuls, there arose discords and civil seditions, which brought the republic to the brink of ruin.

"The city became divided as it were into two, by a rivulet that passes through it;[1] on one side it was called the New

* Muratori, *Annal.* anno 1183.
[1] Imperoche si come la città in due parti dal fiumicello Cremonella vien divisa, così si divisero anche i cittadini.

City, and on the other the Old, though all the popular men of the old city joined with the new; in short, the division was between the gentlemen and the populars[1] at bottom. The new city arose in tumults, and were joined by all but the gentlemen in the old, made new magistrates and governors, and congregated together to constitute a new general council at Sant' Agata.

"1210. The old city and the new, each, made its podestà, and many quarrels and civil wars followed; and the hatred between persons and parties increasing, as if they had not been born in the same city, but had been most cruel enemies, they soaked the bosom of their common mother with blood, and had no mercy on her houses or riches, which they consumed by fire. But with much pains and intercessions of the bishop a peace was made, by which the podestà of the new city submitted to the podestà of the old, and swore obedience to him, with this reservation, however, that he was to remain podestà of the people.

"The civil war was renewed in 1211, between the citizens of the old and the new city. The two factions proceeded to a sharp conflict, and after having killed an infinite number of citizens, those of the old city set fire to the houses in the neighborhood of the scene of action, and consumed every thing in them. The year before Otho had been excommunicated by Innocent, the pope, and deprived of the empire, and Frederic Roger was elected in his place; for this reason the Cremonese went this year in favor of the Marquis of Este, and drove out of Ferrara Uguccione de' Guarnesi, who was podestà there in the name of Otho."

In 1212, civil discords were somewhat appeased, and consuls were appointed. The wars between Cremona, and Milan, and Placentia, may be read by those who are curious, but are not to our purpose. They lasted till 1217, in the beginning of which year civil discords and seditions increased, because the people could not agree in creating the magistrates; and it was not till after a long delay, and the interposition of the pope, with apostolical exhortations by letter, that they were persuaded to lay aside their hatreds and discords, so far as to appoint a podestà.

---

1 "i popolari."

"In 1221, the most terrible discords and civil wars, between the gentlemen[1] and the common people in Placentia, were accommodated for a time under the mediation of Sozzo Coglioni, podestà of Cremona. The substance of the peace, to which each party swore, was to lay aside their discords and contentions, and forgive the injuries, damages, and mischiefs, mutually committed and received."

But of what avail are oaths and treaties, which the nature of man and the form of the government will not permit to be observed?

"1222. This year two noble citizens of Cremona were made, one after the other, podestàs of Placentia.

"In the beginning of the year 1229, the discords among the citizens prevailed so far, that they created consuls, and those only for six months; and this year there was a confederacy of Verona, Modena, and Parma, against Cremona.

"There arose, in 1232, in the city of Cremona, seditions and civil wars.

"1233. The Cremonese united with the popular party in Placentia, in favor of whom Uberto Pallavicino, from Cremona, went with a hundred light-horse to oppose the noble exiles.

"1234. The Milanese and Brescians, joining the noble exiles from Placentia, went with a powerful army against Cremona, and deformed the whole country with blood and fire.

"In the year 1242, there began to take root in Cremona those abominable and pernicious factions of Guelphs and Ghibellines, and to infect it to such a degree, as occasioned an infinite expense of the blood of the citizens, an inestimable destruction of wealth, an unspeakable perdition of families, and a most melancholy and miserable ruin of the country."

The city was, in 1246, divided between the two factions; but the Ghibellines had the majority, and obtained the appointment of a podestà. This year the Emperor Frederic was excommunicated by the pope and council at Lyons, in France, and Henry Duke of Thuringia was elected.

The two factions daily increased in violence. The old city, that is the gentlemen, were favorers of the Ghibellines, and adherents of Frederic, the schismatical emperor; and the new

---

[1] "I popolari e i nobili."

city, that is the common people, were partisans of the Guelphs, who adhered to the holy see. The bloody wars occasioned by this division, between Frederic and Innocent, and their respective followers, can be read at leisure, and may cause a laugh at the terrible disgrace of Cremona in the loss of their triumphal chariot,[1] an infamy which none but the gentlemen could obliterate. The Marquis Uberto Pallavicino, a most powerful man, and of great reputation, but a zealous Ghibelline and old-city-man, was appointed podestà; he fought a memorable battle, made two thousand prisoners, retook the *carroccio*, and returned in triumph to Cremona."

Campo begins his third book in the manner of Machiavel, with deep, grave, and formal reflections, as if a diversity of sentiments, contradictory principles, inconsistent interests, and opposite passions among the citizens, could be reconciled and united by declamations against discord and panegyrics upon unanimity, without a balance, in a government possessed of sufficient force.

According to him, "disunion of the citizens is, indeed, the worst evil in a city; for what mortal pestilence can bring upon them greater damage than discord? This not only precipitates noble and illustrious families to ruin, but exterminates powerful and famous cities; nor is there any principality or kingdom so stable or well founded that it may not be torn up by factions."

If this is true, it is still an argument against constituting a city in such a manner that it must necessarily be destroyed by factions.

" All things are maintained and increased by concord, and go to ruin by disunion; union brings victory, and discord defeat; enemies are easily resisted when you agree among yourselves; when members are disunited from the body, the person loses both strength and beauty. When Cyrus divided the Euphrates into three hundred rivulets, a child might ford the largest of them, though his favorite had been drowned in attempting the united water. Italy, the lady and the queen of the world, after infinite conflagrations, sacks, slaughters, pillages, subversions, and ruins, has finally been degraded, by the discord of her sons, into a servant and a handmaid."

---

[1] " *Carroccio.*"

All this may be true; but how long will republicans be the dupes of their own simplicity! how long will they depend upon sermons, prayers, orations, declamations, in honor of brotherly love, and against discords, when they know that, without human means, it is but tempting and insulting Providence, to depend upon them for the happiness of life, or the liberty of society!

"The city of Cremona, to come to the present point, by its discord and divisions, suffered intolerable evils, and ultimately lost her liberty, falling under the power and domination of Uberto Pallavicino; who, taking the opportunity from the controversies, which went on every day increasing among citizens, disunited and divided into divers factions of new city and old, gentlemen and common people, Guelphs and Ghibellines, of Capelletti, of Barbarasi, and of Maltraversi, in the year 1251, from podestà, made himself absolute lord, patron, and master, of the commonwealth, by the assistance of the Ghibellines, who in the old city were very numerous and powerful.

"Sozzo Vistarino, a principal nobleman of the city of Lodi, maintained, as a guard of his person, a company of soldiers from Cremona; but the whole family of Vistarino being soon afterwards banished and expelled by the people of Lodi, Pope Innocent endeavored to negotiate their restoration. But the people would accept of no conditions of peace until Milan and Cremona made war upon them, and unitedly compelled them to receive the Vistarini into their city. At the end of the same year the Marquis Pallavicino, at the requisition of the people of Placentia to oppose their noble exiles, went, with many of Cremona, to the siege of Rivergaro, to which those nobles had retired.

"The Cremonians about Rivergaro, in 1252, compelled the noble exiles of Placentia to surrender, and that castle was destroyed, with some other great places. Pallavicino, not content with having made himself master of Cremona, or rather of the old city, aspired to the dominion of Placentia, and to this end gave trouble enough to the podestà of that city. While Pallavicino was master of the old city, his rivals Bosio Doara, first, and Azzolino of the same family, were successively made lords of the new city.

"Uberto Pallavicino, in 1253, was created by the Placentians podestà of that city; but as the affairs of Cremona were in a

critical and fluctuating posture, he left a vice-podestà at Placentia.

"The Marquis Pallavicino, having arranged affairs as he liked
in Cremona, returned to Placentia in 1254, and, by favor of the
Ghibellines, was created perpetual governor and lord of that city.

"1256. Uberto Pallavicino, with the Ghibellines of Cremona
and Placentia, went to the assistance of Ezzelino of Romagna,
the most cruel of tyrants, and confederating with him against
the Mantuans, consigned the whole territory to fire and sword,
and laid siege to the city for three weeks, and would have taken
it, if the Marquis of Este, and the Bolognese, had not come to
its relief.

"1258. A kind of triumvirate was formed between Ezzelino,
Pallavicino, and Doara, who aspired at the domination of Lombardy. 1259. The triumvirate disagreed, and a new league was
formed between Pallavicino, Doara, and Cremona, on the one
part, with Azzo, Marquis of Este, and Ancona, Louis, Count of
Verona, and the cities of Ferrara, and Padua, on the other part,
against Ezzelino."

The particulars of the war, and the success of Pallavicino
against Ezzelino, the conquest of Bresca, and the subsequent
persecutions of the Guelph party in that kingdom, may be omitted; but in the year 1260, the rage of factions and seditions
were so distressing to all the cities, that there arose a new species of pilgrimage and penitence, whose object was to restore
peace among the parties, and obtain the return of the exiles to
their proper cities. The number of these pious and charitable
people grew to be prodigious in Tuscany, Romagna, and Lombardy, and very austere were their penitences, and very affecting their cries of "Mercy! mercy!"

"Pallavicino was alarmed, and prohibited, under severe penalties, these kind of pilgrimages in Cremona and Bresca, because
he feared they would prove the ruin of those seditions and divisions by which he maintained the domination of those cities.
He grew proud and insolent, plundered the bishopric, and drove
the bishop into exile.

"1261. Pallavicino having recovered the city of Placentia by
means of the Ghibellines, went, with a noble company of Cremonians, and established a government, making podestà Visconti
Pallavicino, a son of one of his brothers.

"1263. Gandione Doara, a noble Cremonese, was, in the name of Pallavicino, podestà of Placentia; but the Guelph exiles making an insurrection, he was driven out with his garrison. Pallavicino began at this time to be uncommonly jealous of Bosio Doara.

"1264. Pallavicino fell into a controversy with Philip della Torre, and detained in Cremona all the merchants of Milan, with their effects, pretending that Philip was his debtor, for having given him assistance, with his Cremonese soldiers, to recover the castle of Arona, occupied by Otho Visconti, archbishop of Milan.

" Pallavicino, in 1266, grew odious, and the factions of the Barbarasi, as well as the Ghibellines, had plundered the church, so that the city was laid under an interdict; and the pope's nuncios had influence enough with the people to produce a revolution, a deposition of Pallavicino, and a restoration of all the exiles, by the general council.

"1267. After the deposition of Pallavicino, Bosio Doara occupied the government of Cremona, but did not retain it long; for, upon the return of Amatino de gli Amati, the proper head of the contrary faction, from exile, Doara, with his followers, was driven out of the city; but he only went to Placentia, and there held the dominion, and appointed to the government a podestà, Gerardino Doara, a relation.

"1269. Uberto Pallavicino having lost the lordship of the principal cities of Lombardy, died miserably in Sisaligo, his castle, in which he was besieged by the Parmesans and Placentians.

"1270. Bosio Doara, with the Ghibelline exiles from Cremona, went in support of Napoleon della Torre, against his enemies at Lodi. This year they began in Cremona to create captains of the people.

"1273. Pontio Amato, a citizen of Cremona, being podestà of Milan, was killed in a battle between the Torriani, and Otho Visconti, Archbishop of Milan.

"1278. The Torriani having taken Crema, set fire to it. The Cremonese of the Guelph faction gave assistance to those of Torre, against Otho and the other Visconti, with whom was Bosio Doara of the Ghibelline faction, who prepared employment enough to the Torriani.

"1281. The Cremonese and Parmesans, desirous of effacing the memory of the injuries done to each other in times past, restored their respective triumphal chariots, which had, in former days, been taken. Great joy was discovered upon this occasion, and the two cities entered into a strict confederation with the Modenese and Reggians, and the Marquis of Este. The principal article of this league was, that they should assist the inhabitants of Lodi, who were molested by the Milanese, who favored the party of the Visconti, of which the Marquis of Monferrato was captain. Bosio Doara, and Gabrino di Monza, who were also of the faction of the Visconti, entered into Crema with four hundred soldiers on horseback, and as many on foot, the Guelphs having fled.

"1282. The Torriani, being exiled from Lodi, took refuge in Cremona, and at the same time Bosio Doara, sallying out from Crema, took by stratagem Soncino and Romanengo, castles in the jurisdiction of Cremona. The Cremonese of the Guelph faction, then dominant, fearing that their affairs would grow worse, assembled their army, and called a diet of the cities their confederates. The ambassadors therefore of Placentia, Reggio, Parma, Modena, Brescia, Bologna, and Ferrara, assembled at Cremona; and the Marquis of Este, wrote that he would come in person. Florence, and the other cities of Tuscany, offered to lend their aid; the same offer was made by John Appiano, procurator of Romagna. They sent also a noble embassy to the pope, to inform him of the situation of affairs in Lombardy, and in how much danger the cities affectionate to his highness were. Otho Visconti perceiving these movements, entered into a closer league with the Marquis of Monferrato, and they, collecting as many armed men as they could, marched out with the triumphal chariot of Milan, and united with Bosio Doara. The Cremonese conducted their army, now very powerful by the additions of the confederates, partly to Castellione, and partly to Paderno, castles of Cremona; and while the two armies stood fronting each other, they began to treat of peace, which was finally concluded, by means of the ambassadors of Placentia and Brescia. The conditions of this peace were, that all the cities should expel each other's exiles. Otho Visconti easily complied with the conditions of this convention, because he had already conceived no small jealousy of the Marquis of Monfer-

rato, and a most violent hatred against Bosio Doara, who, being
excluded from this confederation and peace, and having too much
confidence in himself, refused to surrender Soncino and Romanengo. The Cremonese therefore called another diet, who sent
an army and expelled him, not only from those two castles, but
from Crema. William and Ugolino Rossi, noble and most powerful citizens of Parma, having contracted marriage, the first with
Donella Carrara, of the signori of Padua, and the other with
Elena Cavalcabò of the family of the Marquis of Viadana, these
cities had made peace, and were full of rejoicings on the union.

"1285. William, Marquis of Monferrato, having made war
upon Otho Visconti, Archbishop of Milan, the Cremonese sent
some companies of soldiers to his assistance. At this time the
triumphal chariot began to be disused, as very inconvenient in
battle; they retained only the general standard in white, with a
red cross, to which Otho, who was the first not to use it, added
the image of St. Ambrose.

"A peace was concluded, in 1286, between the Visconti, the
archbishop, and the exiles of Milan. The numerous family of
Sommi had a confirmation of certain rights, anciently granted
to the family by the Bishop of Cremona.

"A new confederation was formed, in 1288, between Otho
Visconti, Archbishop of Milan, and the cities of Cremona, Pavia,
Placentia, Brescia, Genoa, and Asto, against the Marquis of Mon-
ferrato; but the marquis, having made himself sovereign lord of
Pavia, a new diet was assembled at Cremona, and another con-
federation formed.

"Matthew Visconti, who had been declared imperial vicar of
the city of Milan, by Adolphus, King of the Romans, called a
diet in that city, to deliberate on a war against the Torriani.
The ambassadors of Cremona were there, and promised to send
their forces to the aid of Visconti; but the Torriani made no
movement, and Visconti did not long hesitate to break with
Cremona and Lodi; for, impatient to enrich his followers, he
began to discover an intention to impose taxes on those cities.
The Torriani, too, began to complain, and were supported by the
patriarch of Aquileia; the Torriani came to Cremona, and began
to prepare war against Matthew Visconti.

"1295. The Torriani removed from Cremona to Lodi, where
they met many of their friends, and soon received the news that

Matthew Visconti had taken Castellione from the Cremonese; the Torriani, with some soldiers from Cremona and Lodi, and a gross multitude of Milanese exiles, their adherents, went to meet Visconti, but were attacked and routed by him.

"1299. The ambassadors of Cremona, of the Marquis of Monferrato, of the Marquis d'Este, of Novara, of Casale, of Bergamo, and of Vercelli, all congregated at Pavia, and made a league against Matthew Visconti. The Cremonese, not long afterwards, with the Marquis d'Este, were routed by Visconti. This year, however, a peace was concluded between Milan and Cremona, in which no mention is made of Visconti.

"A league was made, in 1302, between Cremona, Placentia, and Pavia, and they chose for their captain-general Alberto Scotto, then Lord of Placentia; these having hired a good body of soldiers, and united with the Torriani, went under the walls of Milan. Matthew Visconti, seeing that he was hated by his fellow-citizens, went out of Milan, and renounced all his authority to Scotto; and while they were treating of peace, the Torriani entered Milan, and drove off Matthew and all his partisans. After having expelled the Visconti from Milan, a new congress met at Placentia, of ambassadors from Cremona, Milan, Pavia, Lodi, Como, Novara, Vercelli, Tortona, Crema, Casale, and Bergamo, and concluded to hire, at the common expense, and for the common defence, a thousand horse and a thousand foot.

"A tumult in Parma, in 1303, was occasioned by an attempt of Giberto di Correggio to restore the Parmesan exiles. Giacopo Cavalcabò, Lord of Viadana, Amato, Persico, and Sommo, all noble citizens of Cremona, and old friends of Correggio, transported themselves to Parma, were elected arbitrators, and soon decided the controversy in favor of their friend Correggio. This year controversies and enmity arose between the Cremonese, and Alberto Scotto, Lord of Placentia.

" There was a diet of confederate cities, in 1304, against Alberto Scotto. A powerful army was collected, and the Marquis of Monferrato and the Marquis of Saluzzo were created captains; and having passed the Po, and taken many castles in the neighborhood, laid siege to Placentia; but the Cremonians and Lodians, considering the danger they might be exposed to, if that noble and powerful city should fall into the hands of the Marquis of Monferrato, began to withdraw their troops. They were followed by those of Pavia, and the others, and the army was dispersed, and Placentia delivered from the siege. A new league was made against Scotto, the head of which was Visconti Pallavicino; and the next year the Torriani made themselves masters of Placentia.

"1307. Giacopo Cavalcabò, a most noble citizen of Cremona, and Lord of Viadana, a man of ingenuity and an elevated spirit, was created podestà of Milan. The Fulgosi, Scotti, and Palastrelli, noble families of Placentia, with the assistance of William Cavalcabò and the Cremonians, expelled Lando and Visconti Pallavicino from Placentia.

"1308. Guido della Torre, Lord of Milan, made Persico, a noble Cremonian, podestà of that city. This year a controversy arising between the Parmesans and Giberto di Correggio, the Rossi, the Lupi, and other noble exiles, who had taken refuge in Cremona, were summoned by their countrymen to return; and they instantly obeyed, and carried with them the assistance of Tignaca Pallavicino, who at that time was podestà of Cremona, and the Cremonian soldiers, and having driven Correggio from Parma, Giacobo Cavalcabò was created podestà of that city. A confederation was also made between Guido della Torre, and the city of Cremona, to which Lodi, Bergamo, Placentia, and Crema acceded.

"1309. Giuliano Sommo, a noble Cremonian, was made podestà, and captain of the commons and people of Placentia, for months, according to the custom of those times.

" Henry VII. the Emperor came, at the end of 1310, into Italy to be crowned, and he called together all the Ghibellines of Lombardy, among whom Matthew Visconti held the first place. At that time the authority and influence of William Cavalcabò, brother of Giacopo, was so great in Cremona, that all public affairs were administered according to his will; but as these brothers were the heads of the Guelph faction they were little friendly to the emperor.

" Cremona, in 1311, tasted more than ever the bitter fruits of faction, civil discord, and unbalanced government, with which, however, it had been vexed and distressed for many years; it was now, besides infinite proscriptions of property and slaughter of citizens, upon the brink of total ruin from Henry. Fachetto, Marquis of Canossa, had been sent with the title of imperial vicar, but had been refused and expelled by the Guelphs, who then had the domination in Cremona. The emperor's indignation was excited, and he gave orders to Matthew Visconti to pass the Adda, and assault Cremona with an army of Ghibellines, who, collecting together from every quarter, were increased to a great number. The emperor himself, with the empress his consort, departing from Milan, removed to Lodi. Gulielmo Cavalcabò, to whom the absolute dominion of Cremona had been given by the Guelphs, perceiving such formidable preparations for war, knowing his own city to be nearly divided into equal parties, and having little confidence in his own faction, quitted the city, and went to Viadana, followed by the Picenardi, Sommi, and Persichi, with many others, nobles and populars, his adherents. And the city would have been wholly evacuated and abandoned, if the citizens had not been dissuaded by Sopramonte Amato, who went into the middle of the multitude, exhorted them to stay, and throw themselves on the mercy of the emperor, whom he painted as pious and clement, and offered himself as one of the principal intercessors. The people being comforted by his speech, it was ordered that two hundred of the principal men should go to meet Henry, who, hearing of the flight of Cavalcabò and his adherents, removed towards Cremona, and was already arrived at Paderno, eight miles distant from that city; there he was found by the Cremonians, who had been sent with Sopramonte Amato; and, in miserable habits, with their heads uncovered, with naked feet, and cords about their necks, when they came before the emperor, they fell upon their knees, and cried out, 'Mercy!' (*misericordia!*) and, with tears and lamentations, endeavored to recommend themselves and their country to the clemency of the conqueror. Such a spectacle of misery might have moved to compassion the heart of cruelty itself; it had not, however, the force to move in the smallest degree to mercy the most inhuman soul of Henry, who, with a cruelty more than barbarous, rolling his eyes another way, that he might not see them, commanded, with a voice of ferocity, that they should be all sent to prison; which was instantly executed by his ministers, and they were soon after put to death.

"Henry entered Cremona, assembled the council, and ordered that the walls of the city should be thrown down. This order was executed. And Henry desired to have the houses demolished; but at the prayer of some of his lords and barons, he was diverted from this malicious purpose; but they could not hinder many from being burned by Cremonian citizens, who had been exiles for being of the Ghibelline faction, and who sought every cruel method of revenge for the injuries they had received. The city was therefore filled with misery; the Germans and Italians all robbed alike; and nothing was heard but violence, murder, rapine, and extortion. The most rich were sure to be declared guilty, and their estates to be confiscated. At last, the emperor came to the public palace, and caused a most severe sentence to be published, in which he condemned the Cremonians to pay a hundred thousand golden florins, confiscated the public revenue, and ordered that the walls and bulwarks of the city should be ruined, and the ditches filled up. These hard conditions were accepted, and the fulfilment of them sworn to by Frederick Artezaga, syndic of the commons of Cremona, in whom was placed the government of the faction of Ghibellines, favored and exalted by the emperor, who left one of his vicars and departed. The Guelphs, thus ill treated, now concerted another confederation, and called in to their aid Robert, King of Apulia. Into this league all the cities of Romagna and Tuscany entered. The principal were Florence, Lucca, and Siena; and of those of Lombardy, Bologna, Reggio, and Parma, whose sovereign lord was Giberto di Correggio. The Torriani and the Cavalcabòs, with the rest of the Milanese and Cremonian exiles, joined the confederacy; and all these united, after having made themselves masters of the bridge of Dossolo over the Pò, took also Casalmaggiore, driving out the Ghibellines.

William Cavalcabò, having learned that John Castiglione, Podestà of Cremona, in the name of the emperor, was gone with the militia to Pozzobaronzo, a place subject to the Cremonians, in which were some Guelphs, taking advantage of this opportunity, flew with wonderful rapidity to Cremona, and entering the city by the gate della Mosa, arrived without opposition to the piazza, where he was encountered by Galeazzo Visconti and Manfredino Pallavicino; but these not being able to sustain the impetuosity of the soldiers of Cavalcabò, not without a great slaughter of Ghibellines, among whom Giacomo Redenasco was slain, they betook themselves to flight, and Galeazzo saved himself in Crema. Soon afterwards, as an insurrection was expected in Cremona, Giberto di Reggio went thither from Parma, where he was received with tokens of the greatest joy; and having quieted with great prudence the controversies, he established Cavalcabò in the lordship of the city, making Quirico Sanvitale, his son-in-law, podestà. The inhabitants of Soncino having also expelled the imperial governor, surrendered to Cavalcabò, who, fearing that the enemy would encamp at that post, suddenly went thither with Venturino Benzone, head of the Guelphs of Crema, and with Venturino Fondulo, one of the principal men of Soncino. The Barbuoi and other families of Soncino, of the opposite faction, having conveyed intelligence of this to the emperor, he gave Soncino to the Count Guarnero, his general in Lombardy, who went and laid siege to the place. There were in Soncino, besides the Terrazzani, the Guelphs of Cremona, Crema, and Bergamo; and with the Count Guarnero, besides the German troops, were the Ghibellines of Cremona, Bergamo, and Crema. The inhabitants of Soncino defended themselves on the first assault with great activity, encouraged by the valor of Cavalcabò, Benzone, and Fondulo; but, seized with a panic, upon some advantage gained by Galeazzo Visconti, the soldiers, who came to their assistance from Cremona, shamefully abandoned their defence, and retreated into the houses. Cavalcabò, seeing such cowardice or treachery, consulted with Benzone to get out of that place as soon as possible. Collecting their soldiers in a compact body, they rushed into the midst of the enemy, combating with wonderful intrepidity; but Cavalcabò being killed, and Benzone and Venturino Fondulo, with his two sons, made prisoners, the Ghibellines remained victorious. Benzone, falling into the hands of the Ghibellines of Crema, was miserably assassinated; and Fondulo, with his two sons, by the orders of Guarnero, was hanged before the gate of Soncino. The news of this defeat filled Cremona with terror and confusion. But Giberto Correggio, with a company of Parmesans coming in, their fears subsided, and the enemy having intelligence of this succor, had not the courage to approach the walls. The Cremonians, to recompense the benefit received from Correggio, gave him the government of the city for five years. The Guelphs took Castellione, in which was Manfredino Pallavicino, who was made prisoner. And Castelnovo, the mouth of the Adda to the Guelphs, was taken by the Ghibellines.

" Passarino della Torre had the government of Cremona in 1313, with the title of Vicar of Robert, King of Apulia.

" Giacopo Cavalcabò, Marquis of Viadana, was, in 1315, by the common consent of the people, elected to the government of Cremona. Ponzino de' Ponzoni, his brother-in-law, whether from private envy or republican jealousy, was enraged beyond all measure at this, and he stirred up insurrections against Cavalcabò, many other noble families, the Ponzoni, the Guazoni, the Amati, and the Picenardi, who went out of Cremona, and made a league with the Visconti, and occasioned much mischief and ruin to their country, against which they took up arms.

" Ponzino Ponzone and all his adherents, having made a league with Cane della Scala, Lord of Verona, and with Passarino Buona-cossi, Lord of Mantua, came to Cremona, and laid siege to it; but by the valor of those within they were repulsed; yet they did much damage in the territory. A peace, or the appearance of a peace, between those in the city and the exiles, was then made; and, by common consent, Egidiolo Piperaro was deputed to the government of the city, with the title of Abbate of the People; and then the Ponzoni, with their partisans, returned to the city.

" The whole city, in 1317, arose in arms, excited by Giacopo and Luigi Cavalcabò, and Gregorio Sommo, and others, their partisans of the Guelph faction, with whom were the Brusati, Lords of Brescia, with all their followers. These entering the great piazza of Cremona, slew Egidiolo Piperaro, who had mounted the rostrum to still the tumult. Leonard and Baccanino Picenardi, though one of them was a brother-in-law of Louis Cavalcabò, were both assassinated; the Pedecani, Malombra, Alemanni, and others innumerable, both of the noble and popular families of the Ghibelline faction were murdered; and the whole faction was, in fact, driven out of the city, Ponzone taking his flight with some others of the principal citizens who fled with him. He was received into Soncino by Philip Barbuò, and soon obtained Castellione, and all the Guelphs were driven out of both these places. Ponzone, who had first holden with the Guelph party, now conjured up another faction, by the name of the Maltraversi, of whom he was the head," (for every faction had its podestà, little council, and great council, its king, lords, and commons,) " and in a short time made himself master of almost all the Cremonese territories in the country. Finally, the Ghibellines and Maltraversi made a coalition, and constituting Ponzino their head, entered into close alliance with Cane della Scala, Lord of Verona, and Passarino Buonacossi, Lord of Mantua, and with Matthew Visconti, Vicar-General of Milan. These came, therefore, to the assistance of the Ghibellines and Maltraversi, against the Guelphs, in Cremona, Cane, and Passarino, with their people, and Matthew sent them Luchino, his son, with the Milanese cavalry and infantry, with whom were some companies of Pavians, Placentians, Parmesans, Bergamans, and others, from Coma, Novara, Vercelli, Crema, and Monferrato. All these people, uniting together, encamped against Cremona. The siege continued twenty-eight days, without any event of consequence, excepting their depredations upon the territory in the country, and destruction of all the estates of the Guelphs.

" 1318. Ponzone, having made a breach in the wall, entered the city with his Ghibellines and Maltraversi, and reached the piazza without being discovered. The Guelphs, when they saw him, were astonished and fled, and with them Giacopo Cavalcabò and Gregorio Sommo. Ponzone was proclaimed Lord of Cremona by the Ghibellines and Maltraversi. At the same time, the partisans of Cavalcabò took Robecco, and went to Olmeneta, eight miles from Cremona, and ruined a certain tower of the Zucchelli, in which was Niccolò Borgo, with some others of the faction of Ponzone, who, upon hearing of the destruction of his friends, went with a body of soldiers to those places, and made much havoc among the people of Cavalcabò.

"Giberto Correggio, captain-general of the Guelph league, with Cavalcabò, and all those of their faction, broke down the walls of the city in 1319, entered, and by force of arms drove out the Ghibellines, and Ponzino Ponzone, with his league of Guelph Maltraversi.

" This Ponzone appears to have joined any side, as his circumstances gave him opportunity; for in 1321, he made a coalition with Galeazzo Visconti, son of Matthew, and Lord of Placentia, entered, with the Ghibelline faction, by force of arms, into Cremona, and drove away the Cavalcabòs, with all the real Guelphs, their partisans. There was afterwards published a proclamation, in the name of Galeazzo, that it should be lawful for all, of whatever faction, to inhabit the city of Cremona, excepting the Cavalcabòs, and certain other citizens, suspected of having concerted a plot against Galeazzo and his partisans.

"1324. Alberto Scotto, of Placentia, head of the Guelphs, took the castle of Malamorte, which was on the bank of the Po, directly opposite to the city of Cremona, and more than three hundred Ghibellines who were within were slain. Raimondo Cardona was sent by the pope, John XXII., with a powerful army, to the assistance of the Guelphs, who, assembling all of his faction in Lombardy, went against Galeazzo Visconti, and shutting him up in Milan, laid siege to it.

"1327. Louis IV., of Bavaria, set up an anti-pope against John.

"1329. Louis confirmed to the Cremonians all the privileges granted to them by his predecessors.

"1330. Guido de Camilla, imperial vicar, had the government of the city, and a truce was established between the community of Cremona and Gregory de' Sommi, by which it appears, that Cremona was not at that time subjected to the Visconti. The city was governed by Ghibellines, who were the majority, or predominant party; and Gregory Sommo was one of the principal heads of the Guelph party.

"1335. Azzo Visconti, son of Galeazzo, having made a peace with the Cremonians, gave them the dominion of Crema, which, after the death of Pope John, had subjected itself to the Visconti. This year, according to some historians, the lordship of Cremona was given by its inhabitants to the same Azzo Visconti.

"1339. Azzo Visconti, Lord of Cremona, died without sons, and to him succeeded in the dominion of Milan and of Cremona, Luchino Visconti, and John his brother, who, from Bishop of Novara, was a little afterwards made Archbishop of Milan, so that he became in that city lord both in spiritual and temporal affairs. Cremona enjoyed a state of tranquillity under the joint lordship of Luchino and John the archbishop.

"Luchino Visconti died in 1348, and for his rare and excellent qualities very much regretted by the people his subjects. He left no son, and therefore the Archbishop obtained the sole lordship of Milan and Cremona, and of many other cities acquired by the virtue of Luchino. John and Luchino had obtained from Benedict XII., pope, the title of Vicars of the Holy Apostolical See.

" 1350. Bernabò and Galeazzo, brothers of the Visconti, nephews of John, the Archbishop and Lord of Milan and Cremona, both married; the first to Regina della Scala, daughter of the Lord of Verona and Vicenza; and Galeazzo married a sister of the Duke of Savoy, named Bianca.

" John Visconti, Archbishop and Lord of Milan, after having greatly amplified his dominions, died in 1354, leaving as his heirs Matthew, Bernabò, and Galeazzo, sons of Stephen his brother. The extent of absolute dominion already acquired by this family over the ruins of so many commonwealths, ruined by their unbalanced factions, appears by the division made upon this occasion. To Matthew were assigned Placentia, Lodi, Bologna, Massa, Lugo, Bobio, Pontremolo, and Borgo San Donino; to Galeazzo, the cities of Como, Novara, Vercelli, Asti, Alba, Alessandria, Tortona, Castelnuovo di Scrivia, Bassignana, Vigevano, St. Angelo, Montebuono, and Mairano; to Bernabò were given Cremona, Bergamo, Brescia, Crema, Valcamonica, Lonato, with all the river dal Lago di Garda, and other places. The lordship of Milan and Genoa remained to them all united.

" 1355. The Emperor, Charles IV., came into Italy to receive the imperial crown, and was crowned with the crown of iron at Milan, by Robert Visconti, archbishop of that city, and he there created knights, John Galeazzo, a boy of two years old, who was afterwards the first Duke of Milan; and Marco, who was not two months old, both sons of Galeazzo Visconti. The Emperor gave also the title of Imperial Vicars in Italy to the three brothers, Galeazzo, Matthew, and Bernabò. The dominion of Cremona remained alone in Bernabò.

" 1365. Bernabò married Verde, his daughter, to Lupoldo, brother of the Archduke of Austria; and the wedding was celebrated at Milan, before a congress of ambassadors from Cremona and all the other cities subject to him; and he gave his daughter a dower of a hundred thousand florins.

" 1368. Violante, daughter of Galeazzo, was married to a son of the King of England, with another dower of a hundred thousand florins, and an annual pension of twenty-four thousand more, assigned upon some city of Piedmont.

" 1372. Isabella, the first wife of John Galeazzo, Conte di

Virtù, the first-born son of Galeazzo Visconti, before mentioned, died, and left an only daughter, called Valentina. At this time Bernabò gave great signs of an inhuman and cruel nature.

"1377. La Verde, daughter of Galeazzo, was married to a son of the Marquis of Monferrato, who was assassinated by his subjects. She was then married by her father, with a dispensation from the pope, to a son of Bernabò.

"1378. Galeazzo died, and left two sons, John Galeazzo, Conte di Virtú, and Azzo. John Galeazzo, who was the eldest, succeeded his father in the dominion of the state.

"1380. Catherine Visconti, daughter of Bernabò, was, by her father, married to John Galeazzo, Conte di Virtù, her cousin, with a dispensation from the pope.

"1381. Azzo died, brother of John Galeazzo, to whom alone remained the government of their paternal state.

"1385. Cremona gave itself voluntarily to John Galeazzo Visconti, Conte di Virtù, under whose dominion came all the other cities and places subject to Bernabò, his uncle and father-in-law; Bernabò having been made a prisoner, with Ludovico and Rodolfo, his sons, by the same John Galeazzo, who, having learned from his wife, the daughter of Bernabò, that her father had several times attempted to put him to death, in order to rule alone, resolved to relieve himself from anxiety and suspicion. To this end he went to Pavia, and affected a retired life, and pretended to go a pilgrimage to St. Mary del Monte. Bernabò, with his two sons, went to meet him, and all three were taken by the soldiers of John Galeazzo, and confined in the castle of Trezzo, where they all died of poison, as it is supposed, sent them by his nephew and son-in-law. John Galeazzo was immediately accepted by the Milanese as their lord; and the Cremonians spontaneously gave themselves up to Giacopo Virino, the captain and counsellor of the same John Galeazzo, and soon after sent sixteen ambassadors to Milan with a capitulation, which was accepted and confirmed by him, article by article, with some limitations. The first article was, that the city of Cremona gave itself voluntarily and by a common concord of all the people.

"1388. Bianca, mother of John Galeazzo, died, and Valentina his daughter, by Isabella, his first wife, was married to Louis Duke of Orleans, brother of Charles VI., King of France; and this year was born John Maria, son of John Galeazzo, by Catherine his consort.

" Philip Maria, second son of John Galeazzo, was born in Milan, in 1392.

"John Galeazzo, Conte di Virtù, obtained the title of Duke of Milan, of Wenceslaus the emperor. He received all the ensigns of the ducal dignity, and that with admirable pomp, before a congress of the ambassadors from all the cities subject to him, among whom were those from Cremona, those from Venice, Florence, the Marquis di Ferrato, the Lords of Forli and Urbino, and the sons of the Lords of Padua, with a multitude of others. He gave to the Emperor an hundred thousand ducats for the ducal dignity. In 1399, the Duke obtained the domination of the city of Pisa; in 1400, that of Perugia; and in 1402, Bologna.

" 1403. Factions arose again in this province, out of which were engendered seditions, civil discords, and rebellions, by which John Maria, second Duke of Milan, lost the ample dominion that had been left him by his father. Seditions arose in Milan, in which they expelled the ducal lieutenant; which, being understood by the other cities, they all arose, driving off the ducal officers. John Castiglione, a Milanese, was then in Cremona, with the title of Ducal Vicar, but he was now expelled by the fury of the people; and, at the same time, John Ponzone, and Ugolino Cavalcabò, Marquis of Viadana, most noble and powerful citizens, and heads of the factions of Guelphs and Maltraversi, drove the Ghibellines from the city, and made themselves masters of it. There followed, at this time, innumerable homicides and burnings of houses, both in the city and country, there not being a village in which there were not the two parties."

But passing over the horrid detail of particulars, we may pass to the year 1404, when " Ugolino Cavalcabò, having seized the dominion of Cremona, conceived suspicions of some of the principal citizens, and caused their heads to be struck off, as guilty of plotting against him, and endeavoring to restore the city to the duke. Tyranny and cruelty are always the effect of such a state of affairs in all parties; and the Duke John Maria grew every day more cruel. He imprisoned his own mother, Catherine Visconti, in the castle of Monza, and caused her to be there strangled. Ugolino, coming to battle near Brescia with Estore Visconti, was taken prisoner with Marsilio and Cæsar Cavalcabò and many other citizens of their faction. Ugolino was conducted to Soncino, and then to Milan, where he remained many months in prison; and Cabrino Fondulo, his captain, saved himself in that conflict by flight to Cremona. The captivity of Ugolino being known, Charles Cavalcabò, of the same family, seized the government of Cremona.

"Francesco Gasoni, a knight, and heretofore podestà of Cremona for Ugolino Cavalcabò, and afterwards made captain-general in that city, by Charles his successor, was beheaded for being suspected of holding a correspondence and concerting a conspiracy with Estore Visconti. A league was published this year between Charles Cavalcabò, Pandolfo Malatesta, Vignati, Lord of Lodi, and Bartolomeo and Paolo Benzoni, Lords of Crema; and Charles took Piadena, whose citadel was surrendered to him by William Picenardo.

"1406. The Visconti castle was this year fortified by Charles Cavalcabò, and Ugolino escaping from prison, went to Mancastorma to find Cabrino Fondulo, who came with him to Cremona, to enter into the castle, in which was Charles, who had an understanding with Fondulo. Ugolino was therefore received into the castle, but his foot was scarcely within the gate before he was made prisoner; for these people were not much more inclined to surrender their power to their own families than to strangers. A little afterwards Fondulo, having fraudulently invited to supper with him, in the castle of Mancastorma, Charles and Andreaso Cavalcabò, made them both prisoners, and cruelly murdered them. He came soon after to Cremona with many armed men, entered the castle and the other fortresses, and made himself master of the city, and of all the lands and castles possessed by Cavalcabò, except Viadana, which would not submit to him. Cabrino, little grateful to that family by whom he had been elevated to an honorable rank, defaced all the arms of the Cavalcabòs which appeared in public places, and miserably murdered Ugolino, by whom he had been made captain.

"Fondulo, in 1407, caused to be beheaded two sons of Picenardo, in the piazza of Cremona, and cast cruelly from the ruins of a tower two of the family of Barbuò. This year Pandolfo, the son of Fondulo, was born. A truce, made between the Duke of Milan and Cabrino Fondulo, Lord of Cremona, was renewed for four months.

"1408. John Maria, Duke of Milan, married, in the city of Brescia, Antonia, daughter of Malatesta, Lord of Rimini. Cabrino Fondulo caused to be burned John de' Sesto, for having made false money; and buried alive John Lantero, for having slandered Cabrino; he hanged Lorenzo Guazzoni, and beheaded Rubertino of the same family, for having been found on the land of Gazzo, which had rebelled against him.

"1409. Another son was born to Cabrino Fondulo, Lord of Cremona. He had taken Gazzo, which had rebelled against him, and destroyed it; and was this year made a knight in the city of Milan, by Bucicaldo, Governor of Genoa for the King of France.

"1411. John da Terso, Lord of Soncino, was taken and assassinated by the people of Cabrino near Brescia; and Cabrino obtained from the inhabitants of Soncino the land and fort.

"1412. John Maria Visconti, Duke of Milan, while he was at mass, was murdered by Trivulzio, Guerrino, and Baruchino, and other conspirators of several conspicuous families, and Estore Visconti, son of Barnabas, maternal grandfather of John Maria, was proclaimed by the conspirators Lord of Milan: but these were driven out by Philip Maria, Lord of Pavia, brother of the deceased duke, who entered Milan with the forces of Facino Cane, and Estore being fled to Monza, was pursued by Philip, besieged, fought, and slain. Whereupon Philip Maria was proclaimed Duke of Milan, and married Beatrice, formerly wife of Facino Cane, and availed himself of her dower, and of the soldiers of her late husband, to recover the state from the hands of the tyrants who, from the death of his father, had possessed it. At the end of this year a truce was made between the Duke Philip Maria and Cabrino Fondulo.

"1416. A confederation was made between Fondulo, Malatesta, the Marquis of Ferrara, and Philip Arcelli, Lord of Placentia, on one part, and Philip Maria, Duke of Milan, and his adherents, on the other. The friends of the duke were Vignati, Lord of Lodi, Rusca, Lord of Como, Benzone, Lord of Crema, and Orlando, Marquis Pallavicino. This convention lasted not long, though it was made for two years.

"1417. The Duke Philip Maria, having broken the truce and confederation, sent his forces, under Carmagnuola, his captain-general, to commit depredations on the Cremonians. Going afterwards to Placentia with part of his people, he was met by Cabrino, Lord of Cremona, with a few infantry of Malatesta, and defeated.

"1418. Philip Maria, Duke of Milan, caused to be beheaded Beatrice his wife, for no other reason but because she was grown old and he was weary of her, although he propagated against her suspicions of adultery.

"1419. The Count Carmagnuola returned to the Cremonian territory with the ducal army, took Castellione and all the other castles, destroyed the vines and corn, and laid siege to the city. Cabrino Fondulo, seeing that he could not resist the forces of the duke, endeavored to sell the city of Cremona to Pandolfo Malatesta. But the duke sent Carmagnuola upon the territory of Brescia, and soon had all its fortresses in his possession. Cabrino, seeing that the assistance of Malatesta would fail him, began, by the means of Carmagnuola, to treat of an agreement with Philip Maria, who, knowing the difficulty of taking the city from so powerful and sagacious a man as Fondulo, finally agreed with him.

"1420. Cabrino agreed with the duke to surrender Cremona and all its country, reserving only Castellione, of which he was invested in fee, with the title of marquis, by the duke, for which he paid forty thousand ducats.

"1421. The duke recovered Genoa, Albenga, Savona, and Brescia.

"1424. Fondulo, desirous of regaining the domination, made an agreement with the Florentines against the duke.

"1425. The duke condemned to death Cabrino Fondulo, and beheaded him."

The rest of this history may be consulted at leisure. It was at this time, and had been long, an absolute monarchy. While it was a republic it was a continual struggle between the families of Pallavicini and Doara, Cavalcabò and Visconti, Ponzoni and Cavalcabò, Visconti and Fondulo. The family of Visconti acquired in Lombardy a sovereignty like that of the Medici in Tuscany, and by the same means. And both because there was no balance in the governments, and because the executive power and judiciary power were elected in the legislative assembly; that is, precisely, because all authority was attempted to be placed in the same centre. Is it worth while, merely for the whistling of the name of a republic, to undergo all the miseries and horrors, cruelties, tyrannies, and crimes which are the natural and inevitable fruits of such a constitution?

CHAPTER NINTH.

The elements and definitions in most of the arts and sciences are understood alike, by men of education, in all the nations of Europe; but in the science of legislation, which is not one of the least importance to be understood, there is a confusion of languages, as if men were but lately come from Babel. Scarcely any two writers, much less nations, agree in using words in the same sense. Such a latitude, it is true, allows a scope for politicians to speculate, like merchants with false weights, artificial credit, or base money, and to deceive the people, by making the same word adored by one party, and execrated by another. The union of the people, in any principle, rule, or system, is thus rendered impossible; because superstition, prejudice, habit, and passions, are so differently attached to words, that you can scarcely make any nation understand itself. The words monarchy, aristocracy, democracy, king, prince, lords, commons, nobles, patricians, plebeians, if carefully attended to, will be found to be used in different senses, perpetually, by different nations, by different writers in the same nation, and even by the same writers in different pages.

The word *king*, for example. Ask a Frenchman, What is a king? His answer will be, A man with a crown and sceptre, throne and footstool, anointed at Rheims, who has the making, executing, and interpreting of all laws. Ask an Englishman. His idea will comprehend the throne, footstool, crown, sceptre, and anointing, with one third of the legislative power and the whole of the executive, with an estate in his office to him and his heirs. Ask a Pole; and he tells you, It is a magistrate chosen for life, with scarcely any power at all. Ask an inhabitant of Liege; and he tells you, It is a bishop, and his office is only for life. The word *prince* is another remarkable instance. In Venice, it means the senate, and sometimes, by courtesy, the doge, whom some of the Italian writers call a mere *testa di legno*. In France, the eldest sons of dukes are princes, as well as the descendants of the blood royal; in Germany, even the rhingraves are princes; and in Russia, several families, not descended from nor allied to royal blood, anciently obtained, by grant of the sovereign, the title of prince, descendible to all their posterity; the consequence of which has been, that the number of princes in that country is at this day prodigious; and the philosopher of Geneva, in imitation of the Venetians, professedly calls the executive power, wherever lodged, the Prince. How is it possible that whole nations should be made to comprehend the principles and rules of government, until they shall learn to understand one another's meaning by words?

But of all the words in all languages, perhaps there has been none so much abused in this way as the words *republic, commonwealth*, and *popular state*. In the *Rerum-Publicarum Collectio*, of which there are fifty and odd volumes, and many of them very incorrect, France, Spain, and Portugal, the four great empires, the Babylonian, Persian, Greek, and Roman, and even the Ottoman, are all denominated republics. If, indeed, a republic signifies nothing but public affairs, it is equally applicable to all nations; and every kind of government, despotisms, monarchies, aristocracies, democracies, and every possible or imaginable composition of them are all republics. There is, no doubt, a public good and evil, a commonwealth and a common impoverishment in all of them. Others define a republic to be a government of more than one. This will exclude only the despotisms; for a monarchy administered by laws, requires at least magistrates to register them, and consequently more than one person in the government. Some comprehend under the term only aristocracies and democracies, and mixtures of these, without any distinct executive power. Others, again, more rationally, define a republic to signify only a government, in which all men, rich and poor, magistrates and subjects, officers and people, masters and servants, the first citizen and the last, are equally subject to the laws. This, indeed, appears to be the true and only true definition of a republic. The word *res*, every one knows, signified in the Roman language wealth, riches, property; the word *publicus*, quasi populicus, and per syncope *pôplicus*, signified public, common, belonging to the people; *res publica*, therefore, was publica res, the wealth, riches, or property of the people.[*] *Res populi*, and

* See any of the common dictionaries, Soranus, Stephens, Ainsworth.

the original meaning of the word *republic* could be no other
than a government in which the property of the people predomi-
nated and governed; and it had more relation to property than
liberty. It signified a government, in which the property of the
public, or people, and of every one of them, was secured and
protected by law. This idea, indeed, implies liberty; because
property cannot be secure unless the man be at liberty to acquire,
use, or part with it, at his discretion, and unless he have his
personal liberty of life and limb, motion and rest, for that purpose. It implies, moreover, that the property and liberty of all
men, not merely of a majority, should be safe; for the people,
or public, comprehends more than a majority, it comprehends
all and every individual; and the property of every citizen is a
part of the public property, as each citizen is a part of the
public, people, or community. The property, therefore, of every
man has a share in government, and is more powerful than any
citizen, or party of citizens; it is governed only by the law.
There is, however, a peculiar sense in which the words *republic,
commonwealth, popular state*, are used by English and French
writers; who mean by them a democracy, or rather a representative democracy; a "government in one centre, and that
centre the nation;" that is to say, that centre a single assembly,
chosen at stated periods by the people, and invested with the
whole sovereignty; the whole legislative, executive, and judicial
power, to be exercised in a body, or by committees, as they shall
think proper. This is the sense in which it was used by Marcha-
mont Nedham, and in this sense it has been constantly used from
his time to ours, even by writers of the most mathematical precision, the most classical purity, and extensive learning. What
other authority there may be for this use of those words is not
known; none has been found, except in the following observations of Portenari, in which there are several other inaccuracies;
but they are here inserted, chiefly because they employ the words
republic, commonwealth, and *popular state*, in the same sense with
the English and French writers.

" We * may say with the philosopher,[1] that six things are so
necessary to a city, that without them it cannot stand. 1. The

---

* *Della Felicità di Padova*, di Angelo Portenari, Padovano Agostino, libro
nove, in Padova per Pietro Paolo Tozzi, 1623, p. 115.
[1] Aristot. *Polit.* b. 7, c. 8.

first is provisions, without which its inhabitants cannot live.
2. The second is clothes, habitations, houses, and other things,
which depend upon the arts, without which civil and political
life cannot subsist. 3. The third is arms, which are necessary
to defend the city from its enemies, and to repress the boldness
of those who rebel against the laws. 4. The fourth is money,
most necessary to a city in peace and in war. 5. The fifth is
the care of divine worship. 6. The sixth is the administration
of justice, and the government of the people. For the first are
necessary, cultivators of the land; for the second, artificers; for
the third, soldiers; for the fourth, merchants and capitalists; for
the fifth, priests; for the sixth, judges and magistrates. Seven
sorts of men, therefore, are necessary to a city: husbandmen,
artificers, soldiers, merchants, rich men, priests, and judges.

"But, according to the same philosopher,* as in the body
natural not all those things, without which it is never found, are
parts of it, but only instruments subservient to some uses, as in
animals, the horns, the nails, the hair, so not all those seven sorts
of men are parts of the city; but some of them, namely, the
husbandmen, the artificers, and the merchants, are only instruments useful to civil life, as is thus demonstrated. A city is
constituted for felicity, as to its ultimate end; and human felicity, here below, is reposed, according to the same philosopher,
in the operations of virtue, and chiefly in the exertions of wisdom and prudence; those men, therefore, are not parts of a city,
the operations of whom are not directed to those virtues; such
are the husbandmen who are occupied, not in wisdom and prudence, but in laboring the earth; such are the artisans, who
fatigue themselves night and day to gain a livelihood for themselves and their poor families; such, finally, are the merchants,
who watch and labor continually, not in wisdom and prudence,
but in the acquisition of gold. It is therefore clear, that neither
husbandmen, artificers, nor merchants, are parts of a city, nor
ought to be numbered among the citizens, but only as instruments which subserve certain uses and conveniences of the
city."

We must pause here and admire! The foregoing are not
only the grave sentiments of Portenari and of Aristotle, but

---

* Arist. Polit. lib. vii. c. 9.

form the doctrine almost of the whole earth, and of all mankind; not only every despotism, empire, and monarchy, in Asia, Africa, and Europe, but every aristocratical republic, has adopted it in all its latitude. There are only two or three of the smallest cantons in Switzerland, besides England, who allow husband-men, artificers, and merchants, to be citizens, or to have any voice or share in the government of the state, or in the choice or appointment of any who have. There is no doctrine, and no fact, which goes so far as this towards forfeiting to the human species the character of rational creatures. Is it not amazing, that nations should have thus tamely surrendered themselves, like so many flocks of sheep, into the hands of shepherds, whose great solicitude to devour the lambs, the wool, and the flesh, scarcely leave them time to provide water or pasture for the animals, or even shelter against the weather and the wolves?

It is, indeed, impossible that the several descriptions of men, last enumerated, should, in a great nation and extensive territory, ever assemble in a body to act in concert; and the ancient method of taking the sense of an assembly of citizens in the capital, as in Rome for example, for the sense of all the citizens of a whole republic, or a large empire, was very imperfect, and extremely exposed to corruption; but, since the invention of representative assemblies, much of that objection is removed, though even that was no sufficient reason for excluding farmers, merchants, and artificers, from the rights of citizens. At present a husbandman, merchant, or artificer, provided he has any small property, by which he may be supposed to have a judgment and will of his own, instead of depending for his daily bread on some patron or master, is a sufficient judge of the qualifications of a person to represent him in the legislature. A representative assembly, fairly constituted, and made an integral part of the sovereignty, has power forever to control the rich and illustrious in another assembly, and a court and king, where there is a king. This, too, is the only instrument by which the body of the people can act; the only way in which their opinions can be known and collected; the only means by which their wills can be united, and their strength exerted, according to any principle or con-tinued system.

It is sometimes said, that mobs are a good mode of expressing the sense, the resentments, and feelings of the people. Whig mobs to be sure are meant! But if the principle is once admitted, liberty and the rights of mankind will infallibly be betrayed; for it is giving liberty to tories and courtiers to excite mobs as well as to patriots; and all history and experience shows, that mobs are more easily excited by courtiers and princes, than by more virtuous men, and more honest friends of liberty.

It is often said, too, that farmers, merchants, and mechanics, are too inattentive to public affairs, and too patient under oppression. This is undoubtedly true, and will forever be so; and, what is worse, the most sober, industrious, and peaceable of them, will forever be the least attentive, and the least disposed to exert themselves in hazardous and disagreeable efforts of resistance. The only practicable method, therefore, of giving to farmers, &c. the equal right of citizens, and their proper weight and influence in society, is by elections, frequently repeated, of a house of commons, an assembly which shall be an essential part of the sovereignty. The meanest understanding is equal to the duty of saying who is the man in his neighborhood whom he most esteems, and loves best, for his knowledge, integrity, and benevolence. The understandings, however, of husbandmen, merchants, and mechanics, are not always the meanest; there arise, in the course of human life, many among them of the most splendid geniuses, the most active and benevolent dispositions, and most undaunted bravery. The moral equality that nature has unalterably established among men, gives these an undoubted right to have every road opened to them for advancement in life and in power that is open to any others. These are the characters which will be discovered in popular elections, and brought forward upon the stage, where they may exert all their faculties, and enjoy all the honors, offices, and commands, both in peace and war, of which they are capable. The dogma of Aristotle, and the practice of the world, is the most unphilosophical, the most inhuman and cruel that can be conceived. Until this wicked position, which is worse than the slavery of the ancient republics, or modern West Indies, shall be held up to the derision and contempt, the execration and horror, of mankind, it will be to little purpose to talk or write about liberty. This doctrine of Aristotle is the more extraordinary, as it seems to be inconsistent with his great and common principles, "that

* Aristot. Pol. lib. iv. c. 11.

a happy life must arise from a course of virtue; that virtue consists in a medium; and that the middle life is the happiest.

" In every city the people are divided into three sorts, the very rich, the very poor, and the middle sort. If it is admitted that the medium is the best, it follows that, even in point of fortune, a mediocrity is preferable. The middle state is most compliant to reason. Those who are very beautiful, or strong, or noble, or rich, or, on the contrary, those who are very poor, weak, or mean, with difficulty obey reason. The former are capricious[1] and flagitious; the latter, rascally and mean; the crimes of each arising from their different excesses. Those who excel in riches, friends, and influence, are not willing to submit to command or law; this begins at home, where they are brought up too delicately, when boys, to obey their preceptors. The constant want of what the rich enjoy makes the poor too mean; the poor know not how to command, but are in the habit of being commanded, too often as slaves. The rich know not how to submit to any command; nor do they know how to rule over freemen, or to command others, but despotically. A city composed only of the rich and the poor, consists but of masters and slaves, not free-men; where one party despise, and the other hate; where there is no possibility of friendship, or political community, which supposes affection. It is the genius of a free city to be composed, as much as possible, of equals; and equality will be best preserved when the greatest part of the inhabitants are in the middle state. These will be best assured of safety as well as equality; they will not covet nor steal, as the poor do, what belongs to the rich; nor will what they have be coveted or stolen; without plotting against any one, or having any one plot against them, they will live free from danger. For which reason, Phocylides * wisely wishes for the middle state, as being most productive of happiness. It is plain then that the most perfect community must be among those who are in the middle rank; and those states are best instituted wherein these are a larger and more respectable part, if possible, than both the other;

---

* Πολλὰ μέσοισιν. ἄριστα· μέσος θέλω ἐν πόλει εἶναι.
Which Dr. Gillies interprets thus:
      " How happy is the middle walk of life,
            O! may it be my portion in the state!"
[1] ὑβρισταί, in the original, " insolent."

or, if that cannot be, at least than either of them separate; so that, being thrown into the balance, it may prevent either scale from preponderating. It is, therefore, the greatest happiness which the citizen can enjoy, to possess a moderate and convenient fortune. When some possess too much, and others nothing at all, the government must either be in the hands of the meanest rabble, or else a pure oligarchy. The middle state is best, as being least liable to those seditions and insurrections which disturb the community; and for the same reason extensive governments are least liable to these inconveniences; for there those in the middle state are very numerous; whereas, in small ones, it is easy to pass to the two extremes, so as hardly to have any medium remaining, but the one half rich, and the other poor. We ought to consider, as a proof of this, that the best lawgivers were those in the middle rank of life, among whom was Solon, as is evident from his poems, and Lycurgus, for he was not a king; and Charondas, and, indeed, most others. Hence, so many free states have changed either to democracies or oligarchies; for whenever the number of those in the middle state has been too small, those who were the more numerous, whether the rich or the poor, always overpowered them, and assumed to themselves the administration. When, in consequence of their disputes and quarrels with each other, either the rich get the better of the poor, or the poor of the rich, neither of them will establish a free state, but, as a record of their victory, will form one which inclines to their own principles, either a democracy or an oligarchy. It is, indeed, an established custom of cities, not to desire an equality, but either to aspire to govern, or, when they are conquered, to submit."

These are some of the wisest sentiments of Aristotle; but can you reconcile them with his other arbitrary doctrine, and tyrannical exclusion of husbandmen, merchants, and tradesmen, from the rank and rights of citizens? These, or at least, those of them who have acquired property enough to be exempt from daily dependence on others, are the real middling people, and generally as honest and independent as any; these, however, it must be confessed, are too inattentive to public and national affairs, and too apt to submit to oppression. When they have been provoked beyond all bearing, they have aimed at demolishing the government, and when they have done that, they have

sunk into their usual inattention, and left others to erect a new
one as rude and ill-modelled as the former. A representative
assembly, elected by them, is the only way in which they can
act in concert; but they have always allowed themselves to be
cheated by false, imperfect, partial, and inadequate representations of themselves, and have never had their full and proper
share of power in a state. But to proceed with Portenari.

"The other kinds of men," says he, "namely, the rich, the
soldiers, the priests, and the judges, are parts of the city, and
properly citizens. The first, because riches are instruments for
generating and conserving virtue in the citizens. The second,
because it is necessary that military men, besides the virtue of
fortitude, should be adorned with prudence, to know the times
and occasions proper for undertaking an enterprise. The third,
because the priests ought to be examples of every virtue to the
people, and give themselves to the contemplation of divine
things. The fourth, because the judges and rectors of a city, to
judge and govern rightly, have occasion more than all the others
for science and prudence, which are the true lights and guides
of human actions."

If these are proper arguments for admitting these descriptions
of men into the order of citizens, instead of being reasons for
excluding merchants, &c. they are of proportional weight for
admitting them.

"As to the form of government, which is the other part of the
animated city, let us say with those wise men who have written
of civil dominion and public administration, as Plato,* Aristotle,†
Polybius,‡ Plutarch,§ and others,‖ that the simple forms of
good government are three, to which are opposed three other
forms of bad government. The first form of good government
is monarchy, or kingship, and is the absolute and independent
dominion of one man alone, who has for the ultimate end of his
operations the public good, and the best state of the city, and
who has the same relation to his subjects that the shepherd has
to his flock, and the father to his children. Such were the monarchies of the Assyrians, Medes, Persians, Macedonians, Scy-
thians, Egyptians, and Romans, from the beginning of their

---

* 4 & 8 *De Leg. & in Civili, seu De Regno.*   † 3 *Polit.* c. 7, 8, & 8 *Eth.* c. 10.
‡ Lib. vi.   § *De Unius in Repub. Domin.*
‖ Sigon. *De Ant. Jur. Civ. Rom.* lib. i. c. 1.

reign to the creation of the consuls, and, after the extinction of the Roman republic, under the empire of many Cæsars. To monarchy is opposed* that form of government which is called tyranny, in which one lords it alone, who has no thoughts of the public good, but whose aim is to depress and exterminate the citizens, to whom he shows himself a monster, rapacious after their property, and a cruel wild beast after their lives; such were Phalaris in Agrigentum,† Dionysius in Syracuse,‡ and Nero in Rome.§

" The second form of good government is aristocracy, according to which the dominion is held by those who, above all others, are adorned with virtue, prudence, and benevolence; who directing all their actions to the utility and common dignity of the city, procure it a happy and blessed state. This species of government is called also the regimen of the better sort, (*optimates*,) either because the best men of the city bear rule, or because they look, in all their operations, to the best and most perfect state of the city. This manner of government was used by the Spartans. To this form of government is opposed oligarchy, which is a principality of the most rich and powerful, who, for the most part, are few; who, by depressing and robbing of their property the less rich, and crushing the poor with intolerable weight, make a government full of arrogance and of violence, and are like wolves among lambs. Such was the dominion of the Triumvirs in Rome, who having oppressed the republic, proscribed and put to death many good citizens, and plundered their property; exalting the seditious and perverse, and abasing good men, they distempered Rome with their contagious wickedness; and of a city, the capital of the world, they made it a den of robbers.‖

" The third form of good government, not having a proper name, was called by the Greeks *politeia*, and by the Latins, *respublica*, names common to every species of government. *This is the dominion of the multitude, namely,—of the whole body of the city, composed of all sorts of citizens, rich and poor, nobles and*

---

* Plutar. *Loc. Cit. Beros.* lib. iv.   Diodor. lib. i. 3.   10 Justin. lib. i. 2, 3.   Oros. lib. i. & seq.   Herod. lib. i. 2.   Liv. et alii script. *Rom. Hist.*
† Val. Max. lib. ix. c. 2.   Cic. in Verr. 5.
‡ Cic. 2, *De Offic.*   Plat. *Epist.* vii.   Diodor. lib. xiv.
§ Suet. *in Neron.*   Tacit. 14 *Annal.*
‖ Appian. 4, *De Bel. Civ.*   Plutarch *in Ant.*

*plebeians, wise and foolish, which is also called a popular govern-
ment.* All this body, which contains men, some endowed with
prudence and wisdom, some inclined to virtue and persuadable
to all good works, by the conversation and familiarity which
they have with the prudent and learned, employ all their care,
labor, and industry, to the end that the city flourish in all those
things which are necessary and convenient for living well and
happily, such as was at one time the government of the Athenians.* To this species of good government is opposed democracy; according to which the most abject plebeians, and the
vilest vulgar, hold the domination for their own private interest,
by which they oppress the rich and the noble, and aggrandize and
enrich the poor and the ignoble, as the two brothers, the Gracchi,
began to do in Rome.†

"Three, therefore, are the simple forms of good government,
monarchy, aristocracy, and that which by a common name is
called a republic; and from these, mixed together, four others
may result. The first is compounded of all the three, as was
that of the Lacædemonians, instituted by Lycurgus,‡ who, *se-
lecting the good from the three former, composed out of them one
of the most perfect kind.* Such, also, was the Roman republic,§
in which the power of the consuls was like the regal authority;
that of the senate was aristocratical; and that of the people
resembled the popular state. The second form of mixed government is composed of monarchy and aristocracy, such as, according to some, is the most serene republic of Venice,‖ in which
the annual podestàs have a power similar to a regal authority,
and the senate are an assembly or collection of the optimates;
although others contend that it is a perfect aristocracy. The
third is mixed of a monarchy and a republic; and the fourth of
a republic and an aristocracy; of which two species of mixed
government we have no examples to allege.

"But to return to the three simple forms; it is the common
opinion of the learned,¶ that monarchy holds the first rank

* Plut. *De Unius in Rep. Dominio.* Thucyd. lib. ii. in *Orat. Periclis.* Sig. *De
Repub. Athen.* lib. i. c. 5.
† Appian. 1, *De Bel. Civ.* Plutarch in *Gracchis.*
‡ Polyb. lib. vi. Sigon. *De Ant. Jure Civ. Rom.* lib. i. c. 1.
§ Bellarm. *De Roma.* ‖ Boter. *Relat. Venet.* p. 1. Sabellic. lib. iii. lec. 2.
¶ Plat. in *Civili vel De Reg.* Arist. 8 *Ethic.* c. 10. & 3 *Polit.* c. 10. Philo. lib.
De Conf. Linguar. Senec. 2 *De Benef.* Herod. lib. iii. Hom. 2 *Iliad,* v. 204.

above all others, resembling the power of God Almighty, who alone governs the world; resembling the heart, which alone vivifies all the parts of the animal; and resembling the sun, which alone illuminates the celestial bodies, as well as the lower world. It is very true, that to a monarchy ought to be elevated only that citizen, according to the philosopher,* who, exceeding others in the ordinary course, in riches, wisdom, prudence, and benevolence, is like a god upon earth; such as would be the man who should be adorned with heroic virtue, according to which, performing all the labors of virtue in the utmost perfection and supreme excellency, he would appear to be not the son of a mortal, † but of God. But it being impossible, or at least most difficult, to find a man so rare, it has happened, that, laying aside monarchy, the philosophers have disputed which of the other two forms of good government is better accommodated, more practicable, and more profitable, for the regimen of cities and of peoples. Some were of opinion that this praise was due to an aristocracy; nevertheless Aristotle confutes them, because in the aristocratical government the magistracies and the honors being always in the hands of a few, there is great danger that the multitude, perpetually excluded from public management, should be tumultuous, and conspire against the lives of the principal men, to the great damage of the whole city; because in these revolts the force and violence of the people regard friends no more than enemies; it is mad, and most horribly pillages, murders, and abuses, all that comes in its way. It remains, then, that the third species of good government, which is the popular government, in which the citizens alternately command and obey, must be the most useful, and better adjusted to the nature of man, in whose soul the Divinity has stamped the desire of ruling; with such limitations and temperaments, however, as, says the same philosopher, that the vile plebeians may not have magistrates appointed for their ignorance and imprudence, which are the two fountains of all civil calamities; but that the plebeians may not be totally despised, and that all occasion of insurrections may be taken away, power should be given them of joining with the other citizens in the election of magistrates, and of calling them to account for their administration."

* Aristotle, 3 *Polit.* c. 11.　　　　† 7 *Eth.* c. 1.

"All these opinions appear to be not unbecoming; for, although the plebeians be not qualified of themselves to judge who are fit for the administration of the affairs of the city, and to know the failings of those who have governed, nevertheless, by the conversation and practice which they have in such things with the wise men, it is presumed that, from daily intercourse with these, and from common fame and public reputation, which daily circulates concerning men who are wise and good in government, they may have so much light, that they may discern the apt from the inept, and good behavior from bad. This may suffice to have said concerning the different forms of government according to the writers before cited, in order to explain the following account of the form of government in Padua, and the various changes it passed through.

"In the four hundred and fifty-second year of the Christian era, Padua was miserably destroyed by Attila, King of the Huns. The Paduans, who then fled for safety to the islands in the Adriatic, could not return for fifty years to rebuild their city, for the many armies of barbarians who infested Italy till 493, when Theodoric, King of the Ostrogoths, killed Odoacer, King of the Heruli, and remained unrivalled in the dominion of Italy. But Justinian, the emperor, having, in 535, sent Belisarius, and afterwards, in 552, Narses, to drive away the Goths from Italy, Padua, in that war, which lasted with alternate victories and defeats of the Goths and the Greeks, eighteen years, was subjected sometimes by one and sometimes by the other. Afterwards, under the government of exarchs, till 601, it was a second time burned and destroyed by Aginulphus, King of the Lombards. It was afterwards restored by the Paduans, assisted by the Venetians, and remained under the dominion of the Lombards, till they were exterminated by Charlemagne, King of France, in 774. It became subject to the Kings of France of the race of Charlemagne, and after them to the Berengarii, and finally to the emperors of Germany, from Otho I. to Henry the Fourth, according to the German, and the Third, according to the Italian historians. In a word, Padua lived under foreign law six hundred and twenty-nine years, namely,—from 452 to 1081; thirty-three years before which period, namely,—in 1048, a few rays of liberty began

Lib. iv. cap. 2, p. 123.

to dawn, because the Emperor Henry III., (as appears by public instruments preserved in the archives of the cathedral of Padua,) granted, for the repose of his soul, and that of Agnese his wife, to Bernard Maltravers, Bishop of Padua, the prerogative of coining money, building fortresses and castles with towers and ramparts, erecting mills, and to be, as it were, prince of the city. Afterwards, Henry IV., his son, at the solicitation of the Queen Bertha, his wife, and on account of the prayers of Milo, Bishop of Padua, his relation, gave liberty, in 1081, to the Paduans, conceding to them, that, for the future, they might live according to their own laws, and have a triumphal chariot, (*carroccio*,) which was the principal sign of a free city.[*] This *carroccio*, for a perpetual memorial of the benefit received by the intercession of Queen Bertha, was called by the Paduans by her name. Henry also granted them the faculty of making of the body of their nobility a senate, who, for the government of the city, created annually two consuls.[†]

" There was, therefore, formed a government mixed of monarchy and aristocracy, says the historian ; of monarchy, because the consuls, according to the manner of kings, had the power of life and death ; and of aristocracy, because the senate, exclusively of the plebeians, was composed only of patricians or nobles. These, as the desire of enlarging dominion is insatiable, not contented to have the government of the city, procured, partly by imperial grants, and partly by other means, jurisdiction of blood in their castles situated in the country of Padua, assuming the titles of *proceri*, peers or barons, and a little afterwards the yet higher ones of marquises, counts, and castellans. Padua was ruled by this form of government about eighty years, in peace and tranquillity ; but peace being the nurse of riches, and riches of ambition, the consular dignity began to be ardently desired by all men, and caballed for by every artifice. In the progress of these contests, as one would not give way to another, and as it all depended on a few of the most powerful, the city became divided into factions, which finally, in 1177, came to arms, and civil wars ensued, which for some years filled the city with slaughter, burnings, revolt, and confusion ; so that the con-

[*] See a description and stamp of the Paduan carroccio, in Portenari, lib. v. c. 5 and 6.

[†] Sigonius, *De Reg. Ital.* lib. ix. an. 1081.

D 2

sulate, becoming feeble, was now intermitted, and then exercised, according as the power of different parties prevailed. But finally, this magistracy, serving no longer for the maintenance of the public good, but merely as an instrument of revenge against enemies, and having become most pernicious, not less to the plebeians than to the patricians, was, in 1194, abrogated and totally extinguished.

"The good government,[1] composed of monarchy and aristocracy," as our author calls it, though nobody will agree with him in opinion at this day, "being changed, by the malice of men, into the bad one of oligarchy, and this by its noxious qualities being in a short time annihilated, there arose another species of government, mixed of monarchy and a republic, in this form :— The Paduans instituted four councils ; the first was of eighteen, whom they called the *Anziani*, three of whom were drawn by lot every three months. They were afterwards reduced to the number of sixteen, and then drawn to the number of four every four months. The office of these magistrates was, together with the podestà, to exert themselves with all their influence and power to conciliate and appease all discords and dissensions among the citizens, not only in civil affairs, but in criminal prosecutions ; to see that the decrees of the senate regarding the public utility were observed ; that the buildings going to decay should be rebuilt or repaired ; that the streets, public roads, and walks should be kept in order, free, and unincumbered with obstructions ; that in the principal quarters of the city instruments should be provided for extinguishing or preventing the progress of fire, such as buckets, vessels and ropes for drawing water, ladders, hatchets, pickaxes, iron bars, &c.; and, finally, to suggest to the other councils all those things which might be of public utility. And that they might be enabled to do this, all public letters from foreign princes, and from all magistrates within the dominion of Padua, were read in their presence. No man was admitted to this council of the anziani who was not a Paduan by birth, and an inhabitant of the city for at least thirty years without interruption, and who had not a foundation of property among his fellow citizens of at least two hundred pounds a year.

The second council was called *the lesser*, which at first con-

---

[1] Cap. xiii. p. 124.

sisted of forty citizens, partly noble, and partly plebeian, but afterwards was increased to the number of sixty. The authority of this council was such, that nothing could be treated in the greater council if it were not first discussed and agitated here, and from hence proposed to the greater council. The mode of discussing and consulting upon business was by the way of orations or harangues made by the senators, after which they proceeded to a vote, and two thirds of the suffrages determined the question. This rule was also observed in the greater council. This council was changed every four months, and the senators who had once been in it must be excluded for eight months. Father and son, brothers, and uncle and nephew, were not permitted to sit together in it. To be of this council, it was necessary to be a Paduan born, to have a father who was a Paduan born, to have inhabited in Padua with a family at least for forty years continually, to have an estate of fifty pounds income, and to have served in the ordinary charges of the commons of the city.

" The third council was called the *Greater Council* and *Parliament*. It was at first of three hundred senators, one moiety nobles, and the other moiety plebeians ; it was afterwards increased to the number of six hundred, and finally, in 1277, to a thousand. The magistrates were chosen, and all affairs relative to peace and war were debated in it. By these two councils, the greater and the less, were made, at divers times, various municipal laws and statutes, of which, by a determination of 1263, four copies were made. The first was deposited in the monastery of St. Benedict, the second in that of St. John, the third in that of St. Mary, and the fourth in that of the fathers of St. Mary di Porciglia.

The fourth and last council was common to all the people of the city, into which, the doors being open, every one might enter. But this council was very seldom assembled, and never but for things of the utmost importance. The Paduans desirous of providing a remedy against the disorders and mischiefs occasioned by the consulate, and to extinguish in the citizens all occasions of ambition to enjoy the government of the city, invented the annual magistrate of the podestà, which was the best medicine that could be thought of by them to cure the disorders already felt, and prevent the greater that were apprehended. They established, therefore, as ruler of the city, a person who should be a foreigner, of noble blood and excellent reputation for virtue, who, by the weight and eminence of his authority in cases of life and death, and from his superintendence over all the judicial authority, civil and criminal, from the more absolute obedience paid him as the supreme head of all the other magistracies, of the patricians, of the plebeians, and of the rustics, and, in a word, from his absolute power, as it is called, over the city and its territory, was called, by way of eminence, by the name of Podestà.

" This manner of government continued happily enough, as it is said, till 1237, when the city was subjected by Ezzelino da Romano, who most terribly afflicted and most cruelly tormented it for the space of nineteen years; in which time there was no sort of torment, inhumanity, or cruelty, which it did not suffer from that infernal monster, during whose tyranny that most malignant pestilence, the factions of Guelphs and Ghibellines, which, under the names of *the Imperial party* and *the party of the Church*, infected many cities of Italy, among others, distempered Pistoia, and did inestimable mischief.

" Before we pass on, it may be well, for the more complete information concerning this magistrate of the podestà, to relate a few particulars. The podestà was obliged, three months before the end of his government, which lasted one year, to assemble the greater council, and cause to be elected eight citizens, four noble and four plebeian, of more than thirty years of age. These elected twelve senators of the same council and of the same age, six of the patricians and six plebeians; who, in like manner, elected eight others of the same council, age, and condition, the office of whom was to elect the new podestà. These were shut up together in one apartment, and could not speak to any one, or have more than one repast a day, that they might the sooner agree in the nomination of three personages, who were afterwards carried to the greater council, who proceeded to the election in this manner. All three were separately balloted for, and he who had the most suffrages was the new podestà; he who had the next number of votes held the second place; and he who had fewest, the last, in such election. The syndic of the city was sent in haste with public letters to him who had been honored with most votes, who, if he accepted the charge, was understood to be podestà; but if in four days he did not accept it, the syndic was sent to the second; and if he refused, the third was sent to; and if he declined, a new election was made of other three persons; and of the acceptance or refusal of these a record was made by a notary.

" This method of electing the podestà was changed in 1257, whereby the examination of the subjects fit for the post was committed to the lesser council, the election of whom afterwards was made by the greater council, with this condition, however, by virtue of a statute made in 1236, that the electors of the present podestà could not have a vote in the election of the subsequent podestà. No man could be elected podestà who had in Padua, relations, by consanguinity or affinity within the fourth degree, nor who had been banished from his country for forgery or treason; and this was also understood of the court or retinue which the podestà brought with him, which consisted of four judges or assessors, two lieutenants of police, and some other constables. The office of the first judge was to assist the podestà in all things belonging to the government of the city; the other three judges had the charge of hearing and trying the criminal causes, each one for three months, which was ordained to remove all occasion of suspicion that the accused, by length of time, might possibly corrupt the judges. But these orders were afterwards changed, and it was resolved that the first judge, who must be an eminent doctor of laws, should be the vicar of the podestà; that the second should judge criminal causes; the third should have the charge of the provisions; and that the fourth should be questor and receiver of the public money. The podestà, judges, and lieutenants, could not have with them in Padua their wives, nor other ladies their relations, unless for fifteen days, on occasion of sickness, nor even their brothers, sons, or nephews, above twelve years of age, nor servants who were Paduans. The podestà was obliged to bring with him his two lieutenants, twelve bailiffs, twelve horses, twelve valets and servants, and to maintain all this family and these horses at his expense, for the public service of the city. His salary was two thousand five hundred *lire* a year, and was afterwards increased to four thousand. The podestà was required to come to Padua eight days at least before possession was given him of the post, in which time he was obliged to take the oath of office, namely, — to swear that he, with his judges, would govern without ambition and justly, and that they

would give the greatest attention to the affairs of the public, and
with all their power would conciliate and pacify the controversies
and discords of the citizens. The podestarate began on the first
of July ; but in 1280, it was decreed to begin the first of January.
This magistracy at first continued for a year ; but in 1294, a law
was made that it should endure only six months, and that two
podestàs should be created each year, one of whom should begin
his administration with January, the other with July ; which law
was observed as long as the republic of Padua remained. But
after Padua became subject, now to the emperor, Henry VII.,
now to Frederic, Duke of Austria, now to his brother Henry,
Duke of Carinthia, now to the Scaligeri, Lords of Verona, then
to the Duke of Milan, and finally to the Carrara family, this
custom of two podestàs went into desuetude.

" The podestà, when once in possession of his office, was bound
to execute the following orders : — First, in the space of eight
days, to cause to be read, and afterwards to cause to be punctually observed, the papal constitutions against heretics. Secondly,
to reside continually in the city, and rule it until the arrival of a
successor. Thirdly, during the whole time of his administration,
to hear the causes of all persons indifferently, to which end the
gates of the palace, except at the hour of dinner, always stood
open. Fourthly, that, together with the *anziani*, he should use
all his endeavors that the canonicates and the other ecclesiastical
benefices of the bishopric and diocese of Padua should be conferred on citizens of Padua or of the district. Fifthly, to elect
eight citizens, men of prudence and experience, two for each
quarter, who should make choice of four or five hundred able
men, who, when they should hear the sound of the palace bell,
were to come armed, under their standards, to the palace of the
pretor, and to the Piazza del Vino, for the defence of the podestà.
Sixthly, to give orders that, at the sound of the great bell of the
tower of the palace, all the citizens and inhabitants of Padua,
from sixteen to sixty years of age, should run armed to the piazza
to defend the common liberty. Seventhly, to create a captain,
who, with some soldiers, should have the custody of the city and
its suburbs. Eighthly, to hold, night and day, guards at the gates
of the city. Ninthly, to give orders that in the city and in the
suburbs should be kept crossbows and other weapons to exercise
the soldiers. Tenthly, to cause to be enrolled in the militia many

men of the villages, who, according to occurrences, should come armed to the city. Eleventhly, in all great tumults, to order into the piazza the standard of the community; in which case, all the *gastaldi* of the arts, at the sound of the bells of the palace, were held to go to the Piazza del Vino, with the men under their command, armed, ready to obey whatever orders the podestà should issue, and there assemble, to be formed into a body, under the ensign of the community, which could not depart from the piazza without the express command of the podestà himself, for whose guard there were always five hundred soldiers chosen, one hundred from the body of the patricians, and four hundred from the plebeians, and distinguished into four squadrons, under four standards. Twelfthly, that for eight days before the arrival of a successor, the podestà cannot give sentence in civil or criminal causes. Thirteenthly, that having finished his podestarate, he, his assessors, and court, should remain fourteen days in Padua, to render an account before the syndic of their administration, which is done in this manner: — For the first three days, it was lawful to every one to accuse the podestà, assessors, and court, before the syndics, of any wrongs or injuries done them. In the eight following days these complaints were determined by the votes of the major part of the syndics; and if, by the multitude of complaints, or by differences of opinions among the syndics, or through other reasons, the business could not be finished, three other days were added, in which the syndics were obliged to determine it. From the defence against the complaints made of the podestà, all his favorites, friends, and relations were excluded, and all advocates; his own judges and assessors were alone admitted, and were thought sufficient for his defence. At the end of the fourteenth day the podestà might depart with his family. He could not be confirmed in the post for the next year, nor for the five following years; neither himself, nor any of his relations, could hold any office, dignity, or honors, in the city of Padua; and this was understood of the assessors, lieutenants of police, and other officers. But this statute was very often not observed. As population augmented, and causes and controversies multiplied, and, therefore, the podestà and his assessors could not determine the whole, certain other judges were instituted, and called Judges of the Lower Courts, and were distinguished from each other by the names of animals, for the most part, as

the bear, the horse, the leopard, and others. For the suits arising
between relations, two judges were instituted as arbitrators, who,
in the space of two months, were to give sentence, and terminate
the controversy. And if they could not agree, they called in ten
jurors for each party; and if these disagreed, the podestà himself, in the space of fifteen days, sat in judgment with the rest,
and decided the cause.

[1]"As to the government of the territory, it is to be observed,
that some of the most rich and powerful citizens of Padua had
the name of *proceres,* noblemen or barons, and in some of their
landed estates and places they exercised the jurisdiction of blood,
that is, the power of life and death; and to ennoble their dominions, manors, or lordships, with the magnificence of titles, in
the year 1196, they distinguished themselves into marquises,
counts, and castellans. The lords of Este were entitled marquises; the lords of Anguillara, Abano, Arquà, Baone, Bibano,
Borgoricco, Calaone, Rusta and Cerro, Calcinara, Caldenazzo,
Candiana, Carturo, Castelnuovo, Cortaloro, Fontaniva, Honara,
Limena, Lozzo, Montebello, Montebuso, Montemerlo and Man-
dria, Nono, and Piazzola, were called counts; the lords of Carrara, Camposanpiero, Montagnone, Peraga, Pievedisacco, Publica, Revolone, Ronchi de' Campanili, Stra, Selvazzano, Tertula,
Tribano and Galzignano, Noventa, Treville, and Villa Nova,
were denominated castellans. But the Castellan of Selvazzano
having caused the eyes of a certain woman to be put out for theft,
who afterwards came, deprived of her eyes, to Padua, the cruelty
of this action displeased the republic so much that, in the year
1200, a law was made, that under pain of death, no man should,
for the future, exercise any jurisdiction in the territory of Padua;
which law was reënacted and confirmed in 1205. The jurisdiction of life and death, and all other jurisdiction, being taken away
from these grandees, (*magnati,*) the whole territory was governed
by the Podestà of Padua; and afterwards, in the course of time,
the republic of Padua sent a podestà into the following districts
of land, namely, — Conselve, Lonigo, Montagnana, and twenty-
four other districts. The custom of sending podestàs into those
districts continued till 1290, when a statute was made, that
places which were not walled should not have a podestà, but
that into some of them vicars only should be sent.

[1] Cap. v.

" Such, then, was the government of Padua, from the year 1194 to the tyranny of Ezzelino, mixed of monarchy and a republic, and this constitution was restored after the delivery of the city from that fierce and cruel oppression, and lasted happily for fifty years, with a remarkable increase of the city in riches and power; and it would have lasted much longer, if the cursed factions of Ghibellines and Guelphs had not disturbed the peace of the citizens, which afterwards, by little and little, after the fashion of poison, creeping in their hearts, afflicted the city to such a degree that, at last, in the year 1318, it took away their vital spirits, depriving them of their beloved liberty.

" The parties of Ghibellines and Guelphs, under the names of the Empire and the Church, sown in the hearts of men by the enemy of the human race, had poisoned Italy, and distempered the city of Padua."

So says the historian; and, without denying to the devil his share in the instigation of all such party distinctions and animosities, it must be still insisted on, that the essential defect in the constitution of every Italian republic was the greatest cause, and the instrument with which the infernal agent wrought. The parties of rich and poor, of gentlemen and simplemen, unbalanced by some third power, will always look out for foreign aid, and never be at a loss for names, pretexts, and distinctions. Whig and Tory, Constitutionalist and Republican, Anglomane and Francomane, Athenian and Spartan, will serve the purpose as well as Guelph and Ghibelline. The great desideratum in a government is a distinct executive power, of sufficient strength and weight to compel both these parties, in turn, to submit to the laws.

" The mischiefs of these contagious parties were greatest under the tyranny of Ezzelino, who, being standard-bearer and head of the Imperial or Ghibelline party, exerted all his force to extirpate the Guelph party, followed by the people and a great part of the patricians. After his death, the Guelph party rose, and with all their power persecuted the Ghibellines, driving them from the city, and spoiling them of all their goods; and, as the plebeians of Padua were devoted to the Guelph party, whether from their natural inclinations, or because the Guelphs had delivered the city from the empire of Ezzelino, upon this occasion certain profligate popular men, made through their favor heads of the Guelph faction, became proud, arrogant, and presumptuous, desiring that all the affairs of the republic should depend upon their will; but suspecting that some of the principal gentlemen, to whom, although Guelphs, so much pride had become disgusting, would oppose their ambitious enterprises, they gave the plebeians to understand, that those gentlemen intended to make themselves sole masters of the government. So great a commotion was excited, that the plebeians, who, servile in adverse fortune, as insolent in prosperity, demanded in a turbulent manner, and obtained by threats of force, the institution of a magistrate, according to the usage of the Roman republic, like a tribune of the people, (the Paduans called these magistrates *Gastaldi dell' Arti*,) who should defend the rights of the plebeians, and have authority to rescind all those determinations of the senate, (as was the custom in Rome,) which could occasion any prejudice to the jurisdiction of the plebeians. Wherefore, in testimony of the power granted to the tribunes, it was, in 1293, ordained by a decree of the senate, that every podestà, in the beginning of his administration, should consign to each of the *gastaldi of the arts* the standard of that art; and this tribunitian magistracy advancing every day in power, caused to be made in its favor, in the year 1296, a statute, that, on the first Sunday in every month, the *gastaldi* should all assemble in the church of the palace of the commons, and treat fully of all things that belonged to the state of the city.

" The whole government of the city, by this alteration, devolved into the hands of the tribunes; because, as has been said before, they annulled or confirmed at their pleasure, the determinations of the greater council; and because they carried up to the council whatever they had concluded among themselves, with a certainty of obtaining their concurrence, by the dependence which they had upon the *popular*[1] senators, and also upon the less powerful of the noble senators, whose devotion they had secured by electing them to the honors of the city, and by assuming some of them into the number of the tribunes, from which magistracy, as universally from all the greater honors, they always most arbitrarily excluded the most powerful.

" From this disorderly and violent domination of the tribunes,

---

[1] "*popolari*," "of the popular party."

who had, for the most part, greatly enriched themselves, grew intestine hatreds and terrible seditions between the first class of persons and the heads of the popular party, with whom the patricians of middling power, exalted by the people to honors, joined. And, finally, some of the gentlemen and most powerful patricians, not being able any longer to bear to be neglected by the tribunitian power, took up arms, killed the principal heads and defenders of the plebeians, and so far intimidated those patricians who adhered to the plebeians, that, after many engagements, and a profuse effusion of blood, the tribuneship of the people was abolished in the year 1314, and the government and the public authority were transferred to the patricians, excluding totally the plebeians. These, in order to keep down the Ghibellines, increased the senate (which, from the time of the extinction of the house of Honara, had been only of three hundred members) to the number of a thousand, incorporating seven hundred Guelphs; and, wishing that all questions and matters relative to peace or war should depend wholly on the Guelph faction, and the better to establish the superiority of their party, they instituted another council, wholly of Guelphs, which had authority to approve or reject the decrees of the greater senate. From the body of this lesser council were created the four *anziani*, conservators of liberty, and eight secretaries for the care of the city. This mode of government continued till the year 1318, when Padua began to lose her liberty, which she afterwards wholly lost, remaining subject sometimes to the Germans, sometimes to the Scaligeri, sometimes to the Carrari, until, finally, after infinite calamities, she was benignly received into the pious bosom of the most serene republic of Venice, in the year 1405." [*]

Such, as has been related, were the vicissitudes of the government of the city of Padua after the tyranny of Ezzelino, which may be recapitulated thus. According to the historian, at first, it was a mixture of monarchy and a republic; afterwards it was changed into a democracy, for such he denominates the tribuneship of the plebeians, in which the people attempted the abasement and annihilation of the grandees; and, finally, it terminated in a government mixed of monarchy and aristocracy, having the senate of the optimates, and creating the podestà an-

* Laugier, vol. v. p. 236.

nually; for the major part of the time, from 1081 to 1318, it was governed by one or other of the two best species of mixed government, as our historian thought, which are composed of monarchy and aristocracy, and of monarchy and a republic.[1]

This sovereignty of Padua was, for the most part, in one assembly; for, although a check was aimed at by the law, that nothing should be done in the great council, which had not been previously debated in the little council, yet, when any thing was proposed by the latter to the former, they sat together and voted as one assembly. At some times the sovereignty was clearly in one assembly of optimates or patricians; at another, in one assembly of plebeians, as that of the tribunes was. At last, two assemblies were formed, with each a negative; but there being no third power to mediate between them, no balance could be formed or maintained between them. At no time had the monarchical power, either under the consuls, anziani, or podestàs, a negative; for, though the podestà was an office of great dignity and splendor, he never had the whole executive power, nor a negative on the legislative. The nobles and commons were mixed together in both councils; and the executive power, the appointment of officers, &c. was always in one or other of the assemblies; and the consequence was instability to the laws, insecurity to life, liberty, and property; constant rivalry between the principal families, particularly the Scaligeri and Carrari, which ended in conquest and subjection to Venice.

From 1103 to 1194, the government of consuls continued; from 1195 to 1236, the government of podestàs, under the republic of Padua. From 1237 to 1256, the tyranny of Ezzelino

---

[1] Sismondi traces the vicissitudes of the government directly to the ill-regulated impulses of the people.

"Les Padouans, dans l'ensemble de leur conduite, méritoient souvent tous les reproches qu'on a faits aux démocraties absolues. Le sénat même étoit démocratique, car il étoit composé de mille citoyens qu'on élisoit chaque année; et le peuple, toujours passioné, n'agissoit point avec suite, ou d'après les règles qu'auroit prescrites la prudence la plus commune. Une jalousie violente lui faisoit écarter du gouvernement les nobles, qui, par leurs richesses, leurs talens, leur courage, et l'illustration de leur nom, auroient donné du relief à l'administration; une prévention non moins déraisonnable lui faisoit confier aveuglément une autorité dangereuse à une seule de ces familles nobles, celle qui, plus qu'aucune autre, auroit mérité sa jalousie, et qui en restoit seule exempte, la maison de Carrara. Les plus légers succès inspiroient à ce peuple une présomption insensée, et un orgueil ridicule; les plus légers revers abattoient son courage, et le disposoient à se soumettre aux dernières humiliations."

Rép. Ital., tome iv. p. 382.

was supported. From 1257 to 1294, the government of podestàs, under the republic, was revived and maintained. From 1295
to 1311, they had two podestàs. In 1312, Gerardo de gl' Inzola
da Parma was imperial vicar for the Emperor Henry VII., to
whom the Paduans began to yield obedience; though they rebelled again this year against his authority, and the podestàs and
republic were revived and continued till 1318, in which year
Giacomo Grande da Carrara was made the first Lord of Padua.
He governed one year and three months, and then renounced
the dominion, and died in 1324. In 1319, a podestà again for
one year. In 1320, the city of Padua, to deliver itself from the
siege of Cane Scaligero, Lord of Verona, gave itself to Frederic III., Emperor and Duke of Austria, who afterwards gave it
to his brother Henry, Duke of Carinthia, under whom they were
governed by podestàs, who were, at the same time, imperial
vicars, till 1328. The podestà of this year was dismissed by
Marsilio da Carrara, who had been elected by the people Lord
of Padua, who, however, made Pietro de i Rossi, of Parma,
podestà; but he, not being able longer to resist in the war with
Cane della Scala, married Tadea, daughter of Giacomo Grande
da Carrara, first Lord of Padua, to Mastino dalla Scala, nephew
of Cane, giving him Padua in dower. From 1329 to 1337, Padua was governed by podestàs, under the dominion of the Scali-
gers. In 1337, Marsilio da Carrara, having expelled the Scali-
gers, was made the second Lord of Padua, and governed in 1338.
In 1338, Marsilio da Carrara, second Lord of Padua, died; and
to him succeeded Ubertino da Carrara, third Lord of Padua.
From 1339 to 1345, the government of podestàs continued
under the Princes Carrara. In 1345, Ubertino da Carrara, third
Lord of Padua, being sick, caused to be elected for his successor
Marsilietto Papafava da Carrara, who was the fourth Lord of
Padua, and died; but the same year, Marsilietto was killed by
Giacomo da Carrara, who became the fifth Lord of Padua; and
under him the government of podestàs continued till 1350, when
Giacomo da Carrara, the fifth Lord of Padua, was assassinated
by William da Carrara, a natural son of Giacomo Grande, the
first lord; to whom succeeded Giacobino da Carrara, his brother,
the sixth lord, and Francesco da Carrara, surnamed the Old, his
son, and seventh Lord of Padua. Under these, the government
by podestàs continued till 1362, when Francesco da Carrara the

Old imprisoned his uncle, Giacobino da Carrara, because he had conspired his death, and reigned lord alone till 1388, when Francesco da Carrara renounced the dominion of this city to his son, Francesco da Carrara, called the New, eighth and last Lord of Padua. The same year, in November, both the father and the son were deprived of the government of this state by John Galeazzo Visconti, first Duke of Milan, who governed it by podestàs, for the years 1388 and 1389, when Francesco da Carrara, called the New, drove out the people of the Duke of Milan, and recovered Padua and its district, except Bossano. From 1390 podestàs were continued till 1405, when the Carrara were conquered, and Padua admitted into the republic of Venice. In 1393, Francesco da Carrara, surnamed the Old, seventh Lord of Padua, died in a prison in Monza, to which he had been sent by John Galeazzo Visconti, Duke of Milan.

CHAPTER TENTH.

EQUICOLA[1] concurs with Leonardo Aretino and all the other Italian writers, in his account of the antiquity, riches, and power of the Tuscans, Etruscans, Etrurians, Tyrrhenians, or Dodeca-poli, (for by all these names they were known); their original emigration from Lydia; their government of Lucumoni; their twelve confederated peoples; their subjection, in a course of time, to the Romans, Goths, Lombards, and Charlemagne, who, for his merit, was, in the year 800, created emperor, with the titles of Cæsar and Augustus, by the Pope Leo III., who understood the effect upon the minds of the people of words and titles so anciently beloved, as well as dreaded, in Italy. He gave him also the title of Great, which had been before given only to three princes, Alexander, Pompey, and Constantine. The authority which the Roman senate and people had anciently exercised, of electing and confirming the emperors, was now by Charlemagne transferred to the Roman pontificate; and, to prevent seditions, the power of confirming the pontiff was given to the emperor; a promising alliance!

"Afterwards, Gregory V., in 1002, ordained a constitution, which continues to this time, that the election of future emperors should be free in the power of the Germans, and the ecclesiastical and temporal electorates were then created.[*]

" In 1111, Mantua fell into discords, threw off her subjection to Matilda, and assumed an independence; but being besieged and reduced to great distress, was obliged, in 1114, to submit again to that princess.

" Sigebert, an enterprising man, took the opportunity of the troubles in Italy to aggrandize himself, and going from Lucca, he made himself lord of Parma and Reggio. He was a Lom-

* Equicola, p. 25.
1 Dell' Istoria di Mantova, libri cinque. Scritta in Commentari da Mario Equicola d'Alveto. Quarto. Seconda impressione, in Mantova, 1610.

bard by descent, and was prefect or lord of the aforesaid city.
Sigebert had three sons, Sigebert II., Atto, and Gerardo; two of
them died, and Atto alone remained, who, by the change of the
letters, was afterwards called Azzo.   He fortified Canossa, in
Reggiano, and dwelt there as his principal seat, whence his descendants were called *da Canossa*.   He had two sons, the first
of whom was named Tedaldo, and the other, uniting the names
of his grandfather and father, was called Sigebertazzo, although
it was afterwards corruptly called Albertazzo.   This person was
sent into Germany, and recommended himself to Otho the emperor so effectually, as to obtain a grant for his services of Calaone, Monselice, Montagnana, Arqui, and *Este*, with the title
of marquis.   He married Alda, a natural daughter of the emperor.   From this match there issued two sons, Ugo and Folco;
the latter remained in Germany with his mother; Ugo came into
Italy with his father, and succeeded to the lands above mentioned, and to the marquisate of Este.   From this Ugo are
descended the illustrious lords of the house of Este, who reigned
so long in Ferrara; and from them were descended the family
that was called *the Canossi* of Verona.

"There were in Mantua, in 1265, four most powerful families,
and four others their adherents, of somewhat less influence.   The
Bonacossi and Grossolani inhabited one quarter; the Arlotti and
the Poltroni another; these not long before had driven out the
Calorosi.   In a third quarter were the Casaloldi and those of
Riva; and in the fourth, the Zenacalli and the Gaffari."

The government was, as in all the other cities of Italy, in one
centre, a general council, who first appointed consuls, then podestàs, then gonfaloniers, captains of the people, &c., which produced
the usual struggles for power.

"In the year 1266 the Gaffari entered into a secret conspiracy
to deliver the city of Mantua into the hands of the Estensi, Lords
of Ferrara.   The treason was discovered; those who saved their
lives by flight were banished forever, and the others instantly put
to death, and the houses of all who were accomplices or privy to
the crime were burnt and demolished.   The power of individual
citizens increased every day, and parties and factions in consequence.   The podestà, though a foreigner was usually appointed to that office, administered its functions according to the will
and pleasure of a small number of the principal men.   Justice

was oppressed by power, and equity gave way to violence.* In such a tumult of the factious, the prudent men called a convention, to deliberate on a new form of government. Some were for *ephori*, as in Sparta; others for *cosmi*, as in Crete; others for *suffetes*, as in Carthage; but the most were for *hypati*, as in Greece, or rather for two consuls, as in Rome. Two magistrates were, therefore, created; and that they might be sure to guard against ambition, they must be chosen in rotation every six months, two at a time, from each of the four quarters of the city. These were to be called *captains of the people*, and were to be the protectors of the plebeians, and defenders of their liberties. Two magistrates, therefore, from the body of the nobility, were elected, in the nature of tribunes of the people, and those were Pinamonte, of the family of Bonacossi, and Ottonello, of that of Zenecalli, in the year 1274.

" These had not continued one month in office together, before such animosities arose between the two families, that Zenecalli was treacherously called in the night into the palace of Bonacossi, under pretence of consulting upon some sudden affair of the last importance, and there murdered. The next morning Bonacossi called together the principal nobility, and, with fictitious grief and pharisaical tears, communicated the fact, and exhorted the people to revenge, wishing that every one might believe that the deceased magistrate had been assaulted and put to death by some private enemy. An inquiry was ordered, which engaged so much attention, and took up so much time, that no man spoke of any successor, and therefore Pinamonte governed alone."

The scramble for power was as yet altogether among the gentlemen.

" Benvenuto da Imola, in his Commentaries upon Dante, where he discourses of Mantua, writes, that this city had been inhabited by gentlemen of Riva, of Mercaria, and of the Casaloldi; and that Bonacossi had agreed with these houses to expel from the city every other nobleman; and that afterwards, forming a particular agreement with two of them, he drove out the third; and then uniting with the Casaloldi, he banished the

---

* Cresceva ogni dì più la potenza de' particolari, & augumentavansi le fattioni & parti. Il podestà, quale forastiere si soleva creare, ad arbitrio di alcuni pochi amministrava il suo officio; la giustitia dalla forza era conculcata, & l'equità cedeva alla violenza. *Commentari Mantouani*, di Equicola, pp. 47, 48.

second; and, finally, driving out the Casaloldi, he remained alone, and, by artifice assisted with force, continued without a colleague in the magistracy; and taking for his podestà Alberto della Scala, for a stricter union he obtained the place of podestà in Verona for Giannino de' Bonacossi, not failing to maintain a good intelligence with the Marquis of Este. By all these arrangements he easily obtained from his followers the prolongation of his own power for another six months; and when he had thus laid his foundations sufficiently strong to support any edifice, he assumed the title of captain-general. These encroachments were very uneasily supported by the nobles, who perceived that from free citizens they were become, by little and little, the subjects of a tyrant. Whereupon the Arlotti, the Casaloldi, the Agnelli, and the Grossolani, conspired together to throw off the yoke; but Pinamonte, being informed of the plot on the very day on which it was to have been executed, and being well prepared, fell unexpectedly on the conspirators separately, a part of whom he took prisoners; others were killed, many wounded, and the great multitude saved themselves by flight. Many suspected persons were sent out of their beloved home, and confined in various places. Pinamonte did not cease to persecute his adversaries, until all things in the city appeared to be quieted under his dominion.

" The miserable Mantuans were dispersed in various places, and particularly in Gonzaga; but the tyrant had the art to hold out temptations of lands, restitution of property, and restoration to their country, to these, till they surrendered to him that Gonzaga, which had often defended itself both against popes and emperors. Pinamonte then established a friendship with Venice and Padua, but was interrupted in his career, in 1289, by death."

The family of Bonacossi, with Pinamonte at their head, had, by forming a popularity among the vilest plebeians, been able to expel the other noble families, and make themselves absolute. So complete was their ascendency over the minds of the rabble, that, upon the death of Pinamonte, the minority were not able to obtain any regular election or rational reform of the government; but,

" Bardello Bonacossi was set up by his party for a successor, a man universally hated, a monster without virtue, wholly without capacity, insolent, without judgment or experience; equally ignorant and arrogant, vile and suspicious, yet credulous, and a slave to adulation; devoted to cruelty and lust. This pestiferous tyrant governed in Mantua five years, according to Platina; but the plebeians themselves could bear him no longer, and set up another of the same family against him. Bottigella Bonacossi with little difficulty was able to expel him, and Tamo, his brother, one of whom died miserably at Padua, and the other at Ferrara."

We pass over the actions of Bottigella, and his wars with Cremona and with Azzo of Este, &c. In 1308, Bottigella died, as well as his enemy Azzo; to the latter succeeded his son Flisco, and to the former Passarino, his brother; for this plebeian tyranny was already become hereditary in the family. Although the government of Passarino was not remarkable for folly or severity, yet Luigi Gonzaga, who had connected himself in marriage with the Bonacossi, being a man of abilities, and knowing the general discontent of the people, and the universal hatred of the nobility against that family, entered into concert with some of the neighboring lords, as Cane della Scala, &c., found little difficulty to depose and expel Passarino, put him to death, and reign in his stead. The family of the Gonzaghi were named from the place of their ancient residence, which was Gonzaga. A multitude of conjectures and fables, collected from various authors, concerning the origin of this family, we pass over. Guido Gonzaga, who fought against Manfred, King of Naples, had five sons, the first of whom was Luigi, the author and founder of the lordship and marquisate of Mantua.

In 1328, it is said, that " by the consent of the people, according to the laws and good custom, one was elected, after the death of Passarino, to whom, and to his successors, the whole empire was given for perpetuity, as was usual in the heroic times. The Mantuans reasoned in this manner: The mode of making a commonwealth perpetual, or of any long duration, is by prudence, which disposes and rules with manly energy, as well as with wise discernment. This can alone be performed in a state by means of justice, which distributes to every one his deserts; to the good, rewards and honors; to the wicked, punishment and infamy. As the virtue of clemency is the daughter of magnanimity, and participates of divinity, we always applaud it when it extends only to offences committed against ourselves;

and it is commended in princes whenever pardon and mercy cannot cause an injury to the public, and give insolence to the daring to rise against the laws. It should be a pleasure to princes to remit private injuries; but skilful in the healing art, they should not be so partially compassionate as to heal one wound at the hazard of destroying the whole body. The liberty of the people consists in two things, in the laws and the tribunals; when these prevail in a city, without favor, respect, or partiality, that city and its citizens are free.

Upon these principles the Mantuans, finding that liberty never had been enjoyed by them under their uncouth government of a republic, strange to relate! adopted voluntarily an absolute monarchy. Louis Gonzaga was elected and constituted upon these principles and for these reasons, and began his reign by an assiduous attention to the revival of laws which had been trampled under foot, and by a diligent solicitude that all the good customs should be observed with equality. And this is sufficient for another example of the struggles of a few families, in an unbalanced government, for preëminence, and of the final triumph of the Gonzaghi over the Bonacossi, in a monarchy erected on the ruins of a republic.

MONTEPULCIANO.

Chiusi, the country and residence of Porsenna, the ancient king to whom Tarquin fled for hospitality, was one of the most ancient and powerful cities of Tuscany or Etruria. As Chiusi was in a low situation and a bad air, Porsenna chose, for his pleasure and his health, a mountain in the neighborhood, where was a salubrious atmosphere and an admirable prospect; an ample plain, the lake of Thrasimene, and the river of Chiane, with hills and valleys loaded with every production of the earth, in grapes, grains, and fruits, in the most perfect elegance and abundance, were around it.[1]

" In after ages, upon a civil war in Chiusi between the gentlemen and plebeians, in which the former were expelled, they retired to this mountain, and gave it the name of Mons Politicus, which was corrupted afterwards, in the vulgar pronunciation, into Monspolitianus, and since into Montepulciano. The plebei-

---

[1] *Storia della città di Montepulciano*, di Spinello del Capitano Marcello Benci. 4to. In Fiorenza. 1641.

ans of the same city passed the river, took possession of another elevated situation, where they built a castle, and called it Castrum Plebis."

Though Florence and Siena have, at different times, pretended that Montepulciano was in their dominion; yet it is certain that, for three hundred years at least, it was an independent sovereign republic. At an expense of continual wars, it maintained its liberty. Its government was by podestàs and general councils like all the other cities; and its whole history is made up of revolutions, from nobles to plebeians, and from plebeians to nobles, Florence and Siena taking the parties of opposite factions. Even in this little village, there were great families as well as little ones, the Guidos, Ugolinos, the Bulgarellos, and Rinieri, continually struggling for precedence.

"In the year 1328, the Rinieri, or rather the family del Pecora, were accounted noble, because they were rich, and powerful in followers, adherents, and relations; they had increased in reputation and power to such a degree, that they domineered, at their discretion, over all their compatriots. The heads of the house were Jacob and Nicholas de' Cavalieri, who governed in concurrence, with prudence and good order, till 1352, when dissensions and discords began to arise between them.

"Jacob concerted with Peter Sacconi, who governed in Arezzo, a project to make himself master of Montepulciano; but Nicholas, his colleague, revealed it to the governor of the people, who excited an insurrection, and expelled Jacob, with twenty of his followers; and afterwards, with the influence and counsels of Nicholas, the government was reformed, and all the friends of Jacob were excluded from any share in it,"[*] according to the custom and nature of all majorities, when there is no power but a minority to rebuff their pretensions. "Jacob then intrigued with Visconti, Archbishop of Milan, and his allies, and, corrupting a notary, an officer on guard, broke down a gate in the night, entered with all his men, and excited a tumult. Nicholas, a knight of great spirit, seized his arms, and mounting his horse, with a few of his companions, waiting for no further help, attacked the enemy with such impetuosity that they fled in a panic. Jacob, with twenty-five horsemen, escaped; the others were taken, to the number of seventy-five, together with the

[*] Matt. Vill. lib. iii. c. 10, f. 146, an. 1352.

41 *

notary and the guard. The governors of the people hanged thirty, and released the rest, having first marked them forever, by slitting their noses and cutting off their ears.

"Jacob then fled to Siena, and there attempted to form connections and obtain auxiliaries; and Nicholas, and the governors of the people of Montepulciano, applied to Perugia. A war was excited between those two cities, which was terminated by ambassadors, upon these conditions, that Montepulciano should remain under the government of the people, under the protection of the commons of Siena, for twenty years; Jacob and Nicholas were to be indemnified for the expenses, and their estates restored, and the commons of Florence and Perugia were to be guarantees. Tommasi adds, that another condition was, the restoration of all the refugees.*

"The next year the peace was broken, and Nicholas sent into banishment; but, collecting his friends without, and concerting measures with his partisans within, he found means to enter Montepulciano, with two hundred horse and five hundred foot; but he met with such a resistance from his enemies in the place, and their Sienese allies, that he perceived he could not overcome them. He therefore took the barbarous resolution to burn the town, and retire; his party set fire to as many houses as possible, and, while the people and soldiers were intent upon preventing the progress of the flames, he retreated. Nicholas and Jacob, at length finding that they gained nothing and lost much by continual quarrels, came to an agreement, and solicited the emperor to hold the government of Montepulciano as imperial vicars; but the people would not admit them, because the Sienese would not receive such vicars. This occasioned a fresh war between the commons of Montepulciano and those of Siena, on one side, and the Perugians, in conjunction with the Pecora family and their adherents, on the other. In this war a memorable battle was fought, and the Montepulcians distinguished themselves by so much valor, that the Perugians created four of them cavaliers, namely,—John, the son of Nicholas, and Gherard, the son of Jacob, and two of their nephews, Berthold and Corrado, all of the family del Pecora; and the Perugian conquerors, with their Montepulcian cavaliers, committed the customary depredations and devastations.

* Tom. lib. x. fo. 319, an. 1353.

" The government of the land being in the hands of the people, for the sake of the public tranquillity, Jacob and Nicholas del Pecora remained abroad in banishment, inhabiting Valiano, a strong place, and a plentiful situation. The latter, knowing the nature of the citizens of Montepulciano, accustomed to hope more than they ought, and to tolerate less than was necessary, discontented and prone to novelties, vacillating between the commons of Siena and those of Perugia through alternate envy, jealousy, and resentment, and being never at rest, entered into a secret correspondence with them, in order to return to his country. His purpose was in time accomplished, and he was joyfully received by the people, and mutual forgiveness of injuries and affronts was stipulated. Recollecting that the rupture between him and Jacob had been the cause of all the evils, he sent a messenger to him, and a reconciliation was effected between them for the common benefit of their country. All was now joy, friendship, and festivity, in appearance, but the secret causes of discord were still at work, and before the year 1363 produced another revolution, and Nicholas and his friends were again exiled.

" Five years afterwards the exiles from Montepulciano, with some assistance from the grandees of Siena, entered and conquered their country, and sent Jacob, who had made himself lord and master, to prison. But the plebeians and others, who had been oppressed by him, and mortally hated him, could not satiate their vengeance merely by burning and plundering all his property; they broke open his prison, and tore him into pieces so small, that no part of his body could ever be collected for sepulture. The grandees were so transported with indignation at this infamous barbarity, that they put to death a great part of the plebeians, and banished the remainder. They reformed the government of the land, however, into a popular state, and banished the Cavalieri as rebels."

Not to pursue this relation to any greater length, it may be observed in general, that this little hill maintained its independence for three hundred years, by the mutual jealousies of Florence, Siena, and Perugia; but it was by uninterrupted wars with one or the other of them, all in their turn seeking its alliance or subjugation, and all in their turn taking its part when in danger of being subdued by any one. This occasioned a continual vacillation of its friendship and enmity with those cities, and constant revolutions of government at home upon every change. There was no balance in their government by which parties or powerful individuals might be restrained, and a few families were continually scrambling for superiority. There were no nobles by name, that is, there were no marquises, counts, or barons; but there were gentlemen and common people, and the gentlemen were called cavaliers, because they could afford to keep a horse, or at most, three horses to each man. The family del Pecora was the principal one of these cavaliers, and they enslaved their country of course, as the Medici did in Florence.

Perhaps it may be said, that in America we have no distinctions of ranks, and therefore shall not be liable to those divisions and discords which spring from them; but have we not laborers, yeomen, gentlemen, esquires, honorable gentlemen, and excellent gentlemen? and are not these distinctions established by law? have they not been established by our ancestors from the first plantation of the country? and are not those distinctions as earnestly desired and sought, as titles, garters, and ribbons are in any nation of Europe? We may look as wise, and moralize as gravely as we will; we may call this desire of distinction childish and silly; but we cannot alter the nature of men; human nature is thus childish and silly; and its Author has made it so, undoubtedly for wise purposes; and it is setting ourselves up to be wiser than nature, and more philosophical than Providence, to censure it. All that we can say in America is, that legal distinctions, titles, powers, and privileges, are not hereditary; but that the disposition to artificial distinctions, to titles, and ribbons, and to the hereditary descent of them, is ardent in America, we may see by the institution of the Cincinnati. There is not a more remarkable phenomenon in universal history, nor in universal human nature, than this order. The officers of an army, who had voluntarily engaged in a service under the authority of the people, whose creation and preservation was upon the principle that the body of the people were the only fountain of power and of honor; officers, too, as enlightened and as virtuous as ever served in any army; the moment they had answered the end of their creation, instituted titles and ribbons, and hereditary descents, by their own authority only, without the consent or knowledge of the people, or their representatives or legislatures. If these gentlemen had been of opinion that titles and ribbons were necessary in society, to have been consistent, they should have taken measures for calling conventions of the people, where it should have been determined, first, whether any such distinction should be introduced; secondly, how many such orders; thirdly, what number of individuals of each; and, lastly, there should have been in convention a general election of noblemen for each of the thirteen states. As great injustice may be done by giving too much honor to one, and too little to another, as by committing trespasses upon property, or slanders upon reputation; the public good requires justice in the distribution of fame as well as fortune; and the public, or some tribunal erected by the public, can be alone competent to the decision.[1]

As there is no instance more parallel than this of Montepulciano, where the people who owned horses agreed together to call themselves cavaliers, and thus created a distinct order in the state, this opportunity has been taken to make an observation upon an institution, which ought not to be passed over in considering the subject of these labors. It is greatly to be wished that the officers would voluntarily discontinue their societies, and lay aside their eagles, which will do them, as well as the community, much more hurt than good; they have already excluded many excellent men from places in civil life, to which their merit in other respects entitled them; they have excited disputes which are very pernicious; they are founded on no principle of morals, true policy, or our own constitution.[2]

[1] Of the feeling which was excited throughout the country by the establishment of the order of the Cincinnati, there is abundant proof in the publications of the time. The moderation of Washington in recommending a modification of the objectionable features of the institution, and the wisdom of the society in yielding at once to public opinion, smoothed all difficulties. Nevertheless it may be doubted whether the institution ever had in it the seeds of any mischief, for it was not based upon a distinction of property, without which no aristocratic class can really continue. The statute of distribution of estates is the most solid pillar of a republican edifice.

[2] This volume contains all of that part of the Defence, devoted by the author to a review of the domestic history of some of the Italian Republics in the Middle Ages; a portion to the perusal of which it is difficult to attach great interest, and yet not without its value to those disposed to study faithfully the working of popular forms of government. M. de Sismondi has since given to the public a more extended and perfect sketch of the Italian history for the same period, and has endeavored to analyze the causes, as well of the prosperity as of the decline of the republican states. His hundred and twenty-sixth chapter is devoted to an examination of their ideas of liberty, and to a comparison of them with those established at the present day. He considers the former as embraced in three propositions, which are equally considered as axioms among the people of the United

States. The first is, that all authority exercised over the people emanates from the people. Secondly, That the power conferred should return at stated intervals to its source. Thirdly, That the recipient of the power must be responsible to the people for its exercise. These axioms M. de Sismondi considers as sufficient to account for the great impulse given to the energy and activity of those communities at that time.

But they do not supply the regulating principle which should have prevented them from falling into disorders and excess. The truth seems to be, that no well defined ideas of human rights were entertained in any quarter, and consequently there were no limitations of the power of majorities over minorities. The histories consequently show nothing but a series of struggles for the control of the government between factions all equally disposed to abuse their power whenever they succeeded in securing it. In these contentions the safety and happiness of the individual citizen were made of no account. He rose or fell, with the success or defeat of the faction to which he attached himself. With such a state of things, continued for any length of time, it could not fail to happen that a great number would gradually be led to prefer the more durable authority emanating from the will of one. It is, therefore, no great cause of surprise to find that, in course of time, the people of each separate city voluntarily submitted to the unrestrained will of some single person powerful enough to compel the maintenance of order for their protection.

To remedy the dangers attendant upon the arbitrary use of power, checks, however multiplied, will scarcely avail without an explicit admission of some limitation of the right of the majority to exercise sovereign authority over the individual citizen. The modern theory of republicanism rests upon the axioms that, in the eye of the state, certain natural rights belong equally to all men; and that these rights cannot be annihilated at the mere pleasure of the greater number. Without some such securities, there is no protection from social tyranny, whatever may be the form it takes. In popular governments, minorities constantly run much greater risk of suffering from arbitrary power than in absolute monarchies. For the majority which wield the power against the smaller number, at the same time create the public sentiment that will sustain them, at least for the moment, in a despotic act; whereas, under single rulers, although individual cases of oppression are more likely to happen, public opinion will yet be left free to censure or correct them. The only cure for this is in the recognition of the right of every individual citizen to complete protection, so long as he conducts himself like a good citizen. Hence spring all the safeguards so carefully introduced into the constitutions and the declarations of rights in America, which are, however, after all dependent for their force mainly upon the establishment of a sound public opinion. The use of checks and balances in the forms of government, is to create delays and multiply diversities of interests, by which the tendency on a sudden to violate them may be counteracted. In the cities of Italy, there was no effective barrier between the passions of the majority and their object, but physical force. Hence the minority was always driven to violence to protect itself.

It is a little singular that the course of education generally pursued in America, especially among those destined to make and to expound the laws, should be almost exclusively devoted to the consideration of those precedents in history in which the inequality of ranks is an acknowledged and vital element; whilst very little attention has been paid to the observation of those phenomena which the legislation and the social systems, by analogy most nearly approximating our own, almost uniformly present. It must be conceded that, as yet, philosophical generalization upon abstract questions of the highest class is not the characteristic of the American mind. But the time may come when it will be pushed to a higher point in some departments connected with practical results than has yet been anywhere reached.

APPENDIX.

POSTSCRIPT.

THE following was appended to the first volume of the original edition of the Defence, which made its appearance alone. As it seems to have no necessary connection with that place, it has been transferred to this, where it seems equally appropriate, and where it serves more nearly to equalize the size of the volumes.

THE foreign gazettes and journals have announced to the world that the Abbé De Mably was applied to by the United States of America for his advice and assistance in the formation of a code of laws.[1] It is unnecessary to say any thing to this, only that it is a part of a million volumes of lies, according to the best computation, which are to be imposed upon posterity, relative to American affairs. The Abbé himself, in his observations, has said that I desired his sentiments. This is true ; but the manner of the request ought to be known, that those who think it of any consequence may understand in what sense it is true. Upon my arrival in Paris, in October, 1782, upon the business of the peace, the Abbé de Mably's book, upon the manner of writing history, was put into my hands. At the conclusion of that publication, he declared his intention of writing on the American Revolution. Meeting the Abbé soon afterwards, at dinner, at Monsieur De Chalut's, the farmer-general, my friends, the Abbés De Chalut and Arnoux, who were of the party, informed me that their friend was about writing the history of the American Revolution, and would be obliged to me for any facts or memorials that might be in my power. The question was asked, What part of the revolution he intended to write ? The whole. Where had he obtained the materials ? It was supposed they might be obtained from the public papers, and inquiry of individuals. In answer to this a few difficulties were started, and the conversation spun into length. At last the gentlemen asked to have, in writing, what had been then said upon the subject, as, the conversation being in

1 This statement is made by Baron de Grimm in his Literary Correspondence for the month of January, 1783, and corrected in his review of de Mably's " Observations sur le Gouvernement et les Lois des États-Unis d'Amérique," in October, 1784. The story was revived in some of the American newspapers in 1816, which drew from the author a note to the editor of the North American Review, inclosing a copy in English of the letter to the Abbé de Mably, and both were published in that Magazine for the month of November, 1816, together with two notes of acknowledgment, one from the Abbé himself, and the other from Marmontel, which are now appended.

French it might not have been fully comprehended. Accordingly, in a few days, I wrote the Abbé a letter, the translation of which, by a friend, into French, is here inclosed; the original, in English, not being in my possession. By this it will be seen, that the request to the Abbé to write upon American affairs, was a mere civility; and rather a desire that he would not expose himself, by attempting a history that he was altogether unprovided for, than any formal request that he should write at all. We ought to be obliged to any gentleman in Europe who will favor us with his thoughts; but, in general, the theory of government is as well understood in America as it is in Europe; and by great numbers of individuals is every thing relating to a free constitution infinitely better comprehended than by the Abbé De Mably or M. Turgot, amiable, learned, and ingenious as they were.[1]

TO THE ABBÉ DE MABLY.

IT is with pleasure that I have learned your design to write upon the American Revolution; because your other writings, which are much admired by Americans, contain principles of legislation, policy, and negotiation, which are perfectly analogous to their own; so that you cannot write upon this subject, without producing a work instructive to the public, and especially to my fellow-citizens.

But I hope, sir, you will not accuse me of presumption, of affectation, or of singularity, if I venture to express my opinion, that it is yet too soon to undertake a complete history of that great event; and that there is no man, either in America or Europe, at this day, capable of performing it, or who is in possession of the materials requisite and necessary for that purpose.

To engage in such a work, the writer ought to divide the history of America into several periods.

1. From the first establishment of the Colonies, in 1600, to the commencement of their disputes with Great Britain, in 1761.

2. From the commencement of those disputes in 1761, occasioned by an order of the board of trade and plantations in Great Britain, sent to the officers of the customs in America, to carry into execution in the strictest manner the acts of trade, and to apply to the courts of judicature for writs of assistance for that purpose, to the commencement of hostilities on the nineteenth of April, 1775. During this period of fourteen years, there was little more than a war of the quill.

3. From the battle of Lexington to the signature of the treaty with France, on the sixth of February, 1778. During this period of three years, the war was exclusively between Great Britain and the United States.

4. From the treaty with France to the commencement of hostilities between Great Britain and France, in the first place; afterwards, with Spain; then to the gradual progress of the armed neutrality, and the war of England against Holland. Finally, all these scenes have their catastrophe in the negotiations of the peace.

----

[1] In the original edition of this work, the letter was in French; but as it was not so written by the author, and as an authorized English version has been since published, that has been adopted in the present instance.

Without a distinct knowledge of the history of the colonies in the first period, a writer will find himself embarrassed, from the beginning to the end of his book, to account for events and characters which will present themselves in every step of his path, as he advances to the second, third, and fourth periods. To acquire a sufficient knowledge of the first period, it will be necessary to read all the charters granted to the colonies, and the commissions and instructions given to governors, all the codes of laws of the different colonies, (and thirteen volumes in folio, of dry, disgusting statutes, cannot be read with pleasure, or in a short time,) all the records of the legislatures of the several colonies, (which cannot be found but in manuscript, and by travelling in person from New Hampshire to Georgia); the records of the board of trade and plantations in Great Britain, from its institution to its dissolution; as also the files in the offices of some of the Secretaries of State.

There is another branch of reading which cannot be neglected, if the former might be omitted. I mean those writings which have appeared in America from time to time. I pretend not, however, in the place where I am, at a distance from all books and writings, to make an exact enumeration. The writings of the ancient Governors Winthrop and Winslow, Dr. Mather, Mr. Prince, Neal's History of New England, Douglas's Summary, the Progressive Amelioration of the Lands and the present state of the British Colonies, Hutchinson's History of the Massachusetts Bay, Smith's History of New York, Smith's History of New Jersey, the Works of William Penn, Dummer's Defence of the New England Charters, the History of Virginia, and many other public writings. All these were anterior to the present quarrel, which began in 1761.

During the second period, the writings are more numerous, and more difficult to be procured. There were then given to the public, works of great importance. In the controversies between those who were actors in this scene, as writers, there are some who ought to be distinguished. Among them are the Governors under the king, Pownall, Bernard, and Hutchinson, Lieutenant-Governor Oliver. Mr. Sewall, the Judge of Admiralty for Halifax, Jonathan Mayhew, D. D., James Otis, Oxenbridge Thacher, Samuel Adams, Josiah Quincy, Joseph Warren; and perhaps the following have not been less important than the foregoing, namely, — the writings of Mr. Dickinson, Mr. Wilson, and Dr. Rush, of Philadelphia; of Mr. Livingston, and Mr. McDougall, of New York; of Colonel Bland and Arthur Lee, of Virginia, and of many others. The records of the town of Boston, and especially of the Committee of Correspondence, the records of the Board of Commissioners of the Customs in Boston, the journals of the House of Representatives, and of the Council of Massachusetts Bay. Moreover, the gazettes of the town of Boston, not forgetting those of New York and Philadelphia, ought to be collected and examined from the year 1760. All this is necessary in order to write with precision, and in detail, the history of the discussions, before hostilities commenced, during the period from the year 1761, to the nineteenth of April, 1775.

During the third and the fourth periods, the records, pamphlets, and gazettes of the thirteen states ought to be collected, as well as the journals of Congress, (of which, nevertheless, a great part is still secret,) and the collection of the new constitutions of the several states. The Remembrancer, and the Annual Register, periodical papers, published in England. The *Affaires de l'Angleterre et de l'Amérique*, and the *Mercure de France*, published in Paris, and the *Politique*

Hollandois, printed at Amsterdam. The whole course of the Correspondence of General Washington with Congress, from the month of July, 1775, to this day, which has not yet been published, and which will not be published till Congress shall order or permit it. Allow me to say, that until this vast source of information shall be opened, it will be scarcely possible for any man to undertake the history of the American War. There are still other writings of importance, in the office of the Secret Committee of Congress, in the Committee of Foreign Affairs, in the Committee on the Treasury, in the Marine or Naval Committee, in the Board of War, as long as it existed, and of the Departments of War, of the Navy, the Finances, and of Foreign Affairs, from their institution. There are also letters of American ministers in France, Spain, Holland, and other parts of Europe.

The greatest part of the documents and materials being still secret, it is premature to undertake a general history of the American Revolution. But too much labor and care cannot be employed in making collections of those materials. There exist, however, in part, already two or three general histories of the American War, and the American Revolution, published in London, and two or three others published in Paris. Those in the English language are only materials, indigested and confused, without discernment; and all these histories, both in French and English, are only monuments of the complete ignorance of the writers of their subject. The whole of a long life, to begin at the age of twenty years, will be necessary to assemble from all nations, and from all parts of the world in which they are deposited, the documents proper to form a complete history of the American Revolution, because it is indeed the history of mankind during that epoch. The histories of France, Spain, Holland, England, and the neutral powers, must be united with that of America. The materials ought to be assembled from all those nations; and the documents, the most important of all, as well as the characters of actors and the secret springs of action, are still concealed in cabinets, and enveloped in ciphers. Whether you, sir, undertake to give a general history, or only observations and remarks, like those you have published concerning the Greeks and Romans, you will produce a work very interesting and instructive in morality, policy, and legislation; and I shall esteem it an honor and a pleasure to furnish you with any little assistance in my power to facilitate your researches.

It is impossible for me to say whether the government of France would wish to see any work profoundly written, and by an author of great celebrity, in the French language. Principles of government must be laid open, so different from those which we find in Europe, especially in France, that such an essay, perhaps, would not be seen with indifference; but of this I am not a competent judge.

Permit me, sir, before I finish this letter, to point at a key to all this history. There is a general analogy in the governments and characters of all the thirteen states; but it was not till the debates and the war began in Massachusetts Bay, the principal province of New England, that their primitive institutions produced their first effect. Four of these institutions ought to be amply investigated and maturely considered by any person who wishes to write with correct information upon this subject; for they have produced a decisive effect, not only in the first determinations of the controversies in writing, and the first debates in council, and the first resolutions to resist in arms, but also by the influence they had on the minds of the other colonies, by giving them an example to adopt more or

less the same institutions and similar measures. The four institutions intended
are : —

1. The towns or districts.	3. The schools.
2. The congregations.	4. The militia.

The towns are certain extents of country, or districts of territory, into which
Massachusetts Bay, Connecticut, New Hampshire, and Rhode Island, are divided.
These towns contain upon an average, say, six miles or two leagues square.
The inhabitants who live within these limits are formed by law into corporations,
or bodies politic, and are invested with certain powers and privileges, as, for example, to repair the great roads or highways, to support the poor, to choose their
selectmen, constables, collectors of taxes, and above all, their representatives in
the legislature; as also, the right to assemble, whenever they are summoned by
their selectmen, in their town halls, there to deliberate upon the public affairs of
the town, or to give instructions to their representatives in the legislature. The
consequences of these institutions have been, that the inhabitants, having acquired from their infancy the habit of discussing, of deliberating, and of judging
of public affairs, it was in these assemblies of towns or districts that the sentiments of the people were formed in the first place, and their resolutions were
taken from the beginning to the end of the disputes and the war with Great
Britain.

2. The congregations are religious societies, which comprehend the whole
people. Every district contains a parish or religious congregation. In general,
they have but one, though some of them have several. Each parish has a temple for public worship, and a minister, maintained at the public expense. The
constitutions of these congregations are extremely popular, and the clergy have
little influence or authority beyond that which their own piety, virtues, and
talents naturally give them. They are chosen by the people of their parishes,
and receive their ordinations from the neighboring clergy. They are all married,
have families, and live with their parishioners in an intimate and perfect friendship. They visit the sick; they are charitable to the poor; they solemnize mar-
riages and funerals, and preach twice every Sunday. The smallest imputation on
their moral character would destroy their influence, and ruin them forever. They
are, therefore; wise, virtuous, and pious men; their sentiments are generally conformable to those of their people, and they are jealous friends of liberty.

3. There are schools in every town, established by an express law of the
colony. Every town containing sixty families, is obliged, under a penalty, to
maintain constantly a school and a schoolmaster, who shall teach his scholars
reading, writing, arithmetic, and the rudiments of the Latin and Greek languages. All the children of the inhabitants, the rich as well as the poor, have a
right to go to these public schools. There, are formed the candidates for admission as students into the colleges at Cambridge, New Haven, Princeton, and Dart-
mouth. In these colleges are educated future masters for these schools, future
ministers for these congregations, doctors of law and medicine, and magistrates
and officers for the government of the country.

4. The militia comprehends the whole people. By virtue of the laws of the
country, every male inhabitant between sixteen and sixty years of age, is enrolled in a company, and a regiment of militia completely organized with all its
officers. He is enjoined to keep always in his house, and at his own expense, a

firelock in good order, a powder horn, a pound of powder, twelve flints, four-and-twenty balls of lead, a cartridge box, and a knapsack; so that the whole country is ready to march for its own defence upon the first signal of alarm. These companies and regiments are obliged to assemble at certain times in every year, under the orders of their officers, for the inspection of their arms and ammunition, and to perform their exercises and manœuvres.

Behold, sir, a little sketch of the four principal sources of that prudence in council and that military valor and ability, which have produced the American Revolution, and which I hope will be sacredly preserved as the foundations of the liberty, happiness, and prosperity of the people.

If there are any other particulars, concerning which I can give you any information, be so good as to point them out.

I have the honor to be,

1782.   JOHN ADAMS.

This letter was privately communicated to M. Marmontel, who seems to have had some intention of writing on America, as well as the person to whom it was addressed, and it drew from both the following acknowledgments.

L'Abbé de Mably est bien fâché de ne s'être pas trouvé chez lui quand Monsieur Adams lui a fait l'honneur d'y passer. Il a celui de lui remettre l'écrit qu'il lui a addressé. Jamais l'Abbé de Mably ne s'est proposé d'écrire l'histoire de la révolution d'Amérique; il seroit mort avant que d'avoir rassemblé la moitié des materiaux d'un si important ouvrage. Il sera tres obligé à Monsieur Adams s'il veut avoir la bonté de lui faire tirer une copie de la dernière partie de cet écrit, en y joignant quelques remarques sur le génie et les intérêts de quelques-uns des premiers confédérés, et surtout sur l'état actuel des richesses ou fortunes des particuliers, et sur la nature du luxe connu en Amérique.

M. Marmontel a l'honneur de faire milles complimens à Monsieur Adams, et de lui renvoyer l'excellente lettre qu'il a eu la bonté de lui confier. Elle lui fait sentir plus que jamais l'extrême besoin qu'il a de ses secours et de ses lumières pour être en état d'écrire passablement l'histoire de la grande révolution, qui fait la gloire de l'Amérique septentrionale et qui assure son bonheur.

Ce 8 Mars, 1783.

END OF VOLUME V.

Printed in the United States
134597LV00006B/78/A

9 780559 692277